THE STATE OF THE WORLD'S CHILDREN
1985

Oxford University Press, Walton Street,
Oxford OX2 6DP
London Glasgow New York Toronto
Delhi Bombay Calcutta Madras Karachi
Kuala Lumpur Singapore Hong Kong Tokyo
Nairobi Dar es Salaam Cape Town
Melbourne Auckland
and associates in
Beirut Berlin Ibadan Mexico City Nicosia

Oxford is a trade mark of Oxford University Press
Published in the United States by Oxford University Press,
New York

©United Nations Children's Fund 1984
All rights reserved. No part of this publication may be reproduced, stored in a retrieval system, or transmitted, in any form or by an means, electronic, mechanical, photocopying, recording, or otherwise, without the prior permission of Oxford University Press.

British Library Cataloguing in Publication Data
The state of the world's children.—1985
1. Children-Care and hygiene
613' 0432 RJ101
ISBN 0-19-828497-7 Cloth
ISBN 0-19-828496-9 paperback

UNICEF, 866 U.N. Plaza, New York, N.Y. 10017
U.S.A.
UNICEF, Palais des Nations, CH. 1211
–Geneva 10–Switzerland.

Cover and design: Miller, Craig and Cocking, Woodstock, U.K.
Charts and tables: Stephen Hawkins, Oxford Illustrators, Oxford, U.K.
Typesetting and Printing: Burgess & Son (Abingdon) Ltd, U.K.

Edited and produced for UNICEF and Oxford University Press by P & L Adamson, Benson, Oxfordshire, U.K.

THE STATE OF THE WORLD'S CHILDREN 1985

James P. Grant
Executive Director of the
United Nations Children's Fund
(UNICEF)

PUBLISHED FOR UNICEF

Oxford University Press

I THE STATE OF THE WORLD'S CHILDREN 1985

A Revolution Beginning

A revolution in child survival is beginning to go into action around the world. But if its low-cost techniques are to fulfil their potential to save millions of children's lives, then the focus of health care must be shifted from institutions to families. Enough of the capacity to reach and support these families is now in place in most nations of the developing world. A drastic improvement in 'the state of the world's children' is therefore possible – if the world wants it.

page 1

Protection in Poverty

The poorest women and children have taken the brunt of the world recession. For those who are so poor that their children cannot grow and develop normally, a minimum 'safety net' of health and nutrition is needed. The cost is now so low that it would be unconscionable not to afford such basic protection to children.

page 16

Going into Action

With falling rates of child deaths, falling birth rates can also be expected. The basic child survival techniques of growth monitoring (page 39), oral rehydration therapy (page 23), the protection of breast-feeding (page 27), and expanded immunization (page 31), are now beginning to go into action on a significant scale in some parts of the world.

page 21

The Disproportionate Benefit

Because of the synergistic alliance between malnutrition and infection, illness is frequent, recovery times are inadequate, and assaults on a child's growth therefore become cumulative. By the same token, a relatively small number of interventions can break this cycle, allow fuller recovery, reduce infection's frequency, and therefore have a disproportionately beneficial effect on child health.

page 42

Marketing Survival

The two most relevant precedents for putting new knowledge and new techniques at the disposal of the majority are the Green Revolution and the campaign to promote family planning. Success in both depended on political commitment, the mobilization of all channels of support, and the use of 'social marketing'.

page 47

A Health Service for All

With relatively little training in basic techniques, voluntary and community health workers could help mothers to bring about a revolution in child survival and development. Given even a small reallocation of resources towards primary health care, plus a partnership with traditional midwives, the idea of a trained health worker for every community is not an impossible dream.

page 57

Women's Time

All of the child survival revolution strategies demand more of women's time, energy, and knowledge. Mothers therefore need practical support as well as information if they are to bring this change about. Basic amenities such as water supply and sanitation would also help families to take more control of their own health.

page 64

Changing Perceptions

Changing perceptions of what is normal, what is possible, and what the individual can do to improve family life, is both the means and the end of the revolution in child survival and development.

page 72

II LIFELINES

Extracts and summaries from recent research and writing on cost-effective strategies for protecting the lives and normal development of the world's children.

Growth monitoring
malnutrition's many causes □ the growth monitoring approach □ the involvement of mothers □ the growth standards debate.
page 77

Oral rehydration therapy
impact of diarrhoeal disease □ causes and prevention □ oral rehydration therapy □ home remedies □ new developments.
page 82

Breast-feeding
dangers of bottle-feeding □ decline of breast-feeding □ advantages of breast-milk □ promotion and support □ the importance of weaning.
page 87

Immunization
vaccine preventable diseases □ vaccine effectiveness, schedules and storage □ side-effects □ costs and coverage □ supply problems □ creating the demand □ immunization and primary health care.
page 93

Female education
maternal education and child survival □ education as an independent force □ possible explanations of the link □ progress in female education.
page 98

Family spacing
effects of births too close together □ health benefits of family planning □ unmet demand for family planning methods.
page 100

Food supplements
causes and consequences of low birth-weight □ preventing low birth-weight □ food fortification □ prevention of anaemia □ prevention of IDD □ prevention of Vitamin A deficiency.
page 103

III STATISTICS

Economic and social statistics on the nations of the world, with particular reference to children's well-being.

Graphics on trends in infant mortality — page 110
Alphabetical index to countries — page 111

Basic indicators
infant mortality rate □ total population □ annual no. of births and child deaths □ GNP per capita □ life expectancy □ adult literacy □ school enrolment □ income distribution
page 112

Nutrition
low birth-weight □ breast-feeding □ malnutrition □ food production □ calorie intake
page 114

Health
access to water □ immunization of children □ immunization of mothers □ life expectancy
page 116

Education
male and female literacy □ primary school enrolment and completion □ secondary school enrolment
page 118

Demographic indicators
total and child populations □ population growth □ infant and child mortality □ death rate □ birth rate □ fertility rate □ urbanization
page 120

Economic indicators
GNP per capita □ growth rate □ inflation □ poverty □ government spending on health, education, defence □ aid □ debt servicing
page 122

Basic indicators for less populous countries
infant mortality rate □ total population □ annual no. of births and child deaths □ GNP per capita □ life expectancy □ adult literacy □ school enrolment □ income distribution
page 124

Signs and explanations, general note on the data — page 125
Footnotes to all tables — page 126
Definitions — page 128
Main sources — page 129
Note on variations in IMR within countries — page 130

PANELS

Colombia: immunizing 800,000	**1**
***El Tiempo* reports:** 'A triumph for all Colombia'	**2**
Africa: the permanent crisis	**3**
India: reaching 10 million	**4**
Bangladesh: surviving the autumn	**5**
Nigeria and the Sudan: immunizing more for less	**6**
Cheraga: child deaths down 60%	**7**
The Recession: women and children last	**8**
Disabilities: the preventable burden	**9**
Population growth: survival helps slow-down	**10**
The West: a return to breast-feeding	**11**
The Code: action in 130 nations	**12**
India: creating the demand	**13**
Matlab: providing the proof	**14**
China: a generation ahead	**15**
Delhi: mothers monitor growth	**16**
Protecting growth: a graphic presentation	**17**
Tanzania: a literacy revolution	**18**
Bangladesh: teaching two million	**19**
Gambia and Honduras: marketing ORT	**20**
Thailand: PHC goes national	**21**
Tanzania: saving on essential drugs	**22**
Diarrhoeal disease: briefing the professionals	**23**
Rural poverty: trial by seasons	**24**
Oral rehydration: story of a breakthrough	**25**
Bhutan: ending the IDD tragedy	**26**

TEXT FIGURES

Fig. 1   Developing countries producing oral rehydration salts
Fig. 2   Global supply of oral rehydration salts (WHO/UNICEF formula)
Fig. 3   Effect of birth spacing on infant and child survival, Bangladesh
Fig. 4   Impact of malnutrition during pregnancy on perinatal mortality
Fig. 5   Number and percentage unable to meet basic needs, 1974–82
Fig. 6   Health and wealth
Fig. 7   Impact on population growth of a reduction in child deaths
Fig. 8   Impact of ORT on hospital treatment of diarrhoea
Fig. 9   Average duration of breast-feeding
Fig. 10 Duration of breast-feeding in rural and urban areas of Bangladesh by age and education of mother
Fig. 11 Influence of breast-feeding on interval between births
Fig. 12 Percentage of pregnant women immunized against tetanus
Fig. 13 Percentage of children immunized in the first year of life
Fig. 14 Coverage and drop-out rates in DPT vaccination programmes
Fig. 15 Number of deaths from selected vaccine-preventable diseases
Fig. 16 Impact of hand-washing on transmission of diarrhoeal infections
Fig. 17 Child growth to age six
Fig. 18 Child death rates in nine months following acute phase of measles, the Gambia
Fig. 19 Effect of ORT on weight-gain and on duration of diarrhoeal illness
Fig. 20 Health expenditures and population served
Fig. 21 Availability of doctors and traditional midwives
Fig. 22 Seasonal pattern of diarrhoeal infections in rural Gambia
Fig. 23 Prevalence of anaemia among women of the developing world
Fig. 24 Effect of poverty on weight-gain in pregnancy
Fig. 25 Impact of improved water supply on health and nutrition

A note on famine in Africa

UNICEF, together with many other agencies, is doing all it can to bring immediate relief to the victims of Africa's famines. For many months, we have been appealing for emergency assistance. By November 1984, special funding of more than $15 million had been raised to help meet emergency needs in the 13 most critically affected countries.

At the same time, UNICEF believes that the time has come to appeal for an extension of the concern which has been shown in response to this emergency.

In late 1984, pictures of camps in the north of Ethiopia were shown in almost every country of the world. And the world was rightly moved. UNICEF offices everywhere received generous donations of money and offers of help in response to the visible fact of child starvation and child death.

In some of those camps, approximately 40 children died each day. In the poor world as a whole, approximately 40,000 children died each day – every day of 1984.

Because those 40,000 children were dispersed throughout the world's poor and underdeveloped communities, their suffering and their deaths became invisible. They nonetheless suffered. And they are nonetheless dead.

This wider tragedy is what UNICEF has long called 'the silent emergency'. And while responding to the 'louder' emergencies, whether in Kampuchea or Lebanon or Ethiopia, UNICEF must also make a more difficult appeal – an appeal for a longer term commitment to saving the lives and protecting the normal growth of children whose malnutrition goes unseen and whose deaths go unannounced.

In many countries this year, the public itself has made it clear to governments that it does not regard the suffering seen on its television screens as acceptable in the one world of the last quarter of the 20th Century. If that same concern were to be maintained on behalf of the children of the 'silent emergency', if the public at large were to make it clear that their suffering too was unacceptable in a world which could now prevent it, then action might also be taken to save the health and the lives of children in need wherever they may be.

Such action could not only save many thousands of lives each day. It would also help to prevent much of the hidden malnutrition which now stops many more thousands of children from growing and developing normally. It would therefore also mean that those children would eventually be able to contribute more fully to, and benefit more fully from, the development of their nations. And that in turn might mean that the 'loud emergencies' themselves would become both less frequent and less severe.

At this time in particular, extraordinary new opportunities are arising for drastically reducing child malnutrition and child death in the world's poorest communities. This year's *State of the World's Children* report describes some of those opportunities as they are now beginning to go into action in different countries of the world. For there is good news to report as well as bad, and hope is as necessary as outrage if a commitment to protecting the world's most vulnerable children is to be maintained.

This report is therefore a contribution to the extension of a sustained public concern which will one day declare the silent emergency of 40,000 children dying invisibly each day – and millions more living on in malnutrition and ill-health – to be just as unacceptable as the more visible crises by which it is now so rightly moved.

I
THE STATE OF THE WORLD'S CHILDREN 1985

James P. Grant

A Revolution Beginning

Protection in Poverty

Going into Action

The Disproportionate Benefit

Marketing Survival

A Health Service for All

Women's Time

Changing Perceptions

I THE STATE OF THE WORLD'S CHILDREN 1985

Infant Mortality Rate

The infant mortality rate (IMR) is the number of deaths before the age of one year – per 1,000 live births.

Figures given for the infant mortality rates of particular countries, in both the text and statistical tables of this report, are estimates prepared by the United Nations Population Division on an internationally comparable basis, using various sources. In some cases, these may differ from national estimates.

Most national IMR figures, being for 1982, do not yet reflect the impact of any of the recent campaigns and child survival programmes mentioned in the text.

A Revolution Beginning

In the last twelve months, the lives of an estimated half a million children have been saved by oral rehydration therapy (ORT). Yet as the year comes to an end, less than 15% of the world's families are using this revolutionary low-cost technique for preventing and treating diarrhoeal dehydration – the biggest single killer of children in the modern world.*

But this picture is rapidly changing as ORT begins to capture the imagination both of governments and of a world-wide public. In total, 38 nations have begun large-scale production of the oral rehydration salts (fig. 1) and national ORT campaigns have been launched in more than 20 countries, including Pakistan, Thailand, the Philippines, Indonesia, Bangladesh, Laos, Viet Nam, Nigeria, Tanzania, the Gambia, Algeria, Egypt, Morocco, Colombia, Honduras, Haiti, Nicaragua, Jamaica, Brazil, and Mexico. In the past year, UNICEF itself has supplied 78 nations with approximately 65 million sachets of the salts and total annual production by developing countries themselves is now estimated at 100 million packets (fig. 2).

Previously, dehydration could only be treated intravenously by medical personnel in clinics. Now, it can be prevented orally by parents in the child's own home – using the mass-produced 10-cent sachets of pre-packed salts or the even cheaper home-made solutions of sugar, salt, and water.** Either way, it is ORT's cheapness and its manageability-by-parents which holds out the hope of its being made universally available.

"In the next few years," says the Director of the International Centre for Diarrhoeal Disease Research, Bangladesh, "ORT has the potential to save the lives of enormous numbers of people around the world. It is truly an incredible concept that something as simple, inexpensive and effective has emerged from the laboratory into people's homes on such a large scale".

Given the mobilization of all possible resources to support parents in the use of this technique, UNICEF believes that ORT can become available to half the world's families within the next five years. And at that point, it will save the lives of some two million young children a year.

A low-cost revolution

ORT is the most dramatic in a range of low-cost methods now available for protecting the lives and health of children in low-income communities. For the last two years, the *State of the World's Children* report, with the help of the mass media,

---

* Oral rehydration therapy (ORT) is a technique for preventing and treating the dehydration which can result from diarrhoeal infections. Estimates of the use of ORT, and of the deaths it prevents, are of necessity approximate. The figures do not include China. Because of the infrequency of data collection, it will be some time before the impact of ORT can be seen in national infant and child mortality statistics.

** For prevention, an effective oral rehydration solution can be made in the home using water, salt, and the glucose found either in sugar or in starchy cereals such as rice or starchy vegetables such as yams or carrots. For the treatment of dehydration, solutions made from pre-packed sachets of salts made up to the precise WHO/UNICEF formula should be used wherever possible.

I THE STATE OF THE WORLD'S CHILDREN 1985

Colombia: immunizing 800,000

In the last few months, Colombia has immunized three-quarters of its young children against five major diseases in a massive campaign spread over three National Vaccination Days.

The campaign was the opening shot in the child survival revolution launched by Colombia's President Betancur earlier this year. Citing oral rehydration therapy, breast-feeding, growth monitoring and immunization, the President announced to the nation:-

"Thousands of children still die whose lives could be saved by very simple measures... I propose to all of you to take the decision to reduce infant mortality by half in the near future – thus avoiding the loss of 50,000 children a year."

At 8 a.m. on the morning of June 23rd, the President immunized the first child in the Presidential Palace in Bogotá. By 7 p.m. that evening, over 800,000 children had been vaccinated against measles, polio, diphtheria, tetanus, and whooping cough. And the turn-out increased with each vaccination day. In the process, the campaign also achieved its second major objective – strengthening the immunization system itself.

To achieve this result, over 120,000 volunteers were mobilized and over 10,000 vaccination posts were set up in schools, parks, town halls, market-places and health clinics. General-election style, the results were broadcast every two hours over 90 radio stations. At the immunization sites themselves, candy stalls, music groups, and fireworks provided a carnival atmosphere.

As in most countries of the developing world, Colombia's health services do not yet have the outreach to either create or meet a nation-wide demand for immunization. To overcome this problem, every conceivable organization in the country was asked to lend its resources to the campaign.

To create the demand, the country's biggest daily newspaper, *El Tiempo*, joined forces with the national broadcasting network Caracol to inform all parents about the three National Vaccination Days. On April 6th the campaign mascot – a cartoon character called Pitín, symbolizing the healthy Colombian child – was born in the pages of *El Tiempo* and was soon adopted by 20 other newspapers. One of the country's largest private banks, the Banco del Estado, distributed many thousands of calendars showing the figure of Pitín next to the dates of the National Vaccination Days – June 23rd, July 28th and August 25th.

On the vaccination days themselves, popular entertainers broadcast hourly calls to immunization on the Caracol radio network – reaching an estimated 10 million mothers. Organizations from the the Boy Scouts to the Street Vendors Association reached out to their own constituencies. In the *barrios* of Bogotá, touring puppet theatres played dramas with immunization themes.

On each Sunday before the National Vaccination Days, priests in most of Colombia's 2,280 parishes gave sermons about child health and the importance of having children immunized. The Ministry of Education called on its 200,000 teachers to promote the campaign and the Ministry of the Interior requested all governors and the mayors of 950 municipalities to take the lead in local campaigns.

To ensure supply, the health services enlisted the support of the Colombian Red Cross Society, which trained more than 13,000 of its members to be vaccinators and fielded another 16,000 volunteers to help with organization and record-keeping. The United Nations Development Programme, WHO, and UNICEF provided the vaccines and syringes and helped maintain the 'cold chain'. Over 500 police and army medics joined the campaign and the Ministry of Defence made planes and helicopters available to get vaccines to remote immunization centres in all corners of the country.

Every parent bringing a child for immunization has been given a growth chart with the child's immunization record – plus advice on breast-feeding, nutrition, and the treatment of diarrhoeal illness.

(See next panel for the *El Tiempo* editorial commenting on this campaign.)

has drawn world-wide attention to the fact that just four relatively simple and inexpensive methods could now enable parents themselves to halve the rate of child deaths and save the lives of up to 20,000 children each day.

In brief, those methods are:-

○ **Growth monitoring** – which could help mothers to prevent most child malnutrition before it begins. With the help of a 10-cent growth chart, and basic advice on weaning, most mothers could maintain their child's healthy growth – even within their limited resources.

○ **Oral rehydration** – which could save most of the more than 4 million young children who now die each year from diarrhoeal dehydration.

○ **Breast-feeding** – which can ensure that infants have the best possible food and a considerable degree of immunity from common infections during the first six months of life.

○ A full $5 course of **Immunization** – which can protect a child against measles, diphtheria, whooping cough, tetanus, tuberculosis, and polio. At present, these diseases kill an estimated 5 million young children a year, leave 5 million more disabled, and are a major cause of child malnutrition.

In this year's report, it is possible to begin reporting on the progress of these strategies.* In the words of the Secretary-General of the United Nations, Javier Pérez de Cuéllar:-

"... the world-wide response has been encouraging. There are unmistakable signs that a veritable child survival revolution has begun to spread across the world and offers the hope that the rates of infant and child mortality, still so deplorably high, may be reduced drastically in the foreseeable future."

Citing the four low-cost methods outlined above, the Secretary-General concludes:-

"Evidence accumulates that these and other such simple low-cost interventions are being extended both by governments and community action groups, with the co-operation of the media and other forms of mass communication. In spite of the continuing and serious constraints of world recession, such action is proving possible and cost-effective."

Some examples of this child survival revolution as it begins to go into action around the world:-

Fig.1 Developing countries producing oral rehydration salts

REGION	COUNTRY
AFRICA	BURUNDI ETHIOPIA KENYA LESOTHO MOZAMBIQUE BURKINA–FASO* ZAIRE
AMERICAS	ARGENTINA BRAZIL COLOMBIA COSTA RICA DOMINICAN REPUBLIC EL SALVADOR HAITI HONDURAS MEXICO PARAGUAY PERU VENEZUELA
EASTERN MEDITERRANEAN	AFGHANISTAN EGYPT IRAN (ISLAMIC REPUBLIC OF) PAKISTAN SYRIAN ARAB REPUBLIC TUNISIA
EUROPE	MOROCCO
SOUTH-EAST ASIA	BANGLADESH* BURMA INDIA INDONESIA NEPAL MONGOLIA* THAILAND
WESTERN PACIFIC	CHINA* KAMPUCHEA* MALAYSIA PHILIPPINES REPUBLIC OF KOREA

*Indicates a cottage industry approach
Source: WHO/CDD/84.10 World Health Organization, Geneva, 1984.

---

* As a mnemonic, these four low-cost techniques have become collectively known as GOBI – for Growth monitoring, Oral rehydration, Breast-feeding and improved weaning, and Immunization.

I THE STATE OF THE WORLD'S CHILDREN 1985

El Tiempo reports: 'A triumph for all Colombia'

Editorial from *El Tiempo*, one of Colombia's leading dailies, on the morning of 29 August 1984

The third National Vaccination Day came to a highly successful culmination last Saturday. The outcome of this campaign should be a source of pride to all Colombia, for by its actions, as several spokesmen for international organizations working on this commendable effort have pointed out, Colombia has set an example of mass infant immunization for the international community. The Executive Director of UNICEF, James Grant, compared the success of this campaign with man's landing on the moon because it, too, demonstrated that something was possible – in this case, that it is possible to conduct massive vaccination campaigns providing protection for large numbers of children.

We, the organizers of this project, never suspected how important it would be nor how successful. It seemed to us that this initiative could turn into just another good idea that would get lost in the bureaucratic shuffle and general indifference. Fortunately, however, things did not turn out that way. From the outset, the idea of protecting Colombian children from five diseases which take many lives among the infant population caught on and stirred a degree of enthusiasm rarely seen in our community. Perhaps it was the campaign's objective – children. Or perhaps it was the country's prevailing mood – a weariness of violence and bad news Whatever it was, the fact is that people rallied around this idea and worked unselfishly, without the egotism that has done us so much harm in the past. Here lies the importance of this campaign, and here lies the fundamental impetus behind its success.

The list of organizations and people who made it possible to immunize more than 800,000 children is endless, for the simple reason that everyone contributed what they could. From the President of the Republic to the owner of the canoe that transported children from our indigenous tribes out of the inhospitable jungles in the remotest areas of Colombia – everyone played an important part in this noble effort. It was not a triumph for Caracol and *El Tiempo* alone, since other sectors of the mass media also helped publicize this campaign. Neither was it the exclusive success of the government, UNICEF or the Pan American Health Organization, which worked so hard and so enthusiastically on this campaign. *It was a triumph for all Colombia, and it helps make up for the many difficulties and troubles we have experienced and strengthens our faith in our nation's destiny.*

In Indonesia, the fifth largest nation in the world, 400,000 volunteers in over 31,000 villages are managing a national programme including the monthly growth monitoring of children, oral rehydration therapy, the promotion of breast-feeding and safe weaning, the use of immunization services, and birth spacing. The aim is to reduce the overall infant death rate by approximately half – from 90 to less than 50 deaths per 1,000 live births – over the next fifteen years.

Fig.2 Global supply of oral rehydration salts (WHO/UNICEF formula)

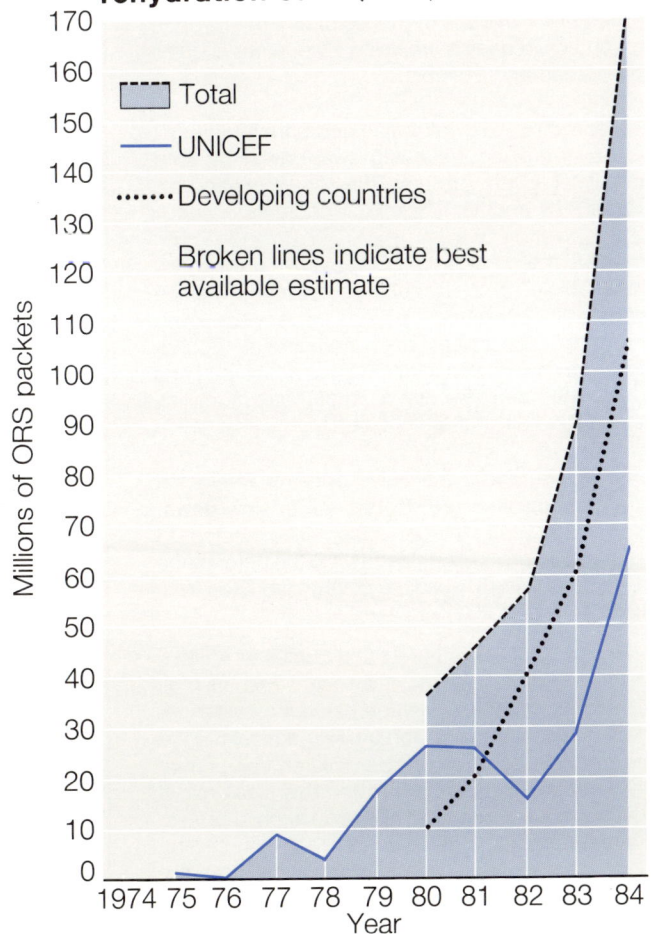

Legend:
- Total
- UNICEF
- Developing countries
- Broken lines indicate best available estimate

Y-axis: Millions of ORS packets (0 to 170)
X-axis: Year (1974 to 84)

Note: Figures exclude commercial production. In addition to the above figures, an estimated 10 million packets are supplied by other international and bilateral aid agencies.

Source: UNICEF

In Pakistan – where half a million children have been dying every year from diarrhoeal dehydration and 'immunizable' diseases alone – an Accelerated Health Programme has lifted the immunization rate from 5% to almost 50%, produced 30 million sachets of oral rehydration salts in 1984, and trained over 12,000 traditional birth attendants in low-cost techniques for protecting the lives and growth of Pakistan's children.

In India, the programme for Integrated Child Development Services – using a similar range of low-cost techniques – is operating in one-fifth of India's 5,000 development 'blocks' and reaching almost 10 million young children (see panel 4).

In Baguio City, the Philippines, a campaign centred on growth monitoring, the promotion of breast-feeding, immunization, oral rehydration therapy, and birth spacing has helped to reduce infant and child death rates by 50% over the last five years.

In Colombia this year, over 800,000 young children have been immunized on each of three National Vaccination Days as part of a campaign to bring about a revolution in child survival (see panel 1).

In Brazil, 1984 has also seen 2 million under-twos vaccinated against measles, 1.5 million immunized against diphtheria, whooping cough and tetanus, and almost all the nation's children protected against polio – through the mobilization of over 400,000 volunteers manning over 90,000 vaccination posts on two separate National Vaccination Days.

In Tanzania, a campaign based on oral rehydration therapy and growth monitoring has been launched as the first stage of a nutrition programme which aims to halve the death rate among the 50,000 children living in 167 villages of Iringa province.

In Ethiopia, the city of Addis Ababa has taken the first steps in a campaign to halve its infant and child death rates over the next three years.

In Nigeria, a campaign has just been launched to try to repeat on a national scale the successes of the new-style vaccination campaign in the Owo area – where immunization coverage has

I THE STATE OF THE WORLD'S CHILDREN 1985

Africa: the permanent crisis

Exactly one hundred years after the colonial powers divided up the continent at the Congress of Berlin, Africa finds itself in a state of permanent crisis. Twenty-nine of the world's 36 poorest nations are to be found south of the Sahara and 24 of them are now appealing for emergency aid to ward off famine.

The crisis goes deeper than present drought. Africa is the continent with the lowest incomes, the lowest economic growth rates, and the lowest levels of life expectancy and literacy. It is also the continent with the highest rates of population growth, the least political stability, and the most severe environmental problems.

As a reflection of these ills, Africa also has the highest rates of child deaths. This year, nearly 5 million African children have died and another 5 million have been disabled by malnutrition and disease.

The optimism which followed independence for so many African nations began to evaporate in the 1970s. When exports prospered, they had taken out loans to invest in development. But then fuel prices rose and the prices paid for Africa's raw materials fell.

New loans had to be taken out – but this time to import food and fuel and to service past debts. Today, fuel imports cost 40% of Ghana's export earnings, debt repayments claim a third of the revenues of Burkina-Faso, and food imports cost Nigeria more than $2 billion a year.

To earn the necessary foreign exchange, most agricultural investment goes to cash crops for export. But devoting the best land to export crops has meant growing food on more and more marginal lands. The result is environmental deterioration, greater vulnerability of the poor and pastoralists, and increasing dependence on imported food. Today, Africa barely grows half its own food and has to import over 20 million tonnes of grain annually.

Superimposed on this pattern is the drought which now affects a third of Africa's population and the floods which have ruined crops in Swaziland and Mozambique. In 1983, per capita food production was down by a disastrous 14% on the 1981 figure as whole crops of millet and sorghum parched in the fields. This year, the appeal has gone out for millions of tonnes of emergency food aid and child deaths are rising in countries such as Mali, Chad and Ethiopia.

Meanwhile, soils left brittle and bare by drought and over-grazing are being swept away by wind and water. Every year now, the Sahara expands its frontiers by another 1.5 million hectares.

Nor is the continent's political environment any more stable. In the last 25 years, more than 70 leaders in 29 African nations have been overthrown by assassination or coup d'état. Boundaries drawn by colonial rulers have not helped and today the continent as a whole has 5 million refugees – half of them children.

Finally, Africa is the only continent where the rate of population growth has yet to slow down. Within 25 years its population is expected to double to over 1 billion. Meanwhile the percentage of Africans living in absolute poverty has risen from 82% in 1974 to 91% in 1982.

Inevitably, it is the minds and bodies of Africa's children which are most at risk. And just as drought may become self-perpetuating by denuding the land of soil for tomorrow's agriculture, so the damage done to today's children can permanently erode the capacity of tomorrow's parents. In Africa's hour of need, a revolution in child protection is therefore more necessary than ever before. Given present advances in knowledge, it is also more possible than ever before. Oral rehydration and immunization, for example, could together save the lives of perhaps half the African children who now die each year.

been lifted from less than 10% to 83% in the twelve months since the campaign began (see panel 6).

In Turkey, the launching of a five-year Turkish Child Survival and Development Revolution is planned for 1985 to try to repeat, nation-wide, the successes achieved in Van province where the same combination of low-cost techniques has reduced infant deaths by 65% in the last four years.

In Cheraga district, Algeria, the infant mortality rate has already been cut by 60% (from 103 to 43 per 1,000) in only five years, using a combination of low-cost techniques including the promotion of breast-feeding, better weaning, growth monitoring, oral rehydration therapy, and immunization (see panel 7).

In Algiers itself, the country's newly appointed Health Minister has pledged to halve the nation's infant death rate in the next five years. The campaign will be spearheaded by a nation-wide ORT programme to combat the diarrhoeal dehydration which now accounts for nearly 40% of all child deaths in Algeria.

Not all of these campaigns will succeed. Some will fail to maintain the initial enthusiasm. Some will rest content to have reached 50% instead of mobilizing all possible resources to reach 80% and 90% of the population. Some will fail to reach the poorest families. Some will fall victim to recession and cut-backs in government spending. But some *are* succeeding in achieving higher levels of children's health and well-being. The child survival revolution is no longer a theory. Many thousands of children's lives are being saved. And there is now a realistic basis for hope that, over the next 10 to 15 years, infant death rates will fall by as much as 5% or more a year in countries such as Tanzania, Nigeria, Algeria, Turkey, India, Pakistan, Indonesia, Haiti, Nicaragua, Brazil and Colombia.

Self-health

Breakthroughs in knowledge and technique have been made before. Usually, they have reached only a minority of the developing world's people: either they were too expensive, or they could only be made available via the hospitals, doctors and clinics which are just not available to the majority. But the four basic strategies of the child survival revolution represent advances of an altogether different order. And what gives them their unique potential is that:-

○ They can be distilled down to an essence of simple practicable information and advice which almost all parents can understand and act on. They are therefore not dependent only on the extension of health services.

○ They are so inexpensive that almost any family and any nation can afford to put them into practice. For all four, the average additional cost would probably not be more than $10 per child.

○ They are so universal in their relevance, and so synergistic in their relationship with each other, that they would strike at the heart of the child health and malnutrition problem in almost every poor community in the developing world.

○ They are not dependent on profound changes in values nor do they go against the grain of people's own priorities. Rather, they offer a means by which parents can realize their own wishes for healthy surviving children.

Drastically improved child health and survival is therefore made realistic by shifting its operational centre of gravity from health institutions to the family itself. And in that sense, the child survival revolution can be seen as part of an even broader global trend towards returning the primary responsibility for health to the individual.

In the industrialized world itself, the investment of extra billions of dollars in medical technology is yielding ever more marginal gains in human health. Low-cost changes within the power of the individual, on the other hand, could lever health to new levels. It is now known, for example, that an American male can add approximately 11 years to his life expectancy by not smoking, drinking only in moderation, eating wisely, and taking regular exercise. In response to the promotion of this kind of knowledge, literally millions of people in the industrialized world have improved their own health by their own actions

I THE STATE OF THE WORLD'S CHILDREN 1985

India: reaching 10 million

India has more children than all the 46 countries of Africa put together. The majority of those children are living in poverty: one in three is born underweight, one in seven dies before the age of five, and an estimated 3 million die each year from conditions which could be prevented by oral rehydration and immunization alone.

Over the years, successes in improving the health of Indian children have been chalked up in pilot projects and small-scale government programmes. But there are now signs that the government is setting in place a matrix of basic child health strategies on a scale commensurate with the problem itself:-

○ Following successful local campaigns (see panel) which have raised child immunization rates to over 80%, several state governments are now moving to immunize all children. UNICEF's regional office in New Delhi estimates that if all state governments follow through on this commitment, then India can achieve its goal of vaccinating 85% of all infants by the year 1990.

○ A national code on the marketing of breast-milk substitutes is soon to become law.

○ A national programme to prevent disability has been launched – including massive distribution of vitamin A to prevent blindness in children.

○ Government outlays on clean water and sanitation are to be almost quadrupled over the next five years.

At the heart of these activities lies the massive programme for Integrated Child Development Services (ICDS), centred on the *anganwadi* – literally, a courtyard for child care. The *anganwadis* each cover a population of about 1,000 and serve simultaneously as a pre-school for children up to six, as a supplementary feeding centre for pregnant and nursing women and for poor children, as the focal point for children's immunizations and for regular check-ups on their health, and as a centre for literacy, health and nutrition courses for mothers. Along with village health guides, the *anganwadi* workers – women recruited from the community and trained for several months – are the community's primary link with the health centres and all other services for young children.

From experimental beginnings ten years ago in 33 of India's 5,000 administrative 'blocks' (each with an average of 100,000 people), the ICDS programme will by mid-1985 be active in 1,000 blocks containing some of India's poorest villages and slums. At that point the *anganwadi* workers, currently some 60,000 strong, will be organizing immunizations and check-ups for 10.3 million children, classes for 3.4 million mothers, and supplementary feeding for 6.1 million children and 1.1 million women. Another 1,000 blocks will be covered by 1990, and the programme as a whole is due to reach every poor child aged six and under by the turn of the century.

Already, the immunization rates have doubled and tripled in ICDS blocks. A survey of the children in 15 of the original project blocks has shown that severe malnutrition fell from 21.9% to 5.4% over 21 months. Among children up to three, usually the hardest group to reach, malnutrition fell from 29.2% to 6%. Even though the children in rural ICDS blocks are among the most deprived in the country, their infant mortality rate is steadily falling: a study of 200 ICDS blocks found an infant mortality rate in 1982-1983 of 89 deaths per 1,000 live births in rural blocks, as compared with the national figure of 124 per 1,000 in rural areas.

Remarkably, the current 1,000 ICDS projects cost out at only 0.13% of the country's gross domestic product. And the cost will still be well below 1% even when all India's children in need have been reached.

– especially in giving up cigarettes and taking daily exercise.

In the very different circumstances of the developing world, where health has also tended to become associated only with white coats and hospitals, a new perception of the family as the prime guardian of its own health is also the precondition for a dramatic advance. And in most developing nations today, the frontiers to a healthier society can also be crossed by knowledge which enables families themselves to protect the lives and the health of their children by changes which are within their own power to realize.

But if this potential is to be fulfilled, then a very much more difficult breakthrough must now be made – a breakthrough not in knowledge, but in ways of putting what is already known at the disposal of many millions of families. How that task is being attempted in many nations of the world will be one of the principal subjects of this year's *State of the World's Children* report.

Health services

Clearly, the health services are essential. Equally clearly, they are not enough. In the developing world today, two-thirds of the population has no regular access to modern health facilities. If the child survival revolution is to be a revolution for the majority, it must therefore depend more on ordinary families than on medical institutions.

This, in turn, means that our mental map of child health care needs to be radically revised. In the conventional 'circle of health', it is the paediatricians, the doctors and the hospitals which are seen as 'the centre'. Less well-qualified health workers and village volunteers are known as 'workers at the periphery'. Mothers and children, needless to say, are the periphery itself.

To further the present potential, it will be necessary to turn this circle inside out. The mother needs to be seen as the centre of child health care. It is she who is the highest-level health worker – not in training or in qualifications but in time and love, in the special knowledge of her own children, in the breadth of 'integrated services' she provides, and in the permanent presence she brings to her child's life.

The empowering of the mother, and the building of concentric circles of support around her, is therefore the only approach which can realistically hope to bring the benefits of a child survival revolution to the majority of the developing world's children. For it is the mother who is usually responsible for deciding whether or not she will be immunized against tetanus during her pregnancy; whether or not a trained person will be present at the birth; whether oral rehydration therapy will be used to prevent dehydration; whether to breast-feed and for how long; when to wean and with what foods; whether hands and cooking surfaces are frequently washed; whether bouts of diarrhoea will be treated by withholding food or by continued feeding; whether a child will be taken for a full course of immunization; and whether there will be an adequate interval before the next child is born.

Empowering mothers with present knowledge and techniques of child protection is therefore the key to unlocking the present potential for a revolution in child health. But the responsibility for turning that key rests with the whole of society. For the mother cannot act alone, should not bear the responsibility alone, and cannot be empowered by information alone.

To use new knowledge and techniques, the mother needs the moral encouragement and practical support of all the concentric circles around her. She needs the partnership of her husband and the co-operation of her parents-in-law; she needs the solidarity and example of her friends and neighbours; she needs the advice of a trained and trusted person in her own locality; she needs to feel that she has the sanction of her spiritual and political leaders; and she needs the confidence of knowing that what she is doing has the blessing of those whom she trusts and respects.

On another plane, she needs more access to education and income-earning opportunities; she needs a little more say in the allocation of the family's food, money and work; and she needs basic technologies to relieve her of drudgery and give her more energy and time.

I THE STATE OF THE WORLD'S CHILDREN 1985

Bangladesh: surviving the autumn

Extracts from a speech made by Bangladeshi Health Minister Major-General Shamsul Haq to the Consultative Group of the International Centre for Diarrhoeal Disease Research, Bangladesh (ICDDR,B)

Oral rehydration therapy (ORT), developed in its present form at the ICDDR,B in Bangladesh, can rightly be called the medical miracle of this century. For it has proven to be the most successful tool for combating a curse that has stalked mankind from earliest times down to the present.

In Bangladesh, where diarrhoea continues to be endemic, we have an old adage: "If you survive one autumn, you will survive another year." This is because the incidence of diarrhoeal diseases peaks as flood waters recede in the autumn. However, we now have the technology with which to combat diarrhoea. This technology is simple, effective and cheap; and with its timely administration, most deaths due to diarrhoea can be avoided.

Lest there be any doubt about the importance of ORT, let me point out that in many areas of Bangladesh where the government has collaborative programmes with the ICDDR,B, deaths due to cholera, the most dreaded of the diarrhoeal diseases, have been reduced by over 50%.

Moreover, I am proud to say that before the development of ORT, it was the ICDDR,B that developed the first effective intravenous fluid preparations widely used to prevent diarrhoeal dehydration deaths. Yet intravenous therapy was not the answer for a country such as Bangladesh: it requires qualified medical personnel and must be administered at static health facilities.

To reach such facilities, diarrhoeal disease victims have to be taken long distances, using primitive means of transport. All too often diarrhoeal dehydration kills swiftly – and victims often die travelling the last hundred yards to a treatment clinic. In our country, where there is only one doctor for 20,000 persons, the only answer for successful treatment of diarrhoeal disease is to teach people to treat their families at home. Community studies in Bangladesh have shown that home-based ORT can easily be taught to a family member. This self-management of problems is also a crucial background for the development of effective primary health care.

There is another benefit to home-based ORT: that is the release of scarce hospital facililities which otherwise would be occupied by diarrhoeal disease patients.

With all these advantages, there is, however, still a problem. Oral rehydration salts are usually made available in plastic packets – to be mixed with water. Such packets, though easy to use, are still not readily available in rural areas of developing countries. Though they are cheap, they are still beyond the purchasing power of most poor people, people who are struggling for their very survival.

To overcome these problems, ICDDR,B scientists have developed a highly simplified oral solution, which can be produced at the lowest possible cost. This new solution is based on cereals, and uses ingredients readily available in all households. In addition, the cereal-based mix may contribute to improved nutritional status of those most vulnerable to diarrhoea – poor, young children.

For developing-country peoples in Asia, Africa and Latin America, ORT holds the promise of healthier childhoods and more productive adult lives. A country such as Bangladesh, whose prime asset is its human resources, hardly can afford to allow diarrhoea to sap the vitality of its population. To deliver a nation from the curse of diarrhoea will truly be a major step towards that nation's economic emancipation.

Wider still, the mother also needs the support of the mass media and communications industries, of all departments of government, of financial and development policies, and of aid, trade, and financial policies in the industrialized world itself.

In particular, recent research in the developing world has highlighted three kinds of support for women which are of such potential significance for their own and their children's health that they must also now be counted among the breakthroughs in knowledge which could change the ratio between a country's health and wealth. These changes are sometimes known as the three Fs:-

○ **Female education:** even within low-income communities, a child born to a mother with no education has been shown to be twice as likely to die in infancy as a child born to a mother with even four years of schooling.

○ **Family spacing:** infant and child deaths have been found to be, on average, twice as high when the interval between births is less than two years (fig. 3).

○ **Food supplements:** a handful of extra food each day for at-risk pregnant women has been shown to reduce the risk of low birth-weight – a risk which carries with it a two or three times greater likelihood of death in infancy (fig. 4).

Although more difficult and costly to bring about, such changes would not only slow population growth and improve the health and well-being of millions of the world's children, they would also represent a step forward in justice and human rights for the majority of the world's women.

The capacity to reach

Like all 'knowledge breakthroughs', the currently available techniques for improving child health depend upon equivalent 'social breakthroughs' in the capacity to organize and communicate. Low-cost techniques are, in themselves, not enough; there must also be mechanisms and channels for reaching out to inform and support parents in the management of those techniques.

By dint of tremendous efforts over the last twenty years, most nations of the developing world have now made that 'social breakthrough'. Twenty years ago, for example, the proportion of girls who had the chance to go to school was less than one-third: today it is over 80%. Twenty years ago, the radio was a rarity: today there are over 8,000 radio stations broadcasting to over 1 billion transistors. Twenty years ago, the printed mass media were relatively undeveloped: today the developing world has 8,000 daily newspapers and one-third of the world's readership (excluding China). Twenty years ago, there were hardly any trained paramedics or community development

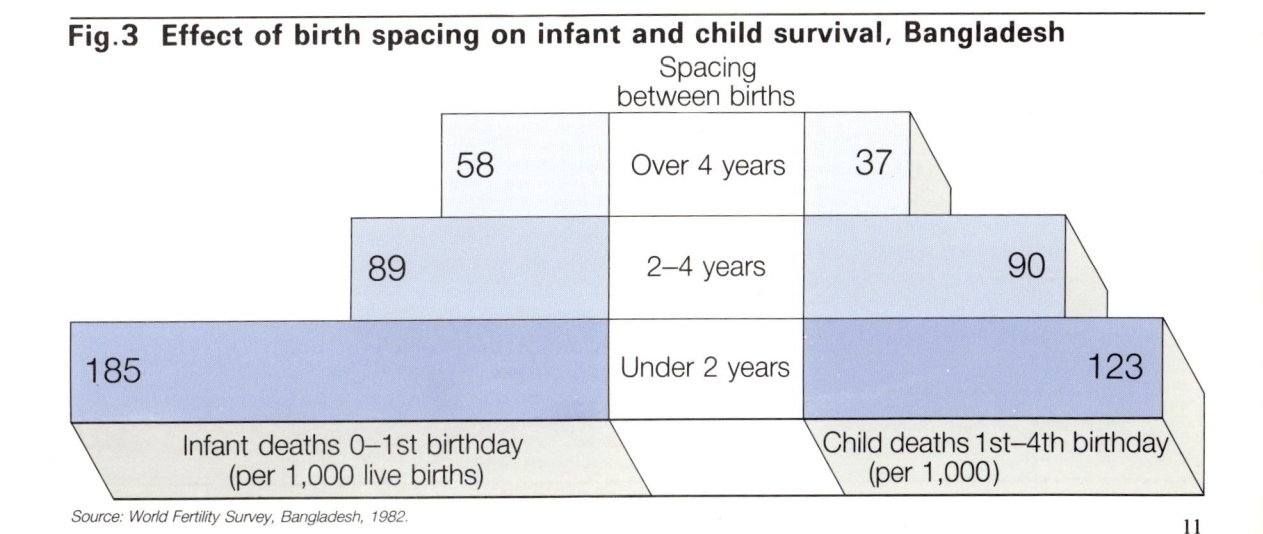

Fig.3 Effect of birth spacing on infant and child survival, Bangladesh

Infant deaths 0–1st birthday (per 1,000 live births)	Spacing between births	Child deaths 1st–4th birthday (per 1,000)
58	Over 4 years	37
89	2–4 years	90
185	Under 2 years	123

Source: World Fertility Survey, Bangladesh, 1982.

I THE STATE OF THE WORLD'S CHILDREN 1985

Nigeria and the Sudan: immunizing more for less

Years of experience with immunization have shown that simply making it available is not enough. Often, only half of the children are brought along to the vaccination centre and only half of those return for the second and third 'shots'.

For immunization to work, parents need to understand what it has to offer. And they must also be able to get their children immunized without making major sacrifices in the time and effort needed to cope with the day-to-day business of survival in poverty.

This year, two campaigns in Africa have shown what can be achieved when these two conditions are met:-

By July 1983, immunization had been 'available' for seven years to the 335,000 people of Owo district in Ondo state, Nigeria. But only 9% of the children had been vaccinated – partly because Owo's 15 clinics lacked reliable supplies of fuel to keep vaccines refrigerated.

Towards the end of 1983 the state authorities launched a new kind of immunization campaign. Within a month, nearly 30% of children had been vaccinated. Within twelve months, the campaign had surpassed its target of 80%. And as the vaccination tally rose, the cost per child diminished.

Technical breakthroughs played their part, notably the use of improved cold boxes. Cheap, large, light, and able to keep vaccines cool for a week, the boxes and their cargo were swiftly shipped in and out from a single refrigeration depot.

But 'social breakthroughs' were even more crucial. Before starting the campaign, the organizers enlisted the support of all the community leaders. So the campaign was promoted not only by the health services but by the *oba* and *kayibesi* traditional chiefs, the schoolteachers, the Chief Imam, the Catholic bishop, by information leaflets and posters, by radio and television, and by loudspeaker vans touring the villages.

Soon the clinics, used to only a trickle of 'customers' on immunization days, were besieged by mothers and children. More parents knew about the *need* for immunization. And because immunization posts were also set up in marketplaces, schools and churches, more parents were *able* to bring their children for a full course of vaccines.

Two thousand miles away, in the city of Juba, Sudan, similar methods have been scoring similar successes.

After two years of Juba's expanded immunization programme, a survey was commissioned to assess its impact. The findings were depressing. Only 8% of the city's young children were immunized. And only 40% of the parents even knew that immunization was available.

The Public Health Department decided to try a different approach – starting in the Kator district of the city.

Realizing that its own outreach was limited, the Department invited other organizations to join in the campaign, including the Department of Youth and Sports, several non-governmental organizations and the informal leaders of Kator district itself. Next, the council's extension workers were given a month's in-service training in *communications*, specializing in low-cost and traditional methods such as story-telling, drama and group discussion. Backed by weekly radio programmes, articles in the *Nile Mirror*, and a touring loudspeaker car, the council workers have been visiting every home to encourage parents to bring their children to the immunization centres and to stress the importance of a full course of injections.

The result so far: the proportion of Kator's children under two fully protected by immunization has risen from less than 10% to more than 40%.

In both of these cases, success has been a spur. Since January 1984, the Juba authorities have been extending the campaign to the entire city. And in October 1984, Nigeria's Head of State personally launched a programme to try to repeat – on a national scale – the successes of the Owo campaign.

workers: today the governments of the developing world have trained over 3 million paramedics and unknown numbers of community workers, water engineers, extension workers, and village volunteers.

As never before, these and other mechanisms by which parents might be informed, involved and supported in bringing about a child survival revolution are now in place in most nations of the world. Too numerous to list, some examples of these mechanisms can be drawn from among those already working in the service of child survival strategies:-

The rapid expansion of primary-school education has enabled a country like Nigeria to call upon its 230,000 primary-school teachers to promote knowledge about ORT and immunization to many millions of children and their parents.

The existence of several thousand family planning workers in Indonesia has made it possible – with retraining – to carry child survival strategies into millions of homes.

The training of 86,000 village hand-pump caretakers in Karnataka, India, has meant that the state government can now call on 86,000 more village 'promoters' in its campaign to make ORT available to families.

In addition to these government resources, people's movements in the developing world have grown in both number and organizational capacity over the last two decades. Ten years ago, the New Naam movement in the north of Burkina-Faso (formerly Upper Volta) was only reaching out to a few Mossi settlements: today it has 45,000 members in 700 villages and volunteer Naam workers are being trained to make ORT and other child protection strategies available to all families. Twenty years ago, the Sarvodaya movement was a handful of teachers in a work-camp just outside Colombo, Sri Lanka: today it has 6,000 volunteers, mostly young women, who are now mobilizing to carry the child survival revolution to over 4,000 villages throughout the island.

Also in the last twenty years, the capacity and outreach of organized religion has grown to the point where it has become a major development resource as well as a spiritual force in many developing nations. Today, thousands of imams in Indonesia are promoting the advantages of breast-feeding and growth monitoring. And in the Maldives, child survival messages are now regularly included in the national Friday sermon broadcast by radio to the main mosques on every inhabited island. In Brazil, the Catholic Church now has over 14,000 health workers and the National Conference of Brazilian Bishops has decided to put the child survival revolution into action in almost every diocese within the next three years. (Early indications are that the infant mortality rate has already been reduced by 50% in the pilot area of Florestopolis.)

Similarly, in Colombia, priests are beginning to inform all couples who come for pre-marital and

Fig.4 Impact of malnutrition during pregnancy on perinatal mortality

The winter of 1944–45 was a time of acute food-shortage in the Netherlands. The chart below shows the effect of shortages on those born, and those conceived, during Holland's 'hunger winter.'

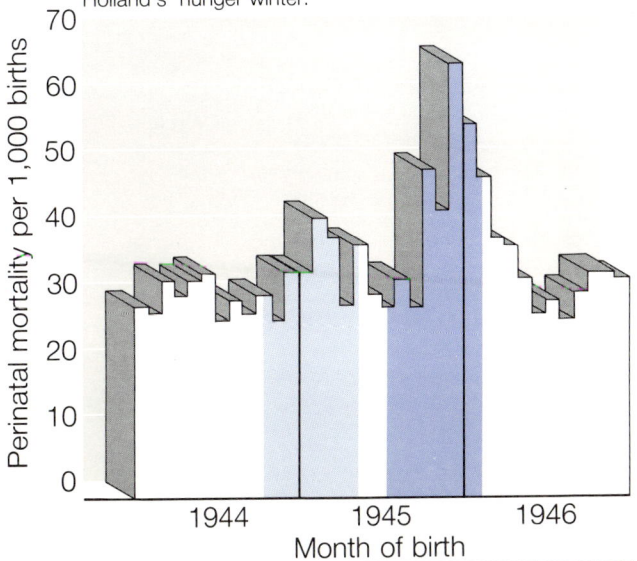

[Bar chart: Perinatal mortality per 1,000 births by month of birth, 1944–1946, showing peaks during and after the food shortage period]

- Born during food shortage
- Conceived during food shortage

Note: The perinatal mortality rate is the total number of deaths, including still births, between the end of the 23rd week of gestation and the end of the first week of life – per 1,000 **total** births.

Source: Adapted from: The Prevention of Handicap of Early Pregnancy Origin, Margaret and Arthur Wynn, Foundation for Education and Research in Child-Bearing, 1981.

I THE STATE OF THE WORLD'S CHILDREN 1985

Cheraga: child deaths down 60%

A child survival revolution has already come to the Cheraga district of Algeria. The rate of infant deaths among the population of 150,000 has been cut by 60% in only five years. Simple, low-cost measures – such as breast-feeding, immunization and vitamin D supplements to prevent rickets, as well as the use of growth charts and education about oral rehydration therapy – have lowered the infant mortality rate from 103 to 43 deaths per 1,000 live births.

This dramatic fall was the direct result of a child health plan designed and implemented by a team of Algerian doctors. Moving away from the centralized hospital tradition, the Cheraga health plan established a network of 18 local health centres close to the homes of the local population.

According to a report on the Cheraga experience by Dr. Emile Gautier of the Vaudois University Hospital Centre in Lausanne, Switzerland, this decentralized approach has the advantage of making parents "more responsible for the health of their children". At the same time, the new approach has also protected the one hospital in the district "from being overwhelmed by large numbers of children in need of primary care and preventive measures," freeing it to care for the more severely ill. During the five-year period from 1976 to 1981, consultations at the health centres rose from 28,171 to 97,662; those at the hospital only rose from 24,346 to 35,713.

The basic strategy was to "capture the births of the children who would live in the district". So the nearest health centre began a medical record for each new-born infant, registering every treatment.

Initially, very few of the children were protected by immunization. Over the next five years, primary health workers visited every child's home to talk to parents about the importance of immunization, and to tell them when and where vaccination was available. By 1981, 90% of the children had been immunized against tuberculosis, 80% against polio, diphtheria, whooping cough and tetanus, and 75% against measles.

When the programme began, 13% of Cheraga's children were afflicted by rickets – a bone disease caused by vitamin D deficiency. By 1981, more than 65% had received vitamin D supplements, usually given with the vaccines.

More than 50% of infant and child deaths were accounted for by diarrhoeal infections and malnutrition. To reduce this figure, campaigns were launched to inform parents about the prevention and treatment of diarrhoea. Families were taught – in classes and in their homes – how to mix and administer oral rehydration solutions. Mothers were also taught that by breast-feeding their babies, they could provide natural immunity for their infants against common infant illnesses.

Health workers and families also paid particular attention to the children's weight curve. The children were weighed at every immunization and every time they were brought to the health centre, so that any early signs of malnutrition or faltering growth could be detected on their growth charts.

Though the centres were staffed by a team of trained medical personnel, it was the more than 40 primary health workers – local people with no previous training in nursing – who had the job of working directly with the families to bring about improvements in child health. Their efforts enabled the health centres to maintain contact with approximately 90% of the children in the Cheraga district.

Nearly 150,000 children under five are now dying in Algeria each year. The government is drawing up plans to halve the infant and child mortality rate within the next five years, and has launched a national oral rehydration programme as the first stage in the new campaign. If the national programme comes close to the success of the Cheraga experiment, the lives of 75,000 children under five will be saved every year.

pre-baptism classes that low-cost techniques are now available for protecting the lives and the health of their children. In 1984, on the Sunday before each of the three National Vaccination Days, the sermon in most of Colombia's 2,280 parishes was devoted to the importance of taking young children to be immunized (see panel 1).

In the Philippines, the President of the Catholic Bishops' Conference has also launched a campaign to begin a child survival revolution, starting with the example of his own diocese.

In Rome, the Holy See has announced that *"the entire Catholic aid network in the various countries of the world, and especially in the developing nations, will lend its maximum support to these important simple proposals to improve the health of hundreds of millions of children"*.

In many nations, voluntary organizations have also now grown in number and capacity to a point where they are among the most important of all organized resources for the national development effort. India alone now has 12,000 private voluntary organizations – often working with innovative ideas among the very poorest people. In neighbouring Bangladesh there are more than 6,000 separate voluntary agencies working for development – among them the Bangladesh Rural Advancement Committee which, by bus, bicycle, and rickshaw, has taken the ORT message to over 2 million homes over the last three years (see panel 19). In Zaire there are over 1,000 hospitals run by voluntary and religious organizations. In Uganda, they provide between 40% and 60% of all modern health services. And in almost all nations, women's organizations have either been founded or rapidly expanded in the last decade. Today, oral rehydration therapy and other low-cost child survival strategies are being promoted by the Organization of Angolan Women, by the Patriotic Women's Association of Laos, by the Revolutionary Ethiopian Women's Association, by the Indonesian National Village Women's Movement, by the Botswana Council of Women, by the Nursing Mothers' Association of the Philippines, by the Women's Unions and Committees for Mothers and Children in Viet Nam, by the 'Women of the South' in the Dominican Republic, by the Federation of Cuban Women (with its 48,000 'health cadets'), by the *mahila mandals* of India, and by the Saemaul Undong Village Women's Movement which counts among its members the women of over 2,000 villages throughout the Republic of Korea.

In some countries, international voluntary agencies also represent a powerful and organized resource.* This year, for example, the League of Red Cross and Red Crescent Societies has launched its world-wide 'Child Alive' campaign based on promoting ORT, breast-feeding, immunization and other low-cost methods of protecting children in poor communities. Already, the potential importance of the Red Cross commitment to a child survival revolution has been dramatically demonstrated in Colombia's immunization campaign (see panel 1). For the three National Vaccination Days, the Colombian Red Cross mobilized 7,000 of its first-aid workers, 5,000 of its youth leaders, and 1,600 of its 'grey ladies' to be trained as vaccinators and organizers in the task of immunizing almost all of Colombia's children. In addition, a total of 16,000 Red Cross volunteers helped with the promotion and administration of the campaign.

In all of this, the health services themselves have the crucial role of providing training, referral services, and essential medical skills to back up the work of all the many other resources which can be mobilized in support of the child survival

---

* Internationally, Save the Children Fund organizations in Sweden (Rädda Barnen), Norway (Redd Barna), the United Kingdom and the United States, are among many organizations now promoting low-cost strategies for child protection. In Gamu Gafu, southern Ethiopia, Oxfam is introducing the rice-based oral rehydration technique developed in Bangladesh. In London, the Teaching Aids at Low Cost (TALC) organization is making available millions of growth charts and double-ended plastic spoons specially designed to measure out the right quantities of sugar and salt for oral rehydration solutions. Other voluntary organizations actively working to bring about a revolution in child survival include Zonta International, Defence for Children International, the International Catholic Child Bureau, Baha'i International, Rotary Club International, Soroptimist International, Catholic Relief Services, CARE, the Christian Children's Fund, World Vision, the World View International Foundation, and the world organizations of the Girl Guides and Scouts. In Indonesia, 10 million Scouts may soon be in line for merit badges for proficiency in oral rehydration therapy.

I THE STATE OF THE WORLD'S CHILDREN 1985

revolution. And with growing acceptance of the idea of primary health care, the professional health services in several nations are beginning to respond to this challenge by deploying their expertise through channels and organizations – be they paramedics or traditional birth attendants or the mass media – which reach out to much larger numbers of people than the health services themselves.

In most nations, the steady development of these ways of reaching people means that another priceless asset has moved into place. Perhaps for the first time, large areas of the developing world have the organizational and communication infrastructure to reach out to inform and support the majority in bringing about change. And it is this new capacity, as much as the low-cost techniques themselves, which now makes possible a revolution in child health and survival.

In most regions of the developing world, therefore, enough of the elusive pre-conditions for such a revolution are now in place. The technologies and the knowledge are available. The idea of primary health care and the empowering of parents rather than institutions has been widely accepted. And the organizational capacity to put these techniques and these ideas at the disposal of the majority, and to achieve a child survival and development revolution, is greater than ever before. In short, it can now be done – if the world wants it.

Protection in Poverty

The front line in the long war on poverty and underdevelopment is and remains the struggle for economic justice and growth. And the fundamental issues of women's rights, land reform, disarmament, income distribution, job creation, fairer aid and trade policies, and a more equitable international order remain fundamental determinants of children's survival, health and well-being (see figs. 5 and 6). But while that struggle is being waged, an extraordinary opportunity has now arisen to strengthen the 'second front'. Most parents in poor communities could now be given the knowledge and the support to enable them to protect their children from the worst effects of that poverty in their most vulnerable, vital years of growth. And in so doing, a long-awaited blow could be struck against development's 'enemy within' – the self-perpetuating cycle of ill-health, poor growth, and lowered potential by which the poverty of one generation casts its shadow on the next.

Ironically, this potential for significantly improving the 'state of the world's children' arises at a time when the economic position of many of the world's poorest families is becoming steadily worse (see panel 8).

Large areas of the developing world are suffering from the backlash of the world's longest economic recession since the 1930s. Rising protectionism, falling imports, and higher interest rates in the industrialized nations have eroded the third world's earnings and deepened its debts. The result is a fall in real incomes for the majority of nations in Latin America (where average per capita incomes fell in 17 out of 19 countries during 1983 and GNP in the region as a whole dropped by over 5%) and in Africa (where drought now adds to the burden of a recession which has reduced already low average incomes by 2.4% a year in 1981 and 1982) (see panel 3).*

This year, UNICEF has published a specially commissioned study of the recession – from the point of view of the children of the world's poorest communities. The study points out that the poorer a family is, the higher the percentage of

---

* In low-income Asia, where many of the most populous nations are more insulated from the effects of recession in the West, average incomes grew by less than 2% a year in 1981-1982 – more slowly than in the 1970s.

its income spent on necessities – food, water, fuel, and health care. Any fall in that income therefore means a fall in the capability to sustain life itself. And in such circumstances, it is the developing minds and bodies of young children which are most at risk.

To compound the hardship of falling incomes, the social services have often been the first to suffer from cut-backs in government spending which recession, debts, or international monetary policy may enforce. And it is again the poorest who are most dependent on the social services.

The conclusion of the study was therefore that the main impact of recession, in the developing countries, is being borne by those least able to sustain it – simply because they have neither the political muscle to prevent it nor the economic fat to absorb it.

Fig.5 Number and percentage unable to meet basic needs, 1974–82

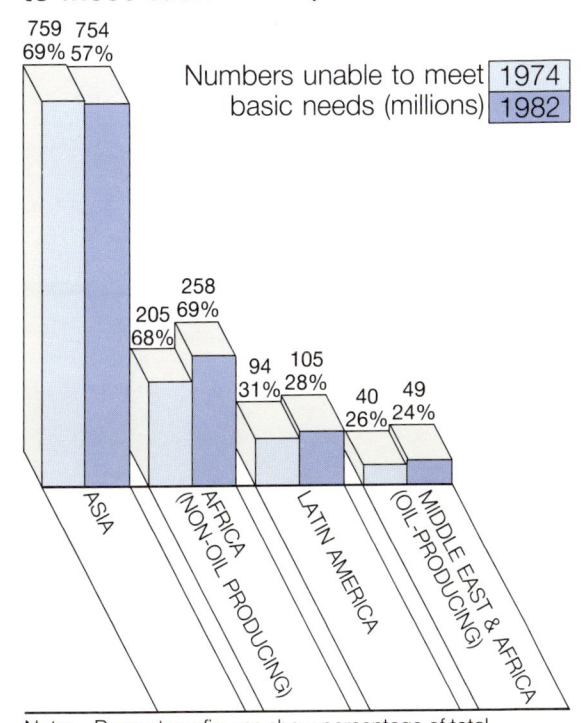

Region	1974	1982
ASIA	759 (69%)	754 (57%)
AFRICA (NON-OIL PRODUCING)	205 (68%)	258 (69%)
LATIN AMERICA	94 (31%)	105 (28%)
MIDDLE EAST & AFRICA (OIL-PRODUCING)	40 (26%)	49 (24%)

Numbers unable to meet basic needs (millions)

Note: Percentage figures show percentage of total population in each region.

Source: World Bank

Safety net

Very few hard facts are known about the effect of all this on the children of the developing world – and that in itself is evidence of how little they are taken into account when calculating recession's cost. But from small gleanings, we do know that average height-for-age has declined among the children of northern Zambia, that low birth-weights (an indicator of malnutrition even before the child is born) are on the increase in certain parts of Brazil, that the number of children being treated for severe malnutrition has trebled in Costa Rica over the last three years (despite a continued commitment to health and social services), and that nutritional 'wasting' has increased among the children of Sri Lanka during the 1980s.

A world which has pretensions towards civilization cannot long allow the severest economic blows to be borne by its poorest women and children. And it is not an immutable law that the poor must always suffer most when hard times become harder. Several times this century, we have seen examples of what governments can do – when the will is there – to protect the most vulnerable members of human society from the most serious consequences of economic hardship.

Out of the economic collapse of the 1930s, for example, arose the 'New Deal' in the United States and the strengthening of the welfare systems in many European countries. Again in the 1940s, war brought destruction and shortages which could have pushed many more Europeans into destitution. But because governments made optimum use of available resources, and made it a wartime priority to ensure a basic level of food and health care for their populations, starvation and destitution was kept to a minimum. In the United Kingdom, for example, the overall level of health and nutrition among the nation's children was maintained at a higher level in the scarcity years of 1940-1945 than in the immediate pre-war or post-war periods when resources were more abundant.

Since the 1930s, a safety net has therefore been in place in the industrialized world. And however imperfect it may be, it protects the majority of the vulnerable from falling into destitution. Now, the

I THE STATE OF THE WORLD'S CHILDREN 1985

The Recession: women and children last

The special study published by UNICEF earlier this year on the impact of the world recession on the world's children uncovered some grim facts about falling family incomes and cut-backs in government expenditure on social services.* Analysing those facts, the study also showed that recession strikes progressively harder at those with the least to fall back on – the developing countries, the poorest population groups in those countries, and finally the most vulnerable group of all – the poorest mothers and their young children.

Since the study was commissioned the recession has begun to lift in the industrialized countries – modestly in Europe, more strongly in the North American economy. The developing countries, too, have begun to show signs of recovery; their GNP per capita, which fell by 2.5% in 1983, was due to rise by 0.5% or 1% in 1984. But so far the improvement is concentrated in the relatively well-off countries of east and south-east Asia. India, for instance, has regained some of its momentum, largely because of improved agricultural production. In the Republic of Korea, GNP has grown rapidly over the last two years and infant mortality has fallen to the lowest level ever recorded.

But elsewhere prospects are bleak. There is no sign of recovery in Africa, the poorest of all the continents, with governments beset by low earnings and high debt and with an estimated 150 million people at risk from the effects of three years of drought. In Nigeria, for example, government revenue has dropped by more than half over the past two years. The numbers of severely malnourished children are rising, and hunger has been a daily theme in newspaper editorials during 1984.

In Latin America, per capita incomes fell in 17 out of 19 countries during 1983, and GNP in the region as a whole dropped by over 5%. Crippling debt repayments have forced massive retrenchments, with social welfare programmes the first to suffer. During 1983, prices more than quintupled in Argentina, more than quadrupled in Bolivia, tripled in Brazil, and more than doubled in Peru: in Mexico they rose by 80% and in Ecuador and Uruguay by more than 50%.

Though statistics are hard to come by, these economic stresses have been levying their toll on children:-

○ Infant mortality is rising sharply in the poorer states of Brazil: in some parts of the north-east, one in five children is dying before reaching the age of one year.

○ In Bolivia, food prices rose tenfold in the year ending June 1984, and drought has reduced the 1984 harvest to an estimated 60% of normal. Infant mortality rates have remained stable, thanks to major immunization and oral rehydration campaigns, but child malnutrition has increased steeply in the drought areas.

○ In Peru, GNP per capita dropped by more than 14% in 1983 and continued to fall in 1984. The Food and Agriculture Organization of the United Nations judges that 63% of households do not earn enough to buy even an adequate diet. Outbreaks of tuberculosis, malaria, and other infectious diseases are increasingly common.

○ In Sri Lanka, inflation and cut-backs in government spending have eroded the food-stamp programme and led to an increase in malnutrition among the children of the poor.

At the start of 1984 the UNICEF study predicted that the worst was yet to come. The prediction holds for those countries which have been unable to improve their economic performance – or to shield their children from the worst consequences of recession.

---

* The study forms Chapter IV of the hardback version of *The State of the World's Children 1984*, published by Oxford University Press. It is also available as an offprint from UNICEF offices.

time has come to fashion the first strands of such a safety net for the poorest and most vulnerable families of the developing world, families who live in the permanent but silent emergency of poverty and underdevelopment, families who each year suffer the deaths of 15 million of their children.

Morally, few people would accept that a small percentage downturn in an $8 trillion world economy should mean an increase in low birthweight, malnutrition, frequency of illness, and poor mental and physical growth among the most vulnerable children in the poorest quarter of human society. And if we do not accept that morally, then the time has come to ask what can be done about it practically. For those families whose standard of living does not allow for the normal development of their children – whether the cause be economic recession or pre-existing poverty – a minimum protection should be provided against the worst effects of economic deprivation. And that can now be achieved at a very low cost to the world community.

The case for such a safety net is a case which rests not only on common humanity but also on common sense. The growth of a human brain is 90% complete by the time a child is four years old. Poor growth during those vital vulnerable years usually means that the child will never fulfil the mental and physical potential with which he or she was born. Many times it has been argued and demonstrated that it is a nation's human resources which are the key to its social and economic progress and that investment in people makes economic sense. In its 1980 *World Development Report*, for example, the World Bank concluded that the right kind of social investment in such things as primary education and health care can yield an average economic return of up to 25% a year – far higher than can be expected from most investments in physical goods. It therefore makes

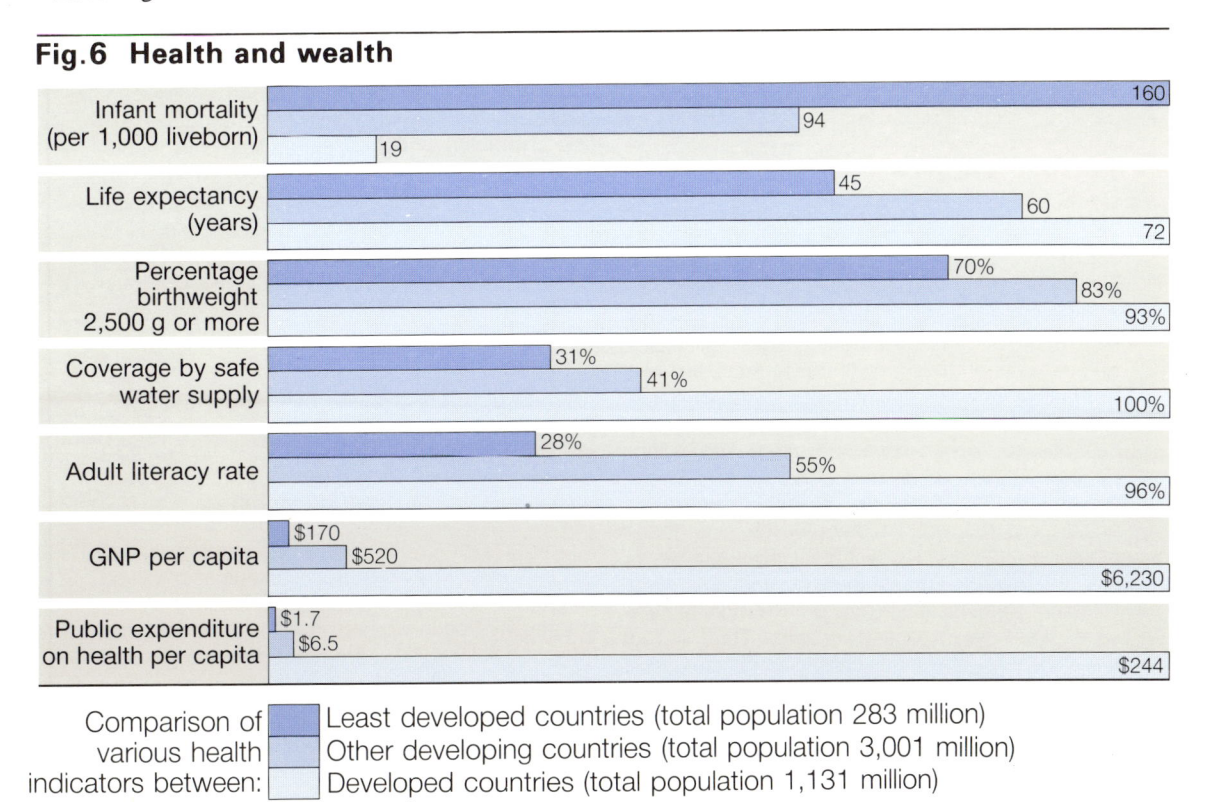

Fig.6 Health and wealth

Indicator	Least developed	Other developing	Developed
Infant mortality (per 1,000 liveborn)	160	94	19
Life expectancy (years)	45	60	72
Percentage birthweight 2,500 g or more	70%	83%	93%
Coverage by safe water supply	31%	41%	100%
Adult literacy rate	28%	55%	96%
GNP per capita	$170	$520	$6,230
Public expenditure on health per capita	$1.7	$6.5	$244

Comparison of various health indicators between:
- Least developed countries (total population 283 million)
- Other developing countries (total population 3,001 million)
- Developed countries (total population 1,131 million)

Note: The figures are weighted averages based on data for 1980 or latest available year
Source: Global Strategy for Health for All by the year 2000, World Health Organization, Geneva, 1981.

I THE STATE OF THE WORLD'S CHILDREN 1985

Disabilities: the preventable burden

One in ten of the world's people – some 460 million – suffer from mental or physical disability. Four out of five live in developing countries. And one-third are children under fifteen. The low-cost child survival techniques discussed in this report would also reduce this unacceptable toll:-

○ Expanded immunization would prevent polio, which cripples half a million children every year. In some developing countries between two and nine of every 1,000 schoolchildren are lame.

○ Measles, a major killer, can also lead to malnutrition and disability. In about 30% of cases, the children who survive the disease fall prey to its complications: conjunctivitis, which can cause blindness; middle-ear infection and subsequent deafness; encephalitis, which can cause permanent brain damage; and severe malnutrition resulting from loss of appetite and diarrhoea.

○ Tuberculosis can eventually lead to meningitis, spinal deformity, swollen joints, and the chronic incapacity of pulmonary tuberculosis.

Not all disabilities are as obvious as deafness or lameness. Many millions of children fall victim to the invisible disability of poor mental and physical development, caused by the frequency of illnesses and assaults on their growth during those first two or three years which are most vital for the evolution of brain and body. Once that growth opportunity has passed, it can never be caught up again. So poor growth in childhood is the most widespread – though the least noticeable – form of disability in the world today. All the main techniques of the child survival revolution – oral rehydration therapy, breast-feeding and improved weaning, immunization, and growth monitoring – save lives by protecting growth. They would therefore also save many millions of children from physical and mental handicap.

Another key element in the child survival revolution is preventing low birth-weight, which carries with it such a high risk of death and poor growth in infancy. Of the 21 million low birth-weight babies born every year, over 19 million are born in developing countries, where two out of three pregnant women are anaemic and many are malnourished. Even a handful of extra rice each day in the last three months of pregnancy can go a long way towards preventing low birth-weight. Better diet or inexpensive iron supplements can ward off anaemia. Once again, such a strategy could prevent disabilities as well as saving lives: children born underweight are four to six times more vulnerable to mental or physical handicap than babies of normal birth-weight.

Other disabilities, too, can be prevented at low cost, although supplying the remedies can prove complex. Iodine deficiency, which in some mountainous parts of the world sets entire populations at risk of stunted growth, deaf-mutism and mental retardation, can be prevented for a few cents by adding iodine to salt and other common foods or by injections of iodated oil. Lack of vitamin A blinds an estimated 500,000 children every year and can be remedied by vitamin supplements costing 20 cents or less a year per person, or by teaching mothers to feed their children green vegetables.

When disability has not been prevented, children who develop impairments need early diagnosis and rehabilitation to help them realize their potential. Yet 98% of the developing world's disabled have no access to trained help.

One solution is community-based rehabilitation programmes, which call on the resources of village health workers and villagers themselves. When community health workers in Toluca, Mexico, had been specially trained, they substantially improved the living conditions of 70% of the disabled in their charge; only 10% needed specialized rehabilitation services. Such programmes cost only $9 a year for each disabled person.

neither economic nor political sense to allow children – the human resources of the future – to grow up with an impaired ability to contribute to and benefit from their nation's development.

An achievable aim

A safety net woven from the strands of minimum wages, unemployment pay, sickness benefit, and family allowances is, unfortunately, some way into the future for most people in the developing world. But a more elementary safety net of minimum food entitlements, primary health care, elementary education, safe sanitation, and clean water, could be put in place by most developing nations – if they can suspend one corner of that net on fair and stable policies of international trade and aid.

The subject of this report – as of its two predecessors – is an even more basic, more modest, and more immediate goal:-

Even in difficult economic times, it can be seen that a combination of changing knowledge and circumstance has opened up the possibility of providing a minimum safety net of the most basic protection for the growing minds and bodies of the world's most vulnerable children. The techniques are known. The organizational capacity is, broadly speaking, in place. The costs, both politically and financially, are absolutely minimal in relation to the benefits such protection would bring.

In short, we are faced not with a grandiose long-term plan dependent upon a thousand doubtful premises, but with a few specific tasks which most nations could realistically expect to achieve within the next few years. Specifically, all families could be enabled to use ORT, all children could be immunized, all mothers could become aware of the importance of breast-feeding and proper weaning, and almost all parents could have the means and the knowledge to prevent malnutrition through the monitoring of their children's growth. It is extraordinary that four such apparently simple propositions could so dramatically improve child health as to halve the rate of deaths, disabilities, and malnutrition. But this is the opportunity which present knowledge has now opened up. And we are therefore left with a stark question – have we the will to do it?

In the developing world, it is clear that the realization of this present potential depends, more than anything else, on the political commitment of a nation's leadership and the mobilization of all its organized resources. But many nations will also still require financial and practical help – especially in the form of foreign exchange. The industrialized world therefore also has an opportunity to demonstrate its commitment to the world's children.

Going into Action

As the basic techniques of the child survival revolution begin to go into action around the world, a body of experience is beginning to build up around them. But before looking at that experience in a little more detail, it is worth recording an important item of news which has emerged from the area of Bangladesh where much of the pioneering work on ORT has been done.

In the Matlab area, where child deaths have already been drastically reduced by ORT and other child survival strategies, the average size of families has begun to fall (see panel 14). With growing certainty that their children will survive, and with growing confidence in their own ability to take decisions which improve their own lives, the parents of Matlab are now making more use of family planning services. On average, the number of children per family is now two less than it was only a few years ago – a result better than that

21

I THE STATE OF THE WORLD'S CHILDREN 1985

Population growth: survival helps slow-down

Low-cost techniques now have the potential to save the lives of approximately 7 million children each year. But would the net result be another surge in world population? Paradoxically, the answer is no.

If reducing child deaths by half had no effect at all on the number of births, then population would increase because more children would survive to eventually have children of their own.* But all the evidence suggests that a reduction in the number of child deaths would also help to bring about a greater reduction in the number of child births:-

○ The death of an infant naturally means the end of breast-feeding – and of the contraceptive protection which breast-feeding provides. So saving a child's life may also help to postpone the next birth. Surveying many recent studies, Population Reports concludes that "breast-feeding makes a substantial contribution to birth-spacing and fertility control in many areas".

○ The greater the chance of a child's survival, the less the parents need to insure against loss by bearing more children than they actually want. Statistically, parents who suffer the loss of a child tend to have 0.5 more 'births' than parents whose children all survive. Saving a child's life might therefore be said to also prevent 'half a birth'. But over time, parents respond not only to their own direct experience but to falling child death rates in the community at large. So in practice, the effect on the birth rate would probably be much greater.

○ One of the key strategies for bringing about a child survival revolution is birth spacing itself, since it is now clear that infant and child mortality is typically one-and-a-half to two times higher when the average interval between births is less than two years than when the average interval is two to four years. Birth-spacing strategies will obviously lead directly to fewer births as well.

○ Rising levels of female education – another key child survival strategy – are also strongly associated with falling birth rates.

○ Probably the most important prerequisite for the acceptance of family planning is the realization by parents that they have the power to take important decisions to improve their own lives. Any change which reinforces parents' confidence in their own ability to improve their own circumstances is therefore a change which makes the acceptance of family planning more likely. As almost all the main strategies of the child survival revolution offer parents more control, so they are all strategies which increase the likelihood of parents opting for smaller families.

For all these reasons, reducing child deaths is likely to cause population growth to slow down and stabilize at an earlier date and at a lower level than would otherwise have been the case.

Broad-based evidence for this conclusion already exists: those countries and regions which have already achieved a revolution in child survival, such as China, Sri Lanka, the Republic of Korea, Cuba, Costa Rica, Singapore, and the state of Kerala, now have birth rates among the lowest in the developing world. If every developing nation had infant death rates and birth rates as low as Sri Lanka's, for example, then there would be 7.5 million fewer child deaths each year – *and 35 million fewer births.*

* Even if a reduction in child deaths had *no* effect on the birth rate, the increase in population would not be very great. Because family size has declined quite sharply in most parts of the world, the long-term population increase caused by saving a child's life today is very much less than in the 1950s or 1960s. Even if child deaths were halved overnight, for example, this would add only 10% to the 10.5 billion people who will finally inhabit the earth in the year 2110 – the point when world population growth is expected to stabilize.

achieved by family planning programmes in any other rural area of Bangladesh.

"What the people of Matlab have shown," says the Director of the International Centre for Diarrhoeal Disease Research, Bangladesh, *"is that a dramatic reduction in child deaths, far from causing a population explosion, will eventually result in lower rates of population growth"* (see panel 10 and fig. 7).

Before her tragic death, this fundamental connection between child survival and fertility decline was also spelt out by India's Prime Minister, Indira Gandhi, who noted that:-

"Parents are more likely to restrict their families if they have reasonable assurances of the health and survival of their two children."

Towards the end of 1984, in Mexico City, the World Population Conference agreed on a resolution to this same effect:-

"Through breast-feeding, adequate nutrition, clean water, immunization programmes, oral rehydration therapy, and birth-spacing, a virtual revolution in child survival could be achieved. The impact would be dramatic in humanitarian and fertility terms."

Oral rehydration therapy

On average, the child living in a poor community in the developing world will suffer an attack of diarrhoeal infection somewhere between two and six times per year. Every episode of diarrhoea lowers the child's nutritional level, and every episode carries with it the risk of death from dehydration. In a country like Bangladesh, for example, diarrhoeal dehydration kills almost 10% of all children.

The cause of diarrhoea is poverty – poor water supply, poor sanitation, poor health education, poor housing. ORT will not change that poverty. But it will provide a remarkable degree of protection from one of poverty's worst effects – and it is an essential strand in the safety net of minimum health and nutrition for children in the world's low-income communities.

In almost all cases, dehydration can be kept at bay by a parent who knows how to manage an episode of diarrhoea. If the parent knows that feeding should continue, that an oral rehydration solution should be given to the child from the beginning of the illness, and that enough should be given to replace the fluids lost during the

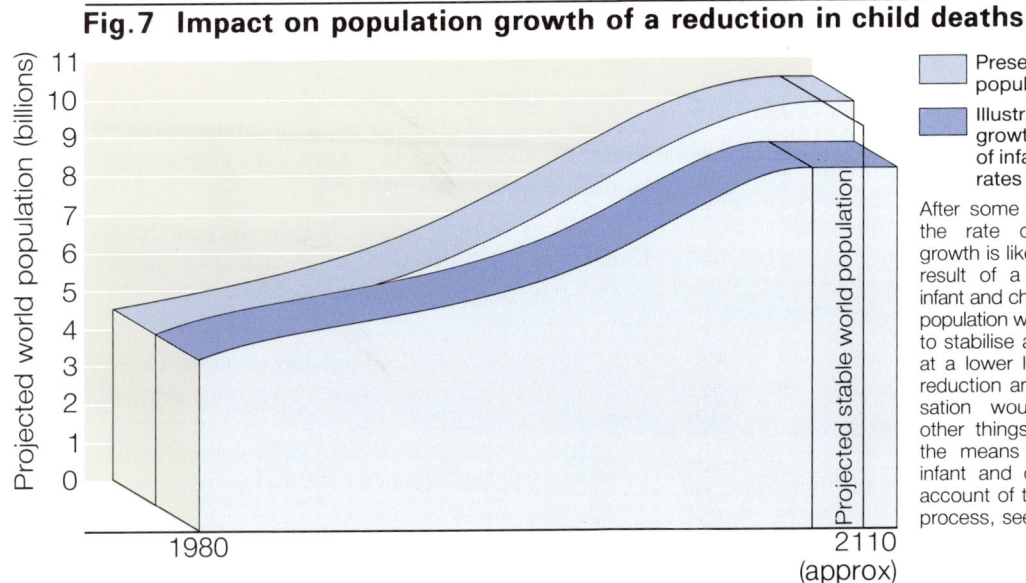

Fig. 7 Impact on population growth of a reduction in child deaths

Presently projected world population growth

Illustrative population growth assuming a halving of infant and child mortality rates over the next decade.

After some small initial increase, the rate of world population growth is likely to slow down as a result of a drastic reduction in infant and child deaths. Total world population would therefore be likely to stabilise at an earlier date and at a lower level. The size of the reduction and the date of stabilisation would depend, among other things, on the speed and the means of the reduction in infant and child deaths. For an account of the forces behind this process, see panel 10.

Source: UNICEF 1984

I THE STATE OF THE WORLD'S CHILDREN 1985

illness itself, and that help should be sought if the diarrhoea persists or if dehydration sets in, then the lives of several million young children a year could now be saved. At the same time, the use of oral rehydration salts can mitigate the impact of the illness on the child's growth.

But whatever the potential of the technique itself, the greatest breakthrough remains to be made: the knowledge of how and when to use oral rehydration therapy must now be put at the disposal of millions of parents the world over.

A similar breakthrough against any of the major causes of illness and death in the industrialized world would have become available throughout Europe and North America in a matter of months. Good news for the poor travels more slowly. But things are beginning to move:-

In one region of Honduras, 1,200 ORT demonstrators, backed by a radio campaign, have taught 93% of mothers how to use sachets of 'Litrosol' for oral rehydration therapy (see panel 20).

In neighbouring Nicaragua, 360 oral rehydration posts have been set up across the country (one for every 2,000 young children) and 5,000 *brigadistas*, backed by People's Health Councils, are carrying the ORT message to people's homes in a nation-wide ORT campaign.

In Haiti, the proportion of mothers using ORT when their children have diarrhoea (which is responsible for almost half of all child deaths in Haiti) has risen from 2% to 34% after only six months of a campaign – including intensive radio advertising – to teach parents how to use the new therapy. In several smaller surveys taken after one year, the proportion had increased to more than 60%.

In Brazil, 14 million sachets of salts were produced in 1983 and 10 million more in the first six months of 1984 to back up ORT campaigns in 16 out of the nation's 23 states and for export to Bolivia, Peru and Suriname. With three laboratories now manufacturing oral rehydration salts, production capacity has risen to 36 million sachets a year.

In Bangladesh, 1,200 workers from the Bangladesh Rural Advancement Committee have personally visited 2.5 million homes to teach parents how to make oral rehydration solutions from ordinary household ingredients (see panel 19).

In Thailand, thanks to the work of over 400,000 village-based health workers, well over half of all families now have access to the new therapy (see panel 21).

In the Philippines, production of oral rehydration salts has now reached 5 million sachets a year – available nation-wide through the health services, village health volunteers, and village drugstores. In total, 83% of all reported cases of diarrhoea in children under five are now being treated with ORT. As a result:-

"...in children under five years, the mortality rate for diarrhoeal diseases has decreased significantly, the proportion of all deaths attributable to diarrhoea has also fallen significantly, and the decline in diarrhoea deaths has been much more rapid than the general decline in mortality".*

In Laos, the government plans to make ORT available to 75% of all families by the end of 1985.

In Mexico, a National Oral Rehydration Project has been launched – and supported by the local production of 14 million sachets of salts a year.

In the Gambia two-thirds of all mothers have become aware of ORT through an intensive radio campaign and almost 40% have started to use the technique (see panel 20).

In Niger, 4,000 village health workers have been trained to teach ORT in an attempt to make it available to half the nation's children over the next three years.

In Egypt, a National Oral Rehydration Campaign is now under way – based on lessons learned from pilot campaigns and backed by $26 million in assistance from the United States Agency for International Development (USAID).

---

* Report of the fifth meeting of the Technical Advisory Group, Diarrhoeal Diseases Control Programme, World Health Organization, Geneva, March 1984.

In Tanzania, an initial 8.5 million sachets of oral rehydration salts have begun to be distributed in the last twelve months, as part of a new essential drugs programme which reaches out to every clinic and health post (see panel 22).

Not all of these campaigns will succeed. People do not suddenly begin to use ORT just because the facts about it are made available to them – any more than people suddenly stop smoking, or change their eating habits, just because new facts become widely known. And before ORT, in all its different forms, becomes the standard way of treating the most common of all childhood illnesses, parents will need to hear a clear and consistent message about the new therapy from all sides – from the media, by word of mouth, from health professionals, from the local imam or priest, from community and government leaders, and from their own friends and neighbours and trusted sources of information. In most cases also, a mother will need to be given a practical demonstration of ORT – and to have the informed support of those around her – before becoming confident enough to actually use the new therapy when her own child has diarrhoea. Of the mothers who now know about ORT in Honduras or the Gambia, for example, 'only' about half are actually using the therapy when their children have an attack of diarrhoea. Similarly in Bangladesh, 'only' about 35% of mothers who have been taught the 'seven points to remember' for making and using home-made oral rehydration salts are confident enough – *so far* – to put what they know into practice when the time comes. As more and more mothers are seen to use ORT successfully, more and more mothers will be encouraged to try it – a process which can be accelerated by using all possible channels of communication and support. Home visits and radio campaigns, voluntary action and government backing, are likely to act synergistically so that the impact of the campaign as a whole is considerably greater than the sum of its parts.

ORT demands time and patience as well as knowledge. Mothers, often overworked and illiterate mothers, have to know what proportions of salt and sugar to use, what quantities of water to dissolve them in, how frequently a fresh solution should be made up, how much should be given to the child, and how often, and for how long. Few mothers in the industrialized world – with all the advantages of literacy, water-on-tap, measuring jugs and refrigerators – are asked to undertake any treatment as demanding as ORT to protect their child's health.

But as the mothers of many nations are now showing, the home use of ORT *is* possible and does open the way for a drastic reduction in child deaths and child malnutrition.

Fig.8 Impact of ORT on hospital treatment of diarrhoea

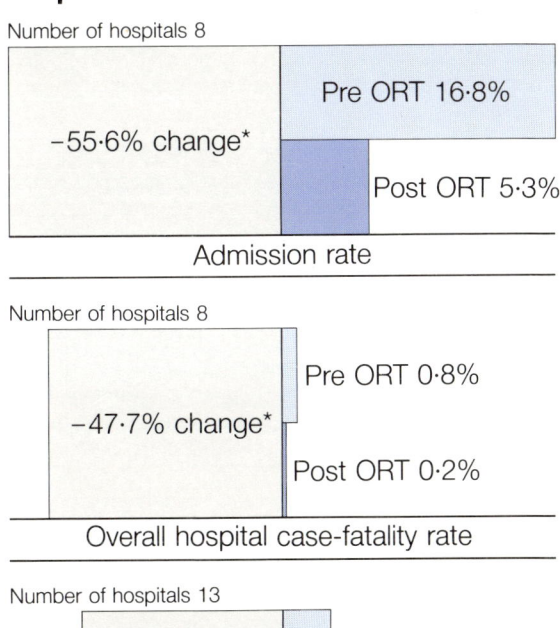

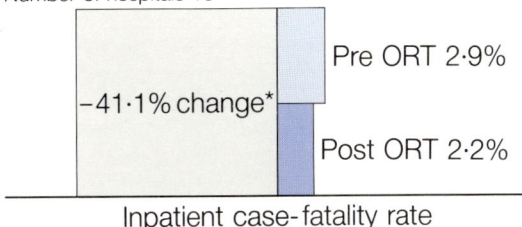

Number of hospitals 8

−55·6% change*
Pre ORT 16·8%
Post ORT 5·3%
Admission rate

Number of hospitals 8

−47·7% change*
Pre ORT 0·8%
Post ORT 0·2%
Overall hospital case-fatality rate

Number of hospitals 13

−41·1% change*
Pre ORT 2·9%
Post ORT 2·2%
Inpatient case-fatality rate

*Percentage change is a median of changes in rates at individual hospitals expressed as a percentage of the pre ORT rate.

Note: Information from major hospitals in Bangladesh, Costa Rica, Egypt, Haiti, Jamaica, Kenya, Nepal, Papua New Guinea, the Philippines, Sri Lanka, Thailand, and Tonga.

Source: Programme for the Control of Diarrhoeal Disease Interim Progress Report 1983 (WHO/CDD/84.1), World Health Organization, Geneva.

I THE STATE OF THE WORLD'S CHILDREN 1985

The West: a return to breast-feeding

Until two generations ago, almost all human infants were breast-fed. Even as late as 1911, two-thirds of America's one-year-olds were still being fed on breast-milk. But by 1973, only a quarter of American infants were breast-fed from birth, and only 10% beyond three months.

Europe soon followed. In Sweden, the proportion of infants exclusively breast-fed at two months dropped from 85% in 1944 to 35% in 1970. In the Netherlands, the 1975 figure for exclusively breast-fed infants (at three months) was only 11%.

The driving force behind this change was modernization. More women began working, and many saw the bottle as a symbol of their liberation. In response, infant-formula companies brought new products onto the market and began advertising them. And in an age which was almost unreservedly enthusiastic about all things modern and 'scientific', the infant formulas appealed to a growing sense of sophistication both in parents and in the medical profession. As more babies were born in hospitals, the emphasis on strict hygiene and spotless order made breast-feeding seem messy or 'unclean'. Most babies were separated from their mothers at birth in the interests of hospital efficiency, and they were fed on schedule rather than on demand.

But in the last decade, breast-feeding has staged a remarkable come-back in the Western world. In Norway, Finland and Sweden, for example, 95% of babies are now breast-fed from birth. In the United States, the proportion of mothers who begin breast-feeding their babies has more than doubled between 1973 and 1980. In the Federal Republic of Germany, almost 70% of babies are still breast-fed at two months.

The trend back to breast-feeding – like the earlier trend away from it – has been led by better-educated mothers. A 1980 survey in the United States, for example, showed that almost 70% of graduate mothers breast-fed their children as opposed to only 25% of mothers with nine or less years of schooling.

What caused the return to breast-feeding in the Western world?

First of all, a conviction about breast-milk's natural superiority led groups of women to start up organizations to support breast-feeding mothers – the La Leche League in America, Ammehjelpen in Norway, the Nursing Mothers Association in Australia.

At the same time, modern technologies were coming to be looked at more critically and respect was beginning to grow again for the natural world. In the 1970s, scientific research reinforced this trend by discovering a great deal about the nutritional, immunological and emotional advantages of breast-feeding. Soon the medical profession and governments began to take notice. Sweden set up a breast-feeding task-force at ministerial level. The United States government, in 1984, has "set the promotion of breast-feeding as a principal canon of United States health policy" – with the aim of raising to 75% the proportion of babies who are breast-fed from birth.

In the developing world, there are now signs of a similar drift away from breast-feeding – again led by the more modern and urban mothers. But poor mothers rarely earn the income needed to buy enough milk powder, and lack not only the clean water to mix it with but the equipment to sterilize bottles and the literacy to read the detailed instructions. A large-scale move away from breast-feeding in the poor world would literally mean the deaths and malnutrition of many millions more infants.

The rapid spread of information on – and support for – breast-feeding is therefore essential if the Third World is to avoid the trap and take less time than the West to realize that breast-milk is the best the world can offer its infants.

Breast-feeding

Almost unnoticed, many nations are also now moving to preserve another vital element of child protection – breast-feeding (figs. 9 and 10).

Breast-feeding is a natural 'safety net' against the worst effects of poverty. If the child survives the first month of life (the most dangerous period of childhood), then for the next four months or so, exclusive breast-feeding goes a long way towards cancelling out the health difference between being born into poverty and being born into affluence. Unless the mother is in extremely poor nutritional health, the breast-milk of a mother in an African village is as good as the breast-milk of a mother in a Manhattan apartment. So even under the poorest roof, a child who is breast-fed in this period is likely to be as healthy and to grow as well as a baby born into a European or North American home. It is almost as if breast-feeding takes the infant out of poverty for those first few vital months in order to give the child a fairer start in life and compensate for the injustice of the world into which it was born.

In recent years, there have been signs that this strand of child protection is beginning to fray. In many cities of the developing world, the incidence and duration of breast-feeding has begun to fall precipitously.

Often encouraged by the example of hospitals, by the acquiescence of doctors, by the advertisements of infant-formula manufacturers, by the demands of wage employment outside the home, and by their own belief that bottle-feeding is more sophisticated, many mothers have either not begun to breast-feed at all or have not persisted beyond the first few weeks. But equally often, mothers in poor communities are unable to afford sufficient quantities of infant formula, unable to read the instructions on the back of the container, unable to obtain clean water, or to sterilize bottles and teats, or to keep the solution cool. They are therefore trapped into spending money they cannot afford on feeding their children with over-diluted milk powder from unclean milk bottles. The result can be a doubling or trebling of malnutrition, infection, and infant deaths.

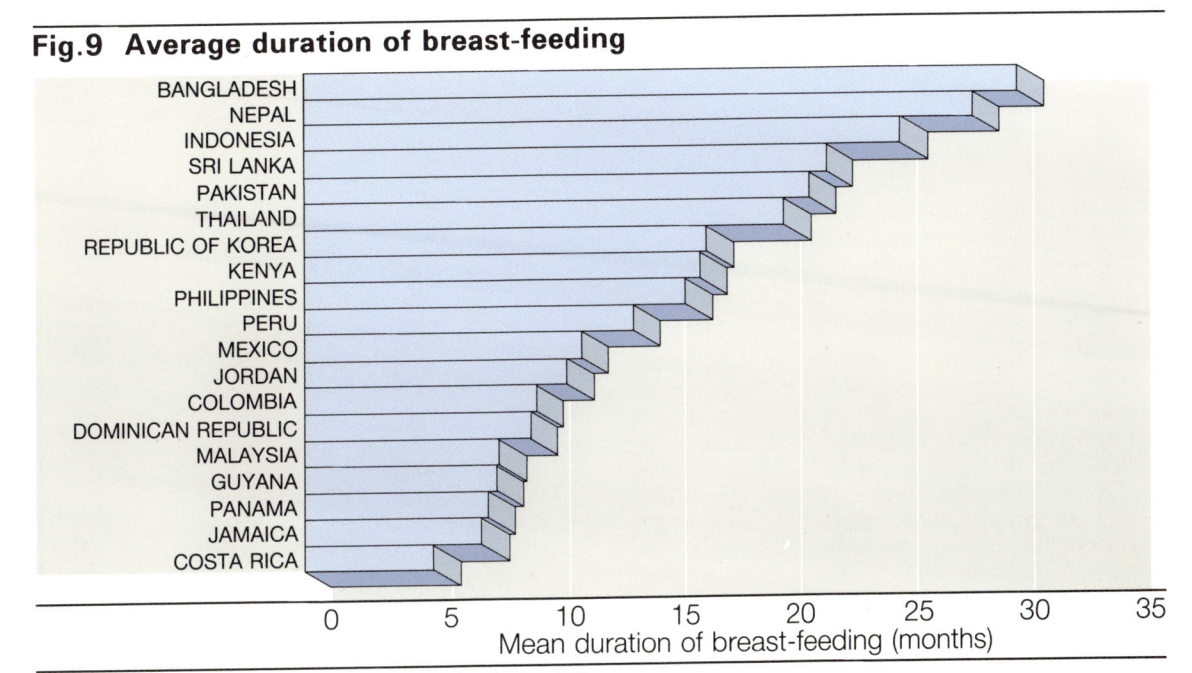

Fig.9 Average duration of breast-feeding

Country	Mean duration of breast-feeding (months)
BANGLADESH	~30
NEPAL	~27
INDONESIA	~24
SRI LANKA	~22
PAKISTAN	~20
THAILAND	~18
REPUBLIC OF KOREA	~16
KENYA	~15
PHILIPPINES	~14
PERU	~13
MEXICO	~11
JORDAN	~10
COLOMBIA	~9
DOMINICAN REPUBLIC	~8
MALAYSIA	~7
GUYANA	~6
PANAMA	~5
JAMAICA	~4
COSTA RICA	~3

Source: World Fertility Survey data, International Statistical Institute, London, 1980.

I THE STATE OF THE WORLD'S CHILDREN 1985

The Code: action in 130 nations

In a poor community of the developing world, a baby who is bottle-fed is two or three times more likely to die in infancy than a baby who is breast-fed. The steep decline of breast-feeding in the cities of the developing world has therefore become a major cause for concern.

One of the most visible forces behind the rise of bottle-feeding has been the advertising of infant formulas by the commercial baby-food companies. In May of 1981, after a ten-year campaign by health professionals, non-governmental organizations and international agencies, the World Health Assembly adopted the International Code of Marketing of Breast-milk Substitutes.

The aim of the Code is "the provision of safe and adequate nutrition for infants, by the protection and promotion of breast-feeding, and by ensuring the proper use of breast-milk substitutes, when these are necessary, on the basis of adequate information and through appropriate marketing and distribution".

By mid-1984, three years after the Code's adoption, the World Health Organization reported that the Code had been translated into 17 languages and that 130 countries had taken some form of action on it. More than 18 industrialized and developing countries have enacted national codes or adapted existing legislation to include the Code's provisions; and at least 34 countries are currently drafting legislation.

Some 33 governments have banned the advertising of breast-milk substitutes to the public, and 17 have actively used the mass media to promote breast-feeding. In the Philippines, for example, the Ministry of Health is leading a national breast-feeding campaign which uses radio and television spots, posters, and manuals and handbooks for health personnel; bottle-feeding publicity is barred from hospitals and health centres. In Brazil, television networks have donated more than $1 million a year in broadcasting time to promote breast-feeding, with leading actresses and celebrities giving their time free of charge.

Most infant-formula manufacturers have now accepted the Code's main provisions and have agreed to abide by them when selling their products in developing countries. Nestlé, which controls over 50% of the infant-formula market, has agreed to comply with the Code's basic provisions and the international boycott of Nestlé products has now been lifted.

But some manufacturers still regard the Code as an unjustified restriction on the marketing of their products, and infringements consequently persist. In one three-week period during 1984, the International Baby Food Action Network reported more than 100 violations of the Code by 22 companies in ten different countries.

Action to encourage breast-feeding needs to be supported by a wider range of measures, as many countries have recognized. Working mothers, in particular, require special arrangements if they are to be able to breast-feed their babies – such as guaranteed, adequate and fully paid maternity leave, arrangements for home help, day-care centres near the work-place, and nursing breaks at work. Viet Nam, for instance, now allows an hour of break for nursing mothers during the working day until the baby is a year old, and Lesotho recently introduced legislation providing for 90 days maternity leave and nursing facilities at or near the work-place.

Many organizations, national and international, have joined forces to publicize the dangers of milk substitutes. National coalitions to protect breast-feeding have been established in Costa Rica, India, Kenya, Malaysia, Peru, the Philippines, and other developing countries. All these organizations are continuing to play a vital role in monitoring the marketing of infant formula.

In 1981, a ten-year campaign against the promotion of bottle-feeding culminated in the adoption, by the World Health Assembly, of the International Code of Marketing of Breast-milk Substitutes (see panel 12). Since then, 18 nations have brought in legal or voluntary codes to prevent the public promotion of breast-milk substitutes and 34 countries are currently drafting legislation. Much of the most blatant advertising has now disappeared and most containers of infant formula now carry the message that 'breast-milk is best'. Nestlé, which controls 50% of the infant-formula market world-wide, has announced its intention to comply with all the Code's main provisions and, in late 1984, the international Nestlé boycott campaign has been ended.

Despite this progress, the infant formula code, as it has come to be known, is still not being observed by all companies in all countries. In the last year, for example, the International Baby Food Action Network has reported over 100 violations by 22 companies in ten different countries during one three-week period.

Stopping the irresponsible advertising of breast-milk substitutes is not enough. In the present climate of conflicting social pressures and growing uncertainties, breast-feeding also needs to be promoted. For at this point of balance, present knowledge about the protection offered by breast-feeding – and the dangers threatened by bottle-feeding – should surely be made available to all mothers who may be in doubt – and to all those who are in a position to influence the mother's decision.

World-wide, the promotion of that knowledge has now begun to gather momentum:-

In the United States, the percentage of mothers who breast-feed their babies from birth has doubled from 26% to 54% in the last decade. In Norway, Sweden and Finland, 95% of all babies are now breast-fed from birth (see panel 11).

Fig.10 Duration of breast-feeding in rural and urban areas of Bangladesh by age and education of mother

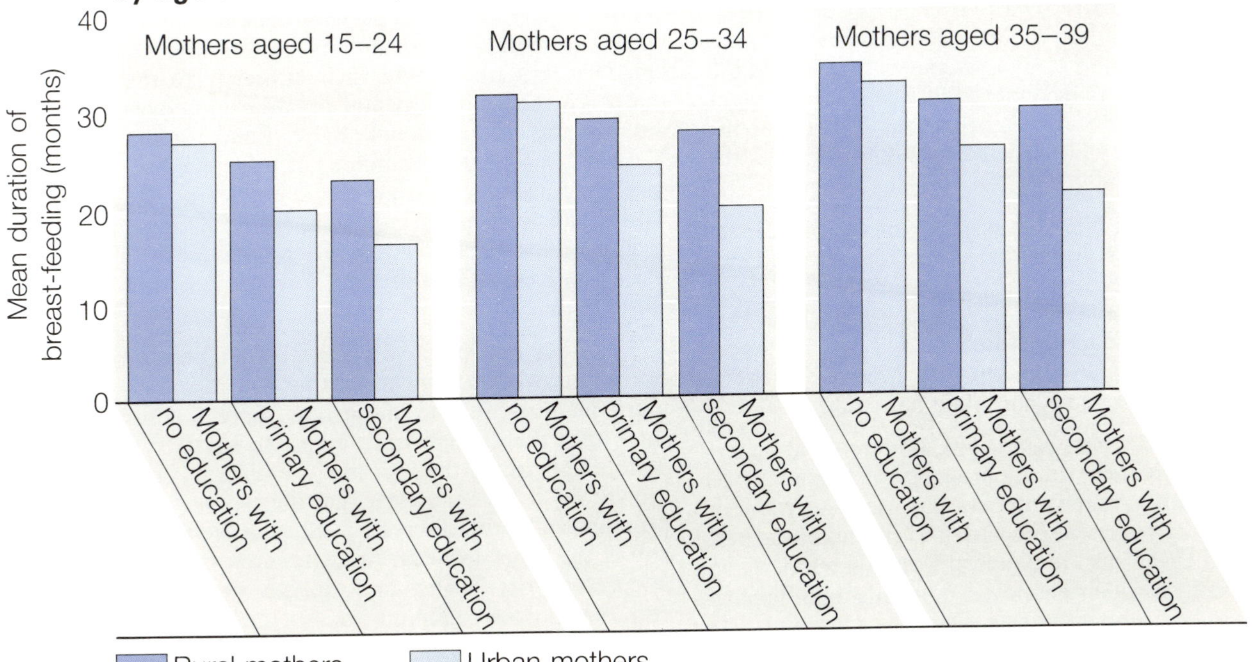

Rural mothers / Urban mothers

Source: World Fertility Survey data, International Statistical Institute, London, 1980.

I THE STATE OF THE WORLD'S CHILDREN 1985

In the Philippines, the Ministry of Health has retrained its personnel and is leading a national campaign using radio, television, and posters to publicize breast-feeding's superiority. Publicizing or supplying infant formula is now banned by the Ministry in all government hospitals and health centres.

In Brazil, over 100,000 health workers and other officials have attended training sessions on the promotion of breast-feeding and national television and radio networks, as well as advertising and communication professionals, have donated air time and services worth well over $1 million to the campaign in the space of one year. In 15 states, education about breast-feeding is now part of the standard school curriculum.

In India, the government has passed an ordinance on the marketing of breast-milk substitutes and now has legislation ready to put before Parliament.

In Sri Lanka, a mass media campaign to promote breast-feeding and a ban on all advertising of infant formula has helped to stop the steep rise in bottle-feeding and seen the incidence of breast-feeding recover to over 70% in urban areas. A study of children born into the poorest sections of society in Sri Lanka has shown that 76% of the breast-fed babies achieved 90% of normal weight gain after the first eight months of life. For the babies who had been fed on infant formula, the figure was only 29%.

In Papua New Guinea, one of the pioneers of legislation to protect breast-feeding, the incidence of bottle-feeding in Port Moresby has been reduced from 35% to 12% in four years. Over that same period, the number of cases of severe malnutrition brought to Port Moresby's general hospital has been more than halved.

In all of these campaigns, hospitals and maternity units have an importance which is out of all proportion to the numbers who use them. Modern hospitals are often regarded as shrines of the best and latest ideas in child care, and therefore set an example which permeates outwards to millions of mothers who will never see inside a hospital. The fact that many maternity units used to separate mothers and infants at birth and encourage bottle-feeding from the first day has been a major factor in the decline of breast-feeding in many of the developing world's cities. More up-to-date hospitals in many countries – both industrialized and developing – have begun changing their standard routines to encourage 'rooming-in' and breast-feeding from birth. Most of the leading hospitals in India, China, the Philippines, Brazil, Indonesia, and Nicaragua, for example, have now changed to these pro-breast-feeding policies. And the Congress of the International Confederation of Midwives, meeting in Sydney in late 1984, has affirmed "*the right of all babies to be breast-fed; the right of all mothers to proper advice, encouragement and counselling; and the right of all families to accurate information*".

In addition to the health services, many other organizations are also supporting the campaign: ministries of education, school principals, and teachers are including the subject in the curricula; employers and trade unionists are becoming involved in discussions about longer maternity leaves and better facilities for breast-feeding at the work-place; traditional birth attendants and paramedical staff are helping mothers to persist with breast-feeding and to cope with common problems; community organizations, priests and Islamic leaders are lending their authority to the campaign; non-governmental organizations have set up the International Baby Food Action Network, made up of hundreds of private voluntary organizations in over 60 countries of the world; and women's groups have set up national coalitions for breast-feeding in the Philippines, Malaysia, Kenya, Trinidad and Tobago, Peru and Costa Rica.

The next few years will tell whether present campaigns will succeed in halting the march of bottle-feeding. But as more and more studies show that the change from breast to bottle can double and treble the risk to the child's life and growth, so it becomes clear that the campaign to promote and protect breast-feeding is as vital as any of the other low-cost strategies now available to protect the health and normal growth of children in poor communities.

In addition, breast-feeding has also been shown to be one of the most important determinants of the average interval between births, especially in poor and rural communities (fig. 11). As an adequate interval between births is also known to be crucial to the well-being of both mother and child (fig. 3), breast-feeding may be even more important to human health than is currently recognized.

But like the campaign to promote oral rehydration therapy, the campaign to protect breast-feeding must also recognize that a great deal is again being asked of the mother. Breast-feeding is not always easy. For some mothers, it can be a painful, tiring, inconvenient, and sometimes embarrassing process. It demands a great deal of the mother's time, patience, and freedom of movement and is also a 'nutritional stress' on the mother herself.

Overcoming these problems is not a task for women alone. An increase in a woman's share of family food, and a lightening of her work-load during periods of pregnancy and breast-feeding, are the two most obvious ways by which the community as a whole – and especially its men – can help to extend the protection of breast-feeding to all children.

Immunization

Earlier this year in Bellagio, Italy, a small meeting was held under the title 'To Protect the World's Children'. Convened by the executive heads of the World Health Organization, the World Bank, the United Nations Development Programme, and UNICEF, its participants included the heads of many of the world's major aid programmes, representatives from developing nations in Africa, Asia and Latin America, plus former World Bank President Robert McNamara, Rockefeller Foundation President Richard Lyman, and several distinguished figures from the world of immunization.

A summary of the present state of immunization world-wide, prepared for the Bellagio meeting, told the story of the gulf between immunization's potential and actual contributions to child health and child survival in the developing world. For a total cost of approximately $5, a child can now be immunized against six of the most common and dangerous diseases of childhood – measles, tetanus, pertussis (whooping cough), diphtheria, poliomyelitis and tuberculosis. But in 1984, less than 20% of the developing world's children were protected against all or most of these infections (fig. 12). The result is that cheaply preventable diseases are being allowed to kill 5 million young children a year and to leave 5 million more mentally or physically disabled (see panel 9 and fig. 15).

Clearly, if the gulf between potential and performance could be bridged, then immunization could take its rightful place as another powerful means of protecting growing children against the worst effects of poverty.

A great deal of recent research has therefore concentrated on technologies which can help to make vaccines more widely available. And on this front, there is also progress to report. More heat-stable vaccines, better and cheaper methods of sterilizing equipment, improvements in cold-chain technology, and the development of colour-change indicators to monitor the potency of vaccines, have all made it more possible to make

Fig. 11 Influence of breast-feeding on interval between births

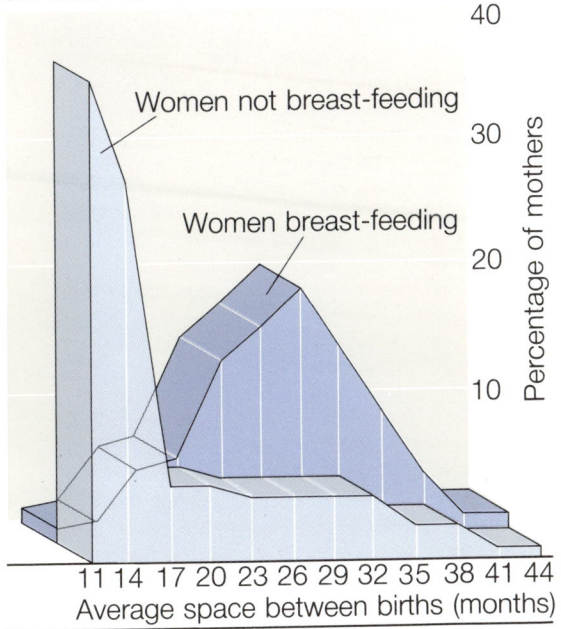

Source: Survey by H van Balen of 259 mothers (209 lactating and 50 after stillbirth) cited in Breast-Feeding, Fertility, and Contraception, IPPF, 1984.

I THE STATE OF THE WORLD'S CHILDREN 1985

India: creating the demand

In the last two years, campaigns in hundreds of Indian villages have shown that immunization rates can be pushed up from under 10% to 80% or more at relatively low cost and in a relatively short time. And in each campaign, success has hinged on ensuring that parents understand the need for vaccination, and on organizing the vaccinations to dovetail with the routines of daily living.

In Dewas district of Madhya Pradesh, immunization had been 'available' for several years. But only 2% of children were protected against polio and only 3.5% had received diphtheria, pertussis and tetanus (DPT) vaccination. Within a year, a campaign in 600 villages had raised these figures to 75% for polio and 41% for full DPT protection.

As in Nigeria (see panel 6), success was achieved both by increasing the incentive and reducing the difficulties. First, parents were empowered with the knowledge of what immunization can achieve. Newspapers, radio, posters, songs, banners, processions, car-stickers, and door-to-door visits by community volunteers brought the message to all households. Plays about immunization were performed on market-days. And in every village, the *chowkidars* or village criers beat the traditional drums to underline the message. Almost everyone became involved – health professionals, district authorities, village leaders, health workers, schoolteachers, Rotary Club members, village volunteers and parents themselves.

To reduce the difficulties, over 250 immunization posts were set up in schools, temples and polling booths as well as health centres, so that few mothers had to travel more than one kilometre with their child. For the first round the organizers expected 20,000 children; 27,900 turned up.

But a major disappointment was waiting in the new year: only 11,400 children were brought for the third shot of DPT vaccine. One reason turned out to be the slackening off of publicity efforts. And the organizers had also overlooked a key fact of life in Dewas: in February, the month chosen for the third immunization round, many people were away seeking seasonal employment in the sugar factories.

Nonetheless, the immunization rates had gone up more than tenfold, and the campaign organizers had learned some important lessons. Now, the Madhya Pradesh state government has begun extending the campaign to cover nine more districts in the coming year and the entire state by 1986.

A similar campaign has been mounted in 600 villages of Karnataka state, where immunization was also 'available' but only 15% of children were protected. The campaign was based on the existing health centres. But it did not stop there. Also involved were members of Parliament, local family planning associations, non-governmental organizations, the Methodist churches, *panchayat* (local government) members, the *tahsildar* (revenue officer), the *mahila mandal* (village women's organizations), schoolteachers, and the *anganwadi* workers of the programme for Integrated Child Development Services (see panel 4). Films, tape-recordings, slide advertisements in local cinemas, touring public address systems – all were used to inform parents of the campaign and its benefits for children under two. The day before each immunization 'camp', every home was visited by a health worker, or family planning worker, or *mahila mandal* member, or schoolteacher, or *anganwadi* worker, to remind parents that 'tomorrow was the day'.

Four immunization days were held between December 1983 and March 1984. The result has been the protection of 95% of children against tuberculosis, diphtheria, whooping cough and tetanus.

Similar strategies have also worked in Delhi, where puppet shows, banners, posters and plays heralded an immunization campaign which used the *anganwadi* workers and other staff of the programme for Integrated Child Development Services. In poor communities totalling nearly a quarter of a million people, immunization rates have been pushed from 20% to over 80%, and the strategy is being duplicated in other slum areas served by *anganwadis*.

immunization available to more people.

But the gap between immunization's potential and performance will never be bridged by technology alone. For there is mounting evidence that even widening the availability of vaccines is, in itself, not enough.

Bluntly stated, the most significant breakthrough in knowledge about immunization is the realization that present immunization rates could be doubled, and in many cases trebled, if parents took advantage of *existing* immunization services and if those who brought their child for the first immunization were also to turn up for the second and third injections. In 81 immunization campaigns in Africa and Asia surveyed by WHO between 1979 and 1983, for example, the average drop-out rate between the first and third 'shots' of DPT vaccine was almost 40% (fig. 14).

Immunization is therefore as much a question of demand as of supply. And if 'the world's greatest public health tool' is to play its part in low-cost protection against malnutrition and disease – and fulfil its potential for bringing about a reduction of up to one-third in the rate of death and disability among the world's children – then parents must be empowered with the information to make sure that their children are immunized. And by means of new-style immunization campaigns, that is what countries like Pakistan, India, Nigeria, Colombia and Brazil are now beginning to do.

But before looking at this element of the child survival revolution as it begins to go into action, it would be unjust not to put into context the low turn-out and high drop-out rates of many immunization campaigns in the developing world.

In most industrialized countries, a baby is practically born onto a conveyor belt of immunization. Every birth is registered and every child's vaccination record is on file. Health visitors call on the new mother at her home to remind her about vaccinations and to make her appointments at health clinics. Every appointment ends in a new appointment for the next stage of immunization.

Fig. 12 Percentage of pregnant women immunized against tetanus

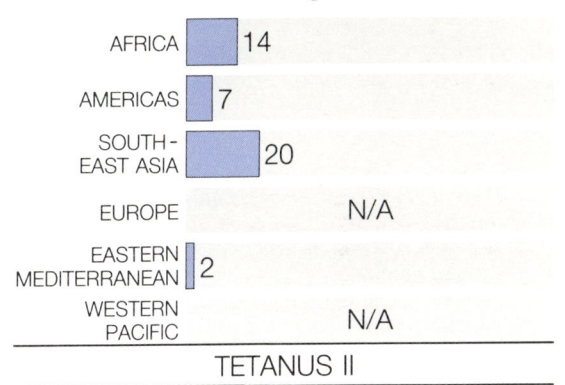

Region	TETANUS II
AFRICA	14
AMERICAS	7
SOUTH-EAST ASIA	20
EUROPE	N/A
EASTERN MEDITERRANEAN	2
WESTERN PACIFIC	N/A

Source: Report of the Expanded Programme of Immunizations Global Advisory Group Meeting, 31 Oct.–4 Nov. 1983, Manila, EPI/GEN/83/7, WHO, Geneva.

Fig. 13 Percentage of children immunized in the first year of life

Region	BCG	DPT III	POLIO III	MEASLES*
AFRICA	34	24	21	42
AMERICAS	53	58	71	39
SOUTH-EAST ASIA	24	33	14	1
EUROPE	77	76	81	74
EASTERN MEDITERRANEAN	9	13	16	15
WESTERN PACIFIC	80	70	63	46

Note: DPT = Diphtheria, Pertussis (Whooping cough) and Tetanus
Source: Report of the Expanded Programme of Immunizations Global Advisory Group Meeting, 31 Oct.–4 Nov. 1983, Manila, EPI/GEN/83/7, WHO, Geneva.

*Measles: Coverage data for children up to 60 months are included for countries recommending immunization at, or later than, 12 months (excluding USA data).

I THE STATE OF THE WORLD'S CHILDREN 1985

Matlab: providing the proof

In the low-lying, flood-prone district of Matlab, Bangladesh, scientists at the International Centre for Diarrhoeal Disease Research have been preventing deaths from diarrhoea for more than twenty years at their treatment centre in Matlab Bazar. They have also been studying changes in population growth since 1966. The name of Matlab is therefore famous among researchers the world over as one of the most closely studied areas of the developing world.

Field data collected from 1975 to 1977 found that children under five represented only a sixth of Matlab's population of 260,000 but accounted for more than half of all deaths. One child in every four was dying before the age of five.

What did the children die of? Once the researchers had taken into account the lives saved by the Matlab Bazar treatment centre, their figures revealed that infants in their first year died primarily of neonatal tetanus, which accounted for 26% of deaths. Diarrhoea, fever and respiratory infections caused another 26%.

Among the one-to-four-year-olds, diarrhoea caused 44% of deaths. Measles, which also concentrated its ravages in this age group, accounted for at least 13% of deaths. Fevers and respiratory infections killed a further 13%.

From these grim figures, the researchers moved on to consider what measures could do most to reduce the death toll. Clearly, immunizing mothers-to-be against tetanus would have the greatest impact, followed by measles vaccination. When whooping-cough and tuberculosis vaccination had been added to the list, the researchers concluded that a basic immunization programme could prevent 25% of all children's deaths before the age of five.

They also calculated that home-based oral rehydration therapy, backed up by intravenous treatment, could prevent 75% of child deaths from diarrhoea.

When immunization and oral rehydration were considered together, they carried the potential for cutting infant mortality by as much as 40%, and mortality among under-fives by more than a third.

Evidence to support some of these hypotheses was collected over the following three years, from October 1977 to 1981, when a health and family planning programme was launched in one area of Matlab with a population of 90,000. A similar population was used for comparison.

The programme's field-workers reached 80% of women of child-bearing age. The rate of contraceptive use, originally 7%, rose within eighteen months to a steady 33%. Tetanus immunization for pregnant women was introduced later on, in June 1978, but made slower headway because of the mothers' fears of injection during pregnancy. Nevertheless, by the end of the study period one in three pregnant women had been vaccinated.

The effects of these two measures did not take long to show up. By late 1978 and throughout 1979 there were consistently fewer deaths in the study population as a whole; the crude death rate fell by 21%. The birth rate also fell, by 21%, to 36 births per 1,000 population compared with 46 per 1,000 in the comparison area.

Most significant of all, the infant mortality rate began to drop even before the tetanus shots had been introduced. By the end of the study it had fallen by 11%, averaging 103 deaths per 1,000 live births in the project area in contrast to 116 per 1,000 in the control area. When the mothers had had tetanus shots during pregnancy, infant mortality was 45% less than for infants whose mothers had never been immunized. And in the years since that first phase of the health and family planning programme in Matlab, years in which parents have grown more confident that their children will survive, average family size is now two children less than when the programme began.

Fig. 14 Coverage and drop-out rates in DPT vaccination programmes
(Graph illustrates 30 immunization programmes listed)

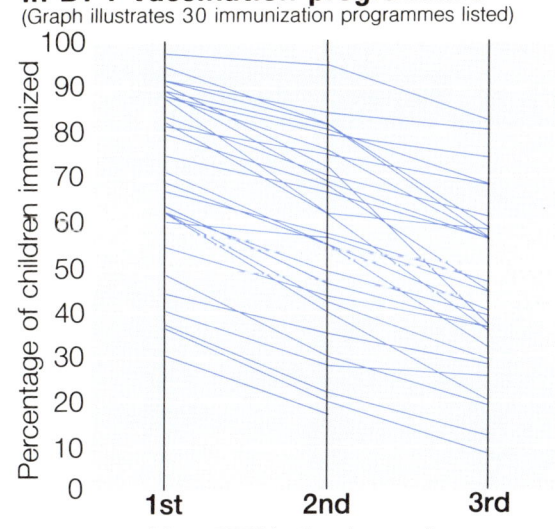

A full course of three DPT injections is normally necessary for immunity against Diphtheria, Pertussis (whooping cough), and Tetanus

Survey date	Country/Area	DPT I	DPT II	DPT III	Drop-out rate
1978	Tanzania/Iringa	54%	43%	36%	33%
1979	S. Leone/Bo	48%	30%	19%	60%
1979	Sudan/Wadmedani	37%	22%	12%	68%
1979	Turkey/Nevsahir	69%	55%	32%	54%
1980	Gambia/National	89%	80%	68%	24%
1980	Bahrain/National	81%	75%	68%	16%
1980	Nepal/Kathmandu	40%	28%	26%	35%
1981	Iv. Coast/Ferke	60%	56%	44%	27%
1981	Mauritania/Gorgol	87%	61%	35%	60%
1981	Ecuador/Chimborazo	90%	72%	36%	60%
1981	Somalia/Johar	67%	57%	46%	31%
1981	U.A.E./Al-Ain	89%	69%	56%	37%
1981	Sri Lanka/Kurunegala	91%	81%	58%	36%
1982	Burundi/Kirundo	82%	62%	58%	29%
1982	Gambia/National	91%	84%	80%	12%
1982	Lesotho/National	75%	67%	56%	25%
1982	Mozambique/National	62%	40%	20%	68%
1982	Colombia/Huila	60%	49%	39%	35%
1982	Uruguay/Montevideo	83%	70%	61%	27%
1982	Jordan/Amman, rural	88%	79%	74%	16%
1982	Yemen/Rural	36%	20%	8%	78%
1982	Indonesia/S. Sulawesi	30%	17%	—	43%
1982	Thailand/Chumporn	79%	68%	44%	44%
1982	Botswana/National	97%	94%	82%	15%
1983	Rwanda/National	63%	46%	36%	43%
1983	Sao Tome/National	44%	35%	28%	36%
1983	Togo/Kara	61%	42%	29%	52%
1983	Oman/National	71%	55%	40%	44%
1983	Burma/Irrawaddy	94%	81%	56%	40%
1983	P.N. Guinea/Chimbu	88%	76%	56%	36%

Note: The sample size was over 200 children in all but one of the areas surveyed. All children were older than one year and most were in their second year of life.

Source: Adapted from: Results of EPI sample surveys of immunization coverage performed during reviews of national programmes, by year, 1979–83, EPI, WHO, Geneva.

A missed appointment means a postal reminder and repeated absence means a further visit from the health services. In the Netherlands, for example, a computerized system tracks every child's immunization status from birth and automatically sends the appropriate reminder to all parents until all children are fully immunized. A high level of literacy, good roads and cheap transport, awareness of the value of vaccines – all this smooths immunization's path. Even so, the proportion of children immunized against measles in New York State, for example, did not rise above the 65% mark until the 1970s when legislation was introduced to the effect that unvaccinated children would not be registered in primary school.

In the developing world, immunization is a different story. And it is not because of any greater carelessness that a child is not vaccinated when immunization is theoretically available.

Perhaps the mother has already taken the child for three immunizations. But when the baby is nine months old, she has to decide whether to go back yet again (usually for measles vaccine). She has been told she ought to go. But she does not know why. There was a notice in the clinic, but she could not read it. No-one around her is encouraging her to go, because no-one seems to know anything more about it than she does. Her working day starts at five in the morning and does not end until she goes to sleep at nine or ten o'clock at night. Going to the clinic will mean finding somebody else to do her work in the home and missing a whole day in the fields, perhaps at the busiest time of the year. At nine months, the child is just getting to the awkward age when it is too old to carry and too young to walk. The clinic is 4 kilometres away, and there is no money for a bus fare. Besides, last time she walked all the way to the clinic she had to wait in line for an hour and a half in the sun with nowhere to sit down. When she finally got to the front, the young doctor had been rude and snapped at her when she asked about the baby's cough. She had felt humiliated. That evening, after she got back, the baby began running a fever and cried almost the whole night. They had said that that might happen after the injection, but all of them sleep in one room and her husband had lost his temper at being kept awake. Now, the child seems perfectly well, and surely three injections is enough?

And so the day goes by, the appointment is missed and another child goes unprotected.

If vaccines are to play their vital part in bringing about a revolution in child survival and development, then immunization must be made available in practice and not just in theory. And that means taking into account the poverty of circumstance, the lack of information, and the unfair burden of work which effectively deprive many women of the power to protect their children by immunization.

In practice, this 'slack' between available immunization services and the proportion of children actually immunized can be taken up in two ways. First, empowering parents with information about what immunization offers – a reduction of at least a quarter in the risk of child death – can increase the distance which parents *are prepared to travel*. Second, making immunization available at times and places more convenient to working people can reduce the distance which parents *need to travel*. Both bring immunization nearer.

At Bellagio, these strategies were summed up by the experienced voice of Donald Henderson, now Dean of the Johns Hopkins School of Hygiene and Public Health and formerly director of WHO's successful smallpox campaign:-

"Not surprising is the fact that successful prevention programs have required a different approach in providing services than those concerned with curative interventions. Such programs are characterized by two principles: (1) Provision of the services at a convenient location near the residence of the recipients and at a convenient time; (2) Active promotion of the service being offered.

"When immunization, for example, is brought to the residents at a time of day when villagers are not in the fields or at the market, acceptance by 90% or more is common. Comparable results are obtained if immunization is offered at convenient assembly points which are not too distant provided that the program is well organized and promoted... Remarkably high levels of acceptance have been achieved when educational and promotional methods have been imaginative."

Taking advantage of these two main lessons of recent experience, immunization coverage can be drastically increased in a very short time, and at very little extra cost.

Fig.15 Number of deaths from selected vaccine-preventable diseases

Estimated annual deaths in thousands

	Neonatal Tetanus[a]	Measles[b]	Pertussis[c]	Total
INDIA	298	782	189	1,269
PAKISTAN	132	163	66	361
BANGLADESH	119	173	69	361
INDONESIA	71	218	63	352
NIGERIA	64	171	68	303
MEXICO	31	57	19	107
ETHIOPIA	16	60	25	101
ZAIRE	21	45	19	85
PHILIPPINES	12	59	12	83
BRAZIL	28	34	18	80
BURMA	20	43	16	79
THAILAND	10	57	11	78
VIETNAM	12	46	19	77
KENYA	9	37	15	61
EGYPT	16	32	13	61
SOUTH AFRICA	11	35	14	60
SUDAN	8	36	15	59
AFGHANISTAN	11	27	11	49
IRAN	17	19	9	45
ALGERIA	10	25	8	43
MOROCCO	10	21	5	36
TURKEY	8	16	5	29
COLOMBIA	9	14	6	29
TANZANIA	6	7	6	19
REP. of KOREA	5	10	2	17
Total	954	2,187	703	3,844
All other developing countries	181	411	139	731
Grand total	1,135	2,598	842	4,575

Note: Figures exclude China

a Based on survey data or in absence of survey data, neonatal tetanus deaths are estimated from countries with similar socio-economic conditions.

b Based on immunization coverage data reported to EPI/WHO, assuming vaccine efficacy of 95% and that 90% of unimmunized children will acquire measles. Coverage is assumed to be zero in countries from which data are not available.

c Based on immunization coverage data reported to EPI/WHO assuming vaccine efficacy of 80% and that 80% of unimmunized children will acquire pertussis. Coverage is assumed to be zero in countries from which data are not available.

Source: World Health Organization, Geneva

In the Owo area of Ondo state, Nigeria, for example, the attempt to put this knowledge into practice has quickly doubled and redoubled the rate of immunization while actually reducing the cost per child immunized (see panel 6).*

In India, similar strategies are now being used, and with remarkable success rates, in the states of Karnataka and Madhya Pradesh, and in the city of Delhi itself (see panel 13).

In Dewas district of Madhya Pradesh, three-quarters of all children have been protected against polio and almost half against diphtheria, whooping cough and tetanus, in a campaign which is now to be extended to the entire state by 1986.

In a similar campaign across 600 villages of Karnataka this year, 95% of all the children have been protected against polio, tuberculosis, diphtheria, whooping cough and tetanus – saving approximately 500 lives and preventing an estimated 30,000 cases of serious illness or disability.

Also in 1984, similar strategies have gone into action in Delhi via the programme for Integrated Child Development Services (see panel 4). In poor communities totalling nearly a quarter of a million people, immunization rates have been pushed from just 20% to over 80% of all children.

Similar attempts to make immunization universally available are now planned by several states including Himachal Pradesh, and by the central government in 30 other districts.

In the Kator district of Juba, Sudan, the proportion of under-two-year-olds fully protected by immunization has risen from less than 10% to more than 40%. In January 1984, Juba town council decided to extend the campaign to the other eight districts of the city (see panel 6).

In Zimbabwe, promoting nation-wide awareness of immunization through radio advertising and through popular folk songs by rural groups has helped to more than double immunization rates from 25% in mid-1982 to 52% today.

In Lesotho, similar campaigns run by the maternal and child health services have raised the proportion of children protected by immunization to over 50% for the six main target diseases.

In the Gambia, more than 80% of all children are now immunized against all six diseases covered by WHO's Expanded Programme on Immunization.

In Pakistan the Accelerated Health Programme has boosted the *supply* of immunization through a 50% increase in the number of immunization centres across the country. At the same time, a mass media information campaign has also increased the *demand* for immunization. After one year, the proportion of Pakistan's children fully immunized has risen from less than 5% to more than 25% and the campaign is now likely to go close to its target of full protection for 50% of the nation's children by the end of 1984.

But in the last twelve months, the largest of the new-style immunization campaigns have been seen in the two most populous nations of the South American continent – Brazil and Colombia.

Last year, the *State of the World's Children* report recorded the success of Brazil's National Vaccination Days which have virtually wiped out poliomyelitis among Brazil's 19 million under-fives. This year, the campaign has been dramatically extended to include vaccination against diphtheria, whooping cough, tetanus and measles. On the same two National Vaccination Days — June 16th and August 11th – a total of 450,000 volunteers again manned over 90,000 immunization posts across a country larger than Western Europe.

Those 90,000 vaccination posts, set up in schools and community centres as well as in the clinics, drastically reduced the distance which parents had to travel. At the same time a massive public information campaign made sure that almost all parents in Brazil knew where and when and why their children should be immunized. Four short TV videos were distributed by satellite to all local stations and shown 12 times a day on prime-time television. Eight separate advertise-

---

* Certain fixed costs are incurred in making immunization available whether the number of children actually immunized is one or 1,000. Increasing the 'take-up' of available services can therefore reduce the cost per child immunized.

I THE STATE OF THE WORLD'S CHILDREN 1985

China: a generation ahead

In recent years, several internationally sponsored workshops have been held in China to promote oral rehydration therapy (ORT) in the country which houses a quarter of the world's children. The workshops, held in hospitals, were attended by paediatricians who were using intravenous therapy to treat diarrhoeal dehydration.

At about that time, in 1979, survey results began to come in from Shanghai county showing that although diarrhoeal disease was common, deaths from dehydration were not. At the time no-one could account for this finding, which flatly contradicted the experience of most developing nations.

In 1982, the Ministry of Health began working with UNICEF to promote maternal and child health in ten 'model counties'. During the initial research for the project, a village barefoot doctor was asked how she would treat a child with diarrhoea. After mentioning various treatments, she added – "and of course we also make sure that the mother is giving the child a salt and sugar solution."

It was assumed that she was an exception, but her reply prompted researchers to include the question in a survey of barefoot doctor practices.

Over 100 barefoot doctors in all ten counties – from Jilin province in the north to Yunan in the south, from Guangdong in the east to Sichuan and Shanghai in the west – were questioned about what they advised for the treatment of diarrhoeal disease. Many preferred intravenous therapy for dehydration. But nine out of ten said that they advised the mother to give a salt and sugar solution. Some said that they did not even need to advise ORT, since it was already common knowledge among mothers.

Clearly, ORT is being used in China and, along with generally satisfactory nutritional levels, helps to explain the rarity of deaths from dehydration. Neighbouring India, by contrast, loses an estimated 1.8 million children a year to diarrhoeal dehydration. But it would be wrong to assume that all Chinese mothers use ORT as a traditional remedy. In fact the origins of ORT seem to go back to a deliberate act of mass-promotion which has now been almost forgotten.

The story begins as far back as 1956, when a severe epidemic of diarrhoeal disease overwhelmed children's hospitals in Beijing. Lacking the intravenous facilities to cope, Chinese doctors developed an oral treatment using tablets of sodium and potassium chloride dissolved in water.

As an oral rehydration solution, this would not work without glucose or sugar. But the doctors found that Chinese mothers routinely sweetened the salty solution before giving it to their children just as they traditionally sweeten all medicines.

Throughout the late 1950s and 1960s, the salt-sugar solution was widely promoted in health education programmes through the schools, radio, and the printed media – and by the waves of young doctors and mobile hospital teams who went out to work in the countryside during and after the 'Great Leap Forward'. In the years that followed, most barefoot doctors and many mothers remembered and carried on using ORT while the hospitals themselves quietly reverted to intravenous therapy. Only recently have some of China's hospitals begun using ORT as a first choice – with a resulting fall in case-fatality rates.

Today, millions of young Chinese mothers are using ORT without depending on the health services. That is the ultimate aim of the campaign to promote ORT world-wide. If it succeeds, the day will come when it seems strange that a massive international promotional effort was necessary for something so ordinary and everyday as ORT. In that sense, China can be said to be a generation ahead of the rest of the world in using what the *Lancet* has called "potentially the greatest medical advance this century"

ments were distributed to all radio stations and broadcast 20 times a day in the weeks leading up to the National Vaccination Days. Posters and pamphlets – printed in their tens of millions at 26 printing centres across the country – reinforced the message. Advertisements were published not only in newspapers and magazines, but on public buses, on pay-slips, bank statements, lottery tickets and electricity bills. And announcements were made not only on radio but on almost 4,000 public address systems in rural areas, shopping centres, football stadiums, and supermarkets throughout Brazil.

When the final results of 1984's National Vaccination Days are recorded, the Brazilian Ministry of Health expects to be able to announce that 2 million under-twos have been vaccinated against measles and 1.5 million against diphtheria, whooping cough and tetanus.

In Colombia, this year, an equally spectacular and even more comprehensive campaign has succeeded in mobilizing over 120,000 people, including almost 30,000 volunteers from the Colombian Red Cross, to assist the health services in vaccinating more than three-quarters of a million under-four-year-olds on each of three National Vaccination Days (see panel 1).

It is always possible that enthusiasm for such campaigns will fade with the declining visibility of the target diseases, especially where they are not yet built into a permanent primary health care system. But in some cases – and the Colombian campaign is such a case – the mobilization of communities for immunization can strengthen the organizational infrastructure of primary health care itself.

In the longer term, it is public understanding itself which is the best guarantee of immunization programmes. As WHO's Director-General has said: *"You can't keep up the enthusiasm unless people understand and demand that their children are immunized"*.

Growth monitoring

Exclusive breast-feeding offers protection against both infection and malnutrition in the first six months of life. Taking a child to be immunized offers protection against six of the most dangerous diseases. Oral rehydration therapy protects against dehydration. But if the growing mind and body of the young child is to be protected from the worst effects of poverty, then a fourth wall of protection must be built around the child's life. Somehow, malnutrition itself must be kept out.

Malnutrition may be an age-old scourge. But it is a relatively new field of scientific study. And in recent years, there has been a quiet revolution in our understanding about what causes child malnutrition – and what can be done to prevent it:-

○ Most malnutrition is invisible and most parents of malnourished children do not know that there is anything wrong.

○ Most malnourished children live in homes where there is no absolute shortage of sufficient food to provide an adequate diet for a small child.

○ Most malnutrition is caused not so much by lack of food as by repeated infections which burn up calories, depress the appetite, drain away nutrients in vomiting or diarrhoea, and often induce mothers to stop feeding while the illness lasts.

In this context, the two most common failings of present efforts to combat child malnutrition are that they concentrate on the treatment of malnutrition rather than its prevention, and that they do not sufficiently involve the mother in learning how to prevent malnutrition from recurring.

If the early signs of faltering growth could be made visible to the mother, and if at the same time she could be made aware of the special food needs of the very young child, then it would be possible to prevent perhaps half or more of all the child malnutrition in the developing world even within existing family resources.

The low-cost technology for making that malnutrition visible already exists in the form of growth charts which are now coming into use in over 80 countries. By weighing the child each month and entering the results on the chart, the first signs of poor growth are made visible to both mothers and health workers. If a mother can see

I THE STATE OF THE WORLD'S CHILDREN 1985

Delhi: mothers monitor growth

A group of Indian mothers from the poorest communities of Delhi have shown that they can dramatically reduce malnutrition among their children by using growth monitoring charts and by learning how to make better use of the food they have available.

The mothers were attending the clinic attached to the Srimati Sucheta Kripalani Hospital in Delhi. Their children – a total of 120 under-fives – were all malnourished, some of them severely.

Normally, the treatment would have been supplementary foods, a routine check-up, and some verbal advice to the mothers. But in this particular case, a group of paediatricians from one of Delhi's medical colleges attempted a different approach. They were convinced, as they wrote later, that "if the mother is charged with the responsibility of managing her malnourished child by herself, under periodic and regular supervision, her child's nutrition will improve."

Each mother was given a 'Road to Health' growth chart to keep at home. Its use was explained and, at every visit, the child was weighed and its growth curve plotted on the chart.

If the chart showed the child gaining weight, this was treated not as routine but as a cause for complimenting the mother. If the chart showed no gain or a fall in the child's weight, then the problem was discussed with the mother. In addition to checking for infections, the staff discussed the child's diet in detail – what the child ate, how much, and how frequently – and advised the mother both on more frequent feeding and on improvements to the child's diet which the mother could make within her limited resources.

Perhaps as many as two-thirds of all mothers of malnourished children do not know that there is anything wrong. In the Delhi clinic, all the mothers were taught to recognize the subtler signs of malnutrition – including listlessness and lack of energy, irritability or frequent crying. Food supplements were not given.

The progress of all 120 children was followed over periods ranging from five months to one year. No fewer than 103 of the children – approximately 85% – showed a significant improvement, as defined by their reaching at least 80% of the average weight for their age. Only 13 showed no improvement and only four fell further behind.

According to Dr. Sudarshan Kumari, who initiated the Delhi experiment:-

"These results show the striking effectiveness of this approach in tackling the problem of malnutrition in the most vulnerable age group, viz. children under the age of five years. The nutritional status of 85.8% of severely malnourished children was brought to normal or near-normal by this method. Such an approach is cheap, administratively easy to organize, does not require extra personnel, does not subject these children and their families to heavy financial burdens and avoids the risks of hospitalization. No new set-up, as in the nutritional rehabilitation centre, is required. Any outpatient-based clinic, e.g. a primary health centre, can utilize this approach effectively. Nutrition education requires just an elementary knowledge of the dietary requirements of the growing child and any person with a little extra training can be involved in this programme, e.g. community health worker, schoolteacher, public health nurse and secondary-school children. As the mother herself is involved in the child's care, her confidence improves, her changed nutritional outlook helps to prevent a relapse in the child, and her outlook towards the family diet is also changed. Nutrition education becomes a part of a package of programmes to improve the total well-being of the child. The whole community also benefits indirectly since the effect on the child's nutrition through an improvement in his diet has the effect of a live demonstration for the whole community."

Fig.16 Impact of hand-washing on transmission of diarrhoeal infections

Impact of hand-washing programme on incidence of diarrhoeal disease in day-care centres in the United States

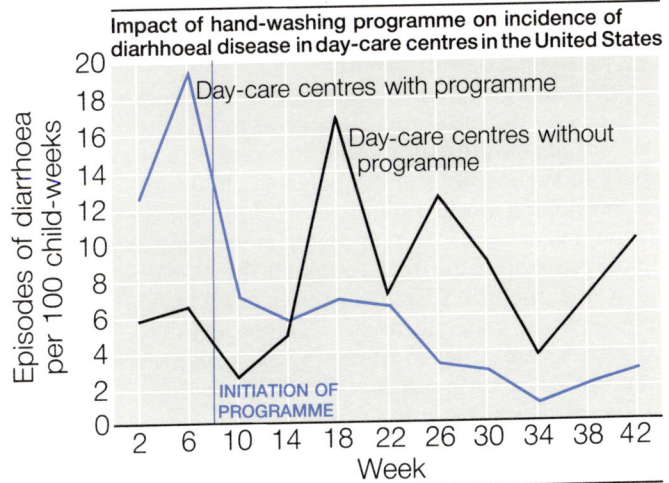

Note: Child-weeks are the number of children present for at least two of five days in a week

Source: Handwashing to Prevent Diarrhea in Day-care Centers. Robert E. Black et. al. American Journal of Epidemiology, Vol. 113, No 4, 1981.

Impact of hand-washing programme on intra-family transmission of diarrhoeal infection in Bangladesh

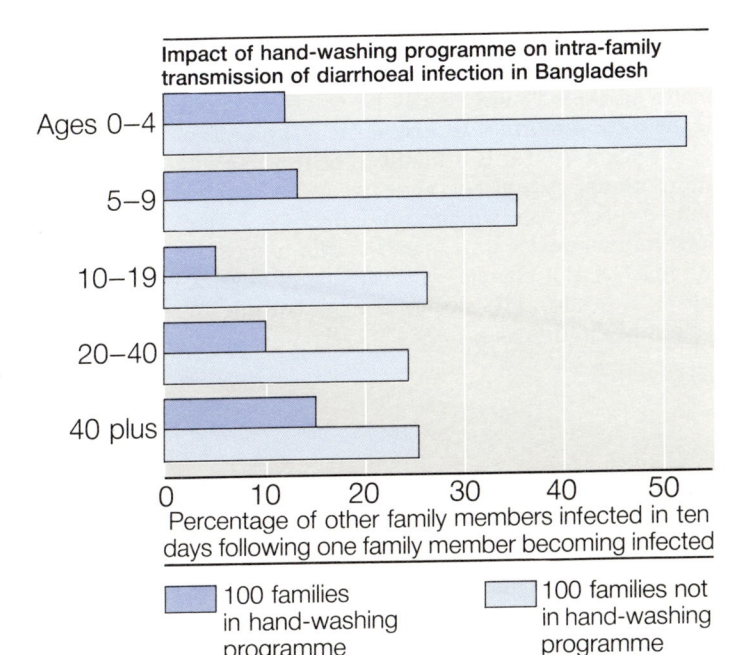

Percentage of other family members infected in ten days following one family member becoming infected

■ 100 families in hand-washing programme
□ 100 families not in hand-washing programme

Note: Diarrhoeas due to causes other than shigella were also reduced by 37% by the use of soap and water

Source: Adapted from Moslem Uddin Khan, "Interruption of Shigellosis by Handwashing", International Centre for Diarrhoeal Disease Research, Transaction of the Royal Society of Tropical Medicine and Hygiene, vol.76, No 2, 1982.

her child's progress beginning to falter, she will take action to put the child back on course. Sometimes, she needs no further information. More often she will need, and seek, advice on how to maintain the child's normal healthy growth.

That advice might include:-

○ Keep on breast-feeding until the child is at least one year old.

○ At the age of four or five months, begin giving the child other foods – whatever is in the family pot, plus a little oil and some skinned and mashed vegetables.

○ Children have small stomachs, so feed a child often – even if it is only a small amount.

○ Persist in feeding during illness or diarrhoea – even though the child has no appetite.

○ The three to five days after an illness are a special time for catching up on lost growth – frequent feeding in these few days will help towards a complete recovery.

○ Wash hands often, and especially after defecating and before preparing food. Keep food clean (fig. 16).

Some households are so deprived of basic foods that this information would be of limited use. Some mothers have so little decision-making power over the allocation of the family's food that they would not be able to make these small but vital changes. Some women have so little time and so many responsibilities that advice about more frequent feeding of specially prepared weaning foods would be just insensitive to their circumstances.

But in the majority of cases, a growth chart which makes the problem of malnutrition visible, and some basic advice which makes that information practicable, could enable millions of mothers to prevent child malnutrition (see panel 17).

Over 200 different kinds of growth chart are now in use. They can be made of virtually indestructible plastic-paper, they cost only a few cents and they can also carry other vital messages about immunization, weaning, breast-feeding, birth spacing, and how to make an oral rehydration solution. In short, they can become a parent's

I THE STATE OF THE WORLD'S CHILDREN 1985

guide to protecting the life and normal healthy growth of children.

Growth charts have been in limited use for many years. But with the spread of a new understanding about malnutrition, some countries are now beginning to use growth charts on a scale commensurate with the problem.

In Thailand, the number of growth charts in use has risen from 400,000 in 1980 to 2.5 million at the beginning of 1984. In Uganda, 2 million charts have gone into service in the last 12 months. In Botswana, to help cope with a state of nutritional emergency, 95% of all children under five now have growth charts. In Zimbabwe, 500,000 have just been printed for use throughout the health service. In Tanzania, 700,000 are now going into use. In the Republic of Korea, 600,000 have been distributed. And in 1984, Mexico, Pakistan, Bangladesh, Ethiopia, Viet Nam, and Zaire have all been finalizing standard national growth charts with the intention of providing one for each child under the age of three.

There are very great difficulties to be overcome if growth monitoring of children is to fulfil its potential as a dramatically effective low-cost technique for preventing child malnutrition. The need for an accurate weighing of the child each month, and the need for monthly contact with a trained person to assist in plotting the child's growth and giving advice, are severe limitations on the outreach of the growth monitoring idea. In Indonesia, a nutrition improvement programme has tackled these problems by training several hundred thousand village nutrition volunteers or *kaders* who manage the monthly sessions where over 3 million mothers weigh their young children on ordinary market scales. The impact of this imaginative campaign has yet to be measured.

The training of more community health workers is clearly the most important pre-condition for the spread of growth monitoring and growth advice to the majority of mothers and children in the developing world (see pages 57-61). But the second major obstacle to growth monitoring is almost purely technical. Throughout the developing world, there is a desperate need for a cheap, light and accurate means of weighing children. Most scales are either so heavy and expensive that they can only be found in a few fully equipped clinics; or they are so difficult and awkward to use that visiting community health workers sometimes give up in embarrassment; or they are so inaccurate that they cannot detect a change in a child's weight from one month to the next.

So important is growth monitoring to the survival and normal development of many millions of children, that the invention of an appropriate weighing device for use by community health workers would rightly be regarded as one of the most important technical breakthroughs of recent years. And it is difficult to believe that the international scientific and technical profession – a profession which can launch a 2.5-ton $600 million device into space in order to measure the mass of the planets – is incapable of developing a two-kilo, $10 device for measuring the weight of children.

The Disproportionate Benefit

Individually, breast-feeding, growth monitoring, oral rehydration, and immunization therefore offer remarkably cost-effective protection to children in poor communities. But their combined effect could be several times greater than a simple addition of their advantages. To see why the whole is so much greater than the sum of the parts, demands a more sophisticated understanding of the problem itself.

Until very recently, it has been conventional wisdom to say that 2 million children die each year of measles, that a million and a half die from whooping cough, that several million die from diarrhoeal dehydration, and several million more from malnutrition. Every government and every international development agency, including UNICEF, uses such statistics to draw attention to the principal dangers facing children who live in poverty. But only in a relatively superficial sense are such figures true.

Very few children die from malnutrition alone. Very few die from measles alone, or even from respiratory infections or dehydration alone.

Most of the 40,000 young children who are now dying each day are dying not because they lost a battle but because they lost a war – a long losing war against the sheer frequency of the assaults on their growth during their most vulnerable years. Each infection, whether it be measles or diarrhoea or whooping cough, lowers the child's nutritional status, and leaves the child weaker and more susceptible to further infection (see panel 17).

In the industrialized world, too, infection weakens children, burns up calories, reduces the absorption of nutrients, depresses the appetite, and slows the growth. But when the infection itself passes and appetite is regained, the child usually 'catches up' the growth which has been lost. In other words, the part which illness plays in the story of the child's development is that of a temporary set-back from which a full recovery is normally made.

In a poor community of the developing world, the whole relationship between illness, nutrition, and a child's development is fundamentally different. Instead of being a temporary set-back, an illness is often the first step towards an early death or, for the survivors, permanently retarded growth.

Why is illness such a different proposition for a child living in poverty?

First of all, illness is much more frequent because the environment of poverty is shot through with media of infection – unclean drinking water, unhygienic sanitation, lack of soap, inadequate food storage, lack of knowledge about handwashing, and overcrowded living and sleeping conditions.

Second, the child's resistance to this more prevalent infection is usually very much lower – either because the child is not adequately nourished or because he or she has not fully recovered from a previous illness.

Either way, this combination of more prevalent infection and less robust resistance means that illness among young children is very much more frequent. In a poor community in the developing world, for example, a child is likely to be ill for 16 or 20 weeks a year – with three or four bouts of diarrhoeal infection, perhaps four or five respiratory infections, and maybe an attack of measles, or malaria, or other common childhood illnesses. In one study of children in an extremely poor area of Bangladesh, young children were found to be ill for three-quarters of their lives.

This difference in frequency amounts, in practice, to a difference not just in degree but in kind. Incomplete recovery between illnesses means that successive illnesses undermine the child's growth, lowering resistance and making subsequent illness both more likely and more severe. Far from being a temporary set-back, illness at this level of frequency becomes cumulative in its impact. And the child is now on a steepening downward slope.

In perhaps 2 million of these cases, the child dies with the late symptoms of measles. In more than a million cases it is the racking cough of pertussis or the inflamed lungs of pneumonia which finally prove too much for a weakened body. And in more than 4 million cases a year, the child dies in the stupor of dehydration. But what kills most of these children is not only the particular illness they happened to have at the time of their deaths but the frequency of illness during their lives.

Even for the survivors, the impact on growth can often be permanent. Constant illness and malnutrition, in the years when mind and body are scheduled to develop most rapidly (fig. 18), mean that children are smaller, weaker, and often lacking in the energy to play, to explore, to demand and receive the stimulus which is so vital to the development of mental, physical and social skills.

Protection against all of the illnesses and dangers of growing up in poverty will only happen when poverty itself is overcome. But

I THE STATE OF THE WORLD'S CHILDREN 1985

Protecting growth

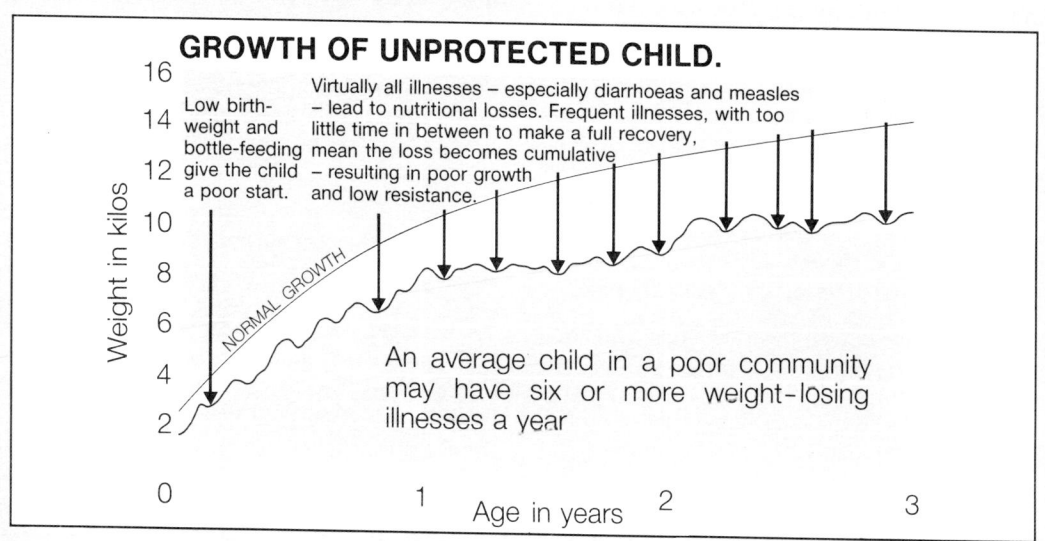

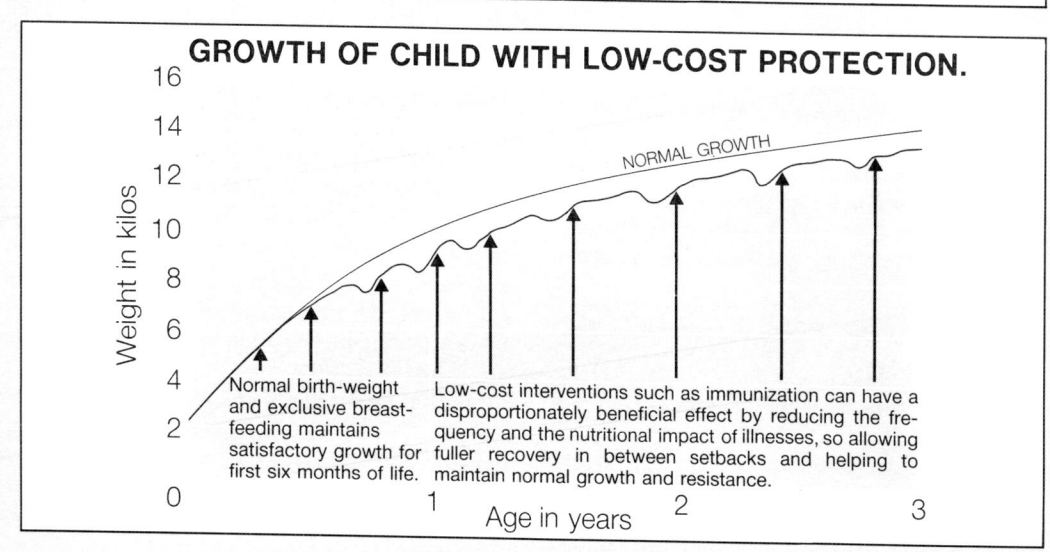

GROWTH OF UNPROTECTED CHILD.

Low birth-weight and bottle-feeding give the child a poor start.

Virtually all illnesses – especially diarrhoeas and measles – lead to nutritional losses. Frequent illnesses, with too little time in between to make a full recovery, mean the loss becomes cumulative – resulting in poor growth and low resistance.

An average child in a poor community may have six or more weight-losing illnesses a year

GROWTH OF CHILD WITH LOW-COST PROTECTION.

Normal birth-weight and exclusive breast-feeding maintains satisfactory growth for first six months of life.

Low-cost interventions such as immunization can have a disproportionately beneficial effect by reducing the frequency and the nutritional impact of illnesses, so allowing fuller recovery in between setbacks and helping to maintain normal growth and resistance.

protection against a few specific illnesses can *help to break the cycle*, by reducing the number and frequency of illnesses, allowing longer periods of recuperation in between, and so pulling the child away from the steepening slope. That is why a limited number of basic interventions can have a disproportionately beneficial effect.

This is the context in which a combination of available strategies could provide such a remarkable protection to the lives and the growth of children in the poor world. It is the self-perpetuating cycle of frequent illness and malnutrition which poses the main threat. And that cycle can now be broken by putting low-cost techniques in the hands of the world's parents.

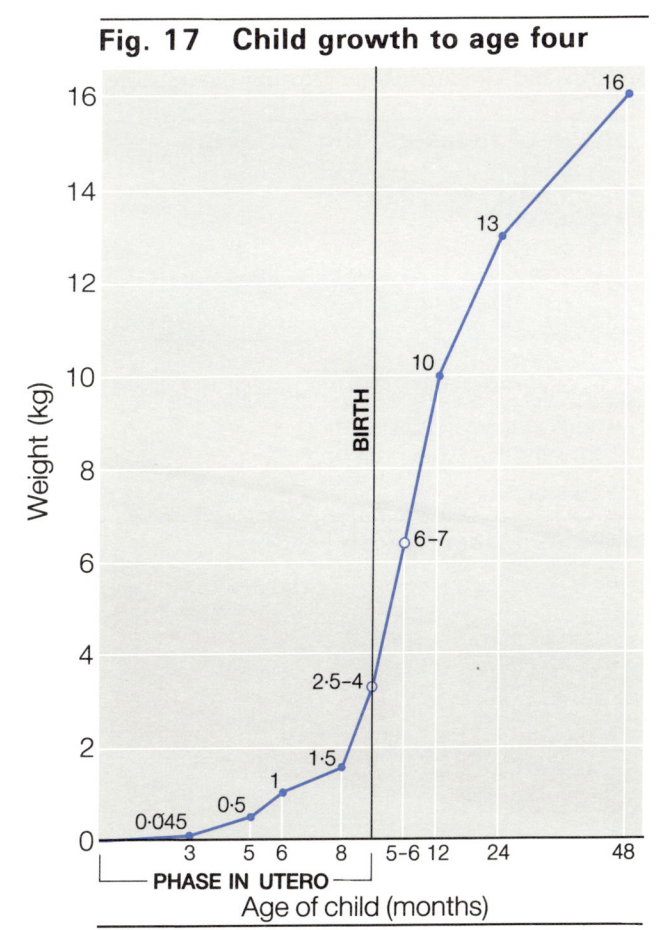

Fig. 17 Child growth to age four

[Graph showing weight (kg) vs age of child (months). Values plotted: 0.045 at 3, 0.5 at 5, 1 at 6, 1.5 at 8, 2.5-4 at birth, 6-7 at 5-6, 10 at 12, 13 at 24, 16 at 48. Phase in utero marked before birth.]

Source: Children in the Tropics No 138–139–140, International Children's Centre, Paris, 1982.

Measles immunization, for example, can achieve very much more than the prevention of measles. In one study of a measles outbreak in the Gambia, it was found that 5% of the children with measles died during the outbreak itself. But nine months later, 10% of those who had survived the measles were dead from other causes (fig. 17). Measles is a major cause of diarrhoea and malnutrition, often causing a serious loss in body weight. Recovering that loss of growth can take anything between 6 and 12 weeks – weeks of malnutrition and weakness which open the way for other infections and further malnutrition. Immunization against measles might therefore have saved not just the 5% of children who died of measles itself but also many of the much larger number who died during the following year. As the World Health Organization has also said this year:-

"Immunization services are effective in preventing specific diseases which can precipitate malnutrition and, by permitting the child a longer recovery period between the events, can prevent this downward spiral and contribute significantly to the overall reduction of childhood mortality.

"By preventing some of these events, immunization services can help reverse this cycle, and their contribution to the prevention of infant and childhood disability and death can therefore extend beyond the prevention of the individual target diseases."

And just as immunization can have an effect beyond the particular disease it is aimed at, so all four of the main low-cost interventions discussed in this report can achieve much more than seems to be the case when looking only at their direct effects. Together, breast-feeding, growth maintenance, oral rehydration, and immunization would, for example, also offer considerable protection against the acute respiratory infections which rank alongside diarrhoeal dehydration as a major cause of illness and death among the developing world's children.

Similarly, oral rehydration therapy itself can do much more than prevent death from dehydration. Diarrhoeal infection is a major cause – in some cases *the* major cause – of child malnutrition. Studies in Guatemala, Bangladesh, Uganda, Brazil, and the Gambia, have all shown that young

I THE STATE OF THE WORLD'S CHILDREN 1985

children typically spend 12% to 14% of their lives suffering from diarrhoeal infections. In one study in Bangladesh, the average child was found to suffer almost 50 days of diarrhoeal infection a year. During those 50 days, the child's appetite is reduced and the mother's inclination is to withhold food. Even when the child does eat, the illness itself severely restricts the body's absorption of nutrients. The result is the loss of perhaps 1 kilo of weight gain over the year, from diarrhoeal disease alone.

Given such a rate and frequency of nutrient loss, it is not hard to see why diarrhoeal infections are coming to be seen as one of the most important causes of child malnutrition. Similar studies in the Gambia, for example, have shown that almost all cases of child malnutrition have been preceded by frequent bouts of diarrhoea.

Oral rehydration therapy drastically reduces the risk of death from dehydration. But it also reduces the nutritional impact of the illness itself. Studies in the Philippines, Bangladesh, and Turkey have shown that children treated with oral rehydration salts during bouts of diarrhoea showed better weight gain than children to whom ORT was not available (fig. 19).

The full potential of the low-cost interventions now available can only be seen in the context of this synergism. For with a few decisive interventions like ORT, immunization, and practicable advice on infant feeding, the downward spiral of malnutrition and infection can be broken and, in its place, an upward spiral can be set in motion – less frequent illness leading to more complete recovery leading to more normal growth leading to less frequent illness....

Growth itself is the aim and the measure of this process, and the growth monitoring chart is the

Fig. 18 Child death rates following acute phase of measles, the Gambia

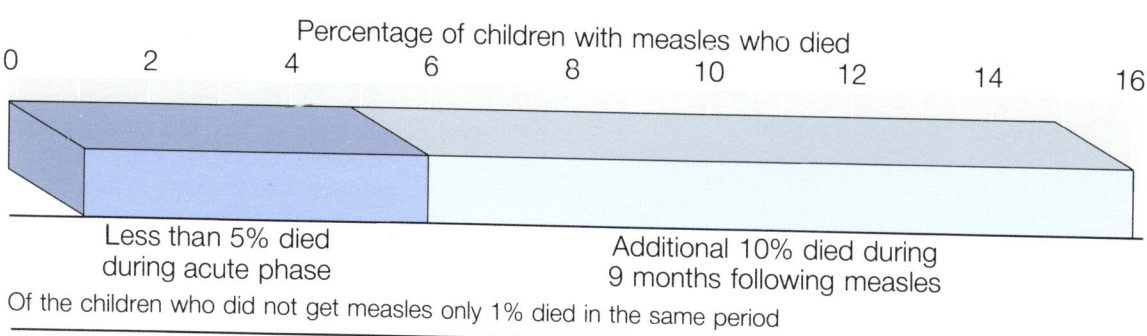

Percentage of children with measles who died
0 2 4 6 8 10 12 14 16

Less than 5% died during acute phase

Additional 10% died during 9 months following measles

Of the children who did not get measles only 1% died in the same period

Child death rates during acute phase of measles infection

Measles may be responsible for far more deaths than those attributed to the acute phase of measles, itself. Often, it is measles which pushes young children into the downward spiral of diarrhoea, malnutrition, lowered resistance, respiratory infections, and further malnutrition.

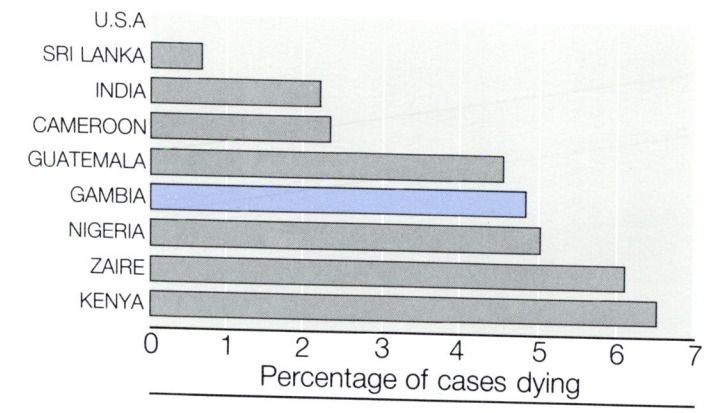

U.S.A
SRI LANKA
INDIA
CAMEROON
GUATEMALA
GAMBIA
NIGERIA
ZAIRE
KENYA

0 1 2 3 4 5 6 7
Percentage of cases dying

Source: Adapted from 'Impact of Vaccine Preventable Diseases in Developing Countries', Timothy J Dondero, Jr, MD, Centre for Disease Control, Presentation to the Conference of the American Public Health Association, Dallas, Texas, November 1983.

simple piece of technology which can reveal to mothers, and to community health workers, whether a child's growth is faltering or whether the child is on the way to healthy normal development.

That is why David Morley, Professor of Tropical Child Health at the University of London and one of the pioneers of low-cost ways of protecting the growth of children, has concluded:-

"The potential impact of growth charts is nothing less than revolutionary ... understanding that it is infection which is the cause can lead to a mother understanding the health workers' advice about the necessity of feeding even during diarrhoea; about the use of oral rehydration solutions; about the importance of measles immunization; or the introduction of weaning foods.

"It is this informed involvement of the mother in the struggle to make sure that the child puts on weight each and every month which is perhaps the greatest contribution the growth charts can make to child development and child health".

Marketing Survival

In summary, growth monitoring charts, sachets of oral rehydration salts, and vaccines, are low-cost, life-saving, growth-protecting technologies which can enable parents to protect their children against the worst effects of poverty. Similarly, a matrix of up-to-date and down-to-earth information about pregnancy, breast-feeding, weaning, feeding during and immediately after illness, child spacing, and how to make and use home-made oral rehydration solutions, could also empower parents to protect the lives and the health of their children.

But how can these technologies and this information be put at the disposal of millions of families in the low-income world? For at least the next quarter of a century, significant improvement in the health of the poor world's children will depend on how well that question can be answered.

The initial task of the child survival revolution is the communication of what is now possible. Yet in a world where information technology has become the new wonder of our age, shamefully little is known about how to communicate information whose principal value is to the poor.

There are perhaps only two large-scale precedents:-

The first is the Green Revolution, which, in many cases, succeeded in putting into the hands of thousands of small as well as large farmers the techniques and the knowledge which enabled them to double and treble the yields from their lands.

Like the present potential for a revolution in child health, the Green Revolution in agriculture also began with a series of technical breakthroughs. But it could not have succeeded outside the laboratory without reaching out to millions of farmers to give them the knowledge and the confidence to try the Green Revolution for themselves and the technical and financial support to make it work. Somehow, that difficult task was achieved in Turkey, in the Punjab of both India and Pakistan, in the Philippines and most recently in Indonesia and Sri Lanka. And in each successful case, the keys to the achievement can now be seen to have been: the commitment of a nation's political leadership; the involvement of all branches of government and not just the ministry of agriculture; and the mobilization of all possible organized resources and channels of communication from the local farmers' association to the national mass media. And in each case, success was achieved by a combination of the farmers' *own* decisions to change the way they worked their land and the government's commitment to providing the necessary support for farmers to implement that decision.

I THE STATE OF THE WORLD'S CHILDREN 1985

Tanzania: a literacy revolution

In 1971 the Tanzanian government declared its intention of wiping out illiteracy within five years. With 70% of its population illiterate and its economy languishing among the 15 poorest in the world, this 'literacy revolution' seemed unlikely.

By the end of 1975, the target had not been met. But over 5 million Tanzanians had enrolled in adult classes and illiteracy was down from 70% to 40%. By 1977 it had fallen to 27% and by 1981 to 21%. In other words, the last decade has seen Tanzanians bring down their illiteracy rate by more than 10% a year – the steepest sustained fall in illiteracy ever achieved by any nation.

What made this achievement possible was, first and foremost, the political commitment of the nation's leadership – a commitment arising from the belief that the development of 'human resources' is both the end and the means of development itself. As Tanzania's President Nyerere said in preparation for the campaign:-

"First we must educate our adults. Our children will not have an impact on our economic development for five, ten or even twenty years. The attitudes of the adults, on the other hand, have an impact now."

But to have mounted an adult literacy campaign while neglecting the primary schools would have been like attempting to blow up a tyre with a slow puncture. And over that same ten years, Tanzania also managed to quadruple the number of 6-to-11-year-olds in its primary schools – from just over 1 million in 1971 to just under 4 million in the early 1980s.

Apart from the political commitment from the top, it was Tanzania's *ingenuity* in finding low-cost solutions and its success in mobilizing all possible resources which made this literacy revolution possible.

It was financially out of the question, for example, to suddenly double the number of school buildings. It was therefore decided to double the capacity of the existing schools by operating a shift system – half of the pupils having their school 'day' in the morning and half in the afternoon. It was not ideal – but best was not allowed to become the enemy of better.

The next major problem was the shortage of teachers. At a training cost of 30,000 Tanzanian shillings each, the country could not afford to train more than 5,000 primary-school teachers a year – not nearly enough to meet the needs of a literacy revolution. One solution was to mobilize university students, retired teachers, and older secondary-school pupils to act as assistant teachers. It helped. But it was not enough.

The answer produced in Tanzania was the distance training programme, a three-year course by correspondence and radio, backed by touring village tutors and followed by six weeks' residence in a teacher-training college. Students stayed at home instead of in halls of residence and were given 150 shillings a month as a student grant.

Of the 45,000 men and women who enrolled in the distance training programme, 35,000 passed the final examination and went out to teach in the nation's primary schools. So far, follow-up research has detected no major difference in performance among teachers trained in the new way – and at less than one-third of the normal cost.

For both adults and children, the literacy revolution has not been without its problems – especially the shortage of books, paper, and spare parts for printing presses. Nor are all the problems yet solved – literacy is the beginning, not the end, of education. But a revolution in education has been brought about at a relatively low cost and in a relatively short time. In discussions this year on the present opportunity for another social revolution – a low-cost revolution in child survival and development – President Nyerere has again said: "We will do it."

An independent evaluation of the Green Revolution in Turkey, for example, paid this tribute to the Turkish farmer:-

"The most important conclusion ... is that the Turkish farmer changed....He had to change his seed bed preparation practices, adopt new fertilizing techniques and usage, plant his grain at a lower rate, and on top of all this, borrow more than he had ever borrowed before to accomplish this new change".

But there is a second and even larger-scale example of large numbers of people being empowered to use new techniques for improving their own circumstances through their own decisions. Twenty years ago, there began a campaign to put the knowledge and the means of family planning at the disposal of many millions of people in the low-income world. And that too was a campaign to promote low-cost technologies with the potential to give people more power to improve their own and their children's lives.

At first, the official health services were thought to be the only proper channel for putting the knowledge and means of contraception at people's disposal. As a result, the practice of family planning spread only slowly in the late 1950s and early 1960s. But in the 1970s, countries like Thailand and Indonesia began to pioneer ways of breaking family planning out of the medical chest and turning it into a people's technology. Soon, pills and condoms were being sold in pharmacies and bazaars, corner-stores and cigarette kiosks, vending machines and gas stations. Adverts in cinemas and newspapers, phone-in advice services and mail-order contraceptives, question-and-answer shows on radio and TV, spot advertisements repeated dozens of times a day – all were used to put the knowledge and the means of birth control into the hands of the people.

Demystified and deprofessionalized, family planning began to gather pace. World-wide, a majority of parents now have access to modern means of controlling the number and spacing of their births.

There are two great lessons to be learned from

Fig.19 Effect of ORT on weight-gain and on duration of diarrhoeal illness

In a study of ORT administered at home by trained midwives in a rural area of Turkey, a total of 1,237 children aged 0–5 years were monitored over a 16 month period. 746 were in the ORT treatment group and the rest in a control group. The results:–

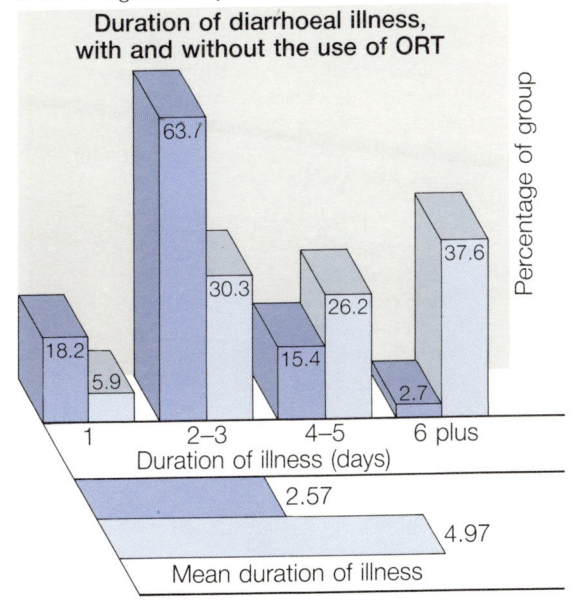

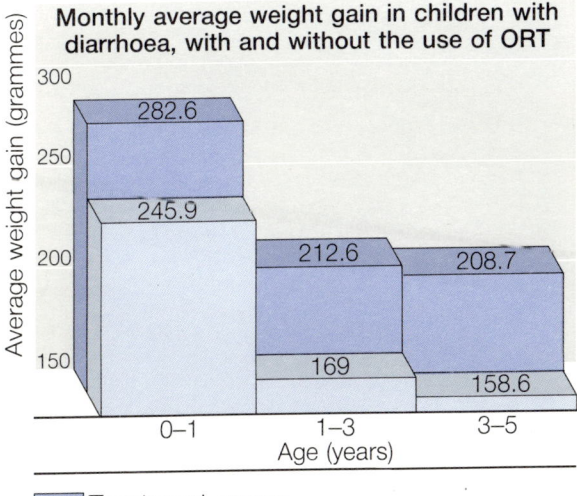

Duration of diarrhoeal illness, with and without the use of ORT

Duration of illness (days)	Treatment	Control
1	18.2	5.9
2–3	63.7	30.3
4–5	15.4	26.2
6 plus	2.7	37.6

Mean duration of illness: 2.57 (treatment), 4.97 (control)

Monthly average weight gain in children with diarrhoea, with and without the use of ORT

Age (years)	Treatment	Control
0–1	282.6	245.9
1–3	212.6	169
3–5	208.7	158.6

■ Treatment group
□ Control group

Source: Bulletin of the World Health Organization, 58(2):333–338 (1980).

# I THE STATE OF THE WORLD'S CHILDREN 1985

Bangladesh: teaching two million

In Bangladesh, almost 10% of all the children born die before reaching the age of five from the dehydration and malnutrition brought on by diarrhoea. And for those who survive, diarrhoeal disease is a major cause of malnutrition.

Most of the deaths could be prevented by the simple means of packets of oral rehydration salts mixed with water. But cheap though the packets are, supplying them to the 15 million mothers of young children in Bangladesh sets almost insurmountable problems. The country would need to produce 90 million packets a year instead of today's 10 million; over 80% of Bangladeshi women are illiterate and cannot read the instructions; health services reach only 20% of the population; and many rural families do not earn enough to buy the packets.

The Bangladesh Rural Advancement Committee (BRAC) recognized that a solution was needed which every rural household could afford. After a year's experimenting it came up with the answer – a set of simple messages called 'seven points to remember' which teaches mothers how to ward off dehydration by mixing a set amount of water with a three-finger pinch of salt (*lobon*) and a four-finger scoop of *gur*, the local unrefined sugar.

BRAC launched its oral rehydration programme in mid-1980. Nine hundred field-workers organized in teams of ten – seven women oral rehydration workers, two male team co-ordinators and a cook – fanned out through five of Bangladesh's 20 districts. Within three years the team had taught 2.5 million women in 20,700 villages how to prepare the *lobon-gur* mix.

The team co-ordinators visit the villages first, to pave the way with government officials and village leaders; they also meet with the men of the village and organize diarrhoea control campaigns in local schools.

The oral rehydration workers then call on each family door-to-door, explaining the 'seven points to remember' to mothers, showing them how to prepare the *lobon-gur* mix, and watching while the mothers make it.

A month later, a monitoring team questions 5% of the mothers on the 'seven points' and asks them to prepare the mix. The responses are graded and the oral rehydration workers paid according to how much the mothers have learned – 16 cents for a perfect score, 8 and 4 cents for lower scores, and nothing if the mother has forgotten how to make the mix. Even after six months, 98% of mothers can still prepare the mix accurately.

The monitoring teams also test how often the mothers actually give the mix to their children when they have diarrhoea. The initial responses were disappointing; usage rates were as low as 8%. With diarrhoea such an everyday event, mild attacks received no treatment at all.

After studying the problem, BRAC concluded that oral rehydration needed more support from husbands and male community leaders. So BRAC included two more men in each monitoring team to speak to the men of the villages – individually and in groups, at the mosques and market-places – and to hold special seminars for the traditional healers, who are also usually men.

The result was improvement in the use of *lobon-gur*, although the rate has yet to rise above 60%. But BRAC is confident that the rates will continue to grow as the message is repeatedly brought home through the schools and traditional healers, and by a media campaign which uses posters, leaflets, television and radio spots.

As it enters its fifth year, the programme has increased the number of its field-workers to 1,200 and has every chance of achieving its interim target of reaching 6.5 million mothers by 1986.

both of these precedents. First, they have shown that the way to promote a people's technology and to put information at the disposal of the majority is by mobilizing all possible resources and working through all possible channels both to create the *demand* and to meet it. Second, hindsight clearly shows that neither the Green Revolution nor the family planning movement really took off until they were seen as political and economic priorities and given the full backing of a nation's political leadership. When the weight of the president or prime minister was put behind the campaign, when the ministries of labour and finance and education as well as the ministries of health or agriculture became involved, it then became possible to mobilize more of the resources of government and of society.

Nowhere are these two lessons more clearly illustrated than in present-day Indonesia. Because the campaign for family planning was given high personal and political priority by the President, and because 85% of all family planning services were made available *outside* the formal health services, almost all Indonesian parents today have access to the knowledge and the means of contraception. A similar combination of presidential leadership and the use of all available channels was responsible for Indonesia's successful Green Revolution of the late 1970s and early 1980s.

In stark contrast, oral rehydration salts have been 'passively' available for the last ten years through health clinics which serve only about 20% of the people. Between 1974 and 1979, approximately 10 million sachets were used and, undoubtedly, many lives were saved. But in that same period no less than 3 million Indonesian children died of dehydration.

There is no convincing medical reason why oral rehydration salts should only be available through clinics or health centres. And if the salts are to become available to the majority then the time has come for mass information campaigns to create the demand and for the product itself to be available – as easily as matches, soap, razor blades, soft drinks, cigarettes, tea, cooking oil, or batteries – from grocery stores, vending machines, street hawkers, *sari-sari* stores, bazaars, supermarkets, barber's shops, tea stalls, gas stations, and bars.

Although the task of making the knowledge and the means of family planning universally available is far from completed, the story of family planning over the last ten years is a story of great hope for the child survival revolution. Exactly a decade ago, at the first World Population Conference in Bucharest, it was resolved by the international community that *"all couples and individuals have the basic right to decide freely and responsibly the number and spacing of their children"*.

In 1984, as the second World Population Conference met in Mexico City, it could look back on a decade of rapid progress in translating that human right into a human reality. The majority of parents now have the knowledge and the means of birth control. Now, the time has come to also give parents the knowledge and the means of death control.

Social marketing

Inasmuch as the prospects for a revolution in child survival depend on the communication of practicable information to millions of parents, the modern mass media are clearly a powerful resource for helping to bring that revolution about. And it is perhaps in this specific area of 'social marketing' that the present campaign has most to learn from the family planning experience.

Over the last twenty years, the developing world has transformed its capacity to communicate with its own people. The consolidation of national languages, the installing of national road and rail networks, the increasing concentration of peoples in towns and cities, and the dramatic rise in school enrolment have created a new potential for mass communications. Radio remains of paramount importance for reaching the majority. But the printed media are important in urban areas and television and video have spread more quickly than anyone would have imagined: by the end of the present decade, for example, almost three-quarters of India's 700 million people will have access to television.

In the industrialized world, the modern media's capacity for mass communication is increasingly being deployed to bring about changes in behaviour and improvements in society. The National

The Gambia and Honduras: marketing ORT

Armed with the knowledge of oral rehydration therapy (ORT), parents themselves can now defeat the diarrhoeal dehydration which is the main cause of child deaths – and a major cause of child malnutrition – in the developing world. At the moment, less than 15% of parents know about ORT. So the question mark over this major medical breakthrough is: how can it be put into the hands of the vast majority of the world's parents?

One possible answer is 'social marketing' – promoting ORT by the same methods which have put drinks like Coca-Cola into almost every village in the third world.

To try out the idea, the governments of two countries – the Gambia and Honduras – enlisted the help of an experienced social marketing team – the American non-profit Academy for Educational Development.

Today these campaigns represent the world's first experience of mass-marketing ORT. The story so far:-

In Honduras, the campaign opted to promote Litrosol – brand name of the locally manufactured sachets of WHO/UNICEF oral rehydration formula. The target population was 400,000. Seven months of careful audience research gradually shaped the marketing plan. Radio was selected as the one medium which reaches most mothers and several 60-second ORT 'ads' were developed for use on 30 commercial radio networks.

Within a few months, the ORT theme song was nationally popular and almost three-quarters of all mothers knew the words.

But it was also found that most mothers needed a one-to-one demonstration of ORT. So doctors and nurses were enlisted to train 1,200 'red heart ladies' – village demonstrators from whose homes flew flags bearing the campaign's symbol of a red heart.

The campaign opened amid nation-wide publicity in 1981. Less than a year later, 93% of the population knew about Litrosol and 48% had used it at least once. After eighteen months, a survey was undertaken in homes where a child had suffered from a diarrhoeal infection in the two weeks prior to the survey. Almost 40% had been treated with ORT. The cost of the campaign was 25 cents per mother reached.

In the Gambia, it was decided that pre-packed sachets of oral rehydration salts would be beyond the financial reach of too many of the nation's mothers. So the campaign set out to teach mothers to forestall dehydration by making up their own solution from ordinary household ingredients. Careful research turned up a bottle for a local soft drink – 'Julpearl' – as the one measuring device available to almost everyone in the country. Eight Julpearl bottle-caps of sugar plus one of salt, added to three Julpearl bottles of water, was found to make a satisfactory oral rehydration formula.

In a largely illiterate population, radio was again selected as the main medium for reaching the nation's mothers. Free air time was given to the campaign by Radio Gambia – listened to by 75% of mothers in 98% of villages.

Soon, radio advertisements were explaining 'do-it-yourself' ORT. At the same time, almost all of the country's health workers and nurses were involved in giving demonstrations in villages and reinforcing the radio message. A total of 11,000 women entered the Happy Baby lotteries which offered plastic measuring jugs and bars of soap as prizes for village mothers who could answer basic questions on ORT. Community prizes of sugar and rice went to the villages where the highest proportion of mothers knew how to prepare an oral rehydration solution.

Within eight months, two-thirds of the nation's mothers knew how to mix the solution and almost 40% had started to use home-made ORT when their children had diarrhoea.

High Blood Pressure Education Program in the United States, for example, has helped to reduce stroke deaths by over 5% a year, leading to an overall reduction of 40% in the rate of stroke deaths during the 1970s. Other media campaigns in the industrial world have helped to tackle the problems of breast cancer, drug abuse, road safety, energy conservation, and home-accident prevention. Inevitably, such mass media campaigns have adopted and adapted many of the techniques of the commercial marketing world and have therefore attracted the label of 'social marketing'.

In the developing world, the new capacity for mass communications has also opened up a potential for social marketing campaigns. And in the last few years, much has been learned about the potential – and the limitations – of social marketing as a means of bringing about improvements in the field of health and nutrition.

Most of the experience of social marketing in the developing world has accumulated around the promotion of family planning. But successful campaigns have also been geared to other goals. In Ecuador, a campaign to prevent goitre – based on a one-minute radio advertisement repeated several times a day for twelve months – has increased the number of households using iodized salt from 5% to 98%. In the Philippines, 250 radio stations broadcasting daily messages for three months about improved agricultural techniques have significantly increased both the rice yields and the incomes of the 50,000 participating farmers. Also in the Philippines, a radio campaign to persuade mothers to enrich weaning foods has succeeded in increasing the percentage of women who add oil to the usual porridge from less than 1% to more than 20% in the first eight months of the campaign.

Today, the resources of the mass media – and the techniques of social marketing – are already beginning to be used to put the techniques of a child survival revolution at the disposal of millions of parents:-

In Honduras and the Gambia, social marketing campaigns have promoted ORT to hundreds of thousands of mothers (see panel 20). Within one year, almost 100% of mothers knew about ORT and almost half of them had used it.

Similarly in Nicaragua, a government radio station in partnership with a commercial advertising agency has taught 70,000 mothers that 'Super Limonada' (the name given to oral rehydration salts) will prevent dehydration. One-quarter of the mothers were reported to be actually using the salts and the cost of the campaign is between 65 cents and $1.75 per mother reached.

In Brazil, the equivalent of $1 million a year in radio and television advertising time has been put behind a nation-wide campaign to promote breast-feeding. Virtually everyone in Brazil is now aware that mother's milk provides the best possible nutrition and protection for babies, though it is not known whether the campaign has yet reversed the recent rapid slide towards bottle-feeding in so many of Brazil's cities.

In India, child survival messages are being proclaimed by advertisements on buses and billboards. In Nigeria, groups of doctors are literally 'marketing' health by setting up health stalls in market-places. In Ghana, a group of young doctors has even begun giving child survival information talks on country buses. In Indonesia, commercial marketing techniques were used to research and design the growth chart which now monitors the nutritional status of over 3 million children and is currently being adapted for use in Ethiopia. In Haiti, demand for oral rehydration salts is being created by a nation-wide advertising campaign and the sachets themselves are being supplied through corner-shops and grocery stores plus 2,000 village outlets.

In India, magazine advertisements promoting information on breast-feeding brought 4,000 letters a month into UNICEF's New Delhi offices and child survival revolution messages on radio are reaching audiences of up to 200 million people.

The potential of social marketing is only just beginning to be explored. But already, there is a body of experience available to guide future efforts. First, it is clear that people's lives and behaviour cannot be transformed simply by waving the magic wand of social marketing. Mass media messages about the need to boil water or to breast-feed or to feed a child more frequently cannot solve the problems of firewood shortage or

I THE STATE OF THE WORLD'S CHILDREN 1985

maternity leave or give a mother more energy or more hours in the day. Reviewing several attempts to use social marketing for nutritional improvement, for example, Richard K. Manoff* has written:-

"The nutrition-educator-turned-advertising agent, cognizant of this new-found power but mindful of its limitations, has the responsibility of never permitting its use as a substitute for necessary social policy initiatives."

Secondly, it has proved important to recognize the differences as well as the similarities between commercial and social marketing. Most commercial advertising aims to promote brand-name consciousness in a competitive market and to associate products with moods and emotions. Such advertising is often deliberately devoid of substance or rationality. By contrast, social marketing usually depends on the substance of its message and the rationality of its presentation. A campaign designed to help a community and its parents learn how to make and use oral rehydration solutions, for example, is a different marketing proposition from a campaign to persuade a community to drink Coke rather than Pepsi.

Because social marketing campaigns usually seek a more important change in behaviour and attitudes than a change in loyalties to a particular brand name, mass media messages in themselves are usually not enough. In the promotion of a more complex process such as ORT, for example, mass media campaigns can be an important complement to, but not an adequate substitute for, practical face-to-face demonstrations by health workers or trained volunteers.

So far, the commonest mistake of social marketing campaigns seems to be a concentration on the superficial aspects of commercial marketing techniques at the expense of its deeper disciplines. Research into how a target audience perceives its own problems and needs, into what sources of information have credibility, into what kinds of presentation are acceptable and what kinds of information are practicable, are all essential to campaigns which seek to bring about complex changes in human behaviour. In developing such campaigns, considerable resources of time, money, and creativity need to be invested in message selection, media planning, analysis of message resistance and monitoring of message response. A lack of professionalism in any one of these disciplines can easily cut in half the effectiveness of a social marketing campaign.

Careful market research in the campaign to promote breast-feeding in Brazil, for example, suggested that it would be wrong for the campaign to dwell on the idyllic aspects of breast-feeding or on the idea that breast-feeding is the symbol of 'love, nutrition and protection'. From careful sampling and interviewing, it was shown that:-

"Such an emphasis could seriously dismay a mother having routine problems with breast-feeding, by arousing in her intense anxiety about her potential inability to provide 'love, nutrition and protection'. A message simply extolling breast-feeding could actually contribute to sharpening normal anxiety and consequently diminish the mother's all-important lactation reflexes."

Similar research also proved important in the campaign to promote ORT in Honduras, where attitude surveys showed that mothers were very strongly predisposed towards treatments with a sophisticated, urban image. It was therefore decided that, on balance, the promotion of ORT would be significantly more likely to succeed if the campaign were to promote the foil-wrapped sachets of oral rehydration salts rather than the use of home-made salt and sugar solutions.

Constant monitoring of the campaign's effect quickly revealed another potentially disastrous problem. The nurses themselves – on whom the training of village women depended – were so unenthusiastic about ORT that many were unwilling to go out and recommend the therapy to mothers. The reasons given were usually vague. But persistent research revealed the problem. The commonest local measure of a litre of water was a soft-drink bottle with a very narrow neck. Moth-

---

* Richard Manoff has been consultant to many social marketing and nutrition education projects in Latin America, Asia and Africa. He has also acted as special adviser to WHO and UNICEF in the development of the International Code of Marketing of Breast-milk Substitutes (see panel 12).

ers always rinsed the bottle before handing it to the nurse to demonstrate 'Litrosol'. When the nurse tried to pour the contents from the foil sachet into the bottle, the salts caked on the wet narrow neck. So getting the salts into the bottle was a difficult and fussy process which the nurses found embarrassingly difficult to perform in front of the mothers.

On this one detail, the campaign could have foundered. But once the problem was known, the solution was not far away. A Honduran laboratory technician suggested changing the shape of the foil sachet so that one end was long and pointed: when opened at the pointed end, the foil sachet became a funnel for pouring the salts cleanly into the bottle. As a bonus, mothers are also left with a useful item of kitchen equipment. Says the technical report on the Honduras programme: *"it is perfectly clear to us now that if the nurses' concern had gone unnoticed, or had been ignored, the whole programme could have been endangered"*.

It is already possible to say that social marketing is one of the most important tools for taking child protection strategies out of the medical chest and putting them into the hands of parents. But there is a great danger that this potential will be squandered in facile imitation of the more visible techniques of commercial marketing, while ignoring the painstaking research, the professionalism, and the attention to detail, which successful marketing demands.

The industrialized world

Rightly or wrongly, the industrialized nations also possess remarkable power to promote new norms and new attitudes – especially in the field of health. It was the industrialized world which set the example of bottle-feeding and the separating of mothers and babies into different rooms in hospital maternity units. On a more general level, it is the industrialized world which has made health care almost synonymous with dependence on medical professionals and expensive curative care.

In promoting the methods and attitudes which could help to bring about a child survival revolution, therefore, the industrialized world has a responsibility which goes further than the financial resources which it could make available. And there are some definite signs that a better model of health care is now beginning to emerge. To begin with, the basic tenet of the child health revolution – the idea that primary responsibility for health can be taken by the individual – is an idea that is now gathering momentum in many industrialized nations. The support of professional health services is of course essential, but the millions of individuals in the rich world who are taking up regular exercise, stopping smoking, and being careful with food and drink, are reclaiming the primary responsibility for their own physical well-being.

More specifically, many industrialized nations are themselves using some of the low-cost methods discussed in this report. In recent years, for example, there has been a very pronounced trend back towards breast-feeding, with over 90% of babies being breast-fed from birth in some northern countries (see panel 11). This practical demonstration of the fact that breast-milk is best for all babies and that breast-feeding is not 'just for the poor' will undoubtedly fortify the campaigns to promote breast-feeding in the developing world.

The industrialized world is not quite so advanced in the use of ORT. Probably a majority of hospitals are still using intravenous therapy for dehydration, even though ORT has been shown to be more effective in most cases. Several major hospitals have made the change, including the East Birmingham Hospital in England where a senior paediatrician has commented that *"in Birmingham, as in Bangladesh, the use of oral fluid has revolutionized the management of acute infant gastroenteritis"*. If all mothers and family doctors in the industrialized world also knew about ORT, then most cases of dehydration could be prevented, rendering hospital admission unnecessary.

In the training of health professionals, the publishing of standard texts, and the setting of standards for paediatric and hospital practice, the industrialized world's medical institutions also have a direct influence on approaches to health in the developing world. Yet only in the 1980s have the main paediatric textbooks in the United States

I THE STATE OF THE WORLD'S CHILDREN 1985

accepted and promoted ORT as the best method of preventing, or treating, most cases of dehydration. Similarly in maternity units, 'rooming in' and the active encouragement of breast-feeding are still not standard practice in many of the more old-fashioned but still influential hospitals.

In addition to the power of example, the governments and organizations of the industrialized world could obviously play a major part in the child survival revolution by making more money available to governments and organizations in the developing world which are trying to bring that revolution about. Aid programmes in particular could be increased to the internationally agreed target of 0.7% of the donor nations' GNPs. Today, the figure for the free-market industrialized nations stands at 0.37% of their GNPs – about the same as in 1974 and considerably less than in 1964.

Within those aid programmes, particular attention could also be given to strategies which would benefit both the poorest countries and the poorest people within countries. At the moment, a significant percentage of the industrialized world's aid is devoted to capital-absorbing high-tech programmes which confer their benefits on an urban minority and run counter to the ideal of making low-cost basic health care available to all. Similarly, the international financial institutions could also play their part by adopting the radical idea of taking the needs of the poorest women and children into account when discussing conditions of financial support. In particular, it is essential that financial arrangements should actively seek to protect low-cost services and programmes which benefit the poorest women and children. By any unblinkered calculation, such services are not 'unaffordable consumption' but essential and highly cost-effective investments in the present and future human resources of a nation.

The promotion of low-cost strategies to help build basic protection for the poorest is beginning among the governments of the industrialized world. The development aid agencies of Canada and Sweden, for example, are actively promoting low-cost techniques like ORT. In Washington, the United States Agency for International Development (USAID) has also made a major commitment to the promotion of oral rehydration therapy world-wide. Through its long-time sponsorship of the International Centre for Diarrhoeal Disease Research in Bangladesh, through its initiative in calling the highly successful International Conference on Oral Rehydration Therapy in 1983, and through a rapid increase in its financial support to many governments in launching ORT campaigns, USAID is doing a great deal to bring within reach the "universal availability of ORT within ten years" which AID's Administrator believes to be an attainable goal.

By the voluntary organizations of the industrialized world, and by all the millions of individuals who support them with their money and their time, a major contribution is already being made to the prospects for a change in child well-being. Through financial support of counterpart organizations such as the Colombian Red Cross (see panel 1), thousands of lives have already been saved by low-cost techniques being put into action on a massive scale. And in almost every industrialized country, there are organizations such as Oxfam, Save the Children Fund, a great many church-based organizations, and UNICEF's National Committees, which are working to make available both knowledge of, and resources for, the child survival strategies which so many voluntary organizations have also helped to pioneer over recent years. It is organizations such as these who are doing most to put into practice Swedish Prime Minister Olaf Palme's comment on the prospects for a child survival revolution:-

"Responsibility does not only rest with the governments in the afflicted countries; we – the rich industrialized nations – must also share this responsibility."

A Health Service for All

So far, little mention has been made of the health services themselves. But if health services could reach out to anything like a majority of the world's poor, then they would clearly be one of the strongest layers in the laminate of support which mothers need to improve their children's chances of survival and healthy growth.

In particular, it is the community-based health worker who, even with only a few months of training and a minimum of equipment, can be the mothers' most important source of information and practical support. In practice, such health workers are often volunteer village women.

Most mothers want and need a one-to-one demonstration on how to make up oral rehydration salts and when to use them. Similarly, most mothers need someone to turn to for reminders about immunization schedules; for advice and support on the question of birth spacing; for reassurance about breast-feeding (and for help with problems which may arise); for help with weighing and growth monitoring; for advice on how and when to begin weaning; for checking on tetanus immunization and weight gain during pregnancy; and for help in getting to more qualified services should that be necessary.

As part of the process of empowering mothers, the availability of local, qualified, trusted advice is therefore crucial. A mother may hear about ORT on the radio, or even be taught the technique in her own home. But when, some weeks later, her own child suddenly becomes ill with acute diarrhoea, she needs someone in her neighbourhood – at the time – to reinforce both her knowledge of the therapy and her confidence to use it. Similarly, a mother who may be living in the same house as her parents-in-law may need the moral and practical support of a respected community health worker if she is to make changes in the way her children are cared for – changes such as breast-feeding from birth (rather than discarding the colostrum which precedes breast-milk in the first few days) or changes such as beginning to wean the child at five months rather than one year.

Such community health workers are not expensive. Nicaragua is training village health workers for less than $100 each. Colombia gives three months' training to village *promotoras* for less than $1,000 each. Haiti is training health agents for less than $300 each. World-wide, the cost of basic training for a community health worker is usually in the range of $100 to $500. The cost of training a fully qualified doctor, by contrast, is at least $60,000, and, in some countries, very much more.

Yet equipped with only a few weeks' training, and a few inexpensive items of equipment, a primary health care worker can now bring to a community the knowledge and the technology to help parents halve the rate of deaths and malnutrition among their children.

If that community health worker is also selected and supported by the community's own organization, and backed by efficient referral services offering more specialized care when necessary, then the basic elements of primary health care (PHC) are in place.

Primary health care is beginning to be put into practice. Out of 122 nations recently surveyed by the World Health Organization, PHC is now official policy in 78. Nor is the commitment to the

Fig. 20 Health expenditures and population served

85% / 15%
WHERE THE MONEY IS SPENT
(as a percentage of the national health budget)

10% / 90%
HOW MANY PEOPLE ARE SERVED
(as a percentage of population)

■ PRIMARY HEALTH CARE
□ HOSPITAL CARE

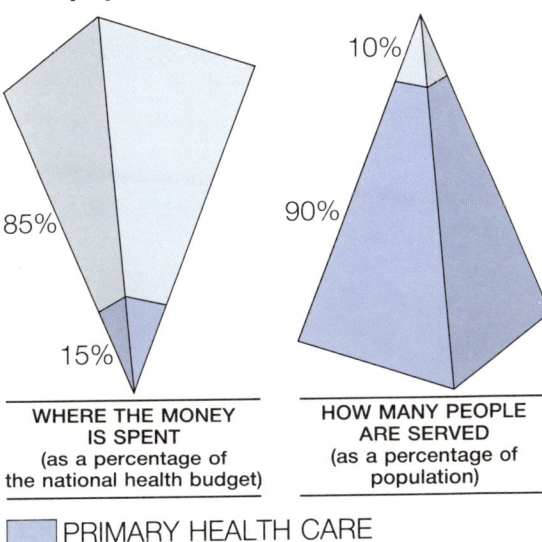

Source: Adapted from: A Primary Health Care Strategy for Ghana, April 1978, Ministry of Health, Accra, Ghana.

I THE STATE OF THE WORLD'S CHILDREN 1985

Thailand: PHC goes national

In a 1983 survey of 122 nations, the World Health Organization found that 78 had committed themselves to attaining 'health for all by the year 2000' by implementing primary health care.

In many of those 78 nations, action lags a long way behind the words. But some developing countries are putting primary health care into practice – and on a scale commensurate with the problems it is designed to tackle. One such nation is Thailand.

Primary health care became Thailand's national health policy in 1977, finding natural roots in Thailand's rural tradition of voluntary work for the community. By mid-1984, almost 40,000 village health volunteers (VHVs), assisted by over a third of a million village health communicators (VHCs), were in place in almost three-quarters of Thailand's 55,772 villages. Today, the VHVs are monitoring the growth of over a third of Thailand's 6.5 million under-fives, and a survey of over a million children has shown a 60% fall in acute malnutrition and a 30% fall in moderate malnutrition over the past four years. Also thanks to the volunteers, immunization against diphtheria, whooping cough, tetanus and tuberculosis has improved from 35% coverage in 1978 to more than 50% in 1982. The programme now includes oral polio and measles vaccines, and by 1986 the government expects 80% of Thailand's children to be fully immunized.

The 384,000 village health communicators (VHCs) are selected by the cluster of 15 or so households where they live and given five days of informal training. Afterwards, they pass on to their neighbours what they have learned – especially knowledge about nutrition and hygiene, the advantages and the means of family planning, the importance of getting children immunized, and ways to prevent and control disease.

Groups of ten VHCs – the norm for an average village – then choose one of their number to go on for 15 days' further training as a village health volunteer (VHV). In addition to monitoring children's growth and organizing immunization campaigns, the VHVs give supplementary food to children whose growth is faltering and to pregnant women who are at risk of giving birth to underweight babies. The VHVs also administer first aid, distribute family planning pills and condoms, and dispense basic drugs for common illnesses.

The VHVs are trained to deal with an estimated 60%-65% of village illnesses: they refer more serious cases to the nearest health centre or district hospital. Each *tambon*, or grouping of six to ten villages, has a health centre staffed by a trained midwife and a sanitarian. The health centres in turn are backed by doctors and higher-level medical services based in the country-wide network of district and provincial hospitals.

The problem of access to basic drugs at cheap prices – a problem which faces primary health care programmes throughout the developing world – has also been tackled on a massive scale in Thailand – and by an unusual method. Throughout the country, over 16,000 village drug banks have been set up under the supervision of the VHVs. Village households buy shares (worth 45 to 90 US cents) in the drug bank. With the money, drugs are bought from the government at a discount and sold at an official retail price. The profits go to buying further supplies and subsidizing medicines for the poorest villagers.

Building a nation-wide primary health care system through the people's own participation has therefore made an impressive start in Thailand. And this year, the seeds of future participation will be sown in Thailand's schools: after a massive campaign to train schoolteachers by radio, primary health care is now to become part of the regular curriculum in the primary schools, which are attended by 96% of Thailand's children.

idea purely rhetorical: India has trained 340,000 health guides and volunteers, for example, and Thailand has trained 384,000 health communicators (see panel 21). In Tanzania, almost every village now has one health post attended by a trained person; in Botswana, 80% of the villages have village health committees; in the Republic of Korea, 2,000 community health practitioners will be available to two-thirds of the population by the end of 1985. In Burma, 13,000 community-based health workers are being trained in five years.

The idea that every village and neighbourhood should have a trained community health worker is therefore by no means an impossible dream. But literally millions of such health workers need to be trained and supported in the use and promotion of low-cost child protection strategies such as immunization and oral rehydration therapy. And there is today little sign that the financial resources are going to be made available on a scale commensurate with the need.

In part, the lack of money for primary health care is a result of international forces – falling exports, declining terms of trade, high interest rates, and international lending policies which tend to discriminate against social spending on programmes of primary importance to the poor.

But whether the money is made available to train and equip community health workers is also a question of how existing health resources are used (fig. 20). At the moment, the World Health Organization estimates that approximately three-quarters of all health spending in the developing world is being used to provide relatively expensive medical care for a relatively small minority in the towns and cities. Over half of the national health budget in Senegal or the Philippines or Tanzania, for example, is spent on urban hospitals. In the Congo, only 1.5% of the Ministry of Health's annual budget is being spent on preventive medicine. In Ghana, 40% of the national health expenditure is devoted to specialist hospital care for less than 1% of the population; a further 45% of the budget is allocated to ordinary hospital care serving 9% of the population; and the remaining 15% is allocated to the community health workers and related programmes serving 90% of the population.

At the moment, there are few signs of a significant change in this pattern. Despite the fact that as many as 50 to 100 community health workers can be trained and equipped for the cost of one doctor, the majority of countries, according to WHO, "*still fall into the pattern of a top-heavy pyramid with most manpower being of the higher professional categories*".

Often, a relatively small shift in this pattern of spending could release the resources to train large numbers of community health workers. In Latin America, for example, the medical schools are scheduled to produce an additional 200,000 fully qualified doctors by 1990. For the same cost, it would be possible to train a few less doctors – say a total of 150,000 – plus one million primary health care workers to live in poor communities and help make available the knowledge and the techniques for drastically reducing child illness and death among the majority of the population.

From its survey of 122 nations, WHO concludes that there is as yet little evidence of this shift and that primary health care, in most countries, still tends to be interpreted not so much as a change of priorities as a 'grafting on' of lower-level health workers to existing systems – if there is anything left after the bills for high-technology hospitals and sophisticated medical colleges have been paid.

At the moment, approximately three-quarters of the developing world's health budgets – and a similar proportion of the industrialized world's health-related aid – is devoted to capital expenditure on modern hospitals and costly medical technologies, with all the long-term recurrent expenditures which such spending patterns dictate.

With a more determined commitment to primary health care than these figures suggest, it would be by no means impossible to think of every community having access to a trained health worker within the next few years. And few measures could do so much to empower and support parents in drastically reducing the incidence of child death, the frequency of child illness, and the severity of poverty's grip on the growing minds and bodies of the rising generation.

I THE STATE OF THE WORLD'S CHILDREN 1985

Tanzania: saving on essential drugs

In many developing countries, 60% to 80% of the population are deprived of basic drugs vital to primary health care. At the same time, much money is often wasted on expensive, sometimes dangerous drugs, inadequately controlled and over-prescribed, or on useless tonics. In some countries, 80% of the health budget is spent on pharmaceuticals destined mainly for city hospitals.

In Tanzania, where up to 75% of all deaths are attributed to poverty-linked diseases, the government has long stressed the importance of village-level primary health care. The Arusha Declaration, which was adopted in 1967 and has formed the basis of government policy ever since, spelt out the inequity of the health services:
"All our big hospitals are in towns and they benefit only a small section of Tanzania; it is the overseas sale of peasants' produce which provides the foreign exchange to repay loans raised to build them. Those who do not get the benefit of the hospitals thus carry the major responsibility for paying for them."

Despite good intentions, though, Tanzania's urban hospitals, serving only 14% of the population, continued to drain 60% of the national health budget. In 1979, the main hospital in the capital, Dar-es-Salaam, was allocated 14% of the national drug budget, while all the village dispensaries together received only 15%; many went without drugs.

But now a new essential drugs programme, backed by the Tanzanian and Danish governments, UNICEF, and the World Health Organization (WHO), aims to give Tanzanians more health for less money.

Firstly, the programme concentrates on providing just 35 drugs – selected from the WHO essential drugs list, and including oral rehydration salts, penicillin, and anti-malarials. All are bought as basic generic drugs rather than as the more expensive 'brand-name' equivalents. Further savings are made by UNICEF buying the drugs in bulk in various countries on a system of international competitive bidding.

Secondly, the programme puts priority on getting a supply of the drugs each month to the country's 2,557 rural dispensaries and 239 health centres, bypassing the hospitals. Distribution is a major problem in a country of 360,000 square miles (945,000 square kilometres) with few good roads. Where there are vehicles, often there is no fuel or spare parts to keep them running. Buses, bicycles and even mules are being used to ensure the drugs arrive regularly.

The problems lie not only in shortages of drugs but in the way they are used by health workers and the general public. One of the legacies of the high-technology curative approach to health has been an 'antibiotic mentality', with health workers and patients alike regarding antibiotics as 'cure-alls'. Often it is pressure from patients, who believe that strong drugs are most effective for every ailment, however minor, which encourages health workers to misprescribe or over-prescribe.

So the other two strategies of the essential drugs programme have addressed the attitudes and understanding of both patients and health workers. Between October 1983 and April 1984, 3,700 health workers went through a week's training in the use and storage of essential drugs. For the general public a country-wide information campaign is announcing the new availability and proper use of the selected essential drugs.

In cost-saving terms, Tanzania's essential drugs programme is already a huge success: the Danish government's contribution of $30 million, intended to support the project for three years, is likely to stretch to five, as the cost of importing drugs has now been reduced by almost 50%.

Primary health care and the training of community health workers is essentially a simple and obvious idea for improving the health of the majority. But as J.M. Keynes said in the introduction to his revolutionary work on economics: *"The difficulty lies, not in the new ideas, but in escaping from the old ones"*.

Traditional birth attendants

The fact that two-thirds of the developing world's poor do not have access to modern medical services does not mean that they have nowhere and no-one to turn to when they need help. And for the great majority of mothers in the developing world, it is the local midwife or traditional birth attendant who is the most important source of support in pregnancy, childbirth, and early child care.

Known in different parts of the world as the *daya* (Middle East), *dai* (India, Bangladesh, Pakistan), *matrone* (West Africa), *dukun bayi* (Indonesia), *hilot* (Philippines), *moh tam yae* (Thailand), *partera empírica* (Latin America), or *curiosa* (Brazil), the one common characteristic of traditional midwives, amid a wealth of different cultural practices, is that they are the ones to whom poor people turn in times of need.

In India, for example, an estimated 600,000 *dais* attend 80% of all births. In Thailand, 17,000 *moh tam yae* attend 80% of births; in Nicaragua, the *parteras* deliver 68% of all babies. In total, between 60% and 80% of all mothers in the developing world turn to traditional midwives for help with the process of bearing and caring for children.

Unlike modern health practitioners, traditional midwives are concentrated among the poor and in the rural areas. Over 90% of the 38,000 *hilots* in the Philippines live in the rural areas. In Haiti, almost all of the country's 11,000 *sages-femmes* live in the countryside. In Egypt, 10,000 *dayas* serve mainly the rural and urban poor. In Indonesia, the 70,000 to 80,000 *dukun bayis* attend over 90% of births to poor mothers.

To simplify, the traditional birth attendants *are* the mother and child health services for the vast majority of the poor (fig. 21). In many poor communities, they are therefore one of the greatest of all potential resources for empowering mothers with knowledge and practical on-the-spot help in the task of protecting their children's lives and health.

Experience has shown that most traditional birth attendants welcome training in new techniques – when it is offered. Modern health services can provide that training. But in the modern health establishment, there has been a pronounced tendency to look down on the traditional birth attendants as ignorant and superstitious practitioners of unscientific and unhygienic methods for dealing with pregnancy and childbirth. Commonly, they have been accused of performing dangerous abdominal massages during pregnancy, or of advising mothers to discard the colostrum which precedes the breast-milk

Fig. 21 Availability of doctors and traditional midwives

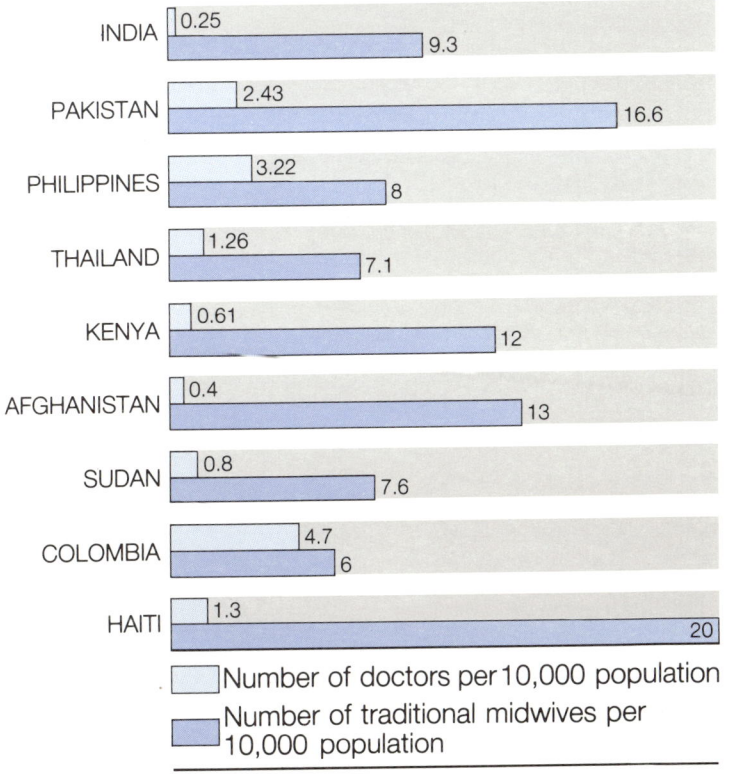

Country	Doctors per 10,000	Traditional midwives per 10,000
INDIA	0.25	9.3
PAKISTAN	2.43	16.6
PHILIPPINES	3.22	8
THAILAND	1.26	7.1
KENYA	0.61	12
AFGHANISTAN	0.4	13
SUDAN	0.8	7.6
COLOMBIA	4.7	6
HAITI	1.3	20

Source: Adapted from Population Reports, Series J, Number 22, May 1980. Population Information Program, The Johns Hopkins University, Maryland, USA.

Diarrhoeal disease: briefing the professionals

World-wide, it is probably true to say that a majority of doctors, community health workers and pharmacists do not yet know about – or do not accept – the breakthrough of oral rehydration therapy (ORT). Many still prescribe drugs and advise mothers to withhold food during diarrhoea attacks. In Egypt, preliminary research for the national ORT campaign found that nearly one in five mothers consulted pharmacists when their children had diarrhoea and that almost all pharmacists advised anti-diarrhoeal drugs. In the United Kingdom, more than a third of all family doctors are still prescribing unnecessary drugs for childhood diarrhoea.

In most parts of the developing world, modern health services reach only perhaps one-third of the people. Nonetheless, their *sanction* is necessary for campaigns which attempt to influence the majority. One of the main reasons for the failure of a recent attempt to introduce ORT into villages of Egypt's Nile Delta, for example, was the fact that the local doctors were not consulted and did not give their backing to the campaign.

If ORT is to fulfil its potential and save the lives of millions of children, then it is essential for knowledge about the new therapy to permeate every pore of the professional health services – from the hospitals and the medical schools to the paediatricians and the doctors, from the nurses and the midwives to the paramedics and the village pharmacists.

But how? Knowledge of ORT – and of developments like the breakthrough with cereal-based solutions – is usually only available in relatively obscure research papers or specialized journals which are strongly English-language-centred, highly technical, difficult to obtain, and very expensive.

In May of 1980, one attempt to overcome this problem was launched by a volunteer group of diarrhoeal disease specialists. From offices in central London, this team of doctors and researchers began issuing a slim quarterly newsletter with the unlikely title of *Diarrhoea Dialogue*. Its aim was to make knowledge about ORT available in a cheap, simple but authoritative form to thousands of parents, community health workers, doctors, paediatricians, ministries of health, voluntary agencies, pharmacists, midwives – in short, everyone involved in the question of how to deal with childhood's commonest disease.

Four years later, *Diarrhoea Dialogue* is going out in English, French, Spanish, Arabic and Portuguese to 46,000 people in over 100 developing and 17 industrialized countries.

The newsletter provides developing-country doctors with reviews of the latest research. Occasional issues are devoted to studying one topic in depth. For example, one issue has focused on the role of breast-feeding in preventing diarrhoea and malnutrition. Another issue has discussed the value of immunization as an ally against diarrhoea.

At the same time, *Diarrhoea Dialogue* also translates specialist information into the simple health messages needed by communities, and provides a forum for readers who need practical advice or who can offer it from their own experience.

The readers range across the spectrum to include teachers, water engineers, field botanists and rural development workers. As the newsletter's executive editor, Denise Ayres, said at an international conference in 1983: "Anyone who requests *Diarrhoea Dialogue* receives it because we feel it is as important that someone running an agricultural extension project reads the newsletter as the district medical officer. It is only through familiarity with the subject that oral rehydration will become commonplace."

Diarrhoea Dialogue is published quarterly by AHRTAG, 85 Marylebone High St., London W1M 3DE.

(and which contains valuable immunological properties), or of failing to cut and dress the umbilical cord hygienically, or of advising mothers to eat less in pregnancy, or of not knowing what to do in the 10% to 20% of births when complications arise. In some cases, these accusations are well-founded. Some traditional birth attendants do promote and practise many dangerous and ill-founded ideas during pregnancy, delivery and infancy.

Clearly, modern health practitioners have much to teach the traditional village midwife. But they may also have much to learn. For it would be a mistake to assume that the majority of village women go to traditional birth attendants only because they are there. In many countries, the poor prefer traditional birth attendants – even when more modern health care is available.

To begin with, many millions of poor women have a great deal more trust and confidence in – and feel very much more comfortable with – the village midwife than with modern health workers. The traditional midwife is almost always a village woman herself – who thoroughly understands the nuances of language, beliefs, and behaviour in her community. She is usually well-known to the family she serves and regarded with confidence and trust rather than with the inferiority and anxiety which so many poor and illiterate women feel when they finally get to the front of the line at the antenatal clinic.

To many women, sharing something as intimate and personal as childbirth with somebody who is a complete stranger and whose interest in the mother seems to be confined to the clinical, is an unaccustomed notion. Some traditional midwives concern themselves not only with all aspects of pregnancy and childbirth, but also with child care up to and beyond the first month of life and with the more rounded needs of the mother herself – with her emotional life, her family relations, and with the necessary rituals, prayers, and social obligations of childbirth itself. In many cases, village midwives also clean the house and wash the bed-linen after the birth. Some take on the cooking and household chores to give the mother time to rest and be with her baby. Some may even act as god-parent. Of the *daya* in Egypt, for example, it has been written:-

"Village women feel that the daya is available whenever they need her, at any time of day or night, and that the daya is able to share with them their joys and sorrows, comforts and pains ... Pregnant women ask for advice on when their babies are due and mothers seek help with their newborns. She is an important source of news and entertainment and a disseminator of information on personal and public events".

And of a particular midwife in a village of the Nile Delta:-

"Zeinab accepts whatever payment is offered her in either money or in kind. She says that she would fear God's punishment if she did not respond to the calls of the poor before those of the rich."*

Since the early 1970s, attitudes towards traditional birth attendants have been slowly changing. In 1972 only about a third of developing countries offered any official recognition to traditional midwives in the form of registration or training. Today, more than three-quarters of all developing countries have training programmes for traditional birth attendants. Pakistan is basing its Accelerated Health Programme on the training of traditional midwives. Bangladesh will have retrained one midwife for every village by 1985 – a total of 68,000. In Afghanistan, the aim is also 'one trained *dai* per village' and 7,500 are now attending courses. In India, over half a million *dais* have been registered and given basic training.

Because of recent breakthroughs in knowledge, even a few weeks' training in low-cost methods of child protection can enable a traditional midwife to drastically reduce the incidence of child deaths and child illness in poor communities. And training those to whom the majority of the poor already turn for help in the task of bearing and caring for children is therefore one of the most cost-effective of all methods for making new knowledge available to the vast majority of parents in the poor world.

---

* Marie Assaad and Samiha El Katsha, "Villagers' use of and participation in formal and informal health services in an Egyptian Delta village", in *Contact*, no. 65, World Council of Churches, Geneva, December 1981.

I THE STATE OF THE WORLD'S CHILDREN 1985

Women's Time

Of the many problems which beset the great opportunity for a revolution in child health, two are so profound and pervasive as to demand acknowledgement even in a report which traditionally emphasizes opportunities rather than constraints.

First, there is the fact that so many mothers in poor communities are already so overwhelmed by work, and so unsupported by male-dominated societies, that they have little time and energy left to put into action the child protection strategies which might now be placed at their disposal.

Second, there is the problem that slow progress towards basic services – and especially clean water and safe sanitation – is still acting as a brake on almost all other child survival strategies.

Women's work

Almost without exception, low-cost strategies for promoting the health and growth of children demand more of their mothers. It is therefore without apology that we return for a moment to the question of a mother's time.

Longer breast-feeding consumes time and energy; oral rehydration therapy demands time and patience to mix up a fresh solution each morning and administer it slowly several times a day to a sick child; preventing malnutrition will mean taking a child to be weighed each month and spending more time in the preparation of the four to five feeds a day which are necessary for safer weaning; and making sure a child is immunized means repeated trips to health clinics or vaccination posts.

Yet many of the women of the poorest communities in the developing world are already working 12 to 16 hours a day. Often spending many more hours in the fields than men, women are responsible for at least 50% of family food production in the developing world. Once the harvest is in, it is also the woman's job to do all the pounding, winnowing, grinding, boiling, straining, drying and storing of the family's staple foods. On top of that, women are normally responsible for collecting firewood and drawing water, gathering fodder and looking after animals, tending kitchen gardens and marketing any surplus, cooking and washing up after meals, cleaning and washing clothes, sewing and weaving, maintaining social

Fig. 22 Seasonal pattern of diarrhoeal infections in rural Gambia

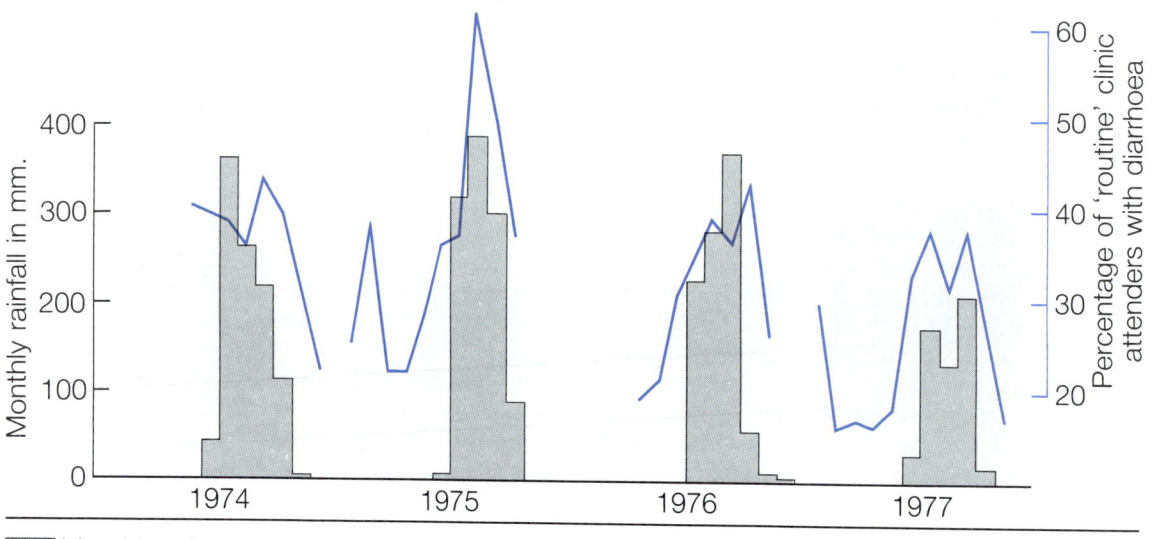

▨ Monthly rainfall in mm.   ── Monthly prevalence of weanling diarrhoea

Source: Infant feeding practices and the development of malnutrition in rural Gambia, R. G. Whitehead, Food and Nutrition Bulletin, vol. 1, No. 4, 1979.

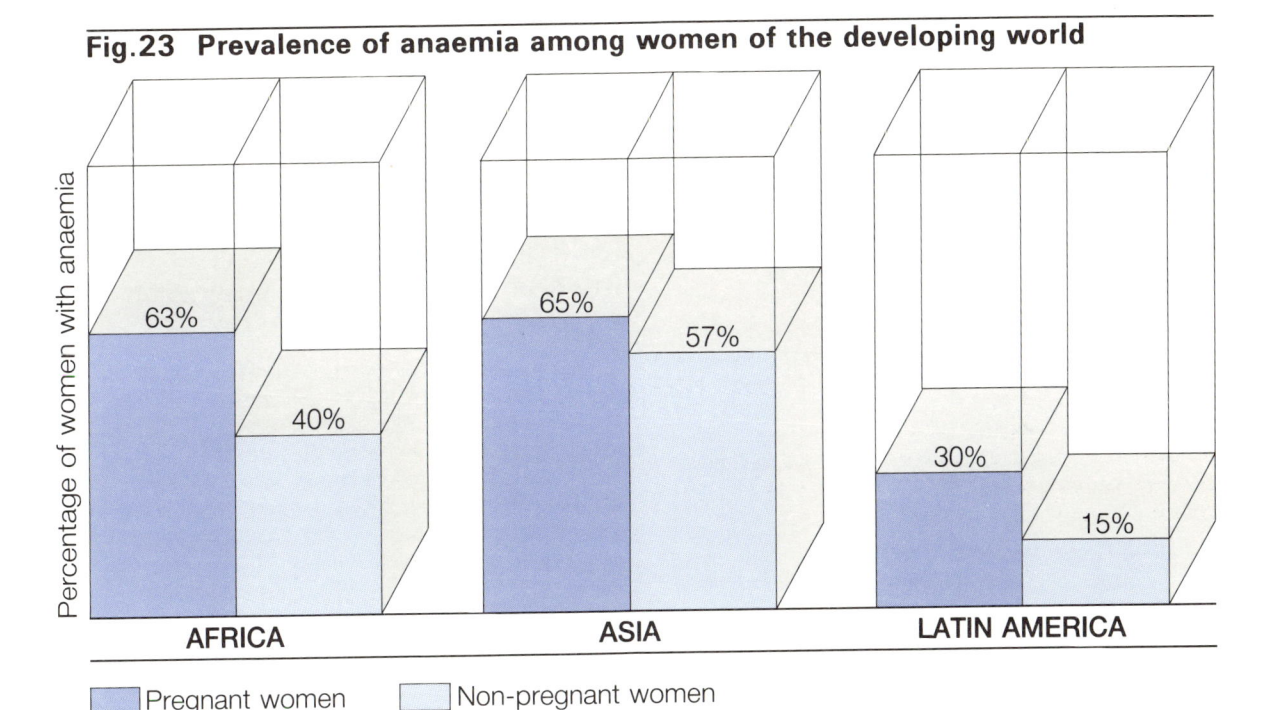

Fig. 23 Prevalence of anaemia among women of the developing world

Percentage of women with anaemia

- AFRICA: Pregnant women 63%, Non-pregnant women 40%
- ASIA: Pregnant women 65%, Non-pregnant women 57%
- LATIN AMERICA: Pregnant women 30%, Non-pregnant women 15%

■ Pregnant women   □ Non-pregnant women

Source: Erica Royston, The Prevalence of Nutritional Anaemia in Women in Developing Countries: A Critical Review, World Health Statistics Quarterly, Vol. 35, No. 2, 1982.

obligations and attending to the sick and the elderly – and all of this is on top of the tasks of bearing and caring for children.

If the mother lives in one of the slums or shanty towns which now house almost a quarter of the developing world, then she may also face the special difficulties of depending entirely on the market-place for her family's food, of long hours away from home as she struggles to earn an income, and of an overcrowded and dangerous environment in which to bring up her children. In the five largest cities of India, for example, 60% of all families live in one room – and most have neither safe water nor hygienic sanitation.

In a rural area, the mother is likely to face different problems. Usually, diarrhoeal and other infections come during the busiest season of the agricultural year (fig. 22). Once the rains have begun, hoeing and planting cannot wait. Once the crop has ripened, the harvest must be gathered in. At these times, mothers cannot keep returning to their homes to administer more oral rehydration solution or to prepare one of the small and frequent meals which a weanling child needs. In one African nation, for example, surveys have shown that women's work in agriculture means that many small children are fed, on average, only 1.6 times a day.

As important as a mother's time is her energy. And again the unequal standing of women, and sometimes their out-and-out exploitation, means that the mother is frequently ill and tired, devoid of the capacity for extra effort which improvements in her child's well-being may demand. Of the 464 million women in the third world, for example, no less than 230 million are estimated to be suffering from energy-sapping anaemia (fig. 23).

To the long hours of physical toil in fields and homes, must be added the physical burdens and nutritional stresses of repeated pregnancy and of breast-feeding. At the age of thirty, a woman has often spent 80% of her adult life in the stressful processes of reproduction and breast-feeding. The result is that too many women are worn out by work and by child-bearing. Every year, half a

I THE STATE OF THE WORLD'S CHILDREN 1985

Rural poverty: trial by seasons

For many millions of the world's children, malnutrition and illness are concentrated into the wet season of the year.

The time of the rains is usually the time of heaviest work in the fields, the time when the ground is prepared for planting. But it is also the time of greatest food scarcity, when the last year's harvest is beginning to run out and the next is not yet ready.

This seasonal coinciding of more work with less food weighs heaviest on mothers and their young children. The press of work in the fields reduces the time a mother can spend on the needs of her family: a study in rural Gambia, for example, has shown that six-to-nine-month-old babies receive 40% less breast-milk in the rainy season than in the dry season – because the mother has less time to suckle her infant. In the all-important weaning period, a young child may be given perhaps only two feeds a day instead of the four or five necessary for health and normal growth.

With food at its scarcest, prices are at their highest. And what food is available usually goes first to the men. The 'savings' are made by women eating less, even though they may be working as hard, if not harder, than their husbands. In that same study in the Gambia, the food intake of women was found to be as much as 40% less in August – the middle of the rains – than in November or December.

To make matters worse, this is also the time when illness is most frequent – especially if the wet season is also the hot season. Malaria, diarrhoeal disease, skin infections and parasitic diseases reach their height during the rains. And they are all exacerbated by the mother's shortage of time and energy for the frequent water-carrying, washing, boiling, and cooking which could help keep disease away.

As if in conspiracy against the mother and her unborn child, this season of greatest hunger, illness and work-load is also the season when more women are in the last stages of pregnancy (as most weddings, festivities, and conceptions happen in the months immediately following the harvest). All women should gain about a kilo a month during pregnancy. But the Gambian study found that, during the rainy season, women in the last three months of pregnancy were *losing* weight through the combination of harder work and less food. Almost inevitably, this failure to gain weight in pregnancy means more low birth-weight babies, more maternal malnutrition, and more infant deaths. In this way, the worst effects of the 'poverty season' are passed on to the most vulnerable – the mother and the young child.

There are two obvious ways to blunt this sudden, seasonal sharpening of poverty. Day-care centres could be provided in villages during the peak time when all hands are needed in the fields. And for the poorest groups, extra food or food subsidies could be specially geared to this time of the year.

For the poor and the landless, the rainy season is also the time when they are most vulnerable to political and economic exploitation. As Robert Chambers has written in *The Seasonal Dimensions to Rural Poverty*:-

"Seasonal stress drives them into debt and dependence. The knowledge that there will be future seasonal crises constrains them to keep on good terms with their patrons. They are thus screwed down seasonally into subordinate and dependent relationships in which they are open to exploitation. Stress is passed down to the weakest – women, children, old people and the indigent. Sometimes the screw becomes a ratchet, an irreversible downward movement into deeper poverty as assets are mortgaged or sold without hope of recovery. This is, then, a time when poor people are kept poor and a time when they become poorer.''

million mothers die from causes related to maternity. And for every mother who dies, many struggle on in a state euphemistically known as 'maternal depletion'.

If mothers in poor communities are to put into practice the strategies now available for protecting the lives and the growth of their children, then they will need more than just information – they will need practical support from their men, their communities, their leaders, and their governments. They will need, for example, technologies which relieve them of the hours a day spent collecting wood for an inefficient open stove, or the hours a day pounding grain with a pestle and grinding it with a stone, or the miles and hours a day spent carrying water. They will also need a fairer division, within the family, of labour and of food. The woman, often working longer and harder, often eats last and least. In her own childhood, the future mother usually has less to eat than her brothers with the result that her growth is impaired and her own children may be born – and may grow up – underweight. In pregnancy, the mother is often left too small a share of the family pot with the result that her baby is malnourished even before it is born (fig. 24). In times of breast-feeding, the mother often does not eat the extra 500 calories or so of food each day which she needs, with the result that her own body becomes depleted by the protection she gives to her child.

In short, progress in women's rights is possibly the most important of all advances for improving the lives of women themselves *and* for supporting mothers in the task of using the new techniques to bring about a revolution in child survival.

Water and sanitation

The second fundamental problem is the lack of basic amenities – especially of water supply and sanitation – in so many of the world's poorest communities. In the rural areas of the developing world as a whole, for example, three-quarters of the population does not have access to either safe water or sanitation. In general, the towns and cities are better served, but at least a quarter of the urban population have no dependable supplies of good water and almost half have no means of safe sanitation.

It has long been known that three-quarters of

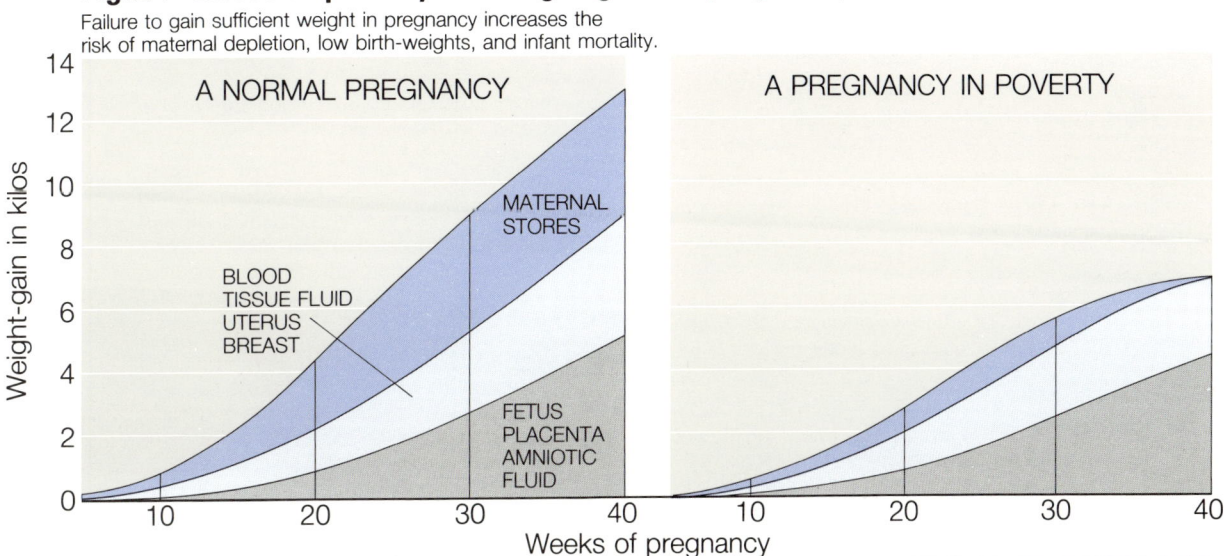

Fig.24 Effect of poverty on weight-gain in pregnancy

Failure to gain sufficient weight in pregnancy increases the risk of maternal depletion, low birth-weights, and infant mortality.

A NORMAL PREGNANCY: MATERNAL STORES; BLOOD TISSUE FLUID UTERUS BREAST; FETUS PLACENTA AMNIOTIC FLUID

A PREGNANCY IN POVERTY

Weight-gain in kilos vs. Weeks of pregnancy

Source: Breast-Feeding, Fertility and Contraception, edited for the International Planned Parenthood Federation by Ronald L. Kleinmann and Pramilla Senanayake, IPPF, 1984.

I THE STATE OF THE WORLD'S CHILDREN 1985

Oral rehydration: story of a breakthrough

Water, salt and sugar seems a simple formula. But the scientific development of oral rehydration therapy (ORT), the treatment that can prevent millions of deaths from diarrhoeal dehydration, was anything but straightforward. Naomi Rock Novak's history of ORT, soon to be published by UNICEF, details the work involved in discovering precisely how diarrhoea causes fluid and salt loss, and how to replace the losses.

Interest in rehydration was sparked by cholera. Starting in 1818, lethal epidemics swept across four continents.

It took over 100 years to prove the value of intravenous rehydration:-

○ 1832: Thomas Latta, an Irish physician, gives a saline solution by injection to 15 dying cholera victims. He stops the treatment too soon at first and only the last five survive. The Lancet, leading British medical journal, praises his work, but for 80 years the medical profession balks at a remedy it considers questionable.

○ 1908-1915: Leonard Rogers, an English pathologist working in Calcutta, gradually reduces cholera death rates from 60% to 20% using intravenous saline solution. Bicarbonate is added in 1915. Even so, the high salt content of 'Rogers' solution' often kills.

○ 1949: Daniel Darrow and Edward Pratt at Yale University add potassium.

○ 1958: Robert Phillips and Raymond Watten, United States Navy researchers in Bangkok, set the correct balance for intravenous rehydration. Essentially the same solution is used today.

Oral rehydration took longer to develop:-

○ 1830: W. Stevens, in the West Indies and London, gives his diarrhoeic patients water and salts to drink. But the conviction that cholera destroys the gut wall – which would prevent rehydration by mouth – persists for another century.

○ Late 1940s: R.B. Fisher and D.S. Parsons, two Oxford University researchers who are not studying cholera, make a crucial discovery; when glucose is absorbed through the walls of the small intestine, it carries salts and water with it.

○ 1968: building on years of international research, Michael Field of Harvard and William Greenough at Johns Hopkins University prove how cholera provokes fluid loss and confirm the value of glucose transport.

These pathology studies provided the scientific underpinnings for ORT. Concurrent experiments supplied the empirical evidence:-

○ 1962: Robert Phillips, now in Manila, successfully mixes salts and glucose to maintain hydration orally in cholera patients. But after five patients die in one trial from sodium overload, Phillips, distressed, abandons his experiments.

○ 1966-1968: appointed director of the Cholera Research Laboratory in East Pakistan (now Bangladesh), Phillips returns to ORT studies. At the Laboratory, scientists develop a formula which passes its first large-scale test during a local cholera epidemic. A Laboratory team reports that ORT reduces the need for intravenous treatment by 80%; moderately dehydrated patients can recover on ORT alone.

○ 1971: fanned by civil war in East Pakistan, cholera rages in the refugee camps of neighbouring India. Nearly one in three victims dies and intravenous supplies run short. A team from the Johns Hopkins research centre in Calcutta, led by Indian scientist Dilip Mahalanabis, treats 3,700 patients with ORT alone. Only 3.6% die.

The story of oral rehydration does not end there. Many scientists – more than there is space to name – helped to develop ORT and are continuing work to perfect it, both at the Cholera Research Laboratory, now the International Centre for Diarrhoeal Disease Research, Bangladesh, and elsewhere. The greatest task of all still remains – how to make ORT known and available to those who most need it.

all the illness in the developing world is associated, in one way or another, with inadequate water supply and sanitation. And until relatively recently, it has been assumed that providing good water and sanitation facilities would therefore wash away a similar proportion of the poor world's health problems.

In practice, clean water by itself has been shown to have disappointingly little effect on the health of low-income communities. In the light of the industrialized nations' own experience, this should not have been surprising. The city of London had put piped water into almost every home by the middle of the last century. But it was not until early this century that the incidence of diarrhoeal infection began its steep decline. It was the educated *use* of water to improve hygiene which finally brought about the decline – over half a century after the water supply itself was installed.

In practice, the results of water supply projects have been greeted with some alarm by governments and international agencies who are now investing substantial sums of money in such programmes throughout the developing world. But at this time of new opportunities for advances in health, it is more important than ever to keep faith with the importance of water and sanitation services (fig. 25).

For it remains a fact that most illness *is* related to unsafe excreta disposal, poor hygiene, and water supplies which are inadequate in either quantity or quality. And it remains a fact that few changes can bring as many potential benefits to a community as ample quantities of clean water and safe and hygienic methods of sanitation:-

With clean water and sanitation, a community can drastically reduce the incidence of the parasitic diseases which sap the energy of hundreds of millions of adults and affect the nutritional health of large numbers of children. In a country like Bangladesh, for example, over 85% of five-year-olds are carrying a medium-to-heavy worm load in their bodies. Apart from causing internal damage, such heavy parasitic loads also consume calories and are therefore another cause of malnutrition.

With clean water and sanitation, a community can also drastically reduce the incidence of diarrhoeal infection. Even if ORT is available to protect the child against the worst consequences of diarrhoeal infections, four or five such infections a year are a major burden for both mothers and children and a serious set-back to growth. Reducing the frequency, as well as the severity, of diarrhoeal diseases is therefore an important part

Fig.25 Impact of improved water supply on health and nutrition

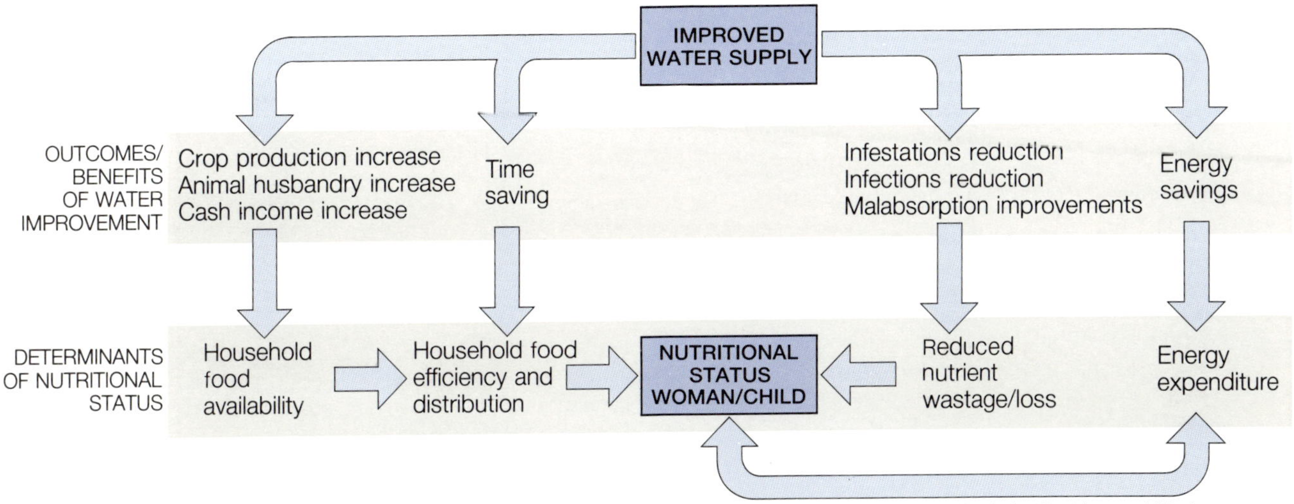

Source: L. Chen, Evaluating the Health Benefits of Improved Water Supply through Assessment of Nutritional Status in Developing Countries, unpublished paper, Harvard School of Public Health, Boston, 1980.

I THE STATE OF THE WORLD'S CHILDREN 1985

Bhutan: ending the IDD tragedy

Across the 'goitre belt' of the Himalayas – northern India, Nepal, Bhutan and southern China – an estimated 10 million people are afflicted with iodine deficiency disorders (IDD). The consequences range from the disfigurement of goitre – an enlargement of the thyroid gland that results in a swelling at the front of the neck – to severe mental and physical retardation. In Bhutan, 60% of the 1.3 million population suffer from goitre – and more than 5% are born with retarded mental development because of lack of iodine in their mothers' diets.

In areas where goitre is endemic, the lack of iodine affects the foetus in the womb. The damage done – especially during the 12 weeks after conception – is virtually irreversible. Usually, the result is a child who is born disabled – with a 90% chance of being either deaf or mute, or both – and a 40% chance of motor abnormalities, such as a halting gait or even severe spastic paralysis. Physical as well as mental growth is retarded – 75% of children with severe iodine deficiency never grow to normal size.

This tragedy is utterly unnecessary. For of all known health problems, iodine deficiency is one of the easiest to prevent. The most widely used, safe, cheap, and technically simple means of supplementing staple diets with iodine is to iodate salt.* In 1983, the Kingdom of Bhutan, one of the world's most seriously affected nations, began planning a nation-wide programme to control IDD by providing an adequate supply of iodated salt.

Iodating the salt used by Bhutan's 1.3 million people will, almost overnight, put a stop to any further iodine deficiency disorders. And it is made possible by the fact that all Bhutan's salt is imported from India through only five different border crossing posts. From November 1984 onwards, instead of going straight to the markets and being dispersed throughout the population, all the imported salt is being taken first to Phuntsholing on the southern border – where a central processing plant adds 30 grammes of iodine to every ton of salt. The import or sale of non-iodated salt is thereafter a punishable offence, a fact clearly advertised at every border post.

Defeating iodine deficiency is almost as simple as that – but not quite.

Most of Bhutan's population live in the villages of the Himalayan foothills, visiting the southern market towns once a year to buy what they cannot produce for themselves. Many people therefore buy a whole year's supply of salt at one time. As it is currently packed and stored in 75-kilo jute bags which have to be loaded and unloaded using steel hooks, the salt is exposed to the air. Over the course of a year, a great deal of moisture is absorbed from the atmosphere and the salt may retain only 10% of the iodine which has been added. To prevent iodine deficiency, the salt must somehow be made to hold on to at least 50% of the added iodine for at least a year.

To solve this problem, the iodated salt leaving the processing plant in Phuntsholing is being packed in smaller quantities using air-tight polythene bags – bags which also carry printed messages about immunization and oral rehydration therapy.

By the end of the century Bhutan will have wiped out iodine deficiency disorders. And if all goes according to plan, then from mid-1985 no more Bhutanese children will be born or grow up mentally and physically retarded by the lack of iodine in their diets. And now that the initial investment has been made, the running costs of the whole operation will be less than 10 cents per person per year.

* In countries where iodating salt is impracticable because salt distribution is too diversified, injections of iodated oil can offer women and children several years' protection at a relatively low cost.

of child protection strategies – and it cannot be achieved without a high standard of both personal and domestic hygiene. Achieving that standard requires that approximately 20 to 25 litres of water per person per day be available close to the home at all hours and on all days of the year.

With clean water and sanitation, a community can also improve its level of nutrition – by irrigation of crops and kitchen gardens, by reducing the infections and parasitic loads which 'waste' the food that is eaten, and by preventing the contamination of food itself.

With a clean water supply, a community can also reduce the daily burden of fetching and carrying water – a burden which frequently takes four hours a day in rural areas of the developing world. Water supply can therefore save the most valuable of all strategic resources for bringing about a revolution in child health – the time and energy of mothers.

For all these advantages, the cost of water supply is not excessive in a society committed to meeting the basic needs of its people. UNICEF's regional office in New Delhi has calculated that the average cost for the installation and use of hand-pumps supplying fresh water close to people's homes in hard-rock areas of India is less than 60 cents per person per year.

If safe water and sanitation can offer so much for so little, why have actual large-scale water projects proved to be so disappointing in their effect on community health? Once again, the discrepancy between potential and performance is a measure of the difference between availability and use. Even when piped water is available it will not reduce illness unless a community uses it for frequent washing of hands and bodies and for the cleaning of utensils and cooking surfaces. And even with improved sanitation, illness will not decline unless latrines are kept clean and used by everybody – including the children. It is widely believed, in developed as well as developing countries, that it is not so important for children to use latrines or to wash their hands afterwards. But the fact is that children are the main sources as well as the main sufferers of diarrhoeal infections.

In other words, the promotion of knowledge and the informed involvement of families and communities are just as important for making water supply effective as they are for making ORT and immunization effective. It is not water or sanitation which washes away illness, it is people's informed use of those facilities which can improve community health and magnify the effect of all other attempts to protect the lives and the growth of children.

These lessons are now beginning to permeate water supply and sanitation projects throughout the developing world – projects to which UNICEF now devotes more than one-quarter of its financial resources each year. An example is the drinking water and sanitation project in Imo state, Nigeria, which has so far drilled 490 boreholes, trained 1,200 village-based workers (VBWs), built or begun the building of 1,500 latrines, and brought improved water supplies to a quarter of a million people.

The Imo project is too new to evaluate its impact on health. But all those who are involved in supporting the project – the Federal Government of Nigeria, the state government of Imo, the World Health Organization, the Ross Institute of Tropical Hygiene, two Nigerian universities, and UNICEF – are fully aware that it is the informed involvement of the community which will make the difference between success and failure. According to progress reports from UNICEF's Lagos office:-

"The most visible participatory elements of the project occur at the village level where VBWs work, steering committees meet, villages make decisions about borehole siting and payment of VBWs, mothers monitor diarrhoea episodes in their young children, and money and labour are contributed to construct the pump platforms and latrines... The project is targeted at women because, in their role as water collectors, food handlers, and child rearers, women initiate behaviour that holds the key to better health."

I THE STATE OF THE WORLD'S CHILDREN 1985

Changing Perceptions

A child survival and development revolution, if it is to succeed in the coming decade, will be achieved by ordinary people doing what it is possible for them to do here and now. For present knowledge could enable the parents of the poor world to improve their own and their children's health in ways which are affordable, practicable, and which achieve results in their own lifetimes.

This is primary health care beginning with people, primary health care shedding the medical mystique, primary health care learning to walk before it can run, primary health care which is as much the concern of the schoolteacher, the volunteer, the religious leader, the water engineer, the mass media, and the ordinary citizen as it is of the official health services themselves.

Present health services – even primary health services – are not easily accessible to, and cannot be depended on by, the majority of the developing world's people. Health education campaigns, if they are to serve that majority, should therefore concentrate on promoting those actions which people can undertake for themselves and those actions which have the greatest impact at the least cost. Recent breakthroughs now offer a group of such actions which are together so powerful that they could enable parents to revolutionize child survival and child health in the developing world.

The more government provides the services which support this parental action – by the training of community health workers, or the deployment of referral services, or the setting up of immunization posts, or the installing of clean water supply – the more dramatic the results will be. But the process clearly begins with the empowering of people. And as the health ministry of one developing country has recently said:-

"This cannot and will not ever be a quiet, uneventful process; quite the contrary can be expected... The more people know, the more they will expect, and demand, of the health services. At the same time, they will be able to solve more of their health problems by themselves, and they will be more capable of assessing their health needs and evaluating the appropriateness of the health care system. In other words, health education will pave the way to community participation in the fullest sense." ★

If it can succeed, the process of empowering parents – whatever its genesis – is unlikely to be confined to matters of health alone. The belief that life can be improved and circumstances changed by one's own actions is both an end and a means of development itself, an essential prelude to political participation, to the struggle for land reform and economic justice, and to new attitudes towards family size and a further fall in the rate of population growth.

As both a cause and a consequence of this process, a people's perception of what is normal and what is acceptable may also undergo a profound change. As Tarzie Vittachi has written:-

"When we talk about a child survival and development revolution we are talking about bringing about a mass ripening for change, about opening people's mental boxes in which habitual acceptance of a low level of health and a high rate of death among their children is locked up as socially or fatefully decreed inevitabilities. We are talking about transforming deeply inlaid attitudes and practices and helping people to see over the hill. What needs to be done then is to present new knowledge to people as a way to empower themselves to change their perception of 'normality' or 'inevitability'."

In the years to come, it will not be accepted as normal that more than 10,000 children die each day from a process which parents can prevent by using simple ingredients found in almost every home.

In the years to come, it will not be accepted as normal that many millions of children should die, and many more be left disabled, for the lack of a $5 course of immunizations.

In the years to come, it will not be accepted as normal that half a million children lose their eyesight each year for the lack of a vitamin A tablet, or of a few greens in their evening meal, or that tens of thousands should be mentally retarded for the lack of a few milligrammes of iodine in their diet.

In the years to come, it will not be accepted as

★ "Health education and community participation – principles and priorities", Ministry of Health, Belize, 1982.

normal for 10 million babies a year to be born malnourished because their mothers did not have enough to eat, or that millions of children, small for their age, should sit listlessly in the shade instead of playing, learning, and growing to their full potential.

Over the next few years, it will not be easy to mount the massive effort to change this 'normality'. It will require, as this report has tried to show, both political commitment at the highest levels and the mobilization of all possible resources – nationally and internationally – to empower and support parents with the knowledge and the means to bring about such a change. But by the same token, there is now an opportunity for any government, and almost any organization or individual, to play a part in bringing about this significant improvement in the lives of the world's children.

If, in the face of this opportunity, we continue to allow so many millions of young children to die and so many millions more to become disabled and malnourished, then there will indeed be cause to ask for whom so many bells toll. For what realistic hope will there be left for a more just, more humane, more peaceful world, and what price the 'sanctity' of human life, if that world ignores such an opportunity as this to save the lives and health of so many of its most vulnerable members?

If, on the other hand, this challenge were to be accepted, then it would be a sign of hope as much for the adult world as for its children. For although in one sense what is at issue is a relatively modest set of practical objectives which can be achieved over a reasonably short period of time, in another sense we are talking about nothing less than a genuine step forward for civilization itself.

In our national societies, and in the international community, we have the knowledge, we have the techniques, we have the organizational capacity. We are therefore confronted with a stark question: do we have the will?

And of those who would argue that it is not a matter of will but of resources, it must now be asked – how low does the cost have to fall before the will is found? We are now talking about a particular opportunity to save the lives of approximately 7 million young children a year, and to protect the normal development of many millions more, at a cost which certainly does not exceed a fraction of 1% of the world's gross international product. If the will to accept that challenge is missing, then perhaps it will never be there. For in all realism, it is unlikely that there will ever again be such an opportunity to do so much for so many, and for so little.

II
LIFELINES

Extracts and summaries from recent research and writing on strategies for protecting the lives and normal development of the world's children

Growth Monitoring

Oral Rehydration Therapy

Breast-feeding

Immunization

Female Education

Family Spacing

Food Supplements

Lifelines: an introduction

The central theme of the "State of the World's Children" report is that a few relatively simple and inexpensive methods could now enable parents themselves to bring about a revolution in child survival and development. Part II of the report sets out, in more detail, present knowledge about these low-cost methods. Each section brings together, in an accessible 'notes and quotes' format, the findings and conclusions from recent research and writing on one of the 'lifeline' techniques.

Primary health care is the idea which makes possible this revolution in child survival and child development. The spread of education, communications, and social organization is the new circumstance which makes it achievable. Growth monitoring, oral rehydration therapy, breast-feeding, and immunization are the techniques which make this revolution affordable even with very limited resources.

It is important to recognise that, within any campaign to improve child survival and growth, priorities will differ according to national and local circumstances. The four principal 'lifeline' techniques discussed in Part II of this report are chosen because they are low-cost, they are available now, they achieve rapid results, they are almost universally relevant, and they promote primary health care by involving people in taking more responsibility for their own health. And in combination with each other, they offer a considerable degree of protection against the synergistic alliance of malnutrition and infection which is the central problem of child health and child development in the world today (see pages 42 to 47).

In addition, recent research has shown that three other changes—female education, family spacing, and food supplementation—are also among the most powerful levers for raising the level of child survival and child health. Although more costly and more difficult to achieve, these changes in the lives of women are of such potential significance that they must also now be counted among the breakthroughs in knowledge which could change the ratio between the health and wealth of nations.

Growth Monitoring

Malnutrition in childhood can permanently affect mental and physical development. The root of malnutrition is poverty and its long-term solution depends on economic growth and social justice. In the meantime, however, low-cost methods are available to significantly reduce the incidence and severity of malnutrition – and its impact on child health and development.

Malnutrition has many causes – of which frequent infection is probably the most important. The invisible slowing down of normal growth happens long before a child becomes malnourished. Regular monthly weighing and the use of a child growth chart can make visible this faltering growth and so provide an early warning to mothers and health workers. At this stage, malnutrition can be relatively easily and cheaply prevented. With basic advice, growth monitoring can therefore help mothers themselves to prevent most child malnutrition. More than 200 different growth charts are now coming into use in over 80 countries.

Malnutrition and Infection

Lack of food is only one of malnutrition's many causes. Probably the most important cause of all is repeated infection:

Recent research shows that repeated infections – especially respiratory and diarrhoeal infections – play a much greater role in causing malnutrition than was previously supposed. Studies in a Gambian village have shown that frequent bouts of diarrhoea are a common and almost constant illness before a child develops malnutrition. During diarrhoea 500-600 calories may be lost each day in the stools. This cyclical relationship of cause and effect needs to be broken.

Summarized from: David Morley and Margaret Woodland, See How They Grow: monitoring child growth for appropriate health care in developing countries, Macmillan, 1979.

A study of 716 rural Guatemalan children under 7 years showed that those suffering from frequent diarrhoeal infections gained less weight and height than those affected by other illnesses. Apart from impairing the functioning of the gastro-intestinal tract, diarrhoea almost always induces a loss of appetite and a drop in calorie and nutrient intake of 20-30%.

Summarized from: R. Martorell, "Acute morbidity and physical growth in Guatemalan children", American Journal of Diseases of Children, no. 129, 1975.

"All infections have a nutritional impact. They can depress the appetite. They can decrease the body's absorption of nutrients. They can induce rejection of food by vomiting. They can drain away nutrients through diarrhoea. They can induce mothers to stop feeding whilst the diarrhoea lasts. And by any or all of these methods, infections become a major cause - perhaps the major cause – of malnutrition among the world's children."

The State of the World's Children 1984, Oxford University Press

"With weaning on contaminated foods and loss of passive immunity, the incidence of infectious diseases, particularly diarrhoea, attained rates of the order of seven to eight episodes per child per year in Cauque (Guatemala) children, during the first three years of life. Acute infections, mainly of the upper respiratory tract, were the most common, followed by diarrhoea, but the latter was more important in view of its adverse effect on host nutrition... The implications of diarrhoea and other infectious diseases are: reduced food consumption, nutrient losses, metabolic alterations, hormonal imbalance, and alterations in immune function; they manifest themselves as wasting, stunting, reduced activity, impaired learning and creativity, and acute malnutrition and death...

"It is then evident that infection and infectious diseases are the main determinants of acute and chronic malnutrition and death among children in societies not suffering from persistent food shortages or famines."

Leonardo Mata, "The evolution of diarrhoeal diseases and malnutrition in Costa Rica", Assignment Children, vol. 61/62, 1983.

"... an infant or child death usually does not have a discrete cause, but in most cases is the result of a long series of individually minor biological insults which cumulatively retard growth, lead to wasting, and progressively wear down the resistance of the individual. Ultimately an ordinarily minor illness such as respiratory infection or diarrhea results in death.

"Because death is only the end result of a cumulative series of pathological processes affecting the child, it follows that the biological status of the surviving children at any point in their lifetime will reflect where they are along the spectrum from good health to life-threatening disability. The simplest indicator of this is growth faltering and body wasting, which can be measured by relating height and weight to age."

W. Henry Mosley, "Will primary health care reduce infant and child mortality?", paper prepared for IUSSP seminar, Paris, 1983.

"A recent careful survey of young children in Bangladesh revealed that, on average, each child suffered 6.8 episodes of diarrhoea per year. Added up, this meant they had diarrhoea for 55 days or 15% of the year. Such children will end up severely deprived of nourishment if they are starved all the time they have diarrhoea."

K.M. Elliott and W.A.M. Cutting, "Carry on feeding", Diarrhoea Dialogue, no. 15, November 1983.

A year-long study in Bangladesh surveyed deaths from diarrhoea in children up to three years old who had been treated for one attack. The severely malnourished children (below 56% of the international standard weight-for-age) were at 14 times more risk of dying than better-nourished children (over 66% of weight-for-age).

Summarized from: S.K. Roy, A.K.M.A. Chowdhury and M.M. Rahaman, "Excess mortality among children discharged from hospital after treatment for diarrhoea in rural Bangladesh", British Medical Journal, vol. 287, October 1983.

Malnutrition and Weaning

Not knowing when and how to begin introducing other foods, in addition to breast-milk, is also a major cause of child malnutrition in many parts of the world:

WEANING – WHEN

"... between the age of four and six months, the child needs semi-solids and solid foods (though breast-feeding should also be continued for as long as possible). To avoid faltering

II LIFELINES: GROWTH MONITORING

growth, it is essential that parents know that this is the right age for weaning to begin. In some parts of India, only about 2% of infants in villages are receiving semi-solids even at the age of six to eight months."

Kusum P. Shah, "Food supplements", in The State of the World's Children 1984, Oxford University Press, 1983.

"Specially prepared foods are needed in increasing quantity and variety until the child can eat the regular family diet. This occurs between 18 and 30 months of age depending on the nature of the family diet and on food habits in various cultures and parts of the world."

Division of Family Health, WHO, "The prevalence and duration of breast-feeding: a critical review of available information," World Health Statistics Quarterly, vol. 35, no. 2, 1982.

WEANING – HOW

A child needs a higher concentration of protein and calories in food than an adult. But a child's stomach is small and the staple foods of the poor are often bulky and low in both calories and proteins. The result may be that a child's hunger is satisfied – but not his nutritional needs. The solution is more frequent feeding of smaller amounts of more calorie-dense foods. But this can be very demanding of a mother's time, energy, and available food:

"Malnutrition is more common during this transitional period than in the first four to six months, largely because families may not be aware of the special nutritional needs of the child at this time, may not know how to prepare weaning foods from the foods that are available locally, or may be too poor to buy the necessary foods."

Division of Family Health, WHO, "The prevalence and duration of breast-feeding: a critical review of available information," World Health Statistics Quarterly, vol. 35, no. 2, 1982.

"... the food ration, which is the amount of food absorbed in one day by one individual, must be sufficient in quantity; that is, it must contain enough food to calm quantitative hunger or 'felt hunger', resulting from the unpleasant sensations felt when the stomach is empty. It must also be varied and balanced, so as to calm qualitative or 'occult' hunger, which is a hunger which exists when nothing, in appearance, informs one of a lack of proteins or vitamins, for instance."

"As an example, it should be noted that the following amounts of food must be consumed in order to ingest 50g of protein: 250g of fresh fish, 500g of millet or maize, 250g of beans or 5 kg of manioc. This problem of volume must be kept in mind, especially in view of the size of a child's stomach."

A.M. Masse-Raimbault, "How to feed young children", Children in the Tropics, no. 138-139-140, 1982.

"Good weaning practices are a major factor in avoiding faltering growth. The amount of extra local food required is small. Lack of income is not, therefore, the only constraint. There may also be important social and organizational constraints, e.g. lack of knowledge about how to prepare appropriate local foods, mother's time required, lack of community production facilities, e.g. grinders, absence of mothers out working during long hours, too long periods between meals, difficulties of keeping prepared food, shortage of fuel, etc. These problems need to be addressed by various local arrangements, strengthened by appropriate health education."

James P. Grant, "New Hopes in Dark Times: UNICEF's Assessment of Past Experience with a Child Survival Package: Its Effectiveness and its Social and Economic Feasibility" paper prepared for an International Conference on Population, May–June 1983.

CONTAMINATED WEANING FOODS

A mother who is already overworked may not have the time to feed a weanling child frequently enough. In the rainy season when work in the fields is usually at its heaviest, the mother may prepare food in the morning for the whole day. Inadequate storage facilities combined with tropical temperatures means that such food easily becomes contaminated. A sample survey of infant food in Ghana showed that even with freshly prepared food, up to one-third would be condemned as microbiologically unfit for human consumption by international standards, and particularly during the rainy months (see table 1):

Table 1: Percentage of food samples containing unacceptable levels of one or more pathogens according to season.

Time after preparation (in hours)	Wet season June–October	Dry season November–May
0–1	34.9 (43)	6.3 (73)
1–2	52.6 (19)	30.8 (13)
4–6	57.8 (38)	46.3 (41)
8	96.2 (26)	70.7 (41)

Figures in parentheses are the actual numbers of samples studied.

R. G. Whitehead, "Infant Feeding Practices and the Development of Malnutrition in Rural Gambia", Food and Nutrition Bulletin, vol. 1, No. 4.

"The necessity of introducing weaning foods becomes obvious by faltering weight any time during the first year when breast milk alone becomes inadequate. This may be as early as the third month ... and ideally is specifically adjusted to the individual child. The extensive literature in recent years arguing the adequacy of breast feeding is unanimous on the decision that monthly weighing is the best indicator of when weaning foods should be started."

Jon E. Rohde, "Community-based nutrition programs", Management Sciences for Health, July 1982.

(For further information on weaning, see Lifelines no. 3 – Breast-feeding.)

Other Causes

PARASITES

Parasites affect hundreds of millions of people the world over, especially children, feeding on their host's nutrients. Twenty Ascaris roundworms (not a heavy load – some 20 million people in the Philippines alone are estimated to harbour about 20) will steal 2.8 grammes of carbohydrate a day from their host.

Summarized from: Benjamin D. Cabrera, "Ascaris: most 'popular' worm", World Health, March 1984.

"Intestinal parasites compete for nutrients while damaging the intestinal structure and decreasing nutrient absorption. Roundworms, the most common of the helminths, can lead to nutrient wastage: about 3% of calories for light infections, up to 25% for heavy, plus increased nitrogen losses... Hookworm infections also reduce absorption, and result in caloric losses estimated at one calorie per worm per day, or as much as 5%

of a person's daily consumption. Combined with its effect on women's iron supply, this parasite can have especially serious impact on pregnant women."

James Austin and others, Nutrition Intervention in Developing Countries, Oelschlager, Gunn and Hain, for Harvard Institute for International Development, 1981.

LOW BIRTH-WEIGHT

Maternal malnutrition can lead to poor foetal growth and low birth-weight which is, in turn, associated with poor growth in infancy and childhood (see Lifelines no. 7 – Food Supplements).

BOTTLE-FEEDING

The trend from breast-feeding to bottle-feeding in many of the developing world's towns and cities is also an important cause of malnutrition (see Lifelines no. 3 -Breast-feeding).

HUNGER AND POVERTY

"For those who simply do not have enough to eat, the long-term solution lies in having either the land with which to grow food or the jobs and the incomes with which to buy it. But as many as one-third of the Third World's labour force is now unemployed or under-employed.

"Land reforms and economic growth to give the poor access to land, jobs, increased productivity, higher incomes, are an essential part of the long-term solution to the poverty from which malnutrition and ill-health are born.

"... the answer to hunger is ... not ultimately technological. The problem is rather one of what crops are grown by whom on whose lands and for whose benefit. And the solution lies in political and economic change to allow the poor to both participate in, and benefit from, the increases in production which can most certainly be achieved."

The State of the World's Children 1982-83, Oxford University Press.

Growth Monitoring

Most child malnutrition is invisible until it reaches an advanced stage. Growth monitoring – by means of regular monthly weighing and the entering of the results on a child growth chart – makes faltering growth visible long before malnutrition begins. At that stage, prevention is relatively inexpensive and relatively simple. The growth monitoring technique – and some basic advice – can therefore help mothers to prevent much of the child malnutrition in the developing world – even within existing resources.

INVISIBLE MALNUTRITION

"The average moderately malnourished child in the 6-24-month age range looks entirely normal but is too small for his or her age, has lowered resistance to infection, and therefore easily succumbs to illness. The child receiving only 60 percent of caloric requirement may give no outward sign of hunger beyond a frequent desire to breast-feed. In a Philippines study, 58 percent of the mothers of ... malnourished children said they thought their babies were growing and developing well."

James Austin and others, Nutrition Intervention in Developing Countries, Oelschlager, Gunn and Hain, for Harvard Institute for International Development, 1981.

"The concept of growth as such is not necessarily known to everybody. However, growth seen as change in body size is well known to all parents. Any mother in a typical village of developing countries knows that her child will have to grow bigger and taller over time. What is very important is that she does not easily and quickly recognize slowed growth in her child. In other words, by pure observation and without some form of visual aid she cannot see early enough if the child is small or light-for-age and does not gain steadily, or understand the relationship between the child's growth, diet and health."

H. Ghassemi, "Growth charts: one good means for better child health and growth", paper prepared for UNICEF, November 1982.

IMPORTANCE OF GROWTH

Regular monthly weighing, and the entering of the results on a child growth chart, can make faltering growth visible long before malnutrition sets in. Once the mother can see the problem, she will normally take action to correct it. With some basic advice on child feeding, growth monitoring can therefore help mothers themselves to prevent the majority of child malnutrition even within existing resources:

"Monitoring nutritional status has been viewed by pediatricians as their most critical assessment of child health, even in developed Western countries, for the past century."

Jon E. Rohde, "Community-based nutrition programs", Management Sciences for Health, July 1982.

"A child who grows well is probably healthy and adequately nourished. If a child is not growing well there must be some reason: usually some illness or lack of adequate nourishment. A child's growth will slow down or even stop months before there are obvious signs of malnutrition."

"Training in recording the child's growth", WHO, 1983 (EPI/FHW/83/TM.1/Rev.1).

"The role of the weight chart is to identify the potential danger of malnutrition before management becomes too difficult at the primary health care level. The weight curve may identify trouble six months or even a year before the child has obvious signs of malnutrition. The opposite is also true. A child who is gaining weight regularly and whose curve is parallel with the curves on the chart will not develop malnutrition."

David Morley and Margaret Woodland, See How They Grow: monitoring child growth for appropriate health care in developing countries, Macmillan, 1979.

"... in several parts of the world, it is now being shown that even within existing health budgets – or for very little extra in the way of resources – the growth of children can be significantly improved.

"The piece of 'technology' which makes this possible is a simple cardboard or thin plastic growth chart, kept by the mother, and costing between two and ten cents. Through the regular monthly weighing of all young children and the entering up of the results on a growth chart, children at risk of malnutrition can be identified. With the appropriate help and advice from health workers, parents can then protect the development of their children. And in so doing, they can protect and improve the economic and social development of their nations."

David Morley, "Growth monitoring", in The State of the World's Children 1984, Oxford University Press, 1983.

"The growth chart is not an end in itself, but is merely a tool for identifying early malnutrition before signs of overt malnutrition occur. It is an alert signal. The important thing is the response to this signal."

"Promotion of nutrition and growth monitoring", programme manual prepared for UNICEF workshop, Bangkok, July 1984.

"In the Hanover project (in Jamaica) workers felt growth monitoring in itself was an intervention. Mothers learned so

II LIFELINES: GROWTH MONITORING

much about the relation between diet and health by watching their child's growth pattern that this alone led to dietary improvements and substantially reduced malnutrition and mortality. These observations have led some health professionals to conclude that ... in communities where social or cultural factors play a greater role than absolute resource inadequacy in the etiology of malnutrition, nutrition monitoring appears to have the potential for a significant impact on mortality even in the absence of more expensive and more difficult to implement components such as nutrition supplementation or education."

Growth monitoring, Primary Health Care Issues, series I, no. 3, American Public Health Association, October 1981.

The researchers of the Narangwal project in India, one of the largest study projects ever undertaken in the developing world, came to a similar conclusion:

"World-wide experience with road-to-health cards for recording weight gain has been reinforced by experience at Narangwal showing that it is possible to help mothers learn that a child with faltering growth is a sick child. Growth monitoring therefore served both as an educational device and as the principal entry point for active nutritional supplementation.

"At the start of the project we decided against trying to provide supplementation to all children in the villages. It was obvious that mere provision of food was not needed because we were in a food surplus area. However, up to a third of children were malnourished...

"...it is our belief that the most important long-term impact from our nutrition program was in the education of mothers. The nutrition problems in the Punjab result mainly from inappropriate feeding practices and the heavy load of infections. Our results showed that it is a fallacy to assume that if food supplies are sufficient in a village, people will solve their own nutrition problems. In most developing countries, just as important as improving food supplies, is the need for a major effort to help mothers learn how to make better use of food. Much of the childhood malnutrition could be ameliorated by nutrients that are already available in the village."

Arnfried Kielmann and others, Integrated nutrition and health care, vol. I of Child and maternal health services in rural India: the Narangwal experiment, Johns Hopkins University Press, 1983.

See page 41 for a summary of the basic advice which can be given to a mother if the growth chart reveals that her child's progress is beginning to falter.

COSTS OF MONITORING

Costs are minimal, though it should be remembered that growth monitoring represents only a starting-point for teaching mothers about their child's health and nutrition:

"The cost of growth monitoring is extremely low, usually ranging between U.S. $0.02-$0.10 per child per year, depending on equipment, charts, and training needs. The tools are relatively inexpensive to buy or can even be locally made at little or no cost. Moreover, the most expensive equipment should last for many years. This makes the cost per child negligible when divided by the under-five population that will use the equipment over the years. Growth charts range in cost from U.S. $0.03 to $0.33. Since ideally only one chart is used per child over a five-year period, the expenditure per child per year is minimal."

Growth monitoring, Primary Health Care Issues, series I, no. 3, American Public Health Association, October 1981.

"Of all the measurements that can be made on children in the developing countries, weighing is most likely to be useful, and its cost-benefit value is very high. For example, the cost of weighing consists mainly of the salaries of health workers. Other costs are small. Weighing scales have a long life, rarely requiring repair or replacement – at least 100,000 weighings may be possible over their normal life. The time spent by staff on weighing is available simultaneously for other purposes, such as discussion with the mother and general observation of the child."

David Morley and Margaret Woodland, See How They Grow: monitoring child growth for appropriate health care in developing countries, Macmillan, 1979.

ALTERNATIVE METHODS

Measuring the circumference of the upper arm is also a method of monitoring growth:

"The first armband for measuring malnutrition in children (Morley-Shakir) was a single thin band used to measure all children from birth to six years of age. Concerned that a single measuring tape might not be sensitive enough to detect the subtle but important differences in the various growth periods of a child, researchers in Colombia designed and are now using two tapes instead. The two tapes ... divide the first six years of growth into seven stages... When the appropriate age tape is wrapped around the upper left arm of a child, the end of the tape falls into a stripe of color which indicates the child's nutritional status: green – well nourished; yellow – early stages of malnutrition; and red – moderate to severe malnutrition."

LIFE Newsletter (League for International Food Education), September 1982.

"Arm circumference is ... not sensitive enough to monitor an individual child's growth over short periods of time like the weight chart. It is useful, however, in situations where it is not feasible to weigh children, particularly to screen children to identify early, and established, malnutrition..."

"Promotion of nutrition and growth monitoring", programme manual prepared for UNICEF workshop, Bangkok, July 1984.

Mothers' Involvement

There has been considerable debate about the ability of mothers – and health workers – to understand the process of plotting a child's growth on a chart:

"Often health workers think that mothers cannot understand the significance of the growth chart, since it is sometimes difficult for the health workers themselves to understand. However, projects that have measured mothers' understanding of the chart after orientation have concluded that mothers have little or no difficulty understanding the chart.

"Data gathered in Ghana indicate that ... many virtually illiterate mothers had little trouble understanding the chart. Even though only 53 percent of the mothers had more than two years of schooling, after six months in the program, 66 percent of all mothers were able to interpret ... charts correctly.

"The experience of Project Poshak in India confirms that mothers can interpret the charts. In this project mothers received weight charts and instructions about their use. By the time of the project evaluation, all mothers interviewed knew that a downward slope in the child's growth line meant illness. Seventy-six percent ... were able to mark their own child's position and to identify the child's health status correctly."

Growth monitoring, Primary Health Care Issues, series I, no. 3, American Public Health Association, October 1981.

"In Indonesia, where UNICEF has supplied 15 million growth charts and 58,700 weighing scales, studies have shown that 95 per cent of the village volunteers can use the growth charts and a survey of 2,500 mothers indicated 67 per cent understood about child health and growth and the need to weigh children monthly. The national reporting system for the nutritional programme in Indonesia shows that 7.45 million children or 35 per cent of the under-fives are enrolled, 55 per cent of those enrolled attend regular weighing sessions and at least 48 per cent are gaining weight."

The Children's Revolution: the Asian picture, UNICEF (Bangkok), 1984.

"It has been reported that the mothers' enthusiasm and participation in a program increases when they are given the growth cards. Possession of the card is a clear indication to the mother that she shares in the responsibility for her child's health. Other advantages include decreasing the amount of time mothers wait for workers to find and refile records."

Growth monitoring, Primary Health Care Issues, series I, no. 3, American Public Health Association, October 1981.

"Some health workers are concerned that records kept by a mother may be lost, or left at home when she visits the clinic. Indeed, there is some evidence that, when a home-based system first starts, losses may be as high as 5 per cent and failures to bring cards to clinics even higher. But this is only a temporary phenomenon, until the new system becomes familiar. Various careful studies have shown that loss rates soon fall below 1 per cent. Even more important, the loss rates by mothers are likely to be lower than by clinic staff."

David Morley and Margaret Woodland, See How They Grow: monitoring child growth for appropriate health care in developing countries, Macmillan, 1979.

"In the Dr. Efrain C. Montemayor Medical Centre in Baguio (in the Philippines), which gives mothers their copies of growth charts, only 1.05% of its more than 2,000 regular mothers in the Under Six Clinic Program forget to bring their charts. This is attributed to the education campaign given mothers at each visit to the clinic. Because mothers understand and realize its importance, they remember to bring the chart as well as come regularly for their child's weighing."

A situation analysis of growth charts in the Philippines, UNICEF (Manila), October 1983.

The Growth Debate

Growth charts are usually based on average child growth rates in the industrialized world. But is it appropriate to judge the nutritional standing of children in developing countries by the international standards based on North American or European children?

"Monitoring the growth of a child requires comparing changes in the same measure taken at regular intervals. A single measurement only indicates the child's size at the moment; it offers little information about whether the child's size is increasing, entering a period of stability, or declining. Because most children will continue to grow – even if only slightly – unless they are extremely ill, it is easy to mistake some growth for adequate growth unless the child's measurement is compared to a reference population. Which population to use for comparison purposes is a controversial question. The debate continues about whether children from different areas of the world have the same genetic potential for growth."

Growth monitoring, Primary Health Care Issues, series I, no. 3, American Public Health Association, October 1981.

"The controversy over whether or not growth standards for children developed in Europe and North America are universally applicable appears now to be settled in favour of those who maintain that they are. Recent evidence suggests that the growth of privileged groups of children in developing countries does not differ importantly from these standards and that the poorer growth so commonly observed in the underprivileged is due to social factors – among which the malnutrition-infection complex is of primary importance – rather than to ethnic or geographical differences…"

"A measure of agreement on growth standards", Lancet, editorial, 21 January 1984.

"There has been a continuing debate as to whether small size in itself is in any way disadvantageous. Where scarcity of food is the norm, might not the nutritional savings realized from being small be decisive for survival? These questions are difficult to answer because it is difficult to isolate the nutrition factor among the deprivations suffered by affected populations. Many studies have shown, however, that the decrease in growth, in both height and weight, associated with various degrees of malnutrition is accompanied by decreases in the circumference of the head, the size of the brain – amounts of important enzymes and neurotransmitters are decreased - and, even in less-than-severe cases, a lowering of scores on tests of cognitive and sensory ability."

Alan Berg, Malnourished people: a policy view, World Bank, June 1981.

"The most useful indicator of nutrition in a young child is whether growth is proceeding normally, i.e. it is the rate of weight gain that is important rather than the nutritional status measured in relation to a norm, at a particular point in time."

"Promotion of nutrition and growth monitoring", programme manual prepared for UNICEF workshop, Bangkok, July 1984.

The aims of growth monitoring in the Indonesian nutrition improvement programme have been described as follows: "Emphasis is entirely on behavioural change leading to the goal 'every child should gain weight every month'. Mothers can easily understand, appreciate, and achieve this goal monthly. By contrast, improved nutritional status (or maintenance of 'normality') has less psychological attraction, is relatively static, and often leads to complacency or resignation on the part of mothers who see their children classified in a single, broad, nutritional category. Monthly growth is a self-motivating goal with recurring rewards."

Jon Rohde and Lukas Hendrata, "Development from below: transformation from village-based nutrition projects to a national family nutrition programme in Indonesia", in David Morley, Jon Rohde and Glen Williams (eds.), Practising Health for All, Oxford University Press, 1983.

II LIFELINES: ORAL REHYDRATION THERAPY

Oral Rehydration Therapy

Diarrhoeal disease (DD) is the greatest single killer of children in the developing world – and often the chief cause of childhood malnutrition.

The prevention of diarrhoea depends upon improvements in water supply, sanitation, and hygiene. But in the meantime, the majority of deaths from diarrhoeal dehydration can be cheaply prevented by oral rehydration therapy (ORT).

Diarrhoeal infections inhibit the body's ability to absorb salts and water. So fluid is lost faster than it can be replaced – leading to dehydration. ORT is based on the discovery that glucose greatly increases the patient's capacity to absorb salts and water. Drinking a solution of salts, glucose and water can therefore prevent dehydration.

Pre-packaged oral rehydration salts (ORS) cost only about 10 cents. But making the packets available to every household is not always feasible. So many ORT campaigns are concentrating on teaching mothers to forestall dehydration by using household remedies – usually sugar and salt solutions.

The natural reaction of parents the world over is to withhold food and fluids during a diarrhoeal attack. The scientific rationale for ORT, and for continued feeding during diarrhoea, has been established beyond doubt: the challenge now is to place that knowledge in the hands of parents so that they themselves can protect their children against the dehydration and malnutrition caused by childhood's most common disease.

Child Deaths

"In 1980 in the developing countries, an estimated five million children under 5 years of age – about 10 every minute – died as a consequence of diarrhoeal disease. These deaths were an outcome of the some 1,000 million episodes that occurred among the 338 million children in this age group and were undoubtedly more frequent in poorer families."

The management of diarrhoea and use of oral rehydration therapy: a joint WHO/UNICEF statement, WHO, 1983.

"About 10 percent of diarrhea episodes lead to dehydration and, if untreated, one or two percent become life-threatening."

"Oral rehydration therapy (ORT) for childhood diarrhea", Population Reports, series L, no. 2, November-December 1980, reprinted April 1982.

Most diarrhoeal deaths stem from dehydration:

"The serious consequence of acute watery diarrhoea results from the loss of large volumes of water containing electrolytes. In severe cases the blood volume is reduced so much that there are signs of 'shock' with an increased pulse rate and a fall in the blood pressure. The loss of the electrolytes may have serious metabolic effects including acidosis. Those changes are usually more serious in small children since a higher proportion of their body weight is fluid. In severe cases the mouth and eyes become relatively dry, the soft fontanelle on the top of an infant's head may be depressed, and the eyes appear sunken; skin elasticity is decreased and a fold which is pinched up and released does not spring back to the usual contour. In the more serious cases 10 per cent or more of the body weight may be lost because of the fluids lost in the stool. If dehydration is less than 5 per cent the clinical features are difficult to detect, but mild dehydration can be assumed in any child with acute watery diarrhoea and appropriate treatment should be started."

W.A.M. Cutting, "Oral rehydration in acute diarrhoea", Pharmaceutical Journal, 26 June 1982.

Malnutrition

Diarrhoeal diseases are a frequent cause of malnutrition; and malnutrition in its turn makes children more vulnerable to sickness and death from diarrhoea:

"Diarrhoea is ... a major factor in the causation or aggravation of malnutrition. This is because the diarrhoea patient loses his appetite and is unable to absorb food properly, and because it is a common practice to withhold fluids and food (including breast-milk) from him. Such malnutrition is itself a contributing cause to the high number of deaths associated with diarrhoea in childhood."

The management of diarrhoea and use of oral rehydration therapy: a joint WHO/UNICEF statement, WHO, 1983.

"A recent careful study of young children in Bangladesh revealed that, on average, each child suffered 6.8 episodes of diarrhoea per year. Added up, this meant they had diarrhoea for 55 days or 15 per cent of the year. Such children will end up severely deprived of nourishment if they are starved all the time they have diarrhoea. Although digestion is less effective during diarrhoea, there is still a significant amount of absorption of nutrients."

K.M. Elliott and W.A.M. Cutting, "Carry on feeding", Diarrhoea Dialogue, no. 15, November 1983.

"Other studies have recorded a relationship between poor nutritional status and increased duration of diarrhoea... In a prospective study in San Jose, Costa Rica, the average duration of diarrhoea episodes in children aged 12-59 months was significantly longer among those with low weight-for-age than among others.

"If poor nutritional status predisposes to more severe diarrhoea ... then it would be expected that poor nutritional status would predispose to diarrhoea mortality. Chen et al. measured the heights and weights of 2,019 children aged 12-23 months in rural Bangladesh and then recorded mortality among these children over the following 2 years. A striking association between nutritional status (weight-for-age) and subsequent diarrhoea mortality was recorded, with children below 65% weight-for-age having a diarrhoea mortality rate 3.8 times higher than children over 65% weight for age...

"Other prospective studies have also reported an association between poor nutrition and diarrhoea mortality. In rural Punjab, India, 71% of under-3-year-old children dying from diarrhoea were under 70% weight-for-age in the two months preceding death. The mean prevalence of under 70% weight-for-age in children from the same community at the same time was significantly lower (25%). In rural Bangladesh, children aged 0-9 years who died of diarrhoea had a pre-morbid mean weight-for-height of 74% of the standard, compared with 83-

86% of standard for children who died of other causes and 88% of standard for living controls."

R.G. Feachem, "Interventions for the control of diarrhoeal diseases among young children: supplementary feeding programmes", Bulletin of the WHO, vol. 61, no. 6, 1983.

A year-long study in Bangladesh surveyed deaths from diarrhoea in children up to three years old who had been treated for one attack. The severely malnourished children (below 56% of the international standard weight-for-age) were at 14 times more risk of dying than better-nourished children (over 66% of weight-for-age).

Summarized from: S.K. Roy, A.K.M.A. Chowdhury and M.M. Rahaman, "Excess mortality among children discharged from hospital after treatment for diarrhoea in rural Bangladesh", British Medical Journal, vol. 287, October 1983.

Causes of Diarrhoea

Many pathogens give rise to diarrhoea. They are both more prevalent and more harmful in an unhygienic environment:

THE PATHOGENS

"Diarrhoeal disease is associated with poverty and with the environmental and education conditions that accompany poverty. In wealthy communities throughout the world diarrhoeal disease has become a minor public health problem. If we look at Europe and North America, for instance, some infections have become very rare (*Vibrio cholerae*, *Shigella* species other than *sonnei*, *Salmonella typhi* and *paratyphi* and *Entamoeba histolytica*) while other infections continue to occur but cause little disease compared to their status in developing countries (rotaviruses, enterotoxigenic *Escherichia coli*, salmonellae, *Campylobacter* and *Shigella sonnei*)."

Richard Feachem, "Water, excreta, behaviour and diarrhoea", Diarrhoea Dialogue, no. 4, February 1981.

TRANSMISSION

"Water-borne transmission is but one special case of faecal-oral transmission and most authorities would agree that a great deal of the transmission of rotaviruses, *shigellae*, enterotoxigenic *E. coli* and *Entamoeba histolytica* is by non-water-borne routes. There is less agreement on the transmission of cholera...

"Many people drink heavily contaminated water (containing up to 10,000 *E. coli* per 100 millilitres) from open wells, ponds or streams. Replacing these sources by piped water or protected wells will dramatically improve water quality... However, some studies ... have found that such improvements failed to have a marked effect on diarrhoeal disease incidence. One possible explanation ... is that diarrhoeal diseases in the communities studied were mainly non-water-borne."

Richard Feachem, "Water, excreta, behaviour and diarrhoea", Diarrhoea Dialogue, no. 4, February 1981.

THE LINK WITH MEASLES

"A prospective detailed study, in which 5,775 children in 12 villages in Bangladesh were observed for a year, showed that measles and diarrhoea appeared to interact synergistically to increase mortality and the irreversible effects of nutritional deprivation. Thirty-four per cent of diarrhoeal deaths were measles-associated. Measles was the single most important cause of death during the period and diarrhoea or dysentery was the most common complication of fatal measles cases...

"It has been estimated that between 6.4 and 25.6 per cent of diarrhoea deaths could be prevented by measles immunization."

M. and V.I. Mathan, "Priority intervention?", Diarrhoea Dialogue, no. 16, February 1984.

PREVENTION OF DIARRHOEA

"There are three basic approaches: interrupting transmission by the improvement of water supply, excreta disposal and hygiene; improving the general health of children by improved nutrition and reducing the incidence of other infections; and immunization. In the long run control will be achieved by a combination of each of these approaches but it is significant that, in developed countries, and in wealthy communities in developing countries, control has been achieved by a combination of the first two alone."

Richard Feachem, "Water, excreta, behaviour and diarrhoea", Diarrhoea Dialogue, no. 4, February 1981.

Oral Rehydration

Deaths from dehydration can be cheaply prevented by oral rehydration therapy (ORT), using either pre-packed sachets of oral rehydration salts (ORS) or home-made solution. The severely dehydrated require intravenous rehydration:

"A rational response to diarrhoea is as follows:
(a) To *prevent* dehydration using solutions prepared from ingredients commonly found in the home ('home remedies'); this should be the first response;
(b) To *correct* dehydration using a balanced, more complete, glucose-salt solution; ORS is the universal solution of this type recommended by WHO and UNICEF;
(c) To correct severe dehydration (usually defined as loss of 10% or more of body weight) by intravenous therapy; this method should also be used in patients who are unconscious or unable to drink."

The management of diarrhoea and use of oral rehydration therapy: a joint WHO/UNICEF statement, WHO, 1983.

"About 90-95% of all patients with acute watery diarrhoea, including infants, can be treated with ORS alone; in the remainder, most of whom have severe dehydration or are unable to take fluids orally, intravenous therapy is required to replace the deficits rapidly."

The management of diarrhoea and use of oral rehydration therapy: a joint WHO/UNICEF statement, WHO, 1983.

ORAL REHYDRATION SALTS

Oral rehydration salts are formulated to replace the nutrients lost during diarrhoea:

The standard WHO/UNICEF recommended formula for ORS consists of:

"Sodium chloride	3.5 grams
Sodium hydrogen carbonate (Sodium bicarbonate)	2.5 grams
Potassium chloride	1.5 grams
Glucose	20.0 grams

To be mixed with one litre of water

"The presence of potassium in ORS is particularly important for the treatment of dehydrated children, in whom potassium losses in diarrhoea are relatively high. Studies have shown that undernourished children who have suffered repeated bouts of diarrhoea are especially likely to develop a blood level of

II LIFELINES: ORAL REHYDRATION THERAPY

potassium below normal if the potassium is not replaced during rehydration.

"The bicarbonate in ORS is needed for the treatment of acidosis, which occurs frequently with dehydration...

"Glucose is included in the solution principally to help the absorption of sodium and not as a source of energy. Ordinary sugar (sucrose) can be substituted for glucose with near equal efficacy, though twice the amount of sugar is needed. Increasing the amount of sugar in the formula as a means of improving palatability or increasing its nutritive value is potentially dangerous as it can worsen the diarrhoea."

The management of diarrhoea and use of oral rehydration therapy: a joint WHO/UNICEF statement, WHO, 1983.

EFFECTIVENESS OF ORT

"A review of 22,559 pediatric records at the State University Hospital, Port-au-Prince, Haiti, indicated a mortality of 35% among 9,434 patients hospitalized with diarrhoea and dehydration during the period 1969-1979. A program for the management of infantile diarrhoea (based on ORT) was established at the University Hospital in 1980. Mortality fell to 14% during the first year, was 1.9% during the second year, and has been less than 1% since January 1982."

Jean W. Pape and others, "Management of diarrhea in Haiti: mortality reduction in 8,443 hospitalized children", in Richard A. Cash and Judith McLaughlin (eds.), Proceedings of the International Conference on Oral Rehydration Therapy, Agency for International Development (Washington, D.C.), 1984.

"In a number of research studies the use of ORS for treating dehydrated children at the community level has decreased the number of deaths from diarrhoea as much as 50-60% over a one-year period."

The management of diarrhoea and use of oral rehydration therapy: a joint WHO/UNICEF statement, WHO, 1983.

Preliminary research in 1980 for the national diarrhoeal disease control programme in Egypt found that early rehydration by mothers with a salt and sugar mix made at home, backed up by ORS from health care providers, reduced preschool child mortality by 40% and diarrhoea-specific mortality by 50%.

Summarized from: A.B. Mobarak and others, "Diarrheal disease control study: May through October 1980", Strengthening Rural Health Delivery Project, Rural Health Department, Ministry of Health, Egypt, n.d.

"A programme of distribution of oral rehydration packets was established by the government in 1980 in 20 of the 80 Costa Rican municipalities... The sachets were distributed free of charge to mothers with preschool children in the 20 experimental municipalities. The result, after one year of operation, was a 50% reduction of infant diarrhoea deaths in the 20 municipalities; no significant change was detected in the remaining municipalities where the intervention was not effected."

Leonardo Mata, "The evolution of diarrhoeal diseases and malnutrition in Costa Rica", Assignment Children, vol. 61/62, 1983.

ORT AND MALNUTRITION

As well as reducing deaths from dehydration, ORT also reduces the impact of diarrhoea on the child's nutritional status:

"Field studies in the Philippines, Turkey, Egypt and Iran have demonstrated not only a reduction in deaths and hospitalization, but also a positive nutritional impact based on the provision of early rehydration either in a nearby centre or in the home by the mothers. Children receiving ORS showed from 0.25 to 0.5 kg better weight gain over one year in comparison to control groups who received only the nutrition advice. The impact was greater on children experiencing multiple episodes, further supporting the importance of ORS in the improved growth. Coupled with detailed advice to continue feeding the child and provide extra food in the recovery period, the provision of early rehydration may be one of the most effective and pragmatic means of avoiding the occurrence of malnutrition."

Jon Eliot Rohde and Lukas Hendrata, "Oral rehydration: technology and implementation", in D.B. Jelliffe and E.F.P. Jelliffe (eds.), Advances in International Maternal and Child Health, vol. 1, Oxford University Press, 1981.

Home Remedies

When ORS sachets are not available, home remedies can perform a valuable function in forestalling dehydration:

"ORT can be provided in the form of prepackaged salts or as home-prepared solutions; both have important roles to play in the management of diarrhoea... There is an urgent need to accelerate the production of ORS and to disseminate more information about the early treatment of diarrhoea in the home."

The management of diarrhoea and use of oral rehydration therapy: a joint WHO/UNICEF statement, WHO, 1983.

"... there is a strong rationale for beginning ORT early, before obvious signs of dehydration develop. First, within a few hours after diarrhea starts, dehydration amounting to three or four percent of body weight can occur without symptoms. Early use of ORT helps to compensate for this undetected loss as it takes place. Second, early ORT minimizes the symptoms associated with increasing water and electrolyte loss, such as vomiting, lack of appetite, and lethargy. Thus feeding can continue and nutritional damage can be avoided. Third, teaching a family to start treatment as soon as diarrhea begins may be easier than trying to explain the difference between diarrhea with and without dehydration."

"Oral rehydration therapy (ORT) for childhood diarrhea", Population Reports, series L, no. 2, November-December 1980, reprinted April 1982.

"In February 1981, only 2.3% of 500 consecutive hospitalized patients (in the State University Hospital, Port-au-Prince, Haiti) had received ORS at home and 24% were severely dehydrated. One year later, 48% of 500 hospitalized children had initiated fluid therapy at home; 3% of these patients were severely dehydrated, as opposed to 23% of children not receiving this early therapy."

Jean W. Pape and others, "Management of diarrhea in Haiti: mortality reduction in 8,443 hospitalized children", in Richard A. Cash and Judith McLaughlin (eds.), Proceedings of the International Conference on Oral Rehydration Therapy, Agency for International Development (Washington, D.C.), 1984.

"There are two groups of home remedies:

"(a) Household food solutions – fluids or liquids that are normally available in the home and are appropriate for the early home treatment of acute diarrhoea. Such solutions are often prepared from boiled water, thus ensuring safety for drinking, and contain sodium, sometimes potassium, and a source of glucose – such as starches – that can facilitate the absorption of salts in the intestine; they also may contain other sources of energy. Two examples are rice water, often found in homes in Asia, and various soups – e.g., carrot soup, often found in homes in North Africa; other less robust examples include juices, coconut water, and weak tea...

"(b) Salt and sugar solutions – consisting of white sugar (sucrose) and cooking salt (sodium chloride). In a few countries molasses or unrefined sugar is used in place of white sugar; it has the advantage of containing also potassium chloride and sodium bicarbonate... Costs, seasonal shortages, and varying quality of sugar or salt have made it difficult to promote and implement the use of 'salt and sugar' solutions in the home in some areas; in such cases the use of 'household food' solutions should be considered.

"As these home remedies may have a varied composition and usually lack or have insufficient amounts of the ingredients in ORS (particularly potassium and bicarbonate), they are not ideal for the treatment of dehydration at any age. However, they certainly should be used at the onset of diarrhoea to prevent dehydration and in situations where the complete formula is needed but is not available."

The management of diarrhoea and use of oral rehydration therapy: a joint WHO/UNICEF statement, WHO, 1983.

"There is widespread agreement that a complete formula such as that recommended by WHO, including both potassium and bicarbonate, is the best formulation for rehydration of dehydrated children. But is there also a place for home-mixed sugar and salt solution that can be prepared anywhere when prepackaged formulations are not available? The answer seems to be a qualified yes – home formulations using household sugar (sucrose) and salt alone can serve a useful purpose, both as back-up when supplies of ORS packets are insufficient and alone where ORS packets are not used...

"Preparing a sugar and salt solution from household supplies is more difficult than mixing from a packet since not only the water but also the sugar and salt must be measured. At least three techniques have been tested... The first is the pinch-and-scoop method, using the fingers to measure a pinch of salt and a scoop of sugar. The second uses household spoons to measure dry ingredients and available bottles, pans, or glasses to measure water. The third involves distributing to each family a plastic spoon specifically designed for measuring the dry ingredients accurately...

"Results with these three approaches have been mixed. Using either the pinch-and-scoop method or using their own household containers and measuring implements, some of the women studied in Bangladesh, Honduras, Nepal and the US mixed solutions containing excessively high salt levels... With all three techniques some Nepalese women prepared solutions containing so little salt that they would be ineffective for rehydration.

"One difficulty in evaluating the findings of mixing and measurement studies is that no definition of acceptable results has been set forth. Is one dangerously salty solution in 100 acceptable in a community-based program? One in 1,000? Is one solution in 100 with an ineffectively low salt level too many?"

"Oral rehydration therapy (ORT) for childhood diarrhea", Population Reports, series L, no. 2, November-December 1980, reprinted April 1982.

"The strongest conclusion to emerge from studies of mixing is the importance of careful, thorough, and individual instruction. In Indonesia most women who had heard of ORS but not received personal instruction did not know how to mix solutions correctly from packets... In Indonesia few of the people who said they understood the directions on the ORS packet could in fact mix the solution properly... A few more could follow verbal instructions accurately. After the technique was actually demonstrated, however, nearly all mixed the ORS solution correctly."

"Oral rehydration therapy (ORT) for childhood diarrhea", Population Reports, series L, no. 2, November-December 1980, reprinted April 1982.

Continued feeding

Parents' natural reaction is to withhold food and fluids during diarrhoea, but this worsens the impact of the diarrhoea:

"The proper management of diarrhoea in the home also includes, along with the administration of ORT, the promotion of appropriate child feeding, both during and after a diarrhoea episode, to prevent excessive and uncompensated loss of nutrients. In many societies the parent's remedial response to diarrhoea is to withhold food and fluid, including breast-milk, in the mistaken belief that this will stop the diarrhoea and ease the strain on the intestine. This 'treatment' only adds to the dehydration and malnutrition caused by the illness."

The management of diarrhoea and use of oral rehydration therapy: a joint WHO/UNICEF statement, WHO, 1983.

"All agree on one point: the importance of continued breast-feeding, even though breast milk contains lactose. If breast-feeding is discontinued, lactation may cease or be reduced, raising the far greater dangers of malnutrition and infection. Even for children who are not nursing, short-term deprivation of nutrients is serious, since a fasting child loses an estimated one to two percent of body weight daily, even in the absence of fluid losses due to diarrhea. If a child experiences 20 to 30 days of diarrhea annually, the nutritional consequences will soon mount up."

"Oral rehydration therapy (ORT) for childhood diarrhea", Population Reports, series L, no. 2, November-December 1980, reprinted April 1982.

"In infants 4-6 months of age or older who have not previously been given semi-solid foods, this is a good time to start feeding such foods and to emphasize their importance in the prevention of future episodes of diarrhoea. In these infants, and in some of those who have lost their appetite during the diarrhoea, a considerable effort may be necessary to get them to eat. In such cases, frequent small meals should be given...

"In infants especially, after an episode of diarrhoea one extra meal should be given each day for at least one week after the diarrhoea stops."

"A manual for the treatment of acute diarrhoea", Programme for Control of Diarrhoeal Diseases, WHO, 1980 (WHO/CDD/SER/80.2).

Safety

Concern is sometimes expressed about the dangers of using too much salt in oral rehydration solution, especially if given to the very young:

"While experts on fluid and electrolyte metabolism continue to debate the relative theoretical merits of each fluid composition, especially the sodium concentration used for young children, it is interesting to note the wide range of sodium that has given acceptable results in studies around the world... Those using higher concentrations of sodium (90-120 meq/l) for treatment of children advocate offering extra water to the child, while those reporting lower sodium (50-80 meq/l) generally admit these solutions are too dilute for effective rehydration of severe diarrhoea especially in adults... Even young children or infants require a higher sodium level during rehydration to expand extracellular fluid and improve circulation than in the later maintenance phase when more free water is required to offset obligatory water losses... the recent Scientific Working Group convened by the World Health

II LIFELINES: ORAL REHYDRATION THERAPY

Organization to examine the composition of oral rehydration mixtures felt the evidence heavily favoured a sodium level of 90 meq/l as optimum for a solution to be used world-wide."

Jon Eliot Rohde and Lukas Hendrata, "Oral rehydration: technology and implementation", in D.B. Jellife and E.F.P. Jelliffe (eds.), Advances in International Maternal and Child Health, vol. 1, Oxford University Press, 1981.

"... rehydration therapy can usually be achieved orally with ORS solution, except in cases with severe dehydration, uncontrollable vomiting, or another serious complication that prevents successful oral therapy. In these cases intravenous therapy is needed. ORS solution is also the fluid used for maintenance therapy. However, normal daily fluid requirements must be given as fluids of lower salt concentration: e.g., plain water, breast milk, or diluted milk feeds. This is particularly important in infants; due to their large surface area per kg of body weight and their high metabolic rate, under normal conditions they require 2.5 times more water per kg than adults."

"A manual for the treatment of acute diarrhoea", Programme for Control of Diarrhoeal Diseases, WHO, 1980 (WHO/CDD/SER/80.2).

ORT AND UNCLEAN WATER

Only one study so far, in the Gambia, has assessed the risk of using ORS solution that is not bacteria-free: 97 children received ORS solution made with clean water and 87 received ORS solution made with well water. The incidence and duration of diarrhoea and the growth rate in the two groups of children were found to be similar.

Summarized from: M. Watkinson and others, "The use of oral glucose electrolyte solution prepared with untreated well water in acute, non-specific childhood diarrhoea", Transactions of the Royal Society of Tropical Medicine and Hygiene, vol. 74, no. 5, 1980.

"On the basis of the available information, the following recommendations can be made regarding the preparation of ORS solution:

"(1) ORS solution should be prepared with water made potable by recognized methods ... in containers washed with such water... there are as yet insufficient data to show that there is no risk associated with the use of 'usual' drinking water;

"(2) ORS solution, once prepared, should be protected against subsequent contamination...

"(3) If potable water cannot be guaranteed, and ORS solution needs to be administered, the best available water should be used."

"Use of locally available drinking water for preparation of oral rehydration salt (ORS) solution", Diarrhoeal Diseases Control Programme, WHO, 1981 (CDD/SER/81.1).

Costs

A sachet of ORS usually costs only a few cents, and remedies given early in the home even less. Hospitals, too, have reduced their expenses by switching to ORT:

"The average cost of treating one patient with intravenous therapy can be more than $5 as compared with less than $0.50 with ORS. In contrast to intravenous therapy, ORS can be given under simple conditions and does not require any special equipment or highly skilled personnel; thus there is increased access to rehydration therapy."

The management of diarrhoea and use of oral rehydration therapy: a joint WHO/UNICEF statement, WHO, 1983.

A diarrhoea treatment centre in Bangladesh found that despite staff increases, "the replacement of intravenous fluid by ORS led to savings of 33% in the total costs incurred... Use of ORS may prolong the stay of a patient in hospital to some extent, but since mothers can be responsible for this treatment, the overall cost, compared to treatment with intravenous fluid, is less."

A.R. Samadi, R. Islam and M.I. Huq, "Replacement of intravenous therapy by oral rehydration solution in a large treatment centre for diarrhoea with dehydration", Bulletin of the World Health Organisation, vol. 61, no. 3, 1983.

"While the use of ORS may *initially* require more health workers' time to train mothers to give ORS to their children, in the long term it frees hospital and health centre staff for other duties. Of greater importance, ORS involves parents directly in the care of their children and presents an excellent opportunity for health workers to communicate important health education messages on diarrhoea prevention and nutrition."

The management of diarrhoea and use of oral rehydration therapy: a joint WHO/UNICEF statement, WHO, 1983.

New Developments

Scientists all over the world are working to perfect ORT. Some current developments:

STARCH-BASED ORS

Recent experiments using rice-starch suggest that cereal starches, which convert to sugar in the small intestine, may have advantages over glucose or sucrose:

"124 patients with acute diarrhoea due to *Vibrio cholerae* or *Escherichia coli* were treated with either the standard sucrose-electrolyte solution or a cereal-based electrolyte solution, containing 30 g rice powder per litre and electrolytes as recommended by the World Health Organization... The proportions of successfully treated patients in the rice-powder group were 80% for cholera patients and 88% for *E. coli* patients – no different from those in patients receiving the sucrose-electrolyte solution.

"Soaked rice in some form, with added salt or sugar, has been a traditional dietary therapy for diarrhoea in Bangladesh and many other developing countries for centuries, but little attention is paid to the correct concentrations of salts and water. Rice is cheaper and more readily available than glucose or sucrose and, as a familiar component of treatment for diarrhoea, it may be more acceptable... and there may be a benefit of increased calorie intake."

A.M. Molla and others, "Rice-powder electrolyte solution as oral therapy in diarrhoea due to Vibrio cholerae and Escherichia coli", Lancet, 12 June 1982.

CITRATE FORMULA

Recent laboratory studies have shown that ORS made with 2.9 grammes of trisodium citrate dihydrate in place of sodium bicarbonate is not only more stable when packed in conditions of heat and humidity, but also tends to reduce the amount of diarrhoea – in some studies, by as much as 26%-46%.

Summarized from: "Report of the fifth meeting of the Technical Advisory Group", Diarrhoeal Diseases Control Programme, WHO, 1984 (WHO/CDD/84.9).

VACCINES

"The use of vaccines to prevent diarrhea has been limited chiefly to cholera, where it is only moderately effective. Work on rotavirus vaccines is promising but still experimental. In Bangladesh, rotavirus and enterotoxic *E. coli* cause about one-third of diarrhea episodes experienced by children under age 2 but account for more than two-thirds of episodes involving dehydration... The development of effective vaccines against rotavirus and enterotoxic *E. coli* might therefore make a significant impact on diarrhea morbidity and mortality in early childhood – if they could be inexpensively produced and widely distributed."

"Oral rehydration therapy (ORT) for childhood diarrhea", Population Reports, series L, no. 2, November-December 1980, reprinted April 1982.

"By using these two rehydration methods, intravenous for very severely dehydrated patients and ORS for the moderately and mildly dehydrated, no one need ever die of cholera. That is the most important thing we have accomplished in the past 20 years, and it is no small achievement.

"And so, while an effective cholera vaccine appears to be on the horizon for the future, right now we must concentrate our energies on reaching people the world over with the therapy we have at hand – a therapy that has been proven to be 100 percent effective against one of the most deadly diseases mankind has ever known."

William B. Greenough, "Need people die any more of cholera? Causes, concerns and control", Future, no. 8, autumn 1983.

Breast-Feeding

In poor communities, the bottle-feeding of infants sharply increases the risk of malnutrition, infection and death. Yet in many parts of the developing world, the incidence and duration of breast-feeding is on the decline and sales of breast-milk substitutes are rising.

For infants, breast-milk is more nutritious, more hygienic, and provides a degree of immunity from infection. For the mother, breast-feeding is economical – but it also makes heavy demands on her energy, time, and freedom of movement.

Many factors now affect a mother's decision on breast-feeding: the advice and example of hospitals and the medical profession; social attitudes and levels of knowledge; difficulties encountered in breast-feeding itself; price, availability and promotion of breast-milk substitutes; employers' policies and government strategies. For babies who are breast-fed, the weaning period is the time of greatest danger to health and life. Although again making heavy demands of the mother, knowing when and how to wean a child could drastically reduce child malnutrition in the developing world.

Dangers of the Bottle

In developing countries, babies who are exclusively breast-fed are more likely to survive than those who are bottle-fed:

"A study of 1,700 women in rural Chile in 1969 and 1970 found that postneonatal death rates (between the 4th and the 52nd week) were three times higher among infants who started bottle-feeding in the first three months than among those who received only breast milk during that time. Because the infants were less likely to be breast-fed, death rates were higher among children whose mothers had moderate education, higher incomes, better sanitation, and prenatal health care than among those without – a contrast with the influence of socioeconomic factors on mortality in most studies...

"A recent study in Cairo under the auspices of the International Fertility Research Program found that children who were breast-fed for 15 to 20 months had a 93 percent probability of surviving until the birth of the next child, whereas children never breast-fed or breast-fed for less than three months had a survival probability of about 64 percent. Although the educational level of the mother also influenced child survival, the influence of breast-feeding was greater, and the lower the mother's educational level, the more influence breast-feeding had. Among children whose mothers had no education, those breast-fed for 9 to 12 months had a 30 percent higher survival probability than those never breast-fed; among children whose mothers had at least seven years of schooling, the difference was 22 percent."

"Breast-feeding, fertility and family planning", Population Reports, series J, no. 24, November-December 1981.

Studies in four countries in Latin America and the Caribbean - El Salvador, Colombia, Jamaica and Brazil – have shown that infants breast-fed for less than six months (or not at all) were six to fourteen times more likely to die in the second six months of life than babies who were breast-fed for six months or more.

Summarized from: Joe D. Wray, "Maternal nutrition, breast-feeding and infant survival" in W. Henry Mosley (ed.), Nutrition and Human Reproduction, Plenum Press, 1978.

A study of 9,662 newborn babies delivered at the Baguio General Hospital and Medical Centre in the Philippines between 1973 and 1977 found a strong correlation between breast-feeding and decreased morbidity and mortality in infants (see table 2):

87

II LIFELINES: BREAST-FEEDING

Table 2: Infant deaths resulting from diarrhoea in relation to mode of feeding, January 1973–April 1977.

	Mode of feeding		Diarrhoea cases			
	No.	%	Morbidity No.	%	Mortality No.	%
Breast-fed	6,408	66.60	6	4.35	0	0.00
Mixed-fed	611	6.35	8	5.80	0	0.00
Formula-fed	2,603	27.05	124	89.85	38	100.00
Total	**9,622**	**100.00**	**138**	**100.00**	**38**	**100.00**

N. R. Clavano, "Mode of Feeding and its Effect on Infant Mortality and Morbidity", Journal of Tropical Pediatrics, vol. 28, no 6, December 1982.

CONTAMINATION AND OVER-DILUTION

To be used safely, infant formula requires access to a pure water supply, as well as means of sterilization and refrigeration. Mothers must also be able to read and understand written instructions, and have sufficient income to buy adequate amounts of the product. When these conditions are not met, the resulting milk solution is either contaminated or over-diluted:

"For many people in the developing world, however, the hygienic conditions necessary for the proper use of infant formula just do not exist. Their water is unclean, the bottles are dirty, the formula is diluted to make a tin of powdered milk last longer than it should. What happens? The baby is fed a contaminated mixture and soon becomes ill with diarrhoea, which leads to dehydration, malnutrition, and very often death."

Natividad Relucio-Clavano, "The results of a change in hospital practices," Assignment Children, vol. 55/56, 1982.

An Indonesian study sampled fifty-three milk solutions from bottles being used to feed infants in four maternal and child health clinics. The findings:

"One-third were less than 50% of proper strength and only 1/2 were within 20% of recommended concentration according to the manufacturer's label.

Milk sampled from feeding bottles in several MCH clinics was highly contaminated by fecal organisms with only four of 53 samples having fewer than 1,000 organisms per ml."

Dani Surjono, S.B. Ismadi, Suwardji and Jon Rohde, "Bacterial contamination and dilution of milk in infant feeding bottles". Journal of Tropical Pediatrics, April 1980.

The Trend Away

"In South Korea the practice of prolonged breast-feeding - for at least 18 months – declined sharply between 1950 and 1970, from over 55% to about 35% of first births.

"In Thailand between 1969 and 1979 the average duration of breast-feeding declined by almost five months – from 12.9 to 8.4 months in the cities and from 22.4 to 17.5 months in rural areas.

"In Taiwan also, the percentage of infants initially breast-fed fell sharply, from 93% in 1966 to 50% in 1980. During the same period the average duration of breast-feeding of children ever breast-fed dropped from 14.6 months to 8.8 months.

"Less than 5% of the women surveyed in the cities of Sao Paulo (Brazil), Panama City (Panama), and San Salvador (El Salvador) breast-fed for six months or more, and in the state of Sao Paulo, Brazil, less than 50% breast-fed for as long as one month."

"Breast-feeding, fertility, and family planning", Population Reports, series J, no. 24, November-December 1981.

Breast-Milk

Breast-milk's advantages include a perfect infant diet for the early months, some immunity from infection, and a degree of protection against conception:

PROTECTION AGAINST DISEASE

"One of the great arguments in favour of breast-feeding has long been its anti-infectious action. Breast-fed infants develop fewer bacterial and viral infections of digestive and respiratory origin than bottle-fed babies. The bottle and the teat are far greater sources of infection than the breast, particularly for families living under deficient sanitary conditions. The immediate consumption of mother's milk (from the breast to the child's mouth), with no handling avoids the proliferation of the germs present on the nipple and areola of the breast and the penetration of other germs which abound in the environment.

"Above all, mother's milk provides direct protection against infections, and gastro-intestinal infections in particular. The disease rate for infections is also lower in breast-fed newborns in the wealthier classes than in those fed artificially."

A.M. Masse-Raimbault, "How to feed young children", Children in the Tropics, no. 138-139-140, 1982.

Research in India and Canada found that artificially fed infants were three times more likely to contract diarrhoeal infections and twice as likely to suffer from respiratory infections – the two main causes of infant death – as infants who were breast-fed (see table 3).

Table 3: Relationship between method of infant feeding and incidence of disease.

	Number of cases of disease in 24 months			
	INDIA		CANADA	
Ailment	BF	AF	BF	AF
Respiratory infections	57	109	42	98
Otitis	21	52	9	86
Diarrhoea	70	211	5	16
Dehydration	3	14	0	3
Pneumonia	2	8	—	—

BF = Breast-feeding, AF = Artificial feeding
Children in the Tropics, International Children's Centre, Paris, 1982.

"Breast-milk is the best food for infants, and no substitute food exactly duplicates it. Studies of breast milk and breast-feeding show that:

"Breast-milk provides some immunological protection for the infant.

"Breast-milk best satisfies the infant's nutritional needs.

"Breast-feeding costs less than feeding with substitutes.

"Because of the immunological and nutritional advantages of breast-milk and because preparing substitutes properly is difficult in much of the developing world, breast-fed infants are less likely to develop infections or malnutrition.

"Breast-feeding protects against pregnancy, although the length of this contraceptive effect is not predictable.

"Many other advantages have been claimed for breast-feeding ranging from closer emotional ties between mother and child to greater intellectual ability in later life for the breast-fed child. Such possible benefits are difficult to measure, and more research will be necessary before any or all can be accepted."

"Breast-feeding, fertility and family planning", Population Reports, series J, no. 24, November-December 1981.

"In a study of infant feeding practices among mothers who had been identified (as underweight) during pregnancy, a sub-sample of 80 children was followed for four to eight months. Of those exclusively breast-fed, 76% achieved 90% of the expected weight gain for children of that age. In the 'mixed feeding' group, the expected weight was attained by 60% of the children; among those on formula alone, by 29%. The conclusion reached was that under poor socio-economic conditions, formula-feeding is expensive and inadequately carried out, while breast-feeding obviously provides the best answer."

Priyani E. Soysa, "The advantages of breast-feeding – a developing country point of view", Assignment Children, vol. 55/56, 1981.

CONTRACEPTIVE EFFECT

In communities where more reliable forms of contraception are either not widely available or not widely accepted, prolonged breast-feeding offers the mother a considerable degree of protection against becoming pregnant. Breast-feeding therefore has a significant effect on the average interval between births, which in turn has a significant effect on an infant's chances of survival and healthy growth:

"Breast-feeding delays menstruation, inhibits ovulation, and therefore reduces the likelihood of conception. In general, the longer a woman breast-feeds, the longer she will remain infecund. Although the contraceptive effect of lactation has been recognized by various cultures for centuries – at least since the ancient Egyptians – only during the last few decades have biological scientists and demographers focused attention specifically on the length, variations, implications, and causes of lactational infecundity. The overall conclusion is that breast-feeding makes a substantial contribution to birth spacing and fertility control in many areas, but that for an individual woman it is an unreliable method of family planning."

"Breast-feeding, fertility and family planning", Population Reports, series J, no. 24, November-December 1981.

"Studies from many parts of the world show a positive relationship between the duration of breast-feeding and the length of postpartum amenorrhea ... In rural Senegal, where breast-feeding averages over 23 months, amenorrhea lasts almost 18 months. The relationship is least consistent among groups where breast-feeding is either relatively short – 12 months or less – or relatively long – over 20 months. In the intermediate range, however, each additional month of breast-feeding means an average of almost one additional month of amenorrhea.

"The longer a woman breast-feeds, the longer her amenorrhea lasts. For example, while women in these populations who do not breast-feed at all will average up to three months of amenorrhea, women who breast-feed up to 18 months will experience amenorrhea lasting eight to 13 months."

"Breast-feeding, fertility, and family planning", Population Reports, series J, no. 24, November-December 1981.

"If women in Ghana were to stop breast-feeding, the already high fertility rate would increase by at least 40% due to the loss of the natural birth-spacing effect of breast-feeding, with widespread economic implications."

Ted Greiner, "Some Economic and Social Implications of Breast-Feeding", paper prepared for UNICEF/Commonwealth Secretariat Seminar on Breast-feeding, Harare, 1983.

The Costs

Breast-milk has an energy cost to the mother and is therefore not 'free'. But it is many times cheaper than commercial infant formula and therefore represents a very considerable 'saving' to the poor (see table 4):

Table 4: Cost of complete formula-feeding for an infant 2 months of age, expressed as a percentage of salaries for selected jobs in different countries.

Country	Hospital cleaner %	Ministry clerk %	Junior staff nurse %
Burma	73	40	21
Egypt	9	10	8
Guatemala	27	12	10
Indonesia	35	51	21
Nigeria	18	16	6
Philippines (Manila)	28	24	18
Sri Lanka	63	45	43
Sweden	4	4	4
Tanzania	32	32	14
Turkey	21	21	16
UK (London)	6	5	4
Yemen	17	13	11

Summarised from: Margot Cameron and Yngve Hosvander, Manual on feeding infants and young children, draft third edition, 1981.

"Bottle-feeding requires the purchase not only of the breast-milk substitute, but also of the bottle and nipple. It requires fuel for sterilization of the equipment and, ideally, refrigeration. These costs vary, but generally the cost of proper feeding with a breast-milk substitute totals at least US$200-$300 for the first year of life. Among substitutes, commercial infant formula is generally more expensive than modifying and preparing milk products in the home.

"Poor families may spend less than $200-$300 a year on bottle-feeding, but the child may suffer as a result. To save money, families may not give enough formula or may overdilute it. They may use milk from cows or other animals without modifying it. They may even mix flour and sugar with water so that it simply looks like milk. A full estimate of the expense of bottle-feeding should include the cost to the family and to society of resulting increases in infant morbidity and mortality when bottle-feeding is inadequate or improper.

"The only direct monetary cost of proper breast-feeding is dietary supplementation of the mother before and after delivery. These extra nutritional needs can sometimes be met by additional quantities of inexpensive foods already in the woman's diet, which cost less than bottle-feeding. Many women do not or cannot augment their diets while breast-feeding, however, and therefore a full estimate of breast-feeding costs should also include the cost to the family and

II LIFELINES: BREAST-FEEDING

society of related maternal health problems and, if milk supply is inadequate, child health problems."

<small>"Breast-feeding, fertility and family planning", Population Reports, series J, no. 24, November-December 1981.</small>

Mexico: "The average monthly expenditure on milk or formula for all sample households was $7.20 or 10% of the average monthly income of all households. Households reporting the lowest average monthly income ($23) spent $8.00 or 35% of their monthly income on milk or formula. Households reporting the second lowest average monthly income ($57) spent $6.50 or 11% of their monthly income on milk or formula."

<small>Kimberly K. Lillig and Carolyn J. Lackey, "Economic and Social Factors Influencing Women's Infant Feeding Decisions in a Rural Mexican Community", Journal of Tropical Pediatrics, vol. 28, October 1982.</small>

Ghana and the Ivory Coast: "The savings in national goods cost could amount to US$16 to 28 million annually ... At the individual level, by breast-feeding rather than artificially feeding an infant for two years the average family in either country would save between US$600 and 730 in the cost of goods and time, plus any savings that might result from the avoidance of disease or malnutrition caused by artificial feeding."

<small>S. Almroth and T. Greiner, "The Economic Value of Breast-feeding", FAO Food and Nutrition Papers, no. 11, FAO, 1979.</small>

ENERGY COST TO MOTHERS

Breast-feeding makes heavy demands on a mother's energy and nutritional resources. In developing countries the lactation period is usually longer and more costly in terms of nutritional demand on the mother than pregnancy itself:

"... the protein intake of pregnant and lactating mothers in Africa is often extremely low ... Physicians frequently see the 'wreck of a woman' following frequent pregnancies on an unsatisfactory diet. She is usually thin, miserable, anemic and often apathetic, with a dry scaly skin, sometimes rather lusterless hair, often with an ulcer that is reluctant to heal, and some mouth lesions. She is labelled in the clinic as a case of 'general malnutrition', 'multiple deficiency'. There is no universally adopted term for this syndrome, nor a sure guide to its diagnosis; is it not, in fact, caloric protein deficiency disease of adults?"

<small>M.C. Latham, "Maternal nutrition in East Africa", Journal of Tropical Medicine vol. 67, 1964.</small>

"... there is clear recent evidence of a close dependence of breast milk output on energy intake particularly when food energy intake falls to exceptionally low levels, as occurs seasonally in many developing countries. In The Gambia in the dry season, when the mean intake of lactating women was found to be about 1800 kcal/day, mean breast-milk output was estimated at approximately 790 ml/day in early lactation. At the height of the wet season (August-September), when daily energy intake was around only 1200 kcal/day, average breast-milk output had fallen to only about 630 ml/day."

<small>G.A. Clugston, "Lactation – Its Processes and Outcomes and the Effect of Maternal Nutrition", paper presented at WHO Workshop on Breast-feeding, Shanghai, October 1982.</small>

Factors in the Decision

Many factors play a part in a mother's decision to breast-feed her child or not. Among the pressures tending to influence mothers in the direction of bottle-feeding are:

"In Western societies the advertising and marketing of infant formulas were probably secondary reasons for the decline in breast-feeding.

"However, in developing countries they may be primary reasons. Companies producing baby-food have long realized that promising new markets are created by the growing monetarization of the economy of Third World countries. They have launched marketing campaigns that are clearly aimed at persuading mothers to start bottle-feeding. Advertisements show smiling, beautiful mothers bottle-feeding babies who, in sharp contrast with reality for most of the people, are well-fed and complacent. This is followed by a message that this one particular product contains 'everything your baby needs', often with protein, vitamins, or iron added for good measure. This must make a mother doubt that her own, old-fashioned product is good enough for her baby, for whom she wishes the best."

<small>Elisabet Helsing with F. Savage King, Breast-feeding in Practice, Oxford University Press, 1982.</small>

BREAST-FEEDING DIFFICULTIES

'Lack of milk' is usually the most common cited by mothers who discontinue breast-feeding after a short time:

A WHO study of breast-feeding in nine countries – Hungary, Sweden, Ethiopia, Nigeria, Zaire, Chile, Guatemala, the Philippines and India – concluded:

"It is of interest that 'insufficient milk' was a reason given by rural mothers among whom prolonged breast-feeding was usual, as well as by economically advantaged urban mothers who mostly breast-fed for a much shorter time. It would seem that this response was more possibly coloured by cultural factors than by any physiological inability to produce sufficient milk."

<small>WHO Collaborative Study on Breast-feeding, Methods and Main Results of the First Phase of the Study. Preliminary Report, WHO, 1983 (MCH/79.3).</small>

Mexico: "Respondents who regularly bottle-feed milk or formula cited the greatest reason for not breast-feeding was insufficient breast-milk ... Other reasons reported by mothers for not breast-feeding included breast problems, inconvenience and refusal of the infant to suckle the breast."

<small>Kimberly K. Lillig and Carolyn J. Lackey, "Economic and social factors influencing women's infant feeding decisions in a rural mexican community", Journal of Tropical Paediatrics, vol. 28, October 1982.</small>

"... women are losing the art of managing a successful breast-feeding relationship with their babies. Breast-feeding becomes so unnatural that they find it difficult to cope with simple problems – pain or soreness of nipples, breast engorgement and sucking difficulties of babies. But these problems can be solved if mothers understand them and have the opportunity to learn how to cope. Like any other skill, breast-feeding has to be learnt. But for many women, it has become easier to give up breast-feeding than to persevere in it."

<small>Natividad Relucio-Clavano, "The promotion of breast-feeding", in The State of the World's Children 1984, Oxford University Press, 1983.</small>

THE COLOSTRUM PROBLEM

"Breast-milk initially appears as colostrum, a concentrated yellowish fluid measuring approximately 25 ml during the first 24 hours. The small amount and strange colour of the milk at this stage misleads many health workers and mothers into feeling anxious that the mother's own milk might not be enough to feed the baby. Because of this, many women resort to prelacteal or supplemental formula. The result is less suckling and therefore less breast-milk supply. In many cases, this process ends in breast-feeding being abandoned altogether."

Natividad Relucio-Clavano, "The promotion of breast-feeding", in The State of the World's Children 1984, Oxford University Press, 1983.

LACK OF KNOWLEDGE

Mexico: "Respondents were questioned as to whether they believed infants were healthier if they were breast-fed or fed a substitute for breast-milk. 52% of the sample responded that breast-milk was better for the child's health. 24% believed milk or formula made infants healthier while 23% felt that what the child was fed made no difference."

Kimberly K. Lillig and Carolyn J. Lackey, "Economic and social factors influencing women's infant feeding decisions in a rural mexican community", Journal of Tropical Paediatrics, vol. 28, October 1982.

FAMILY SIZE

"In the case of women who formula-fed, family size may have been a determinant in the feeding decision. More formula-feeding mothers had from five to 10 children than did breast-feeding mothers. The demands on the mother's time due to large family size and the convenience of allowing an older child to bottle-feed the infant may have made milk or formula-feeding a more attractive alternative to these mothers. Perhaps more importantly, the effect of a greater number of pregnancies and childbirths on these women's health may have contributed to their reported inability to nurse the most recently born child."

Kimberly K. Lillig and Carolyn J. Lackey, "Economic and social factors influencing women's infant feeding decisions in a rural mexican community", Journal of Tropical Paediatrics, vol. 28, October 1982.

GOING OUT TO WORK

"Lactating women whose employment requires separation from their infants face obstacles in many societies. Managing lactation under such circumstances becomes a complex task requiring hand expression of milk, use of infant formula or cow's milk, or use of a wet nurse. Among the strategies developed by employed women are working at home for the first few months; working flexible hours, part time, or shorter shifts; and breastfeeding at night..."

Penny van Esterik and Ted Greiner, "Breast-feeding and women's work: constraints and opportunities", Studies in Family Planning, vol. 12, no. 4, April 1981.

"Working women reiterate that breast-milk is the best for their children, but have not yet been able to muster the support of society in obtaining a longer maternity leave. Such leave can be viewed not as a privilege accorded to a working mother as an individual, but as an expression of the full responsibility of the entire community to uphold the need for mothers to breast-feed their babies – and that because of the many advantages that human milk can offer society. A well-fed, well-nourished, healthy child is an asset to any society. Maternity leave must be considered a social responsibility that is assumed in the aim of producing a healthy young generation."

Priyani E. Soysa, "The advantages of breast-feeding—a developing country point of view", Assignment Children, vol. 55/56, 1981.

CULTURAL ATTITUDES

"Unfortunately, the West's exaggerated concern with breasts as sexual objects is often forced upon and adopted by other societies. When perceived primarily as sex symbols, the breasts must be 'decently hidden' – which of course makes breast-feeding in public places difficult."

Elisabet Helsing with F. Savage King, Breast-feeding in Practice, Oxford University Press, 1982.

Supporting Mothers

If mothers are to be encouraged to practise breast-feeding, there must be a supportive psychological climate, starting with health workers during and after pregnancy, and extending into the family and the mother's work-place:

ADVERTISING INFANT FORMULA

The International Code of Marketing of Breast-milk Substitutes, adopted by the World Health Assembly in 1981, aims to protect and promote breast-feeding and to reduce the pressures of advertising on mothers to bottle-feed their babies (see page 29).

HEALTH WORKERS

"Physicians, midwives, and other health workers can actively encourage breast-feeding not only by providing information to their clients but also by altering hospital and health center policies that discourage breast-feeding. Since many women in urban areas deliver in hospitals, these policies have wide impact. Studies in Thailand and Malaysia found that women who had delivered in medical facilities were less likely to breast-feed than women who delivered at home even after taking into account the influence of socioeconomic status. This suggests that hospitals may have discouraged breast-feeding, and could be one reason that urban women breast-feed less...

"Restricting the availability and promotion of infant formula in hospitals also may encourage breast-feeding. In some countries representatives of infant formula manufacturers have visited hospitals and given free samples of formula to newly delivered mothers. Representatives often wore nursing uniforms. In addition, maternal and child health centers and 'maternity wards' have displayed posters advertising infant formula. Eliminating these practices should help avoid giving mothers the impression that health workers favor bottle-feeding...

"Family planning and other health workers should know about breast-feeding techniques so that they can teach the 'art of breast-feeding' to women. Several surveys have shown, however, that health professionals are often misinformed about breast-feeding. All health workers should be taught that frequent suckling – the pattern of breast-feeding in many traditional societies – is necessary to maintain a high level of milk production. Frequent suckling is especially critical in the first weeks after childbirth, when lactation is being established. If there are long intervals between feedings or rigid schedules, the reduced suckling causes shortages of milk. A woman may then have to supplement breast-feeding or turn entirely to bottle-feeding. Early supplementation with cow's milk or other foods further limits the production of breast-milk as an infant who is not hungry may be less inclined to suckle. Traditional practices such as delaying breast-feeding for two to four days after birth or nursing with only one breast may also reduce the milk supply."

"Breast-feeding, fertility, and family planning", Population Reports, series J, no. 24, November-December 1981.

II LIFELINES: BREAST-FEEDING

"School teachers and extension agents in contact with the community should also be informed about breast-feeding and weaning, and be able to offer information and advice that is consistent with that provided by the health services.

"This is particularly important for primary and secondary school teachers and for literacy teachers, as many girls enter motherhood within a few years after leaving school. It is thus important to introduce training modules into teacher training colleges, and into the material used in literacy campaigns."

"Programmes proposed by UNICEF in support of breast-feeding", UNICEF Secretariat, Assignment Children, vol. 55/56, 1981.

EMPLOYMENT

"The conditions of employment of women, including legislation to protect and support them, also require attention in many countries. Industrial development should be planned in such a way that it is supportive of family and community life. Maternity leave and better job security should be seen as basic principles of social and economic development; this is especially true of those countries where women have traditionally been the main wage-earner for many families. To facilitate their entry into new types of employment, and to promote their employment, and their economic and professional mobility, women need vocational training and guidance. While this may not be easy under many circumstances, special attention should be given to ensuring that industry tries to accommodate to family patterns and their implications; families ought not to be expected to adapt to industry. Industrial employers could also provide day-care centres close to women's workplaces and allow work-breaks for breast-feeding; and provide appropriate health care for working mothers. Part-time employment might be made more easily available to mothers so that, as so often happens, women are not faced with a choice between full-time employment or total exclusion from industry."

WHO/UNICEF, Infant and Young Child Feeding: Current Issues, WHO, 1981.

Weaning

From the age of four or six months, breast-milk alone is no longer sufficient to meet the needs of a growing child. If supplementary feeding is not now introduced, then weight gain falters and resistance to infection is lowered:

"Both the early and late introduction of foods have been linked with child health problems. Introducing foods before 4 months leads to an increased incidence of diarrhea and may lead to increased mortality. On the other hand, the introduction of foods too late may mean nutrition requirements are not met, beginning the malnutrition process and leaving the child more vulnerable to other common childhood diseases."

World Federation of Public Health Associations, Program Activities for Improved Weaning Practices, July 1984.

Researchers in North India have shown that breast-fed babies were more likely to survive the early months of life, but between the ages of 9 and 24 months mortality was higher among exclusively breast-fed infants and toddlers than among those receiving food supplements:

"Thus, in poor countries as elsewhere, breast-feeding is advantageous early, but is not sufficient as the only source of nutrients beyond the sixth month of life."

Joe D. Wray, "Maternal nutrition, breast-feeding and infant survival", in W. Henry Mosley (ed.), Nutrition and Human Reproduction, Plenum Press, 1978.

"The exact time that weaning should begin is determined by the lactation performance of the mother and the rate of growth and maturation of the infant; it does not therefore depend strictly on age, but for most infants it is between the ages of 4 and 6 months... The late initiation of weaning may lead to malnutrition. This is apparent in data from the WHO Collaborative Study, which show that with low rates of supplementation after the age of 6 months, e.g. among the urban poor and the rural population of India, the rate of growth of infants slowed down to well below the norm for this age.

"The late initiation of weaning was particularly noticeable among the urban poor in India and Ethiopia, where 40% and 15% of infants respectively were still exclusively breastfed at 12 and 13 months; in rural India the proportion was 36%. At 18 months, among the urban poor, 12% of infants in Ethiopia and 20% of infants in India were still not being weaned. Among the urban well-to-do, almost all infants everywhere were receiving regular supplementation at 6 to 7 months of age."

WHO/UNICEF, Infant and Young Child Feeding: Current Issues, WHO, 1981.

"Supplementary food should be composed of a gruel made of local foods, and more specifically of the staple food: this is a locally produced food eaten by the majority of the population and which provides the greatest number of calories within the food ration. They are energy-giving foods, then, and are almost always carbohydrates (grains, roots, tubers). Since these foods are not completely balanced, combinations should be recommended. These should be eaten in a single dish: the body derives much more benefit from a meal composed of several categories of food than from a single-food meal."

A.M. Masse-Raimbault, "How to feed young children", Children in the Tropics, no. 138-139-140, 1982.

(For further information on weaning, see Lifelines no. 1 - Growth Monitoring.)

Immunization

For a cost of approximately $5.00, a child can be immunized against six of the most common and dangerous diseases of childhood. But at present, less than 20% of children in the developing world are immunized against all these diseases. As a result, 5 million children die and a further 5 million are mentally or physically disabled each year.

Many developing countries face serious supply problems with immunization services. Technological developments are helping to overcome some of these but management capacities need further strengthening.

Immunization is as much a question of demand as supply. Recent evaluations have shown that coverage rates could be doubled and in many cases trebled if parents took advantage of existing immunization services and if those bringing their children for the first vaccination were also to return for the second and third.

Demand for immunization can be increased in two principal ways. First, empowering parents with information about immunization can increase the distance which parents are prepared to travel. Second, making immunization available at times and places convenient to low-income, working people can reduce the distance parents need to travel.

The convergence of these strategies would enable immunization to bring about a reduction of up to one-third in the rate of death and disability among the developing world's children.

The six diseases

Each year 5 million children in the developing world die and another 5 million are mentally or physically disabled through six vaccine-preventable diseases: diphtheria, pertussis (whooping cough), tetanus, measles, polio and tuberculosis. Only about 20% of the 100 million children born into the developing world each year are currently vaccinated against all or most of these diseases:

"Only rarely does any of these kill a child in Europe or North America. But in the developing world, measles kills some two and a half million children a year, whooping cough claims the lives of a million and a half more, and tetanus still remains unchecked, killing another million newborns every twelve months. Tuberculosis remains a major problem in most developing countries and diphtheria strikes in isolated but lethal epidemics. Meanwhile, almost 30 years after the vaccine to prevent the disease was discovered, half a million children in the developing world are still being crippled by polio each year.

"These six killer diseases are now the target of the Expanded Programme on Immunization (EPI), in which WHO, UNICEF and many other organizations in almost every nation of the world are now collaborating. The overall aim of the EPI is to make immunization against 'the big six' available to all children in the world by 1990."

Ralph Henderson, "Expanded Immunization", in *The State of the World's Children 1984*, Oxford University Press, 1983.

MEASLES

Measles is a highly contagious disease which 90% of the unprotected under-five population contract in some countries. Poor nutritional status seems to be the main factor leading to the most severe consequences of measles. The common practice of withholding food during a child's illness exacerbates the condition. Death is caused by pneumonia, diarrhoea, or in a small number of cases, encephalitis, in association with the disease. Maternal antibodies transferred through the placenta protect the infant during the first months of life. If measles vaccine is given to the infant before nine months of age, these antibodies may prevent the vaccine from producing immunity in the child. But if the child is vaccinated too late, the period of greatest danger to the child will be past.

Summarised from: World Federation of Public Health Associations, *Immunizations*, 1984.

PERTUSSIS (WHOOPING COUGH)

"An acute bacterial infection affecting the respiratory tract, whooping cough is very contagious in the first week or two of infection. The spasmodic coughing or 'whooping' that characterizes the disease is readily recognized and lasts one to two months. Pertussis is most severe in children under five months of age and many lead to death through pneumonia or other conditions. In very young children, there is no characteristic whoop so the disease may be difficult to recognize."

World Fed. of Public Health Associations, *Immunizations*, 1984.

TETANUS

"Caused by a toxin of a bacterium which enters the body through broken skin, this major killer of infants in developing countries is often caused by infection from the cut umbilical cord. Pregnant women who receive two tetanus toxoid immunizations pass immunity which protects the newborn during the first months of life. Tetanus bacteria reside in soil so, unlike smallpox, there is no hope of eliminating the reservoir of harmful organisms. Instead, protection comes only through immunization against the disease or through improved hygiene."

World Fed. of Public Health Associations, *Immunizations*, 1984.

POLIOMYELITIS

Polio is a viral disease spread by contact with objects, food, or water contaminated with excreta. In a small minority of cases, polio leads to varying degrees of paralysis and, sometimes, death. The older the child at age of infection, the more likely the infection will lead to severe consequences. The use of polio vaccines in the last 20 years in developed countries has markedly reduced the incidence of polio; however, its relative infrequency has led to laxity and occasional outbreaks among the unimmunized.

Summarised from: World Fed. of Public Health Associations, *Immunizations*, 1984.

TUBERCULOSIS (TB)

"TB is a bacterial disease spread by coughing and the sputum of infected persons. The disease takes many forms in

II LIFELINES: IMMUNIZATION

children, infecting the bones, lungs, or brain. Often, it may not be recognized as the same disease that affects adults. TB is particularly common where many persons share the same crowded living quarters. In some cities in developing countries, 1% of the adults may be in the active infective stage of the disease. Improved housing, clothing, diet, early detection, and uninterrupted treatment – all difficult to achieve in many developing countries – are all necessary to effectively control TB. Even though the efficacy of the vaccine, BCG, under certain conditions has been questioned, it remains an important means of protecting many children in developing countries."

World Fed. of Public Health Associations, Immunizations, 1984.

DIPHTHERIA

"A major child killer of the past in temperate countries, the mortality and morbidity of diphtheria are the least well documented of the six diseases in developing countries today. Although typically manifested as an acute infection of the throat, diphtheria can affect the heart or brain of infants and young children."

World Fed. of Public Health Associations, Immunizations, 1984.

Vaccine Management

Vaccines differ according to their effectiveness, recommended age for first dosage and temperature at which the vaccine must be stored to retain potency (see table 5).

SCHEDULES

"Immunization scheduling is affected by two biomedical factors: the age at which the infant can develop active antibodies and the number of vaccine doses which must be given. It is also greatly affected by the capabilities of the health delivery system.

"... the most critical time in the life of an infant occurs after the loss of maternal antibodies and before the acquisition of natural immunity. If an immunization is given too soon, the infant will still have passive immunity and will not develop antibodies. If the immunization is delayed, the infant is vulnerable and may fall victim to disease.

"The productivity or coverage capability of a mobile team or an outreach unit of a health center depends upon how soon the unit must return to its starting point to begin a second, third, or fourth cycle of immunizations to follow up immunization of children and mothers reached during the previous rounds.

"In a fixed facility where immunizations are given on a frequent and regular basis, a short immunization cycle is possible. Ideally, children should be immunized as soon as they attain the minimum ages (see table 5) and should receive successive doses at the intervals shown. However, delays will be inevitable if immunizations cannot be made available on at least a monthly basis, and planners will need to use schedules which best meet their own circumstances.

"Immunization of women of childbearing age is an effective measure in controlling neonatal tetanus. In areas where most pregnant women seek prenatal care early enough to be given two doses of tetanus toxoid, these should be spaced at least four weeks apart, with the second dose at least two weeks before delivery. A third dose should be given at the next pregnancy, and any children born during the following five years will be protected."

World Federation of Public Health Associations, Immunizations, 1984.

COLD CHAIN

In order to maintain their potency, vaccines must be maintained at certain temperatures at each stage of transportation between the manufacturers and the persons using them (see table 6).

SIDE-EFFECTS

As with most drugs, vaccines occasionally have undesirable side-effects. According to the World Health Organization, however, the benefits of immunization far outweigh the risks of adverse reactions:

"Despite the safety of the vaccines used in the EPI, complications do occur. Although their rates are difficult to estimate precisely, it is known that they are far less frequent than the complications caused by the diseases themselves...

"The decision to withhold immunization should be taken only after serious consideration of the potential consequences for the individual child and the community.

"It is particularly important to immunize children suffering from malnutrition. Low-grade fever, mild respiratory infections or diarrhoea, and other minor illnesses should not be considered as contraindications to immunization."

"Indications and contraindications for vaccines used in the EPI", in Weekly Epidemiological Record, WHO, vol 59, no. 3, January 1984.

Table 5: Vaccine effectiveness and recommended ages and intervals for doses.

Disease	Effectiveness	No. of doses	Minimum age of first dose	Interval between doses
Measles	95%	1	9 months*	–
Polio	95%	3	6 weeks	At least 4 weeks
Tuberculosis	See text	1	After birth	–
Diphtheria	95%	2–3	6 weeks	At least 4 weeks
Pertussis	80%	3	6 weeks	At least 4 weeks
Tetanus	95%	2	6 weeks	At least 4 weeks
Tetanus (for women)	95%	2	Child-bearing age	At least 4 weeks

*Malnourished children may lose maternal antibodies somewhat earlier

Summarised from: World Federation of Public Health Associations, Immunizations May 1984; World Health Organization, Weekly Epidemiological Record vol. 59, No. 3, January 1984.

Table 6: Temperature requirements and maximum storage times for five vaccines*

	Measles	Oral polio	BCG	DPT	Tetanus
Central store	2 years at −20°C	2 years at −20°C	8 months at 4–8°C	1.5 years at 4–8°C	1.5 years at 4–8°C
Transport to region	−20°C to 8°C	−20°C to 8°C	4°C to 8°C	4°C to 8°C	4°C to 8°C
Regional store	3 months at −20°C	3 months at −20°C	3 months at 4–8°C	3 months at 4–8°C	3 months at 4–8°C
Transport	−20°C to 8°C	−20°C to 8°C	4°C to 8°C	4°C to 8°C	4°C to 8°C
Static unit	1 month	1 month	1 month	1 month	1 month
Mobile team	1 week at 4–8°C	1 week at 4–8°C	1 week at 4–8°C	1 week at 4–8°C	1 week at 4–8°C

*In theory, if proper storage temperature is maintained, vaccines can be maintained at the periphery just as long as they can at the central store. However, the cold chain is usually weaker at the periphery than it is at the centre, so small quantitites of vaccine should be stored at these levels.

World Federation of Public Health Associations, Immunizations, May 1984.

"Parents should be warned of the common side effects of immunizations; otherwise they may suspect that immunizations cause rather than protect against illness. In some cases, measles vaccination produces a mild fever easily controlled by aspirin and a rash which may occur 8 to 12 days after vaccination. Reactions to oral polio vaccine, including a paralysis similar to poliomyelitis, are very rare – perhaps one in every million doses. BCG vaccination will cause a small sore to develop at the vaccination site – the sore usually disappears after one to two months. Rarely, this sore will become a chronic ulcer.

"In the case of DPT vaccinations, the most frequent reactions are fever and redness, swelling, and pain at the site of injection. The pertussis component, in rare cases, can cause several neurologic reactions, some of which are severe. These severe reactions, greatly publicized recently, occur far less frequently than serious side effects from the disease itself in unimmunized children.

"More common than side effects of vaccines are infections and abscesses caused by contaminated needles and syringes. While more frequently resulting from injections given by local injectionists or folk healers, this problem can also occur in organized health programs. Program personnel should be urged to report all serious side effects".

World Federation of Public Health Associations, Immunizations, 1984.

COSTS

Compared with the cost of treatment of childhood communicable diseases, the cost of immunization is small:

"Several studies have calculated the costs per child protected per death averted. These studies generally show that measles, DPT, polio, and BCG immunizations are highly cost-effective. Immunizations are substantially more cost-effective than such other public health measures as providing curative care or safe water.

"Using EPI costing guidelines, analyses were made of program costs per completely protected child (DPT, BCG) in Indonesia, the Philippines, and Thailand. Costs ranged from US $2.86 to $10.73 and seemed most dependent on program organization, health care input costs and population accessibility.

"EPI planners estimate that development costs in starting up broad coverage immunization programs together with operating costs once they are underway will total $5-15 per fully immunized child in the 1980s. More than half this amount will consist of personnel costs, facilities, and operating expenses. The rest of this amount will be needed for vaccines, cold chain equipment, and transportation. EPI planners believe that many developing countries can supply personnel, facilities and operating expenses, but that external resources will be needed to pay for the latter items in the poorest countries; that is, vaccines, cold chain equipment, and transport will need to come from external donors."

World Federation of Public Health Associations, Immunizations, 1984.

Coverage: Supply

The technical and managerial difficulties in placing immunization at the disposal of parents and children are formidable:

"To organize, on a continuous basis, the immunization of several million children during their first year of life whether they be in city slums or desert camps or mountain villages is a management problem of formidable dimensions. Add to it widespread illiteracy, inadequate roads and transport systems, rising fuel prices, budgetary cutbacks, lack of electricity for cold storage of vaccines, and over-stretched health services often reaching only 25% of the population, and we begin to see the true scale of the difficulties facing those involved in expanding immunization."

Ralph Henderson, "Expanded Immunization", in The State of the World's Children 1984, Oxford University Press, 1983.

A great deal of recent research has concentrated on technologies for making vaccines more widely available. Progress on this front has been considerable and includes:

THE STABILITY OF VACCINES

"The stability of vaccines has been considerably improved. Efforts were first concentrated on stabilizing the BCG, which is a live vaccine, sensitive to light as well as to heat. Present vaccines can last one month at 37°C and are packaged in coloured glass vials to avoid the harmful effects of ultraviolet rays.

"Since 1980, most laboratories manufacture a measles vaccine which may be stored at 37°C for one week. This improvement will probably considerably increase the effectiveness of measles vaccination... The vaccine is more resistant to heat, and while strict vigilance is still required in maintaining a low temperature, a refrigerator breakdown is no longer a catastrophe if it is of short duration."

Nicole Guerin, "Recent progress in immunization", Assignment Children, vol. 61/62, 1983.

NEW VACCINATION TECHNIQUES

"Most vaccinations are still administered subcutaneously, intramuscularly, or intradermally, using either a syringe and a needle or a pedojet. Only the live poliomyelitis vaccine is administered orally. However, trials are now under way to evaluate the effectiveness of such techniques as measles vaccination by inhalation, for example, in the hope of

II LIFELINES: IMMUNIZATION

simplifying the technique and perhaps improving the immune response."

<small>Nicole Guerin, "Recent progress in immunization", Assignment Children, vol. 61/62, 1983.</small>

THE COLD CHAIN

"The quality of the cold boxes has been improved, and their cost reduced; there now exist cold boxes in which vaccines may be stored at 4°C for one week, with an outside temperature of 42°C. The same type of research has been carried out on refrigerators: their qualities have been tested, their faults inventoried, their performance improved, the conditions for greatest effectiveness studied. In many countries, workers have been trained to repair simple breakdowns. New sources of energy are being studied and evaluated as substitutes for petroleum or gas, which are costly and not available everywhere...

"The maintenance and checking of equipment does not suffice, however, to guarantee the quality of the vaccine administered. The most recent research deals with indicators of the vaccines' potency. These indicators change colour when exposed to temperatures higher or lower than those recommended for storage over a period of time long enough to alter the vaccine.

"The stoppers of some vials include coloured time/temperature indicators, which warn when the potency of measles vaccines has dropped below an acceptable threshold by turning from red to black."

<small>Nicole Guerin, "Recent progress in immunization", Assignment Children, vol. 61/62, 1983.</small>

NEW VACCINES

"Improved forms of present vaccines, as well as vaccines against additional diseases, including malaria, are on the way. New developments will also provide the opportunity to reduce the number of doses required to protect children against the six current EPI diseases."

<small>Ralph Henderson, "Expanded Immunization", in The State of the World's Children 1984, Oxford University Press, 1983.</small>

Research is also being carried out on vaccines for respiratory tract infections:

"Two vaccines which must be considered in the future, but which cannot at this stage be advocated as primary care interventions, are pneumococcus and influenza. In the case of pneumococcus, the vaccine is effective in adults, but efficacy in young children needs further evaluation, and its expense makes it as yet unfeasible for use in developing countries. In the case of influenza vaccine, antigenic shift and its short-term efficacy put it generally beyond the resources of developing countries."

<small>R.M. Douglas, "Identification of acute respiratory infections control technologies that can be applied at the primary health care level of developing countries: methods of implementation, monitoring and evaluation", WHO, 1983 (WHO/RSD/83.9).</small>

HUMAN RESOURCES

Lack of adequate management capacities is one of the most serious constraints faced by the EPI:

"Current inadequacies are reflected in the frequent failures experienced in national cold-chain and logistics systems and in the low immunization within national programmes. The low rates reflect the fact that appropriate numbers of staff have not been identified in many programmes, and that those who have been identified have often not been given the responsibility or the authority to complete the tasks essential to the programme's success. Supervisory systems remain weak so that such staff are not held accountable for their performance."

<small>"Expanded Programme on Immunization: progress and evaluation report by the Director-General", WHO, 1982 (A35/9).</small>

The main training needs are for middle- and lower-level health workers:

"The training of 12,000 national and international staff by the EPI is an important start. But few national programmes have so far developed the ways and means to pass on the necessary technical and supervisory skills to hundreds and thousands of middle- and lower-level health workers who must ultimately carry out the immunization programmes on the ground. That is why the World Health Assembly, reviewing the overall progress of the EPI in 1982, identified the lack of human resources in general and management skills in particular as the main programme constraints."

<small>Ralph Henderson, "Expanded Immunization", in The State of the World's Children 1984, Oxford University Press, 1983.</small>

Coverage: The Demand

Immunization is at least as much a question of demand as of supply. A WHO survey of 81 immunization campaigns in 31 countries between 1978 and 1983 found that the drop-out rate between the first and third DPT 'shots' was almost 40%, ranging from 12% in Senegal to 60% or over in nine other countries.

<small>Summarized from: Ralph Henderson, "Results of EPI sample surveys of immunization coverage performed during review of national programmes by year, 1978-1983", report prepared for UNICEF, April 1984.</small>

MOTIVATION

"The high drop-out rates between the first and third doses of DPT and poliomyelitis vaccines bear witness to the fact that the mother has not understood the importance of returning and/or has been discouraged by the long waiting times or other inconveniences experienced during her first visit."

<small>Ralph Henderson, "Vaccine preventable diseases of children: the problem", in Protecting the World's Children: vaccines and immunization within primary health care, Rockefeller Foundation, June 1984.</small>

While parents may be prepared to take sick children 10 to 15 km to obtain curative care, they are generally not similarly motivated where disease-preventative services are concerned:

"For almost every intervention of this type, the benefit-cost ratios are high, often extraordinarily so; the cost of the illness or the death or disability caused by vaccine-preventable disease, diarrhoea or the unwanted pregnancy being far greater than the cost of prevention. Delivering these services, however, poses special problems. Healthy individuals in a community are not strongly motivated to seek such services. In rural areas, for example, few will travel more than a few kilometers to a health clinic in order to obtain vaccination..."

<small>Donald Henderson, "Childhood immunization as an impetus to primary health care", in Protecting the World's Children: vaccines and immunization within primary health care, Rockefeller Foundation, June 1984.</small>

TAKING UP THE SLACK

Taking up the 'slack' between available immunization services and the proportion of children actually immunized can be done in two ways:

"(1) provision of the services at a convenient location near the residence of recipients and at a convenient time; and (2) active promotion of the service being offered. When immunization, for example, is brought to the residence at a time of day when villagers are not in the fields or at the market, acceptance by 90% or more is common. Comparable results are obtained if immunization is offered at convenient assembly points which are not too distant provided that the program is well-organized and promoted... Remarkably high levels of acceptance have been achieved when educational and promotional methods have been imaginative."

Donald Henderson, "Childhood immunization as an impetus to primary health care", in Protecting the World's Children: vaccines and immunization within primary health care, Rockefeller Foundation, June 1984.

Parents need two types of information in order to be able to utilize immunization services:

"General information regarding immunizable diseases, the benefits and possible side effects of inoculations, and the need for repeat doses; and

"Specific dates, times, and locations and clear directions on who should come for each immunization session.

"Parents and others who bring children to be immunized should know the following:

"– which diseases the immunizations protect against, and that immunizations will not protect against all diseases;

"– which age groups are to be immunized and why other age groups are excluded;

"– the need for repeat doses;

"– that immunizations are safe and that side effects, such as fever, are signs that the vaccines are working to build their child's protection; and

"– that vaccines do little or no good once a child has contracted the disease."

World Federation of Public Health Associations, Immunizations, 1984.

Immunization and PHC

Immunization coverage is greatest when offered along with other, mutually reinforcing primary health care (PHC) services:

"While immunization services can be delivered alone, they are best delivered along with other services needed by children in their first year of life, and by pregnant women: the persons who constitute the priority groups for primary health care services in the developing world. In addition to the monitoring of the growth of the child, the use of oral rehydration to treat diarrhoea and the promotion of breast-feeding, these services may include malaria treatment and prophylaxis, and counselling with respect to child spacing, nutrition during pregnancy, weaning, clean water and sanitation."

Ralph Henderson, "Expanded Immunization", in The State of the World's Children 1984, Oxford University Press, 1983.

Furthermore, the combination of immunization with antibiotics can drastically reduce mortality from respiratory tract infections:

Immunization services thus not only contribute to the prevention of infant and childhood disability and death, but also extend beyond the prevention of the six vaccine-preventable diseases:

"This adds to the effectiveness of the EPI, and in this way, the EPI can directly contribute to the strengthening of the other primary health care services."

Ralph Henderson, "Expanded Immunization", in The State of the World's Children 1984, Oxford University Press, 1983.

II LIFELINES: FEMALE EDUCATION

Female Education

Research in many countries shows a clear correlation between high levels of female literacy and low levels of infant and child mortality.

It has usually been assumed, however, that female literacy is merely an indicator of general living standards rather than a factor, in its own right, in determining infant and child health.

Recent research suggests that this assumption is generally untrue. Far from being merely a reflection of living standards, maternal education acts as a powerful independent force in reducing the numbers of infant and child deaths.

A study of 11 Latin American countries, for example, has found that the mortality rate of children whose mothers had ten or more years' schooling was only one-third to one-fifth the rate of children whose mothers were illiterate. Furthermore, the study concluded that maternal education outweighed all other factors – including income differentials – in importance.

The mechanisms linking maternal education with improved child survival have not yet been illuminated by detailed research. But it is already clear that the education of girls is one of the best health investments which a developing country can make.

Education and Survival

Many studies during the past three decades have established that low levels of infant and child mortality are almost invariably associated with high levels of female education. A leading authority in this field, Professor John Caldwell of the Australian National University, has summarized the results of these studies as follows:

"Figures from the 1960 Census of Ghana show very large differences in child survivorship by education of mother. The proportion of children dead was almost twice as high for mothers with no education as for mothers with elementary education, and over four times as high for mothers with no education as for mothers with secondary education...

"Figures from a 1966 survey of Greater Bombay, carried out by the International Institute for Population Studies, showed that the infant mortality rate among mothers with no education was almost double that among mothers who had completed elementary education and almost three times that among mothers with education beyond elementary levels...

"In a United Nations study of 115 countries correlation between literacy and expectation of life at birth was higher than between any other specific factor considered and expectation of life; indeed, the correlation with literacy was only marginally lower than that with the General Development Index.

"It might also be noted that very low infant and child mortality levels have been achieved in some societies where levels of female education are high, health inputs moderate and incomes per head low to moderate: Kerala is a prime example, but Sri Lanka probably also fits the description."

J.C. Caldwell, "Education as a factor in mortality decline: an examination of Nigerian data", Population Studies, vol. 33, no. 3.

A recent study in Bangladesh by the International Centre for Diarrhoeal Disease Research concluded that "... the single most important correlate of child survival is not, as might be expected, the family's wealth or the availability of medical facilities, but the mother's educational level. Thus, during very tough times in Bangladesh – the 1974-77 post-revolution and famine period – under-three children of mothers with no education were five times more likely to die than were children of mothers with seven or more years' education. Why this is so is unknown – and is the subject of on-going research."

Annual report 1983, International Centre for Diarrhoeal Disease Research, Bangladesh, 1984.

The World Fertility Survey found that, in virtually all 42 countries surveyed between 1972 and 1984, both infant and child mortality decreased with increasing years of maternal education: "Overall, the ratios of infant death rates for the highest and lowest educational groups range from about one-third in Benin and Costa Rica to more than two-thirds in Bangladesh and Lesotho."

World Fertility Survey 1972-1984, 1984 Symposium, London 1984.

An Independent Force

It has frequently been assumed that the level of female education is simply a reflection of general living standards, rather than a prime factor in its own right, in reducing levels of infant and child mortality. Recent research, however, proves this assumption to be generally unfounded. A survey of 24 studies in 15 countries showed that, in three-quarters of the cases analysed, infant and child mortality declined unequivocally as educational levels increased.

Summarized from: Susan Hill-Cochrane, Fertility and education: what do we really know?, Johns Hopkins University Press, 1979.

Further evidence is provided by studies in West Africa and Latin America:

"Two surveys carried out in Nigeria as part of the Changing African Family Project have shed considerable light on the relationship between child mortality and education of the mother. They confirm that maternal education is the single most significant determinant of child mortality; moreover, they make it clear that maternal education cannot be employed as a proxy for general social and economic change but must be examined as an important force in its own right."

J.C. Caldwell, "Maternal education as a factor in child mortality", World Health Forum, vol. 2, no. 1, 1981.

"There are now several studies from different parts of the world that demonstrate conclusively the link between a mother's education and her children's chances of survival. One of the pioneering investigations of the connection was carried out by Hugo Behm and his colleagues at the Latin American Demographic Center (CELADE). In studies of the socioeconomic context of infant and child mortality, the researchers found that maternal education showed the strongest correlation of any variable observed... It outweighed rural-urban variations, income differentials, and ethnic origin. In 11 countries studied, the mortality rate of children whose mothers had ten or more years of schooling was only one-third to one-fifth the rate of children whose mothers were illiterate."

Kathleen Newland, "Infant mortality and the health of societies", Worldwatch Papers, no. 47, Worldwatch Institute, December 1981.

A study in Kenya attributed 86% of the decline in infant mortality between 1962 and 1979 to maternal education:

"Nationally, the data indicated that fully 86% of the child mortality decline between 1962 and 1979 may be 'explained' by the increase in maternal education. The remaining 14% can reasonably be attributed to improvement in the household economic situation."

W. Henry Mosley, "Will primary health care reduce infant and child mortality?", paper presented at IUSSP seminar, 1983.

Possible Explanations

The exact nature of the link between female education and child health has been little illuminated by detailed research. Professor Caldwell proposes three possible explanations:

"The first explanation is usually the only reason given: that educated mothers break with tradition, or become less 'fatalistic' about illness, and adopt many of the alternatives in child care and treatment of illness becoming available in a rapidly changing society, thus profoundly influencing their children's chances of survival.

"A second explanation is that an educated mother is more capable of manipulating the modern world. She is more likely to be listened to by doctors and nurses; she can demand their attention even when their reluctance to do anything more would completely rebuff an illiterate. She is more likely to know where the proper facilities are and to regard them as part of her world, and their use as a right, not a boon.

"There is a third explanation that may be more important than the other two combined. It has apparently been almost totally ignored in spite of the fact that it can be seen operating in any West African household that includes educated women. This explanation is that the education of women greatly changes the traditional balance of familial relationships, with profound effects on child care.

"As traditional society becomes transitional society, and as educated people appear within it, those without schooling no longer expect the same adherence to traditional roles from the educated that they do from the illiterate. Everywhere in West Africa the impact of schooling is so decisive because it changes not only the educated but the attitudes of others toward them.

"A woman with schooling is more apt to challenge her mother-in-law, and the mother-in-law is much less inclined to fight the challenge. The younger woman will assert the wisdom of the school against the wisdom of the old. She is more likely to attempt to communicate with her husband, and her husband is less likely to reject the attempt...

"Ultimately, the family may even move toward child-centredness, with all that such development means for reducing child mortality. More of the family resources will be devoted to the children; they may work less hard; they may take fewer risks; they will almost certainly live a healthier life."

J.C. Caldwell, "Maternal education as a factor in child mortality", World Health Forum, vol. 2, no. 1, 1981.

Girls in School

Empowering women through education has enormous potential for raising the levels of maternal, infant and child health. During the past quarter of a decade, the developing countries as a whole have succeeded in more than doubling the proportion of girls who at least start school: in 1960 only 35% of girls aged 6-11 began school; by 1979 the figure was over 80% – an enormous achievement.

Summarized from: The State of the World's Children 1984, Oxford University Press, 1983.

But discrimination against girls still persists:

"Currently in the low-income countries, 90 per cent of the boys aged 6 to 11 are in primary school, but only 64 per cent of the girls are. In another ten years or so, these girls will enter the child-bearing years – and one in three of them will be desperately ill-equipped to keep her children alive and well...

"Discrimination against women in educational systems is a recipe for higher infant mortality – as are most other forms of discrimination against women. The relationship between maternal malnutrition and low birth weight has been established, and yet women, even when they are pregnant, continue to be underfed more commonly than men. Research has shown that it is not only malnutrition during pregnancy that impairs a woman's ability to deliver healthy babies. Chronic undernourishment in childhood leads to growth deficiencies that have an impact on reproductive health in later life."

Kathleen Newland, "Infant mortality and the health of societies", Worldwatch Papers, no. 47, Worldwatch Institute, December 1981.

II LIFELINES: FAMILY SPACING

Family Spacing

Family planning is often regarded as simply a means of population control. Yet even if there were no such thing as a world 'population explosion', there would still be a powerful and urgent case for family planning as a method of improving mother and child health and reducing infant mortality rates.

The more numerous and closely spaced the pregnancies in a woman's child-bearing cycle, the more her nutritional reserves become depleted – and the greater the risks to the health of both mother and child. In poor communities, the infant mortality rate for babies born within one year of a previous birth is usually between two and four times as high as for babies born after an interval of two years or more.

In practice, however, many women do not have either the means or the freedom to decide on the number or the spacing of their children.

Empowering women with the means to control their own fertility could therefore have a dramatic impact on both the health of mothers and the growth and survival chances of their children. At the same time, it could also contribute to a reduction in population growth rates.

The Risks

The spacing, timing and number of births a woman has are crucial determinants of her own health and of her children's chances of survival:

The risks to the health of mothers and infants are greatest in four types of pregnancy: before the age of 18; after the age of 35; after four births; and less than two years apart.

In other words, pregnancies can be considered high-risk if they are 'too young, too old, too many, or too close'.

Summarized from: "Healthier mothers and children through family planning", Population Reports, series J, no. 27, May-June 1984.

INFANT AND CHILD DEATHS

"Recent analyses conducted at Princeton University using data from 25 developing countries illustrate a substantial impact of spacing on child mortality. If all births were spaced at least 2 years apart, infant mortality can be reduced by 10% and child mortality (ages 1-4 years) by 16%."

Sandra L. Huffman, "Child spacing: for maternal and child health", Mothers and Children, vol. 4, no. 1, March-April 1984.

"When a woman has pregnancies close together, the likelihood increases that the pregnancy will end in miscarriage or that an infant born alive will die...

"Studies in Hawaii and Bangladesh found that the highest rates of fetal death are among pregnancies that began less than one year after the end of the previous pregnancy."

Deborah Maine, Family planning: its impact on the health of women and children, Center for Population and Family Health, Columbia University, 1981.

"... irrespective of the age of the mother or birth order, a child with a pre- or post-birth interval of less than 18 months was about three times more likely to die in the first five years than a child with intervals of 42 months or more."

Raymond W. Charlaw and Kokila Vaidya, "Birth intervals and the survival of children to age five – some data from Nepal", Journal of Tropical Pediatrics, vol. 29, February 1983.

LOW BIRTH-WEIGHT

Results from the World Fertility Survey point to a link between insufficient birth spacing and low birth-weight:

"The nutritional drain on the mother of a rapid succession of pregnancies and periods of nursing may affect the survival chances of infants and children through an initial low birth-weight and perhaps through breast-milk of inferior composition."

John Cleland, "New WFS findings prove spacing benefits", People, vol. 10, no. 2, 1983.

"Spacing of less than two years between births is especially hazardous because it means lower birth weights and poorer nutrition, possibly including a shorter period of breast-feeding or more competition for family resources and care. From infancy to adolescence, children born into large or closely spaced families experience more sickness, slower growth, and lower levels of academic achievement. Lower socioeconomic status has similar effects, but birth patterns also are important."

"Healthier mothers and children through family planning", Population Reports, series J, no. 27, May-June 1984.

MENTAL DEVELOPMENT

"Childbearing patterns may influence later intelligence through low birth weight. Low birth weight infants have lower test scores than other children. The difference is marked among children from poor families."

"Healthier mothers and children through family planning", Population Reports, series J, no. 27, May-June 1984.

"As might be expected, the same factors that affect children's health also seem to affect their development. Children in large families and children born close together grow less well, both physically and intellectually, than other children. The decline in intelligence test scores as family size increases has been vividly demonstrated in studies of large numbers of children in Scotland, England, France, and the United States."

Deborah Maine, Family planning: its impact on the health of women and children, Center for Population and Family Health, Columbia University, 1981.

"A study in the US matched births within 1 year of the previous full-term pregnancy to those that were over 1 year. The variables used were hospital of birth, sex, race, and socioeconomic status. The study found a significantly larger mean birth weight in infants born after longer intervals. In the study, short spacing was a result of biological factors, not socioeconomic differences between the two groups. An interesting finding was that intelligence scores for children at four years of age were significantly lower in the short birth interval group..."

Sandra L. Huffman, "Child spacing: for maternal and child health", Mothers and Children, vol. 4, no. 1, March-April 1984.

BIRTH DEFECTS

"Concerning spacing, in a study of US birth certificates, birth defects of all kinds were more common among children born within a year of the previous birth. Birth defects were least common when birth intervals were one to five years."

<small>"Healthier mothers and children through family planning", Population Reports, series J, no. 27, May-June 1984.</small>

MALNUTRITION

"Short birth intervals contribute to malnutrition in young infants by putting an early end to breast-feeding. Field studies in a number of countries have found higher death rates among children weaned early, especially those weaned because the mother was pregnant or had just given birth to another infant. In Senegal children weaned after their mothers had conceived were more likely to die within the following six months than children weaned at the same age but whose mothers were not pregnant."

<small>"Healthier mothers and children through family planning", Population Reports, series J, no. 27, May-June 1984.</small>

"Studies in Candalaria, Colombia, have shown that as the number of children in the family increases, the per capita expenditures on food decrease. When families of similar socioeconomic status with 2 adults and 2 children were compared to those families with 4 children, one study found nearly a 500 kcal. difference in food consumption. Where increases in family size are associated with decreases in food expenditures and food consumption, it is evident that increasing spacing between births will ensure more food availability for children."

<small>Sandra L. Huffman, "Child spacing: for maternal and child health", Mothers and Children, vol. 4, no. 1, March-April 1984.</small>

EFFECTS ON OLDER SIBLING

Insufficient birth-spacing affects not only the newborn but also his or her elder sibling:

"When two children are separated by only a short birth interval, not only the younger of the pair suffers. The health of the older child may be harmed as well. People in some countries have long understood this. For example, the word 'kwashiorkor' is used in Ghana to describe the kind of malnutrition often seen when a child is weaned from the breast too early because the mother is pregnant again. Breast-feeding is now known to be one of the most important factors in infant health in developing countries. Anything which cuts short the period of breast-feeding may endanger the health of the infants. Children who are weaned too early are much more susceptible to malnutrition and infection."

<small>Deborah Maine, Family planning: its impact on the health of women and children, Center for Population and Family Health, Columbia University, 1981.</small>

Maternal Depletion

The health of the infant depends directly upon the health of the mother, and insufficient spacing between births places the health of both mothers and young children at risk.

"Births too close together can produce what is often termed the 'maternal depletion syndrome' resulting from the lack of time for the mother's body to recover adequately from the last pregnancy. This is likely to be particularly important when women who are malnourished breast-feed their children, and perform the heavy physical work typical of life in the Third World."

<small>Davidson R. Gwatkin, "Birth spacing", paper prepared for UNICEF, December 1982.</small>

MATERNAL DEATHS

"Maternal deaths increase with birth order because many complications of pregnancy and childbirth rise sharply among third and later births. An estimated 25 million women in developing countries have such complications every year...

"Deaths from hemorrhage (uncontrolled bleeding) and from pulmonary embolism (blood clots in the lungs) are especially common among fourth and higher order births...

"Other complications that increase with birth order are problems with the placenta and umbilical cord, collapse and tearing of the uterus, abnormal birth position of the fetus, and anemia."

<small>Deborah Maine, Family planning: its impact on the health of women and children, Center for Population and Family Health, Columbia University, 1981.</small>

"Not only age and parity, but also the interval between births has an effect on maternal death rates. In Bangladesh and Indonesia, for example, some of the highest death rates are found in women under age 20 with three or more children. When women under 20 have several children, birth intervals must be short. Thus, while differences in living conditions and health care may also be involved, these studies suggest that short birth intervals lead to high maternal death rates."

<small>"Healthier mothers and children through family planning", Population Reports, series J, no. 27, May-June 1984.</small>

Benefits of Spacing

The timing and spacing of births through family planning enables women to have children when they are best prepared – with clear health benefits for both mother and child:

CHILD SURVIVAL

"It is estimated that, if women chose to use family planning to avoid the four types of high-risk pregnancy identified earlier, in 1984 about 5.6 million infant deaths and 200,000 maternal deaths could be avoided. This estimate is based on the work of James Trussell and Anne R. Pebley, who, using data from 25 developing countries, calculated that infant mortality rates would be reduced by about 5 percent if childbearing occurred entirely within ages 20 to 34, by another 3 percent if all births after the third were avoided, and by about 10 percent if all births were spaced at least two years apart. This is a total reduction of 18 percent."

<small>"Healthier mothers and children through family planning", Population Reports (Population Information Program, Johns Hopkins University), series J, no. 27, May-June 1984.</small>

"The impact of declines in high-risk pregnancies on infant mortality has been analyzed in a number of countries. In Costa Rica, for example, birth rates have declined rapidly in recent years (in large part due to the widespread availability of contraceptives). Between 1960 and 1977, births of fifth and higher order and births among older women decreased sharply. During the same period, the infant mortality rate fell by almost 60 percent. An estimated one-fifth of this decline is due to the changes in child-bearing patterns. In the United States, one-half of the decline in infant mortality during 1960-1970 is attributed to the increasing concentration of births among women of more favorable age and family size."

<small>Deborah Maine, Family planning: its impact on the health of women and children, Center for Population and Family Health, Columbia University, 1981.</small>

II LIFELINES: FAMILY SPACING

MOTHERS' LIVES

"In developing countries today, about 5.6 million infant deaths and 200,000 maternal deaths could be avoided if women chose to have their children within the safest years with adequate spacing between births and completed families of moderate size. This amounts to about half of the estimated 10.5 million infant deaths and 450,000 maternal deaths now occurring and represents the combined effect of fewer births and lower death rates."

"Healthier mothers and children through family planning", Population Reports, series J, no. 27, May-June 1984.

FAMILY BENEFITS

"Increasing spacing between births is an important way to promote the health of young children and mothers, although many of the benefits of birth spacing may be indirect. The mother has more time for each child to breast-feed, to prepare weaning foods, or to care for a sick child. Her other work responsibilities are less of a physical strain if she has fewer young children to care for. Increased birth spacing may also mean that there is more food available for the family, and illness and disease may be reduced because of less crowding in the home."

Sandra L. Huffman, "Child spacing: for maternal and child health", Mothers and Children, vol. 4, no. 1, March-April 1984.

POPULATION GROWTH

"In addition to averting infant and child deaths, of course, a lengthening of the birth interval would result in fewer births. The exact number is difficult to determine, but it would almost certainly be several million. Since this number of averted births could be expected to exceed the number of deaths prevented, an extension of birth intervals would also produce a reduction in population growth."

Davidson R. Gwatkin, "Birth spacing", paper prepared for UNICEF, December 1982.

Unmet Demand

It is often assumed that women in developing countries have large families because they choose to. In many developing countries, however, large proportions of women want no more children:

"World Fertility Survey data disprove the common assumption that poor, uneducated women in developing countries generally want as many children as they can have or 'as many as God sends' ... For example, among women with three living children the proportions who said that they want no more children were 24% in Jordan, 35% in Nepal, 50-60% in Costa Rica and Mexico, and 60-70% in Bangladesh and Thailand."

Deborah Maine and Joe Wray, "Family spacing", in The State of the World's Children 1984, Oxford University Press, 1983.

"Women all over the world know the dangers of ill-timed pregnancies and having many children. In India, Iran, Lebanon, the Philippines, and Turkey, 21,000 women were interviewed in a WHO study. More than nine in ten women said the health of the child and the mother are better if the child is born three years after the previous birth, rather than after an interval of only one year. About nine in ten said that they believe that the health of mother and child are better if the family is small. More than nine in ten know that contraception improves the health of women and children."

Deborah Maine, Family planning: its impact on the health of women and children, Center for Population and Family Health, Columbia University, 1981.

"In developed and developing countries, as contraceptive use increases, women have smaller families and fewer births at unfavorable ages... Given a chance, women can and do avoid high-risk pregnancies."

Deborah Maine, Family planning: its impact on the health of women and children, Center for Population and Family Health, Columbia University, 1981.

Food Supplements

Two specific forms of food supplementation have proved to be highly cost-effective in protecting the lives and health of young children.

First, food supplements for 'at-risk' pregnant women have been shown to be effective in helping to prevent low birth-weight (under 2.5 kilos). As low birth-weight is associated with perhaps one-third of all infant deaths in the developing world, food supplements in pregnancy could be a powerful lever for raising levels of child health and survival.

Second, supplementing diets with specific micronutrients can also be a highly cost-effective way of protecting children's lives and growth. To take three of the most important examples: iron supplements can prevent anaemia, iodine supplements can prevent goitre and cretinism, and vitamin A supplements can prevent blindness.

Low Birth-Weight

In some areas nearly one in three babies is born underweight. Mortality is high for low birth-weight babies, and even if they survive their chances of healthy growth and development are reduced:

A 1983 review by the World Health Organization, based on information from 90 countries, concluded that of the 127 million infants born in 1982, 16% – some 20 million – were born weighing less than 2,500 grammes. The majority were born in developing countries. By region, the proportion of infants with low birth-weight was 31.1% in Middle South Asia (Bangladesh, India, Iran, Pakistan and Sri Lanka) and 19.7% in Asia as a whole, 14.0% in Africa, 10.1% in Latin America, 6.8% in North America, and 6.5% in Europe.

Summarized from: "The incidence of low birth weight: an update", Weekly Epidemiological Record, WHO, vol. 59, no. 27, July 1984.

"The birth weight of an infant, simple as it is to measure, is highly significant in two important respects. In the first place it is strongly conditioned by the health and nutritional status of the mother, in the sense that maternal malnutrition, ill-health and other deprivations are the most common causes of retarded fetal growth and/or prematurity, as manifested in low birth weight (LBW). In the second place, low birth weight is, universally and in all population groups, the single most important determinant of the chances of the newborn to survive and to experience healthy growth and development."

"The incidence of low birth weight: a critical review of available information", World Health Statistics Quarterly, vol. 33, no. 3, 1980.

"Low-birth-weight babies are less likely to survive during the first year of life than babies with a higher birth weight. This human wastage places considerable stress on poor societies, both emotionally and economically. At a rural health unit in India, peri-natal deaths were five times more common in low-birth-weight infants than in the new-borns with normal birth weight, and 70.6% of the neo-nates who died were low-birth-weight babies."

Kusum P. Shah, "Maternal nutrition in deprived populations", Assignment Children, vol. 55/56, 1981.

"... no child in Santa Maria Cauque (a Guatemalan village) died in the first year of life if his birth weight was at least 2750 grams and he was breast-fed, despite an environment of crowding, poverty, poor sanitation, rampant infection, and lack of governmental effort to prevent diseases by vaccination. A better definition of the variable 'birth weight' revealed that about 7% of all births in Cauque were preterm, and an additional 34% were term-small-for-gestational-age (TSGA). If most of the TSGA births had been prevented, the infant mortality would have been reduced by 30%."

Leonardo Mata, "Diarrhoeal diseases and malnutrition in Costa Rica", Assignment Children, vol. 61/62, 1983.

"The effects of malnutrition are most serious in early life and especially during foetal life. Inadequate nutrition in foetal life is a common cause of low birth weight... We know that there is a higher incidence (four to six times normal) of physical and mental handicap in infants of low birth weight. Mortality in the newborn period is also eight to ten times that in infants of adequate weight, and this increased likelihood of death is present up to the age of one year."

G.J. Ebrahim, "Maternity and child health services (MCH) and the prevention of disability", Journal of Tropical Pediatrics, editorial, vol. 28, August 1982.

"Neurological studies have shown that about two-thirds of five-year-old children with LBW had normal motor development and neurological status. The rest suffered from cerebral palsy (3.6 percent), minimal brain dysfunction (3.4 percent) and delayed motor development (27.3 percent). All of them had lower IQs than babies with normal birth-weight. The majority of reports on this subject show similar figures..."

A. Lechtig and others, "Birth-weight and society: the societal cost of low birth-weight", in Goran Sterky and Lotta Mellander (eds.), Birth-weight distribution: an indicator of social development, SAREC (Swedish Agency for Research Cooperation with Developing Countries), 1978.

Causes

The mother's malnutrition, both before and during pregnancy, is the primary cause of low birth-weight. Infection, anaemia and too-frequent pregnancies add to the risk:

MATERNAL MALNUTRITION

"There is great variation in the proportion of LBW infants and there are various reasons for low birth weight, but the available evidence suggests that wherever LBW rates are higher than 10 or 15 per cent it can be assumed that significant undernutrition among mothers is widespread."

Joe D. Wray, "Supplementary feeding of pregnant and lactating women", paper prepared for FAO, 1983.

"In the industrialised world ... weight gain in pregnancy is usually around 12 kilos, whereas in the developing world many women – probably the majority – gain only perhaps 6 kilos or less during pregnancy... It has been observed in a Gambian village ... that weight-gain during pregnancy varies between 2.7 kilos and 5.5 kilos according to the different seasons."

Kusum P. Shah, "Food supplements", in The State of the World's Children 1984, Oxford University Press, 1983.

"In a prospective study in a rural community in India, Shah and Shah found that, among the many environmental factors taken into consideration, maternal nutrition had a significant relationship to birth weight, the pre-pregnancy maternal

II LIFELINES: FOOD SUPPLEMENTS

weight being the determinant factor affecting foetal nutrition. The birth weights of the infants whose mothers weighed 38 kg or less before pregnancy were significantly lower than those of new-borns whose mothers weighed over 41 kg. The major factor contributing to the low birth weight of infants was thus the mothers' chronic malnutrition, probably since their childhood."

Kusum P. Shah, "Maternal nutrition in deprived populations", Assignment Children, vol. 55/56, 1981.

INFECTIONS

"In deprived populations in developing countries, pregnant women suffer frequently from upper respiratory tract infections, malaria, dysentery, diarrhoea, parasitic infestations, pneumonia, and hepatitis... It has been reported that pregnant women suffering from malaria deliver a higher number of low-birth-weight infants than those who do not have malaria. Robinson noticed a reduction of the mean birth weight of between 100 and 300 g when placental parasitism was confirmed."

Kusum P. Shah, "Maternal nutrition in deprived populations", Assignment Children, vol. 55/56, 1981.

ANAEMIA

"It has also been shown that the frequency of low-birth-weight infants is higher among anaemic women. Menon reported an average birth weight of 2.4 kg in infants of mothers whose haemoglobin level was 6.5 g, as compared to 2.8 kg in the infants whose mothers had a haemoglobin level of 10.5 g. In addition, the infants of low-income mothers have been found to have liver stores of iron, folic acid, vitamin B12, and vitamin A representing only 50 to 60% of what is considered to be the required amount."

Kusum P. Shah, "Maternal nutrition in deprived populations", Assignment Children, vol. 55/56, 1981.

FREQUENT PREGNANCIES

"Spacing of less than two years between births is especially hazardous because it means lower birth weights and poorer nutrition, possibly including a shorter period of breast-feeding or more competition for family resources and care."

"Healthier mothers and children through family planning", Population Reports, series J, no. 27, May-June 1984.

"There is no doubt that cycles of pregnancy and lactation deplete the low-income mother nutritionally and result in a high proportion of low-birth-weight babies and in quantities of breast milk considerably below those of well nourished mothers in more privileged circumstances. Low-birth-weight babies show poorer growth and higher morbidity and mortality during the first year of life, and the combination of low nutrient reserves at birth and reduced quantity of breast milk means a need to introduce complementary feeding at an earlier age. This, in turn, adds to the risk of infection with enteric organisms and increases the likelihood of malnutrition beginning relatively early in the first year. Presumably, this adverse sequence of events could be prevented by improving the nutritional status of the mother."

Nevin S. Scrimshaw, "Programs of supplemental feeding and weaning food development", in Nevin S. Scrimshaw and Mitchel B. Wallerstein (eds.), Nutrition Policy Implementation, Plenum Press, 1982.

Food in Pregnancy

Extra food during pregnancy significantly reduces the risk of low birth-weight for the baby:

The participants at an international workshop reviewed eight studies from both developed and developing countries of the effect of food supplements during pregnancy:

"All of the studies ... show that in malnourished populations nutritional supplementation during pregnancy increased birth weight. The fact that each of the studies individually provide data in the same direction is very impressive, particularly given the variety of cultural and socioeconomic situations represented...

"These studies show that supplementation provided during the third trimester of pregnancy will increase birth weight, a finding which is consistent with the rapid increase in fetal weight observed during this period. Several studies reveal benefits from supplementation initiated during earlier periods in gestation."

Aaron Lechtig and others, "Effects of maternal nutrition on infant health: implications for action", Journal of Tropical Pediatrics, vol. 28, December 1982.

"Field studies have shown that supplementation during the last three months of pregnancy is sufficient to increase birth weight, and that 500 calories a day is enough under most conditions."

Joe D. Wray, "Supplementary feeding of pregnant and lactating women", paper prepared for FAO, 1983.

In a study in India in which poor women were fed an additional 500 calories and 10 grammes of protein, raising their total daily intake to 2,500 calories and 60 grammes of protein during the last month of pregnancy, they gained an extra 1.5 kilos compared with a control group of women. Their infants' birth-weight was on average 300 grammes more than the weight of those born to the control group.

Summarized from: L. Iyangar, "Influence of the diet on the outcome of pregnancy in Indian women", Proceedings of the Ninth International Congress of Nutrition, Karger (Basel), 1975.

A classic study of nutrition supplements for pregnant women in four Guatemalan villages found that the percentage of babies with low birth-weight was 21% in the group receiving low supplementation (less than 5,000 calories during the pregnancy) but fell to 4% in the group receiving a high level of supplementation (40,000 calories and over). The researchers also assessed the effects of supplements when the mothers were under 1.47 metres tall, or weighed less than 48 kilos at the start of the pregnancy: in both cases, the percentage of low birth-weight babies born to the mothers in the low-supplement group was three to four times greater than in the high-supplement group.

Summarized from: A. Lechtig and others, "Influence of food supplementation during pregnancy on birth weight in rural populations of Guatemala", Proceedings of the Ninth International Congress of Nutrition, Karger (Basel), 1975.

WOMEN AT RISK

"... the most economical and effective way to use supplementary food is to identify those among the pregnant or lactating women who are malnourished and target the program to them... these women may be identified in several ways:

"... Generally speaking, a woman whose weight is 90 per cent of standard (weight for height) should be considered a candidate for supplementation.

"Where weights and heights cannot be measured, women whose mid-upper arm circumference is less than 22.5 centimeters may be targeted.

"... When a woman becomes pregnant she should be weighed at regular intervals to see that she is gaining sufficient weight – about 1.5 kg per month during the last six months of pregnancy. If she fails to do so, she should be considered for food supplementation.

"... the measures required ... are simple to obtain and not too difficult to apply."

Joe D. Wray, "Supplementary feeding of pregnant and lactating women", paper prepared for FAO, 1983.

"Field studies have provided us with tools and methods to identify nutritionally 'at-risk' women. Simplified techniques, such as weight or arm circumference measured with tri-coloured arm tapes, are the most practical for assessing nutritional status... A simple mother's card, similar to a child's growth chart, can constitute a comprehensive, informative, and simple tool for surveillance. Such a card has been used by community health workers and nurses in some countries with rewarding results."

Kusum P. Shah, "Maternal nutrition in deprived populations", Assignment Children, vol. 55/56, 1981.

COST OF PREVENTION

"Much of the maternal malnutrition could be combated through the training of elderly women and traditional birth attendants to provide nutrition information and to promote beliefs and customs favourable to pregnant and lactating women, as well as to young children, particularly girls. It has been estimated, for example, that rural women in Guatemala could satisfy their needs for additional nutrients during pregnancy through locally available food products. The additional investment required would come to about $0.09 per day, compared to the $1.00 required to use the foods traditionally mentioned in the nutrition education schemes of developed countries."

Kusum P. Shah, "Maternal nutrition in deprived populations", Assignment Children, vol. 55/56, 1981.

"There is extensive evidence of an association between malnutrition of pregnant women and low birth weight of their infants. Supplementation of caloric intake during pregnancy does increase the weight of the infant at birth. This suggests that measures to improve nutrition of the fetus, and thus birth weight, might be more effective in reducing infant mortality and less costly than providing intensive medical care for the mass of underweight and premature babies born to undernourished women."

Alan Berg, Malnourished People: a Policy View, World Bank, June 1981.

Food Fortification

Supplementing diets with specific micronutrients can also be a highly cost-effective method of protecting health and guarding against disability:

"Fortification is defined as 'the process whereby nutrients are added to foods to maintain or improve the quality of the diet of a group, a community, or a population'...

"Fortification aims at remedying specific nutritional deficiencies and is typically used in conjunction with staple foods. Its target populations are thus primarily those groups for whom staples represent important dietary components...

"From an implementation standpoint, the rationale for fortification is that fortifiers can be incorporated into existing diets without requiring major changes in consumption behavior by the beneficiaries.

"This intervention assumes that certain nutritional diseases are directly related to specific nutrient deficiencies in the diet, and that by eliminating these deficiencies through fortification the nutritional problems can be reduced. The three major specific micronutrient deficiencies are iodine (causing goiter), vitamin A (causing sight loss or impairment), and iron or folic acid (causing anemia). Vitamin A and iron deficiencies, even in their less acute forms, may exacerbate the duration and severity of other diseases, even leading to otherwise avoidable death.

"Although the prevalence of these deficiencies is not known with precision, it is fairly certain that (a) large areas of endemic goiter exist, especially in mountainous regions; (b) at least 100,000 new cases of Vitamin A associated vision impairments occur each year; and (c) about 25 percent to 80 percent of pregnant women in their last trimester are anemic. The prevalence of these deficiencies, especially of goiter, has decreased in recent years owing to general economic improvements and specific interventions. Nonetheless, the magnitude remains sufficiently large to classify these as major public health problems."

James Austin and others, Nutrition Intervention in Developing Countries, Oelschlager, Gunn and Hain, for Harvard Institute for International Development, 1981.

Nutritional Anaemia

Women in their child-bearing years and young children are especially vulnerable to iron-deficiency anaemia:

A recent study of 500 million women in developing countries other than China found that 46% – around 230 million – had haemoglobin concentrations below those specified by the World Health Organization as indicative of anaemia. Among pregnant women, nearly two-thirds could be described as 'anaemic':

"Women in the reproductive ages form one of the two main vulnerable groups with regard to anaemia, the second group being very young children. They are vulnerable primarily because of their great nutritional needs, and in the case of young children also because of their complete dependence on the support of others. When this inherent vulnerability is combined with socioeconomic stress factors, such as poverty, ignorance and primitive living conditions, the situations of these groups may become truly precarious.

"Women in the reproductive years are at special risk in two ways: when not pregnant or lactating, regular menstrual blood loss constitutes a continuing drain of nutrients which have to be replaced, while pregnancy increases the requirements of the woman's body to meet the needs of the growing fetus. During lactation, iron and folate are passed to the baby via the breastmilk, to the detriment of the mother...

"The daily requirement for iron, as well as folate, is six times greater for a woman in the last trimester of pregnancy than for a non-pregnant woman. This need cannot be met by diet alone, but is derived at least partly from maternal reserves. In a well-nourished woman about half the total requirement of iron may come from iron stores. When these reserves are already low – from malnutrition and/or frequent pregnancies – anaemia results."

E. Royston, "The prevalence of nutritional anaemia in women in developing countries: a critical review of available information", World Health Statistics Quarterly, vol. 35, no. 2, 1982.

II LIFELINES: FOOD SUPPLEMENTS

"(In infants) a supply of iron is necessary to ... cope with needs imposed by rapid growth... During the first four months, stored iron is used to help meet needs... Even in the most favourable cases, iron stores are exhausted around the fourth or fifth month, whence the evident risk of deficiency in case of exclusive and prolonged milk or milk and starch diet."

S. Hercberg and C. Rouaud, "Nutritional anemia", Children in the Tropics, no. 133, 1981.

Causes of Iron Loss

Infections contribute to iron loss in both women and children. Frequent pregnancies further deplete women's iron stores:

INFECTIONS AND PARASITES

"Measles is a severe debilitating illness in malnourished children and is associated with an enteropathy responsible for the loss of about 20 per cent of the dietary protein intake. It is, therefore, usual to detect anaemia in children suffering from measles in the tropics...

"Diarrhoeal diseases due to bacteria and viruses are frequent in infants and young children, and interfere with nutrition. Bacillary dysentery is accompanied by intestinal bleeding which may contribute to iron loss."

Michael C.K. Chan, "Childhood anaemias in the tropics", in R.G. Hendrickse (ed.), Paediatrics in the Tropics: Current Review, Oxford University Press, 1981.

"In the infected area studied in Venezuela, one-third of anaemias were deemed to be directly attributable to hookworm infection... There is also a strong association between anaemia and malaria."

E. Royston, "The prevalence of nutritional anaemia in women in developing countries: a critical review of available information", World Health Statistics Quarterly, vol. 35, no. 2, 1982.

FREQUENT PREGNANCIES

"In Bangkok, the prevalence of anaemia in pregnant women doubled after the third pregnancy and increased fivefold after the fifth pregnancy."

E. Royston, "The prevalence of nutritional anaemia in women in developing countries: a critical review of available information", World Health Statistics Quarterly, vol. 35, no. 2, 1982.

EFFECTS OF IRON DEFICIENCY

"Anaemia in its severest form can lead to death, but this is rare. It does, however, have a profound effect on the psychological and physical behaviour of the individual. The mild and moderate degrees of anaemia which are much more frequent are, under normal circumstances, more or less well tolerated. Nevertheless they lessen the resistance to fatigue and affect work capacity under conditions of stress. Even very mild forms influence the sense of wellbeing. In pregnancy, anaemia has been shown to be associated with an increased risk of maternal and fetal morbidity and mortality."

E. Royston, "The prevalence of nutritional anaemia in women in developing countries: a critical review of available information", World Health Statistics Quarterly, vol. 35, no. 2, 1982.

"Data from two recent experimental studies indicate that, in pre-school children, particular process features of cognition, such as selective attention, vigilance, or rehearsal strategies for memory function, may be altered by iron deficiency..."

Ernesto Pollitt and Nita Lewis, "Nutrition and educational achievement. Part I: malnutrition and behavioural test indicators", Food and Nutrition Bulletin, vol. 2, no. 3, 1980.

PREVENTING IRON DEFICIENCY

Adding iron to common foods – such as bread, sugar, salt, or fish sauce – has been a successful solution, particularly if backed up by nutrition education:

Besides measures in supplementation and enrichment (fortification), it is indispensable to develop general measures aimed at insuring a nutritional iron supply such as:
- augmenting the availability of proteins of animal origin
- augmenting the utilization of vegetable foods rich in iron, such as green leafy vegetables and beans
- improving the nutritional education of the population and above all learning to better utilize available resources
- improving the distribution of food in the family group so that high-risk subjects (women and above all pregnant women) gain access to animal proteins with a high iron content.

Summarised from: S. Hercberg and C. Rouaud, "Nutritional anaemia", Children in the Tropics, no. 133, 1981.

Iodine Deficiency

Thyroxine, the hormone produced by the thyroid gland, is essential for the physical and mental development of children, and dependent on iodine intake. Iodine deficiency disorders (IDD) include goitre and cretinism:

"In many areas of the world, mainly in mountainous regions, the soil and water are very poor in iodine; if the populations in these areas are dependent primarily on the foods produced locally, they may not have enough iodine in their diet.

"In an effort to compensate for this deficiency, the thyroid gland enlarges so that it can utilize the available iodine more efficiently and produce enough thyroxine. This pathological enlargement of the thyroid gland is known as goiter, which presents as a swelling on the front of the neck."

"Endemic goiter: a brief for policy makers", Sub-committee on Nutrition, United Nations Administrative Committee on Co-ordination, 1979 (ACC/SCN-NS1).

"... endemic cretinism ... is characterised by association with endemic goitre and severe iodine deficiency, by the existence of mental retardation together with a predominant neurological syndrome or a predominant hypothyroidism syndrome or a mixture of the two, and by its preventability with supplementary iodine. The fully developed syndrome is only the most obvious manifestation in a whole range of developmental disorders prevalent in goitrous communities – expressed as combinations of retarded mental development, hearing disabilities, speech disorders, neuromuscular abnormalities, coordination defects, and poor physical growth. The more severe the iodine deficiency, the more frequent is endemic cretinism."

"From endemic goitre to iodine deficiency disorders", Lancet, editorial, 12 November 1983.

"It seems that in severely iodine-deficient areas the iodine stores of the mother's thyroid become more depleted with each successive pregnancy and lactation, and her thyroid accumulates iodine more avidly. It is an old experience that the successive children are usually more retarded and finally only cretins are born."

Josip Matovinovic, "Endemic goiter and cretinism at the dawn of the third millennium", Annual Review of Nutrition, vol. 3, 1983.

PREVALENCE

Though mostly limited to mountainous regions, iodine deficiency affects large numbers of people:

"In 1960, Kelly and Snedden estimated that there were 200 million goitrous persons worldwide. Twenty years later Matovinovic's figure for the less developed regions of the world was 329 million, and this is probably an underestimate. As for endemic cretinism, it is impossible to make even an intelligent guess. There are said to be 1-2 million cretins in China alone. In some South-East Asian localities, up to a third of the population may be hypothyroid."

"From endemic goitre to iodine deficiency disorders", Lancet, editorial, 12 November 1983.

PREVENTING IDD

Iodine deficiency disorders can be prevented at low cost:

"(In Papua New Guinea) a recent evaluation in 1982 revealed an absence of goitre and the disappearance of cretinism under the age of 9 years since iodisation, initially with oil injection and then with salt, became widespread from 1972...

"In northern India, goitre has been controlled over a 16-year period with iodised salt...

"A recent report from Bolivia describes improvement in intelligence tests in goitrous school children following the oral administration of a single dose of iodised oil (374 mg iodine) when followed up for a period of 22 months."

Basil S. Hetzel, "The control of iodine deficiency in South East Asia", paper presented at the Pacific Science Congress, Dunedin, New Zealand, February 1983.

"A single dose of iodised oil can correct severe iodine deficiency for 3-5 years. Iodised oil offers a satisfactory immediate measure for primary care services until an iodised salt programme can be implemented. The complete eradication of iodine deficiency is therefore feasible within 5-10 years."

Basil S. Hetzel, "Iodine deficiency disorders (IDD) and their eradication", Lancet, 12 November 1983.

Vitamin A Deficiency
CAUSES AND CONSEQUENCES

Vitamin A deficiency – often the result of lack of knowledge about nutrition – is a leading cause of blindness:

"Xerophthalmia – from the Greek for 'dry eye' – is nutritional blindness caused by a lack of Vitamin A in the diet. It is the leading cause of preventable blindness among young children in developing countries, who are at greatest risk in the first two or three years of life. In general, the disease is linked to protein-calorie malnutrition – failure to consume Vitamin A-rich foods such as green and yellow vegetables and fish, liver, eggs and milk. Often, however, the unavailability of these foods is less responsible than cultural practices with regard to child feeding. For example, while breast-feeding usually provides a baby with adequate Vitamin A, diluted substitute milk or early weaning food is often lacking in this substance and therefore puts the child at risk...

"Recent data indicate that, in Asia alone, at least five million children develop xerophthalmia every year, and that some 250,000 to 500,000 of them go blind."

"Xerophthalmia", Impact fact sheet no. 2 (Rehabilitation International), 1981.

"Children are born with limited vitamin A reserves and are dependent for the first 6-12 months of life on vitamin A provided in the breast milk. When the mother is deficient in vitamin A the newborn child's reserves are even smaller, and the amount of vitamin A provided in the breast milk is reduced. Bottle-fed children are often at an even greater disadvantage, receiving skimmed milk (already low in vitamin A) that has been overdiluted with water (frequently contaminated). After 6 months of life the child requires supplementary feedings with foods rich in vitamin or provitamin A."

Alfred Sommer, Field guide to the detection and control of xerophthalmia, second edition, WHO, 1982.

INCREASED MORTALITY RISK

"There is a close connection between vitamin A deficiency and protein-calorie malnutrition. Seriously malnourished children cannot utilize the vitamin A stored in the body... Moreover, vitamin A deficiency leads to other infections (diarrhea, respiratory ailments) that affect nutritional status."

James Austin and others, Nutrition Intervention in Developing Countries, Oelschlager, Gunn and Hain, for Harvard Institute for International Development, 1981.

"Among children with severe vitamin A deficiency and xerophthalmia (corneal xerosis, ulceration, and keratomalacia), mortality is extremely high. In-hospital death rates average 15-25%. Mortality among rural cases is probably several times greater.

Alfred Sommer and others, "Increased mortality in children with mild vitamin A deficiency", Lancet, 10 September 1983.

"Case-control analysis suggests that children with a history of diarrhea during the previous month are at 13 times the risk of active corneal disease as children without such a history."

Alfred Sommer, Nutritional blindness: xerophthalmia and keratomalacia, Oxford University Press, 1982.

PREVENTION

The remedies lie in supplementing common foods with vitamin A, vitamin supplements, and nutrition education – all relatively inexpensive solutions:

"Vitamin A fortification has begun more recently in Guatemala (sugar), India (tea), and the Philippines (monosodium glutamate). Previously, several countries were fortifying cereal products, e.g., bread in India and corn flour in Guatemala. Margarine is fortified in most developed countries and in several developing nations, including Brazil, Colombia, Chile, Mexico, Peru, the Philippines, and Turkey."

James Austin and others, Nutrition Intervention in Developing Countries, Oelschlager, Gunn and Hain, for Harvard Institute for International Development, 1981.

"A year's supply of vitamin A in capsule form costs only US$ 0.15. However, the cost of delivering capsules and of any required information support must also be taken into consideration. In programmes in Bangladesh and Indonesia, total costs of delivering vitamin concentrates to children at risk are less than $0.20 a year for each protected child.

"Even less expensive, in areas with favourable growing conditions, is the addition of dark green leafy vegetables and other foods containing vitamin A to the child's diet. This can easily be accomplished at minimal extra cost..."

"Xerophthalmia," Impact fact sheet no. 2 (Rehabilitation International), 1981.

"The same amount of Vitamin A is obtained from 68 g of spinach as from 63 g of calf liver, 227 g of hens' eggs, 1.7 litres of whole cow's milk, or 6 kg of beef or mutton."

Alfred Sommer, Field guide to the detection and control of xerophthalmia, second edition, WHO, 1982.

III
STATISTICS

Economic and social statistics on the nations of the world, with particular reference to children's well-being

Basic indicators

Nutrition

Health

Education

Demographic indicators

Economic indicators

Less populous countries

III THE PATTERN OF CHILD DEATHS

The developing world's share of population, births, and child deaths

- ☐ Developing world's share
- ■ Developed countries' share

WORLD POPULATION 4,607 MILLION
- 3,456 MILLION (75%)
- 1,151 MILLION (25%)

ANNUAL BIRTHS 127 MILLION
- 109 MILLION (86%)
- 18 MILLION (14%)

ANNUAL INFANT DEATHS (0–11 MONTHS) 10.3 MILLION
- 10 MILLION (97%)
- 0.3 MILLION (3%)

ANNUAL CHILD DEATHS (1–4 YEARS) 4.3 MILLION
- 4.2 MILLION (98%)
- 0.1 MILLION (2%)

Source: United Nations Demographic Estimates, July 1983.

Trends in infant mortality in the developing countries, 1950–1980

- ☐ 1950
- ☐ 1960
- ■ 1970
- ■ 1980

IMR (infant deaths per 1,000 live births), scale 0–220

LESS DEVELOPED COUNTRIES

MORE DEVELOPED COUNTRIES

AFRICA
- WESTERN AFRICA
- MIDDLE AFRICA
- EASTERN AFRICA
- NORTHERN AFRICA
- SOUTHERN AFRICA

ASIA
- MIDDLE SOUTH ASIA
- WESTERN SOUTH ASIA
- EASTERN SOUTH ASIA
- EAST ASIA

LATIN AMERICA
- TROPICAL SOUTH AMERICA
- CENTRAL AMERICA
- CARIBBEAN
- TEMPERATE SOUTH AMERICA

Source: United Nations. Infant Mortality Rate by Region and Country, 1950–2025, Medium Variant. Population Bulletin of the United Nations. No. 14. 1982 pp. 36–41.

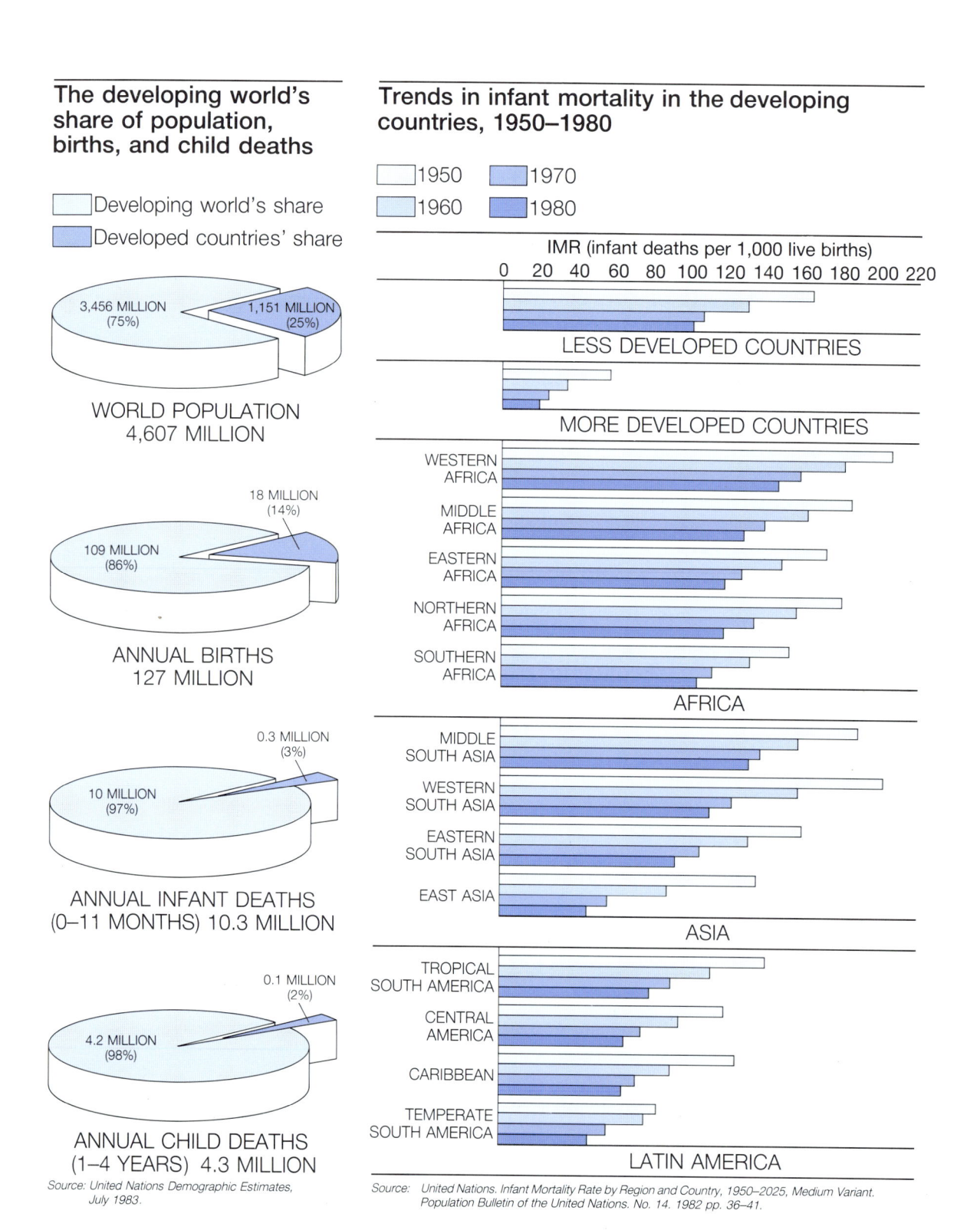

Index to Countries

In the following tables, the countries are listed in descending order of infant mortality. Countries with the same rates are listed alphabetically. The reference numbers indicating that order are shown in the alphabetical list of countries below.

Country	#	Country	#	Country	#
Afghanistan	1	Guyana	87	Pakistan	32
Albania	81	Haiti	36	Panama	98
Algeria	34	Honduras	62	Papua New Guinea	48
Angola	7	Hong Kong*	113	Paraguay	80
Argentina	88	Hungary	103	Peru	49
Australia	120	India	27	Philippines	76
Austria	109	Indonesia	53	Poland	104
Bangladesh	23	Iran, Islamic Rep. of	46	Portugal	99
Belgium	111	Iraq	67	Romania	97
Benin	8	Ireland	116	Rwanda	40
Bhutan	9	Israel	107	Saudi Arabia	50
Bolivia	24	Italy	110	Senegal	20
Botswana	60	Ivory Coast	28	Sierra Leone	2
Brazil	64	Jamaica	96	Singapore	117
Bulgaria	105	Japan	129	Somalia	21
Burkina-Faso	12	Jordan	71	South Africa	56
Burma	44	Kampuchea	3	Spain	121
Burundi	13	Kenya	63	Sri Lanka	84
Cameroon, U. Rep. of	26	Korea, Dem. Rep.	89	Sudan	33
Canada	122	Korea, Rep. of	92	Sweden	130
Central African Rep.	14	Kuwait	91	Switzerland	127
Chad	15	Lao People's Dem. Rep.	29	Syrian Arab Rep.	72
Chile	82	Lebanon	78	Tanzania, U. Rep. of	51
China	83	Lesotho	37	Thailand	77
Colombia	73	Liberia	38	Togo	41
Congo	25	Libyan Arab Jamahiriya	54	Trinidad and Tobago	95
Costa Rica	101	Madagascar	68	Tunisia	57
Cuba	102	Malawi	4	Turkey	42
Czechoslovakia	106	Malaysia	94	Uganda	58
Denmark	124	Mali	10	USSR	100
Dominican Rep.	70	Mauritania	18	United Arab Emirates	79
Ecuador	61	Mauritius	90	United Kingdom	118
Egypt	35	Mexico	74	United States	119
El Salvador	65	Mongolia	75	Uruguay	86
Ethiopia	16	Morocco	47	Venezuela	85
Finland	128	Mozambique	39	Viet Nam	59
France	123	Nepal	11	Yemen	6
German Dem. Rep.	112	Netherlands	125	Yemen, Dem.	22
Germany, Fed. Rep. of	115	New Zealand	114	Yugoslavia	93
Ghana	45	Nicaragua	55	Zaire	43
Greece	108	Niger	19	Zambia	52
Guatemala	66	Nigeria	30	Zimbabwe	69
Guinea	5	Norway	126		
Guinea-Bissau	17	Oman	31	* Colony	

TABLE 1: BASIC INDICATORS

		Infant mortality rate (ages 0–1) 1982	1960	Total population (millions) 1982	Annual no. of births/infant and child deaths (0–4) (thousands) 1982	GNP per capita (US $) 1982	Life expectancy at birth (years) 1982	% adults literate male/female 1980	% of age group enrolled in primary school male/female 1980–1982	% share of household income 1972–1981 lowest 40%	highest 20%
	Very high IMR countries (over 100) Median	140	180	1,362	53,937/9,195	310	46	37/19	82/47	..	..
1	Afghanistan	200	230	14.3	722/212	170x	37	26/6	54/13		
2	Sierra Leone	200	230	3.4	162/55	390	34	31/17	46*/32*		
3	Kampuchea	170	150	6.6	302/..	..	42	78/39	../..		
4	Malawi	170	210	6.4	334/84	210	45	48/25	70/49		
5	Guinea	160	210	5.1	238/72	310	40	35/14	44/22		
6	Yemen	160	210	6.1	297/77	500	44	24*/2*	98*/16*		
7	Angola	150	210	8.1	384/102	470x	42	36/19	../..		
8	Benin	150	210	3.7	188/41	310	42	40/17	88/42		
9	Bhutan	150	190	1.3	51/12	80x	46	../..	15x/7x		
10	Mali	150	190	7.4	374/85	180	42	19/8	35x/20x		
11	Nepal	150	190	15.4	646/138	170	46	25*/4*	94*/36*	13	59
12	Burkina-Faso	150	210	6.5	311/78	210	42	18/5	28/16		
13	Burundi	140	170	4.3	205/43	280	44	35*/13*	41/25		
14	Central African Rep.	140	190	2.4	107/23	310	43	48/19	92/50		
15	Chad	140	190	4.7	208/52	80	43	35/8	../..		
16	Ethiopia	140	180	33.6	1,666/360	140	43	../..	60/33		
17	Guinea-Bissau	140	190	0.8	34/..	170	43	25/13	141/61		
18	Mauritania	140	180	1.7	87/19	470	44	../..	43/23		
19	Niger	140	190	5.6	288/63	310	42	14/6	34/19		
20	Senegal	140	180	6.0	288/70	490	43	31/14	58/38		
21	Somalia	140	180	5.1	230/67	290	43	../..	46*/20*		
22	Yemen, Dem.	140	210	2.0	94/21	470	46	48/16	94/34		
23	Bangladesh	130	160	93.2	4,205/809	140	48	33*/15*	76/47	18	42
24	Bolivia	130	170	5.9	260/50	570	51	79/58	93/78		
25	Congo	130	170	1.6	72/11	1,180	46	70/44	../..		
26	Cameroon, U. Rep. of	120	170	9.0	390/65	890	48	62/36	117/97		
27	India	120	170	717.8	24,044/3,724	260	52	55*/26*	98y/65y	16	49
28	Ivory Coast	120	170	8.9	408/79	950	47	30*/28*	94*/66*	20	50
29	Lao P.D.R.	120	150	4.1	168/34	80x	49	51/36	105/89		
30	Nigeria	120	160	86.1	4,363/766	860	48	66*/38*	../..		
31	Oman	120	190	1.1	51/9.5	6,090	49	../..	90/57		
32	Pakistan	120	160	93.0	3,973/694	380	50	32*/14*	66*/33*		
33	Sudan	120	170	19.8	912/173	440	47	38/14	61/43		
34	Algeria	110	170	19.9	906/147	2,350	58	60/24	106/81		
35	Egypt	110	170	43.4	1,682/269	690	57	56/28	90/65	15	49
36	Haiti	110	180	6.1	253/41	300	53	34/24	74/64		
37	Lesotho	110	140	1.4	59/9.7	510	49	58/81	84x/123x		
38	Liberia	110	160	2.0	98/16	490	49	42/18	82/50		
39	Mozambique	110	160	12.9	568/99	230x	49	36*/18*	90/68		
40	Rwanda	110	150	5.5	283/53	260	49	61/39	75/69		
41	Togo	110	180	2.7	122/23	340	49	33*/20*	135/87		
42	Turkey	110	190	46.5	1,530/215	1,370	63	81*/54*	../..	12	57
43	Zaire	110	150	30.3	1,374/234	190	50	74/37	104x/75x		
	High IMR countries (60–100) Median	90	140	660	24,419/3,035	900	58	69/57	104/94	..	..
44	Burma	100	160	36.6	1,392/187	190	55	86*/70*	75*/70*	21	40
45	Ghana	100	140	12.2	578/84	360	52	59/37	77x/60x		
46	Iran, Islamic Rep. of	100	160	41.2	1,683/243	2,160x	60	55/30	111/78		
47	Morocco	100	160	21.4	950/162	870	58	41/18	97/60		
48	Papua New Guinea	100	170	3.4	139/20	820	53	48/30	73/58		
49	Peru	100	140	18.2	673/84	1,310	58	90*/75*	116/110	7	61
50	Saudi Arabia	100	180	10.0	434/67	16,000	56	35/12	79/54		
51	Tanzania, U. Rep. of	100	150	20.2	1,027/158	280	51	../..	../..		
52	Zambia	100	150	6.0	292/48	640	51	79/58	102/90	11	57
53	Indonesia	90	150	156.7	4,879/653	580	52	80y/64y	123/110	14	49
54	Libyan Arab Jamahiriya	90	160	3.2	148/19	8,510	58	76/36	../..		
55	Nicaragua	90	140	3.0	132/15	920	59	../..	101/107		
56	South Africa	90	130	30.0	1,166/127	2,670	53	81/81	../..		
57	Tunisia	90	160	6.7	230/25	1,390	60	61/34	123/98	15	42
58	Uganda	90	140	14.1	709/115	230	52	50*/29*	62/46		
59	Viet Nam	90	160	56.1	1,789/192	170x	59	../..	120/105		
60	Botswana	80	110	1.0	49/..	900	54	61/61	94/110	8	60
61	Ecuador	80	140	8.5	349/35	1,350	62	82/76	117/113		
62	Honduras	80	140	4.0	175/19	660	60	64/62	96/95		
63	Kenya	80	140	18.2	1,012/124	390	53	61*/38*	114/94	9	60
64	Brazil	70	120	126.9	3,903/388	2,240	63	76/73	93*/93x	7	67

		Infant mortality rate (ages 0-1)		Total population (millions) 1982	Annual no. of births/infant and child deaths (0-4) (thousands) 1982	GNP per capita (US $) 1982	Life expectancy at birth (years) 1982	% adults literate male/female 1980	% of age group enrolled in primary school male/female 1980-1982	% share of household income 1972-1981	
		1982	1960							lowest 40%	highest 20%
65	El Salvador	70	140	5.1	206/20	700	65	70/63	61/61	..	..
66	Guatemala	70	120	7.7	299/26	1,130	60	59/44	73/63	..	..
67	Iraq	70	140	14.2	640/63	3,020ˣ	59	68/32	117/109	..	..
68	Madagascar	70	110	9.2	410/57	320	49	68/55	106ˣ/93ˣ	..	..
69	Zimbabwe	70	120	7.9	375/43	850	55	77/61	130/121	..	..
70	Dominican Rep.	60	120	5.8	194/16	1,330	62	75/73	108/110	15	54
71	Jordan	60	140	3.1	143/12	1,690	64	82*/58*	105/100	..	..
72	Syrian Arab Rep.	60	130	9.5	443/33	1,680	67	72/35	112/89	..	..
	Middle IMR countries (26-50) Median	38	80	1,451	31,198/1,959	1,885	67	90/83	106/103	..	..
73	Colombia	50	90	26.9	839/57	1,460	63	86/84	129/132	..	..
74	Mexico	50	90	73.2	2,508/171	2,270	66	81*/75*	122/120	10	58
75	Mongolia	50	110	1.8	60/3.9	780ˣ	64	93/86	105/108	..	..
76	Philippines	50	110	50.8	1,651/108	820	64	90/88	109/107	..	..
77	Thailand	50	100	48.5	1,398/92	790	63	93/83	99/93	15	50
78	Lebanon	48	70	2.6	79/4.6		65	83/64	122/114	..	..
79	United Arab Emirates	46	140	1.1	30/1.7	23,770	70	30/19	127/127	..	..
80	Paraguay	45	90	3.4	122/6.8	1,610	65	90/83	106ˣ/98ˣ	..	..
81	Albania	44	110	2.9	80/4.4	840ˣ	71	../..	109/103	..	..
82	Chile	41	110	11.5	285/14	2,210	67	94/91	113/110	..	..
83	China	39	140	1,027.5	19,318/1,306	310	67	79*/51*	../..	18	39
84	Sri Lanka	39	70	15.4	419/21	320	67	91*/82*	85*/84*	12*	54*
85	Venezuela	39	80	16.7	591/27	4,140	68	84/78	105/104	15	48
86	Uruguay	38	50	2.9	58/2.6	2,650	70	95/95	116/112	..	..
87	Guyana	37	70	0.9	26/..	670	68	96/93	96/95	..	..
88	Argentina	36	60	29.2	718/31	2,520	70	95/94	120/119	..	..
89	Korea, Dem. Rep.	32	80	18.7	575/23	1,130ˣ	64	../..	../..	..	..
90	Mauritius	32	70	1.0	25/..	1,240	67	86/72	97*/96*	14	55
91	Kuwait	31	90	1.5	57/2.0	19,870	71	72/54	96/93	..	..
92	Korea, Rep. of	30	80	39.2	839/31	1,910	67	96/88	106/103	17	45
93	Yugoslavia	30	90	22.7	374/14	2,800	71	93/81	100/100	19	39
94	Malaysia	29	70	14.5	427/16	1,860	67	79/61	93/91	11	56
95	Trinidad and Tobago	29	50	1.1	27/0.9	6,840	70	97/94	91ˣ/92ˣ	13	50
96	Jamaica	28	60	2.2	63/..	1,330	70	90/93	99/100	..	..
97	Romania	28	70	22.6	395/14	2,560	71	97/94	104/103	..	..
98	Panama	27	70	2.0	58/2.0	2,120	71	87/86	113/108	..	..
99	Portugal	26	80	9.9	176/5.2	2,450	71	85/76	120ˣ/116ˣ	..	..
	Low IMR countries (25 and less) Median	11	31	1,116	17,258/..	7,920	74	../..	100/101	..	..
100	USSR	25	38	270.6	5,068/..	4,550ˣ	71	99/98	../..	..	..
101	Costa Rica	21	80	2.4	74/1.8	1,280	73	92/92	109/107	..	..
102	Cuba	21	70	9.8	166/4.1	1,410ˣ	73	91/91	110/104	..	..
103	Hungary	20	50	10.8	156/3.8	2,270	71	99/98	99/99	26	32
104	Poland	20	60	36.5	679/16	3,900ˣ	72	99/98	100/99	..	..
105	Bulgaria	18	49	9.1	141/3.1	4,150ˣ	72	96/93	100/99	..	..
106	Czechoslovakia	16	26	15.5	252/5.1	5,820ˣ	72	../..	94/96	18	40
107	Israel	15	32	4.0	97/1.8	5,090	74	96/91	103ˣ/102ˣ	..	..
108	Greece	14	50	9.8	154/2.7	4,290	74	94/83	99/98	..	..
109	Austria	13	37	7.5	90/1.5	9,880	73	../..	../..	..	..
110	Italy	13	44	56.4	728/12	6,840	74	96/95	102ˣ/102ˣ	18	44
111	Belgium	12	31	9.9	119/..	10,760	73	99/99	100/101	20	40
112	German Dem. Rep.	12	38	16.7	210/..	7,180ˣ	73	../..	91/97	..	..
113	Hong Kong	12	43	5.3	94/..	5,340	74	94/77	108/104	16	47
114	New Zealand	12	22	3.2	51/..	7,920	73	../..	103/101	..	..
115	Germany, Fed. Rep. of	11	32	61.4	623/..	12,460	73	../..	100/100	20	40
116	Ireland	11	31	3.5	73/..	5,150	73	../..	100/100	20	39
117	Singapore	11	36	2.5	44/..	5,910	72	88/70	106/103	..	..
118	United Kingdom	11	23	55.6	710/..	9,660	74	../..	102/103	19	40
119	USA	11	26	231.8	3,708/..	13,160	74	99/99	../..	14	50
120	Australia	10	20	15.1	245/..	11,140	74	../..	110/109	15	47
121	Spain	10	46	38.1	649/..	5,430	74	96/91	111/109	18	42
122	Canada	9	28	24.7	401/..	11,320	75	../..	106/104	15	42
123	France	9	29	54.1	745/..	11,680	74	99/99	111/112	16	46
124	Denmark	8	22	5.1	58/..	12,470	75	../..	98/98	20	38
125	Netherlands	8	18	14.3	167/..	10,930	76	../..	99/101	22	37
126	Norway	8	19	4.1	51/..	14,280	76	../..	99/100	..	..
127	Switzerland	8	22	6.3	53/..	17,010	76	../..	../..	..	..
128	Finland	7	22	4.8	63/..	10,870	73	../..	96/96	20	38
129	Japan	7	31	118.2	1,501/..	10,080	76	99/99	100/100	22	37
130	Sweden	7	16	8.3	88/..	14,040	76	../..	98/98	20	37

TABLE 2: NUTRITION

		% of infants with low birth-weight 1979–1981	% of mothers breast-feeding 1975–1981 3 months	6 months	12 months	% of children under five suffering from mild-moderate/severe malnutrition 1975–1981	Prevalence of wasting aged 12–23 months (% of age group) 1975–1979	Average index of food production per capita (1974–76=100) 1982	Daily per capita calorie intake as % of requirements 1981
	Very high IMR countries (over 100) Median	16	94	91	82	39/5	..	94	95
1	Afghanistan	..	..	..	..	../..	..	94	72
2	Sierra Leone	..	98*	94	83	24*/3*	26	91	101
3	Kampuchea	..	100*	100*	93*	../..	..	94	95
4	Malawi	..	..	..	95*	../..	..	103	94
5	Guinea	18	..	..	..	../..	..	94	75
6	Yemen	..	80*	70*	55*	54*/4*	17	86	76
7	Angola	19	..	..	..	../..	..	86	83
8	Benin	..	95*	90*	75*	../..	17	102	101
9	Bhutan	..	..	..	..	../..	..	104	103
10	Mali	13	..	..	..	../..	..	100	72
11	Nepal	..	92	90	74	50*/7*	27	84	86
12	Burkina-Faso	21	..	..	..	../40*	17	106	95
13	Burundi	14	..	95*	90*	30*/3*	39x	93	95
14	Central African Rep.	23	..	..	..	../..	..	96	96
15	Chad	11	..	..	..	../..	..	107	76
16	Ethiopia	13	..	97	95*	60*/10*	..	103	76
17	Guinea-Bissau	9	..	..	..	../..	..	82	..
18	Mauritania	..	..	..	..	10*/..	30*	103	97
19	Niger	..	65*	30*	15*	17*/9*	..	122	102
20	Senegal	10	94	94	82	../..	22	72	101
21	Somalia	..	100*	100*	..	16y/..	..	70	100
22	Yemen, Dem.	..	..	..	..	../..	36	83	86
23	Bangladesh	50	98	97	89	63*/21*	53	100	84
24	Bolivia	..	4*	12*	45*	49*/1*	..	90	91
25	Congo	15	97*	97*	85*	30*/1*	..	86	94
26	Cameroon, U. Rep. of	11	..	98	97	../..	5	92	102
27	India	30	..	..	..	33*/5*	..	102	86
28	Ivory Coast	14	93*	90*	50*	23*/28*	21*	116	112
29	Lao, P.D.R.	18	90*	90*	90*	../..	..	129	97
30	Nigeria	18	98*	94*	90*	24*/16*	..	101	91
31	Oman	..	..	..	..	../..	..	..	..
32	Pakistan	27	90*	78*	45*	62*/10*	23	102	106
33	Sudan	17	91	86	72	50*/5*	..	91	99
34	Algeria	10	..	..	..	../..	..	86	89
35	Egypt	14	..	91*	84*	47*/1*	3	94	116
36	Haiti	..	93	85	72	70*/3*	18	88	96
37	Lesotho	15	93	89	75	../..	11	77	111
38	Liberia	..	96	92	64	17*/2*	8	93	114
39	Mozambique	16*	..	..	..	../..	..	80	70
40	Rwanda	17	..	..	..	../..	26	104	88
41	Togo	..	..	99	90	../..	9	103	83
42	Turkey	10*	99*	91*	51*	44y/24y	..	106	122
43	Zaire	16	..	..	..	../..	10	89	94
	High IMR countries (60–100) Median	14	87	78	64	../..	..	92	99
44	Burma	20	90*	90*	90*	50*/1*	44	118	113
45	Ghana	..	..	..	..	../..	..	77	88
46	Iran, Islamic Rep. of	14	..	..	..	../..	..	93	114
47	Morocco	..	93*	93*	93*	40y/5y	..	89	115
48	Papua New Guinea	25	..	..	..	38y/..	..	96	92
49	Peru	6*	80	67	38*	42y/2y	..	87	98
50	Saudi Arabia	12*	..	..	..	../..	12*	..	85*
51	Tanzania, U. Rep. of	13	..	..	..	43*/7*	..	94	83
52	Zambia	14	..	..	93*	../..	33*	71	93
53	Indonesia	18	98*	97*	83*	27*/3*	26	121	110
54	Libyan Arab Jamahiriya	..	..	..	..	../..	..	74	147
55	Nicaragua	..	..	..	71*	65*/3*	..	80	99
56	South Africa	15	..	..	..	../..	..	89	118
57	Tunisia	7	95*	92*	71*	60*/4*	3x	91	116
58	Uganda	10	85*	70*	20*	15*/4*	..	90	80
59	Viet Nam	..	..	..	..	../..	..	113	90
60	Botswana	..	..	..	97*	27y/..	13	70	..
61	Ecuador	..	..	..	57*	40*/..	..	101	97
62	Honduras	..	48*	28*	24*	29*/2*	..	105	96
63	Kenya	18	89	84	44	30*/2*	8	89	88
64	Brazil	9	75*	..	48*	../..	6x	112	107

114

		% of infants with low birth-weight 1979-1981	% of mothers breast-feeding 1975-1981			% of children under five suffering from mild-moderate/severe malnutrition 1975-1981	Prevalence of wasting aged 12-23 months (% of age group) 1975-1979	Average index of food production per capita (1974-76=100) 1982	Daily per capita calorie intake as % of requirements 1981
			3 months	6 months	12 months				
65	El Salvador	13	..	..	..	52*/6*	..	88	94
66	Guatemala	18	..	84	74	69*/4*	..	110	93
67	Iraq	6	..	..	..	../..	..	105	127
68	Madagascar	10	..	..	..	../..	..	89	109
69	Zimbabwe	15	..	..	88*	../..	..	75	90
70	Dominican Rep.	18*	66	47	26	../..	7	94	106
71	Jordan	7	79	70	41	../..	9	96	102
72	Syrian Arab Rep.	..	88	72	41	../..	..	128	120
	Middle IMR countries (26-50) Median	**10**	**63**	**48**	**27**	**../..**		**107**	**114**
73	Colombia	10	62	42	23	43/8	..	115	108
74	Mexico	12	62	48	27	../..	..	102	121
75	Mongolia	..	..	..	..	../..	..	85	111
76	Philippines	20	78	69	53	40/3	16	107	116
77	Thailand	13	82	66	65	51*/2*	18	115	105
78	Lebanon	12	..	..	..	../..	..	127	99
79	United Arab Emirates	..	..	..	..	../..	..	109	139
80	Paraguay	1*	80	77	49	../..	..	107	112
81	Albania	..	..	..	..	../..	..	107	114
82	Chile	13	..	..	..	11/(.)	..		
83	China	6	..	..	..	../..	..	115	107
84	Sri Lanka	21	88	82	60	../..	22	144	102
85	Venezuela	11	50	40	30	../..	..	97	107
86	Uruguay	10	87*	..	..	../..	..	98	110
87	Guyana	..	64	48	21	../..	..	92	..
88	Argentina	6	..	..	..	../..	..	115	125
89	Korea, Dem. Rep.	..	..	..	..	../..	..	108	129
90	Mauritius	..	..	..	..	../..	..	106	..
91	Kuwait	..	..	..	..	../..	..		
92	Korea, Rep. of	8	85*	79*	75*	16*/(.)*	..	111	126
93	Yugoslavia	7	..	..	..	../..	..	112	144
94	Malaysia	9	47x	34x	19x	../..	..	127	121
95	Trinidad and Tobago	..	59	50	14	../..	..	54	121
96	Jamaica	10	57	40	16	../..	..	90	119
97	Romania	..	..	..	..	../..	..	114	126
98	Panama	11	37*	19*	17*	48/3	..	103	103
99	Portugal	..	..	..	..	../..	..	80	110
	Low IMR countries (25 and less) Median	**6.4**	**..**	**..**	**..**	**../..**		**109**	**133**
100	USSR	8	..	..	..	../..	..	97	130
101	Costa Rica	8.5	38	20	9	46*/(.)*	..	92	118
102	Cuba	10	..	..	..	../..	..	129	121
103	Hungary	12	45	21	4	../..	..	119	134
104	Poland	8	42	32	..	../..	..	87	123
105	Bulgaria	..	..	..	..	../..	..	121	146
106	Czechoslovakia	6.1	..	..	..	../..	..	107	141
107	Israel	6.3	..	..	..	../..	..	95	115
108	Greece	..	..	..	..	../..	..	106	150
109	Austria	5	..	..	..	../..	..	123	134
110	Italy	11	..	..	..	../..	1	106	150
111	Belgium	..	..	..	..	../..	..		160
112	German Dem. Rep.	6.3	..	..	..	../..	..	111	144
113	Hong Kong	8	..	18x	..	../..	..	99	129
114	New Zealand	4.9	..	..	..	../..	..	107	129
115	Germany, Fed. Rep. of	6.7	..	..	..	../..	..	115	133
116	Ireland	..	..	..	..	../..	..	98	135
117	Singapore	11	..	..	..	../..	..	228	133
118	United Kingdom	7	..	..	..	../..	..	116	132
119	USA	7.4	33	25	8	../..	..	118	138
120	Australia	5.8	..	..	..	../..	..	89	119
121	Spain	..	..	..	..	../..	..	104	127
122	Canada	6.4	26	13	..	../..	..	121	126
123	France	6.5	9	..	..	../..	(.)	115	133
124	Denmark	6.4	..	..	..	../..	..	115	133
125	Netherlands	4	17	..	..	../..	..	111	133
126	Norway	4.2	..	..	..	../..	..	114	118
127	Switzerland	..	..	..	..	../..	..	113	133
128	Finland	3.9	..	..	..	../..	..	99	103
129	Japan	5.1	56x	..	..	../..	..	91	117
130	Sweden	3.6	35x	14x	..	../..	..	99	119

115

TABLE 3: HEALTH

		% of population with access to drinking water 1975–1980			% of one-year-old children fully immunized 1982 (approx)					% of pregnant women fully immunized against tetanus 1982 (approx)	Life expectancy at birth (years)	
		Total	Urban	Rural	TB	DPT	Polio	Measles	All six diseases		1960	1982
	Very high IMR countries (over 100) Median	23	50	15	32	18	11	20	..	9	38	46
1	Afghanistan	10	28	8	10	5	5	8	5	1	33	37
2	Sierra Leone	14*	52*	2*	30	12	10	23	..	..	30	34
3	Kampuchea	..	..	..	..	..	..	..	..	..	42	42
4	Malawi	41	77	37	86	66	68	65	..	..	36	45
5	Guinea	17	69	2	..	..	..	77	..	..	33	40
6	Yemen	20*	50*	17*	15	3	3	4	..	..	36	44
7	Angola	21	85	10	47*	9*	7*	17*	..	..	33	42
8	Benin	20	26	15	37*	20*	45*	6*	..	..	35	42
9	Bhutan	7	50	5	9	4	4	18	..	(.)	38	46
10	Mali	6	37	(.)	19	..	..	..	..	1	35	42
11	Nepal	11*	83	7*	46*	18*	3*	3*	..	27	38	46
12	Burkina-Faso	30	27	31	16	2	2	23	..	11	33	42
13	Burundi	24	90	20	65	38	6	30	..	..	38	44
14	Central African Rep.	16	..	..	31*	21*	21*	19*	..	24*	35	43
15	Chad	26	..	..	..	..	..	..	..	..	35	43
16	Ethiopia	4*	..	..	10	6	6	7	..	..	36	43
17	Guinea-Bissau	10	18	8	18*	24*	14*	30*	..	..	36	43
18	Mauritania	16*	..	..	57	18	18	45	..	1	36	44
19	Niger	33	41	32	28	6	6	19	..	9	35	42
20	Senegal	42	77	25	..	..	..	..	..	..	37	43
21	Somalia	..	60*	20*	3	2	2	3	..	5	36	43
22	Yemen, Dem.	44	85	25	9	5	5	6	5	3	36	46
23	Bangladesh	43	26	45	3	2	2	2	..	1	43	48
24	Bolivia	37	69	10	33	12	13	16	..	..	43	51
25	Congo	20*	40*	8*	92	42	42	49	32*	44*	38	46
26	Cameroon, U. Rep. of	26	..	..	8	20y	6y	47y	..	..	39	48
27	India	41*	78*	31*	18	39	18	(.)	..	24	42	52
28	Ivory Coast	20*	30*	10*	70*	42*	34*	28*	..	25*	38	47
29	Lao, P.D.R.	..	20*	3*	7*	7*	7*	7*	..	2*	44	49
30	Nigeria	28*	68*	18*	26*	24*	24*	20*	..	11	40	48
31	Oman	..	..	..	71x	40x	40x	47x	32x	27	38	49
32	Pakistan	35	72	20	1	4	4	6	4	1	43	50
33	Sudan	40*	..	..	2	2	4	4	2	1	39	47
34	Algeria	77	..	..	59	33	30	17	..	..	47	58
35	Egypt	75	88	64	62	70	72	59	59	10	46	57
36	Haiti	..	40*	5*	57y	29y	7y	..	..	..	42	53
37	Lesotho	14	37	11	81x	56x	54x	49x	40x	..	40	49
38	Liberia	20	..	..	50*	16*	11*	56*	..	60	40	49
39	Mozambique	13*	50*	7*	62x	20x	20x	25x	11x	..	40	49
40	Rwanda	54	48	55	60x	36x	25x	53x	21x	5	42	49
41	Togo	..	52*	30*	..	..	..	..	..	..	39	49
42	Turkey	63*	63*	63*	47	64	69	52	..	..	51	63
43	Zaire	..	35*	5*	34	18	18	22	..	47*	40	50
	High IMR countries (60–100) Median	46	80	22	56	37	42	42	..	10	46	58
44	Burma	20*	35*	14*	19	9	1	(.)	..	10	44	55
45	Ghana	47	72	33	..	..	..	..	..	..	43	52
46	Iran, Islamic Rep. of	51	..	..	8	35	62	46	..	3	50	60
47	Morocco	35*	63*	15*	66*	44	44	66*	44*	..	47	58
48	Papua New Guinea	16	55	10	51	25	25	..	..	..	41	53
49	Peru	42*	67*	15*	60	22	22	29	..	8*	48	58
50	Saudi Arabia	..	..	..	..	..	..	..	..	..	43	56
51	Tanzania, U. Rep. of	..	85*	41*	55*	58	56	37*	..	35	41	51
52	Zambia	46*	..	..	82y	47y	44y	55y	35y	38*	42	51
53	Indonesia	..	36*	10*	55	29x	3	2	..	15	41	52
54	Libyan Arab Jamahiriya	98	100	90	60	60	60	62	60	7	47	58
55	Nicaragua	38*	70*	7*	82	27	72	40	..	31*	47	59
56	South Africa	..	..	..	..	..	..	..	..	..	44	53
57	Tunisia	58*	86*	27*	65	36	37	65	36	2	48	60
58	Uganda	16*	90*	7*	7*	3*	4*	4*	..	20	43	52
59	Viet Nam	..	..	32	..	..	..	..	..	..	44	59
60	Botswana	..	98*	72*	94x	82x	77x	75x	62x	25*	45	54
61	Ecuador	45	82	16	77	26	26	33	..	4	51	62
62	Honduras	44	50	40	57	53	54	56	..	11	46	60
63	Kenya	26	85	15	..	..	..	..	..	..	42	53
64	Brazil	..	80	3*	61	53	99	64	..	..	55	63

116

		% of population with access to drinking water 1975–1980			% of one-year-old children fully immunized 1982 (approx)						% of pregnant women fully immunized against tetanus 1982 (approx)	Life expectancy at birth (years)	
		Total	Urban	Rural	TB	DPT	Polio	Measles	All six diseases		1960	1982
65	El Salvador	51	67	40	47	44ˣ	44ˣ	45	..	..	50	65
66	Guatemala	..	70*	21*	28	46ˣ	45ˣ	12	..	..	47	60
67	Iraq	73*	97*	22*	76	13	16	33	..	4	49	59
68	Madagascar	38*	70*	30*	13	38*	4*	..	..	..	41	49
69	Zimbabwe	..	..	10*	64ʸ	38ʸ	37ʸ	55ʸ	..	..	45	55
70	Dominican Rep.	59	85	33	52	30	39	26	..	34*	51	62
71	Jordan	89	100	65	(.)	44	44	11	..	2	47	64
72	Syrian Arab Rep.	71	98	54	35*	36*	36*	43*	..	3	50	67
	Middle IMR countries (26–50) Median	80	91	50	75	56	70	36	..	9	59	67
73	Colombia	92	100	79	79*	42*	44*	43*	..	6	55	63
74	Mexico	72*	..	..	25	23	73	8	..	..	57	66
75	Mongolia	..	..	..	50	75	86	96	..	(.)	52	64
76	Philippines	40*	55*	33*	61	51ˣ	44	22*	..	..	53	64
77	Thailand	..	50*	41*	73	53ˣ	33	(.)	..	30	52	63
78	Lebanon	..	..	..	15	11	11	34	4	..	60	65
79	United Arab Emirates	93	95	81	..	..	..	..	..	..	53	70
80	Paraguay	18*	41*	5*	47	39	43	34	..	6	56	65
81	Albania	..	..	..	93	94	92	90	..	..	62	71
82	Chile	76*	93*	20*	94	94	83ˣ	93	..	..	57	67
83	China	..	85*	..	..	..	..	..	..	..	39	67
84	Sri Lanka	19*	49*	10*	64*	56*	56*	(.)	..	47*	62	67
85	Venezuela	81	91	50	..	71	43	36	..	..	57	68
86	Uruguay	78*	93*	13*	31	63	70ˣ	57	..	11	68	70
87	Guyana	72	100	60	78	53	73	68	..	..	60	68
88	Argentina	60*	69*	16*	83	66	100	11	..	..	65	70
89	Korea, Dem. Rep.	..	..	..	..	..	..	..	..	..	54	64
90	Mauritius	95*	95*	95*	88*	91*	91*	33*	..	1	59	67
91	Kuwait	89	..	..	(.)	54	76	66	..	30	60	71
92	Korea, Rep. of	82*	80*	84*	99	61	62	5	..	..	54	67
93	Yugoslavia	..	..	..	100	90	95	95ˣ	..	..	63	71
94	Malaysia	63	90	49	77	47	55	..	..	..	54	67
95	Trinidad and Tobago	98	100	93	..	54	59	..	..	..	64	70
96	Jamaica	86	..	..	27	34	72	12	..	..	63	70
97	Romania	..	..	..	..	..	..	..	..	..	65	71
98	Panama	82	100	65	86	63	63	66	..	..	61	71
99	Portugal	..	..	..	..	90	85	70ˣ	..	..	63	71
	Low IMR countries (25 and less) Median	..	..	..	90	85	94	75	..	..	70	74
100	USSR	..	..	..	..	95	95	95ˣ	..	..	69	71
101	Costa Rica	87*	100*	68*	..	88	100	97	..	..	62	73
102	Cuba	..	..	..	96	67	82ˣ	54	..	..	63	73
103	Hungary	..	..	..	100	100	98	99ˣ	..	..	68	71
104	Poland	..	..	..	95	95	95	65	..	..	67	72
105	Bulgaria	..	..	..	97	97	98	98	..	98	69	72
106	Czechoslovakia	..	..	..	95	95	95	95ˣ	..	..	70	72
107	Israel	..	..	..	65	73	73	69	..	10	69	74
108	Greece	..	..	..	12	31	95	..	..	..	69	74
109	Austria	..	..	..	90	90	90	90ˣ	..	..	69	73
110	Italy	..	..	..	..	..	..	..	..	..	69	74
111	Belgium	..	..	..	..	95	99	50	..	..	70	73
112	German Dem. Rep.	..	..	..	95	80	90	95	..	..	70	73
113	Hong Kong	100	100	95	100	84	94	..	..	..	65	74
114	New Zealand	..	..	..	..	..	..	80ˣ	..	..	71	73
115	Germany, Fed. Rep. of	..	..	..	40	50	80	35ˣ	..	..	70	73
116	Ireland	..	..	..	..	33	65	..	..	..	70	73
117	Singapore	100	..	..	85	81	88	58ˣ	..	..	65	72
118	United Kingdom	..	..	..	..	35	79	50ˣ	..	..	71	74
119	USA	..	..	..	..	..	..	96ˣ	..	..	70	74
120	Australia	..	..	..	..	33	17	..	..	..	71	74
121	Spain	..	..	..	..	..	..	..	..	..	69	74
122	Canada	..	..	..	..	..	..	..	..	..	71	75
123	France	..	..	..	80	79	80	..	..	..	70	74
124	Denmark	..	..	..	..	85	97	..	..	..	72	75
125	Netherlands	..	..	..	..	95	95	91ˣ	..	..	73	76
126	Norway	..	..	..	..	..	..	..	..	..	73	76
127	Switzerland	..	..	..	..	..	..	..	..	..	71	76
128	Finland	..	..	..	90	92	90	70ˣ	..	..	68	73
129	Japan	..	..	..	85	..	..	69ˣ	..	..	68	76
130	Sweden	..	..	..	..	100ˣ	100	56ˣ	..	..	73	76

TABLE 4: EDUCATION

		Adult literacy rate 1970 male/female	Adult literacy rate 1980 male/female	Primary-school enrolment ratio 1960 (gross) male/female	Primary-school enrolment ratio 1980–1982 (gross) male/female	Primary-school enrolment ratio 1980–1982 (net) male/female	% of grade 1 enrolment completing primary school 1975–1982	Secondary-school enrolment ratio 1980–1982 male/female
	Very high IMR countries (over 100) Median	28/10	37/19	45/16	82/47	51/40	50	23/9
1	Afghanistan	13/2	26/6	15/2	54/13	42/11	65	17/5
2	Sierra Leone	18/8	31/17	30/15	46*/32*	37*/26*	46*	23*/10*
3	Kampuchea	71/23	78/39	../..	../..	../..	../..	../..
4	Malawi	42/18	48/25	81/45	70/49	47/39	25	6/2
5	Guinea	21/7	35/14	44/16	44/22	../..	../..	23/9
6	Yemen	9/1	24*/2*	14/(.)	98*/16*	../..	15*	9/2
7	Angola	16/7	36/19	../..	../..	../..	50*	../..
8	Benin	23/8	40/17	38/15	88/42	../..	53	26/10
9	Bhutan	../..	../..	5/(.)	15*/7ˣ	11ˣ/5ˣ	11	2ˣ/1ˣ
10	Mali	11/4	19/8	14/6	35ˣ/20ˣ	../..	61	13ˣ/5ˣ
11	Nepal	23/3	25*/4*	19/1	94*/36*	../..	27*	28*/7*
12	Burkina-Faso	13/3	18/5	12/5	28/16	21*/14*	62	4/2
13	Burundi	29/10	35*/13*	27/9	41/25	22/15	47	4/2
14	Central African Rep.	26/6	48/19	53/12	92/50	73/41	54	21/7
15	Chad	20/2	35/8	29/4	../..	../..	29	../..
16	Ethiopia	9/4	../..	11/3	60/33	../..	50*	16/8
17	Guinea-Bissau	13/6	25/13	35/15	141/61	100/53	39*	33/7
18	Mauritania	../..	../..	13/3	43/23	../..	74	16/4
19	Niger	6/2	14/6	7/3	34/19	../..	75	5ˣ/2ˣ
20	Senegal	18/5	31/14	36/17	58/38	47/31	86	16/8
21	Somalia	5/1	../..	13/5	46*/20*	28/16	33*	24*/10*
22	Yemen, Dem.	31/9	48/16	20/5	94/34	../..	../..	24/11
23	Bangladesh	36/12	33*/15*	66/26	76/47	74/46	20*	24/6
24	Bolivia	68/46	79/58	78/50	93/78	82/72	30ʸ	37/31
25	Congo	50/19	70/44	103/53	../..	../..	73	../..
26	Cameroon, U. Rep. of	47/19	62/36	87/43	117/97	81ˣ/69ˣ	66	25/13
27	India	47/20	55*/26*	80/40	98ʸ/65ʸ	../..	41	39/20
28	Ivory Coast	26/10	30*/28*	68/24	94*/66*	../..	95*	40*/18*
29	Lao, P.D.R.	37/28	51/36	34/16	105/89	../..	../..	22/14
30	Nigeria	35/14	66*/38*	46/27	../..	../..	../..	../..
31	Oman	../..	../..	../..	90/57	69/43	60	30/13
32	Pakistan	30/11	32*/14*	46/13	66*/33*	../..	45*	27/7
33	Sudan	28/6	38/14	35/14	61/43	../..	75	20/15
34	Algeria	39/11	60/24	55/37	106/81	90/71	73	42/29
35	Egypt	50/20	56/28	80/52	90/65	../..	52*	62/46
36	Haiti	26/17	34/24	50/42	74/64	42/38	48	13/12
37	Lesotho	49/74	58/81	63/102	84ˣ/123ˣ	54ˣ/81ˣ	34	13ˣ/20ˣ
38	Liberia	27/8	42/18	45/18	82/50	../..	../..	29/11
39	Mozambique	29/14	36*/18*	60/36	90/68	34/29	9*	9/4
40	Rwanda	43/21	61/39	68/39	75/69	70/65	48	3/1
41	Togo	27/7	33*/20*	63/24	135/87	89/59	41*	46/16
42	Turkey	69/35	81*/54*	90/58	../..	../..	85*	../..
43	Zaire	61/22	74/37	88/32	104ˣ/75ˣ	../..	64	33ˣ/13ˣ
	High IMR countries (60–100) Median	56/37	69/57	66/44	104/94	77/76	71	36/25
44	Burma	85*/57*	86*/70*	61/52	75*/70*	../..	27*	../..
45	Ghana	45/20	59/37	52/25	77ˣ/60ˣ	../..	71	44ˣ/27ˣ
46	Iran, Islamic Rep. of	40/17	55/30	56/27	111/78	../..	70	54/35
47	Morocco	33/11	41/18	67/27	97/60	67/43	84	31/20
48	Papua New Guinea	32/19	48/30	59/7	73/58	../..	67*	17/8
49	Peru	83*/61*	90*/75*	95/71	116/110	94/89	51*	63/54
50	Saudi Arabia	15/2	35/12	22/2	79/54	64/40	72	38/25
51	Tanzania, U. Rep. of	48/18	../..	33/18	../..	73/72	93*	../..
52	Zambia	66/37	79/58	51/34	102/90	85ˣ/79ˣ	80	21/11
53	Indonesia	66/42	80ʸ/64ʸ	86/58	123/110	100/95	79	36/24
54	Libyan Arab Jamahiriya	60/13	76/36	92/24	../..	../..	80	../..
55	Nicaragua	58/56	../..	65/66	101/107	74/76	28	38/45
56	South Africa	70/71	81/81	../..	../..	../..	../..	../..
57	Tunisia	44/17	61/34	88/43	123/98	95/76	71*	40/23
58	Uganda	52/30	50*/29*	65/32	62/46	44/36	78	7/3
59	Viet Nam	../..	../..	../..	120/105	../..	../..	53/43
60	Botswana	41/43	61/61	35/48	94/110	78/90	78	21/25
61	Ecuador	75/68	82/76	87/79	117/113	87ˣ/85ˣ	59	55/54
62	Honduras	55/50	64/62	68/67	96/95	76/75	27*	29/30
63	Kenya	44/19	61*/38*	64/30	114/94	69ˣ/63ˣ	44*	23/15
64	Brazil	69/63	76/73	97/93	93ˣ/93ˣ	76ˣ/76ˣ	30	29ˣ/35ˣ

		Adult literacy rate		Primary-school enrolment ratio			% of grade 1 enrolment completing primary school 1975–1982	Secondary-school enrolment ratio 1980–1982 male/female
		1970 male/female	1980 male/female	1960 (gross) male/female	1980–1982 (gross) male/female	1980–1982 (net) male/female		
65	El Salvador	61/53	70/63	82/77	61/61	56/57	68*	19/21
66	Guatemala	51/37	59/44	50/39	73/63	59/53	37	17/15
67	Iraq	50/18	68/32	94/36	117/109	100/96	93	78/40
68	Madagascar	56/43	68/55	58/45	106ˣ/93ˣ	../..	50	16ˣ/12ˣ
69	Zimbabwe	63/47	77/61	../..	130/121	100/100	../..	18/13
70	Dominican Rep.	69/66	75/73	99/98	108/110	../..	29	40/42
71	Jordan	50*/20*	82*/58*	94/59	105/100	95/90	90	79/76
72	Syrian Arab Rep.	59/21	72/35	89/39	112/89	98/80	81	59/37
	Middle IMR countries (26–50) Median	84/75	90/83	101/93	106/103	90/91	85	57/62
73	Colombia	79/76	86/84	77/77	129/132	../..	37	45/51
74	Mexico	78*/70*	81*/75*	82/77	122/120	../..	83*	54/49
75	Mongolia	87/74	93/86	79/78	105/108	../..	../..	82/90
76	Philippines	83/80	90/88	98/93	109/107	91/92	69	60/64
77	Thailand	86/72	93/83	88/79	99/93	../..	43	30/27
78	Lebanon	74/52	83/64	105/99	122/114	../..	../..	57/59
79	United Arab Emirates	24/7	30/19	../..	127/127	100/100	92	57/66
80	Paraguay	84/75	90/83	105/90	106ˣ/98ˣ	88ˣ/84ˣ	48	26ˣ/26ˣ
81	Albania	../..	../..	102/86	109/103	../..	../..	70/60
82	Chile	90/86	94/91	111/107	113/110	../..	59	56/62
83	China	../..	79*/51*	../..	../..	../..	66*	../..
84	Sri Lanka	86*/71*	91*/82*	100/90	85*/84*	../..	89*	50/55
85	Venezuela	79/71	84/78	100/100	105/104	../..	68	41/38
86	Uruguay	93/93	95/95	111/111	116/112	../..	87	60/67
87	Guyana	94/88	96/93	107/106	96/95	87/88	97	55/59
88	Argentina	94/92	95/94	98/99	120/119	../..	70	54/63
89	Korea, Dem. Rep.	../..	../..	../..	../..	../..	../..	../..
90	Mauritius	77/59	86/72	103/93	97*/96*	89/89	../..	52/49
91	Kuwait	65/42	72/54	131/102	96/93	82/74	98	80/71
92	Korea, Rep. of	92/78	96/88	99/89	106/103	100/99	96*	90/82
93	Yugoslavia	89/74	93/81	113/108	100/100	../..	98	85/80
94	Malaysia	71/48	79/61	108/83	93/91	../..	95	52/50
95	Trinidad and Tobago	95/89	97/94	89/87	91ˣ/92ˣ	76ˣ/78ˣ	../..	63ˣ/62ˣ
96	Jamaica	84/89	90/93	92/93	99/100	92/93	75	54/62
97	Romania	96/91	97/94	101/95	104/103	../..	../..	68/68
98	Panama	81/81	87/86	98/94	113/108	93/93	89*	60/69
99	Portugal	76/66	85/76	132/129	120ˣ/116ˣ	../..	88ˣ	../..
	Low IMR countries (25 and less) Median	95/91	../..	104/103	100/101	97/96	96	83/86
100	USSR	98/97	99/98	100/100	../..	../..	../..	../..
101	Costa Rica	88/87	92/92	97/95	109/107	92/93	../..	44/51
102	Cuba	86/87	91/91	109/109	110/104	97/97	83	72/77
103	Hungary	98/98	99/98	103/100	99/99	97/98	92	33/51
104	Poland	98/97	99/98	110/107	100/99	98/98	92	75/79
105	Bulgaria	94/89	96/93	94/92	100/99	97/96	81ˣ	83/83
106	Czechoslovakia	../..	../..	93/93	../..	34/58	92	../..
107	Israel	92/85	96/91	99/97	94/96	../..	../..	69/80
108	Greece	90/76	94/83	104/101	103ˣ/102ˣ	96ˣ/96ˣ	98	89ˣ/77ˣ
109	Austria	../..	../..	106/104	99/98	86/87	97	71/75
110	Italy	95/93	96/95	112/109	102ˣ/102ˣ	../..	98	74ˣ/71ˣ
111	Belgium	99/99	99/99	111/108	100/101	97/98	../..	90/91
112	German Dem. Rep.	../..	../..	111/113	94/97	../..	../..	92/87
113	Hong Kong	90/64	94/77	93/79	108/104	97/95	88	62/68
114	New Zealand	../..	../..	110/106	103/101	98/97	../..	80/82
115	Germany, Fed. Rep. of	../..	../..	../..	../..	../..	95	../..
116	Ireland	../..	../..	107/112	100/100	90/90	../..	90/101
117	Singapore	82/55	88/70	121/101	106/103	96/96	91	65/65
118	United Kingdom	../..	../..	92/92	102/103	95/95	../..	82/85
119	USA	99/99	99/99	../..	../..	../..	../..	../..
120	Australia	../..	../..	103/103	110/109	100/100	../..	86/89
121	Spain	93/87	96/91	106/116	111/109	100/100	../..	86/90
122	Canada	../..	../..	108/105	106/104	97/96	../..	92/93
123	France	99/98	99/99	144/143	111/112	../..	95	77/79
124	Denmark	../..	../..	103/103	98/98	../..	99	107/104
125	Netherlands	../..	../..	105/104	99/101	90/93	97	97/93
126	Norway	../..	../..	100/100	99/100	98/99	99	92/98
127	Switzerland	../..	../..	118/118	../..	../..	99	../..
128	Finland	../..	../..	100/95	96/96	../..	../..	93/104
129	Japan	99/99	99/99	103/102	100/100	100/100	100	92/93
130	Sweden	../..	../..	95/96	98/98	97/97	100	81/90

TABLE 5: DEMOGRAPHIC INDICATORS

		Total population/ child population (ages 0-4) (millions) 1982	Population annual growth rate (%) 1970-1982	Infant mortality rate (ages 0-1) 1960	Infant mortality rate (ages 0-1) 1982	Child death rate ages 1-4 1960	Child death rate ages 1-4 1982	Crude death rate 1960	Crude death rate 1982	Crude birth rate 1960	Crude birth rate 1982	Total fertility rate 1982	% population urbanized 1982	Average annual growth rate of urban population (%) 1970-82
	Very high IMR countries (over 100) Median	1,362/214	2.6	180	140	42	23	26	19	47	46	6.3	23	5.6
1	Afghanistan	14.3/2.5	2.5	230	200	41	35	31	27	50	50	6.9	17	5.8
2	Sierra Leone	3.4/0.6	2.0	230	200	72	50	35	30	48	47	6.1	26	3.9
3	Kampuchea	6.6/0.6	..	150	170	22	..	21	22	45	44	5.0	15	..
4	Malawi	6.4/1.3	3.0	210	170	58	29	28	20	53	52	7.0	11	6.4
5	Guinea	5.1/0.9	2.0	210	160	65	50	33	24	48	47	6.2	20	5.2
6	Yemen	6.1/1.1	3.0	210	160	60	38	29	22	50	48	6.8	17	8.3
7	Angola	8.1/1.5	2.5	210	150	63	39	31	22	49	47	6.4	23	5.8
8	Benin	3.7/0.7	2.7	210	150	42	23	33	23	47	51	7.0	34	4.4
9	Bhutan	1.3/0.2	2.0	190	150	43	26	25	18	43	39	5.6	4	3.6
10	Mali	7.4/1.4	2.7	190	150	45	27	29	23	50	50	6.7	19	4.7
11	Nepal	15.4/2.6	2.6	190	150	33	22	26	19	46	42	6.3	5	6.7
12	Burkina-Faso	6.5/1.2	2.0	210	150	71	36	31	22	50	48	6.5	7	6.0
13	Burundi	4.3/0.8	2.2	170	140	31	24	25	21	44	48	6.4	2	2.5
14	Central African Rep.	2.4/0.4	2.1	190	140	41	23	30	22	44	45	5.9	43	3.5
15	Chad	4.7/0.8	2.0	190	140	60	37	30	22	46	44	5.9	19	6.4
16	Ethiopia	33.6/6.3	2.0	180	140	42	25	28	22	51	49	6.7	16	5.6
17	Guinea-Bissau	0.8/0.1	..	190	140	..	..	28	22	41	41	5.4	25	..
18	Mauritania	1.7/0.3	2.3	180	140	45	27	28	21	51	50	6.9	30	8.1
19	Niger	5.6/1.1	3.3	190	140	45	27	31	23	46	51	7.1	14	7.2
20	Senegal	6.0/1.1	2.7	180	140	45	34	27	21	48	48	6.5	40	3.7
21	Somalia	5.1/0.9	2.8	180	140	61	47	28	21	47	46	6.1	32	5.4
22	Yemen, Dem.	2.0/0.3	2.2	210	140	59	28	29	19	50	48	6.9	38	3.7
23	Bangladesh	93.2/16.8	2.6	160	130	25	19	22	18	47	45	6.2	11	6.0
24	Bolivia	5.9/1.0	2.6	170	130	40	22	22	16	46	44	6.3	43	3.3
25	Congo	1.6/0.3	3.0	170	130	23	10	25	19	45	44	6.0	38	4.4
26	Cameroon, U. Rep. of	9.0/1.5	3.0	170	120	28	16	25	18	44	43	5.8	38	8.0
27	India	717.8/100.3	2.3	170	120	26	11	24	13	48	34	4.5	24	3.9
28	Ivory Coast	8.9/1.6	4.9	170	120	40	23	26	18	43	46	6.7	39	8.2
29	Lao, P.D.R.	4.1/0.7	2.0	150	120	29	25	19	16	42	41	5.9	14	4.7
30	Nigeria	86.1/17.1	2.6	160	120	50	20	24	17	52	50	7.1	22	4.9
31	Oman	1.1/0.2	4.3	190	120	52	21	28	16	51	47	7.1	8	15.6
32	Pakistan	93.0/16.1	3.0	160	120	25	17	23	15	49	43	5.9	29	4.3
33	Sudan	19.8/3.6	3.2	170	120	40	23	25	18	47	46	6.6	27	5.8
34	Algeria	19.9/3.6	3.1	170	110	39	17	20	12	51	45	7.0	63	5.4
35	Egypt	43.4/7.0	2.5	170	110	23	14	20	13	46	39	5.2	45	2.9
36	Haiti	6.1/1.0	1.7	180	110	47	17	23	14	45	41	5.8	26	4.0
37	Lesotho	1.4/0.2	2.4	140	110	29	17	24	17	43	42	5.8	5	15.4
38	Liberia	2.0/0.4	3.5	160	110	42	16	24	17	46	49	6.9	37	5.7
39	Mozambique	12.9/2.3	4.3	160	110	34	20	23	17	45	44	6.1	16	8.1
40	Rwanda	5.5/1.1	3.4	150	110	40	25	22	17	51	51	7.3	5	6.4
41	Togo	2.7/0.5	2.6	180	110	55	25	26	17	48	45	6.1	19	6.6
42	Turkey	46.5/6.3	2.3	190	110	47	9	16	9	43	33	4.5	46	4.7
43	Zaire	30.3/5.5	3.0	150	110	32	20	24	16	48	45	6.1	42	7.6
	High IMR countries (60-100) Median	660/105	3.0	140	90	27	10	20	11	48	44	6.1	42	4.8
44	Burma	36.6/5.8	2.2	160	100	25	12	21	13	43	38	5.4	28	3.9
45	Ghana	12.2/2.3	3.0	140	100	27	15	21	15	47	47	6.5	38	5.0
46	Iran, Islamic Rep. of	41.2/6.9	3.1	160	100	26	13	19	11	53	41	5.7	52	5.1
47	Morocco	21.4/3.9	2.6	160	100	37	22	21	12	50	44	6.5	42	4.1
48	Papua New Guinea	3.4/0.6	2.1	170	100	26	13	23	14	44	41	6.0	14	6.6
49	Peru	18.2/2.8	2.8	140	100	38	8	19	11	47	37	5.0	66	3.7
50	Saudi Arabia	10.0/1.8	4.8	180	100	48	16	23	12	49	43	7.1	70	7.6
51	Tanzania, U. Rep. of	20.2/4.1	3.4	150	100	31	18	24	15	51	50	7.1	13	8.5
52	Zambia	6.0/1.2	3.1	150	100	38	20	22	15	50	48	6.8	46	6.5
53	Indonesia	156.7/21.9	2.3	150	90	23	13	23	13	44	31	4.0	24	4.5
54	Libyan Arab Jamahiriya	3.2/0.6	4.1	160	90	36	11	19	11	49	46	7.2	60	8.0
55	Nicaragua	3.0/0.5	3.9	140	90	30	9	18	10	51	44	6.0	57	5.0
56	South Africa	30.0/4.8	2.8	130	90	16	5	21	14	41	39	5.1	54	3.2
57	Tunisia	6.7/1.0	2.3	160	90	36	6	19	10	47	34	5.0	54	4.0
58	Uganda	14.1/2.8	2.7	140	90	28	22	21	15	50	50	6.9	13	3.4
59	Viet Nam	56.1/8.6	2.8	160	90	26	4	21	10	42	32	4.4	20	3.2
60	Botswana	1.0/0.2	..	110	80	..	..	20	13	52	50	6.5	17	..
61	Ecuador	8.5/1.5	2.6	140	80	28	7	17	9	47	41	6.0	46	3.8
62	Honduras	4.0/0.7	3.4	140	80	30	8	19	10	51	44	6.6	38	5.5
63	Kenya	18.2/4.0	4.0	140	80	21	13	24	14	57	55	8.1	15	7.3
64	Brazil	126.9/17.2	2.4	120	70	19	8	13	8	43	31	3.8	70	4.1

120

		Total population/ child population (0-4) (millions) 1982	Population annual growth rate (%) 1970-1982	Infant mortality rate (ages 0-1) 1960	Infant mortality rate (ages 0-1) 1982	Child death rate ages 1-4 1960	Child death rate ages 1-4 1982	Crude death rate 1960	Crude death rate 1982	Crude birth rate 1960	Crude birth rate 1982	Total fertility rate 1982	% population urbanized 1982	Average annual growth rate of urban population (%) 1970-82
65	El Salvador	5.1/0.9	3.0	140	70	26	7	17	8	48	40	5.6	42	3.4
66	Guatemala	7.7/1.3	3.1	120	70	10	5	18	9	48	39	5.2	40	4.0
67	Iraq	14.2/2.6	3.5	140	70	28	8	20	11	49	45	6.7	68	5.3
68	Madagascar	9.2/1.6	2.6	110	70	45	23	23	17	44	44	6.1	20	5.2
69	Zimbabwe	7.9/1.5	3.2	120	70	19	14	19	12	47	47	6.6	23	6.0
70	Dominican Rep.	5.8/0.9	3.0	120	60	20	5	17	8	49	33	4.2	53	5.3
71	Jordan	3.1/0.6	2.5	140	60	26	6	20	9	47	45	7.4	62	4.0
72	Syrian Arab Rep.	9.5/1.8	3.5	130	60	25	5	18	7	47	46	7.2	48	4.4
	Middle IMR countries (26-50) Median	1,451/151	1.9	80	38	9	2	11	7	41	28	3.5	52	3.3
73	Colombia	26.9/3.7	1.9	90	50	11	4	13	8	45	31	4.0	66	2.7
74	Mexico	73.2/11.5	3.0	90	50	10	4	12	7	45	34	4.7	68	4.2
75	Mongolia	1.8/0.3	2.9	110	50	11	4	15	7	41	34	4.9	54	4.2
76	Philippines	50.8/7.4	2.7	110	50	14	4	15	7	45	32	4.2	38	3.8
77	Thailand	48.5/6.4	2.4	100	50	13	4	15	8	44	29	3.7	15	4.3
78	Lebanon	2.6/0.3	0.5	70	48	6	3	14	9	43	29	3.8	77	2.8
79	United Arab Emirates	1.1/0.1	15.5	140	46	26	3	19	4	46	27	6.0	80	14.4
80	Paraguay	3.4/0.5	2.6	90	45	9	3	13	7	43	36	4.9	40	3.3
81	Albania	2.9/0.4	2.5	110	44	9	3	11	6	41	28	3.7	38	3.4
82	Chile	11.5/1.3	1.7	110	41	20	2	12	8	37	25	2.9	82	2.4
83	China	1,027.5/96.8	1.4	140	39	26	7	25	7	41	19	2.4	21	..
84	Sri Lanka	15.4/1.9	1.7	70	39	7	3	9	7	36	27	3.4	21	2.5
85	Venezuela	16.7/2.7	3.6	80	39	9	2	11	6	46	35	4.4	84	4.3
86	Uruguay	2.9/0.3	0.4	50	38	4	2	10	10	22	20	2.8	84	0.6
87	Guyana	0.9/0.1	..	70	37	..	..	10	6	42	29	3.3	31	..
88	Argentina	29.2/3.3	1.4	60	36	5	2	9	9	24	25	3.4	83	1.9
89	Korea, Dem. Rep.	18.7/2.6	2.5	80	32	9	2	13	7	41	31	4.1	61	4.2
90	Mauritius	1.0/0.1	..	70	32	..	..	10	6	44	26	2.8	54	..
91	Kuwait	1.5/0.3	6.3	90	31	10	1	10	4	44	37	6.2	92	7.4
92	Korea, Rep. of	39.2/4.0	1.7	80	30	9	2	14	6	43	21	2.6	60	5.0
93	Yugoslavia	22.7/1.8	0.9	90	30	10	2	10	9	23	16	2.1	44	2.8
94	Malaysia	14.5/2.0	2.5	70	29	8	2	15	6	44	29	3.7	30	3.4
95	Trinidad and Tobago	1.1/0.1	0.5	50	29	3	1	8	6	37	25	2.9	22	0.7
96	Jamaica	2.2/0.3	1.5	60	28	4	(.)	9	7	39	28	3.4	51	2.6
97	Romania	22.6/1.9	0.9	70	28	8	2	9	10	20	18	2.5	52	2.7
98	Panama	2.0/0.3	2.3	70	27	6	2	10	5	41	28	3.5	51	3.2
99	Portugal	9.9/0.8	0.8	80	26	9	1	7	10	24	18	2.3	30	2.5
	Low IMR countries (25 and less) Median	1,116/83	0.7	31	11	2	(.)	9	10	19	15	1.8	74	1.5
100	USSR	270.6/23.8	0.9	38	25	2	..	7	9	24	19	2.4	64	1.8
101	Costa Rica	2.4/0.3	2.5	80	21	8	1	10	4	47	31	3.5	44	3.2
102	Cuba	9.8/0.8	1.1	70	21	2	1	9	6	32	17	2.0	70	2.1
103	Hungary	10.8/0.8	0.3	50	20	4	1	10	13	16	15	2.1	55	1.4
104	Poland	36.5/3.3	0.9	60	20	5	1	8	9	24	19	2.3	58	1.7
105	Bulgaria	9.1/0.7	0.4	49	18	3	1	9	11	18	15	2.2	66	2.3
106	Czechoslovakia	15.5/1.3	0.6	26	16	1	1	10	12	17	16	2.2	64	1.8
107	Israel	4.0/0.5	2.5	32	15	2	1	6	7	27	24	3.1	90	3.1
108	Greece	9.8/0.7	1.0	50	14	3	1	8	10	19	16	2.3	64	2.5
109	Austria	7.5/0.4	0.1	37	13	3	1	12	13	18	12	1.6	55	0.7
110	Italy	56.4/3.5	0.4	44	13	3	1	10	10	18	13	1.8	70	1.1
111	Belgium	9.9/0.6	0.2	31	12	2	(.)	12	12	17	12	1.6	89	0.4
112	German Dem. Rep. of	16.7/1.1	-0.2	38	12	3	(.)	13	14	17	13	1.7	77	0.2
113	Hong Kong	5.3/0.4	2.4	43	12	2	(.)	7	6	35	18	2.1	91	2.4
114	New Zealand	3.2/0.3	1.0	22	12	1	(.)	9	8	26	16	1.9	84	1.5
115	Germany, Fed. Rep. of	61.4/3.0	0.1	32	11	2	(.)	11	12	17	10	1.4	85	0.5
116	Ireland	3.5/0.4	1.5	31	11	2	(.)	12	10	21	21	3.2	56	2.5
117	Singapore	2.5/0.2	1.5	36	11	2	(.)	8	5	38	18	1.8	74	1.5
118	United Kingdom	55.6/3.4	0.1	23	11	1	(.)	12	12	17	13	1.8	91	0.3
119	USA	231.8/17.3	1.0	26	11	1	(.)	9	9	24	16	1.9	74	1.5
120	Australia	15.1/1.2	1.5	20	10	1	(.)	9	8	22	16	2.0	87	2.0
121	Spain	38.1/3.1	1.0	46	10	3	(.)	9	9	21	17	2.4	76	2.1
122	Canada	24.7/2.0	1.2	28	9	2	(.)	8	7	27	16	1.8	75	1.2
123	France	54.1/3.6	0.5	29	9	2	(.)	12	11	18	14	1.8	76	1.4
124	Denmark	5.1/0.3	0.3	22	8	1	(.)	9	11	17	11	1.5	85	0.8
125	Netherlands	14.3/0.9	0.7	18	8	1	(.)	8	9	21	12	1.5	90	0.6
126	Norway	4.1/0.3	0.5	19	8	1	(.)	9	11	18	12	1.7	74	2.6
127	Switzerland	6.3/0.3	0.1	22	8	1	(.)	10	11	18	8	1.4	59	0.8
128	Finland	4.8/0.3	0.4	22	7	1	(.)	9	10	19	13	1.6	64	2.4
129	Japan	118.2/8.1	1.1	31	7	2	(.)	8	7	18	13	1.7	76	1.8
130	Sweden	8.3/0.5	0.3	16	7	1	(.)	10	12	15	11	1.6	85	1.0

TABLE 6: ECONOMIC INDICATORS

		GNP per capita (US $) 1982	GNP per capita average annual growth rate (%) 1970–1982	Rate of inflation (%) 1970–1982	% of population below absolute poverty level 1977–1981 urban/rural	% of central gov't. expenditure allocated to health/education/ defence 1981	ODA inflow (million US $) 1982	ODA as % of recipient GNP 1981	Debt service as a % of exports of goods and services 1970	1982
	Very high IMR countries (over 100) Median	310	1.5	11.4	31/61	3.9/15.7/13.1	11,643	9	4.1	7.9
1	Afghanistan	170x	..	..	18/36	../../..	10	(.)x	..	..
2	Sierra Leone	390	−0.3	12.2	../65	../../..	71	6	9.9	20.8
3	Kampuchea	..	..	..	../..	../../..	42	..	..	..
4	Malawi	210	2.0	9.5	25/85	5.2/11.1/8.4	121	10	7.1	22.8
5	Guinea	310	1.2	3.3	../..	../../..	66	4	..	..
6	Yemen	500	5.1	15.0	../..	3.6/14.0/32.6	390	12	..	3.8
7	Angola	470x	−7.2	..	../..	../../..	52	2x	..	..
8	Benin	310	1.2	9.6	../65	../../..	80	7	2.2	..
9	Bhutan	80x	..	..	../..	../../..	11	10	..	..
10	Mali	180	1.7	9.8	27x/48x	3.1/15.7/11.1	194	15	1.2	3.5
11	Nepal	170	−0.5	8.9	55/61	4.1/9.7/6.5	201	9	..	2.3
12	Burkina-Faso	210	1.5	9.7	../..	../../..	206	14	4.0	..
13	Burundi	280	1.7	12.5	55/85	../../..	125	13	..	..
14	Central African Rep.	310	−0.5	12.6	../..	4.9/16.9/9.3	89	12	4.8	2.9
15	Chad	80	..	7.8	30/56	../../..	60	12	3.9	0.4
16	Ethiopia	140	0.7	4.0	60x/65x	../../..	184	4	11.4	9.5
17	Guinea-Bissau	170	..	7.1	../..	../../..	67	45	..	..
18	Mauritania	470	−0.2	8.7	../..	../../..	173	24	3.1	11.8
19	Niger	310	(.)	12.1	../35x	4.1/18.0/3.8	252	13	3.8	..
20	Senegal	490	(.)	7.9	../..	4.3/21.3/15.6	279	11	2.7	..
21	Somalia	290	0.9	12.6	40/70	../../..	382	31	2.1	7.2
22	Yemen, Dem.	470	6.4	..	../20	../../..	136	15	(.)	6.2
23	Bangladesh	140	1.6	14.9	86/86	../../..	1,293	10	..	8.3
24	Bolivia	570	0.8	25.9	../..	7.2/24.4/22.7	148	4	11.3	28.2
25	Congo	1,180	3.2	10.8	../..	../../..	93	5	..	22.6
26	Cameroon, U. Rep. of	890	3.7	10.7	15/40	2.7/7.5/5.1	210	3	3.1	15.6
27	India	260	1.4	8.4	40/51	1.8/1.9/20.4	1,562	1	20.9	7.1
28	Ivory Coast	950	1.1	12.4	30*/26*	3.9/16.3/3.9	136	1	6.8	36.9
29	Lao, P.D.R.	80x	..	..	../..	../../..	37	13	..	..
30	Nigeria	860	1.5	14.4	../..	../../..	35	(.)	4.2	9.5
31	Oman	6,090	1.7	..	../..	3.0/5.3/50.8	128	2	..	2.2
32	Pakistan	380	2.3	12.7	32/29	1.6/3.1/28.5	747	3	..	9.2
33	Sudan	440	2.6	15.2	../85x	1.4/9.8/13.2	702	9	10.7	7.5
34	Algeria	2,350	2.8	13.9	20/..	../../..	250	1	3.2	24.6
35	Egypt	690	5.6	11.9	21/25	../../..	1,433	5	28.7	20.2
36	Haiti	300	1.8	9.2	55/78	../../..	128	8	5.8	5.1
37	Lesotho	510	6.6	11.4	50/55	../../..	89	12	..	2.0
38	Liberia	490	−0.8	8.5	23/..	7.6/16.0/11.3	109	11	..	5.1
39	Mozambique	230x	−5.7	..	../..	../../..	177	6x	..	..
40	Rwanda	260	1.8	13.4	30/90x	4.5/18.8/13.1	145	11	1.3	3.2
41	Togo	340	0.4	8.8	42/..	../../..	77	7	2.9	..
42	Turkey	1,370	2.4	34.4	../..	2.1/16.8/15.2	623	1	16.3	19.6
43	Zaire	190	−2.9	35.3	../80x	../../..	330	5	4.4	..
	High IMR countries (60–100) Median	900	1.9	11.5	23/45	6.5/13.0/11.8	7,700	4	6.4	16.2
44	Burma	190	2.7	9.7	40/40	6.1/10.1/21.7	316	5	15.8	22.0
45	Ghana	360	−3.3	39.5	../..	7.0/22.0/3.7	143	3	5.0	6.8
46	Iran, Islamic Rep. of	2,160x	..	..	../..	5.4/15.9/11.7	3	..	12.2	..
47	Morocco	870	2.5	8.3	28/45	3.0/16.5/16.2	514	3	7.7	36.8
48	Papua New Guinea	820	−0.1	8.1	10/75	9.1/17.7/4.0	311	12	..	10.2
49	Peru	1,310	(.)	37.0	49/..	5.3/11.3/13.8	184	1	11.6	36.7
50	Saudi Arabia	16,000	7.5	22.5	../..	../../..	..	..	..	..
51	Tanzania, U. Rep. of	280	0.6	11.9	10/60	5.5/12.1/11.2	676	13	4.9	5.1
52	Zambia	640	−2.5	8.7	25/..	6.1/11.9/..	237	7	5.9	17.4
53	Indonesia	580	4.8	19.9	28/51	2.5/7.9/12.7	901	1	6.9	8.3
54	Libyan Arab Jamahiriya	8,510	−1.8	16.0	../..	../../..	12	(.)	..	..
55	Nicaragua	920	..	14.3	21/19	14.6/11.6/11.0	118	5	11.0	..
56	South Africa	2,670	0.8	12.8	../..	../../..	..	..	..	..
57	Tunisia	1,390	4.8	8.7	20/15	7.7/15.3/8.3	209	2	17.5	15.1
58	Uganda	230	−4.7	47.4	../..	4.0/10.9/34.5	131	5	2.7	22.3
59	Viet Nam	170x	..	..	../..	../../..	126	1x	..	..
60	Botswana	900	6.5	11.5	40/55	../../..	101	11	..	..
61	Ecuador	1,350	4.9	14.5	40/65	7.9/30.1/11.8	50	(.)	9.1	30.8
62	Honduras	660	0.5	8.7	14/55	../../..	156	7	2.8	18.8
63	Kenya	390	1.9	10.1	10/55	7.8/20.6/10.7	482	7	5.4	20.3
64	Brazil	2,240	4.4	42.1	../..	7.4/3.8/3.4	206	(.)	12.5	42.1

		GNP per capita (US $) 1982	GNP per capita average annual growth rate (%) 1970-1982	Rate of inflation (%) 1970-1982	% of population below absolute poverty level 1977-1981 urban/rural	% of central gov't. expenditure allocated to health/education/ defence 1981	ODA inflow (million US $) 1982	ODA as % of recipient GNP 1981	Debt service as a % of exports of goods and services 1970	1982
65	El Salvador	700	−0.6	10.8	20/32	8.4/17.9/16.8	219	7	3.6	4.6
66	Guatemala	1,130	2.0	10.1	21/25	../../..	64	1	7.4	6.6
67	Iraq	3,020ˣ			../40ˣ	../../..	6	(.)ˣ	2.2	
68	Madagascar	320	−2.2	11.5	50/50	../../..	243	8	3.5	..
69	Zimbabwe	850	0.5	8.4	../..	6.9/19.5/19.9	214	3	..	9.2
70	Dominican Rep.	1,330	2.8	8.8	45/43	9.7/13.9/8.9	136	2	4.1	18.7
71	Jordan	1,690	6.9	9.6	14/17	3.8/7.6/25.3	804	21	3.6	6.1
72	Syrian Arab Rep.	1,680	5.7	12.2	../..	1.1/7.1/37.7	1,138	8	10.8	14.2
	Middle IMR countries (26-50) Median	1,885	3.2	15.9	../..	../../..	2,684	..	9.3	13.4
73	Colombia	1,460	3.5	22.7	34/..	../../..	94	(.)	11.9	17.5
74	Mexico	2,270	3.0	20.9	../..	1.9/18.2/2.5	139	(.)	23.6	29.5
75	Mongolia	780ˣ			../..	../../..				
76	Philippines	820	3.3	12.8	32/41	5.0/14.2/14.2	324	1	7.2	12.8
77	Thailand	790	4.1	9.7	15/34	4.3/19.3/20.6	352	1	3.4	8.4
78	Lebanon	..			../..	../../..	208			
79	United Arab Emirates	23,770	−0.7		../..	7.9/11.7/47.5	5	(.)		
80	Paraguay	1,610	6.0	12.7	19/50	4.5/11.8/13.2	85	2	11.9	10.3
81	Albania	840ˣ			../..	../../..				
82	Chile	2,210	−0.2	44.3	../..	6.4/14.4/12.0	−9	−(.)	18.9	18.8
83	China	310	4.2		../..	3.5/7.2/1.7	510ˣ	(.)ˣ		
84	Sri Lanka	320	3.2	13.3	../..	7.3/18.3/3.9	417	9	10.3	8.3
85	Venezuela	4,140	0.9	12.4	../..	7.3/18.3/3.9	11	(.)	2.9	15.6
86	Uruguay	2,650	2.4	59.3	../..	3.8/7.7/12.9	4	(.)	21.6	13.4
87	Guyana	670	..	9.9	../..	../../..	38	7		
88	Argentina	2,520	−0.3	36.0	../..	1.4/7.3/11.4	27	(.)	21.5	24.5
89	Korea, Dem. Rep.	1,130ˣ			../..	../../..				
90	Mauritius	1,240	3.9	15.0	12/12	../../..	48	4		
91	Kuwait	19,870	2.1	15.6	../..	4.9/9.0/9.8	6	(.)		
92	Korea, Rep. of	1,910	6.4	19.3	18/11	1.3/17.9/35.2	34	(.)	19.4	13.1
93	Yugoslavia	2,800	4.6	20.0	../..	../../50.4	−8	−(.)	8.4	4.6
94	Malaysia	1,860	5.1	7.2	13/38	4.4/15.9/15.1	123	(.)	3.6	5.1
95	Trinidad and Tobago	6,840	4.2	17.8	../39	5.9/11.2/2.0	6	(.)	4.4	2.9
96	Jamaica	1,330	−2.7	16.2	../80	../../..	181	7	2.5	16.8
97	Romania	2,560			../..	../../..				
98	Panama	2,120	2.3	7.5	21/30	13.2/12.8/..	41	1	7.7	13.8
99	Portugal	2,450	2.8	17.4	../..	../../..	48	(.)	..	20.0
	Low IMR countries (25 and less) Median	7,920	2.0	9.9	../..	../../..				
100	USSR	4,550ˣ			../..	../../..				
101	Costa Rica	1,430	1.5	18.4	../..	29.7/23.7/2.6	76	2	10.0	12.5
102	Cuba	1,410ˣ			../..	../../..	16	(.)ˣ		
103	Hungary	2,270	6.7	3.2	../..	../../..				17.0
104	Poland	3,900ˣ			../..	../../..				
105	Bulgaria	4,150ˣ			../..	../../..				
106	Czechoslovakia	5,820ˣ			../..	../../..				
107	Israel	5,090	0.5	52.3	../..	3.5/9.4/39.8	857	4	2.7	20.8
108	Greece	4,290	2.9	15.4	../..	../../..	11	(.)	7.1	13.3
109	Austria	9,880	3.1	6.1	../..	12.9/9.5/2.9				
110	Italy	6,840	2.2	16.0	../..	11.0/9.2/3.4				
111	Belgium	10,760	2.4	7.1	../..	1.7/14.8/5.5				
112	German Dem. Rep.	7,180ˣ			../..	../../..				
113	Hong Kong	5,340	7.3	8.6	../..	../../..	4	(.)	(.)	(.)
114	New Zealand	7,920	0.6	13.1	../..	14.4/13.5/5.4				
115	Germany, Fed. Rep. of	12,460	2.4	4.9	../..	18.5/0.8/9.2				
116	Ireland	5,150	1.7	14.3	../..	../../..				
117	Singapore	5,910	6.7	5.4	../..	7.2/19.1/21.7	20	(.)	0.6	0.8
118	United Kingdom	9,660	1.5	14.2	../..	../../..				
119	USA	13,160	1.8	7.3	../..	10.7/2.5/21.8				
120	Australia	11,140	1.2	11.4	../..	10.1/8.2/9.6				
121	Spain	5,430	2.0	16.0	../..	0.7/7.9/4.4				
122	Canada	11,320	2.0	9.3	../..	6.2/3.5/7.8				
123	France	11,680	2.6	10.1	../..	15.0/8.7/7.5				
124	Denmark	12,470	1.5	9.9	../..	../../..				
125	Netherlands	10,930	1.5	7.4	../..	11.8/12.6/5.6				
126	Norway	14,280	3.5	9.0	../..	../../..				
127	Switzerland	17,010	0.8	4.8	../..	12.7/3.3/10.6				
128	Finland	10,870	2.6	11.7	../..	11.2/14.5/5.1				
129	Japan	10,080	3.5	6.9	../..	../../..				
130	Sweden	14,040	1.3	9.9	../..	2.0/10.5/7.3				

TABLE 7: BASIC INDICATORS ON LESS POPULOUS COUNTRIES

	Infant mortality rate aged 0-1 1982	Infant mortality rate aged 0-1 1960	Total population (millions) 1982	Annual no. of births/infant and child deaths (0-4) (thousands) 1982	GNP per capita US $ 1982	Life expectancy at birth (years) 1982	% adults literate male/female 1980	% of age group enrolled in primary school male/female 1980-1982
Gambia	190	220	0.6	../..	360	35	29/12	71/41
Equatorial Guinea	140	190	0.4	../..	180ˣ	44	../..	../..
Djibouti	130*		0.3*	../..	480*	50	../..	56*/44*
Swaziland	130	150	0.6	../..	940	48	64/58	111/111
Gabon	110	160	1.1	../..	4,000	49	63/44	../..
Comoros	90	140	0.1	../..	340	50	../..	120/85
Cape Verde	80	120	0.3	../1.1*	350	57	54/34	../..
Maldives	80*	..	0.2*	../0.7*	410*	47	82ˣ/82ˣ	../..
Sao Tome and Principe	50*	..	0.1*	../..	370	62	76ʸ/50ʸ	../..
Qatar	46	140	0.3	../..	21,880	70	../..	116/110
Bahrain	38	130	0.4	../0.5*	9280	68	75*/52*	108/95
Belize	38*	..	0.1*	../..	1,080	..	92*/92*	../..
Saint Lucia	35*	..	0.1	../..	720	..	../..	../..
Samoa	35*	..	0.2*	../..	300*	65	../..	../..
Suriname	32	70	0.4	../..	3,030ˣ	69	92/93	103ˣ/96ˣ
Antigua and Barbuda	30*	..	0.1	../..	1,740	..	90*/88*	../..
Fiji	29	70	0.7	../..	1,950	72	88/77	111/109
Barbados	24	70	0.3	../..	2,900	71	98/98	112/108
Seychelles	19*	58*	0.1*	../(.)*	2,220*	66	../..	../..
Cyprus	17	30	0.6	../..	3,840	74	94/85	../..
Malta	14	37	0.4	../..	3800	72	83/80	108/108
Brunei	13	..	0.2	../..	17,380ˣ	..	../..	../..
Luxembourg	12	33	0.4	../..	14,340	73	../..	95/95
Iceland	7	17	0.2	../..	12,150	77	../..	../..
Bahamas	..	..	0.2	../..	3,830	69	../..	../..
Dominica	..	..	0.1	../..	710	58	../..	../..
Grenada	..	..	0.1	../..	760	69	../..	../..
Saint Kitts	..	..	0.1	../..	750	..	../..	../..
Saint Vincent	..	..	0.1	../..	620	..	../..	../..
Solomon Islands	..	..	0.2	../..	660	..	../..	../..
Vanuatu	..	..	0.1	../..	350ˣ	..	../..	../..

General Note on the Data

The data provided in these tables are accompanied by definitions, sources, and explanations of signs and individual footnotes where the definition of the figure is different from the general definition being used. Tables derived from so many sources – nine major sources are listed in the explanatory material – will inevitably cover a wide range of reliability. Official government data have been used wherever possible. In the many cases where there are no reliable official figures, estimates made by the relevant United Nations agency have been used. Where such internationally standardized estimates do not exist, the tables draw on data from relevant UNICEF field offices. All such UNICEF field office sources are marked with * or Y.

The figures for infant mortality rates, life expectancy, crude birth rate, crude death rate, etc. are part of the regular work on estimates and projections undertaken by the United Nations Population Division. These and other international estimates are revised periodically which explains why some of the data differ from those found in earlier UNICEF publications. In the case of GNP per capita and ODA, the data are the result of a continuous process of revising and updating by the World Bank and OECD respectively.

Where possible only comprehensive or sample national data have been used although, as in the table on 'Wasting', there are certain exceptions. Where the figures refer to only a part of the country, this is indicated in a footnote.

In ranking countries by the main indicator used in these tables – the estimate of the infant mortality rate for 1982 – all rates have been rounded to the nearest 10 in the case of countries with a rate of 50 or more. Only in countries with rates below 50, where there is usually a fairly comprehensive registration system, has the figure been rounded to the nearest unit.

Signs and explanations

Unless otherwise stated, the summary measures for the four IMR groups of countries are the median values for each group. The median is the middle value of a data set arranged in order of magnitude.

- ..   Data not available
- *   UNICEF field office source
- (.)   Less than half the unit shown
- X   See footnote at the end of the tables
- Y   UNICEF field office source; see footnote at end of the tables

Most of the IMR figures are estimates prepared by the UN Population Division on an internationally comparable basis using various sources. In some cases, these estimates may differ from national figures.

Footnotes to Tables

Table 1: Basic Indicators

Country	Indicator	Year/Note
Afghanistan:	GNP per capita	1979
Angola:	GNP per capita	1980
Bhutan:	GNP per capita	1981
Bhutan:	Primary enrolment	1979
Mali:	Primary enrolment	1978
India:	Primary enrolment	1979
Lao People's Dem. Rep.:	GNP per capita	1981
Lesotho:	Primary enrolment	1979
Mozambique:	GNP per capita	1980
Zaire:	Primary enrolment	1978
Ghana:	Primary enrolment	1979
Iran:	GNP per capita	1977
Indonesia:	Adult literacy	Age 10 and over
Viet Nam:	GNP per capita	1978
Brazil:	Primary enrolment	1979
Iraq:	GNP per capita	1980
Madagascar:	Primary enrolment	1978
Mongolia:	GNP per capita	1979
Paraguay:	Primary enrolment	1979
Albania:	GNP per capita	1979
Korea Dem. Rep.:	GNP per capita	1979
Trinidad and Tobago:	Primary enrolment	1979
Portugal:	Primary enrolment	1978
USSR:	GNP per capita	1980
Cuba:	GNP per capita	1979
Poland:	GNP per capita	1980
Bulgaria:	GNP per capita	1980
Czechoslovakia:	GNP per capita	1980
Greece:	Primary enrolment	1979
Italy:	Primary enrolment	1979
German Dem. Rep.:	GNP per capita	1980

Table 2: Nutrition

Country	Indicator	Year/Note
Burundi	Wasting	1974
Somalia	Malnutrition	Age 0–6 years
Turkey	Malnutrition	Age 0–24 months
Morocco	Malnutrition	1971
Papua New Guinea	Malnutrition	Age unspecified
Peru	Malnutrition	1972
Tunisia	Wasting	1974
Botswana	Malnutrition	Age 0–5 years
Brazil	Wasting	1974
Colombia	Malnutrition	Age 0–5 years
Philippines	Malnutrition	Age 0–6 years
Chile	Malnutrition	Age 0–5 years
Malaysia	Breast-feeding	1974
Panama	Malnutrition	Age unspecified
Hong Kong	Breast-feeding	1974
Japan	Breast-feeding	1971
Sweden	Breast-feeding	Fully breast-feeding

Table 3: Health

Country	Indicator	Year/Note
Cameroon, U. Rep. of	DPT, polio, measles	1979
Oman	Children immunized	Age 12–23 months
Haiti	Children immunized	Age 0–4 years
Lesotho	Children immunized	Age 12–23 months
Mozambique	Children immunized	Age 12–23 months
Rwanda	Children immunized	Age 12–23 months
Zambia	Children immunized	Age 12–23 months
Indonesia	DPT	Two doses
Botswana	Children immunized	Age 12–23 months
El Salvador	DPT, polio	Two doses
Guatemala	DPT, polio	Two doses
Zimbabwe	Children immunized	Age 1–4 years
Philippines	DPT	Two doses
Thailand	DPT	Two doses
Chile	Polio	Two doses
Uruguay	Polio	Two doses
Yugoslavia	Measles	Age 1–5 years
Portugal	Measles	Age 1–5 years
USSR	Measles	Age 1–5 years
Cuba	Polio	Two doses
Hungary	Measles	Age 1–5
Czechoslovakia	Measles	Age 1–5
Austria	Measles	Age 1–5
New Zealand	Measles	Age 1–5
Germany, Fed. Rep. of	Measles	Age 1–5
Singapore	Measles	Age 1–5 years
United Kingdom	Measles	Age 1–5
USA	Measles	Age 1–5
Netherlands	Measles	Age 1–5
Finland	Measles	Age 1–5
Japan	Measles	Age 1–5
Sweden	DPT	DT only
Sweden	Measles	Age 1–5 years

Table 4:
Education

Bhutan	Enrolment ratios 1980–82	1979
Mali	Enrolment ratios 1980–82	1978
Niger	Secondary enrolment ratio	1978
Bolivia	Completing primary level	1976
Cameroon	Net enrolment ratio	1979
India	Primary enrolment ratio 1980–82	1979
Lesotho	Enrolment ratios 1980–82	1979
Zaire	Enrolment ratios 1980–82	1978
Ghana	Enrolment ratios 1980–82	1979
Zambia	Net enrolment ratio	1979
Indonesia	Adult literacy 1980	Age 10 and over
Ecuador	Net enrolment ratio	1978
Kenya	Net enrolment ratio	1978
Brazil	Primary enrolment ratio 1980–82	1979
Brazil	Secondary enrolment ratio	1978
Madagascar	Enrolment ratios 1980–82	1978
Paraguay	Enrolment ratios 1980–82	1979
Trinidad and Tobago	Enrolment ratios 1980–82	1979
Portugal	Primary enrolment ratio 1980–82	1978
Portugal	Completing primary level	1974
Bulgaria	Completing primary level	1974
Greece	Enrolment ratios 1980–82	1979
Italy	Enrolment ratios 1980–82	1979

Table 5:
Demographic Indicators

There are no footnotes to Table 5

Table 6:
Economic Indicators

Afghanistan	GNP per capita	1979
Afghanistan	ODA as % of GNP	1979 GNP
Angola	GNP per capita	1980
Angola	ODA as % of GNP	1980 GNP
Bhutan	GNP per capita	1981
Mali	Poverty level	1975
Ethiopia	Poverty level	1976
Niger	Poverty level	1975
Lao People's Dem. Rep.	GNP per capita	1981
Sudan	Poverty level	1975
Mozambique	GNP per capita	1980
Mozambique	ODA as % of GNP	1980 GNP
Rwanda	Poverty level	1975
Zaire	Poverty level	1975
Iran, Islamic Rep. of	GNP per capita	1977
Viet Nam	GNP per capita	1978
Viet Nam	ODA as % of GNP	1978 GNP
Iraq	GNP per capita	1980
Iraq	Poverty level	1975
Iraq	ODA as % of GNP	1980 GNP
Mongolia	GNP per capita	1979
Albania	GNP per capita	1979
China	ODA	Excludes Taiwan
Korea, Dem. Rep.	GNP per capita	1979
USSR	GNP per capita	1980
Cuba	GNP per capita	1979
Cuba	ODA as % of GNP	1979 GNP
Poland	GNP per capita	1980
Bulgaria	GNP per capita	1980
Czechoslovakia	GNP per capita	1980
German Dem. Rep.	GNP per capita	1980

Table 7:
Basic Statistics on less populous countries

Brunei	GNP per capita	1981
Equatorial Guinea	GNP per capita	1981
Djibouti	GNP per capita	1981
Maldives	Adult literacy	1977
Sao Tome and Principe	Adult literacy	10 years and over
Suriname	GNP per capita	1981
Suriname	Primary enrolment ratio	1979
Vanuatu	GNP per capita	1981

Definitions

Infant Mortality Rate: annual number of deaths of infants under one year of age per 1,000 live births.

Child Death Rate: annual number of deaths of children aged 1–4 years inclusive, per 1,000 population in the same age group.

Life Expectancy at Birth the number of years newborn children would live if subject to the mortality risks prevailing for the cross-section of population at the time of their birth.

Crude Death Rate: annual number of deaths per 1,000 population.

Crude Birth Rate: annual number of births per 1,000 population

Total Fertility Rate: the number of children that would be born per woman, if she were to live to the end of her childbearing years and bear children at each age in accord with prevailing age-specific fertility rates.

Low Birth Weight: 2,500 grammes or less

Breast-feeding: either wholly or partly breast-feeding

Prevalence of Wasting (acute malnutrition): the percentage of children with greater than minus two Standard Deviations from the 50th percentile of the weight for age reference population i.e. roughly less than 77% of the median weight for age of the US National Centre for Health Statistics reference population.

DPT: Diphtheria, Pertussis (whooping cough) and Tetanus.

Adult Literacy Rate: percentage of persons aged 15 and over who can read and write.

GNP: Gross National Product

Absolute Poverty Level: that income level below which a minimum nutritionally adequate diet plus essential non-food requirements is not affordable.

ODA: Official Development Assistance.

Income Share: the percentage of private income received by the highest 20 per cent and lowest 40 per cent of households

Child Malnutrition: mild or moderate: between 60 per cent and 80 per cent of the desirable weight-for-age; severe: less than 60 per cent of the desirable weight-for-age

Primary and Secondary Enrolment Ratios: the *gross* enrolment ratio is the total number of children enrolled in a schooling level – whether or not they belong in the relevant age group for that level – expressed as a percentage of the total number of children in the relevant age group for that level.

The *net* enrolment ratio is the total number of children enrolled in a schooling level who belong in the relevant age group, expressed as a percentage of the total number of children in that age group.

Children Completing Primary School: percentage of the children entering the first grade of primary school who successfully complete that level in due course

Main Sources

Infant Mortality:	United Nations Population Division and United Nations Statistical Office	**Wasting (acute malnutrition)**	World Health Organization (WHO)
Total Population:	United Nations Statistical Office and United Nations Population Division	**Food Production and Calorie Intake**	Food and Agriculture Organization (FAO) and World Bank
Child Population Age 0–4:	United Nations Population Division	**Access to Drinking Water:**	World Health Organization (WHO)
Annual Number of Births:	United Nations Population Division	**Child Death Rate:**	World Bank
Annual Number of Infant and Child Deaths:	United Nations Population Division and World Bank	**Crude Death and Birth Rates:**	World Bank
GNP per Capita:	World Bank	**Population Growth Rate:**	United Nations Population Division
Life Expectancy:	United Nations Population Division	**Total Fertility Rate:**	United Nations Population Division
Adult Literacy:	United Nations Educational, Scientific and Cultural Organization (UNESCO)	**Urban Population:**	United Nations Population Division
School Enrolment and Completion:	United Nations Educational, Scientific and Cultural Organization (UNESCO)	**Rate of Inflation:**	World Bank
Share of Household Income:	World Bank	**Absolute Poverty Level:**	World Bank
Immunization:	World Health Organization (WHO)	**Official Development Assistance (ODA)**	Organisation for Economic Co-operation and Development (OECD)
Low Birth Weight	World Health Organization (WHO)	**Expenditure on Health, Education and Defence:**	World Bank
Breast-feeding:	World Health Organization (WHO) and World Fertility Survey	**Debt Service:**	World Bank
Child Malnutrition:	UNICEF Field Offices		

Variations in infant mortality rate (IMR) within countries

Like the average GNP per capita, the average IMR for a country can give a misleading picture of the situation. In slums and poorer rural areas, the prevailing IMR is usually considerably above the national average. Conversely the IMR is usually much lower among those with higher levels of education or income. Statistics on the differences in IMR within countries are therefore useful supplements to the national averages.

The attached table presents two sets of measures of IMR variations within countries.

Measure A, columns 2 to 4, shows the estimated percentage of births per 1,000 population occurring in areas where the IMR is more than 25% above, or 25% below, the national average. This measure can be compared to measures of income distribution (or relative poverty), showing the percentage of a country's population receiving incomes some fixed percentage above or below the national average.

Measure B, columns 5 to 8, shows the estimated percentage of the country's population living in areas where the IMR is 150 per 1,000 and over, 100 to 149, 50 to 99, and less than 50. This measure can be compared to measures of absolute poverty, showing the percentage of a country's population living below various poverty lines of increasing severity.

The margin of error involved in the estimates themselves and in the estimating procedures varies widely from country to country, particularly in the case of the second measure, making it important not to draw conclusions from small differences in the figures. But, sensibly used, the data can be an important complement to data showing national IMR averages.

It is interesting to note in the case of the first measure that the degree of regional inequality does not depend on the overall mortality level. Thus Jamaica and Venezuela, with low average mortality levels, show a much greater degree of inequality than is found for example in Indonesia, Morocco or North Sudan where overall mortality levels are much higher. Other recent studies show the role of various social and economic factors in maintaining these differentials. Above all they have clearly established that the more educated the mother, the greater the probability that the child will survive, and this applies to both high and low infant mortality countries. In fact, the variation in child mortality by the mother's education is independent of the overall level of mortality.

Next year's *State of the World's Children* report will look in more detail at this subject of IMR variations within countries. In the meantime, it is hoped that countries will be encouraged to prepare more detailed estimates of internal IMR variations – as well as to monitor the progress in its reduction, especially in the relatively higher IMR states or areas.

IMR Internal differentials by country 1970-1980

In descending order of 1982 national IMR as estimated by the UN Population Division

| | Percentage of births[1] in areas with an IMR more than 25% above or below the national average ||| Percentage of population[2] in areas with an IMR of ||||
Country	More than 25% above	More than 25% below	Total	150 and over	100-149	50-99	Less than 50
Sierra Leone	—	—	—	100	0	0	0
Yemen	—	—	—	57	43	0	0
Benin	25	26	51	25	49	26	0
Nepal	—	—	—	50	50	0	0
Senegal	21	17	38	21	50	29	0
Mauritania	20	15	35	—	—	—	—
Swaziland	—	—	—	27	73	0	0
Bolivia	—	—	—	45	55	0	0
India	—	—	—	23	54	19	4
Ivory Coast	—	—	—	20	63	17	0
Sudan (North)	0	13	13	0	0	100	0
Cameroon, U. Rep. of	5	14	19	0	58	42	0
Egypt	—	—	—	0	67	33	0
Lesotho	—	—	—	0	100	0	0
Turkey	—	—	—	41	59	0	0
Haiti	—	—	—	21	60	19	0
Morocco	12	0	12	0	43	57	0
Ghana	27	10	37	0	27	63	10
Peru	—	—	—	40	27	33	0
Indonesia	0	6	6	0	62	38	0
Tunisia	15	14	29	0	15	85	0
Nicaragua	—	—	—	0	14	86	0
Kenya	30	36	66	0	44	56	0
Ecuador	—	—	—	0	14	86	0
El Salvador	—	—	—	0	0	58	42
Guatemala	—	—	—	0	5	78	17
Dominican Rep.	—	—	—	0	32	68	0
Jordan	—	—	—	0	0	100	0
Syrian Arab Rep.	0	13	13	0	0	87	13
Colombia	—	—	—	0	0	91	9
Mexico	0	2	2	0	0	100	0
Philippines	—	—	—	0	0	90	10
Thailand	—	—	—	0	0	94	6
Chile	—	—	—	0	0	11	89
Sri Lanka	0	0	0	0	0	100	0
Venezuela	21	24	45	0	0	44	56
Argentina	—	—	—	0	0	6	94
Korea, Rep. of	0	0	0	0	0	36	64
Mauritius	—	—	—	0	0	17	83
Fiji	—	—	—	0	0	42	58
Malaysia (Peninsula)	—	—	—	0	0	0	100
Jamaica	25	34	59	0	0	25	75
Panama	—	—	—	0	0	9	91
Costa Rica	—	—	—	0	0	0	100
Cuba	—	—	—	0	0	0	100

[1] Source: World Fertility Surveys.
[2] Source: Population censuses, sample registration data and World Fertility Surveys.

UNICEF Headquarters
866 UN Plaza, New York 10017, USA

UNICEF, Information Division
Palais des Nations, CH 1211, Geneva 10, Switzerland

UNICEF Regional Office for East Africa
P.O. Box 44145, Nairobi, Kenya

UNICEF Regional Office for West Africa
 P.O. Box 443, Abidjan 04, Ivory Coast

UNICEF Regional Office for the Americas
Apartado Aereo 75 55, Bogota, Colombia

UNICEF Regional Office for East Asia and Pakistan
P.O. Box 2-154, Bangkok 10200, Thailand

UNICEF Regional Office for the Middle East and North Africa
c/o UNDP, P.O. Box 35286, Amman, Jordan

UNICEF Regional Office for South Central Asia
73 Lodi Estate, New Delhi 110003, India

UNICEF Office for Australia and New Zealand
G.P.O Box 4045, Sydney NSW 2001, Australia

UNICEF Office for Tokyo, c/o United Nations
Information Centre, 22nd Floor, Shin Aoyama Building Nishikan
1-1, Minami—Aoyama 1-Chome, Minato-ku Tokyo 107, Japan

WORLD KITCHEN

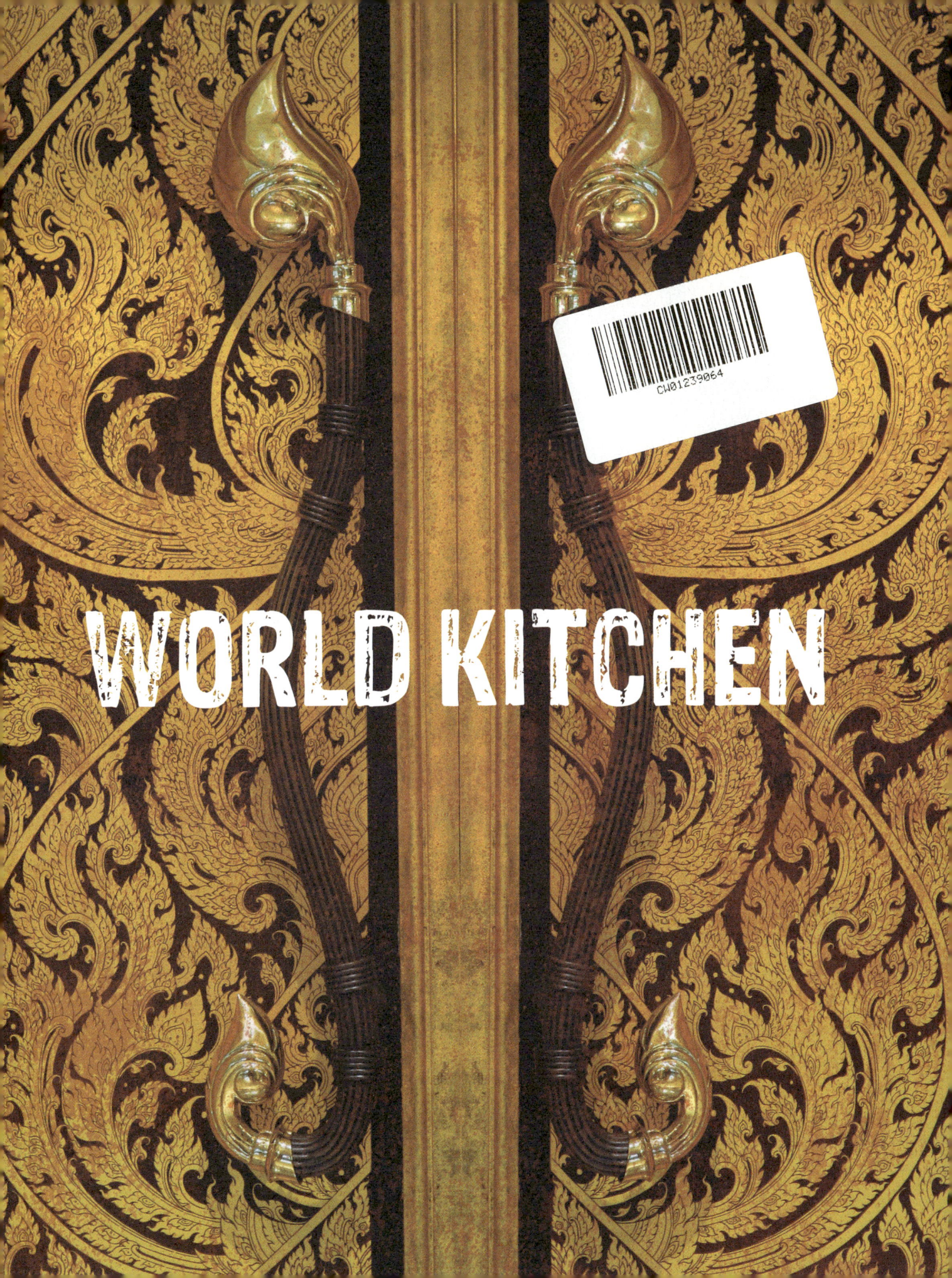

For Mum, who always said, 'Yes, darling, you can help me cook.'
Those were magical words for a child to hear.

Nici Wickes

WORLD KITCHEN
BRINGING GREAT CHICKEN RECIPES BACK HOME TO NEW ZEALAND

Food photography by Shaun Cato-Symonds

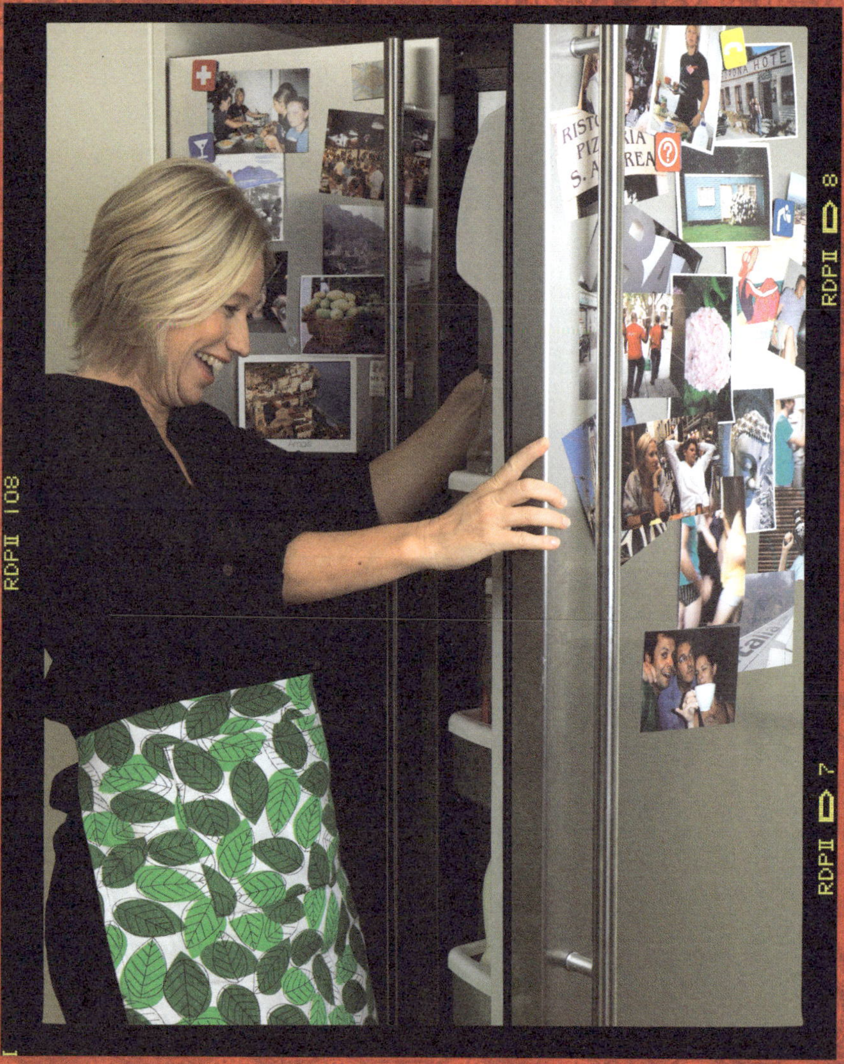
RDPII 108
RDPII 8
RDPII 7

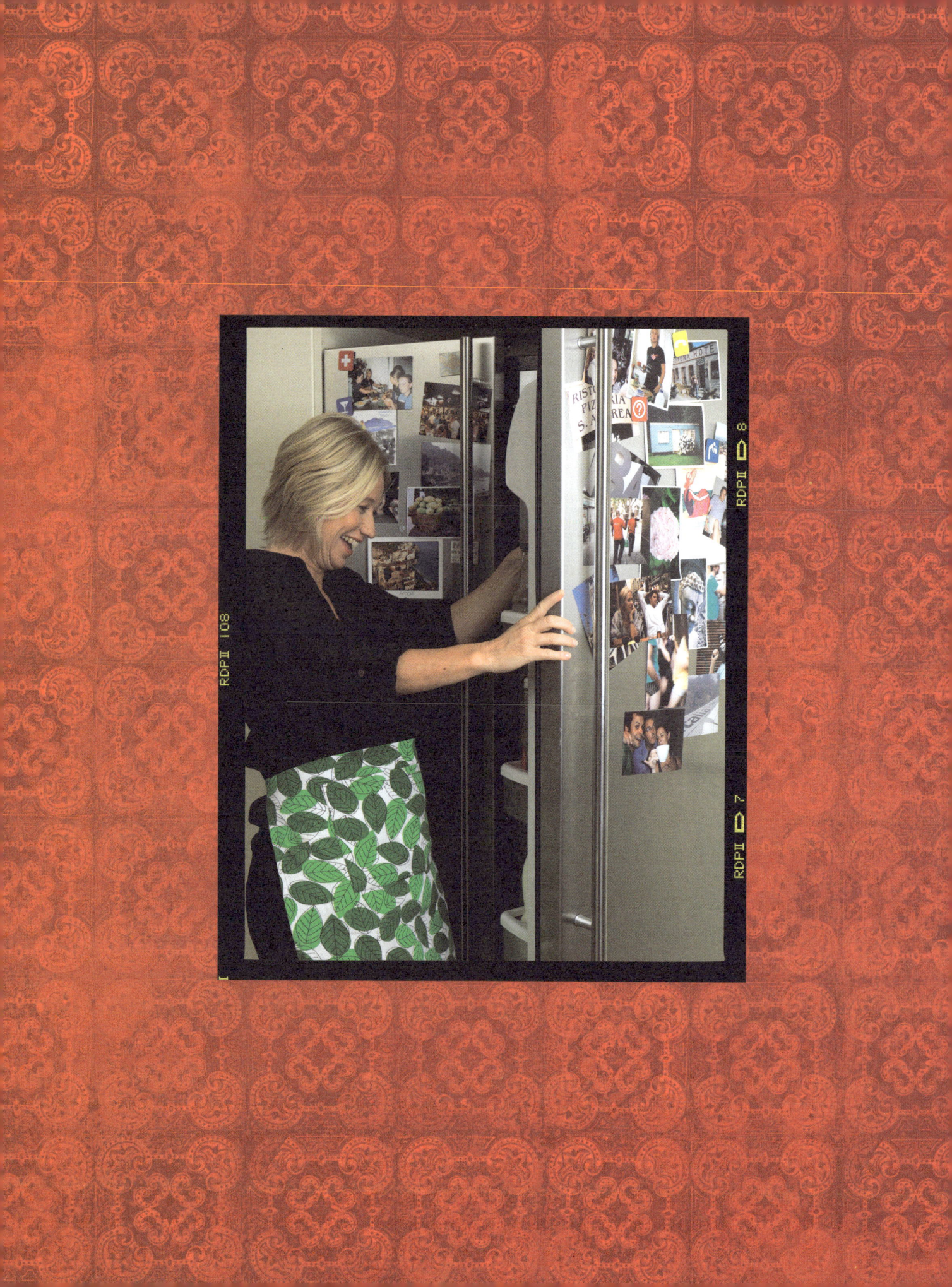

06 **FOREWORD**
07 **INTRODUCTION**
08 **SPAIN** MOREISH BITES IN BARCELONA
32 **ITALY** FRESH AND FLAVOURFUL IN TUSCANY AND AMALFI
56 **FRANCE** INDULGING IN DIJON AND LYON
78 **THAILAND** SPICING IT UP IN BANGKOK AND KO CHANG
102 **VIETNAM** STREET-FOOD HEAVEN IN HANOI
122 **INDONESIA** TASTY FAVOURITES FROM BALI
140 **GLOSSARY**
142 **INDEX**
144 **ACKNOWLEDGEMENTS**

FOREWORD

Chicken is one of the most popular meats around the world as it is so versatile for cooking and simply tastes great. As a consequence, chicken plays a starring role in some of the most amazingly delicious dishes from almost every country's traditional cuisine; from fragrant curries to spicy paellas to hearty casseroles.

World Kitchen is all about finding the very best chicken recipes from around the world and celebrating the unique flavours, textures, aromas and presentation.

We at Tegel Foods Ltd are excited to have supported Nici Wickes in her quest to travel the world's culinary capitals of Europe and Asia, as she has sought out this recipe treasure trove for the *World Kitchen* television series.

Nici is a passionate foodie, driven and creative. She is also a great teacher and has adapted this collection of international recipes to suit the ingredients we can easily source in New Zealand and simplified them to make them easier for us to recreate in our own kitchens. Tegel has loved working with Nici as we share her passion for good food and for helping people to make new and exciting dishes with chicken.

We hope you love this book as much as we do and that you have a go at cooking something new. The recipes are inspiring and innovative and Nici is there all the way through to guide you with simple steps. You'll be producing exotic and utterly delicious dishes in no time. Enjoy!

TEGEL FOODS LTD

INTRODUCTION

The recipes in this book are inspired by the chicken dishes that impressed me most on my recent travels through Europe and Asia making the travel and cooking TV show, *World Kitchen*. They evoke wonderful memories of the food I ate in markets, at roadside stalls and food festivals, in Michelin-star restaurants and in the homes of wonderful local people who invited me in to share their food. I've included some non-chicken dishes too just because I couldn't resist sharing a few more of my favourites with you.

All of the recipes in *World Kitchen* are ones that I cook at home. I have intentionally kept them as simple as possible, incorporating accessible ingredients and limiting methods to a few simple steps because I don't like to overcomplicate cooking. My philosophy is that cooking isn't an exact science and dishes don't have to be fancy to be sensational – they just have to be made with passion and enthusiasm! These recipes are easy to follow and forgiving – if you don't have an ingredient, try leaving it out (within reason of course) and seeing what happens. I'm sure that the dish will survive and so will you.

I have always found cooking (and eating!) immensely enjoyable and for that I thank my grandmother and mother who encouraged us kids into the kitchen and didn't mind the mess. We were allowed to experiment and practise what we'd learnt in 'manual' – cooking classes provided at the local high school – until we produced something edible. I can still remember the first complete meal I cooked for our whole family and the warm feeling it gave me to cook for them. Our family still celebrates with food and we love nothing more than to get together to cook and eat as a way of sharing our lives.

I was 21 when I first took off overseas in search of the flavours of the world and I haven't really stopped since. My way of travelling is not to do art galleries and museums. I do food. I experience a place through tasting the local dishes, by watching who and what's cooking and picking up ideas and tips so I can recreate and relive the experience back home. When I return from a trip I don't bore friends and family with photos, I do it with food: 'Here, try this, it's something I had recently in Thailand at this amazing early morning market.'

I hope you will feel genuinely inspired by this book to recreate a little of Bali or Barcelona, Lyon or Bangkok in your own kitchen and that the results will delight you. It's not every day we get to take our taste buds on a tour of the culinary hotspots of the world – but perhaps this book will offer you the very next best thing. Happy cooking!

NICI WICKES

SPAIN
MOREISH BITES IN BARCELONA

'Among the stalls are small tapas bars, their counters sagging under the weight of little plates of tasty treats, stacked high just waiting to be selected.'

For me, a trip to Spain must start in Barcelona. The population of this late-night city knows how to party and how to eat well.

The morning ritual usually starts later than I am used to, but it's worth waiting for. First up is a visit to a local café nestled in one of the small inner-city squares to devour warm churros – long, sugared Spanish doughnuts – served with a small cup of liquid chocolate for dipping. Sheer pleasure! But don't be tempted to repeat the order – you will be sorry. Trust me, I know from experience . . .

From there it's off to La Boqueria – the market smack bang in the middle of the central city where the freshest of produce explodes in bright, colourful bursts. Among the stalls are small tapas bars, their counters sagging under the weight of little plates of tasty treats, stacked high just waiting to be selected. It's such a sociable way to eat – I love it. Order, eat, exchange news, eat some more, talk about the dishes, eat some more . . . and so it goes until it's time for a cortado – a small glass of strong espresso 'cut' with a shot of warm milk. It's enough to keep you going until another of my favourite Spanish traditions – the siesta. Bliss!

And then it's time for dinner. My strategy is to take a walk around the inner-city alleys looking for the tapas bar with the longest queue. That tells me the food must be good. The conversation is lively as I wait my turn to perch on a bar stool. From there, I can watch the chefs work their magic as I eat my way through a continuous parade of small plates of deliciousness.

Back home I love to cook and serve tapas for my friends. It's a lively way of feeding a large group involving lots of exciting little platefuls of flavour. The Spanish really get it right when it comes to informal party food.

St JOSEP LA BOQUERIA

Bodega Cervecería
CALIDAD EN TAPAS
PAN CON TOMATE
BUEN JAMON SERRANO

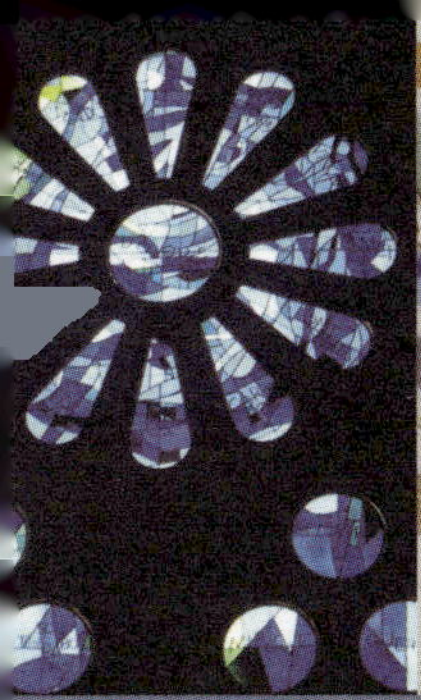
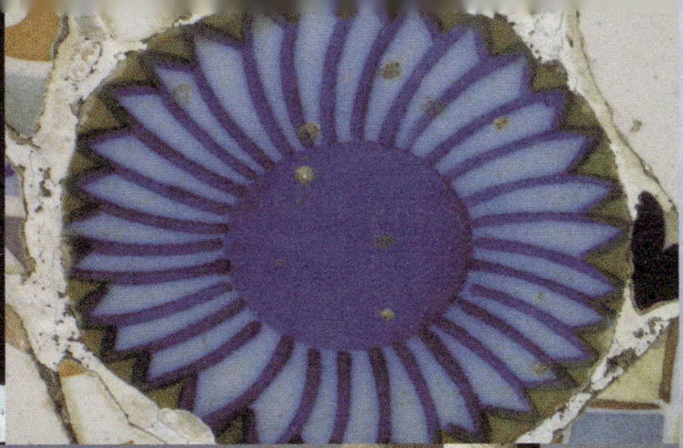
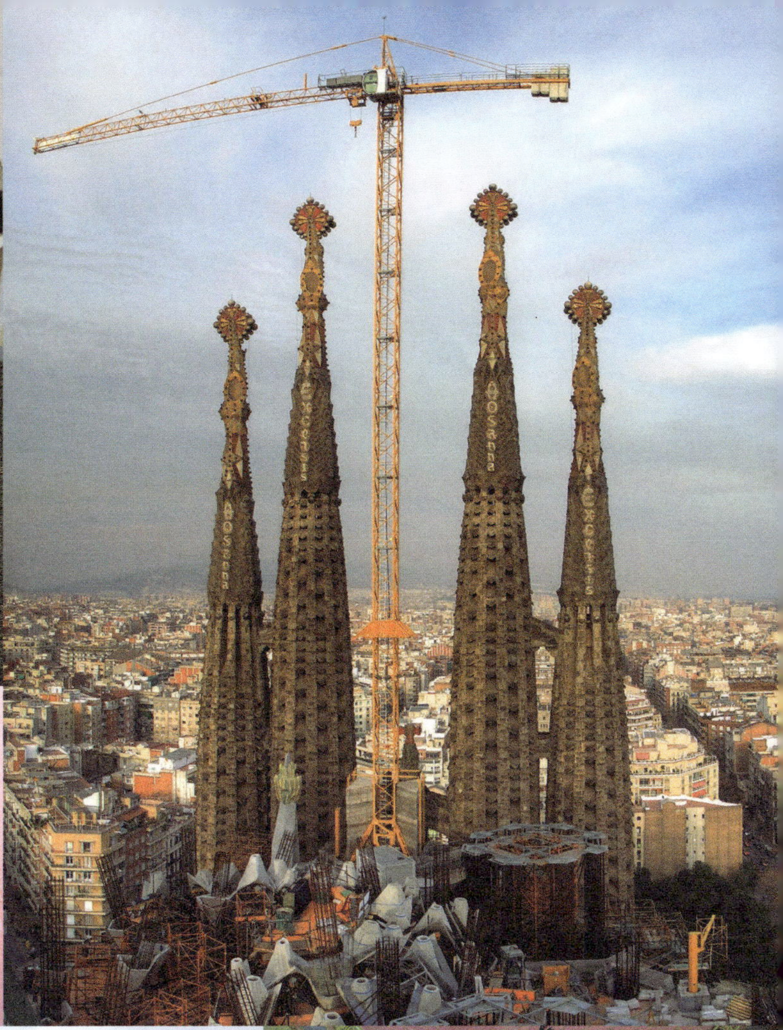
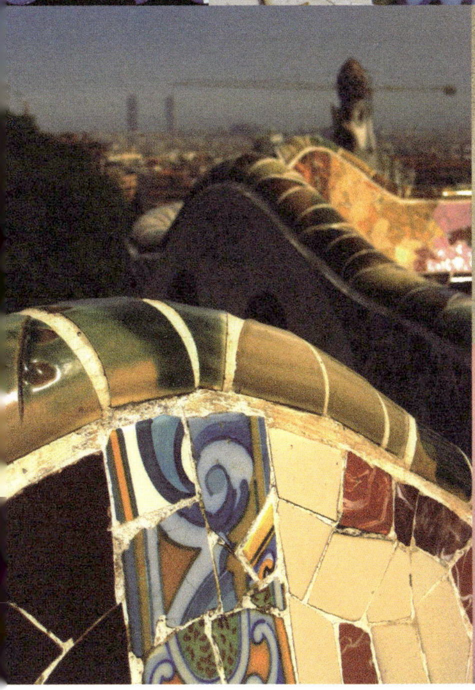
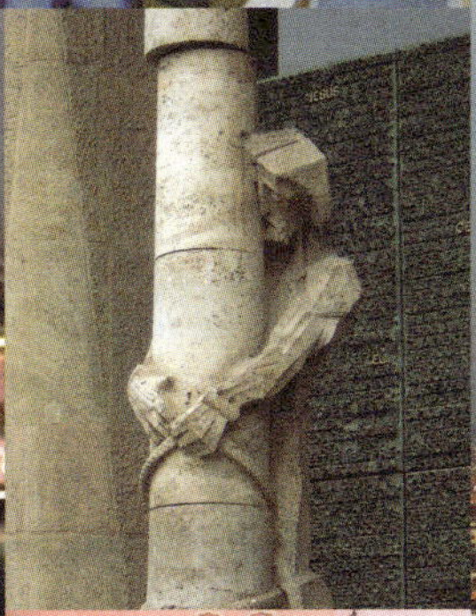
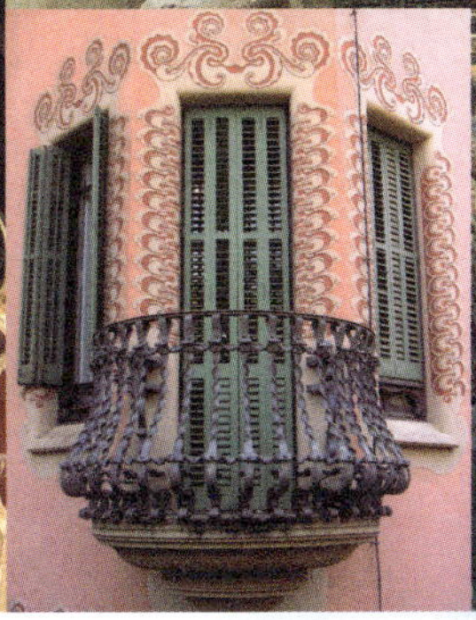
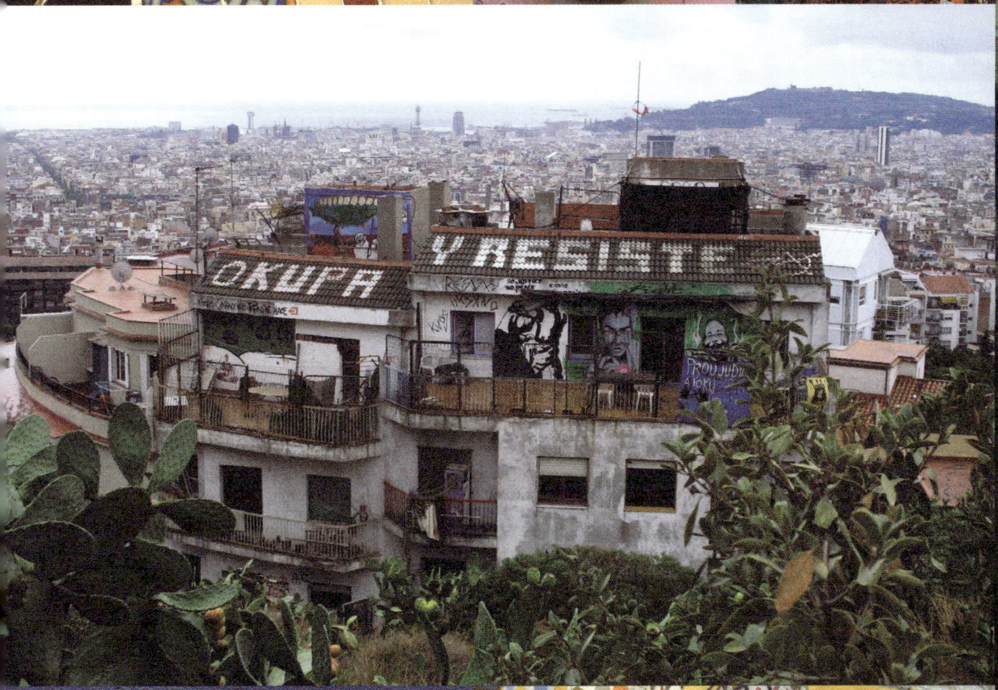
OKUPA
Y RESISTE
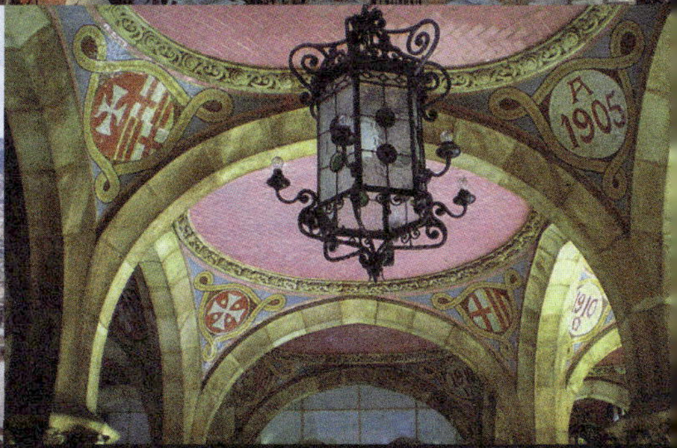
A 1905
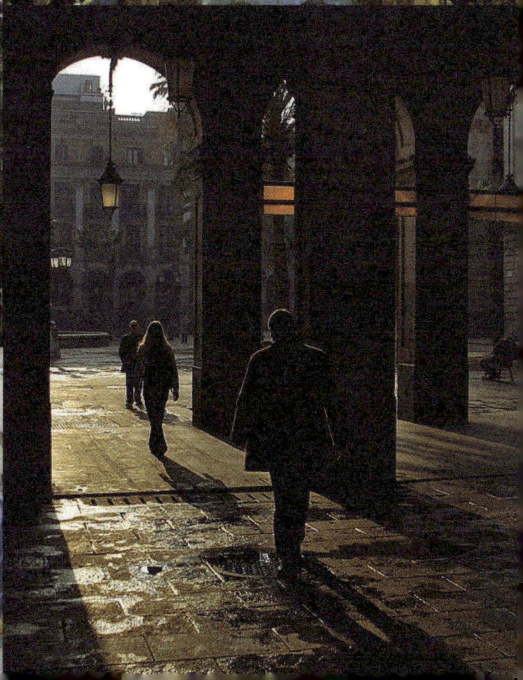

BUZON
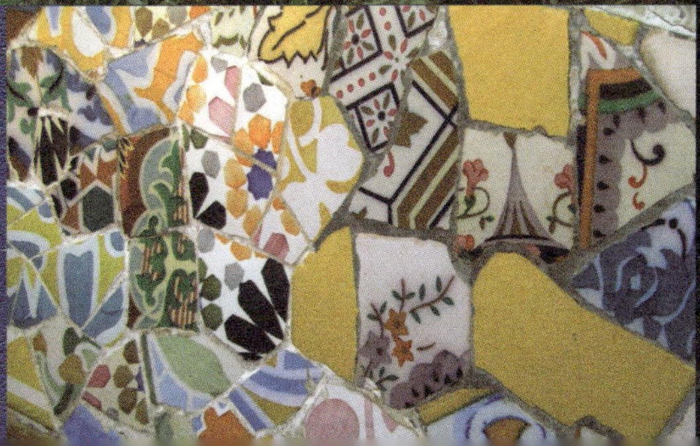

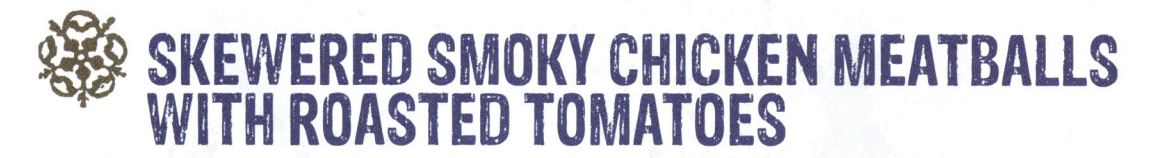

SKEWERED SMOKY CHICKEN MEATBALLS WITH ROASTED TOMATOES

Maybe it's my seventies upbringing, but a party without meatballs is simply not a party!

30 cherry tomatoes
salt and freshly ground black pepper
2 tablespoons olive oil, plus extra for tomatoes and for frying
400g chicken mince
1 small onion, finely diced
2 teaspoons Spanish sweet smoked paprika
1 teaspoon crushed chilli
1 egg, lightly beaten
3 tablespoons flour

30 cocktail sticks or toothpicks

Preheat oven to 150°C and line an oven tray with baking paper.

Cut a small cross in the top of each tomato, place on the tray, sprinkle with salt, black pepper and a little olive oil and bake for 20 minutes.

To make the meatballs, mix the mince, onion, 2 tablespoons olive oil, paprika and chilli together. Add the beaten egg and 2 tablespoons of flour. Stir thoroughly to combine. Season with salt and pepper.

Roll mixture into bite-sized balls (I use about 1 teaspoon of mixture for each). Lightly dust with flour. Heat a little olive oil in a heavy-based frying pan and cook the meatballs in batches. Alternatively, put meatballs on a baking tray lined with baking paper, spray with olive oil and bake at 200°C for 20 minutes or until golden brown and cooked through.

To serve, skewer each meatball with a roasted cherry tomato.

MAKES APPROXIMATELY 30

CLASSIC SANGRIA

Sangria is a refreshing drink with a kick that goes down a treat on a hot, lazy day.

1 cup chopped fruit (whatever is in season)
1 bottle red wine (any will do, but nothing too expensive)
1 cup brandy, Cointreau or white rum
1 litre soda water
¼ cup caster sugar
juice from 2 oranges
juice from 2 lemons
juice from 2 limes
½ cup mint leaves

Half fill a 2-litre capacity water pitcher or carafe with ice and the chopped fruit. Add the remaining ingredients and give it a good stir to dissolve the sugar.

MAKES APPROXIMATELY 2 LITRES

Skewered Smoky Chicken Meatballs with Roasted Tomatoes (front), Classic Sangria (rear)

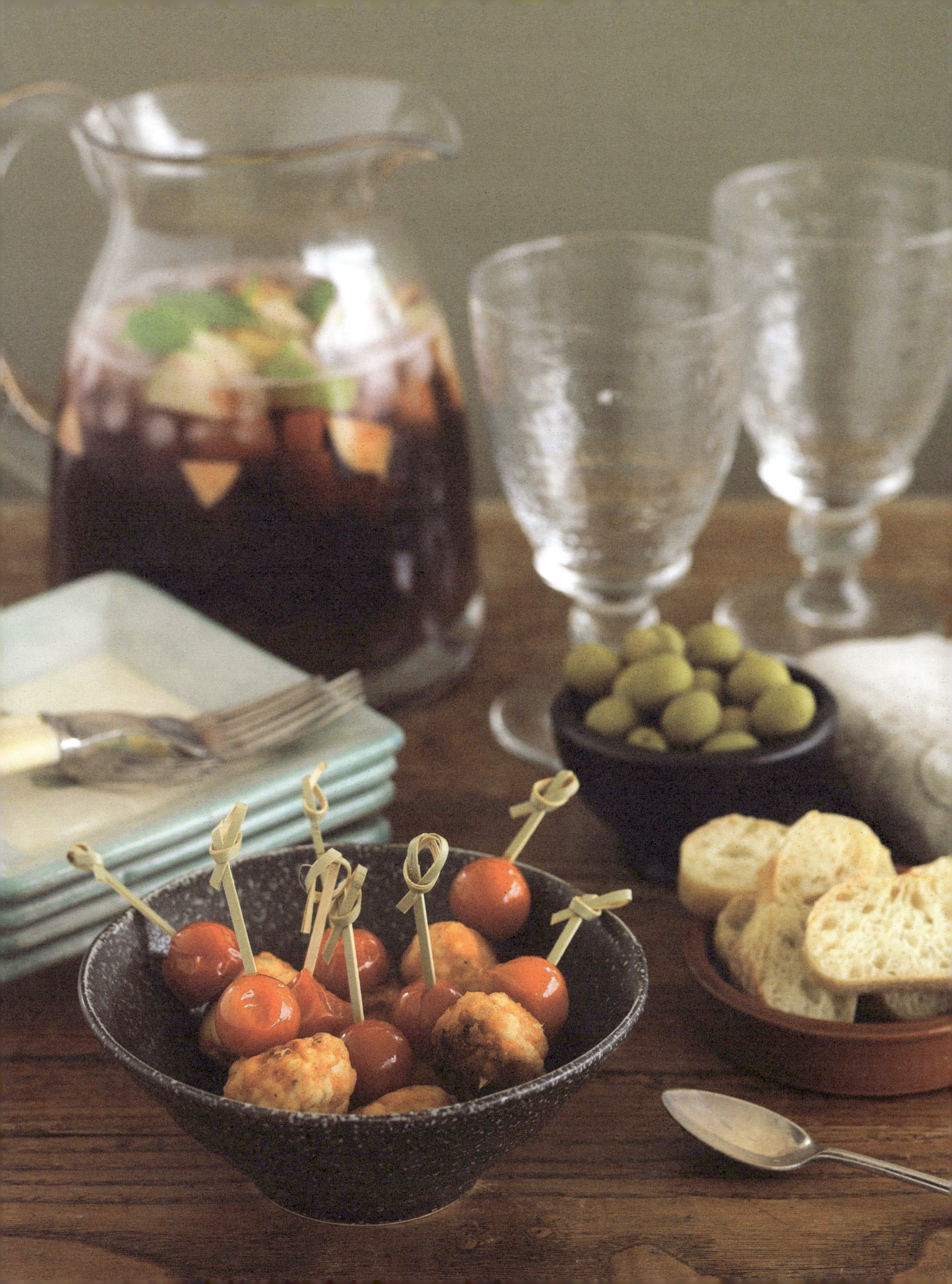

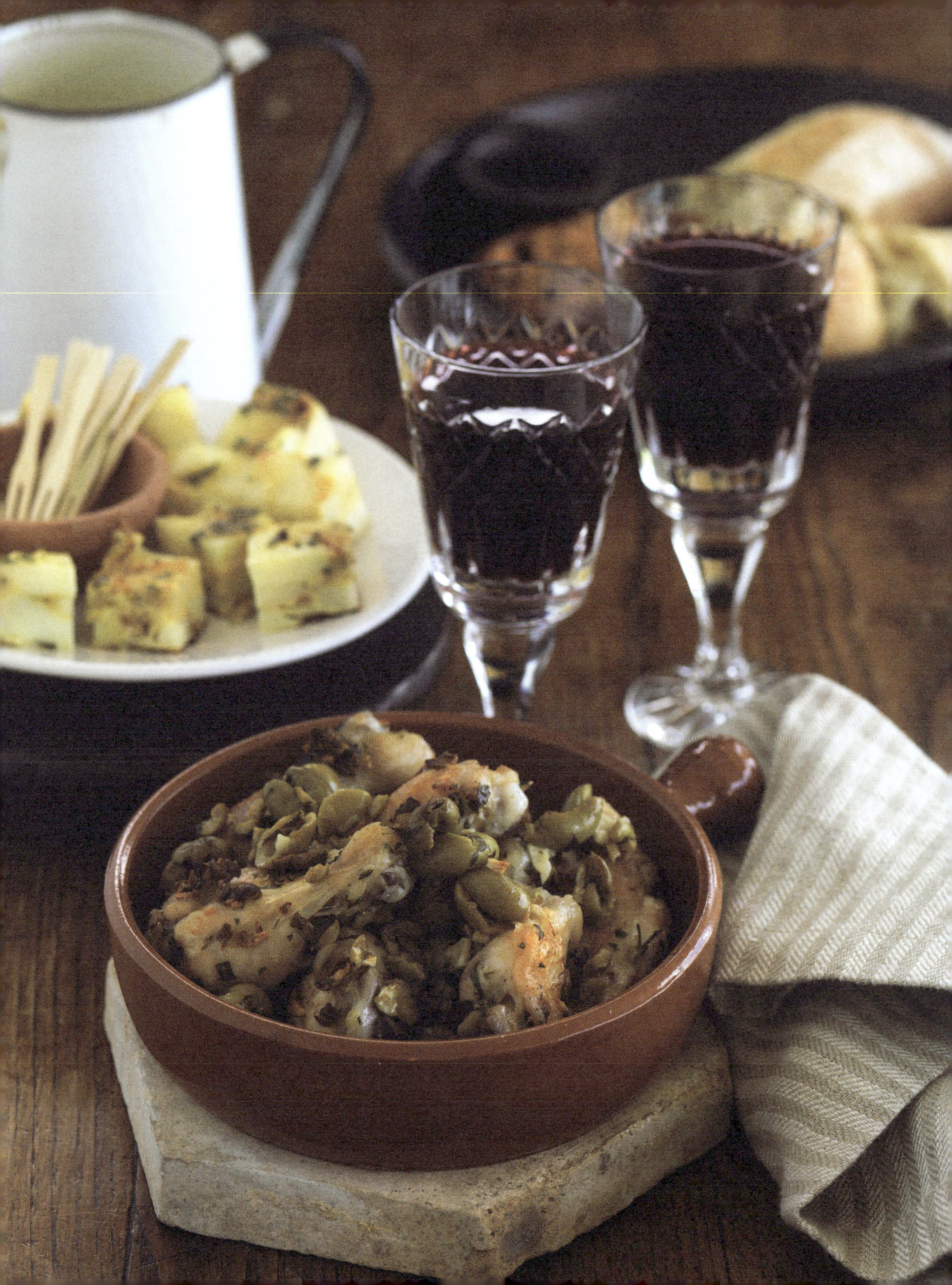

PARSLEY AND GREEN OLIVE CHICKEN NIBBLES

I'm on a mission to bring back white pepper. It has a beautiful, gentle flavour, but has been left behind with the increased popularity of cracked black pepper.

150g Spanish green olives, pitted
20 chicken nibbles, trimmed of excess skin or fat
3 cloves garlic, roughly chopped
2 tablespoons very finely chopped flat-leaf parsley
¼ teaspoon white pepper
1 teaspoon freshly ground black pepper
3 tablespoons olive oil

Preheat oven to 200°C.

Roughly chop half the green olives and leave the rest whole. Mix all ingredients in a large bowl. Put into a roasting pan or two (don't overcrowd the pans) and roast for 30 minutes or until golden and cooked through.

Serve hot on small plates.

MAKES 20

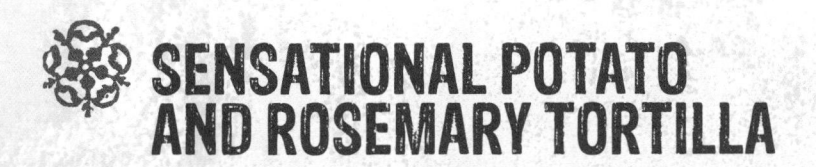

SENSATIONAL POTATO AND ROSEMARY TORTILLA

The Italians call it frittata, the Spanish call it tortilla. Whatever name you give it, this gutsy omelette is perfect for almost any occasion.

5 medium-sized potatoes (old potatoes are good)
½ cup olive oil
2 onions, thinly sliced
6 eggs, lightly beaten in a large bowl
2 tablespoons rosemary, chopped
1 teaspoon salt

Parboil the potatoes (peeled or not, according to your preference) until they are soft on the outside but not cooked all the way through. Drain and when cool enough to handle, slice into rounds.

Heat the oil in a large frying pan and cook the onions until soft. Add potatoes and cook over medium heat for another 5 minutes.

Remove the potatoes and onions from the pan, leaving the oil in the pan, and transfer them to the bowl with the beaten eggs. Stir to cover well with the egg, add the rosemary and season with salt.

Add the egg mixture back into the pan, reduce the heat to low and cook the tortilla slowly until you suspect it is golden underneath and firm enough to flip. Carefully flip, slipping it onto another plate first if necessary, and cook until done.

Cut into wedges or squares and serve either hot or at room temperature.

SERVES 6 AS A SNACK

Parsley and Green Olive Chicken Nibbles (front), Sensational Potato and Rosemary Tortilla (rear)

CHICKEN AND MUSHROOM RICE BALLS

These delicious little morsels make fantastic tapas. They are a bit time-consuming to make but are just the thing to impress guests.

2 tablespoons olive oil
1 onion, finely diced
100g button mushrooms, finely diced
1 clove garlic, crushed
200g (roughly 4 handfuls) Calasparra or arborio rice
½ cup white wine
400g boneless chicken breasts, very finely chopped
2¼ cups chicken stock – use a low-salt version if possible
2 tablespoons butter
¼ cup finely grated Parmesan
2 tablespoons chopped flat-leaf parsley
salt
1 egg, beaten
1 cup fine breadcrumbs
light cooking oil for frying

Heat the olive oil in a heavy-based frying pan or saucepan over low heat. Add the onion, mushrooms and garlic and cook for 4–5 minutes.

Add the rice and turn up the heat to medium. Stir to ensure the rice is evenly coated with the oil and cook for 2–3 minutes.

Add the wine and allow it to bubble away until it is almost all evaporated. Add the chicken to the pan along with enough stock to almost cover the rice. Reduce the heat to low and stir constantly. Add a ladleful of stock at a time as the liquid is absorbed.

After 15–20 minutes, taste the rice to check if cooked. Once cooked, remove it from the heat and stir in the butter, Parmesan, parsley and salt to taste. Allow the mixture to cool slightly.

To make the balls, roll the mixture into walnut-sized balls and dip each ball into egg then breadcrumbs. Add oil to a frying pan to a depth of 1cm. Fry the risotto balls over medium heat until golden brown. Alternatively, fry the balls in a deep fryer. Drain on paper towels and serve immediately, but warn guests that they will be hot!

MAKES APPROXIMATELY 40

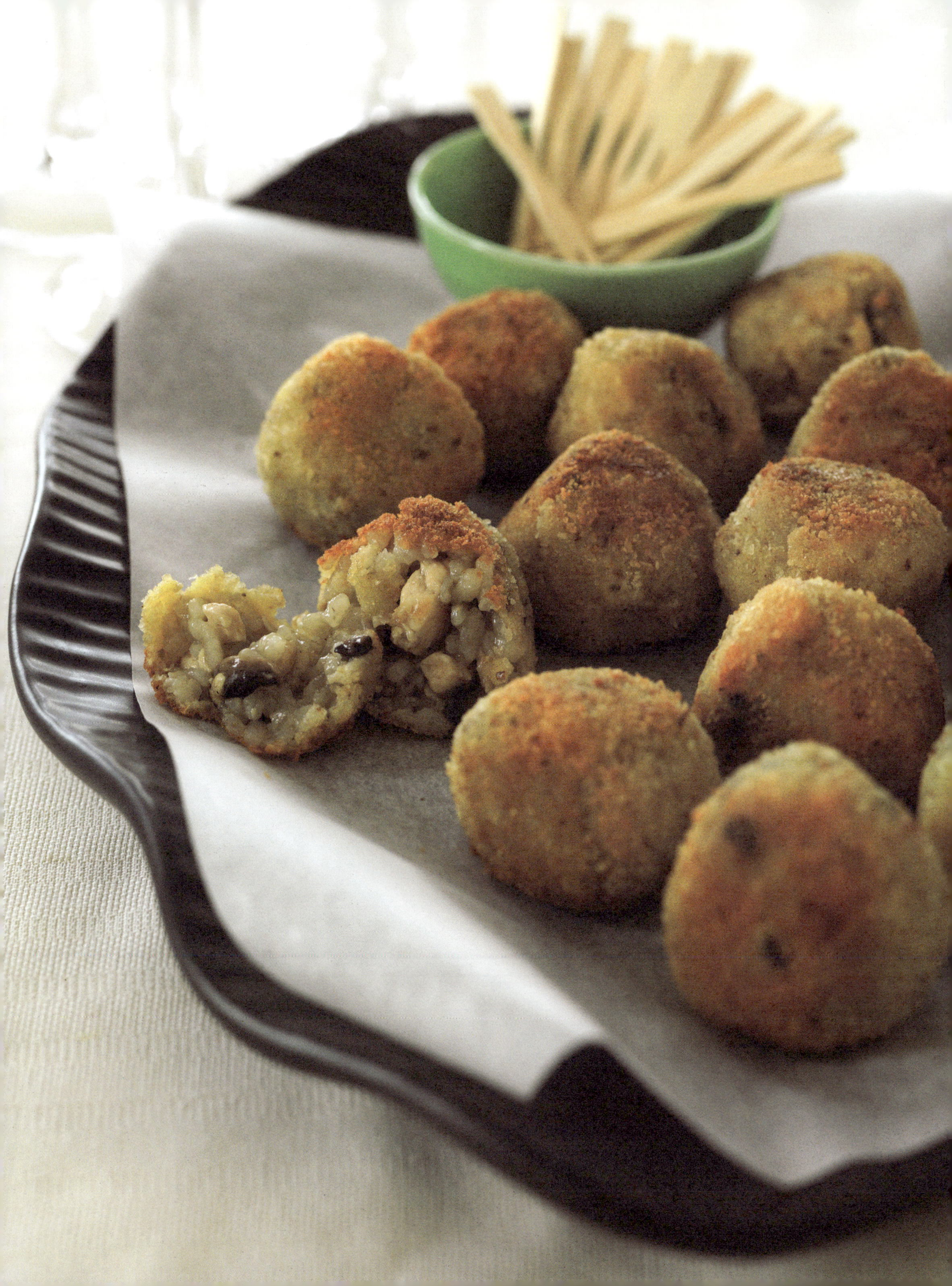

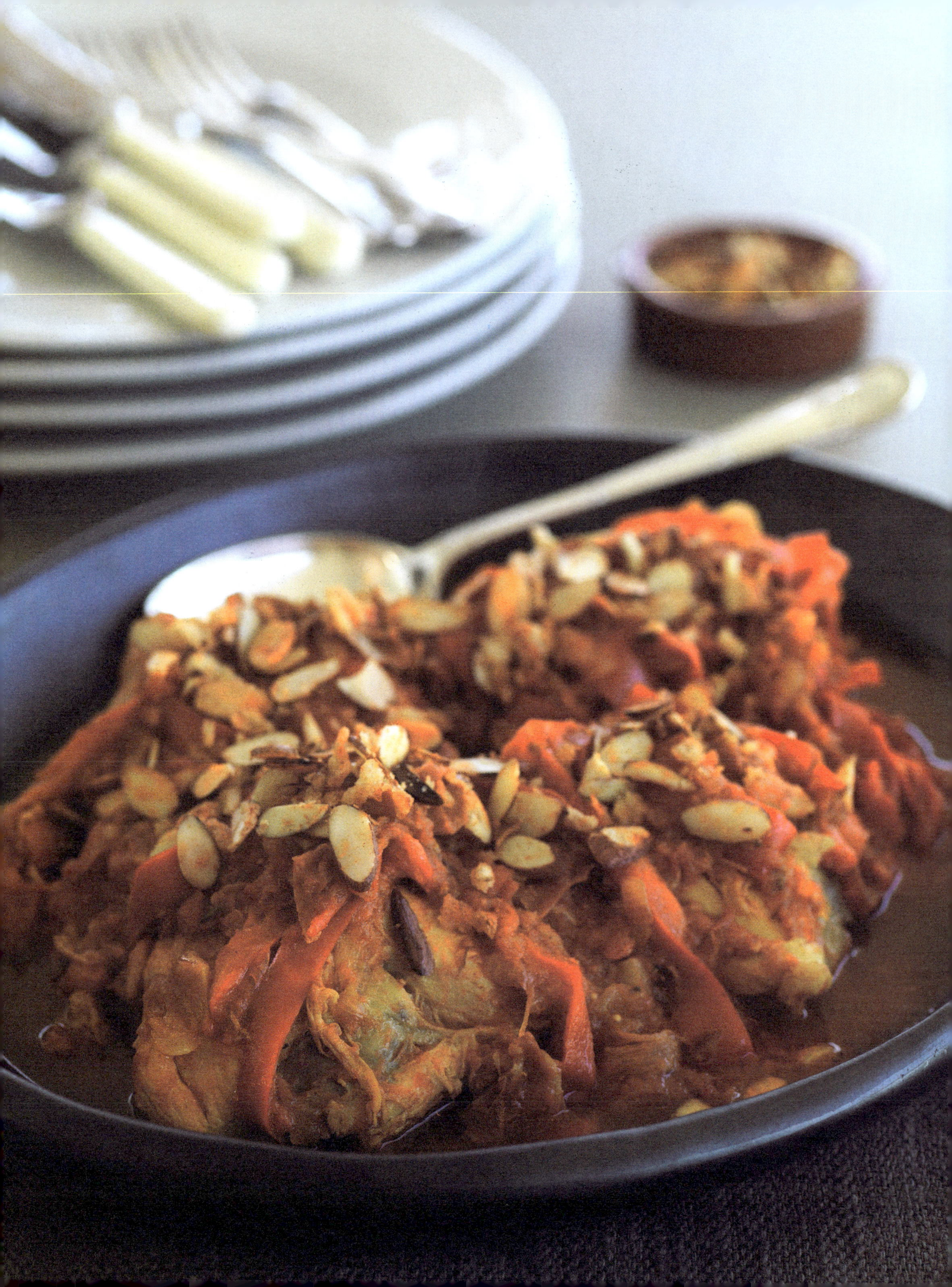

RED CAPSICUM CHICKEN WITH AN ALMOND CRUST

I love the combination of textures in this dish – the chicken soft and falling away from the bone, nestled beneath the golden crunch of the crust.

3–4 tablespoons olive oil
1kg chicken thighs, skinned, bones in
1 onion, finely chopped
4 cloves garlic, roughly chopped
3 red capsicums, deseeded and sliced
400g can chopped tomatoes
½ teaspoon saffron threads, soaked in 1 tablespoon warm water
½ cup Spanish sherry
1 sprig thyme
1 bay leaf
salt and pepper

TOPPING
1 tablespoon olive oil
¾ cup breadcrumbs
¼ cup sliced almonds
½ teaspoon Spanish smoked paprika
salt and pepper

Preheat oven to 200°C.

Heat the oil in a large ovenproof frying pan or casserole dish over high heat and cook the chicken on both sides until browned. Remove the chicken from the pan and set aside.

Add the onion, garlic and capsicums and cook for 2–3 minutes. Return the chicken to the pan along with the tomatoes, saffron and water, sherry, thyme and bay leaf. Season with salt and pepper. Reduce the heat to low and leave to simmer gently while you make the topping.

To make the topping, mix all the ingredients together and sprinkle over the chicken. Cover with foil or a lid and bake for 45 minutes. Uncover and cook for a further 15 minutes or until golden and the liquid has reduced a little.

SERVES 6

EGGPLANTS STUFFED WITH PUMPKIN, PINE NUTS AND SPINACH

These 'purple boats' are so meltingly delicious – they're perfect as a side dish or as a main meal.

2 large eggplants
3 tablespoons olive oil
3 cups diced pumpkin
1 onion, finely chopped
3 cloves garlic, crushed
1 red capsicum, deseeded and finely chopped
1 cup finely chopped spinach
2 tablespoons tomato paste
½ cup water
2 tablespoons toasted pine nuts
2 tablespoons chopped flat-leaf parsley, plus extra for garnish
½ teaspoon Spanish smoked paprika
½ teaspoon salt
½ cup vegetable or chicken stock
1 cup grated Manchego or Tasty cheese

Preheat oven to 180°C.

Cut the eggplants in half lengthwise and remove as much of the flesh as possible without piercing the skin. Place the eggplant skins in a baking dish lined with baking paper. Cut the flesh into small pieces.

Heat the olive oil in a frying pan over medium heat. Add the eggplant flesh, pumpkin, onion, garlic and capsicum and sauté until browned.

Add the spinach, tomato paste, water, pine nuts, 2 tablespoons parsley, paprika and salt and simmer for 10 minutes.

Fill the eggplant skins with the pumpkin mixture. Top with grated cheese. Add stock to oven dish, cover with foil and bake for 60 minutes or until the eggplants are tender. Remove the foil for the last 15 minutes of cooking time so the cheese browns. Sprinkle over chopped parsley before serving.

SERVES 4

Red Capsicum Chicken with an Almond Crust (left)
Eggplants Stuffed with Pumpkin, Pine Nuts and Spinach (overleaf)

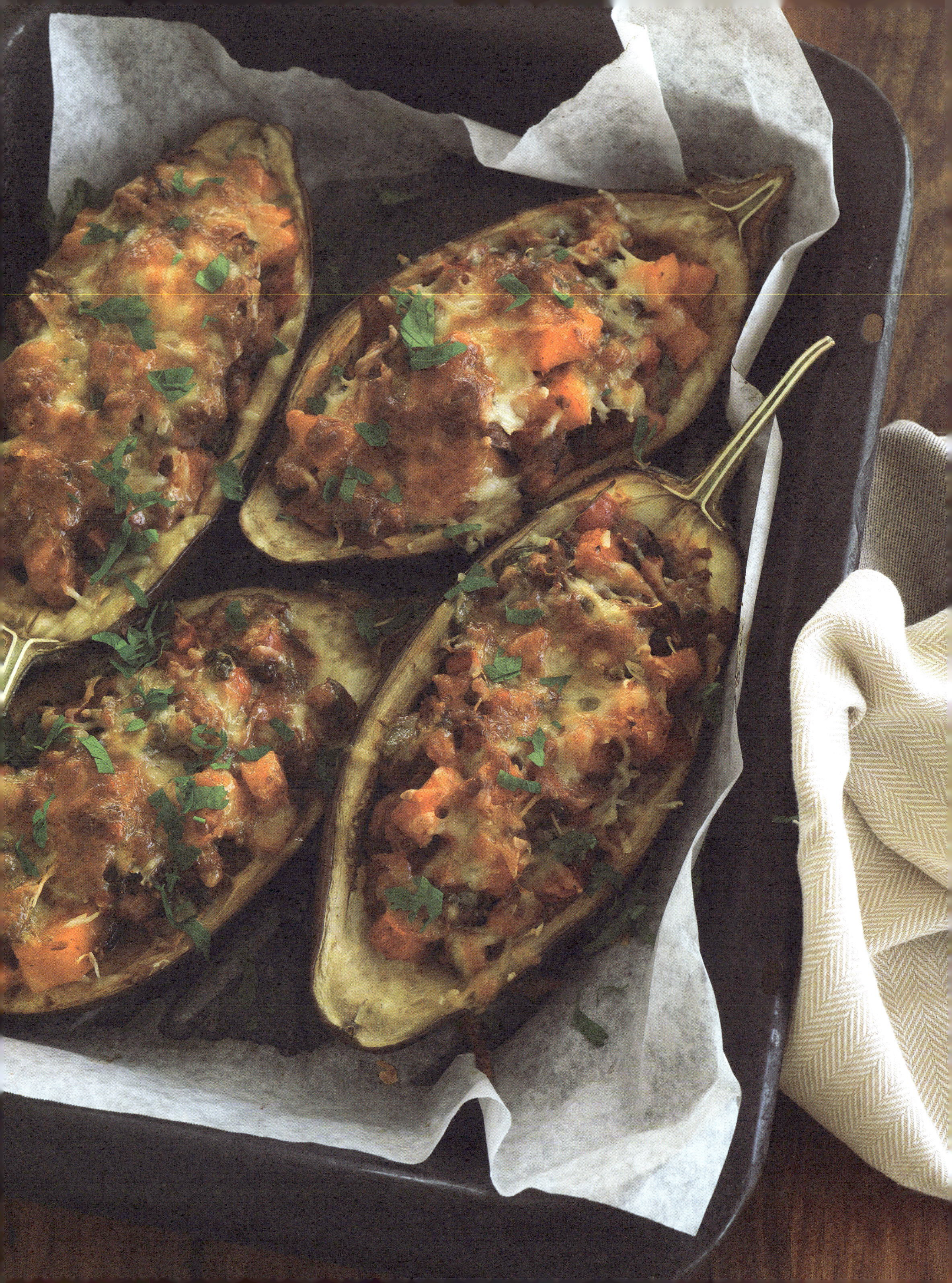

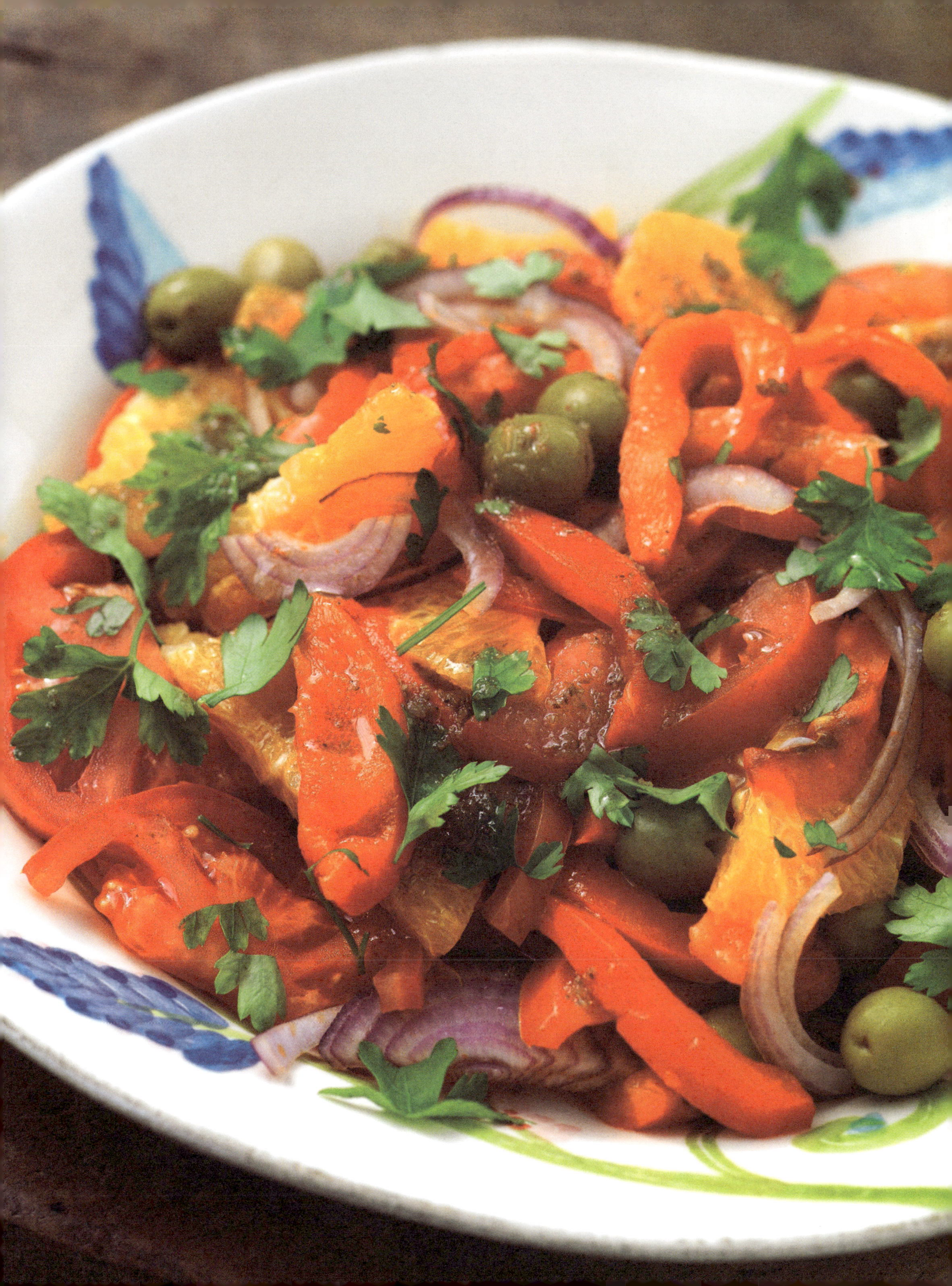

ORANGE AND ROSEMARY CHICKEN

This is one of the quickest dinners to prepare and yet it is positively bursting with the sunny flavours of Spain.

8 chicken thighs, skinned and boned
1 tablespoon olive oil
½ cup orange juice
¼ cup red wine vinegar
1 teaspoon brown sugar
1 clove garlic, crushed
1 tablespoon finely chopped rosemary, plus extra leaves for garnish
½ teaspoon salt
freshly ground black pepper

Cut slashes into the chicken meat to allow the marinade to penetrate and place it in a large shallow dish.

Whisk the remaining ingredients together and pour over the chicken. Cover and refrigerate for 30 minutes.

Preheat oven to 200°C.

Place the chicken and marinade in a large ovenproof dish and bake for 45 minutes or until the juices run clear when pierced with a skewer. Baste occasionally with the marinade during cooking if you feel like it.

Garnish with rosemary and serve with *Red Capsicum, Orange and Olive Salad* (see below).

SERVES 4

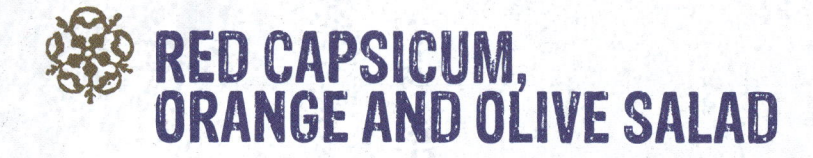

RED CAPSICUM, ORANGE AND OLIVE SALAD

This delicious and colourful salad is perfect with *Orange and Rosemary Chicken* (see above).

DRESSING
¼ cup extra virgin olive oil
2 tablespoons lemon juice
1 clove garlic, crushed
½ teaspoon ground cumin
½ teaspoon salt

SALAD
3 red capsicums, roasted, peeled, deseeded and sliced
2 large oranges, peeled, halved and sliced
1 small red onion, thinly sliced
3 tomatoes, sliced
½ cup green olives
2 tablespoons chopped flat-leaf parsley

To prepare the dressing, combine all ingredients and set aside until required.

Place the capsicums, oranges, red onion, tomatoes and olives into a salad bowl. Add the dressing and toss gently. Sprinkle with the chopped parsley.

SERVES 4 AS AN ACCOMPANIMENT

Orange and Rosemary Chicken (right)
Red Capsicum Orange and Olive Salad (previous page)

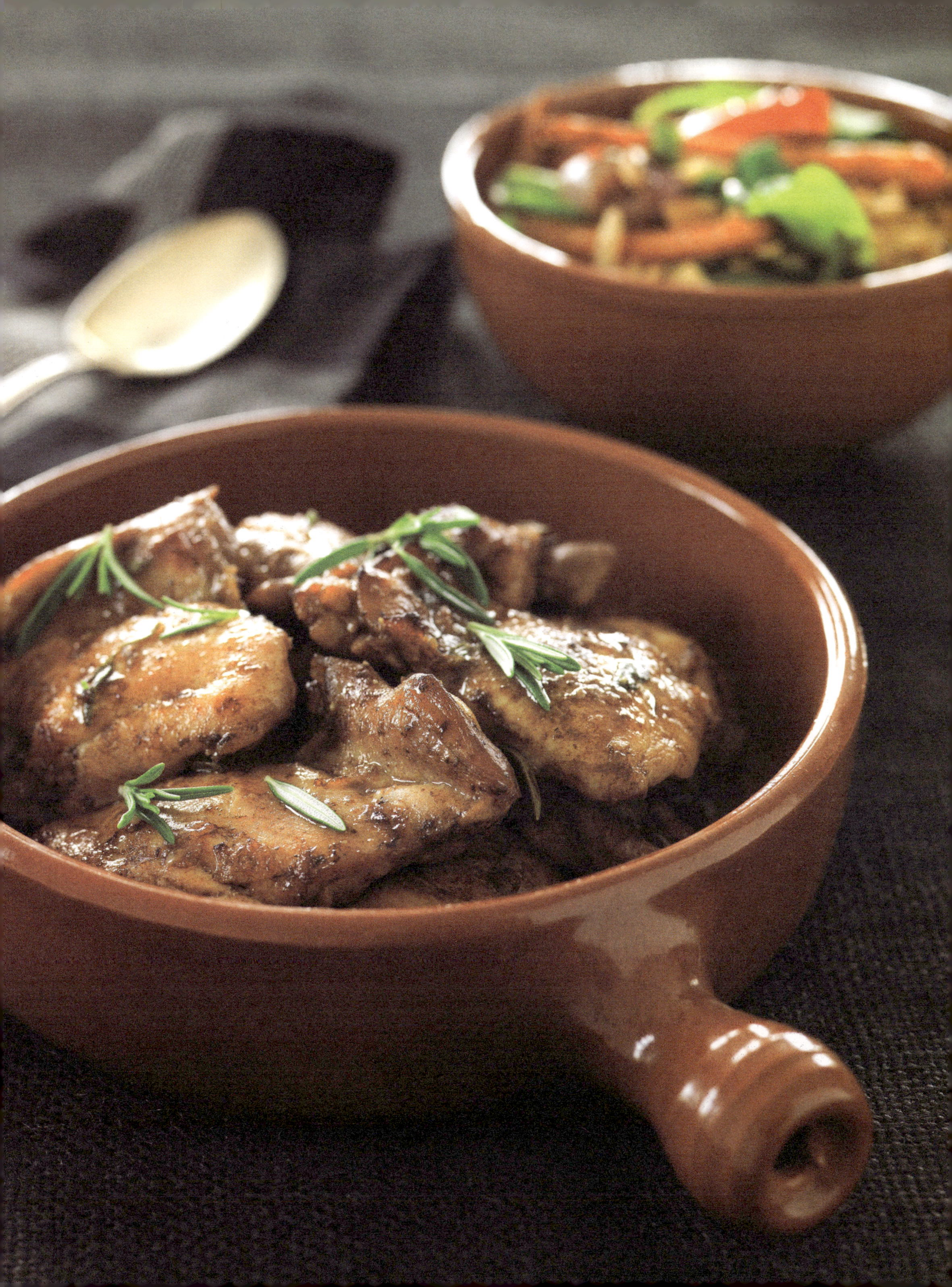

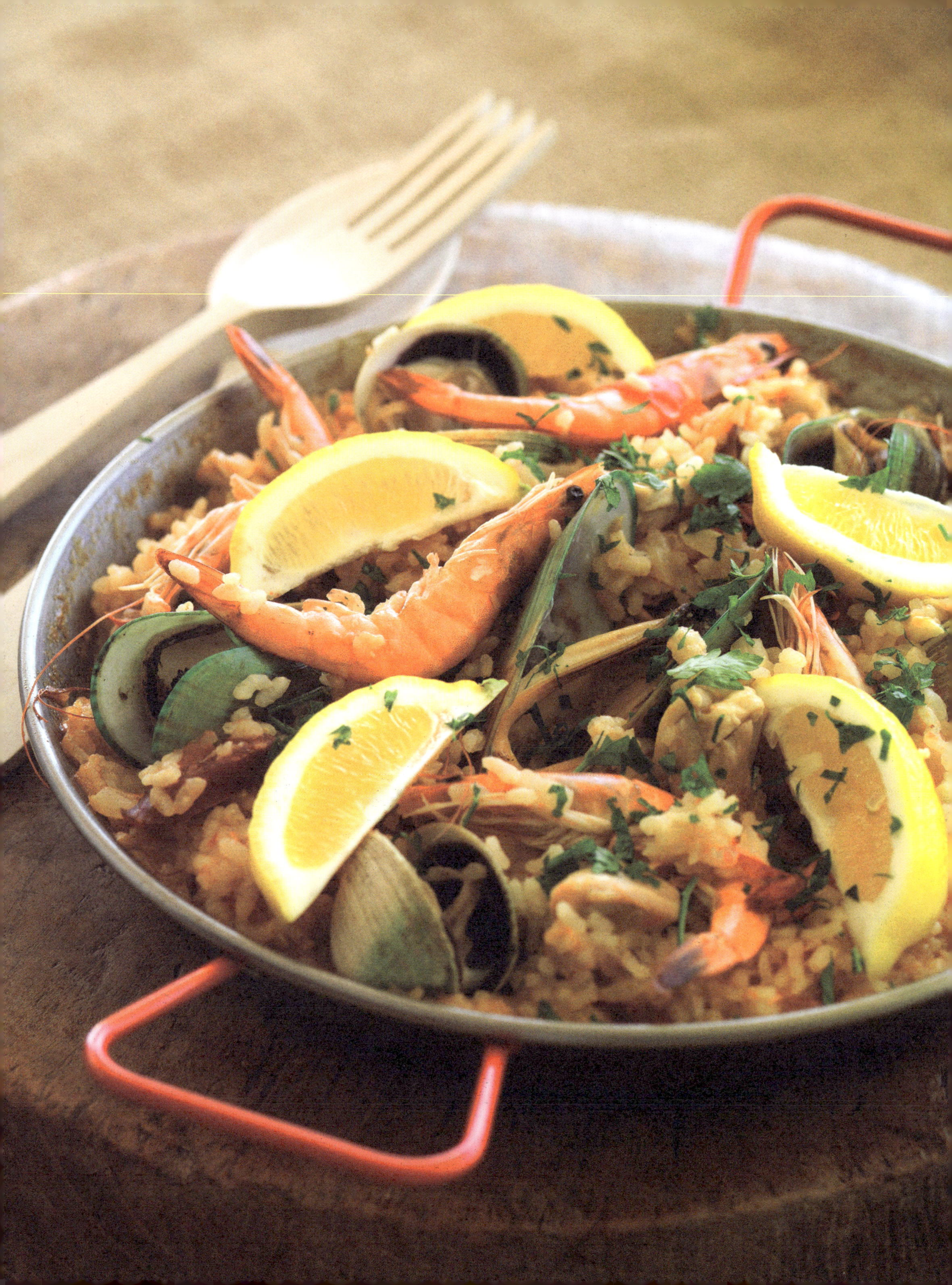

EASY PAELLA

Paella is an ideal dish to cook when feeding a large number of people. Each region in Spain has its own variation depending on what ingredients are nearby. For me, the must-haves for paella are chicken, spicy chorizo, garlic, saffron, tomato and the right kind of rice. The rest is optional!

Unlike risotto, paella is cooked without stirring so that the rice grains remain separate – stirring creates a creamy texture as starch is released from the rice.

6 tablespoons extra virgin olive oil
4–5 boneless chicken thighs, cut into smallish pieces
2 large onions, diced
8 cloves garlic, crushed
3 ripe tomatoes, grated to a mush
3½ cups Calasparra rice (½ cup per person)
salt and freshly ground black pepper
3 chorizo sausages, sliced
½ teaspoon saffron threads, soaked in 1 tablespoon warm water
2 litres vegetable or chicken stock
12 cockles, mussels, clams or pipi in their shells
12 prawns, in their shells
flat-leaf parsley to garnish
lemon wedges to garnish

Use a paella pan if you have one. If not, use your largest frying pan or a saucepan that is not too deep.

Heat 2 tablespoons of the olive oil in the pan. Add the chicken and cook for a few minutes until it begins to turn golden. Remove chicken and set aside. Add the remaining olive oil, onions, garlic and tomatoes to the pan and cook for 5–7 minutes. Add the rice and stir to coat in the mixture. Season well with salt and pepper and sauté for 10–15 minutes.

Add the sliced chorizo and browned chicken to the pan. Add the saffron in its water. Add enough of the stock so that it just covers the rice.

Stir to blend and don't stir again unless absolutely necessary. Bring to the boil, then turn the heat down and simmer gently for about 20 minutes until the rice is cooked and nearly all of the stock absorbed. If it is looking too dry and the rice is still not cooked through, sneak in some more hot stock or boiling water by pouring it around the sides of the pan.

About 5 minutes from the end of the cooking time, add the shellfish and prawns in their shells. Taste paella at this stage and consider whether you need to add more salt or pepper. Continue to cook until the shells open and the prawns are cooked. Discard any shellfish that haven't opened. Gently stir the ingredients around a little.

Scatter with lots of parsley sprigs and garnish with lemon wedges. Bring the paella pan to the table and serve directly from the pan.

SERVES 6–8

CHARGRILLED CHICKEN WITH GREEN OLIVE AND ORANGE SALSA

Fast and fabulous, these chicken breasts will spice up any barbecue.

CHARGRILLED CHICKEN
4 chicken breasts, skinned and boned
2 tablespoons olive oil
2 teaspoons chopped fresh thyme
1 teaspoon finely grated lemon zest
1 clove garlic, crushed
salt and pepper

SALSA
150g Spanish green olives, pitted and roughly chopped
1 orange, segmented and chopped
2 sticks celery, finely chopped
2 teaspoons capers
1 long red chilli, deseeded and finely chopped
1 teaspoon finely grated orange or lemon zest
1 clove garlic, crushed
¼ cup finely chopped flat-leaf parsley
¼ cup olive oil
2 tablespoons Spanish sherry vinegar
salt and pepper

Place a piece of baking paper or plastic food wrap over each chicken breast and gently flatten with a rolling pin to about 1cm thick. Place the chicken in a shallow dish, drizzle with olive oil and sprinkle with the thyme, lemon zest and garlic. Season with salt and pepper. Cover and refrigerate while you prepare the salsa.

To make the salsa, combine all the ingredients in a bowl and stir to combine. Taste and adjust seasoning, if required. How's the heat? Add more chilli. Not sour enough? Add a splash more vinegar. Set aside to allow the flavours to develop while you cook the chicken.

To cook the chicken, preheat a barbecue or ridged grill pan. Cook the chicken for 3–4 minutes on each side until it is cooked through and golden brown.

Serve the chicken with salsa, crusty bread and a green salad.

SERVES 4

CHICKEN AND PROSCIUTTO BIKINI

Available in almost any bar or café in Barcelona, a bikini is the Spanish version of a toasted sandwich. Once you get beyond the embarrassment of asking for one, you'll find they are the best snack to keep you going.

1 tablespoon light cooking oil
1 onion, thinly sliced
½ teaspoon smoked paprika
8 flour tortilla
1 cup grated Manchego or other strong firm cheese
2 roasted red capsicums, peeled, deseeded and thinly sliced
2 cups cooked chicken, shredded
8 slices prosciutto
sour cream to garnish
fresh coriander to garnish
diced tomato to garnish

Heat oil in a frying pan over medium heat and sauté the onions until golden brown. Add the paprika and stir through. Set aside.

Place 4 of the tortilla on a flat surface and top each with grated cheese, roasted capsicums, cooked onions and shredded chicken, finishing with a slice of prosciutto. Cover with the remaining tortilla. Place the tortillas on a sandwich press or in a lightly oiled frying pan and cook over medium heat. Cook for 2–3 minutes each side. Cut each into 4 squares and serve with sour cream, coriander and diced tomato.

MAKES 16 SQUARES

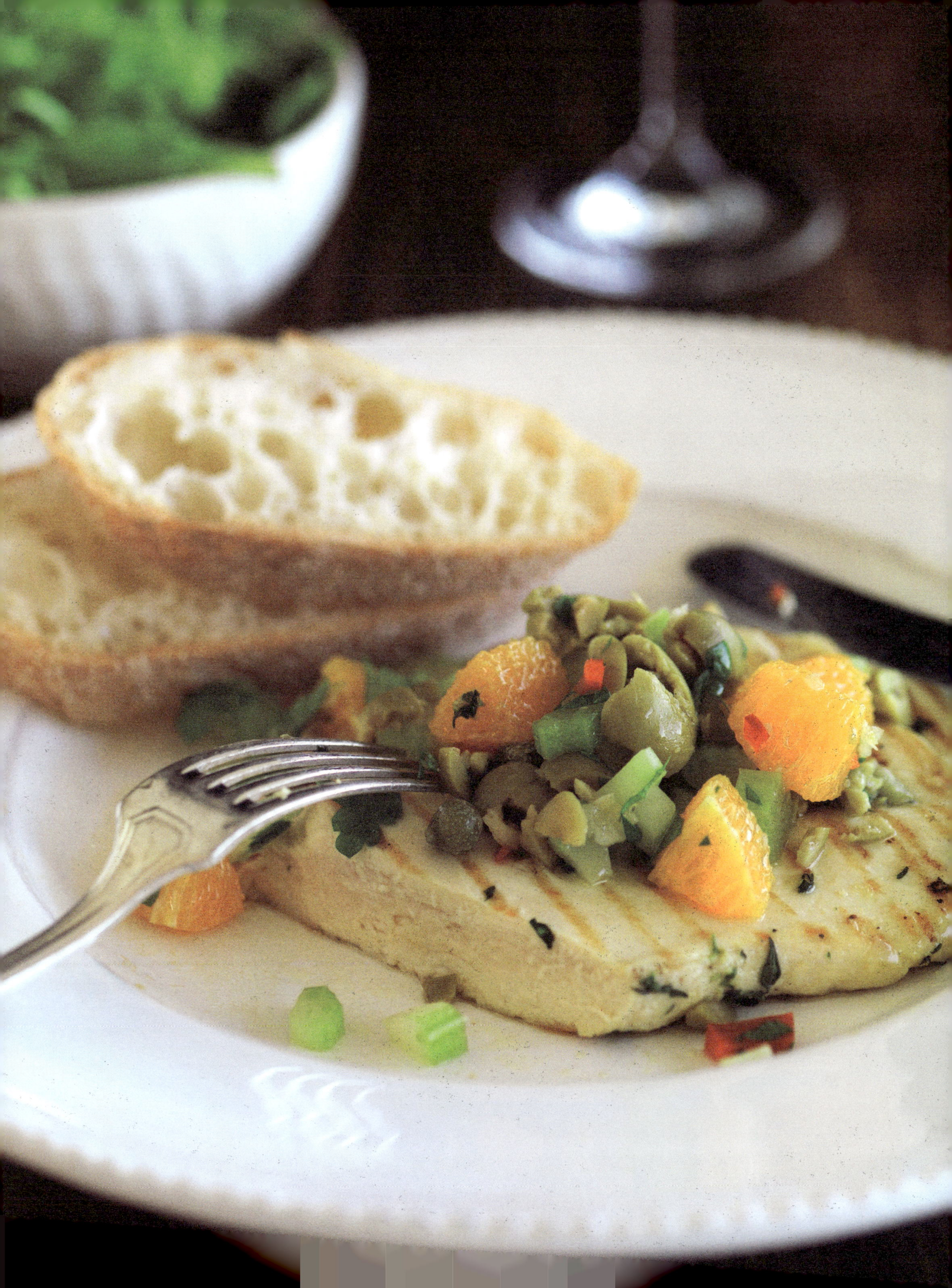

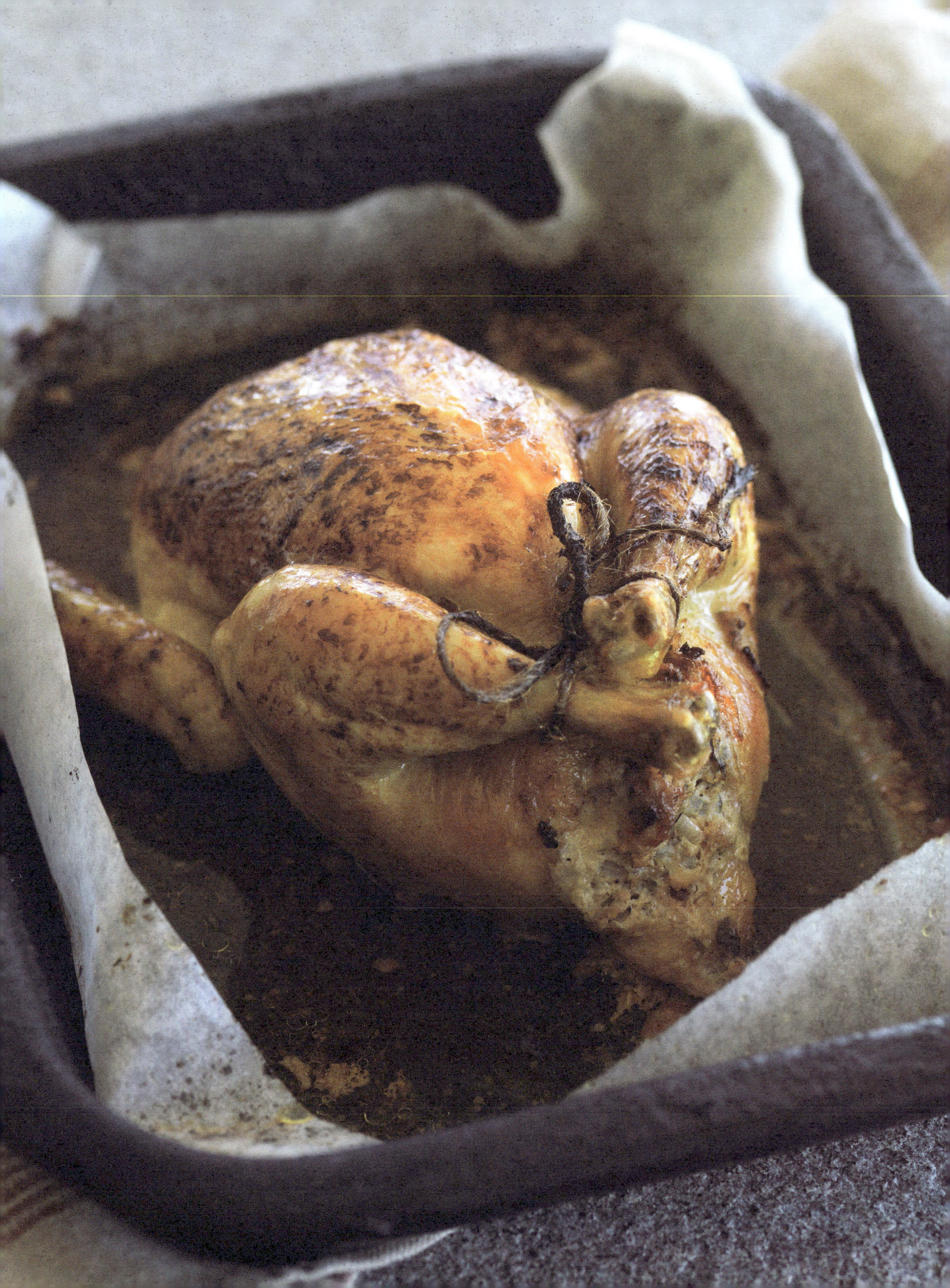

WHOLE ROASTED CHICKEN WITH CHORIZO AND HERB STUFFING

The spicy chorizo in this recipe makes a heart-warming stuffing. For the herbs, I like to use parsley, basil, chives and thyme. When I stuff a bird, I don't do anything fancy like sewing or skewering the cavity closed. I just tie the legs together with a piece of string.

STUFFING
2 tablespoons olive oil
1 red onion, finely chopped
2 cloves garlic, crushed
1–2 chorizo sausages, finely chopped
2 cups breadcrumbs
¼ cup chopped fresh herbs
1 egg
½ teaspoon salt
freshly ground black pepper

CHICKEN
1 whole chicken
2 tablespoons olive oil
salt and freshly ground black pepper
1 cup chicken stock
½ cup dry white wine

Preheat oven to 180°C. Line a roasting dish with baking paper.

Mix all the stuffing ingredients together and fill the cavity of the chicken.

Rub the chicken with olive oil and season with salt and pepper. Place the chicken into the roasting dish. Add the chicken stock and wine to the dish. Cover with foil.

Roast the chicken for 1 hour, then remove the foil and roast for a further 30 minutes or until the juices run clear when pierced in the thickest part. Baste occasionally with the liquid in the pan during cooking.

Serve with crispy potatoes and a salad.

SERVES 4–6

SPANISH BAKED CHICKEN WITH GARLIC AND LEMON

With its sherry and paprika, this chicken has true Spanish flavour. For the herbs, I like to use a mixture of rosemary, thyme and mint.

2 tablespoons olive oil
1 whole chicken, cut into quarters
½ teaspoon salt
3 tablespoons chopped fresh herbs
2 teaspoons paprika
2 medium-sized onions, sliced
8 cloves garlic, peeled but left whole
½ cup dry sherry
½ cup chicken stock
1 teaspoon saffron threads
1 lemon, cut into wedges

Preheat the oven to 180°C.

Heat the oil in a frying pan over high heat. Add the chicken pieces and cook until golden. Remove the chicken from the pan and place in a bowl with the salt, herbs and paprika. Mix well to coat the chicken.

Return the pan to a medium heat and add the onions. Cook until they are just beginning to brown. Add the garlic and cook for a further 2 minutes.

Remove pan from the heat and add the sherry, chicken stock and saffron.

Place the chicken into an ovenproof dish (a large shallow terracotta or ceramic dish is ideal). Pour the onion mixture over the chicken, scraping out the pan to make sure all the pan juices go into the dish. Add the lemon wedges and bake for 45 minutes or until the chicken pieces are golden brown and cooked through.

SERVES 4

SPANISH CHURROS WITH CINNAMON-SCENTED LIQUID CHOCOLATE

Churros are long, sugared doughnuts, commonly served in the morning with a small cup of liquid chocolate scented with cinnamon. In Spain it seems right to eat them for breakfast, but at home my brain shouts, 'Far too indulgent!' Instead I serve them for dessert and guests always love them.

CHURROS
1 cup water
50g butter
2 tablespoons sugar
¼ teaspoon salt
1 cup plain flour
2 eggs
light cooking oil for frying
1 teaspoon ground cinnamon
¼ cup sugar

Line an oven tray with baking paper.

Put water, butter, first measure of sugar and salt in a medium-sized saucepan over medium heat until the butter has melted. Increase the temperature and bring to a boil. Once the mixture is at a rolling boil, remove from the heat and add the flour. Beat with a wooden spoon until the dough forms a ball and comes away from the side of the saucepan. Beat in the eggs, one at a time, until the mixture is smooth (don't worry if it seems that it will never come together as a smooth mixture, just keep beating).

Spoon the dough into a piping bag fitted with a large star nozzle. Pipe fat strips 2.5cm x 10cm onto prepared tray and freeze for 20 minutes.

Alternatively, if you don't have a piping bag, refrigerate the dough for 1 hour and cook the churros by dropping heaped teaspoons of mixture into the hot oil.

Pour oil into a 20cm-diameter saucepan until it is about half full. Heat the oil until almost smoking (approximately 180°C). Drop in 2–3 churros at a time and fry until deep golden brown. Remove churros with a slotted spoon and drain on paper towels.

Put the cinnamon and second measure of sugar in a bowl and stir to combine. Toss the warm churros in the cinnamon sugar and roll around until well coated. Serve with liquid chocolate.

MAKES APPROXIMATELY 30

LIQUID CHOCOLATE
300ml milk
½ teaspoon ground cinnamon
300g dark chocolate (65% cocoa), broken into pieces
3 tablespoons sweetened condensed milk

Put the milk and cinnamon in a small saucepan over low heat until the milk almost reaches boiling point. Watch it carefully and catch it just in time! Add the chocolate pieces and cover with a tea towel. Set aside for 10 minutes. Add the condensed milk and whisk until the sauce is smooth. Serve in little cups or glasses with a plate of warm churros.

MAKES APPROXIMATELY 2 CUPS

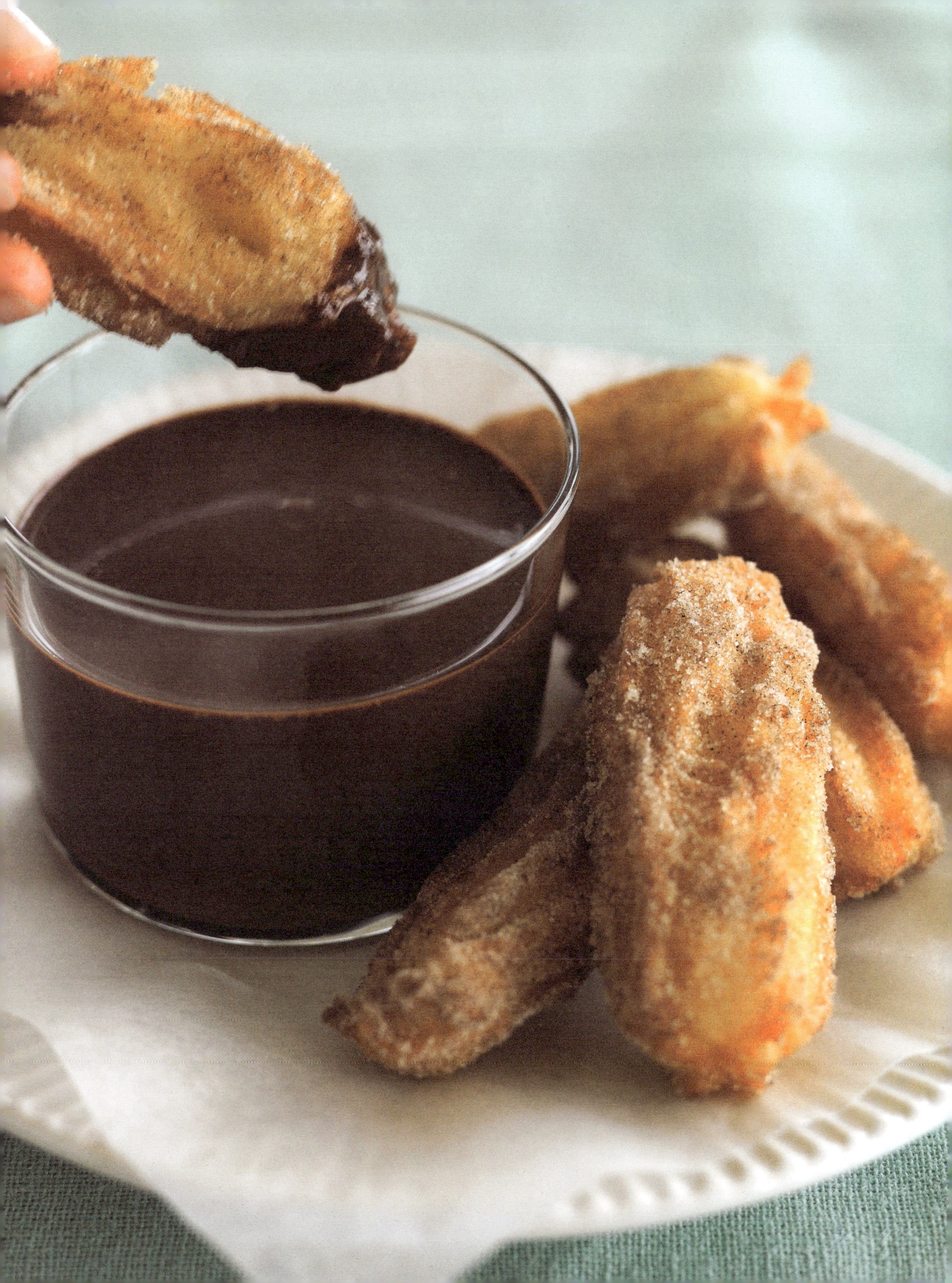

ITALY
FRESH AND FLAVOURFUL IN TUSCANY & AMALFI

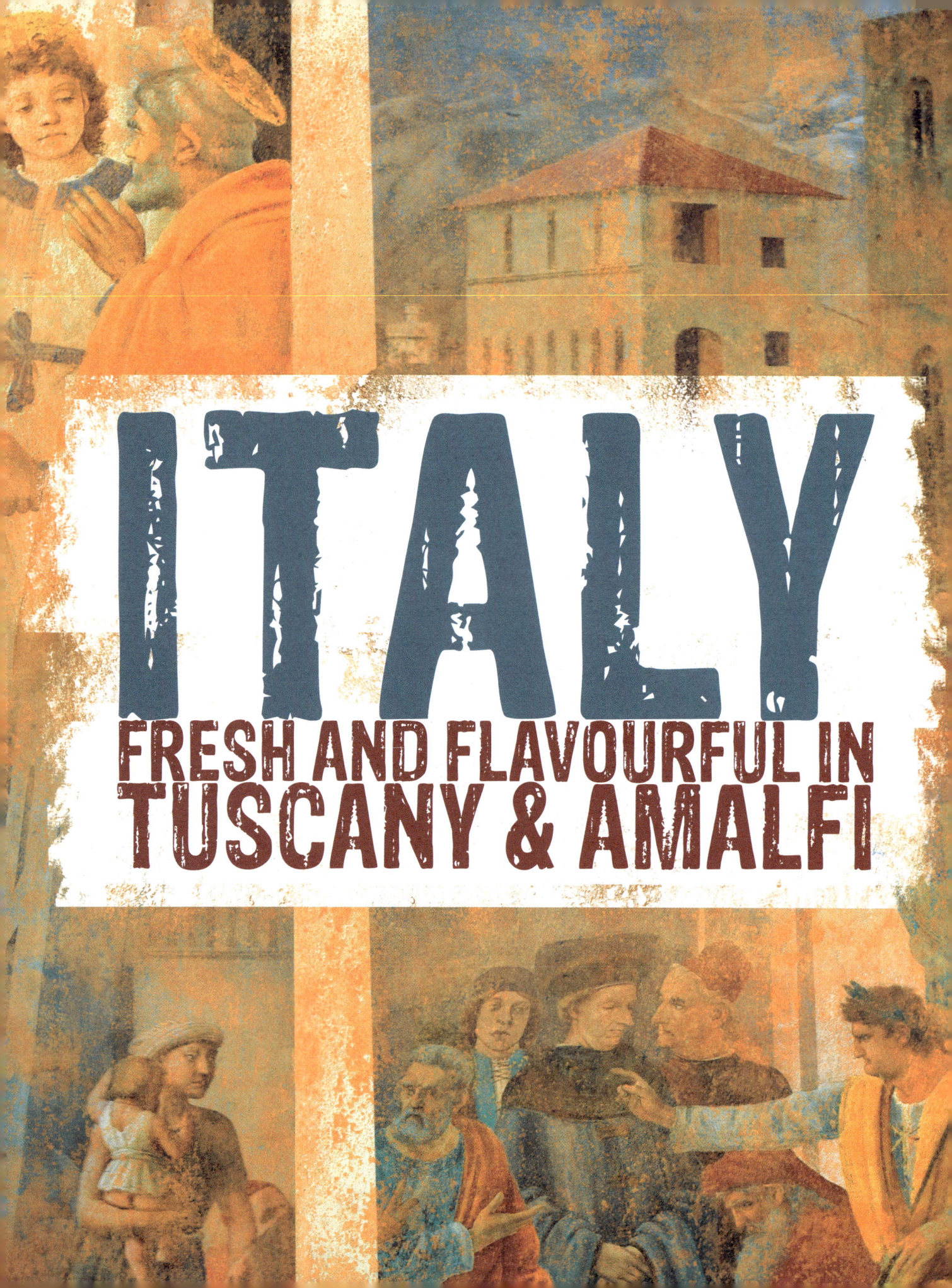

'Sitting around a crowded dining table where the conversation centres on the food is my idea of heaven and Italians have perfected this art.'

On my first visit to Italy I was surprised to find that Italians, known for their gregarious behaviour, are remarkably restrained when it comes to boasting about their cuisine. For years, I had heard of the French master chefs, and I understood the important place that French cuisine held in the world. Arriving in Italy . . . it was as if I was discovering a lost part of my own culinary history.

In Italy, everyone is a foodie and no-one gets bored talking about cooking methods and ingredients, or debating the best way to make a particular dish. Yet, the Italian food culture remains unpretentious. They have the right approach to cooking – they use seasonal ingredients, keep the preparation simple and approach every meal with gusto!

It's all about respecting the ingredients, playing along with their natural form and coaxing them into some of the most wonderful taste combinations I've discovered in all my travels – baked lemons with mozzarella, sun-ripened tomatoes with basil, creamy risotto with the sharpness of Parmesan or pecorino, and olive oil that you can drink it tastes so good.

In Amalfi and Tuscany, I had the pleasure of cooking and eating in locals' homes where the whole family pitches in to create incredible feasts. Sitting around a crowded dining table where the conversation centres on the food is my idea of heaven and Italians have perfected this art – the legendary long Italian lunch is not a fantasy.

On occasion, I was lucky enough to have la nonna – the grandmother – share some, but never all, of her cooking secrets with me. All this, in a country that is so picturesque it makes you want to rent a Tuscan villa just so you can do some cooking!

To recreate Italian-style food back home, I always start with a visit to my local weekend market where I let the stallholders guide me to the freshest and tastiest ingredients. From there I start to plan a menu that will be simple and non-fussy, where the flavours will be the heroes.

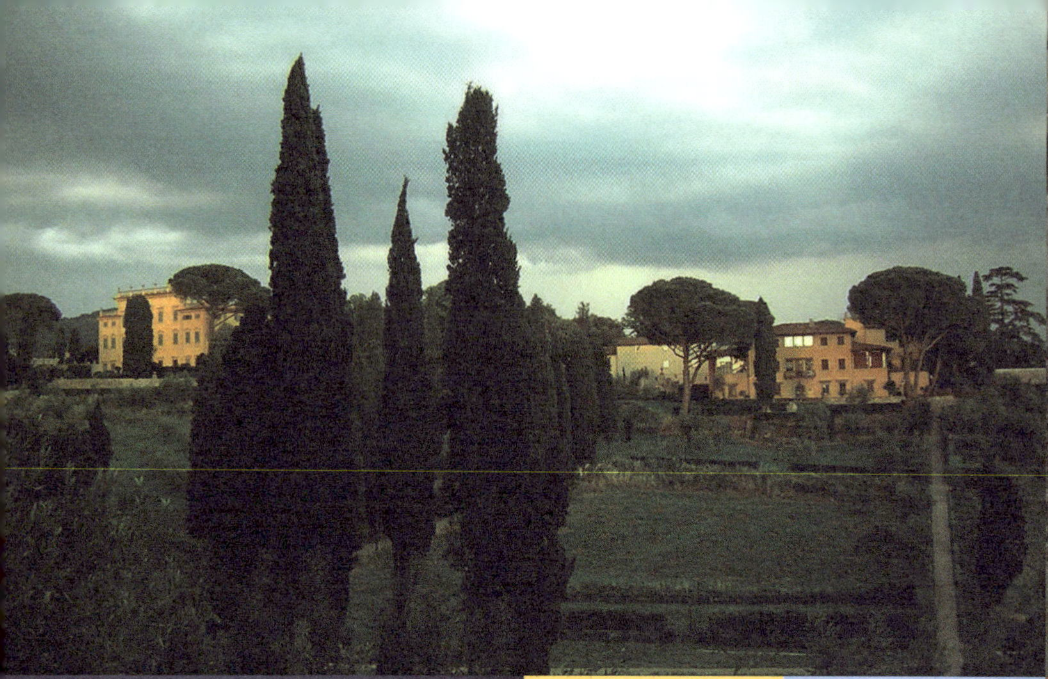
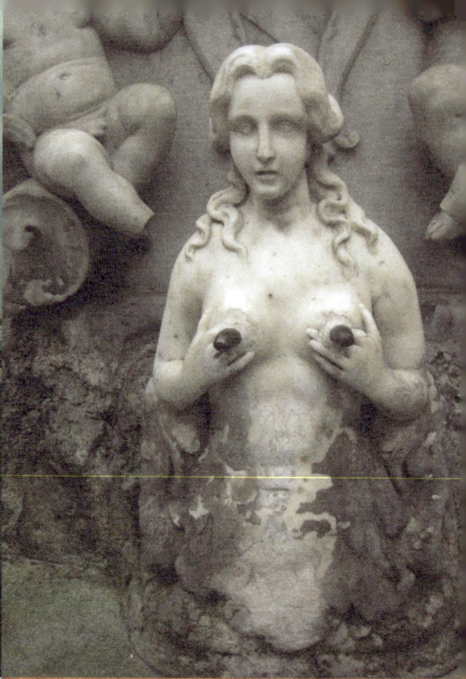
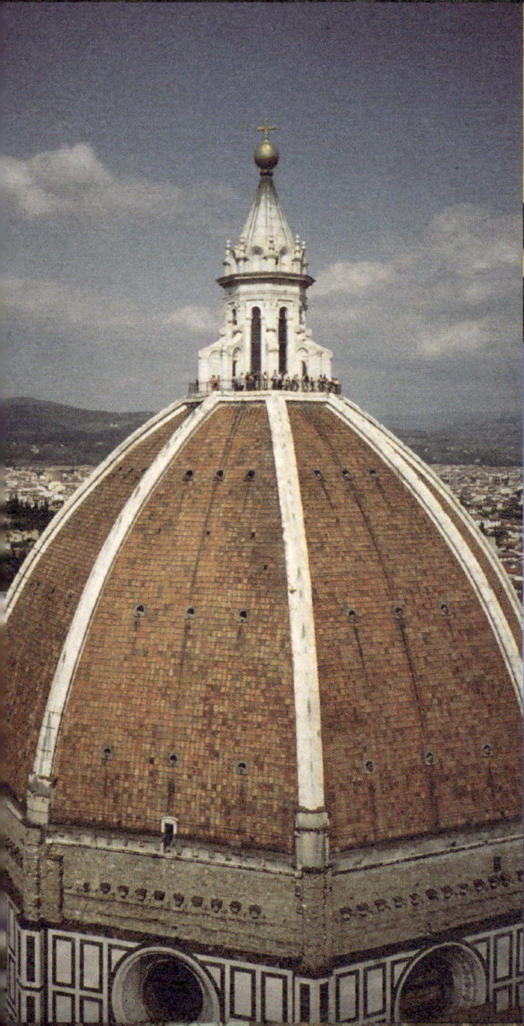
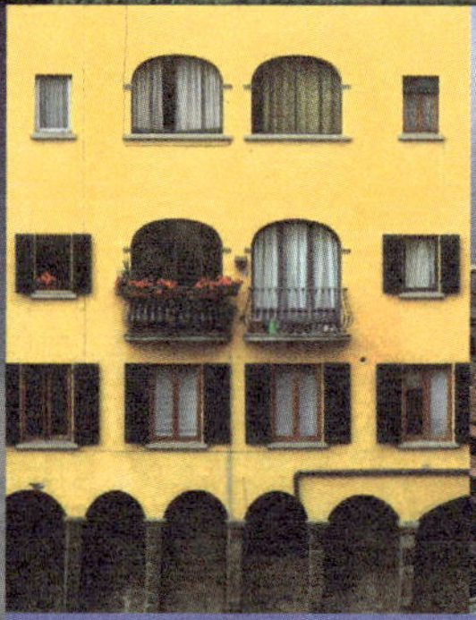
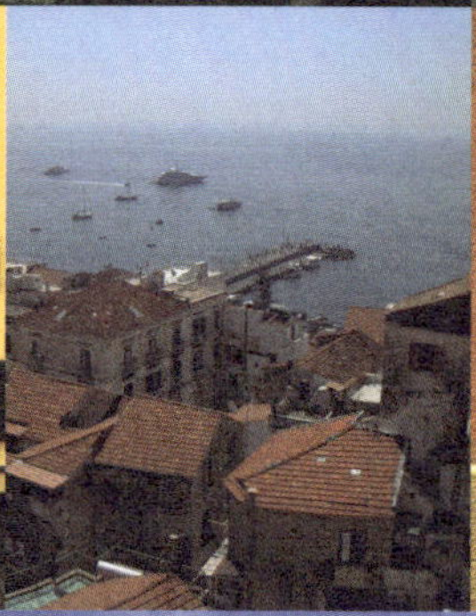

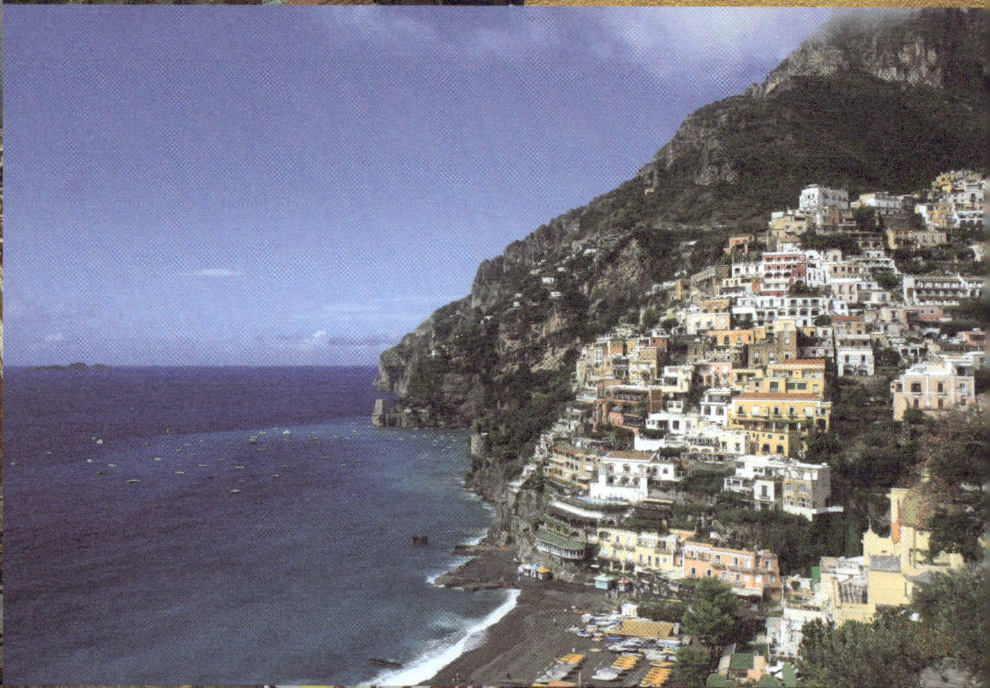
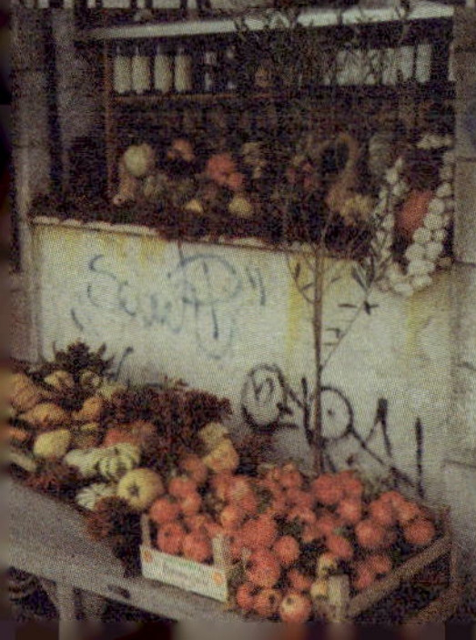
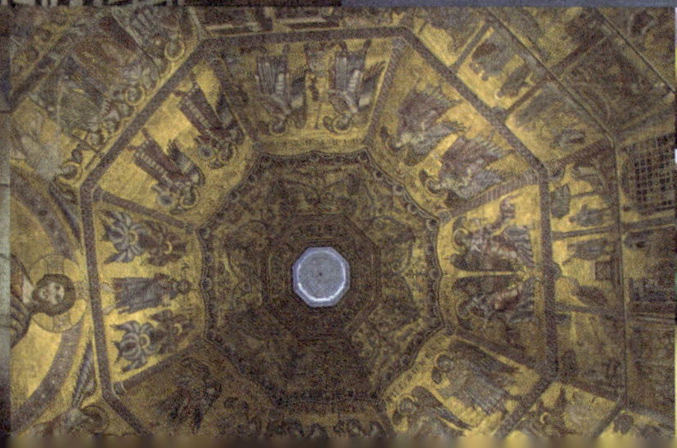
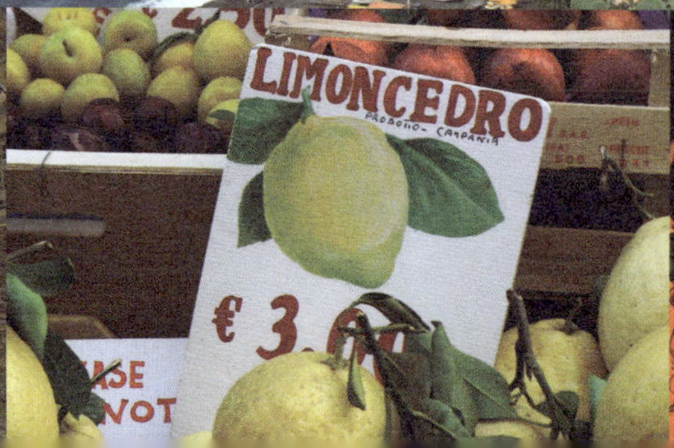
LIMONCEDRO
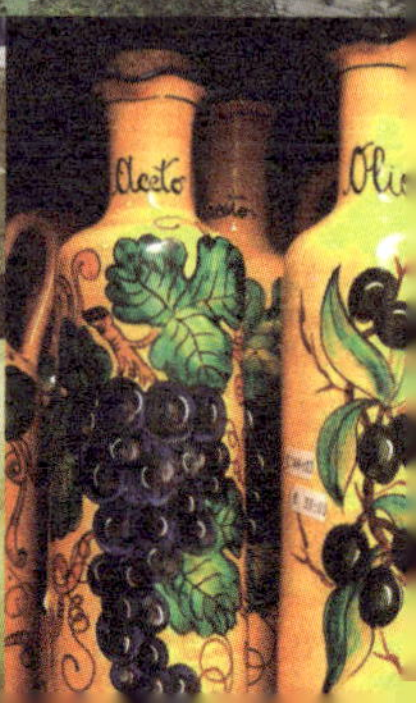

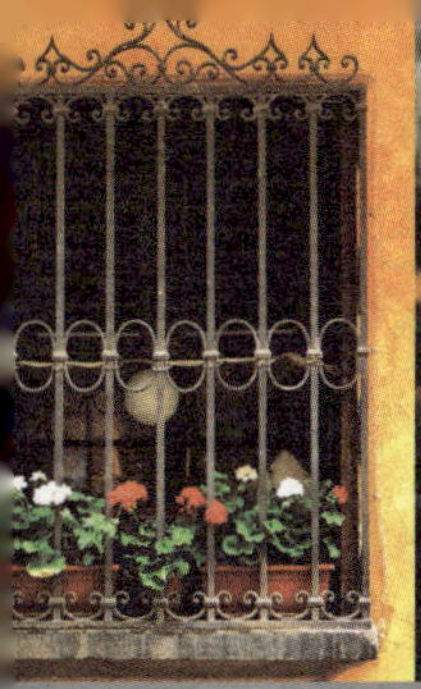
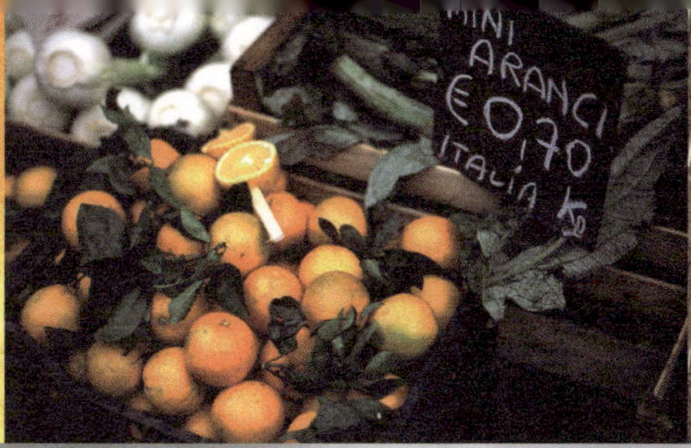
MINI
ARANCI
€ 0,70
ITALIA
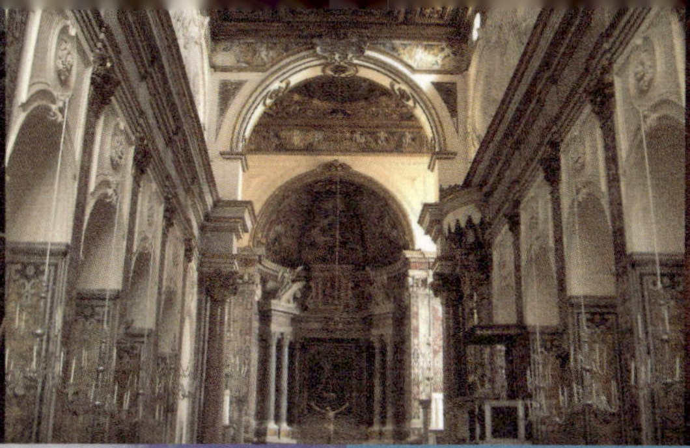
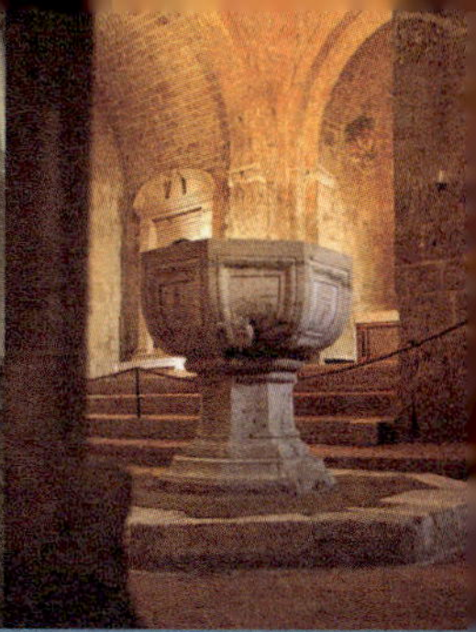
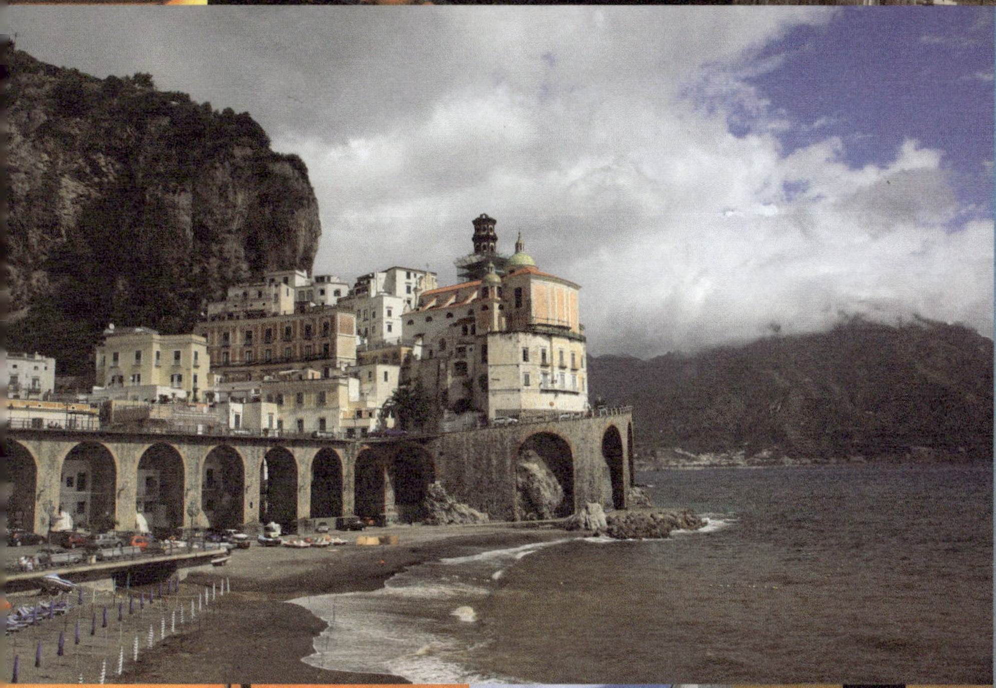
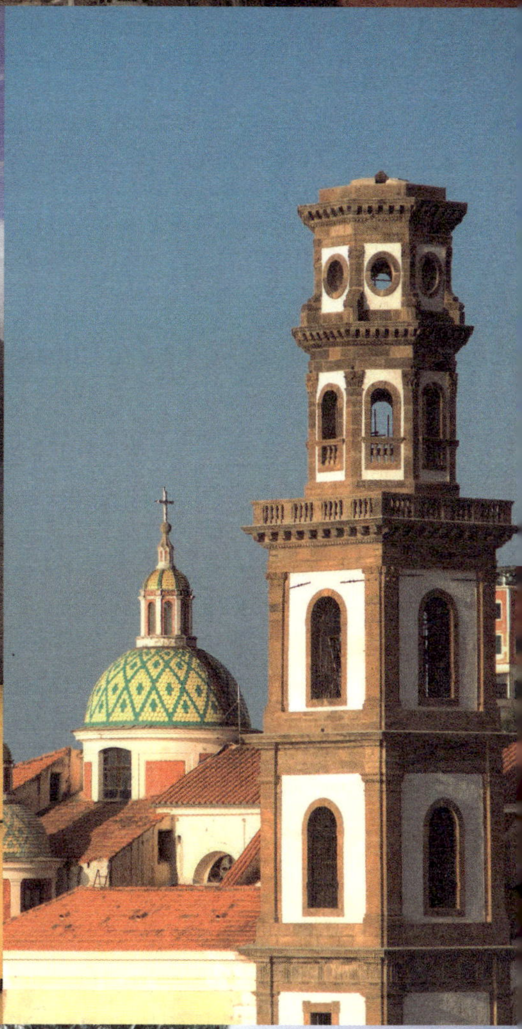
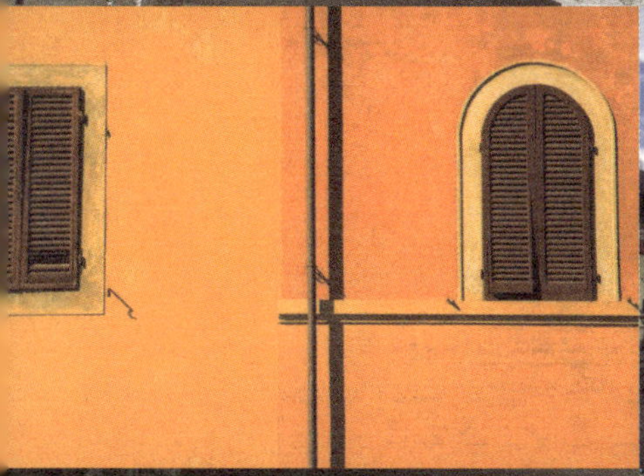
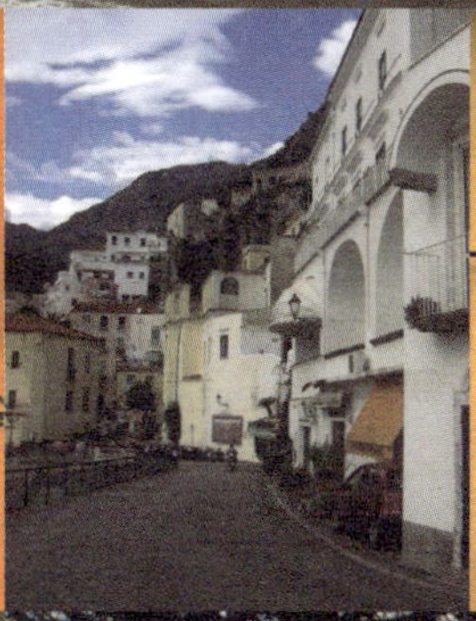
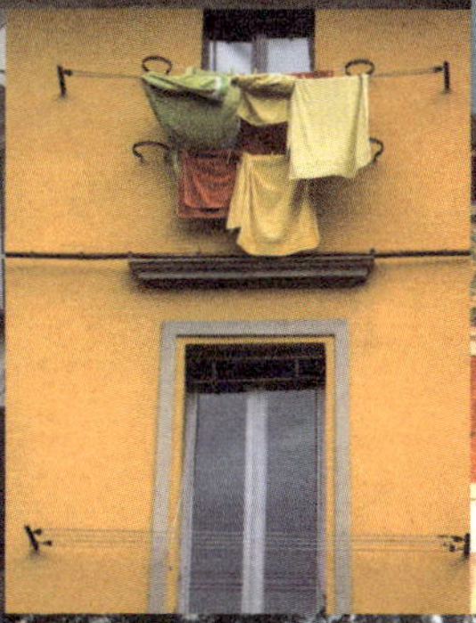
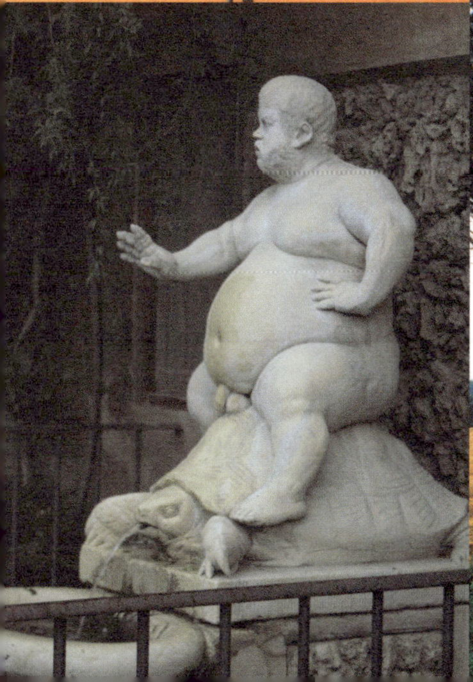
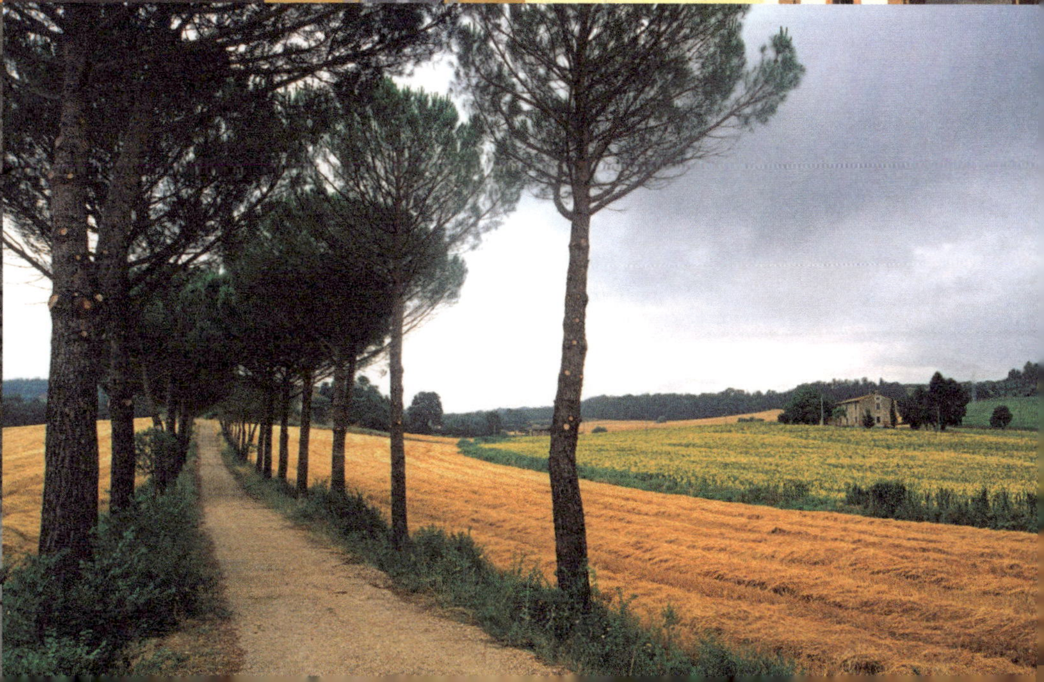

CHICKEN, LEMON, PARMESAN AND PARSLEY SPAGHETTI

This is the easiest and most delicious pasta meal I know – and it's great for lunch or as an entrée or main dish. It will never disappoint.

600g dried spaghetti (buy the best quality you can afford)
2 tablespoons olive oil for cooking
500g chicken tenderloins (or sliced chicken breast)
½ cup good-quality olive oil for dressing
¼–½ cup lemon juice (according to taste)
½ cup chopped flat-leaf parsley
1 cup grated Parmesan
¼ teaspoon sea salt
¼ teaspoon freshly ground black pepper

Cook the pasta according to the directions on the packet (as a rough guide, 100g pasta requires 1 litre of water).

While the pasta is cooking, heat the 2 tablespoons of olive oil in a pan to a medium–high heat. Add half the tenderloins and cook until golden on one side. Turn and cook for 2 minutes or until cooked through. Cook the remaining chicken and set aside until required.

Whisk together the olive oil and lemon juice until well mixed. Add the parsley, Parmesan, salt and pepper and continue whisking until creamy.

Drain the pasta – the better you drain it, the better the sauce will stick to it.

Add the cooked chicken and the sauce to the pasta and toss well so that the pasta and chicken are well coated. Serve immediately.

SERVES 6

GARLIC BRUSCHETTA

These slices of crusty bread are rubbed with olive oil and lightly toasted, then rubbed with garlic and seasoned with sea salt. Grilling the bread on a barbecue or grill plate will add a delicious smoky flavour that's hard to beat.

Toppings are optional – my favourite is thick slices of juicy, sun-ripened tomato and some fresh basil, but you might like to try semi-dried tomatoes with shaved Parmesan or moist buffalo mozzarella with fresh herbs.

1 loaf ciabatta, cut into 8 thick slices on the diagonal
¼ cup olive oil
3–4 cloves garlic
sea salt

Brush each slice of bread on both sides with olive oil and cook on a barbecue, grill plate or in a pan for 1–2 minutes on each side until golden brown – you might even like them to be a little charred. Rub each with a peeled and cut clove of garlic. Season with salt and serve with toppings of your choice or as a side to a hearty stew or soup.

SERVES 4

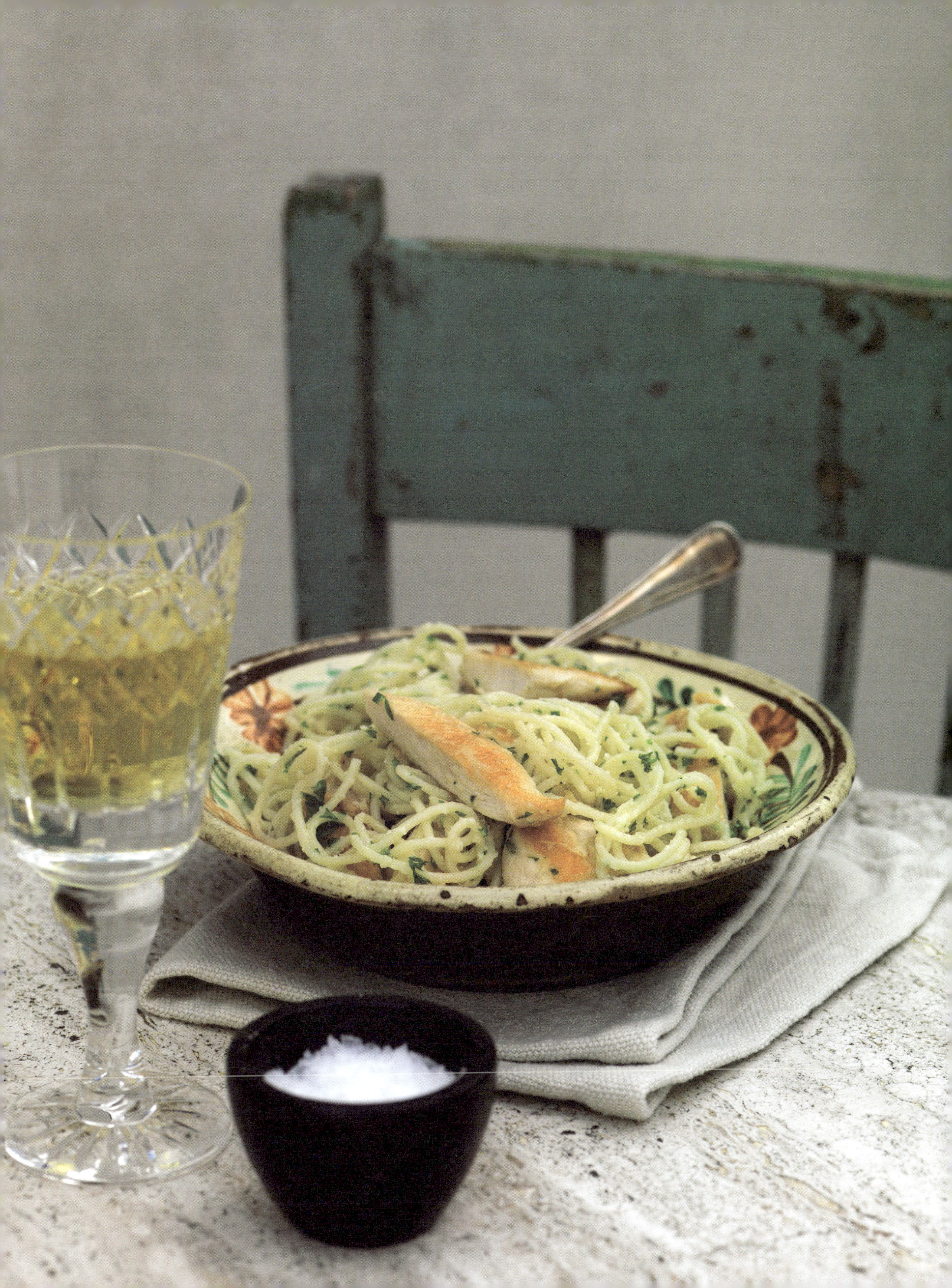

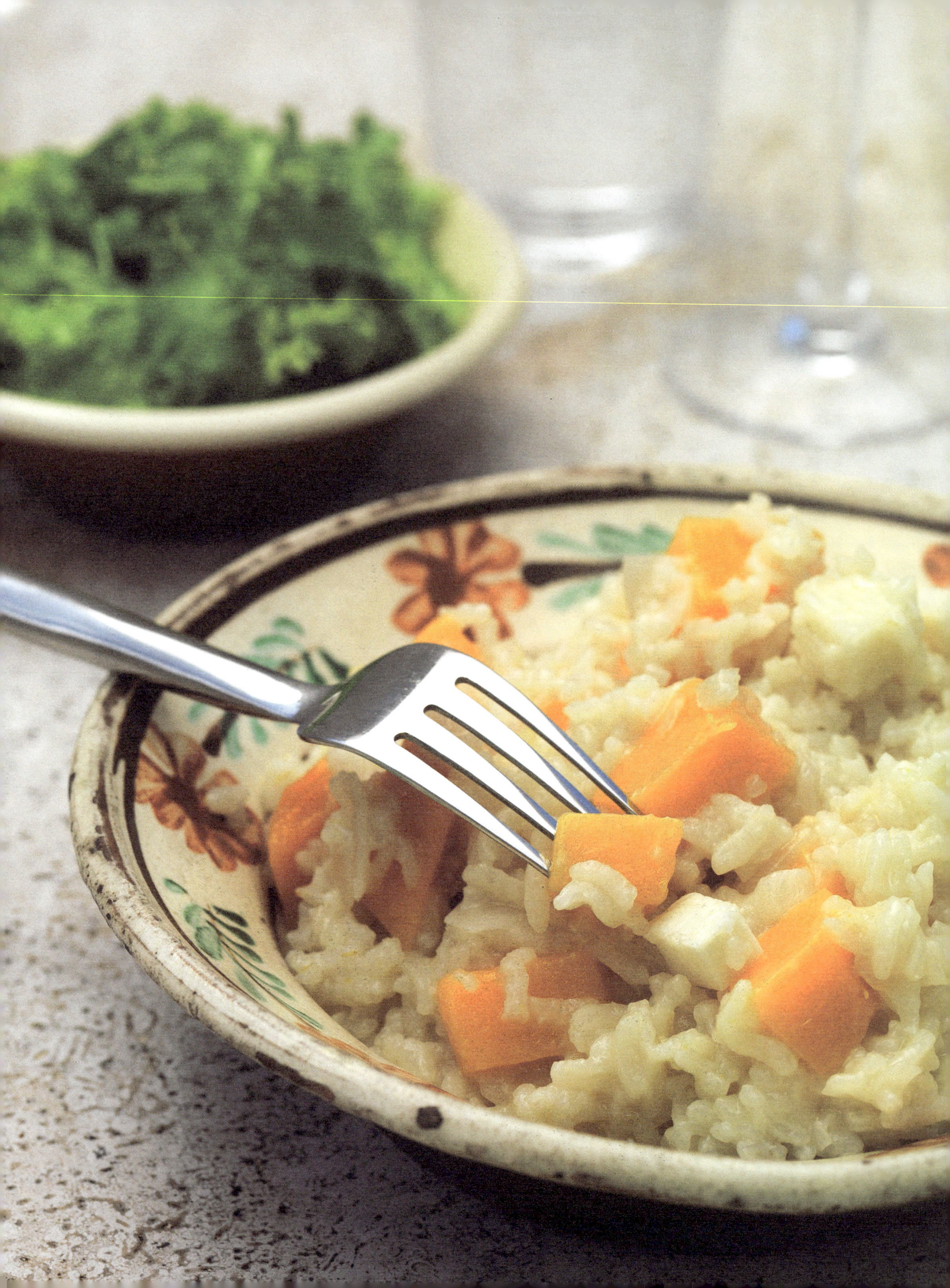

PUMPKIN AND PECORINO RISOTTO

Risotto is not nearly as temperamental as many people think. Although it isn't critical to stir the risotto continuously, it is important to ensure that it doesn't dry out during cooking. The key is to use good-quality risotto rice. With Carnaroli Riso Superfino or arborio you really can't go wrong.

1½ litres chicken or vegetable stock (use a low-salt version, if possible)
50g butter
2 tablespoons olive oil
1 large onion, finely diced
2 cups arborio or Carnaroli Riso Superfino rice
⅔ cup white wine
1 cup diced pumpkin, cut into 2cm dice
zest and juice of 1 lemon
½ cup cubed pecorino (the sharper the better)
salt and pepper
good-quality olive oil to garnish
grated Parmesan to garnish (preferably Parmigiano-Reggiano)

Heat the stock in a large saucepan to a simmer.

Melt the butter and olive oil together in a heavy-based frying pan. Add the onion and cook until soft and translucent.

Add the rice and stir to coat in the oil and butter. Gently sauté the rice for 2–3 minutes, stirring continuously.

Add the wine and allow it to bubble away until it is almost all evaporated. Begin to add the hot stock, a ladleful at a time, allowing it to almost evaporate between each addition – it is important that the rice grains are allowed to absorb most of the liquid before each new addition as this adds to the creaminess of the finished dish.

About halfway through the cooking time (about 10–15 minutes), add the pumpkin pieces.

If you need more liquid than you have stock, add some hot water. Alternatively, the rice may cook before you have used all of the stock and that's okay, too. The rice is cooked when it is firm to the bite but not chalky in the middle.

To serve, stir in the lemon zest and juice and the pecorino and allow risotto to sit for a few minutes. Give it one last stir and spoon onto individual plates and drizzle with extra olive oil and a sprinkle of Parmesan. Serve with a simple green salad.

SERVES 6

BARBECUED TUSCAN CHICKEN WITH CARAMELISED LEMONS

The caramelised lemons in this recipe are a real hit. Encourage your dinner guests to eat them rind and all – they are delicious. Use a decent-sized roasting dish that will fit all the ingredients in a snug-but-not-crowded way.

2 onions, sliced
3 lemons, sliced into thin rounds
1 whole chicken, cut into 8 portions
¼ cup chopped fresh herbs (rosemary, thyme and/or sage are good)
1 teaspoon salt
freshly ground black pepper
3–5 tablespoons olive oil

Arrange the onion and lemon slices in a roasting dish.

Brown each piece of chicken on both sides on a barbecue hot plate or in a frying pan and place on top of the sliced onions and lemons. Sprinkle chopped herbs over and season with salt and pepper. Drizzle over the olive oil and cover with foil. Return to the barbecue or place in a moderate oven (180°C). Cook for 30–40 minutes then uncover – take care to avoid the steam. Cook for a further 15–20 minutes until the onions and lemons are golden and gooey.

Serve with a simple green salad.

SERVES 4–6

CHICKEN THIGHS WITH GREEN CAPSICUM STUFFING

The green capsicum in this stuffing provides a fantastic flavour, which makes a great change from the sweeter red capsicums that seem to be dominating the culinary world lately.

STUFFING
1 green capsicum, deseeded and roughly chopped
½ cup roughly chopped flat-leaf parsley
2 slices bread, ground into breadcrumbs
zest of ½ lemon
3 tablespoons olive oil
salt and pepper

CHICKEN
light cooking oil for greasing roasting dish
6 chicken thighs, skinned, boned and flattened
¼ cup olive oil
12 toothpicks

Preheat oven to 200°C.

To make the stuffing, put the capsicum, parsley, bread and lemon zest in a food processor and pulse until finely chopped. With the motor running, drizzle in olive oil until the mixture begins to form a ball – it will start to clump together. Season to taste.

Lightly grease a shallow roasting dish with light cooking oil.

Put each chicken thigh on a board and place 1–2 tablespoons of stuffing in the middle of each and roll the thigh to enclose the stuffing. Secure with 2 toothpicks to hold stuffing firmly in place.

Place the thighs, toothpick-side down in prepared roasting dish. Drizzle ¼ cup olive oil over the thighs and cook for 30 minutes until golden brown and cooked through.

Serve either whole or cut on the diagonal with green salad and/or risotto.

SERVES 6

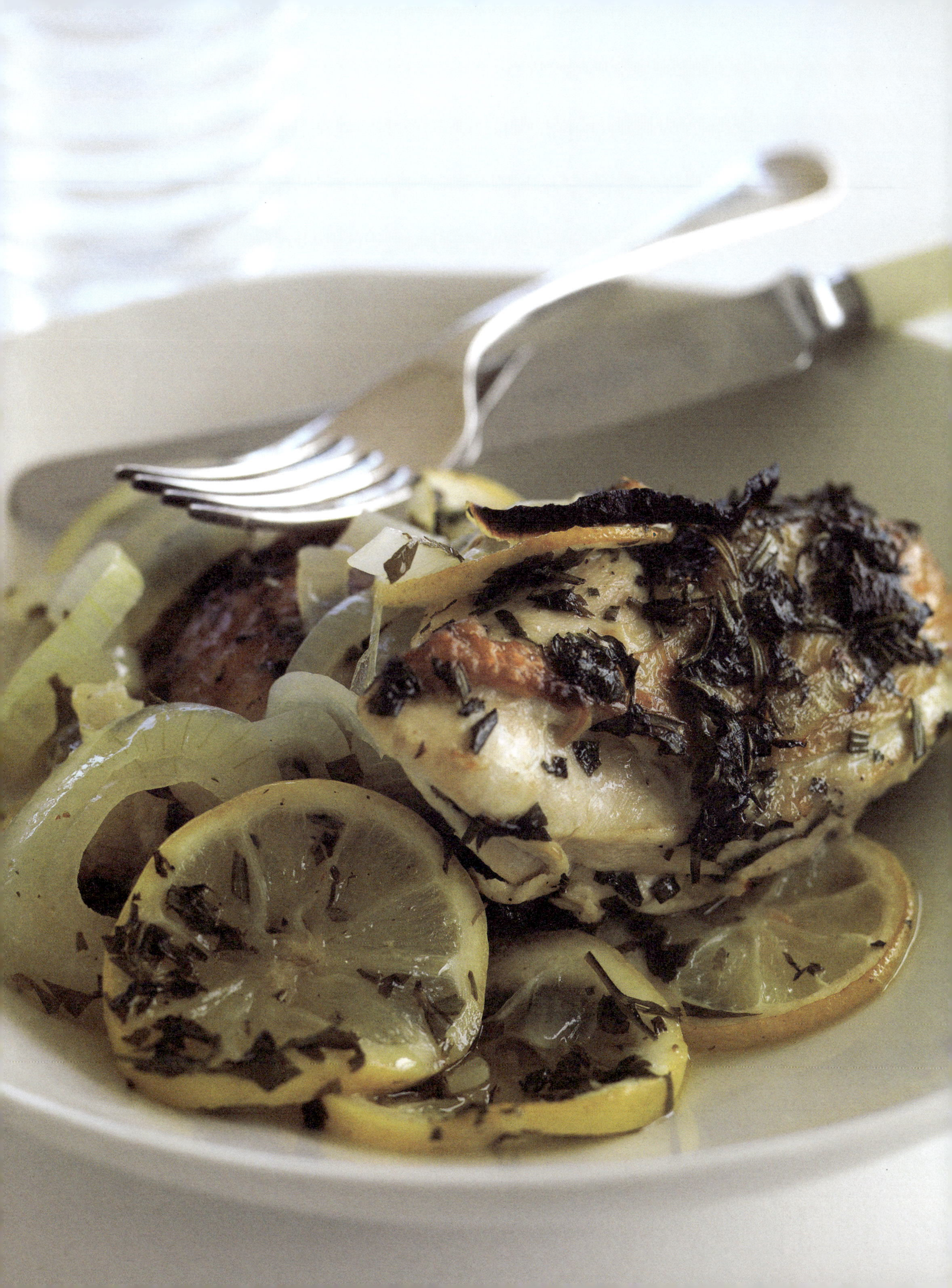

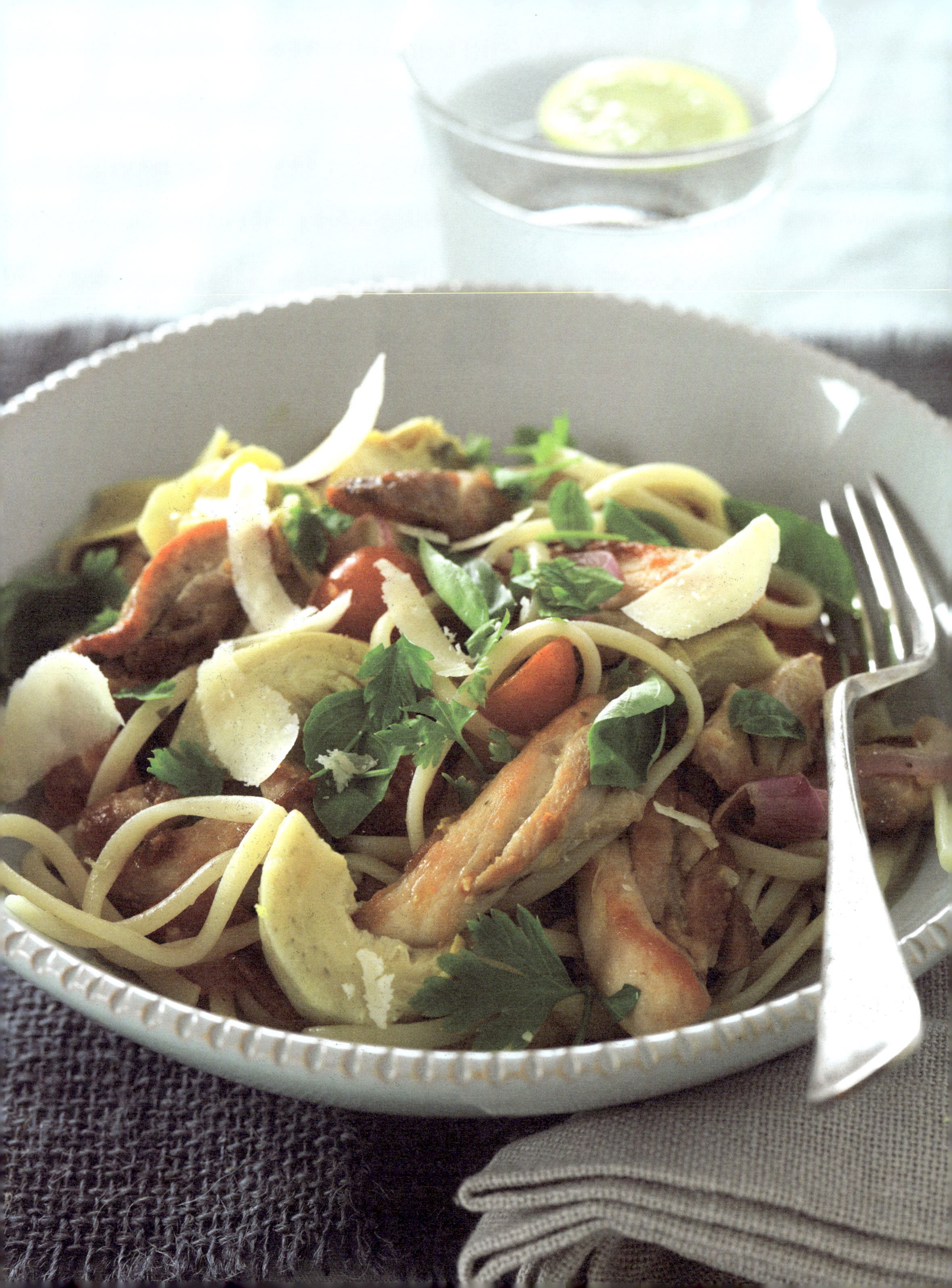

LINGUINE WITH CHICKEN, ARTICHOKES AND CHERRY TOMATOES

This simple dish is easy enough for a midweek dinner, but impressive enough for a dinner party.

400g dried linguine (spaghetti and fettuccine are also good)
2 tablespoons olive oil
400g chicken thighs, skinned, boned and thinly sliced
1 red onion, thinly sliced
2 cloves garlic, thinly sliced
zest and juice of 1 lemon
250g cherry tomatoes, halved
400g jar or can artichokes, drained and halved
¼ cup chopped flat-leaf parsley
¼ cup basil leaves
salt and pepper
¼ cup finely grated Parmesan to serve

Cook the pasta according to the directions on the packet.

While the pasta is cooking, heat the olive oil in a frying pan. Add the chicken and cook over medium heat until golden. Remove from the pan and set aside.

Place the red onion and garlic in the pan and cook over medium heat until golden brown.

Place the chicken back into the pan along with the lemon zest and juice, tomatoes and artichokes. Cook for 2 minutes. Stir in the well-drained pasta, parsley and basil. Season to taste.

Top with the grated Parmesan and enjoy!

SERVES 4

CREAMY PESTO CHICKEN WITH PAPPARDELLE

This is the quickest and easiest dinner and the wide-ribboned pappardelle looks very impressive.

400g pappardelle
2 tablespoons olive oil
500g chicken breasts, skinned, boned and cut into chunks
¼ cup basil pesto
¾ cup cream
¼ teaspoon salt
¼ cup finely grated Parmesan to garnish
basil leaves to garnish

Cook the pappardelle according to the directions on the packet.

While the pasta is cooking, heat the oil in a frying pan. Add the chicken and cook over high heat until golden brown. Reduce heat and add the pesto and cream to the pan. Cook for a further 3–4 minutes until the sauce is thick and creamy and the chicken is cooked through. Season to taste.

Stir the well-drained pasta through the hot sauce. Save a little of the pasta cooking water to thin the sauce, if required.

Place into serving bowls and top with the grated Parmesan and basil leaves. Serve with a green salad.

SERVES 4

Linguine with Chicken, Artichokes and Cherry Tomatoes

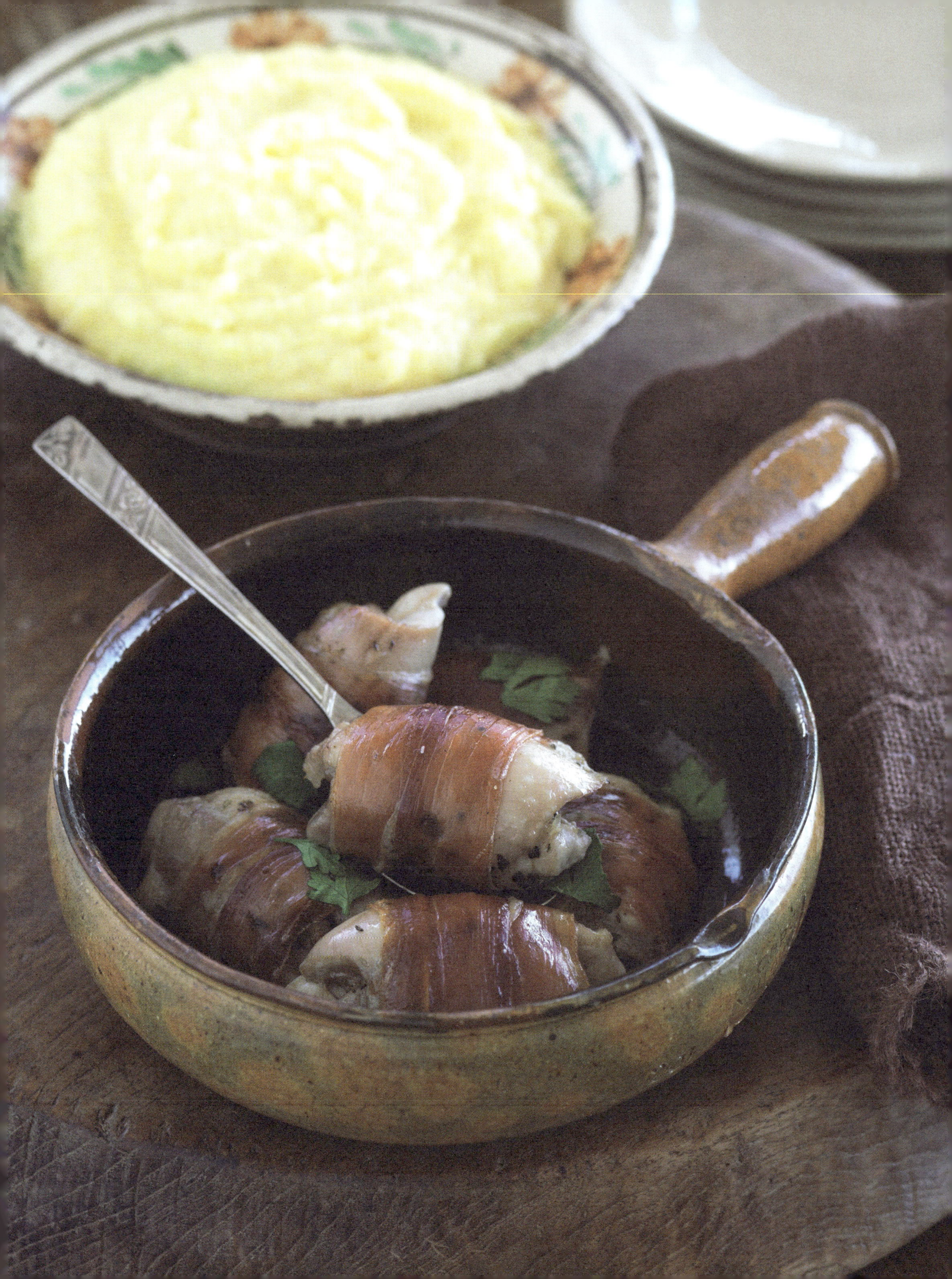

CHICKEN THIGHS WITH OREGANO AND PROSCIUTTO

Wrapping chicken thighs in prosciutto keeps them moist and tasty.

1 tablespoon fresh oregano (or 1 teaspoon dried)
8 chicken thighs, skinned, boned and flattened
salt and pepper
4 slices prosciutto, cut in half lengthwise
1 cup chicken stock
olive oil spray

Preheat oven to 200°C.

Sprinkle a little oregano over flattened chicken thighs and season with salt and pepper. Roll up, pinwheel style. Lay a slice of prosciutto on the board and place a rolled chicken thigh at one end. Roll to enclose the thigh in the prosciutto. Repeat with the remaining prosciutto and chicken pieces.

Place the chicken parcels into an ovenproof dish, spacing them well apart from each other. Pour the stock over the chicken and brush each roll with olive oil.

Bake for 20–25 minutes, basting occasionally, until the chicken parcels are cooked through and golden.

Serve immediately with *Creamy Polenta* (see page 49) and a green salad.

SERVES 4

CHICKEN WITH LEMON AND OLIVES

With this combination of olives and lemons, you will definitely feel as if you're in Italy!

1kg chicken pieces, bone in
1 red onion, cut into wedges
2 cloves garlic, sliced
1 lemon, cut into wedges
½ cup dry white wine
2 cups chicken stock
½ cup pitted green olives, halved
2 tablespoons capers
1 tablespoon olive oil
salt and pepper
¼ cup chopped flat-leaf parsley

Preheat oven to 180°C.

Place the chicken in a large ovenproof dish. Scatter the onion, garlic and lemon wedges over the chicken. Add the wine, stock, green olives and capers. Add a splash of olive oil all over and season with salt and pepper.

Bake uncovered for 1 hour until the chicken is very tender. Increase the oven temperature to 220°C and cook for a further 15 minutes until the chicken is golden brown.

Garnish with parsley and serve with *Creamy Polenta* (see page 49) or mashed potatoes and green vegetables.

SERVES 4

Chicken Thighs with Oregano and Prosciutto (front), Creamy Polenta (rear, recipe page 49)

CHICKEN LASAGNE WITH FRESH BASIL

Fresh basil is like a mouthful of summer and it adds a real freshness to this rich dish.

CHICKEN FILLING
1 tablespoon olive oil
450g chicken mince
1 clove garlic, crushed
a handful of fresh basil, chopped
400g can crushed tomatoes
salt and pepper

WHITE SAUCE
50g butter
1 heaped tablespoon flour
1 bay leaf
¼ cup white wine
1 cup milk

3 large sheets fresh lasagne
½ cup grated Parmesan

Preheat oven to 190°C.

To prepare the chicken filling, heat the oil in a frying pan. Add the chicken mince and garlic and cook for 4–5 minutes over medium–high heat. Mash with a fork to break up the mince as it cooks. Add the basil and tomatoes. Simmer for 5–10 minutes until slightly thickened. Season to taste.

To make the white sauce, melt the butter in a small saucepan. Stir in the flour and cook over medium heat, stirring, until blended. Add the bay leaf and wine and simmer for 3 minutes, stirring constantly. Gradually add the milk, stirring constantly. Continue stirring over medium heat until the sauce boils and thickens.

To assemble the lasagne, lightly grease a 20 x 15cm (or thereabouts) ovenproof dish. Add a spoonful of the chicken mince sauce and spread in a thin layer to just cover the bottom of the dish. Add a sheet of lasagne and top with with one-third of the mince followed by another sheet of lasagne. Add another layer of mince, then another layer of lasagne and a final layer of mince. Top with white sauce and scatter with Parmesan.

Bake for 35–40 minutes until the lasagne is golden brown and bubbling.

Allow to rest for 5 minutes before serving.

SERVES 4–6

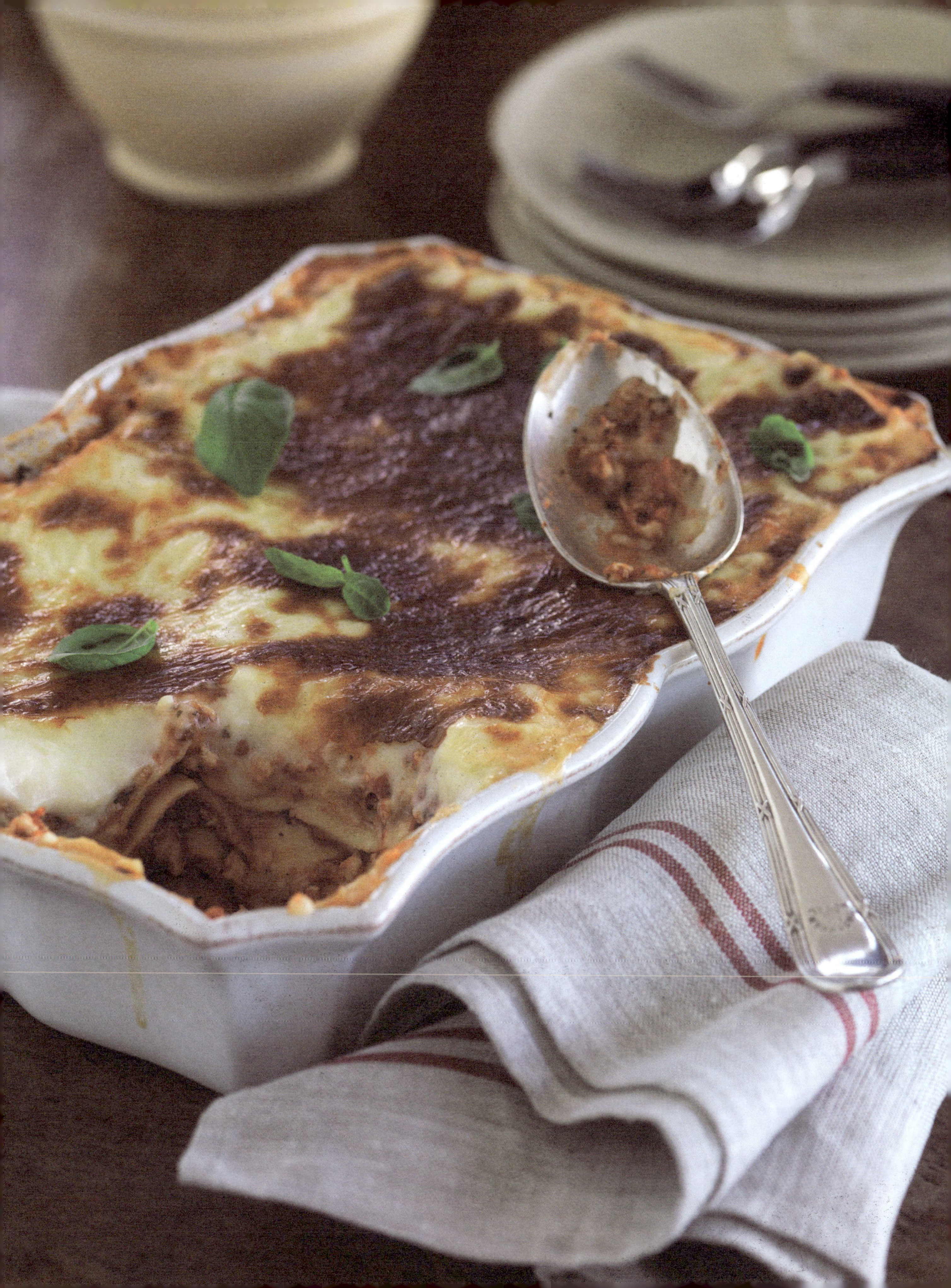

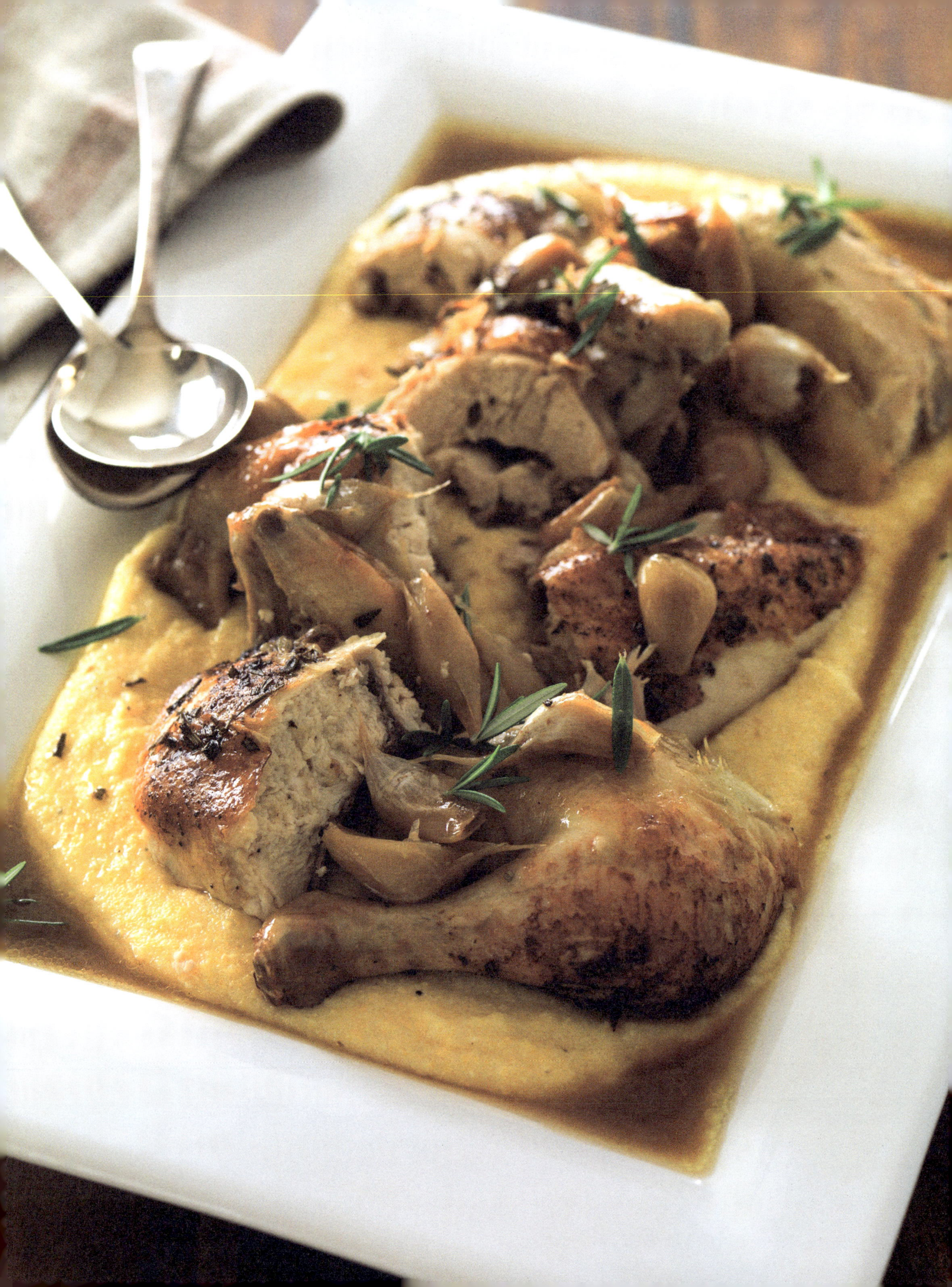

TUSCAN-STYLE ROASTED CHICKEN WITH WINE AND GARLIC

This is a great dish for a cold night and my favourite kind of comfort food, especially when served with *Creamy Polenta* (see below).

1 whole chicken
1 lemon, cut into wedges
1 red onion, cut into wedges
2 tablespoons olive oil
1 tablespoon finely chopped rosemary, plus extra leaves for garnish
½ teaspoon salt
freshly ground black pepper
1 bulb garlic, cloves separated, unpeeled
1 cup chicken stock
½ cup dry white wine
1 quantity of Creamy Polenta to serve

Preheat oven to 180°C.

Dry and generously salt the cavity of the chicken. Place the lemon and onion inside the cavity. Rub the olive oil on the chicken then sprinkle with the finely chopped rosemary and season with salt and pepper. Place the chicken into a roasting dish then add the garlic, chicken stock and wine to the dish.

Roast the chicken for 1½ hours or until the juices run clear when pierced through the thickest part of the thigh. Baste occasionally.

To serve, carve the chicken and arrange on a bed of *Creamy Polenta*. Drizzle the pan juices over the chicken. Squeeze the garlic flesh from the skin and dot cloves over the chicken. Garnish with rosemary leaves.

SERVES 4–6

CREAMY POLENTA

Polenta is a staple of northern Italy. It is good as a side dish to a main, but can also be served as a first course.

2 cups chicken stock
2 cups milk
1 cup instant polenta
½ cup grated Parmesan
2 teaspoons butter
freshly ground black pepper

Heat the chicken stock and milk in a saucepan. Bring to the boil and add the polenta in a steady stream, stirring constantly. Simmer for 3–4 minutes or until it is thick and creamy. Stir in the Parmesan and butter and season with pepper.

SERVES 4–6

Tuscan-Style Roasted Chicken with Wine and Garlic on Creamy Polenta

CHICKEN SCHNITZEL WITH MOZZARELLA, RED CAPSICUM AND BASIL STUFFING

These treats can be served as a substantial party snack – they're easy to eat with your fingers when they have cooled down.

8 slices chicken schnitzel
1 roasted red capsicum, skinned, deseeded and sliced
75g mozzarella, cut into strips
¼ cup fresh basil leaves, plus extra for garnish
1 tablespoon olive oil
½ teaspoon dried oregano
½ teaspoon dried thyme
½ teaspoon dried marjoram
salt and freshly ground black pepper

toothpicks

Preheat oven to 200°C.

Lay each slice of schnitzel on a board. Place a few strips of capsicum, some mozzarella strips and a few basil leaves on one end of each piece. Roll up, pinwheel style, and secure with a toothpick.

Place the schnitzel rolls into a baking dish. Drizzle with olive oil, sprinkle with dried herbs and season with salt and pepper. Bake for 20–25 minutes or until the chicken is cooked through.

Garnish with basil leaves and serve immediately.

SERVES 4

BAKED CHICKEN WITH EGGPLANT, TOMATO AND MOZZARELLA

You've got to love the taste of fresh mozzarella cheese. Buy the best you can afford, I say, and use it sparingly!

2 tablespoons olive oil
1 small eggplant, sliced into 1cm thick slices lengthwise
4 chicken breasts, skinned and boned
400g can Italian diced tomatoes
250g mozzarella cheese, thinly sliced
basil leaves to garnish

Preheat oven to 180°C. Lightly grease an ovenproof dish.

Heat the olive oil in a frying pan. Add the eggplant slices and cook over medium heat for 4–5 minutes on each side or until golden brown and tender.

Place the chicken breasts into the prepared dish. Place a slice of eggplant on each breast, then top each with tomatoes and slices of mozzarella.

Bake for 25–35 minutes or until cooked through and the cheese is golden.

Garnish with the basil leaves and serve immediately.

SERVES 4

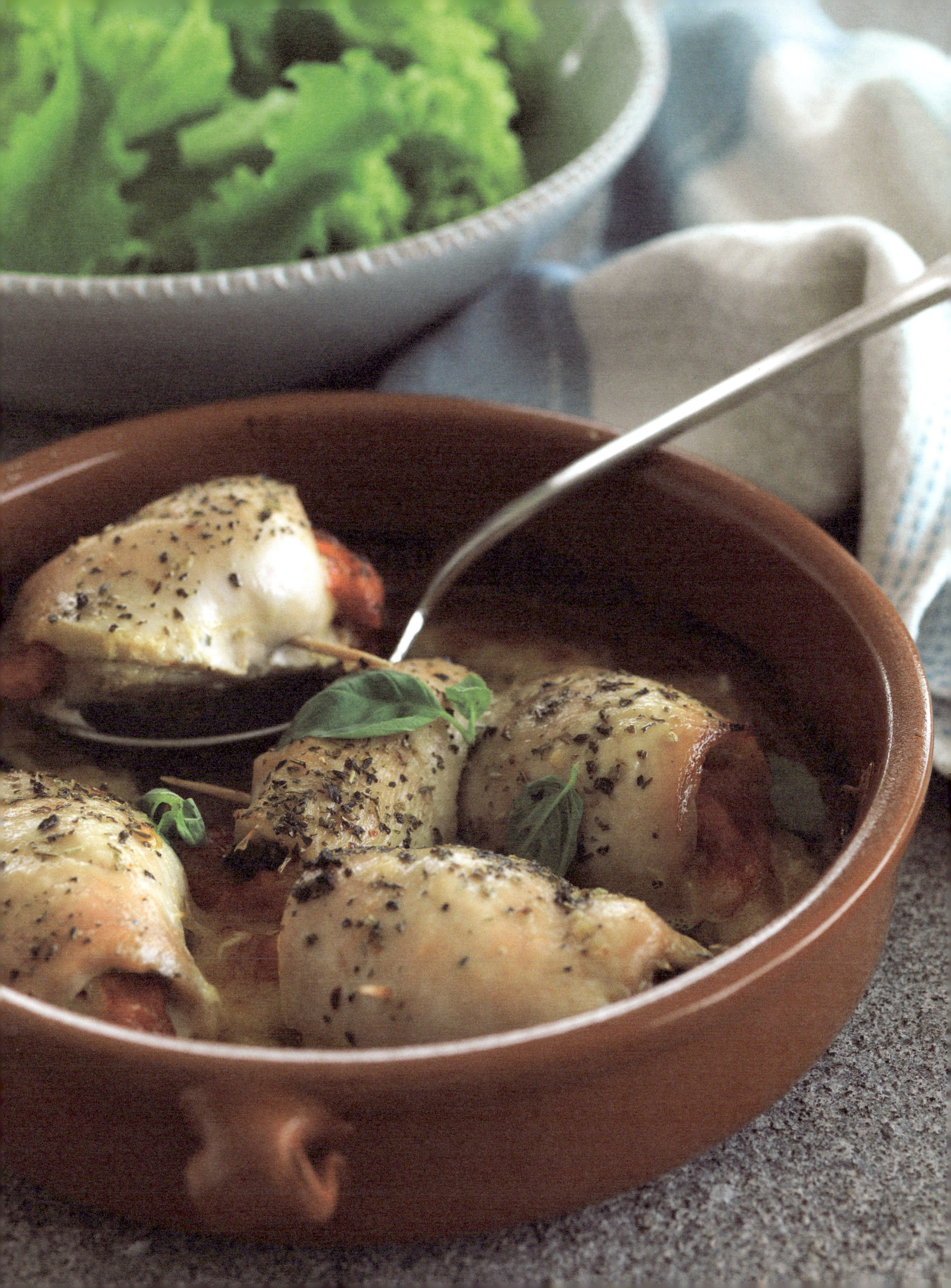

CHICKEN, ORZO AND ROASTED RED CAPSICUM SALAD

Orzo is a rice-shaped pasta that's quick and easy to cook and perfect for salads.

LEMON DRESSING
3 tablespoons extra virgin olive oil
2 tablespoons white wine vinegar
zest and juice of ½ lemon
salt and pepper

SALAD
2 red capsicums, deseeded and sliced
1 red onion, cut into wedges
2 cloves garlic, sliced
3 tablespoons olive oil
2 tablespoons balsamic vinegar
1 tablespoon brown sugar
1 cup orzo
500g chicken breasts, skinned, boned and sliced into strips
2 cups baby spinach leaves
salt and pepper

To make the lemon dressing, whisk oil, vinegar, and lemon zest and juice together. Season to taste with salt and pepper.

Preheat oven to 200°C.

Place the capsicums, onion and garlic in an ovenproof dish and drizzle with 2 tablespoons of the olive oil. Bake for 25–30 minutes until the vegetables are cooked. Stir in the balsamic vinegar and brown sugar and set aside to cool.

Meanwhile, cook the orzo according to the directions on the packet. Drain, rinse and drain again well and set aside to cool.

Heat 1 tablespoon olive oil in a frying pan over medium heat and cook the chicken in batches until golden brown and cooked through.

Put the orzo, roasted vegetables and chicken in a large bowl. Add the spinach leaves and toss gently to combine. Season to taste. Drizzle with the lemon dressing just before serving.

SERVES 4

ROAST CHICKEN BREAST WITH SUN-DRIED TOMATO AND PESTO STUFFING

When ripe tomatoes are dried their flavour intensifies, making them perfect for adding flavour to chicken.

¼ cup ricotta
¼ cup sun-dried tomatoes, drained and chopped
2 tablespoons basil pesto
salt and freshly ground black pepper
4 boned chicken breasts, skin on
2 tablespoons olive oil
½ teaspoon dried rosemary
½ teaspoon dried oregano
½ teaspoon dried thyme

Preheat oven to 180°C.

Combine the ricotta, sun-dried tomatoes and pesto in a small bowl. Season to taste.

Place the chicken breasts on a chopping board. Carefully separate the skin from the breast with your fingers to make a pouch, and gently push one-quarter of the stuffing mixture into each pouch. Place the chicken breasts skin-side up in an ovenproof dish. Drizzle with the olive oil and sprinkle with the dried herbs.

Bake for 30–40 minutes or until the juices run clear when pierced. Remove from the oven and allow to rest for 5 minutes before serving.

SERVES 4

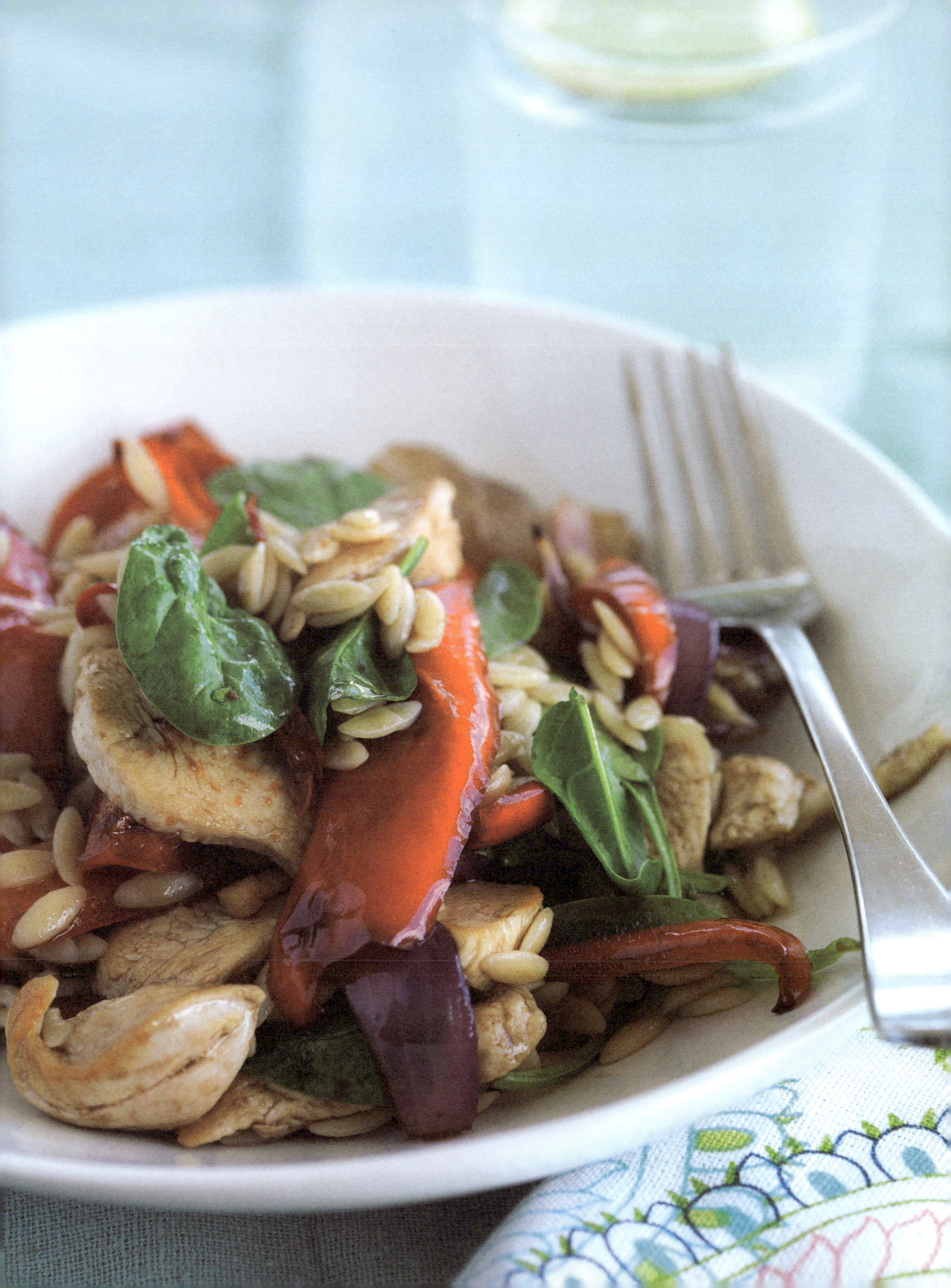

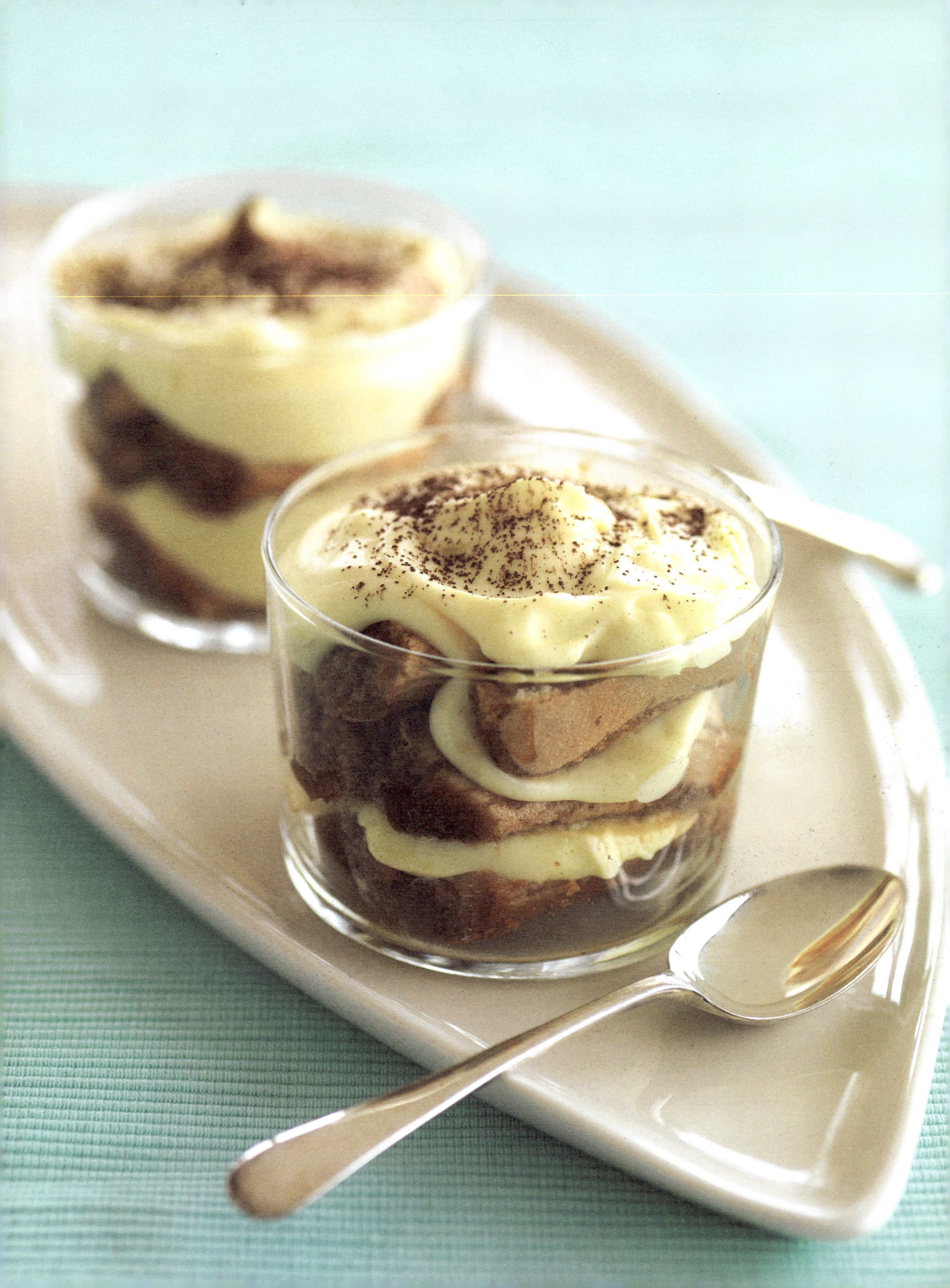

LAZY TIRAMISU

I like to make these individual serves in little espresso glasses or cups and they can be prepared the day before you need them.

24 sponge fingers (store-bought is fine)
2 cups strong espresso, cooled
500g mascarpone
½ cup caster sugar
100ml fresh cream, lightly whipped
cocoa powder to garnish

Dip two sponge fingers into the espresso and arrange on the base of the first ramekin. Repeat with remaining ramekins.

Whisk together the mascarpone and sugar until smooth. Spoon one heaped tablespoon into each ramekin and spread roughly over the espresso-soaked sponge base.

Combine the cream with the remaining mascarpone sugar mix, whisk well and set aside. Dip the rest of the sponge fingers in espresso and add another layer to each ramekin. Top with the creamy mascarpone mixture and refrigerate until required.

Just before serving, dust each dish with cocoa.

MAKES 6 RAMEKINS OR SMALL CUPS

GRILLED NECTARINES WITH VANILLA RICOTTA

This dessert is so simple it barely requires a recipe! Because it's so simple, try to use good quality ingredients so that the flavours really stand out.

GRILLED NECTARINES
3 tablespoons caster sugar
6 firm ripe nectarines, halved and stones removed

TOPPING
1½ cups ricotta
2 tablespoons cream cheese
1 teaspoon pure vanilla essence
¼ cup caster sugar

To grill the nectarines, sprinkle the caster sugar on a saucer and dip each nectarine half, flesh-side down, into the sugar. Place the nectarine halves sugar-side down on a preheated barbecue hot plate or grill plate. Cook them slowly until the sugar begins to burn.

To make the topping, whisk together the ricotta, cream cheese, vanilla and sugar until smooth and creamy.

Top each nectarine with a generous dollop of vanilla ricotta topping and serve immediately.

SERVES 6

FRANCE
INDULGING IN DIJON & LYON

> 'On my first visit to France I was overwhelmed by the cuisine and adored the fact that the French were so passionate and serious about their food.'

My parents' dinner parties in the seventies always seemed to have a French culinary theme – coq au vin, scallops in a white wine sauce, crêpes Suzette, and more. I grew up with these dishes and fell forever in love with French cuisine. The heady aroma of wine cooking, the frantic whisking of a sophisticated crème sauce, the endless flipping of paper-thin crêpes – all held the promise of leftovers the next morning! One of my favourite breakfasts was the gravy from coq au vin heated up and served on buttery toast – a great way to start any day.

On my first visit to France I was overwhelmed by the cuisine and adored the fact that the French were so passionate and serious about their food – from shopping for it, to the careful preparation, to the time they take to eat a meal. Everyone takes absolute pleasure in it and I felt immediately at home.

My mornings in Lyon started with throwing the shutters open from my third-storey room to view the day and watch as people made their way to work along the cobbled streets. I'd join them with a walk down the river for my morning café au lait. Of course my schoolgirl French lessons had taught me how to ask for the important things: 'Un croissant s'il vous plait.' Aah, a buttery feather-light croissant to make my morning complete!

For lunch I liked to visit one of the many restaurants offering two- and three-course lunches. One of my most memorable was a simple salad made with iceberg lettuce, warm chicken livers and a very basic vinaigrette. The flavours rested so delicately on my taste buds and lent themselves perfectly to each other. French food is not all rich and creamy, they do simple very well indeed and it's worth saving space for a small piece of apple tart.

Another of my favourite places to visit in France is Dijon and the surrounding region. Here I can indulge my love of traditional French country cuisine. It's hearty yet not heavy. And it's here that my favourite dinner of all time – coq au vin – is said to have originated.

To recreate the romance of cooking French food when I'm back home, I start early in the day with a coffee and pastry, and plan my trip to a farmers' market. Wine is an essential part of any French meal, of course, so I invite friends who will be happy to join me until the wee hours as we pick our way through the different courses. Oh, and we always finish the meal with cheese . . . followed by dessert!

SANDWICHS
BOISSONS
Fraîches
GLACES

BOCUSE D'OR

RESTAURANT
A
LA CARTE

FOIE GRAS
A LA MODE
DES LANDES

Le TIRE BOUCHON

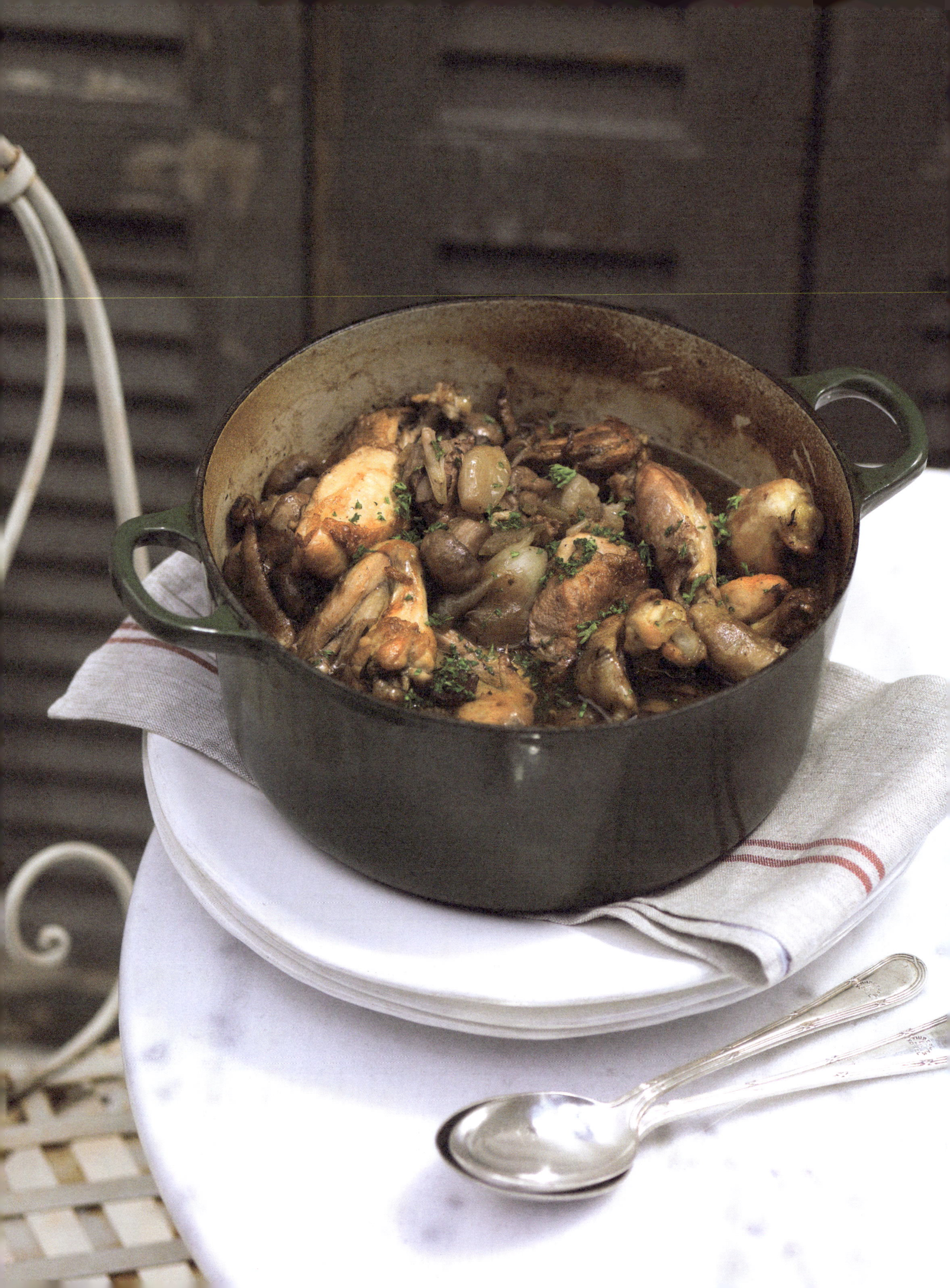

COQ AU VIN

This is an easy variation of a traditional French dish which has many regional interpretations. The key ingredient is always the wine and you will need a large heavy-based saucepan or ovenproof casserole dish with a lid.

Coq au vin is a great dish to make for a large number of guests because the recipe can be multiplied easily, prepared the day before and served at the table.

20g butter
16 baby onions (or shallots), peeled
2 sticks celery, leave whole
3 rashers smoky bacon, diced
24 brown button mushrooms, stalks removed
2 tablespoons olive oil
2 whole chickens, cut into serving-sized portions and excess fat removed (or use chicken pieces)
2 cups red wine (Pinot Noir or Burgundy)
1 cup chicken stock
3 bay leaves
2 tablespoons fresh thyme
1–2 tablespoons plain flour to thicken (optional)
salt and pepper

Melt butter in a saucepan or casserole dish over medium heat and add the baby onions (or shallots), celery and bacon. Sauté until golden, remove and set aside. Add the mushrooms to the pan and sauté for 2–3 minutes. Remove and set aside.

Add the olive oil to the pan and brown the chicken pieces. You may need to do this in 2–3 batches to avoid overcrowding the pan and to ensure the chicken pieces are browned on both sides.

Return the chicken, onions, celery and bacon to the pan. Add the wine and bring to the boil for 2 minutes to cook off the alcohol.

Add the chicken stock, bay leaves and thyme. Bring to the boil, cover then simmer for 1–1½ hours until the chicken is very tender and about to fall away from the bone. Alternatively, cover and cook for 1½ hours in an ovenproof casserole dish, in an oven preheated to 160°C.

Add the mushrooms and season to taste with salt and pepper and continue to cook for a further 20 minutes until the sauce has reduced a little. You want a sauce that is not too thick, not too thin, but just right. If you need to thicken the sauce, mix flour with cold water to form a runny paste and add to liquid in the pan. Stirring occasionally to avoid lumps forming, simmer, uncovered, for 10 minutes.

SERVES 8–10

RATATOUILLE

This traditional French dish is a perfect accompaniment to roast chicken.

¼ cup olive oil
1 red onion, sliced
2 cloves garlic, crushed
2 eggplants, cut into chunks
1 red capsicum, cut into chunks
1 green capsicum, cut into chunks
4 courgettes, sliced
6 tomatoes, skinned, deseeded and chopped
1 teaspoon dried basil
2 teaspoons chopped fresh rosemary
1 teaspoon salt
freshly ground black pepper

Heat the olive oil in a large, heavy-based saucepan. Add the onion and garlic and sauté until soft. Add the eggplants, capsicums and courgettes. Sauté for 5 minutes. Add the tomatoes, basil, rosemary, salt and pepper. Cover and simmer for 45 minutes or until the vegetables are tender.

SERVES 4–6

CHICKEN WITH TARRAGON CREAM SAUCE

This emulates a dish I tried at a restaurant in Lyon that has three Michelin stars. To me it exemplifies the best of French cooking – simple yet elegant and perfect for a quick dinner.

2 tablespoons olive oil
4 chicken breasts, skinned and boned
1 clove garlic, crushed
25g butter
2 tablespoons chopped fresh tarragon (or 1 tablespoon dried)
1 teaspoon Dijon mustard
1 teaspoon lemon juice
¼ cup dry white wine (optional)
½ cup cream
salt and pepper

Heat the oil in a heavy-based frying pan until moderately hot. Add the chicken breasts – they should sizzle mildly when they hit the pan. Cook until golden but not browned. Turn them over, add the garlic to the pan and continue cooking for 4–5 minutes.

Add the butter to the pan. Combine the tarragon, mustard, lemon juice and wine and add to the pan. Simmer for 1 minute to cook off the alcohol, then stir in the cream and simmer for 10–15 minutes to thicken, basting the chicken breasts if you feel like it. Check that the chicken is cooked through – it should be firm to the touch and tender when cut.

Serve with long-grain rice and a simple salad.

SERVES 4

WATERCRESS SALAD

Salads should be simple – most people make the mistake of adding too many ingredients. The pleasure from eating something unfussy should not be underestimated.

2 cups watercress, big stalks removed
juice of 1 lemon
2 tablespoons good-quality avocado or olive oil
¼ cup unsalted roasted almonds, roughly chopped
2 oranges, pith removed, cut into segments

Put all the ingredients in a salad bowl just before serving and toss gently to combine.

SERVES 4

Chicken with Tarragon Cream Sauce served with Watercress Salad

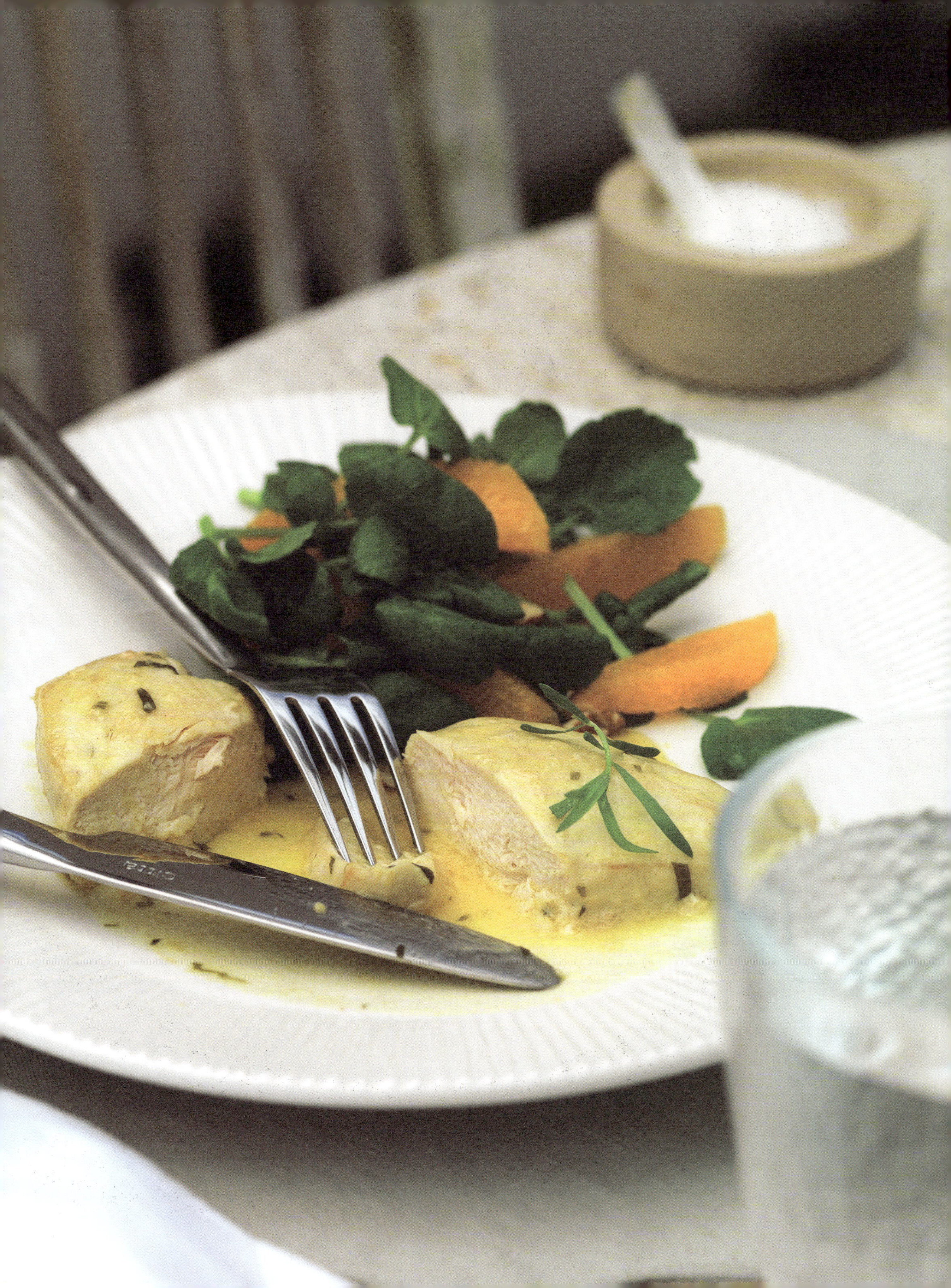

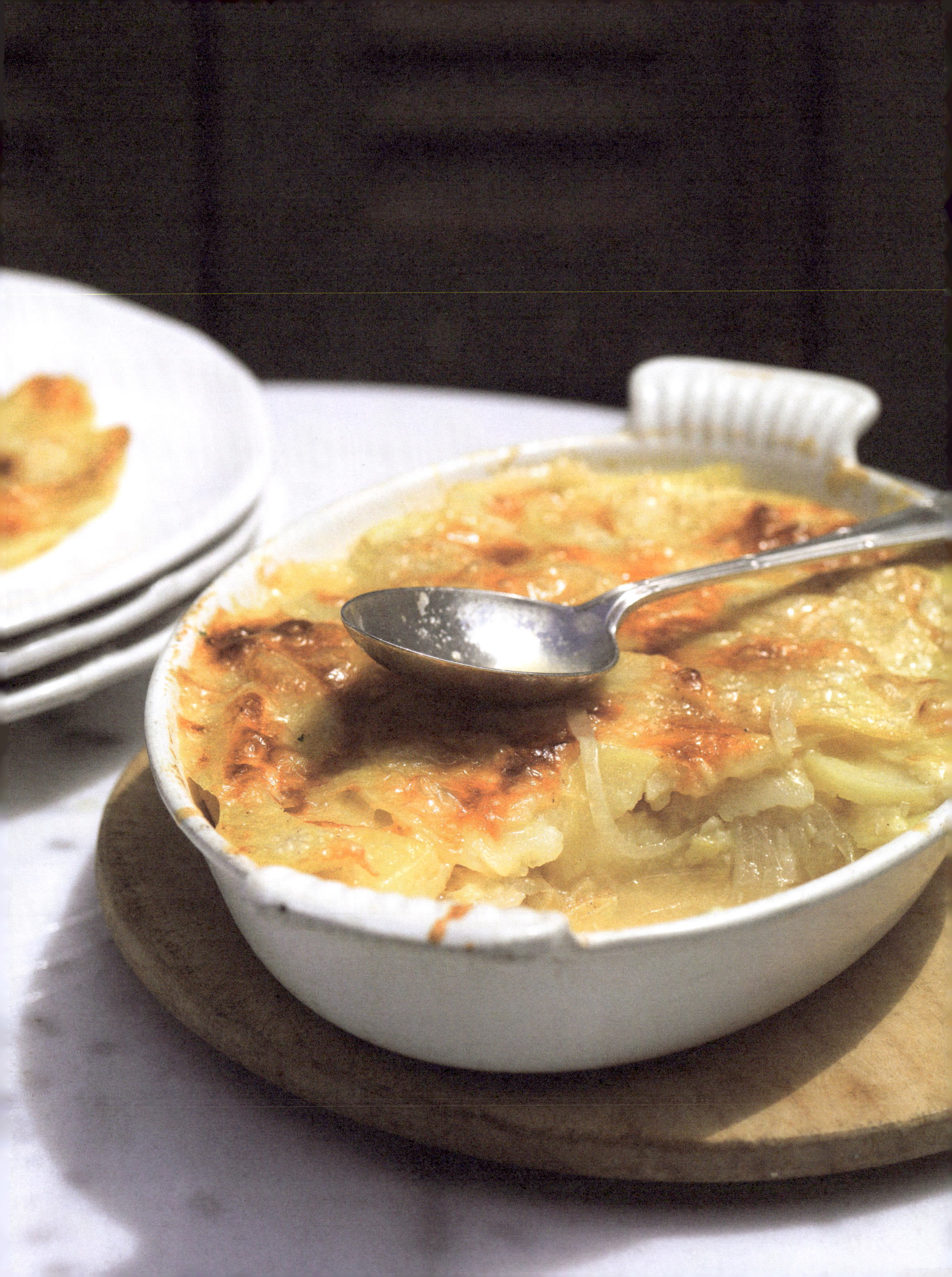

POTATO GRATIN

Who can resist this traditional scalloped potato dish? Make enough to ensure there's leftovers!

75g butter
8 medium–large potatoes (floury variety), thinly sliced
1 large onion, thinly sliced
400ml vegetable or chicken stock (use a low-salt variety, if possible)
salt and freshly ground pepper
1 cup grated cheese (optional)

Preheat oven to 180°C. Grease an ovenproof dish with butter.

Arrange sliced potatoes and onions in layers over the base of the prepared dish. Dot with remaining butter and pour in the stock – if you are in a hurry you can reduce the cooking time by heating the stock first. Season with salt and pepper to taste.

Ensure the potatoes are completely submerged in the stock. Press them down if you need to. Bake for 45 minutes or until potatoes are just tender and beginning to turn golden brown on top.

Sprinkle cheese on top, if using, and grill until golden.

SERVES 8

CHICKEN LIVER PARFAIT WITH ONION MARMALADE

Buttery and light, this parfait makes a welcome change from pâté.

PARFAIT
1 tablespoon butter
1 small onion, finely chopped
1 clove garlic, crushed
1 teaspoon very finely chopped rosemary
350g fresh chicken livers
2 tablespoons redcurrant jelly
150ml cream
½ teaspoon salt
freshly ground black pepper

ONION MARMALADE
2 onions, thinly sliced
¼ cup balsamic vinegar
¼ cup water
¼ cup brown sugar

Preheat oven to 180°C. Butter three 150ml-capacity ramekins.

To make the parfait, heat the butter in a frying pan over low heat. Add the onion, garlic and rosemary and cook for 5 minutes or until the onion is soft and translucent. Allow to cool slightly.

Trim any fat, discoloured spots and membrane from the chicken livers.

Place the onion mixture, chicken livers, redcurrant jelly, cream and salt and pepper in a food processor. Process until the mixture is smooth. Pass the puréed mixture through a fine sieve.

Put the sieved mixture into the prepared ramekins. Cover each ramekin with foil and place in a baking dish. Add almost-boiling water to the baking dish so the water comes halfway up the sides of the ramekins and bake for 20 minutes or until the mixture is just set. Remove from the baking dish, and set aside to cool to room temperature. Cover and refrigerate for several hours.

To make the onion marmalade, put all the ingredients into a small saucepan and bring to the boil, stirring until the sugar has dissolved.

Simmer for 20–30 minutes until the mixture is thick and syrupy. Cool and refrigerate until required, but serve at room temperature.

Serve the parfait with toast, crostini or crackers, onion marmalade and salad greens.

MAKES 3 RAMEKINS

GALETTES WITH CHICKEN, MUSHROOM AND CAMEMBERT

In France, a galette is a main-course crêpe made with buckwheat flour, which gives it a delicious nutty flavour. They are perfect with savoury fillings and are often served for lunch.

GALETTES
¾ cup buckwheat flour
½ cup plain flour
¼ teaspoon salt
1¾ cups milk
3 eggs, lightly beaten
2 tablespoons butter, melted
   plus extra for cooking

FILLING
1 tablespoon butter
1 onion, finely chopped
150g mushrooms, chopped
salt and freshly ground black pepper
2 cups shredded cooked chicken
2 tablespoons chopped flat-leaf parsley
125g Camembert, thinly sliced

To prepare the galettes, place the buckwheat flour, plain flour and salt in a bowl. Make a well in the centre and add the milk, eggs and butter. Whisk vigorously until the batter is completely smooth. Cover and place in the fridge for 1 hour.

Melt a small amount of butter in a crêpe pan or non-stick frying pan over medium–low heat. Add just enough batter to the pan so that when you swirl it, it covers the bottom of the pan thinly with the batter. Cook the crêpe until it is golden underneath then flip and cook the other side. Transfer to a plate to keep warm. Repeat with the remaining batter.

To prepare the filling, heat the butter in a saucepan. Add the onion and cook gently over medium–low heat until soft and translucent. Add the mushrooms and cook for a further 3–4 minutes. Season to taste with salt and pepper. Stir in the chicken and parsley and heat gently until the mixture is warmed through.

To assemble the crêpes, place approximately ½ cup of the chicken and mushroom mixture down the centre of each crêpe. Add a couple of slices of Camembert and fold up one end and loosely roll. Alternatively, tucking in all open sides to form a parcel might make them easier to eat. Serve with a green salad.

MAKES APPROXIMATELY 10 GALETTES

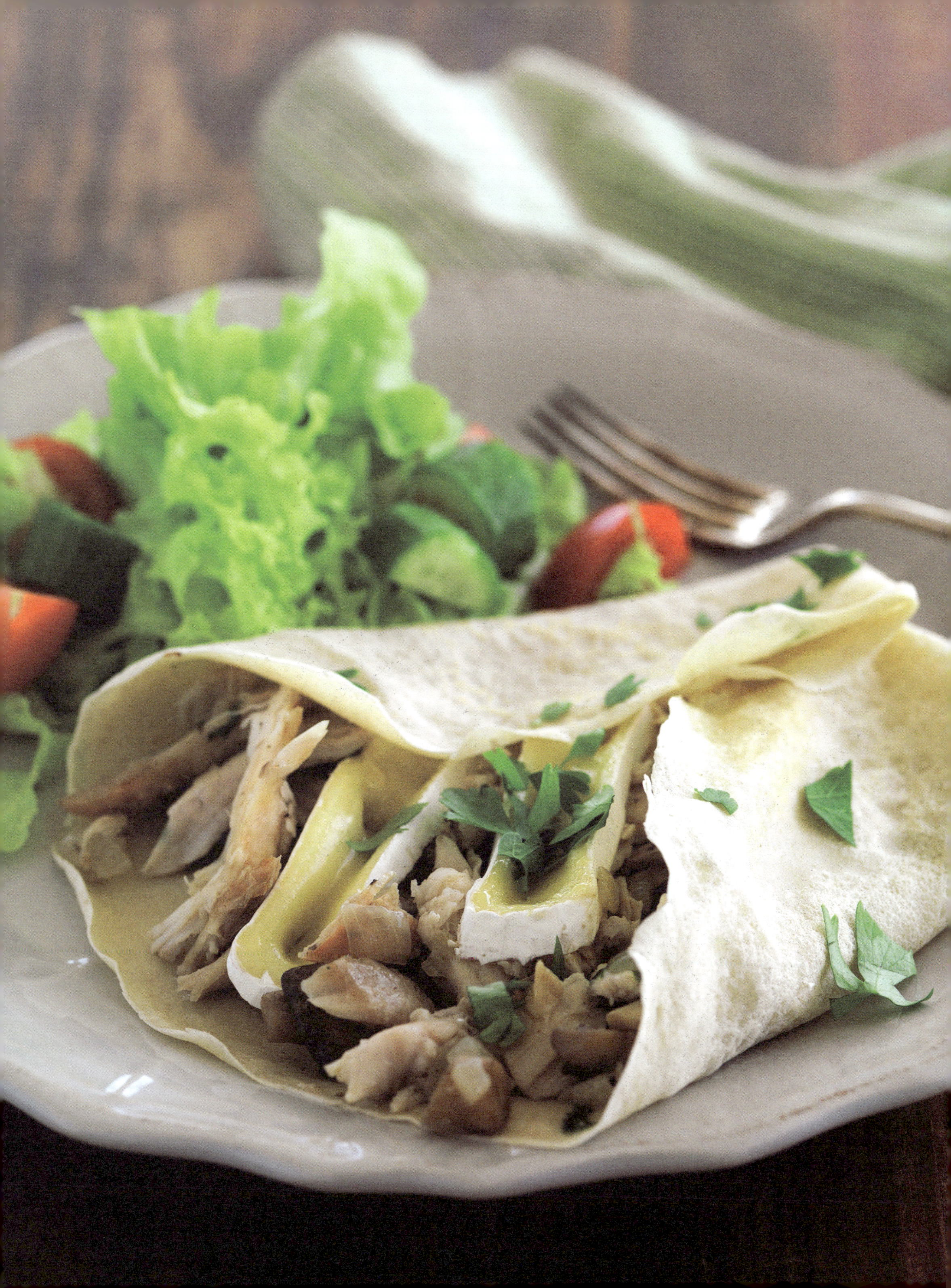

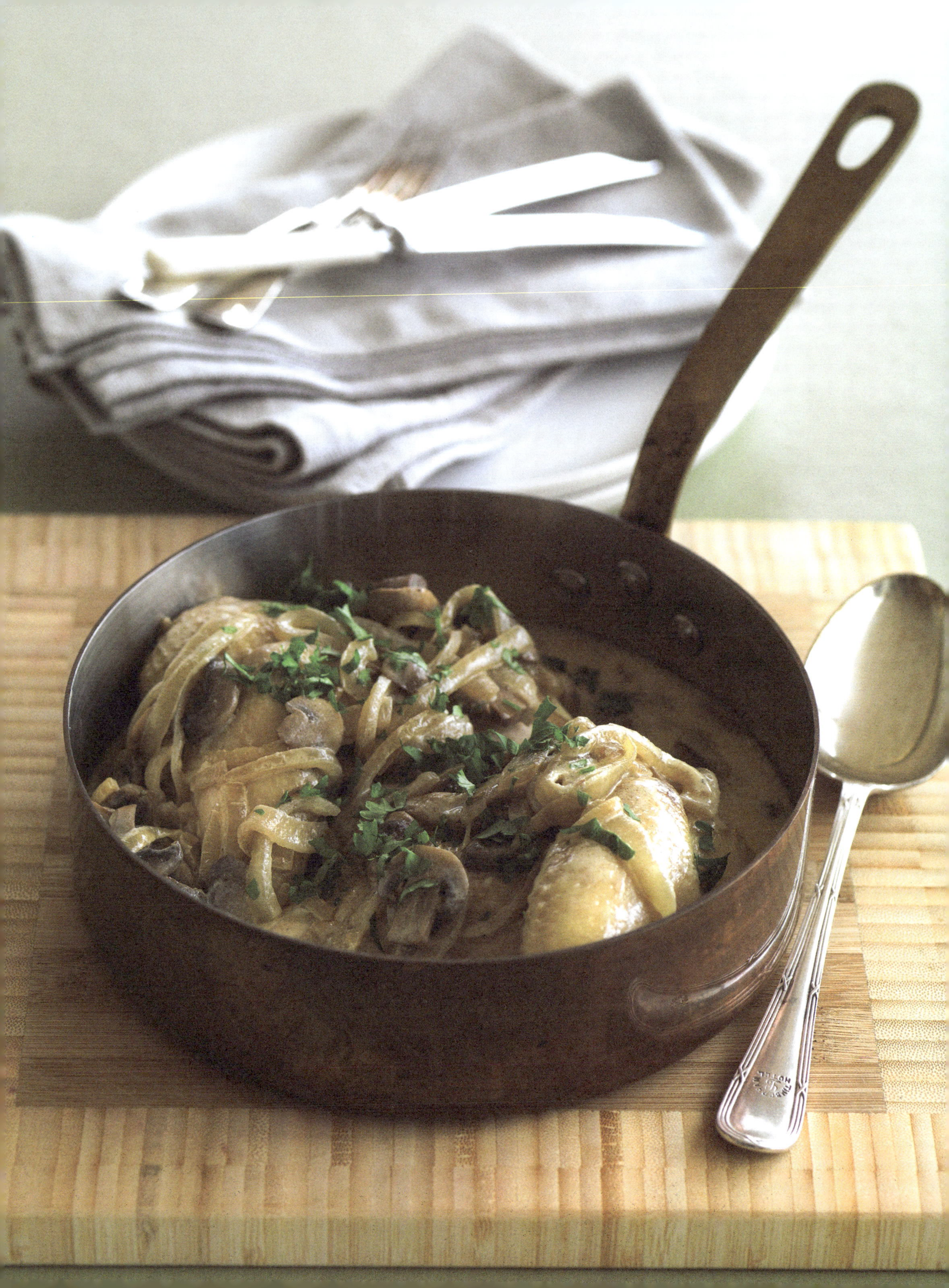

CHICKEN WITH CREAMY MUSHROOM SAUCE

Crème fraîche gives this simple-to-prepare dish a sophisticated flavour – delicious and oh so elegant!

2 tablespoons olive oil
4 chicken supremes (breasts with wing attached)
½ cup white wine
25g butter
1 onion, sliced
500g brown button mushrooms, thinly sliced
½ cup crème fraîche
salt and pepper
chopped flat-leaf parsley to garnish

Heat the olive oil in a heavy-based frying pan over medium–high heat and sauté the chicken pieces until they are golden but not yet browned. Turn and add the white wine. Cover and simmer for 10 minutes. Remove chicken from the pan and set aside along with the pan juices.

Wipe the pan with a paper towel and turn the heat down to medium–low. Melt the butter and add the onion. Gently sauté until soft and beginning to colour. Add the sliced mushrooms and sauté until tender. Allow them to release their juices and then soak them back up again.

Add the crème fraîche and stir the sauce as it simmers for 2–3 minutes. Allow to reduce, but not too much. Season to taste.

Add the chicken and pan juices back into the pan and baste the chicken with the sauce as it cooks for a further 7–10 minutes until cooked through. Add a splash more white wine or water if the sauce reduces too much.

Serve on individual plates with a good drizzle of the mushroom sauce and top with a little parsley.

SERVES 4

CHICKEN WITH TOMATOES, GARLIC AND OLIVE OIL

To peel tomatoes, cut a cross on the top of each tomato and place in a large bowl. Pour boiling water into the bowl ensuring that the tomatoes are all submerged. Leave for 30 seconds then pour off the boiling water. The skins should slip off easily.

4 chicken breasts, skinned and boned
salt and pepper
¼ cup plain flour
2 tablespoons olive oil
1 tablespoon butter
2 cloves garlic, crushed
1 anchovy fillet, mashed to a paste
¼ cup dry white wine
500g ripe Roma tomatoes, peeled, deseeded and finely chopped
¾ cup chicken stock
12 pitted olives, halved
2 tablespoons chopped basil

Season the chicken with salt and pepper then dip in the flour. Shake off the excess flour.

Heat the oil and butter in a frying pan over medium heat. Cook the chicken for 6 minutes on each side, until golden brown and just cooked through. Remove from the pan and keep warm.

Add the garlic and anchovy paste to the pan. Cook for 1–2 minutes until fragrant. Add the wine and bring to the boil. Stir in the tomatoes, chicken stock and olives and simmer for 8–10 minutes until the mixture has thickened. Add the chicken and any juices and simmer for 2–3 minutes until the chicken is heated through.

Sprinkle with basil and serve immediately.

SERVES 4

CHICKEN AND PISTACHIO TERRINE

I love a terrine and they're not nearly as hard to make as people think. They're great served cold for lunch with pickles, relish and breads or cut into small pieces and placed on crostini with baby rocket and relish as finger food.

2 tablespoons olive oil
1 onion, finely chopped
2 cloves garlic, crushed
2 teaspoons very finely chopped rosemary
750g chicken mince
1 cup fresh breadcrumbs
½ cup shelled pistachio nuts
2 eggs
1 tablespoon wholegrain mustard
¼ cup chopped flat-leaf parsley
½ teaspoon salt
freshly ground black pepper
8 slices prosciutto or bacon

Preheat oven to 180°C.

Heat the olive oil in a frying pan over medium–low heat and cook the onion, garlic and rosemary for 3–4 minutes until soft. Place the onion mixture, chicken mince, breadcrumbs, pistachio nuts, eggs, mustard, parsley, salt and pepper in a large bowl. Mix well.

Line a medium-sized loaf tin with the prosciutto or bacon, allowing enough overhang to fold over the top of the terrine mixture.

Spoon the chicken mixture into the prosciutto-lined loaf tin. Fold the overlapping prosciutto over the top of the mixture. Cover with foil.

Bake for 1 hour, removing the foil for the last 10 minutes of cooking to allow the top to brown.

Cool before slicing to serve.

SERVES 4–6

BUTTERFLIED CITRUS AND ROSEMARY ROASTED CHICKEN

This is delicious served with *Potato Gratin* (see page 65) and lightly steamed asparagus or green beans.

1 whole chicken
3 cloves garlic, crushed
¼ cup orange juice
1 tablespoon honey
2 tablespoons lemon juice
2 tablespoons finely chopped fresh rosemary
2 tablespoons olive oil
salt and pepper

Use a pair of kitchen scissors to cut along each side of the backbone of the chicken. Discard the backbone. Place the chicken on a flat surface and press down to flatten it. Cut slashes into the skin of the thighs and drums. Put the chicken into a large ovenproof dish.

Combine the remaining ingredients to make a marinade and pour over the chicken. Cover and refrigerate for 1 hour if you have the time.

Preheat oven to 180°C.

Roast for 1 hour or until the chicken is well browned and cooked through. The more you can baste the chicken during the cooking process the better – as the marinade will have more chance to be absorbed into the flesh.

SERVES 4–6

Chicken and Pistachio Terrine (right)
Butterflied Citrus and Rosemary Roast Chicken (overleaf)

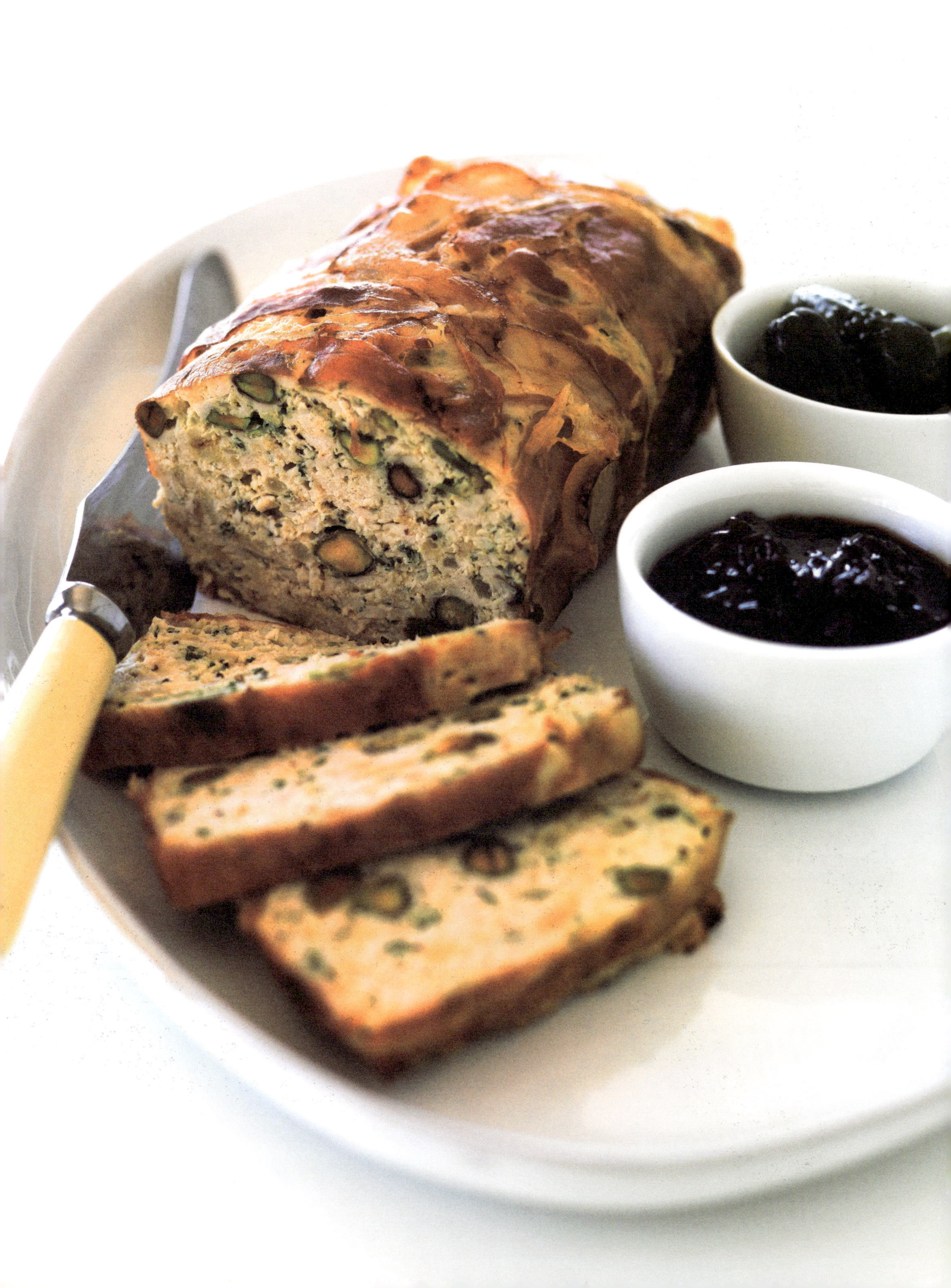

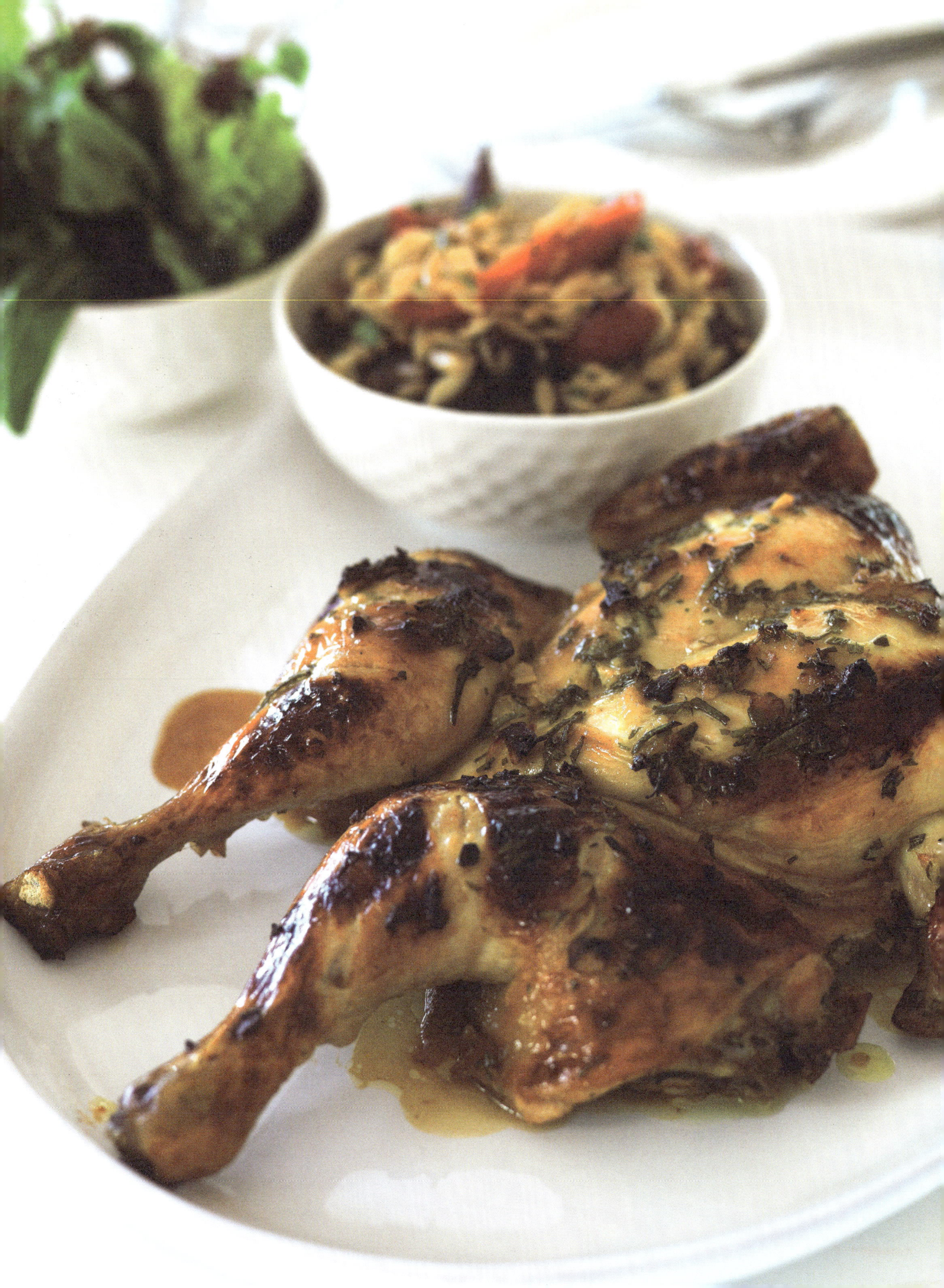

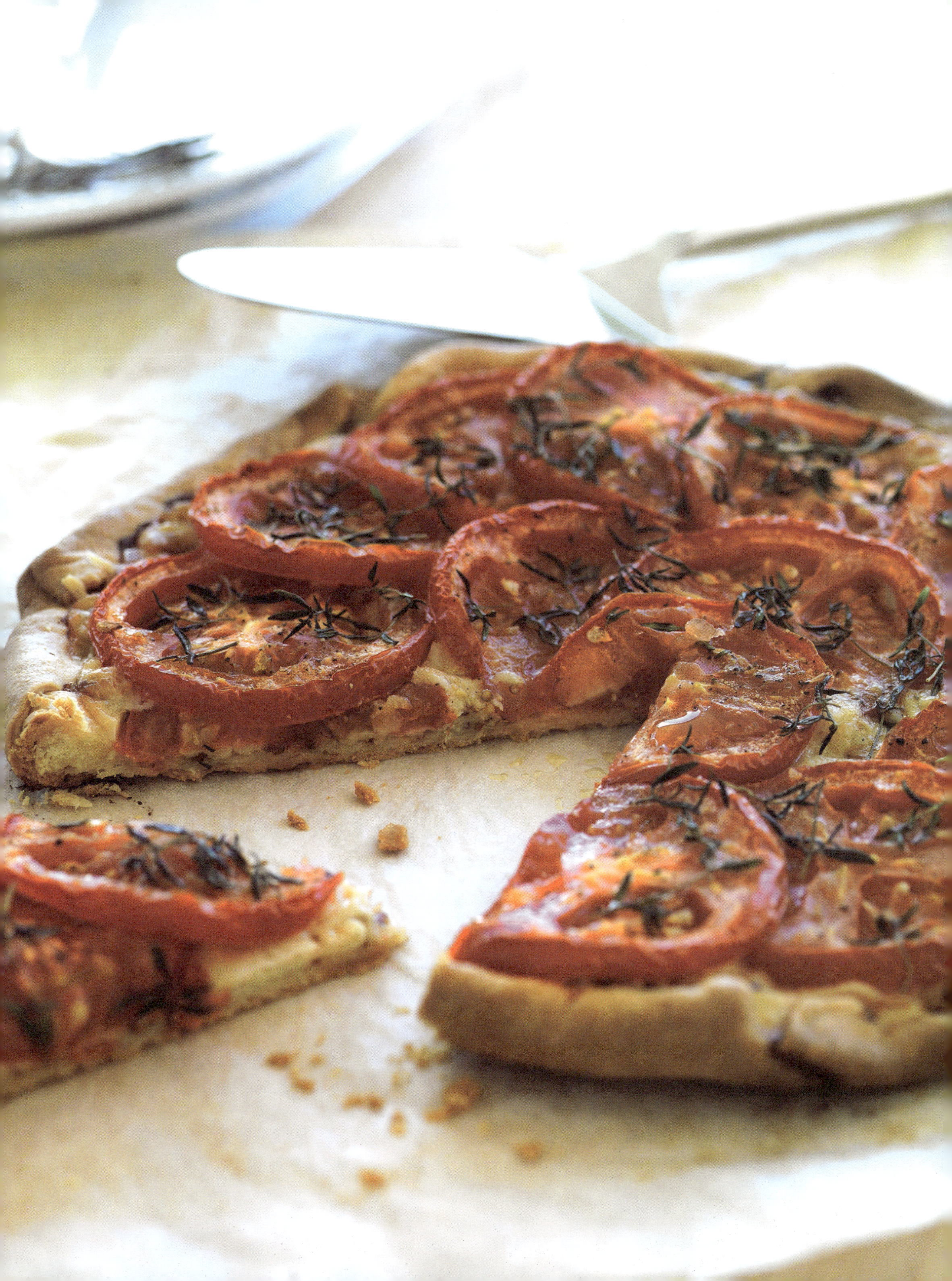

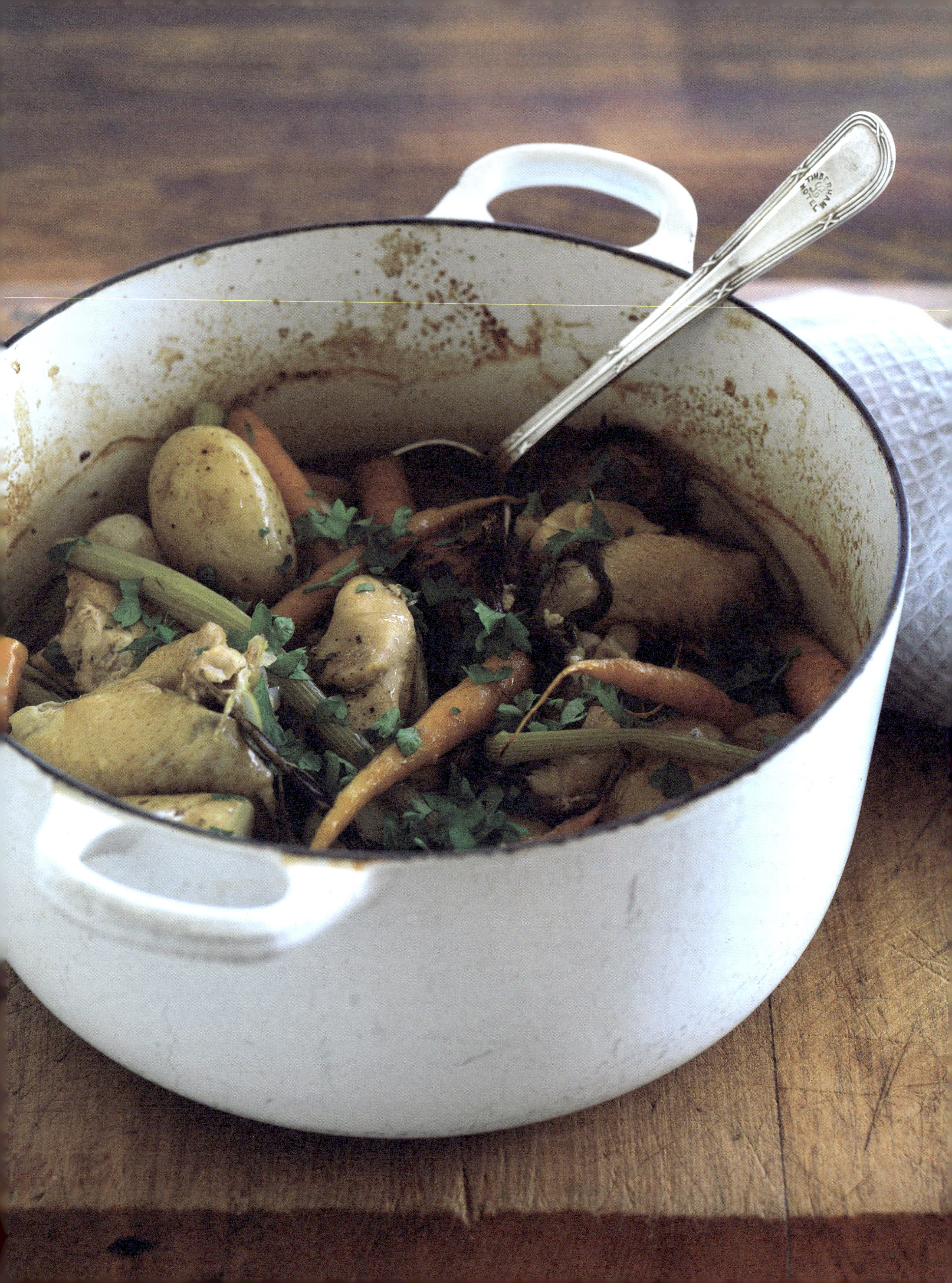

POT AU FEU

This casserole-type dinner is a great way to warm the house and the heart during the colder months.

2 tablespoons olive oil
1kg chicken pieces
1 teaspoon salt
1 teaspoon freshly ground black pepper
4 small parsnips or turnips
8 small potatoes, unpeeled
1 fennel bulb or leek, sliced
6 shallots, unpeeled
8 cloves garlic, unpeeled
4 sprigs rosemary
1 cup white wine
1 cup chicken stock (use a low-salt version, if possible)
12 baby carrots

Preheat oven to 180°C.

Place 1 tablespoon of olive oil in the base of a baking dish or an ovenproof casserole dish. Arrange the chicken pieces in a single layer. Season the chicken with salt and pepper.

Add the parsnips or turnips, potatoes, fennel or leek, shallots, garlic and rosemary. Pour the wine and chicken stock into the dish and drizzle with the remaining olive oil.

Cover with foil and bake for 30 minutes. Add the baby carrots, cover with foil and cook for a further 20 minutes. Remove the foil and cook for a further 20 minutes or until the vegetables are lightly browned and soft – the garlic and shallots will squeeze out of their skins.

Serve with green vegetables.

SERVES 4–6

TOMATO AND MUSTARD TART

This tart is simple and tasty, and it travels well as a picnic item. Don't be put off by the amount of mustard used – it works well.

2 sheets store-bought savoury short pastry, rolled a bit thinner
3–4 large ripe tomatoes, thinly sliced
½ teaspoon salt
¼ cup Dijon mustard
1 clove garlic, crushed
1 cup grated Gruyère
2 tablespoons fresh thyme leaves
salt and pepper
2 tablespoons extra virgin olive oil

Preheat oven to 180°C. Lightly grease a 30cm-diameter pie dish, pizza tray or oven tray and line with pastry. If using an oven tray, you will need to build up the edges of the pastry to form a rustic-looking rim to contain the filling.

Mix together the mustard and garlic and spread over the bottom of the pastry. Sprinkle the cheese over and arrange overlapping tomato slices over on top. Sprinkle with the thyme, salt and pepper and drizzle with olive oil. Bake in the middle of the oven for 30–40 minutes until the pastry is golden brown and the tomatoes are very soft and a deep, rich red. Check after about 25 minutes. If the edges are getting too dark, cover them with foil.

Serve hot, at room temperature or cold.

SERVES 4

Pot au Feu (left)
Tomato and Mustard Tart (previous page)

CARAMELISED APPLE TARTS

This is a simplified version of Tarte Tatin – a caramelised upside-down apple tart made famous by the Tatin sisters from south of the Loire. You can prepare most of this version beforehand, which makes for easy entertaining.

1 sheet store-bought flaky pastry
100g caster sugar
70ml water
100ml cream
20g butter
5 medium apples (any variety), peeled, cored and cut into quarters

Preheat oven to 180°C. Line an oven tray with baking paper.

Cut four 10cm pastry squares and place them on prepared oven tray. Run a knife about 1cm in from the edge around the border of each square to form a rim – do not cut all the way through. Bake until golden. Remove from the oven and set aside to cool. Store in an airtight container until required.

Put the sugar and water in a small saucepan over medium heat. Stir until the sugar has dissolved completely, then bring to the boil. From here on, try not to stir it. Instead, move the saucepan to get the contents swirling if you need to. Cook for 5–7 minutes until golden – you will need to watch it like a hawk as it tends to go from clear to brown to burnt very quickly!

Remove from the heat and add the cream – it may spit when the cream goes in – so be careful.

Return the saucepan to the heat and stir to get rid of any lumps. Add the butter and allow it to melt. Stir to combine. Add the chopped apples and cook gently until they soften slightly. Set aside until required.

To serve, place pastry squares on individual plates and top each with one-quarter of the warmed caramelised apples. Serve with vanilla ice-cream.

SERVES 4

CRÈME BRÛLÉE

'Crème brûlée' translates to 'burnt cream' which doesn't sound very good but this is a fantastic dessert. It's best made a day ahead and finished by 'burning' the tops just before your guests are due to arrive.

800ml cream
1 vanilla pod, split
8 egg yolks
6 tablespoons caster sugar
extra caster sugar to 'burn'

Preheat oven to 150°C. Put eight 150ml-capacity ramekins or one 1.2 litre-capacity ovenproof dish in a roasting tray.

Heat the cream and vanilla pod in a small saucepan to near boiling.

Meanwhile, whisk the egg yolks and sugar together until pale, light and creamy. Slowly pour the hot cream in a steady stream into the egg and sugar mix. Whisk quickly to prevent curdling and to avoid lumps forming.

Pour the custard mixture into prepared ramekins or dish. Pour boiling water into the roasting tray so that the water level comes two-thirds of the way up the sides of the ramekins or dish.

Bake for 30–40 minutes until the custards have set. Remove ramekins from roasting tray and allow to cool.

To serve, sprinkle caster sugar over the top in a thin layer and place under a very hot grill. Watch carefully until the sugar melts, then just begins to bubble and burn. Refrigerate for 30 minutes or until chilled and ready to serve.

SERVES 8

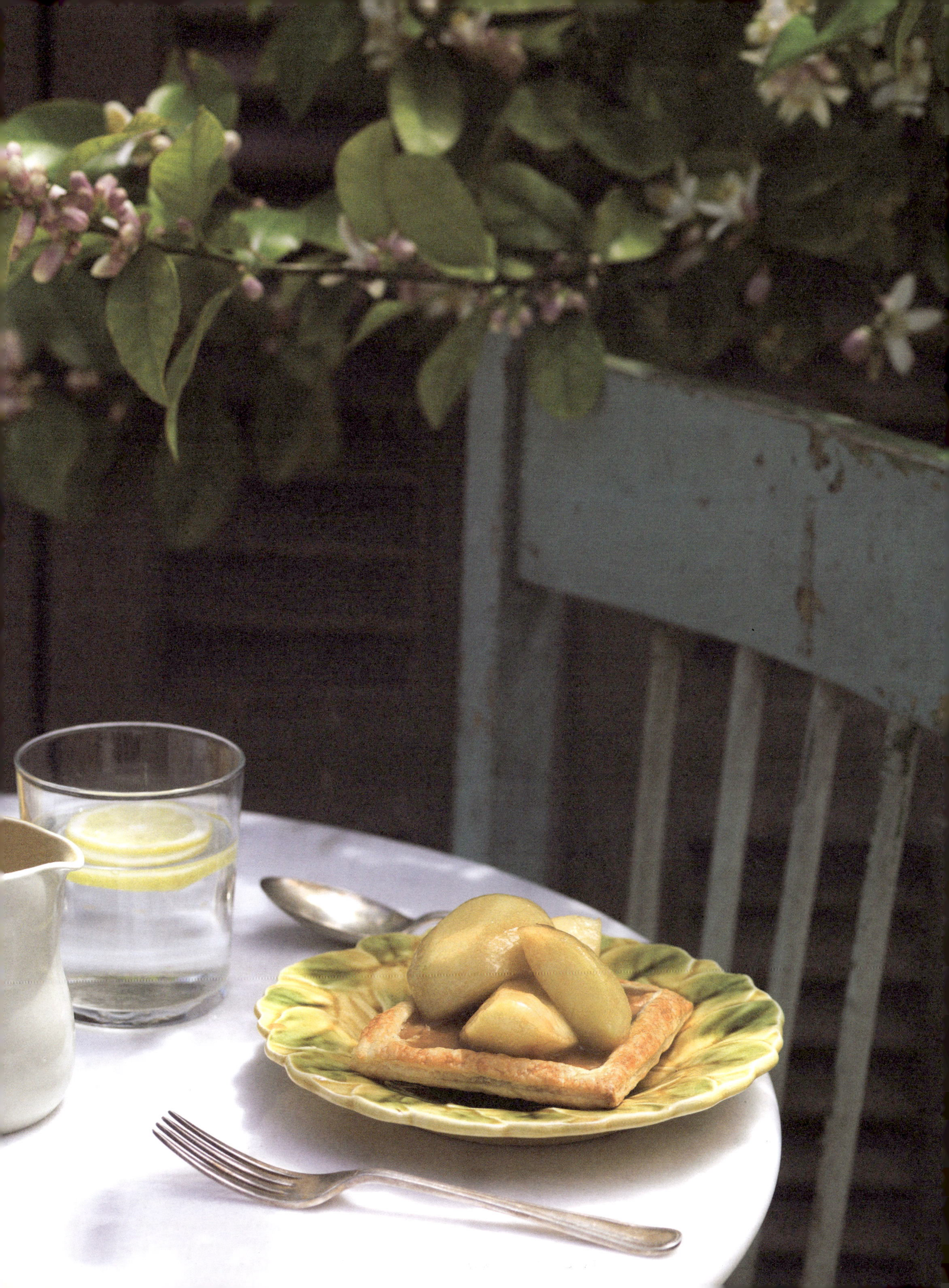

THAILAND
SPICING IT UP IN BANGKOK & KO CHANG

'The folk at this local market, who rarely see tourists, giggle at the blonde foreigner tucking into chicken at 5.30 in the morning.'

On my first visit to Thailand over 15 years ago I hitchhiked over the Malay–Thai border and made straight for the chargrilled chilli chicken stall that was smokin' hot and smelling irresistible! From that moment on I was hooked on the fragrant flavours of Thailand. For the next two months, travelling through this enchanting country, my daily mantra was: I must not have chargrilled chilli chicken today. The little sachets of hot chilli sauce, the packets of sticky rice wrapped in banana leaves, the blackened crispy skin with its magical marinade, the succulent moist chicken meat – it's little wonder my resistance was weak and I invariably failed to abide by my mantra!

A lot has changed in Thailand since then, but I can still catch the river ferry from central Bangkok to the end of the line and I do, on every visit. It takes me to the early morning market where I have chargrilled chicken for breakfast and feel like a young hitchhiker once more. The folk at this local market, who rarely see tourists, giggle at the blonde foreigner tucking into chicken at 5.30 in the morning as they're buying it to take to work for lunch or home for dinner that night – but I'm okay with that.

Once my hunger has been sated I'm free to focus on the rest of the produce – great piles of kaffir lime leaves, huge bunches of coriander, chillies of every variety and freshly made, flat rice noodles.

The only thing I miss in Bangkok is a kitchen to roll up my sleeves and do some cooking in. Instead, I make careful mental notes and store away the flavours, smells, textures and cooking techniques so that when I return home I can set about recreating the many and varied culinary delights from my travels.

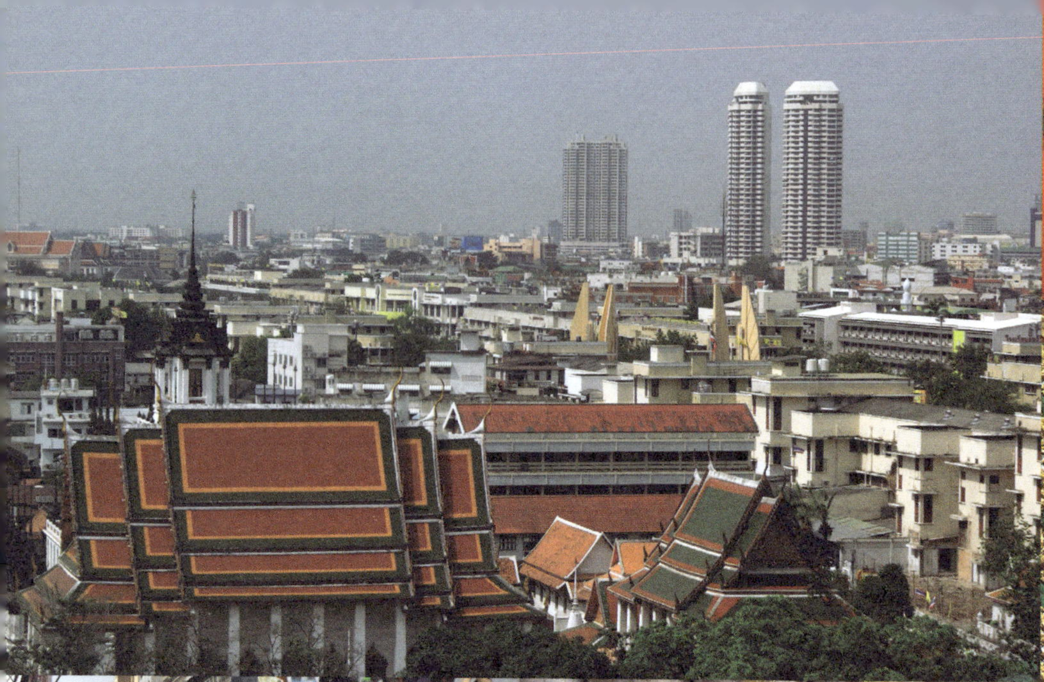
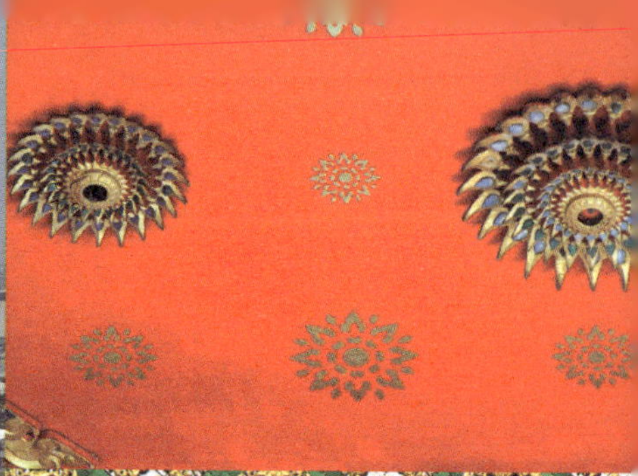
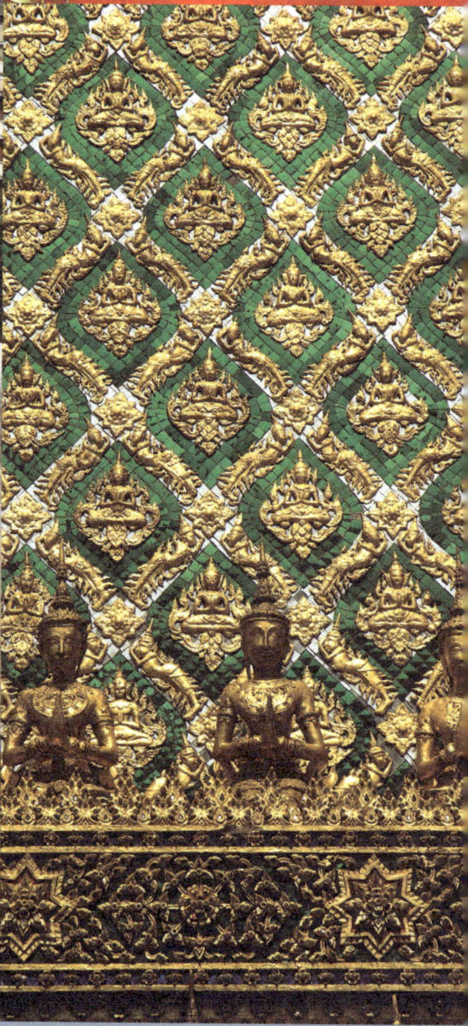
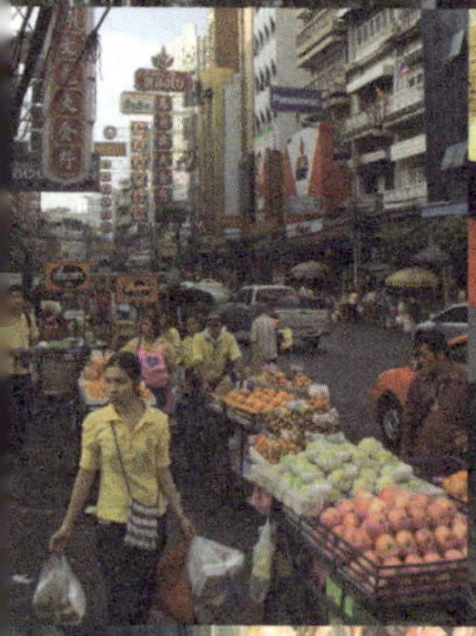
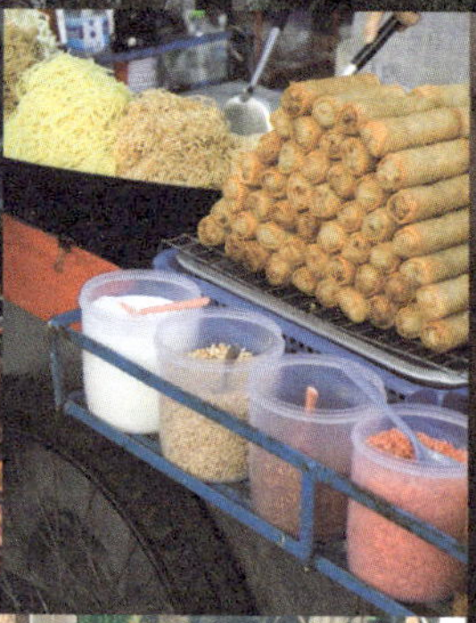
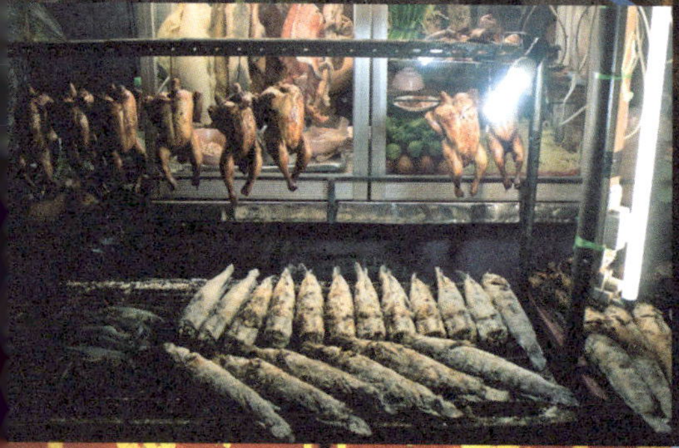
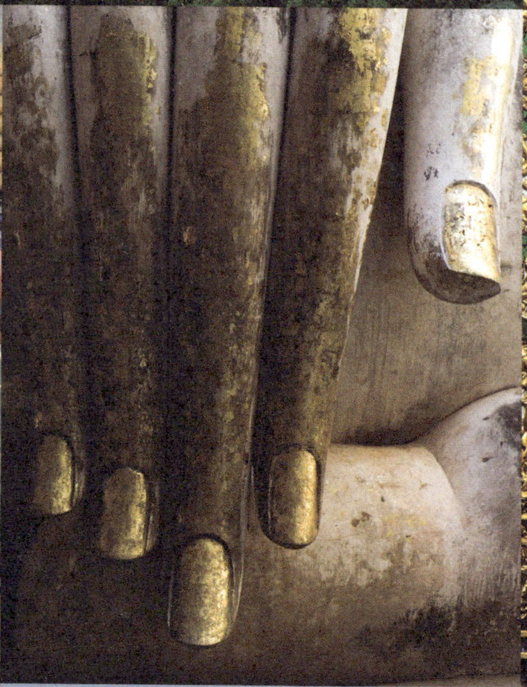

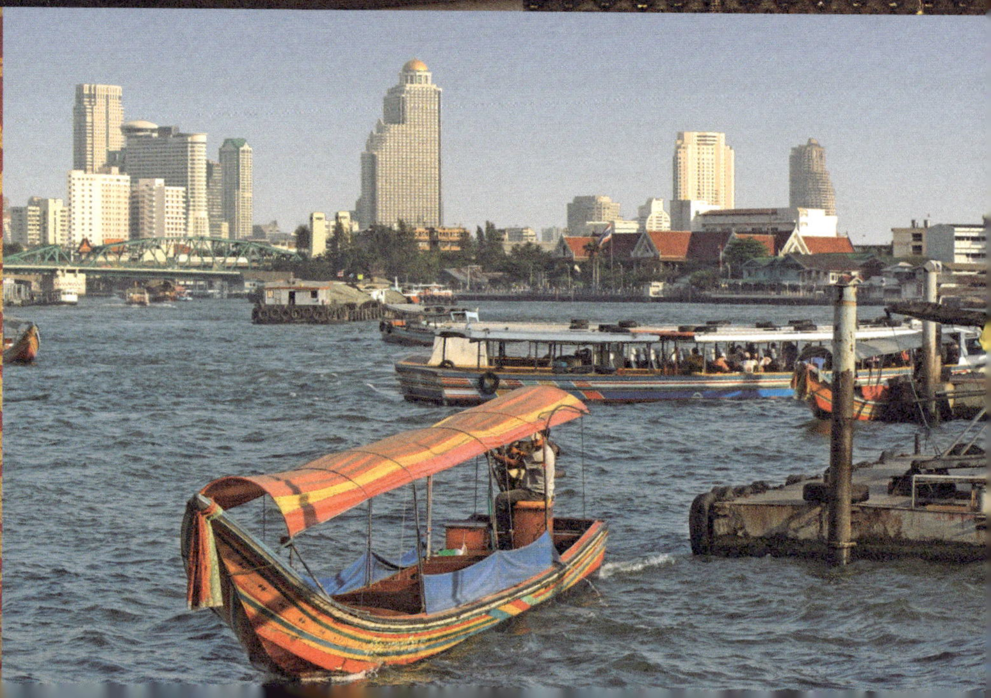

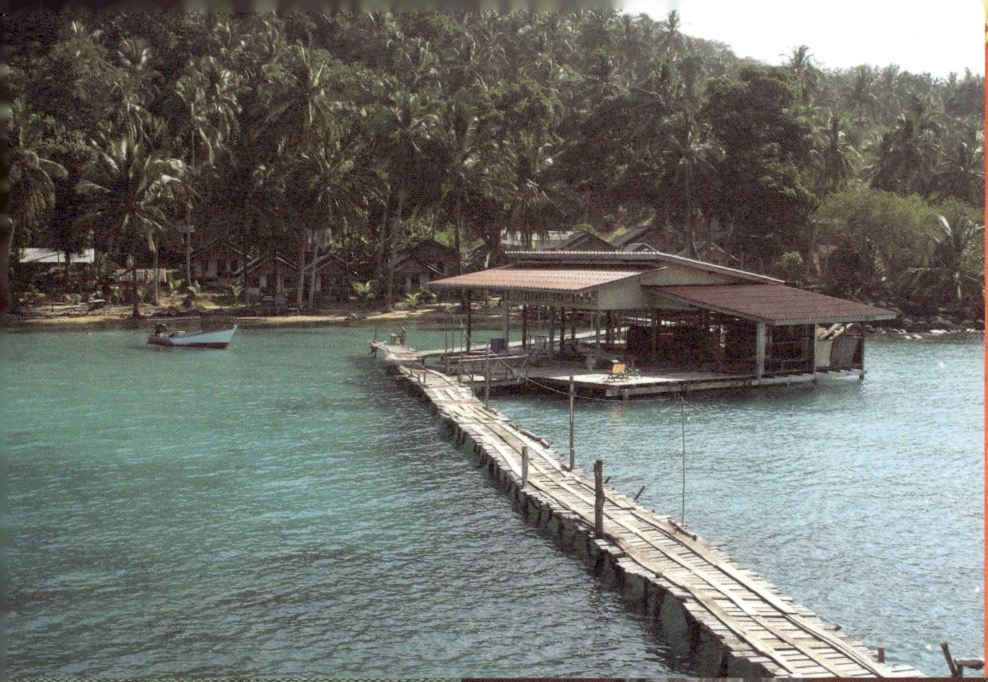
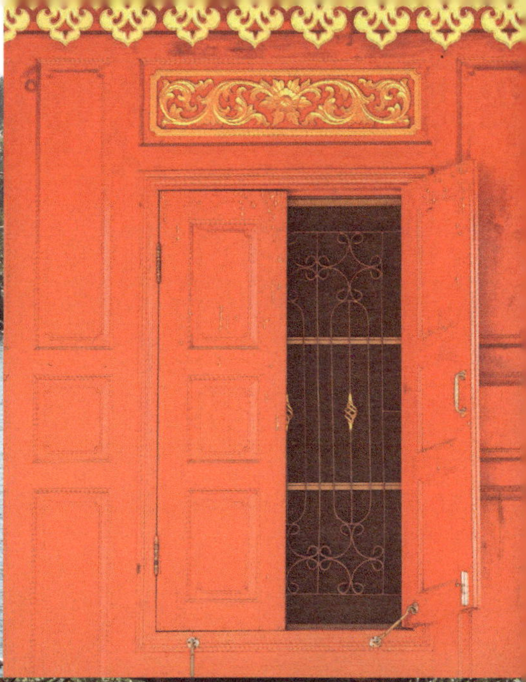
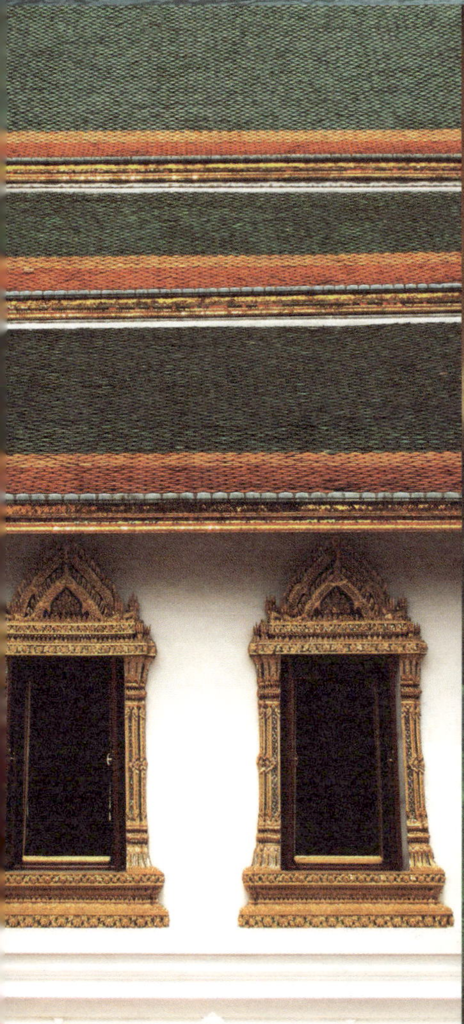
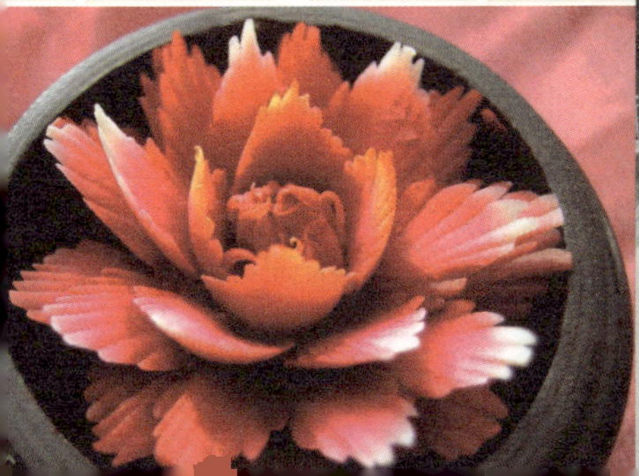
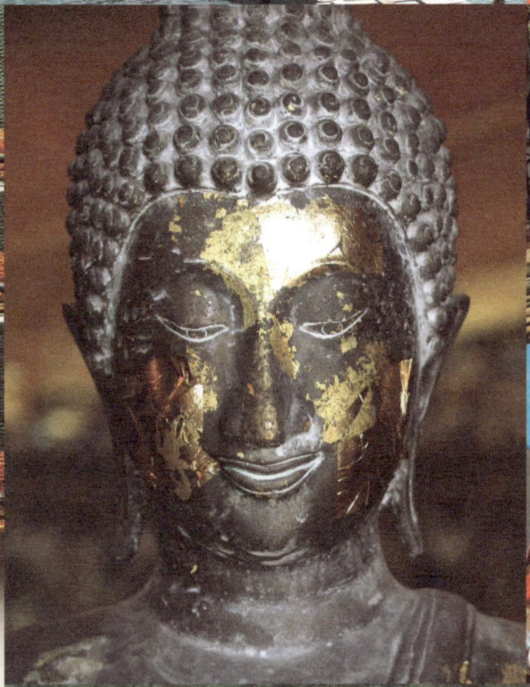
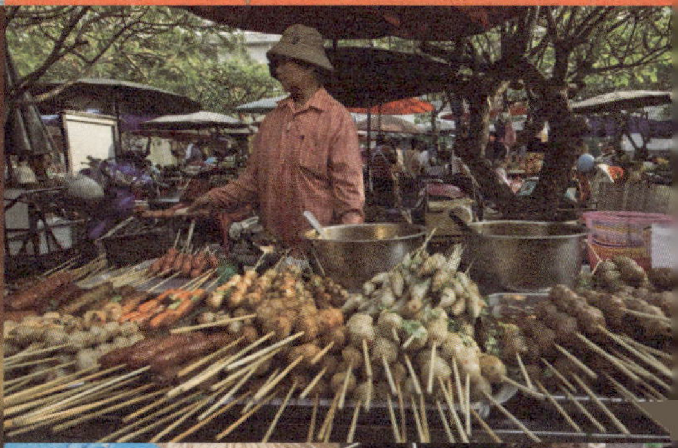
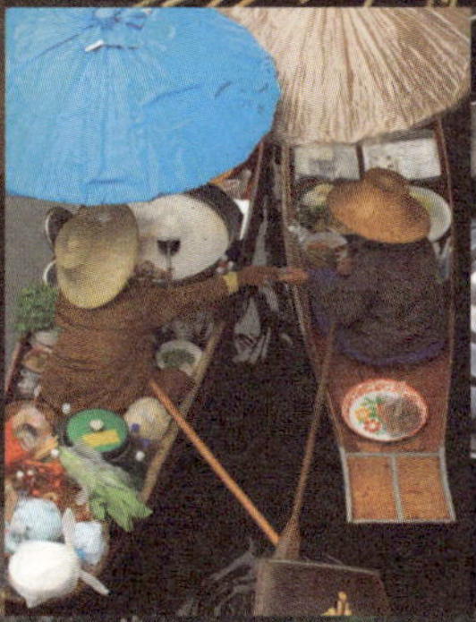
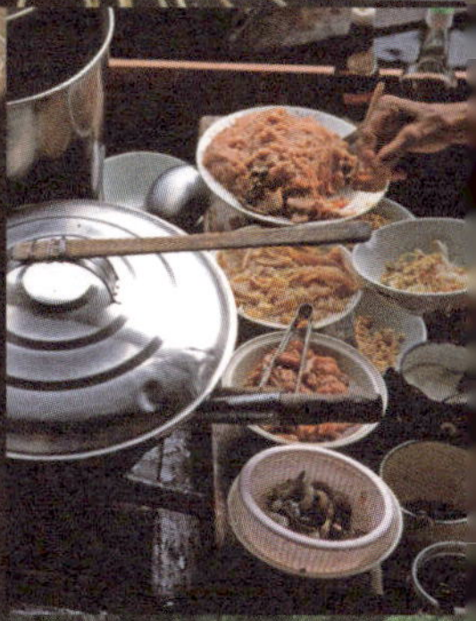
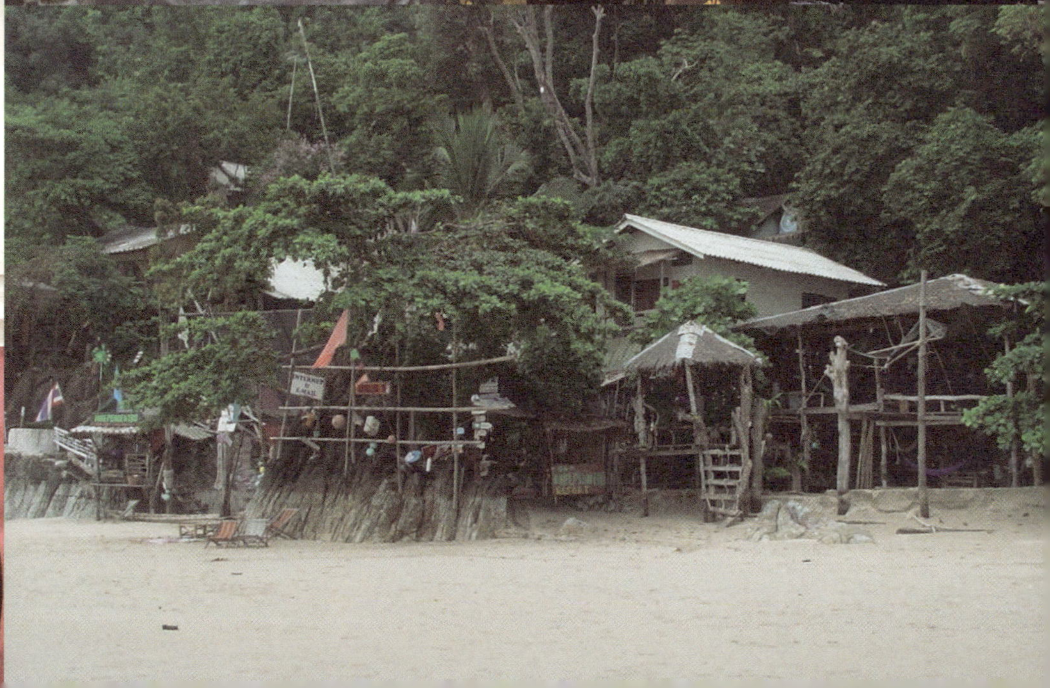

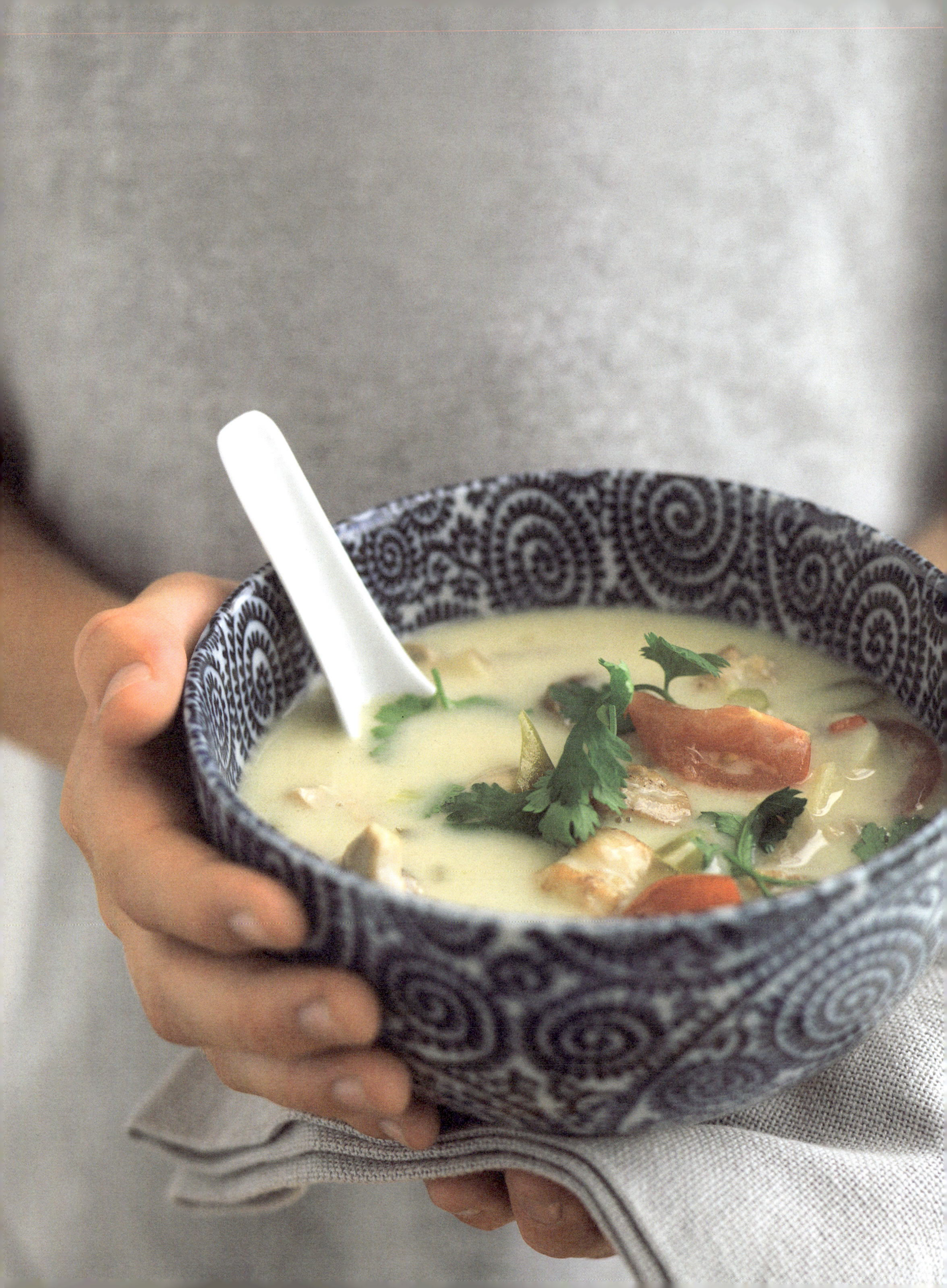

CHICKEN SOUP WITH COCONUT CREAM AND LEMONGRASS

This is an intensely flavoured soup that doesn't require hours of cooking for the flavours to develop. The fragrant broth is best eaten immediately and that suits me just fine.

400ml can coconut cream
1 cup chicken or vegetable stock
2 cups water
2 stalks lemongrass, smashed with a rolling pin but left whole
2cm piece fresh ginger, smashed with a rolling pin
3 kaffir lime leaves, thinly sliced
500g chicken breasts, skinned, boned and thinly sliced
2 medium tomatoes, cut into wedges
200g small button mushrooms
1 large red chilli, deseeded and finely chopped
¼ cup lime juice
2 tablespoons fish sauce
2 tablespoons chopped fresh coriander

Place the coconut cream, stock, water, lemongrass, ginger and kaffir lime leaves into a large saucepan. Bring to the boil and simmer for 5 minutes. If preferred, strain the broth at this point and discard the lemongrass, kaffir lime leaves and ginger. If you leave them in the broth, remember to tell your guests those bits are for flavour only and are not to be eaten.

Add the chicken, tomatoes, mushrooms and chilli to the saucepan. Simmer for 10 minutes or until the chicken is just cooked. Add the lime juice and fish sauce and stir to combine.

Ladle into bowls, garnish with coriander and serve immediately.

SERVES 4 AS A STARTER

TANGY CHICKEN AND RICE NOODLE SALAD WITH TAMARIND DRESSING

Bursting with flavour, this salad makes a unique contribution to a barbecue spread or Thai banquet.

DRESSING
¼ cup orange juice
2 tablespoons soy sauce
3 tablespoons sweet chilli sauce
1 teaspoon tamarind purée
2 teaspoons sesame oil
1 small garlic clove, crushed

SALAD
200g rice stick noodles
1 packet snow peas
1 tablespoon light cooking oil
1 clove garlic, crushed
400g chicken breasts, skinned, boned and sliced
2 carrots, cut into matchsticks
1 Lebanese cucumber, cut into chunks
1 red capsicum, deseeded and cut into strips
1 cup bean sprouts
¼ cup chopped fresh coriander and mint

To prepare the dressing, put all the ingredients in a screw-top jar and shake to combine.

To make the salad, prepare the rice noodles according to the directions on the packet. Drain and set aside.

Blanch the snow peas in boiling water for 30 seconds. Drain and set aside.

Heat the oil in a frying pan. Add the garlic and chicken and stir-fry over high heat for 4–5 minutes until the chicken is golden brown and cooked through.

Place the drained rice noodles on a serving platter, top with the chicken, carrots, cucumber, capsicum, bean sprouts and herbs. Drizzle with the dressing and serve immediately.

SERVES 4

Chicken Soup with Coconut Cream and Lemongrass

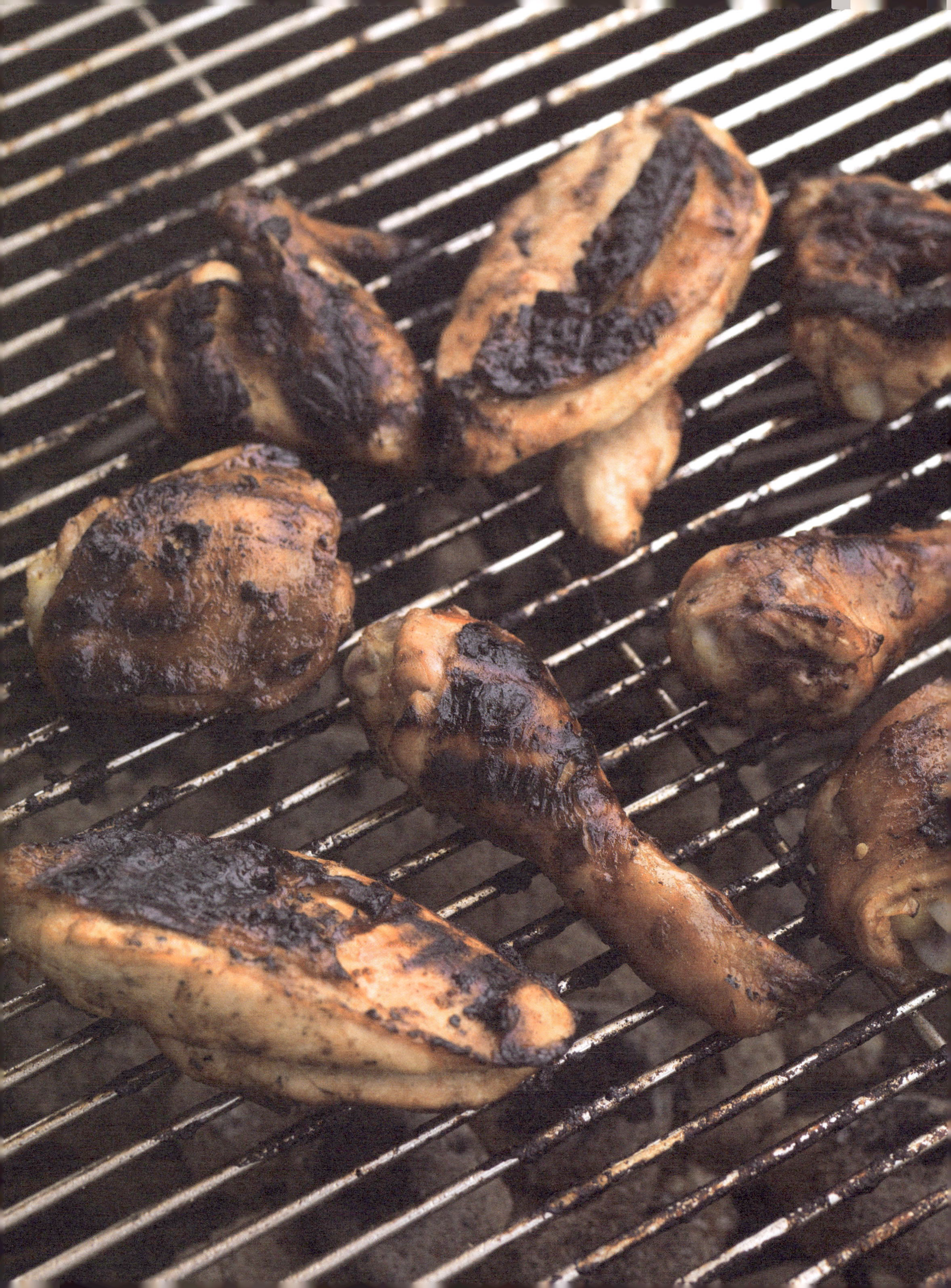

CHARGRILLED CHILLI CHICKEN

This can be prepared ahead of time and served either hot or cold – it's ideal for a crowd. The chicken is pretty spicy but, served alongside a cooling salad or salsa, it's just right.

4 cloves garlic, crushed
1 tablespoon crushed chilli
1 fresh chilli, finely chopped
2 tablespoons crushed lemongrass
2 tablespoons fish sauce
2 teaspoons tamarind purée, soaked in a little warm water to loosen
1 tablespoon brown sugar
2 tablespoons fresh lime or lemon juice
1 teaspoon salt
1 teaspoon sesame oil
1 tablespoon light cooking oil
8 chicken pieces, bone in

Put all the ingredients except the chicken in a bowl and stir to combine until the sugar has dissolved. Add the chicken pieces and stir to ensure they are evenly coated with the marinade. Cover and set aside to marinate for 15–30 minutes or up to 24 hours in the fridge.

Preheat oven grill to 250°C. Line an oven tray with foil.

Arrange the chicken in a single layer on prepared oven tray and place under hot grill. Cook until the pieces are beginning to blacken. Turn pieces over and blacken the other side. Turn the oven to bake and the temperature to 200°C and continue cooking for 20 minutes or until cooked through – the flesh will be opaque and the juices will run clear. Alternatively cook the chicken pieces on a barbecue grill or hot plate.

MAKES 8 TASTY MORSELS

SPICY BAKED CHICKEN PIECES

I love these chicken pieces infused with tasty Thai flavours. You can also use chicken nibbles to make delicious party snacks. Serve hot or cold.

3 tablespoons Red Curry Paste (see page 95)
1 tablespoon light cooking oil
1 kaffir lime leaf, finely shredded
1 tablespoon sesame seeds
2 tablespoons chopped fresh coriander
8 chicken pieces

Preheat oven to 180°C.

Put all the ingredients except the chicken in a bowl and stir to combine. Add the chicken pieces and stir to ensure they are evenly coated.

Line an oven tray with foil. Arrange the chicken in a single layer on prepared oven tray and spread on any remaining paste. Bake for 40 minutes or until the juices run clear.

Serve with rice and salad.

SERVES 4

Chargrilled Chilli Chicken

FRAGRANT LEMONGRASS CHICKEN WITH CHILLI AND PINEAPPLE SALSA

This is a great standby for a quick meal – it's possible to be eating this meal within 30 minutes of thinking about it. Now, that's fast!

CHICKEN
5 chicken thighs (about 600g), skinned, boned and diced
2 cloves garlic
2 tablespoons grated fresh ginger
juice of 1 lemon
2 stalks lemongrass, finely chopped
1 large red chilli, deseeded and finely chopped
1 medium-sized onion, sliced
2 tablespoons light cooking oil
¼ cup grated palm sugar or 2 tablespoons brown sugar
⅓ cup water
salt and pepper to season

SALSA
1 cup cubed fresh pineapple
2 kaffir lime leaves, very thinly sliced
1 red chilli, deseeded and very thinly sliced
splash of rice wine vinegar

To prepare the chicken, put the chicken, garlic, ginger, lemon juice, lemongrass, chilli and onion in a bowl and stir to combine, ensuring the chicken is well coated. Cover and set aside to marinate for at least 15 minutes.

Heat the oil in a heavy-based frying pan until almost smoking. Add the chicken, cook for 3–4 minutes until it is golden on one side. Add the palm sugar, reduce the heat and cook for 1–2 minutes to allow the sugar to caramelise – you may need to stir to loosen the chicken from the pan.

Add the water, salt and pepper and cook for a further 7–10 minutes on a slow simmer.

Meanwhile, place all the salsa ingredients in a small bowl and stir to combine.

Serve the chicken with salsa and a side of sticky or long-grain rice.

SERVES 4–5, MAKES 1 CUP SALSA

STIR-FRIED GINGER CHICKEN WITH SUGAR SNAPS

Delicious and so simple! The sugar snap peas bring a lovely crunchy texture to this dish.

1 tablespoon light cooking oil
500g chicken schnitzel, sliced
2 cloves garlic, sliced
1 tablespoon grated fresh ginger
150g sugar snap peas
2 tablespoons oyster sauce
¼ cup Chinese cooking wine or sherry
1 teaspoon sesame oil

Heat the oil in a frying pan over high heat. Stir-fry the chicken in two batches until golden brown. Remove the chicken from the pan and set aside. Add the garlic, ginger and sugar snaps to the pan and cook for 1 minute.

Return the chicken to the pan along with the oyster sauce, cooking wine or sherry and sesame oil and stir-fry for 2 minutes or until the sauce has thickened slightly.

Serve with rice or rice noodles.

SERVES 4

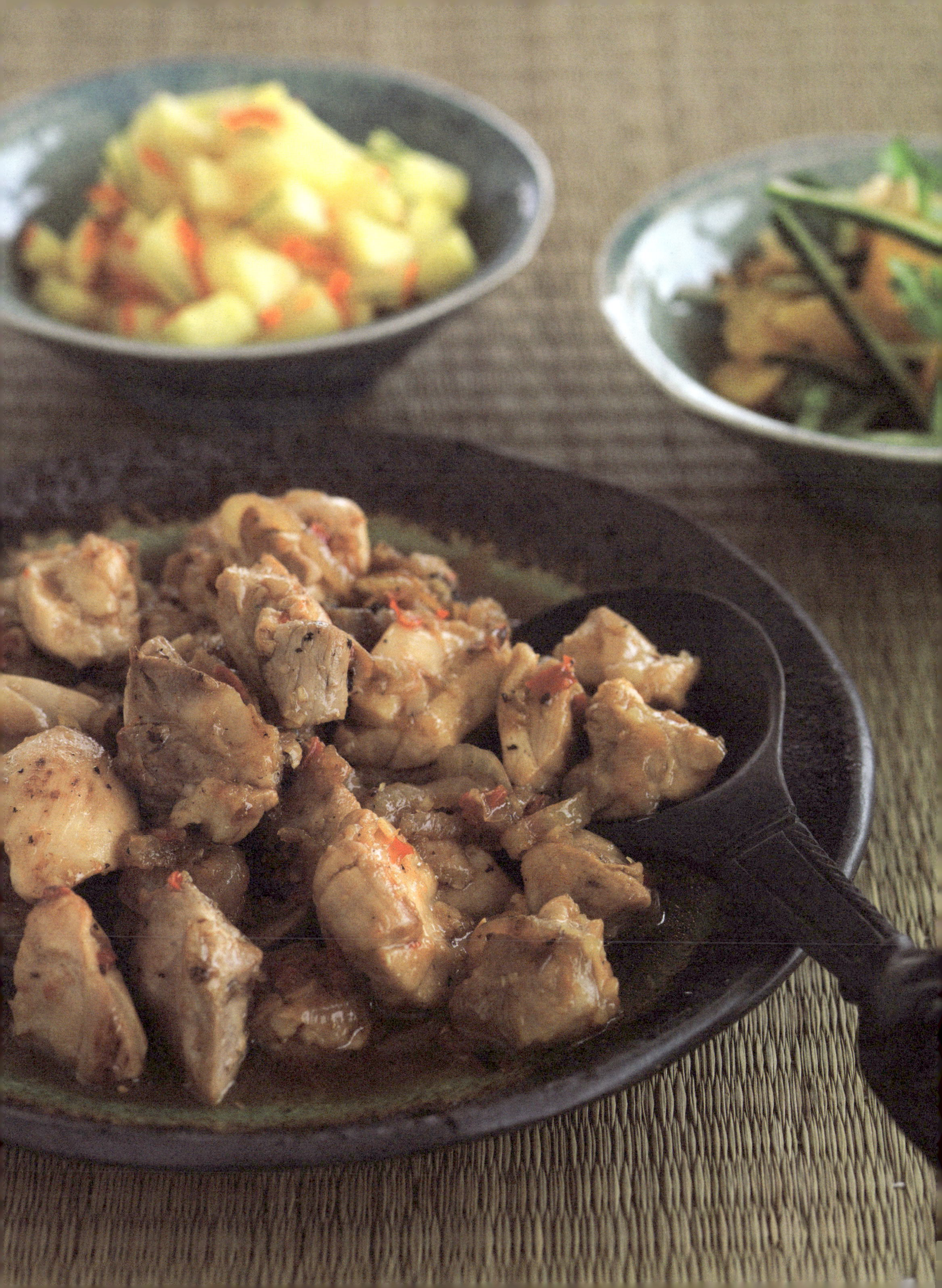

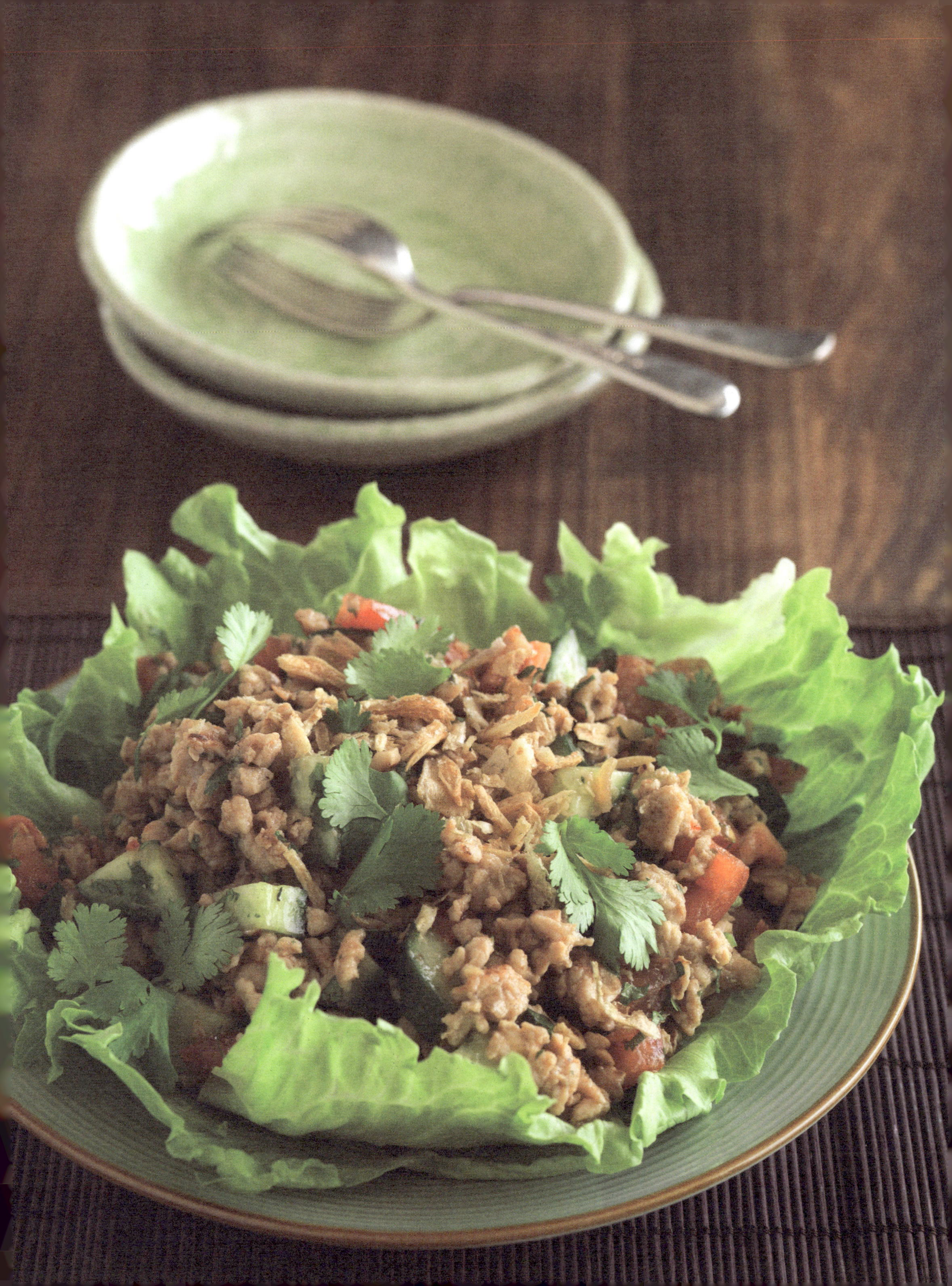

SPICY THAI CHICKEN SALAD

Spicy ground meat salads – usually called larb – are common throughout northern Thailand and Laos. They burst with flavour from lots of fresh herbs and are a surprisingly refreshing dish on a hot day!

500g chicken mince
1 tablespoon rice flour
1 onion, finely chopped
3 cloves garlic, crushed
1 stalk lemongrass, finely chopped
2 red chillies, chopped
2 tablespoons fish sauce
2 tablespoons soy sauce
1 teaspoon ground coriander
2 tablespoons light cooking oil
2 tablespoons lime juice
2 tomatoes, finely diced
½ cucumber, finely diced
¼ cup chopped coriander
2 kaffir lime leaves, very finely shredded
2 tablespoons finely chopped mint
1 iceberg lettuce, leaves removed and separated to form cups
2 tablespoons roughly chopped fresh coriander to garnish
1 tablespoon fried shallots

Combine the chicken mince, rice flour, onion, garlic, lemongrass, chillies, fish and soy sauces, and ground coriander. Cover and refrigerate for 1 hour for the flavours to infuse.

Heat the oil in a frying pan. Add the chicken mixture and cook over high heat until golden brown. Add the lime juice and set aside to cool slightly.

Combine the chicken mixture with the tomatoes, cucumber, coriander, lime leaves and mint.

Place the lettuce-leaf cups on a platter and spoon mince mixture into the cups. Garnish with coriander and fried shallots.

SERVES 4

GRAPEFRUIT SALAD

Fresh and simple is always best for a salad. If you want an amazingly refreshing side dish, this one is hard to beat.

2 grapefruit, peeled, pith removed and cut into segments between the membranes
1 telegraph cucumber, chopped
1 tablespoon brown sugar
1 tablespoon lemon or lime juice
3 tablespoons fresh coriander, roughly chopped
¼ cup roasted, unsalted peanuts, roughly chopped

Place all ingredients in a salad bowl just before serving and toss gently to combine.

MAKES 2 CUPS

PERFECT PAD THAI

Made in the traditional way, pad Thai is true comfort food. You can add chicken and prawns if you want to, but this is a good basic recipe to get you started. It should be cooked quickly, just before eating, but you can soak the noodles and make the sauce in advance.

250g dried flat rice noodles
1 tablespoon tamarind purée (soaked in a bit of warm water to loosen)
2 tablespoons fish sauce
3 tablespoons grated palm sugar
juice of 1 lime or lemon
2 tablespoons light cooking oil
3 fresh red chillies (or green ones if you want a hotter dish), deseeded and chopped
3 tablespoons coarsely chopped garlic
3 eggs
3 handfuls fresh bean sprouts
4 spring onions, including the green shoots, thinly sliced on the diagonal
½ cup coarsely chopped roasted peanuts to garnish
lime or lemon wedges to garnish
1 handful fresh coriander sprigs, roughly chopped, to garnish

Place rice noodles in a bowl and pour enough boiling water over to cover them. Leave for at least 20 minutes until softened – they should still be firm to the bite because they will cook more in the wok or pan.

Drain the noodles and set aside until required.

Meanwhile, mix the tamarind purée, fish sauce, palm sugar and lime or lemon juice in a small saucepan and stir over low heat until the sugar has dissolved. Bring to a gentle simmer while you start the fast and furious cooking process.

Heat a wok or thin-based frying pan over high heat. When hot, add the oil. Add the chillies and garlic, and stir-fry for 1 minute.

Add the drained rice noodles and stir-fry until hot. Add the hot sauce and cook for 3–4 minutes, keeping the noodles moving around the pan to avoid sticking and to get them coated in the sauce. If the sauce evaporates too quickly – before the noodles are ready – add a bit of water and keep stirring. If the noodles continue to stick together, add a bit of oil.

When the noodles are nearly ready – well coated in sauce – push them to one side of the wok or pan and crack the eggs into the space provided. Stir with a fork to scramble the eggs until set. Stir eggs through the noodles then add bean sprouts and spring onions and continue to stir-fry for 1–2 minutes.

Remove from the heat and turn onto a plate.

Garnish with peanuts, wedges of lime or lemon and coriander.

SERVES 6–8

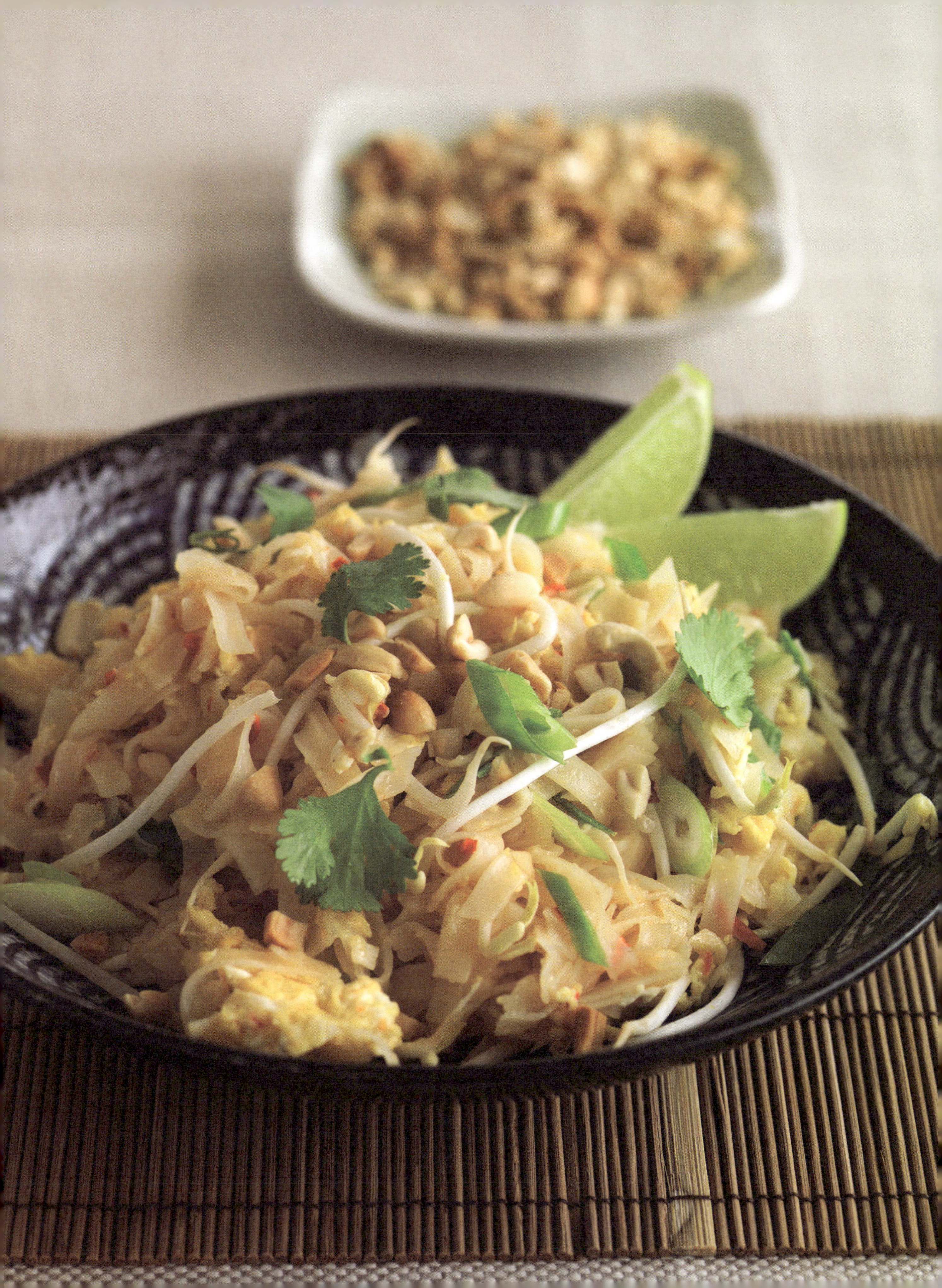

BANGKOK CHINATOWN NOODLES WITH CHICKEN AND PICKLED SQUID

One night in Bangkok's Chinatown, I spotted a lone man working his wok over an open fire as if there was no tomorrow. He produced only this dish and there was a continuous line of hungry people waiting for one of the tiny plastic stools at his stall to be vacated so that they, too, could be served up a steaming plate of these freshly cooked noodles. I like the simplicity of this dish and the squid is quite an unusual addition.

100g fresh squid, cut into strips
3 tablespoons lemon juice
3 tablespoons rice wine vinegar
2 tablespoons light cooking oil
1 chicken breast, thinly sliced
3 garlic cloves, chopped
1–2 eggs
100g dried flat rice noodles, softened in boiling water and drained
1 tablespoon dark soy sauce
3 spring onions, thinly sliced on the diagonal (optional)

Place the squid, lemon juice and vinegar in a bowl and stir to combine. Cover and set aside to marinate for 15–30 minutes.

Meanwhile, get all the other ingredients ready before you begin to cook – once you begin, everything needs to happen quickly!

Heat a wok or thin-based frying pan to a high heat and add the oil, chicken and garlic. Cook for 5 minutes or until the chicken is cooked through.

Push the chicken to one side of the wok or pan and crack the egg(s) into the space. Stir with a fork to scramble the eggs until set.

Drain the squid from its marinade and add to the pan with the noodles, chicken and soy sauce. Keep everything moving around in the wok or pan to coat well in the oil and soy sauce.

Garnish with spring onions – if you're feeling fancy!

SERVES 1–2

CHICKEN CURRY WITH TAMARIND AND KAFFIR LIME

Kaffir lime is a flavour that always brings Thailand to mind.

1 tablespoon light cooking oil
1 onion, chopped
1 tablespoon Mild Curry Paste (see page 95)
3 tablespoons grated palm sugar
500g chicken breasts, skinned, boned and diced
2 tablespoons tamarind purée
1 cup boiling water
4 kaffir lime leaves, finely shredded
1 tablespoon soy sauce
400ml can coconut cream
½ cup finely chopped roasted peanuts to garnish
chopped fresh coriander to garnish

Heat the oil in a frying pan. Add the onion and cook over medium heat for 2–3 minutes. Add the curry paste and palm sugar and cook for 1 minute, stirring.

Add the chicken to the pan along with the tamarind purée, water, kaffir lime leaves, soy sauce and coconut cream. Simmer for 15–20 minutes until the chicken is cooked through.

Turn onto a serving plate and sprinkle with peanuts and coriander leaves. Serve with rice.

SERVES 4

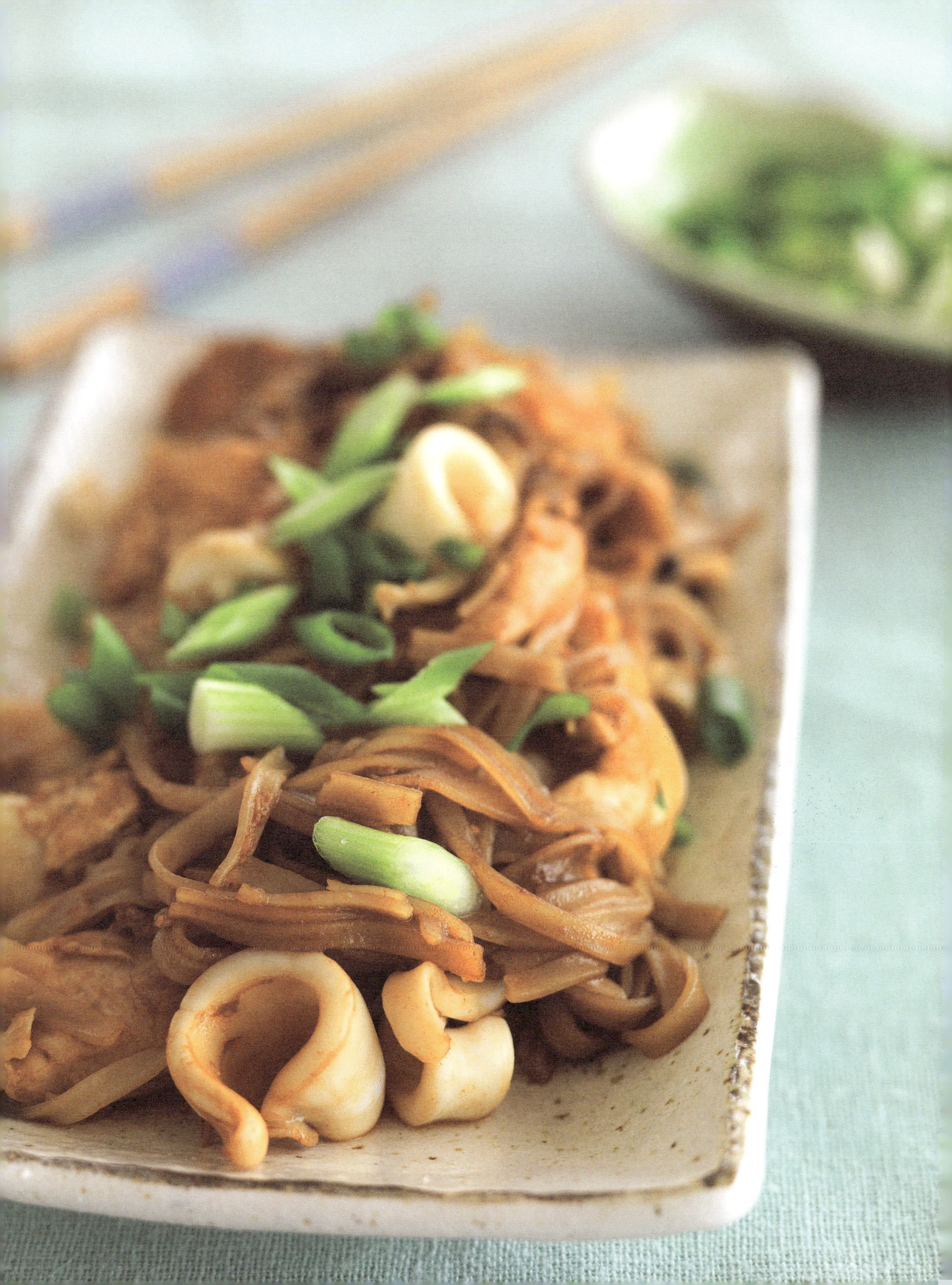

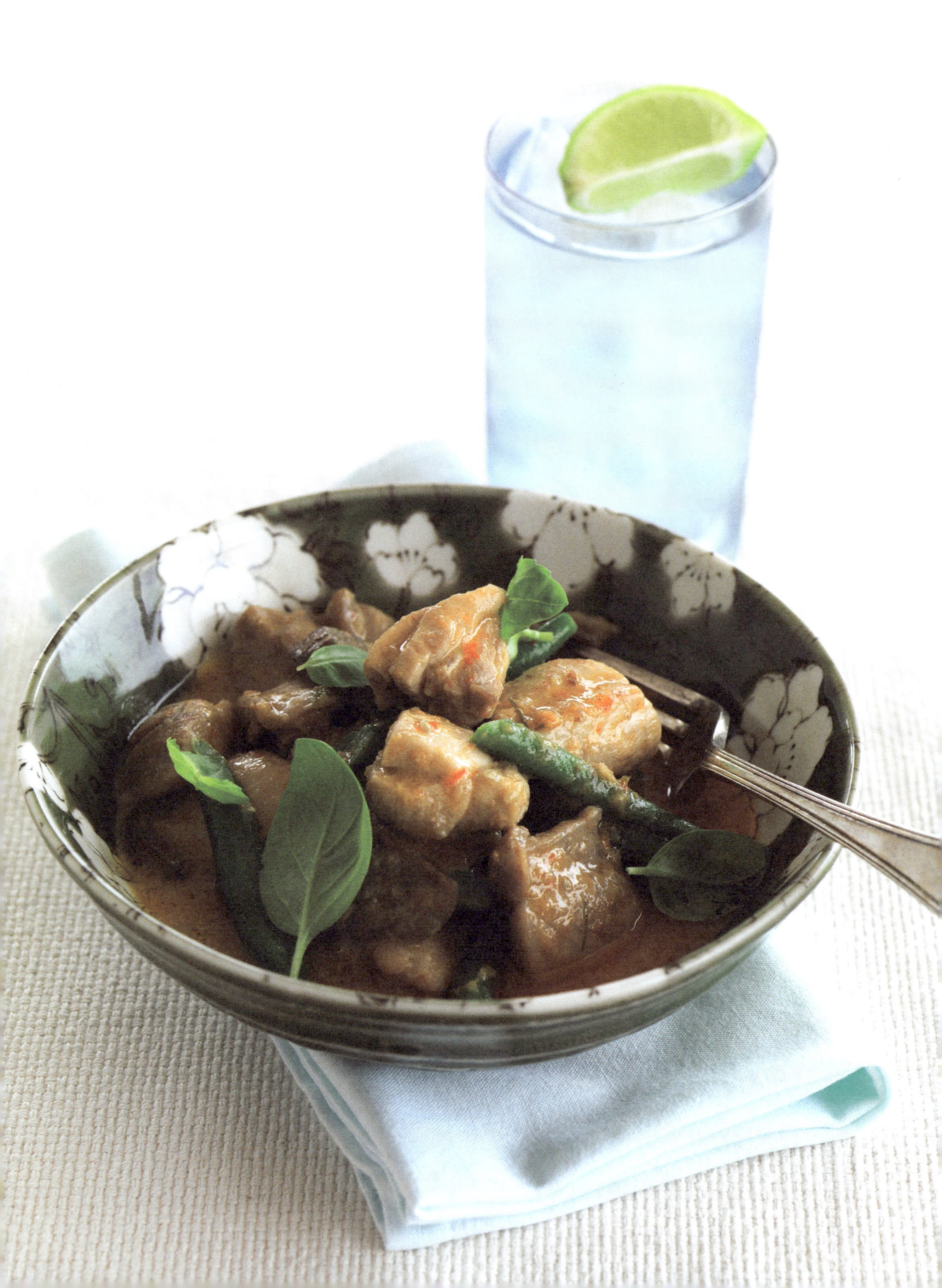

RED CHICKEN CURRY WITH BASIL

A quick dish to make and always bound to please those with a love of spicy food!

1 tablespoon light cooking oil
2–3 tablespoons Red Curry Paste (see below)
500g chicken thighs, skinned, boned and diced
400ml can coconut cream
1 kaffir lime leaf, finely shredded
2 tablespoons grated palm sugar
2 tablespoons fish sauce
100g green beans, sliced
1 tablespoon lime juice
salt and pepper
Thai or regular basil leaves to garnish

Heat the oil in a frying pan. Add the red curry paste and cook over medium heat for 2 minutes until fragrant. Add the chicken and cook for 2–3 minutes until chicken is well coated in the paste.

Add the coconut cream, kaffir lime leaf, palm sugar and fish sauce and reduce the heat. Simmer for 10 minutes or until the chicken is cooked through. Add the green beans and simmer for 5 minutes. Stir in the lime juice and season with salt and pepper.

Garnish with basil leaves and serve with rice.

SERVES 6

RED CURRY PASTE

You can buy red curry paste from the supermarket but you'll get a much more flavoursome result if you make your own. You can adjust the heat of the paste by increasing or reducing the number of chillies.

10 large red chillies, deseeded
2 tablespoons chopped galangal or fresh ginger
2 shallots, chopped
2 tablespoons peanut oil
1 lemongrass stalk, finely chopped
2 teaspoons coriander seeds, toasted
1 teaspoon finely grated lime zest
pinch of salt

Place all of the ingredients in a mortar and pestle or food processor and grind or process to make a smooth paste.

Store in an airtight container in the fridge for up to 3 weeks and use as required.

MAKES ½ CUP

MILD CURRY PASTE

This is a great curry paste that can be used in most Thai curry recipes that call for yellow or green curry paste.

5cm piece fresh ginger
2 cloves garlic, peeled
2 green chillies, deseeded
1 small onion, roughly chopped
1 tablespoon sesame oil
2 tablespoons coriander seeds
juice of 1 lime or ½ lemon
¼ teaspoon turmeric
1 teaspoon fish sauce

Place all of the ingredients in a mortar and pestle or food processor and grind or process to make a smooth paste.

Store in an airtight container in the fridge for up to 3 weeks and use as required.

MAKES ½ CUP

Red Chicken Curry with Basil (left)
Red Curry Paste (overleaf)

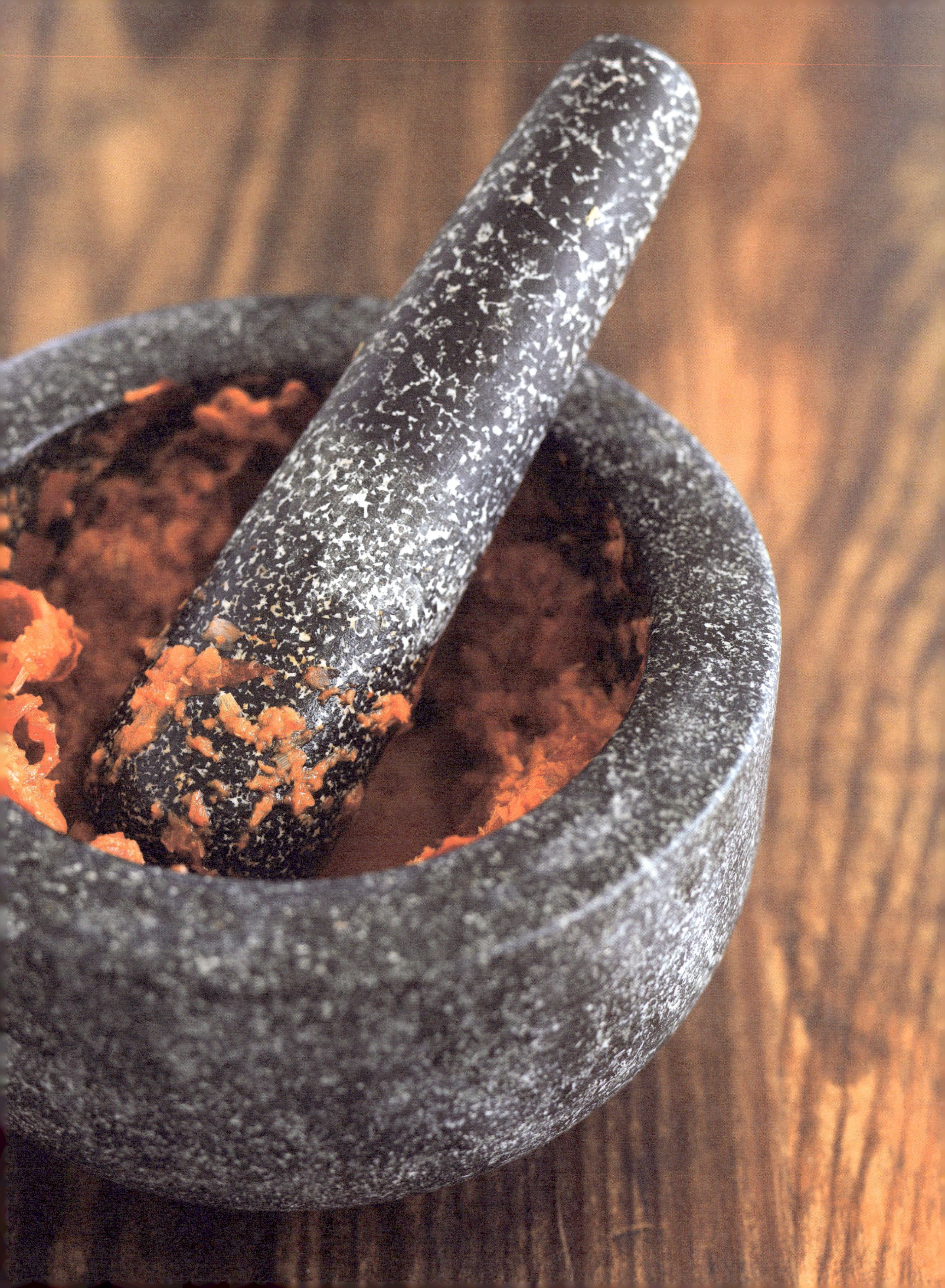

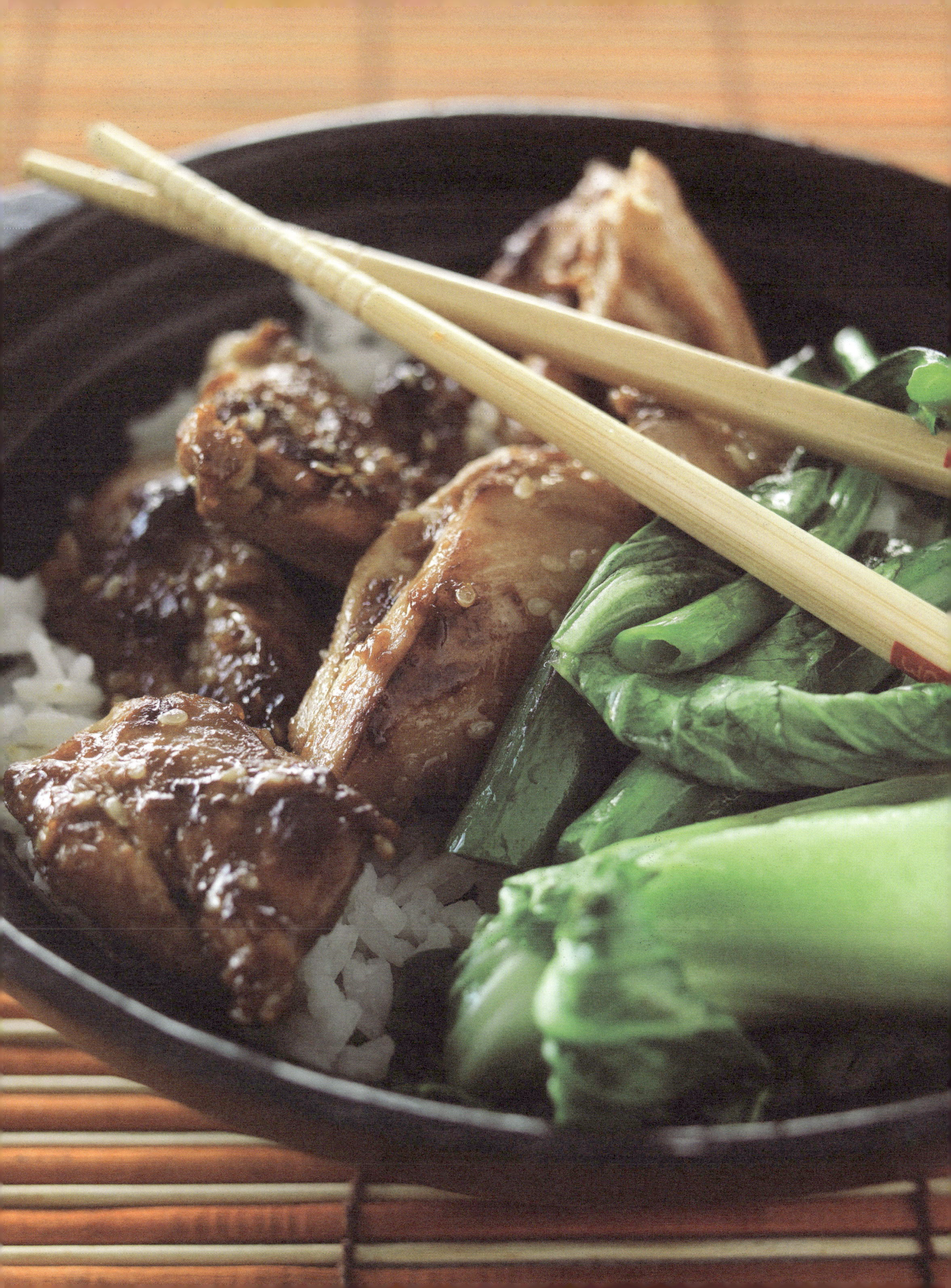

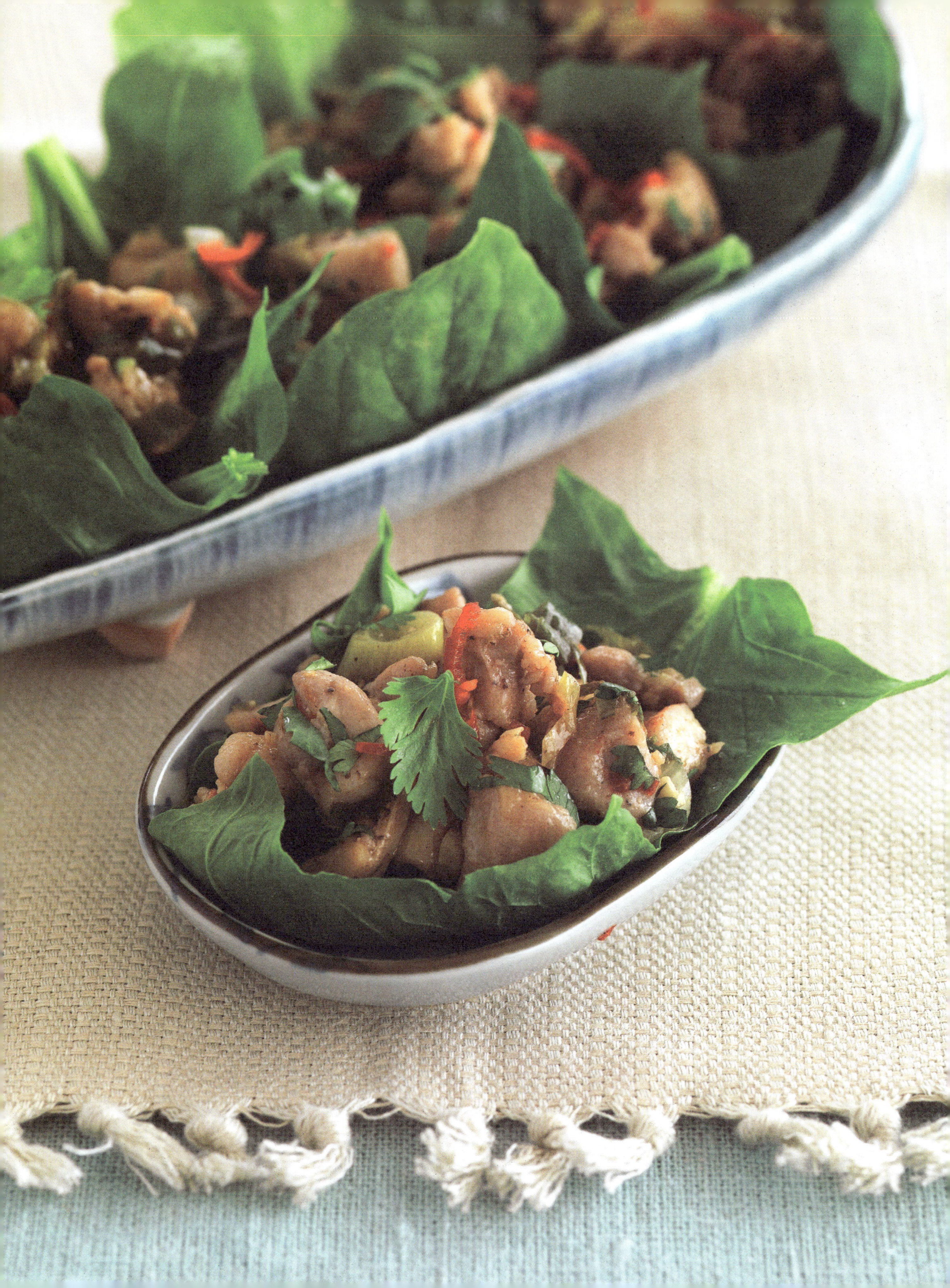

KAFFIR CHICKEN ON SPINACH LEAVES

This delicious, intensely fragrant chicken dish can be served hot or cold. You can wrap the chicken in large spinach leaves or line a platter with baby spinach leaves and pile the chicken on top.

500g chicken thighs, skinned, boned and finely chopped
3 kaffir lime leaves, finely shredded
2 tablespoons fish sauce
1 teaspoon caster sugar
½ teaspoon freshly ground black pepper
1 tablespoon light cooking oil
2 cloves garlic, chopped
2 lemongrass stems, white part only, finely chopped
1 long red chilli, deseeded and finely chopped
2 tablespoons lime juice
5 spring onions, chopped
¼ cup chopped fresh coriander
20 large spinach leaves

Place the chicken into a bowl with the kaffir lime leaves, fish sauce, caster sugar and pepper. Mix well, cover and marinate for at least 30 minutes or overnight in the fridge, if you want to prepare ahead.

Heat the oil in a frying pan over medium heat. Add the garlic, lemongrass and chilli. Stir-fry for 2 minutes. Add the marinated chicken and stir-fry for a further 3–4 minutes until it is cooked through. Add the lime juice, spring onions and coriander.

To serve, place spoonfuls of the mixture into spinach leaves. Fold up and eat with your hands.

MAKES 20 ROLLS

ZESTY CITRUS CHICKEN STIR-FRY WITH ASIAN GREENS

The surprise addition of orange zest and juice gives this stir-fry a wonderfully exotic fragrance.

STIR-FRY
1 tablespoon light cooking oil
500g chicken thighs, skinned, boned and cut into large pieces
1 garlic clove, crushed
1 teaspoon finely grated lime zest
1 teaspoon finely grated orange zest
2 tablespoons lime juice
2 tablespoons orange juice
2 tablespoons soy sauce
1 teaspoon honey
2 teaspoons toasted sesame seeds

ASIAN GREENS
1 tablespoon light cooking oil
1 clove garlic, crushed
1 bunch gai larn, sliced
1 bunch bok choy, sliced

To make the stir-fry, heat the oil in a frying pan and add the chicken thighs. Cook over medium–high heat until golden brown – don't move them around too much as this slows the browning process.

Add the garlic to the pan and cook for 1 minute. Add the lime and orange zests and juice, soy sauce, honey and sesame seeds. Stir-fry for a further 2 minutes or until the chicken is cooked through. Remove the chicken from the pan and keep warm.

Meanwhile, to cook the greens, add oil and garlic to the pan and cook over medium–high heat for 1 minute. Add a little water to the pan and then the vegetables. Stir-fry for a few minutes until they have just wilted – if you are in a hurry cover them with a lid to speed the wilting.

Serve with long-grain rice.

SERVES 4

Kaffir Chicken on Spinach Leaves (left)
Zesty Citrus Chicken Stir-Fry with Asian Greens (previous page)

FRIED SESAME BANANAS

Fried bananas are a common street food in Thailand and it's hard to resist getting some for breakfast and eating them straight from the bag. At home, I serve these delicate morsels drizzled with yoghurt and honey and sprinkled with sesame seeds.

BATTER
½ cup rice flour
¼ cup tapioca flour (or plain flour)
1 tablespoon sugar
2 tablespoons sesame seeds
¼ cup water
¼ cup coconut milk

1 cup light cooking oil for frying
6 finger bananas or 3 regular bananas, peeled and cut diagonally into thick slices
extra sesame seeds to garnish

To make the batter, put the flours, sugar and sesame seeds in a bowl. Make a well in the centre and add the water and coconut milk. Whisk to form a smooth batter that is not too thick and not too thin.

Heat the oil in a small saucepan to just smoking. When it begins to smoke, lower the heat slightly.

Batter each slice of banana and add carefully to the oil. You may need to do this in batches to avoid overcrowding and cooling the oil. Fry until they are golden brown and turn each slice with tongs, if you need to. Remove from the oil with a slotted spoon and drain on paper towels. Keep warm until they are all cooked, garnish with extra sesame seeds and serve immediately with honey and natural yoghurt.

SERVES 6

STICKY RICE WITH MANGO AND COCONUT CREAM

This is another common sweet treat in Thailand. It's an interesting take on Grandma's rice pudding.

1 cup glutinous rice
1 cup coconut milk
2 tablespoons sugar
pinch of salt
1 fresh mango, sliced

Soak the glutinous rice overnight in enough water to cover it – if you are in a hurry, a minimum of 1 hour will do. Drain the rice.

Put water in the bottom of a bamboo or pot steamer and line the steam section with baking paper or a muslin cloth. Put the drained sticky rice into the steamer and cover. Steam over medium–high heat for 20 minutes or until the rice is translucent. Transfer to a bowl.

Heat the coconut milk and sugar in a saucepan over medium heat. Stir constantly and let the coconut milk simmer but not boil to prevent curdling. Add the salt and pour three-quarters of the hot coconut milk over the sticky rice. Let it sit for 5 minutes – the sticky rice will absorb all the coconut milk and become gooey and creamy.

Serve either warm or chilled. Top with the mango and drizzle the remaining coconut milk over the top.

SERVES 6

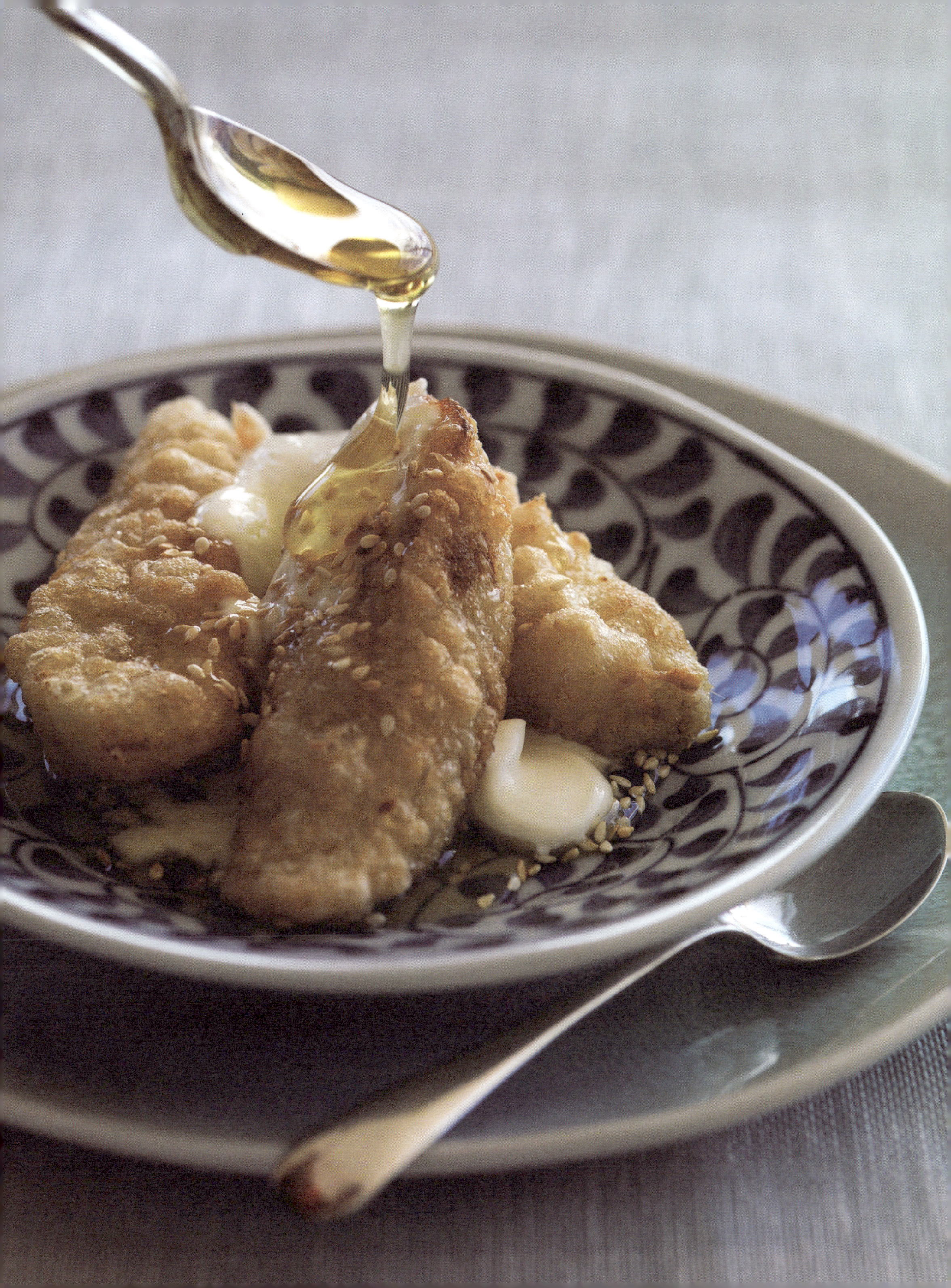

VIETNAM
STREET-FOOD HEAVEN
IN HANOI

'At the bustling markets, food is prepared right in front of you and the counter begins to fill with an assortment of dishes and side dishes.'

If you want to go somewhere where the food is amazing and where you can be sure to experience a starkly different food culture to our own, head to Hanoi, Vietnam. The very best of Vietnam's cuisine is available street-side in this frenetic old city – family-run restaurants spill onto the footpaths with their tiny plastic stools and tables, vying for every square inch of space they can. They open early, and young and old alike pitch in to begin a long and busy day of food preparation and cooking.

Fresh produce from the market is stacked high on a bicycle or motorbike in the small hours to be ferried home, where a team of helpers begin work breaking it down into ingredients for the cooks in the hot seat. So begins the beautiful dance of cooking up some of the world's most delicious and aromatic food using nothing more than a gas cooker and a wok.

Steaming pots of the clean, hot broth called pho are served for breakfast, small doughnuts made with rice flour and filled with sweet bean paste are great for mid-morning snacking, spring rolls – fresh and fried – are to die for all day long, as are the fragrant and moist clay-pot curries . . . it's all there for the eating and that's what I do, from early morning to late into the night, whenever I am in Hanoi.

It's the combination of flavours and textures, brought alive with fresh herbs, especially mint and coriander, chillies, fresh limes – and more – that I adore Vietnamese cuisine for. At the bustling markets, food is prepared right in front of you and the table or counter begins to fill with an assortment of dishes and side dishes, herbs and spices and other condiments – fried peanuts and crunchy bean shoots are always an option. It's a case of perching on a plastic stool and getting stuck in, pointing and eating . . . and pointing and eating some more, until you can't eat any more!

Just make sure you leave enough space to finish with a strong Vietnamese-style coffee – it comes in a glass with a decent dollop of sweetened condensed milk at the bottom. It's gritty, sweet and hot. Sheer pleasure – that's the joy of Vietnamese food.

Recreating the tastes of Vietnam in your own kitchen is easier than ever these days. A quick trip to the local Asian supermarket or supplier to stock up on some of the common ingredients – fish sauce, tamarind purée, palm sugar and fresh coriander – and you've got the beginnings of a taste sensation waiting to happen! Vietnamese food is all about the balance of sweet, salty, sour and spicy hot flavours. Textures are also important and it's best served fresh and fast!

振
乾
坤
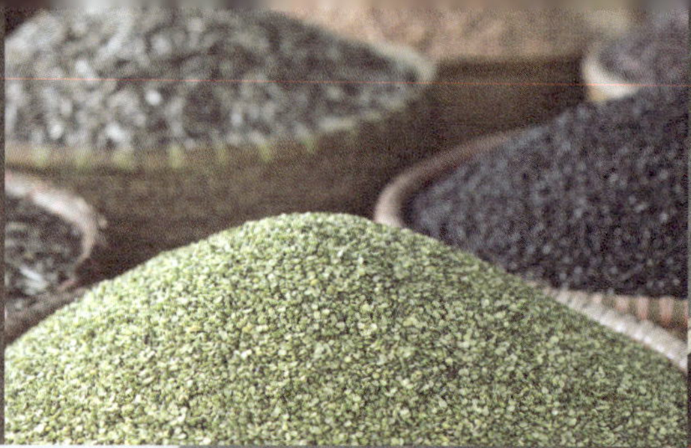
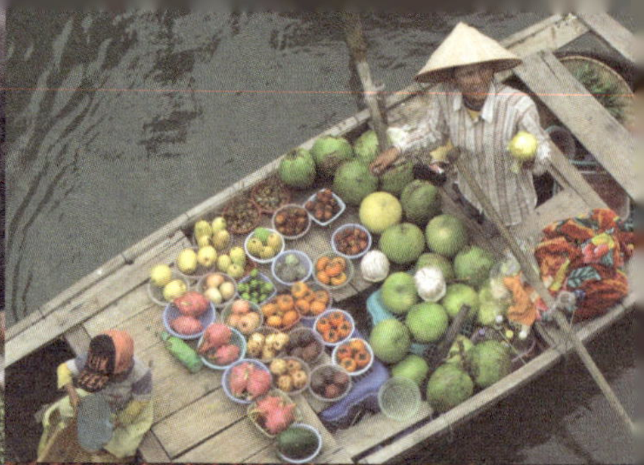
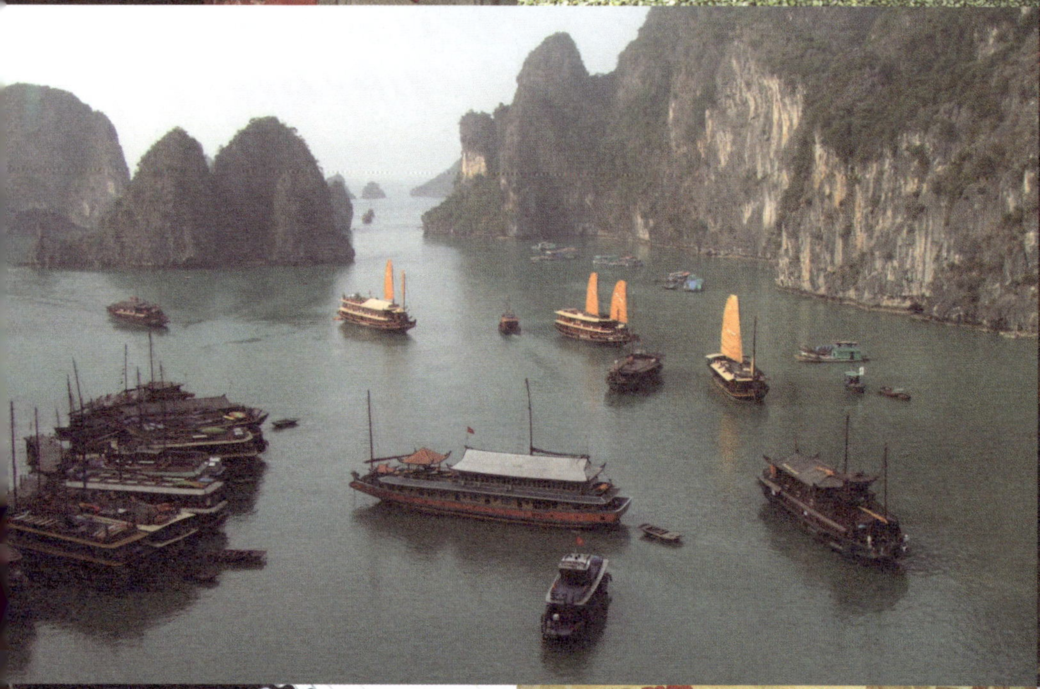
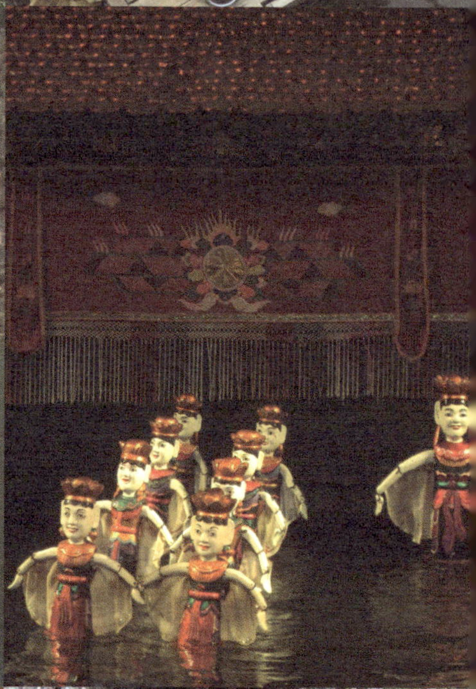
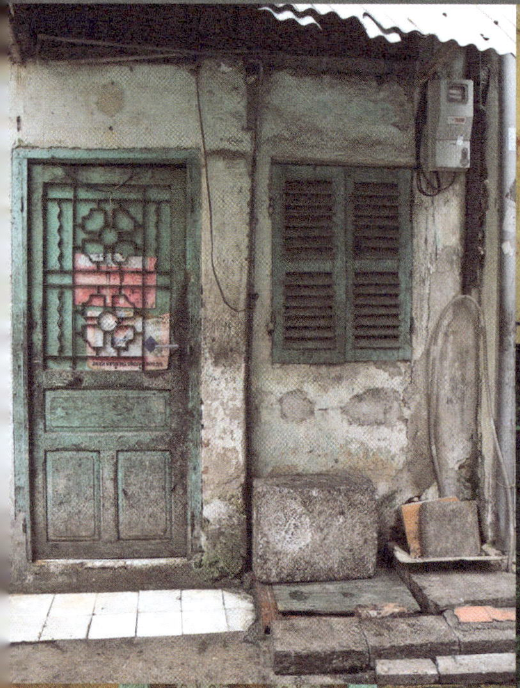
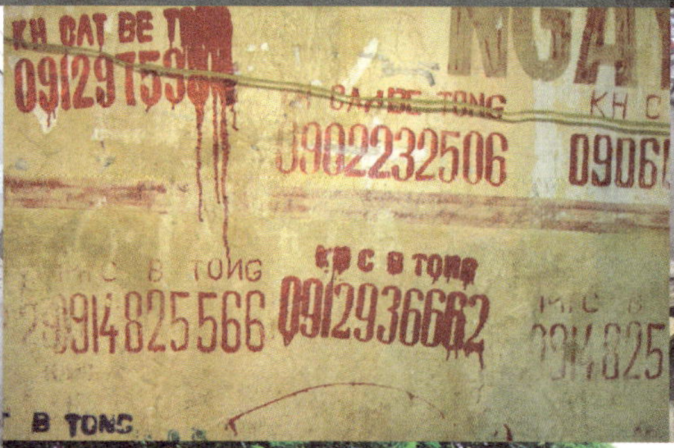
0902232506
0914825566
B TONG
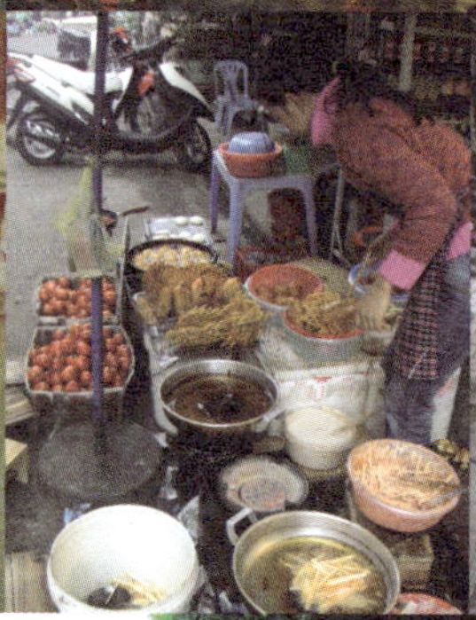
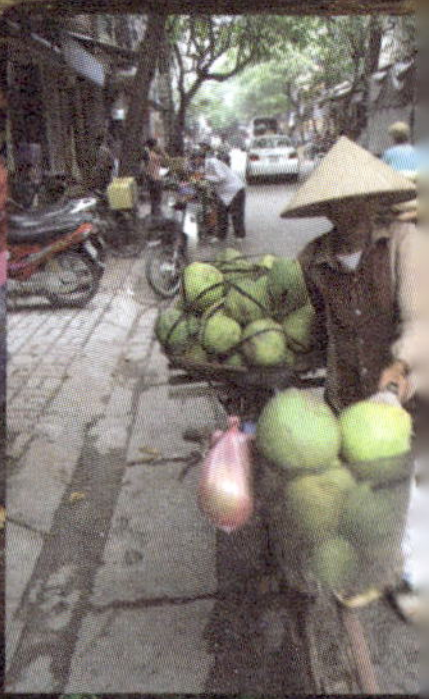
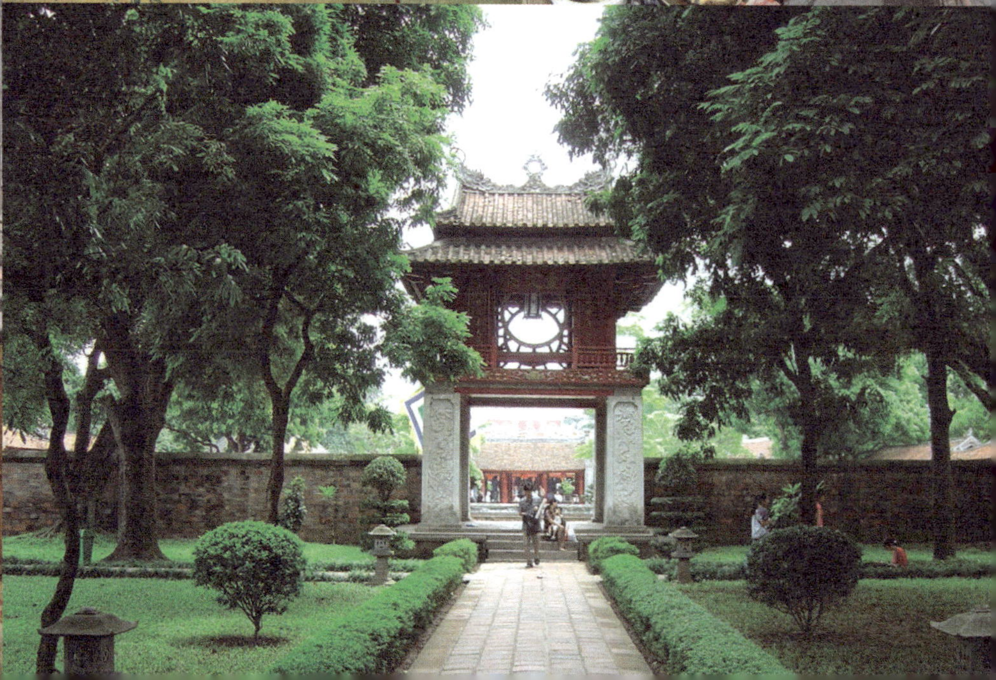
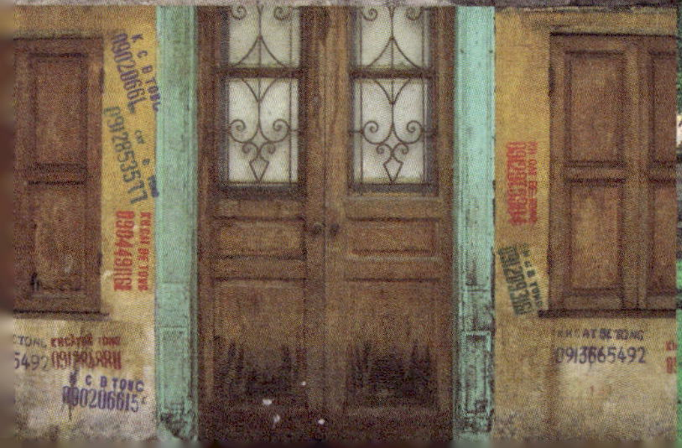
K C B TONG

0936343514
0934 408115
0914608811
0906287679
0916626214
0934 408115
0936343514

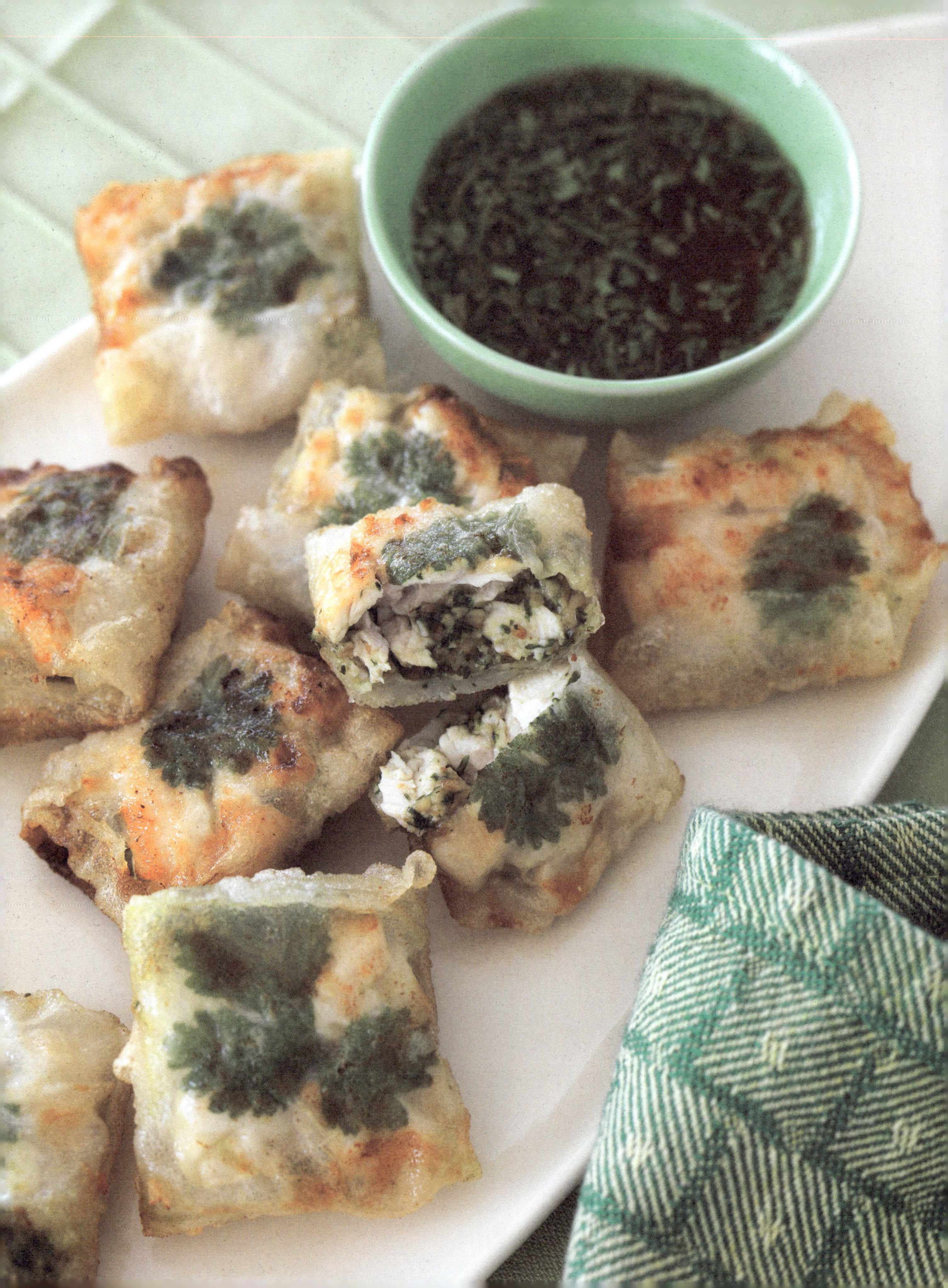

CRISP CHICKEN AND HERB RICE PAPER PARCELS

When I serve these at a party there's never enough – even when I've doubled the recipe!

HERB PASTE
2 cloves garlic, crushed
½ cup roasted cashew nuts
½ cup fresh coriander
½ cup fresh Thai basil or regular basil
¼ cup light cooking oil
salt and pepper

DIPPING SAUCE
3 tablespoons sweet chilli sauce
1 tablespoon fish sauce
1 tablespoon lemon or lime juice
1 tablespoon chopped fresh coriander

RICE PAPER ROLLS
24 small rice paper wrappers
24 coriander sprigs
500g chicken breasts, skinned, boned and finely chopped (or, alternatively, use 500g chicken mince)
light cooking oil for shallow frying

To make the herb paste, place all ingredients into a food processor and process until the mixture forms a smooth paste. Set aside until required.

To make the dipping sauce, put all the ingredients in a bowl and stir to combine.

To assemble the rolls, dip a rice paper wrapper in a bowl of hot water for about 30 seconds or until soft. Pat wrapper dry with paper towel and place on a flat surface. Put a coriander sprig in the centre, top with 2 tablespoons of chopped chicken and 1 teaspoon of herb paste. Fold up the sides of the wrapper to form a square. Place on a piece of baking paper, seam side down. Repeat with remaining rice paper wrappers and filling.

Heat about 1cm of oil in a heavy-based frying pan over medium heat. Cook the parcels in batches for about 3–4 minutes on each side, or until they are golden brown and cooked through. Using a slotted spoon, remove from the oil and drain on paper towels.

Arrange on a platter and serve immediately with a bowl of dipping sauce on the side.

MAKES 24 DELICIOUSLY CRISPY MORSELS

VIETNAMESE-STYLE LETTUCE CUPS

150g rice vermicelli
1 teaspoon light cooking oil
500g chicken mince
1 clove garlic, crushed
2 teaspoons grated fresh ginger
1 tablespoon fish sauce
1 tablespoon lemon juice
¼ cup sweet chilli sauce
2 spring onions, chopped
2 tablespoons chopped fresh coriander
iceberg lettuce leaves
1 Lebanese cucumber, finely diced
2 tablespoons Vietnamese or regular mint, chopped

Prepare the rice vermicelli according to the directions on the packet. Drain well, then cut the vermicelli into short lengths and set aside until required.

Heat the oil in a frying pan. Add the chicken mince and cook over medium–high heat until golden. Add the garlic and ginger and cook for 2 minutes. Add the fish sauce, lemon juice and sweet chilli sauce and continue cooking for 2–3 minutes. Stir in the vermicelli, spring onions and coriander. Set aside to cool.

To serve, spoon the chicken and noodle mixture into lettuce leaves. Top with cucumber and garnish with mint.

MAKES ABOUT 20 (DEPENDING ON THE SIZE OF THE LETTUCE LEAVES)

Crisp Chicken and Herb Rice Paper Parcels

FRESH AS FRESH SPRING ROLLS

There are lots of fried spring rolls in Vietnam, which I love, but after a few days I start to crave the unfried soft ones. You can adjust and add other ingredients, such as shredded chicken, prawns or barbecued pork, but this simple vegetarian version is a good place to start. Your first effort may look a bit raggedy but you will get better with practice.

SPRING ROLLS
1 carrot, cut into matchsticks
½ cucumber, deseeded and cut into matchsticks
1 cup finely shredded lettuce or cabbage
½ cup bean sprouts
¼ cup fresh coriander, finely chopped
¼ cup fresh mint, finely chopped
8 rice-paper wrappers

DIPPING SAUCE
1 teaspoon fish sauce
1 tablespoon white rice vinegar
1 teaspoon sesame oil
juice of 1 lime
1 kaffir lime leaf, finely shredded
1 tablespoon grated palm sugar or 1 teaspoon brown sugar
1–2 red chillies, deseeded and finely chopped (according to taste)

To make the spring rolls, start with a clear bench – you need space to assemble them. Arrange all the prepared vegetables and herbs in a row.

Fill a bowl with hot water. Dip each rice paper wrapper in the hot water for 5 seconds or so and lay them flat on a damp tea towel.

Starting with the first wrapper to have been dipped, and, working in order of dipping, place each wrapper on the bench and place desired amounts of carrot, cucumber, lettuce or cabbage, bean sprouts and herbs horizontally across the centre.

Starting with the edge closest to you, roll it away from you for one complete somersault. Then fold in the left and right sides and continue to roll. You should end up with a tight, neat roll, closed at both ends.

To make the dipping sauce, put all the ingredients in a bowl and stir until sugar has dissolved. Adjust heat to taste – it should be sweet, sour, salty and yummy.

To serve, cut rolls in half on the diagonal and arrange on a platter with a dish of dipping sauce, a dish of hoisin sauce and some crushed peanuts.

MAKES 16 TASTY MORSELS

CUCUMBER, PINEAPPLE AND BEAN SPROUT SALAD

The burst of sweet pineapple combined with the tangy dressing and hint of herbs really makes this simple salad a hit.

DRESSING
½ cup rice vinegar
¼ cup sugar
1 large red chilli, finely chopped
1 garlic clove, sliced
½ teaspoon salt

SALAD
½ telegraph cucumber, halved and sliced on the diagonal
¼ pineapple, cut into 5cm batons
150g mung bean sprouts
fresh coriander and mint leaves to garnish

To make the dressing, put all the ingredients in a small saucepan and bring to the boil, stirring until the sugar has dissolved. Simmer for 2 minutes and set aside to cool until required.

To make the salad, put the cucumber, pineapple and sprouts in a bowl 30 minutes before serving. Add the cooled dressing and toss gently to combine. Garnish with coriander and mint leaves.

SERVES 4 AS AN ACCOMPANIMENT

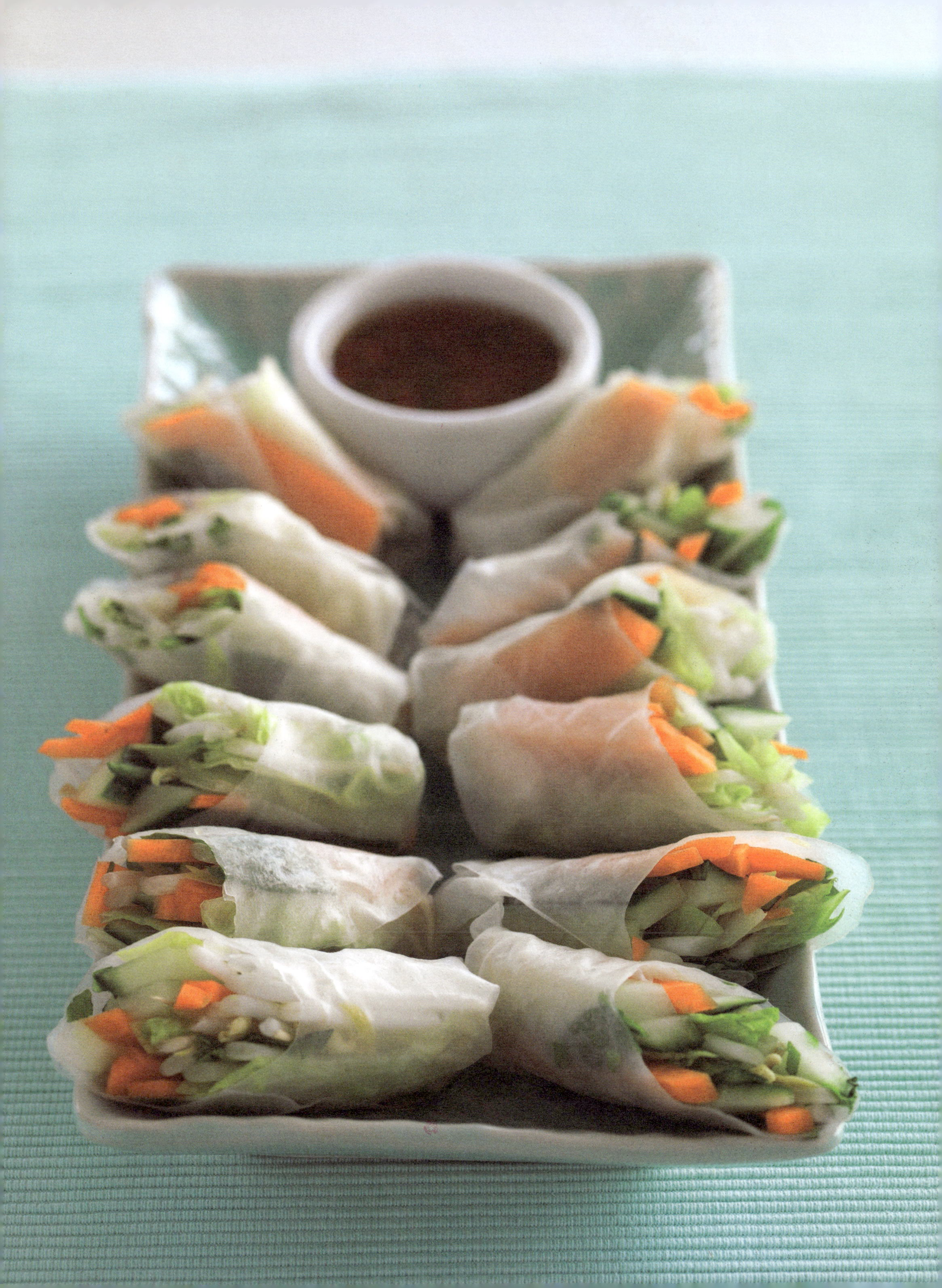

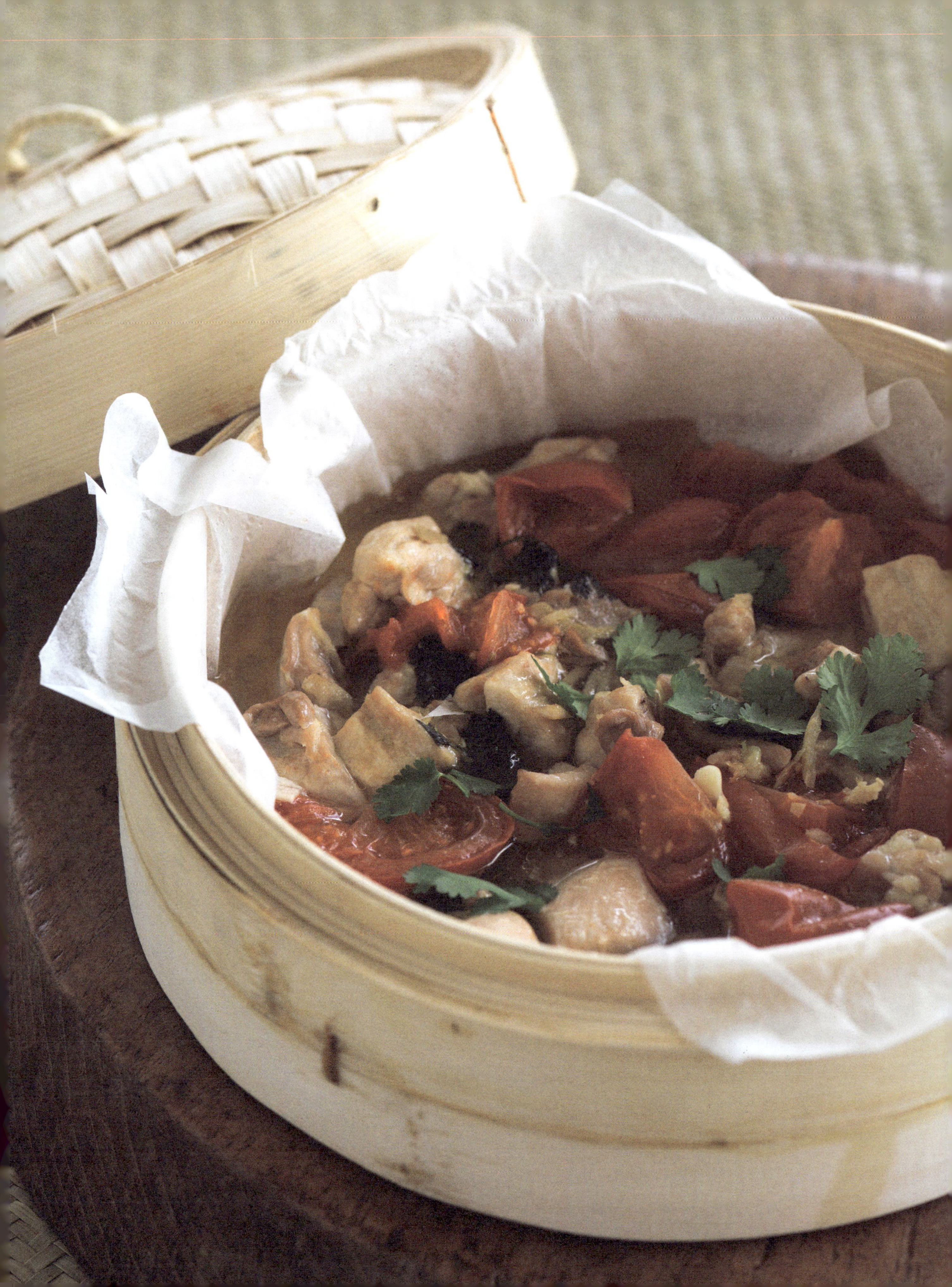

STEAMED CHICKEN WITH TOMATOES AND CORIANDER

Steaming is a great way to create clean-tasting and refreshing food – I love the way that the true flavours of the ingredients are honoured with this method of cooking.

500g chicken thighs, skinned, boned and cut into chunks
1 clove garlic, thinly sliced
1 teaspoon thinly sliced fresh ginger
1 tablespoon fish sauce
1 teaspoon sesame oil
2 teaspoons light cooking oil
3 tomatoes, cut into wedges
2 tablespoons chopped fresh coriander
salt and pepper

Put the chicken, garlic, ginger, fish sauce and oils into a bowl. Mix well.

Line a bamboo steamer basket or regular steamer with baking paper and place the chicken mixture on the paper in a single layer. Add the tomato wedges and coriander. Cover the steamer and place it over a wok or larger pot of boiling water. Steam for 15–20 minutes until the chicken is cooked through. Season with salt and pepper.

Serve with steamed rice.

SERVES 4

CHICKEN, BEAN SPROUTS AND BAMBOO SHOOTS WITH FRAGRANT NOODLES

This recipe is great with either rice, egg noodles or, for a change and if you are in a hurry, crispy noodles.

MARINADE
2 teaspoons light cooking oil
2 teaspoons fish sauce
1 teaspoon sugar
3cm piece of ginger, peeled and cut into thin strips
1 kaffir lime leaf, cut into thin strips
2 cloves garlic, crushed

400g chicken thighs, skinned, boned and finely chopped

NOODLES
200g dried noodles of your choice (see note above)
1 tablespoon tamarind purée
1 tablespoon soy sauce
2 teaspoons sesame oil
1 teaspoon sugar

1 tablespoon light cooking oil
1 small onion, sliced
1 green capsicum, deseeded and thinly sliced
1 yellow capsicum, deseeded and thinly sliced
½ cup drained bamboo shoots, cut into matchsticks
1 cup bean sprouts
fresh coriander leaves to garnish

Put the chicken, garlic, ginger, fish sauce and oils into a bowl. Mix well.

Line a bamboo steamer basket or regular steamer with baking paper and place the chicken mixture on the paper in a single layer. Add the tomato wedges and coriander. Cover the steamer and place it over a wok or larger pot of boiling water. Steam for 15–20 minutes until the chicken is cooked through. Season with salt and pepper.

Serve with steamed rice.

SERVES 4

Steamed Chicken with Tomatoes and Coriander

HEROIC HANOI CLAY-POT CHICKEN

You don't need a clay pot to make this, but a clay pot will add an air of authenticity. Any ovenproof dish will do, as long as you can cover it with foil or a tight-fitting lid.

1–2 large red chillies, deseeded and sliced
1 tablespoon fresh ginger, crushed
1 medium-sized onion, sliced into thin half rounds
2 tablespoons dark soy sauce
½ cup water
1 tablespoon rice wine vinegar
juice of 1 lemon
1 tablespoon fish sauce
1 tablespoon sesame oil
1 tablespoon brown sugar or grated palm sugar
½ teaspoon salt
2 tablespoons light cooking oil
3–4 chicken breasts, skinned, boned and thickly sliced
handful of bean sprouts

Preheat oven to 180°C.

Combine all ingredients except the chicken and bean sprouts in a clay pot or ovenproof casserole dish and stir until the sugar has dissolved.

Add the chicken and stir together, making sure the chicken is well coated with the marinade – there should be enough liquid to almost cover the chicken. You may need to add some water. Bake for 45 minutes.

Remove from the oven, cover and put the hot clay pot on a folded tea towel or wire rack so it doesn't crack. Gently lift lid (to avoid steam burns) and add the bean sprouts. Replace the lid to allow the sprouts to steam – they should, however, remain crunchy.

This is ready to serve and will stay warm for at least 45 minutes.

Serve with rice.

SERVES 4

CARAMEL CHICKEN

Caramelised food has a depth of flavour that is definitely moreish.

500g chicken thighs, skinned, boned and cut in half
2 tablespoons light cooking oil
2 tablespoons fish sauce
3 shallots, sliced
3 cloves garlic, sliced
freshly ground black pepper
¼ cup reduced-salt soy sauce
¼ cup brown sugar
¼ cup water
1 tablespoon lime juice
lime wedges to garnish

Place the chicken in a bowl with the oil, fish sauce, shallots, garlic and pepper and toss to combine. Cover and refrigerate for 30 minutes.

Heat a large frying pan over medium–high heat. Add the chicken mixture and stir-fry for 5 minutes or until the chicken has browned. Add the soy sauce.

Cover the pan, reduce the heat to low and cook for 10 minutes, stirring occasionally.

Increase the heat to high, add the brown sugar, water and lime juice and cook uncovered for 3–4 minutes until the sauce is rich and syrupy.

Garnish with lime wedges and serve with rice and *Cucumber, Pineapple and Bean Sprout Salad* (see page 108).

SERVES 4

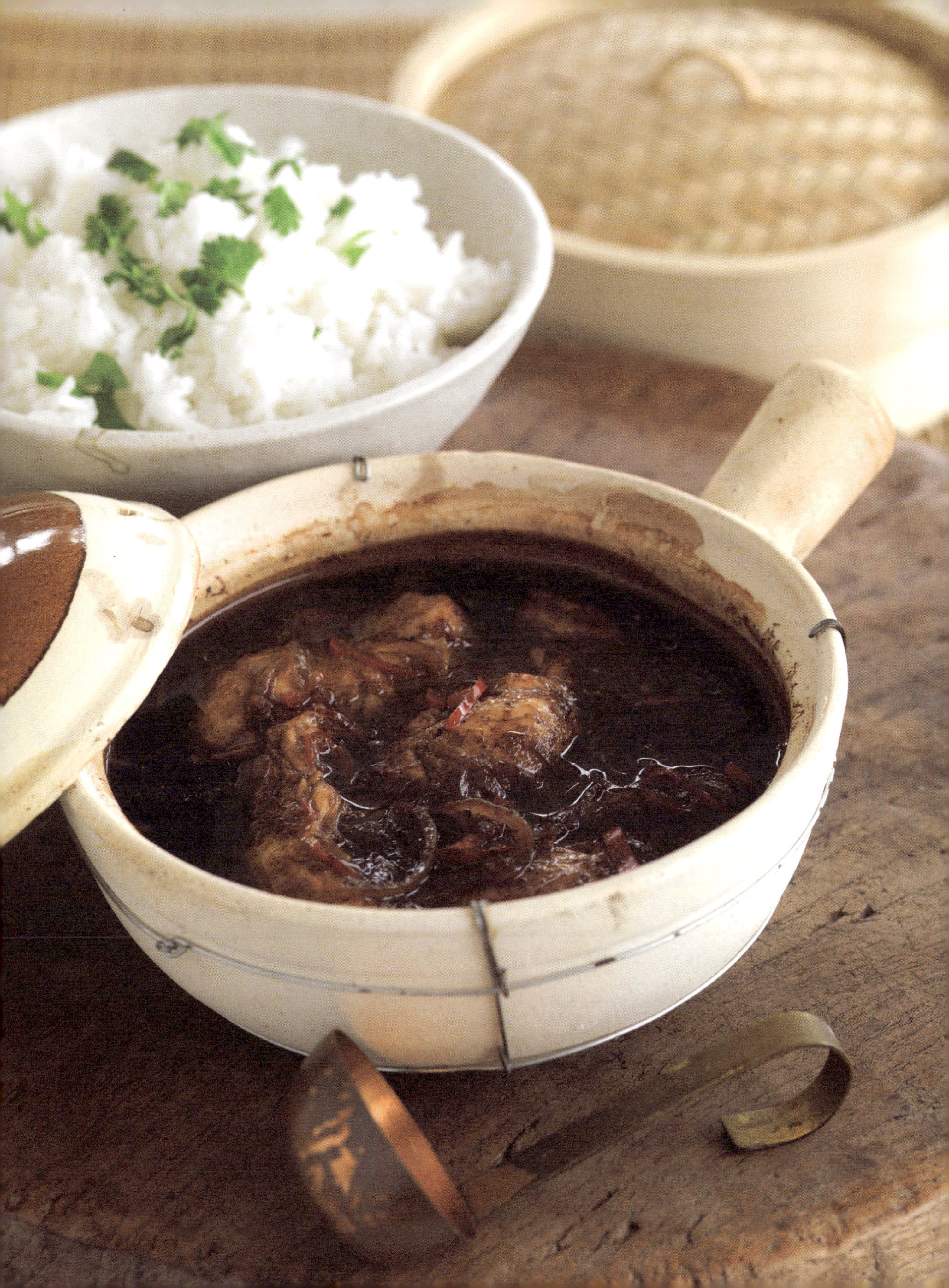

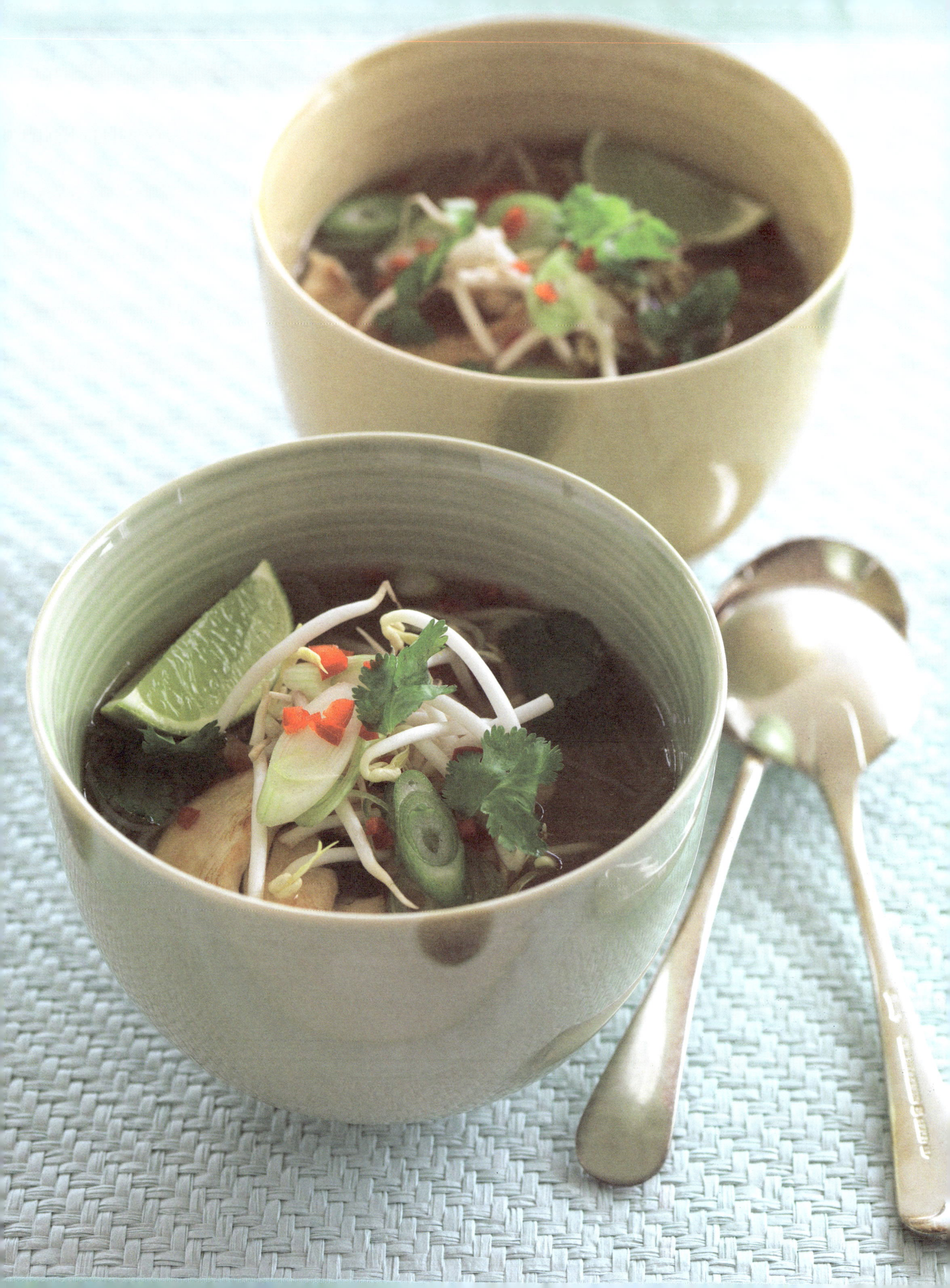

PHO GA

Vietnamese chicken noodle soup is the ultimate in comfort food. It is often served for breakfast in Vietnam, but I love it any time of the day or night. It's especially good if you're suffering from a cold or flu – it's as if the hot and spicy broth burns the bugs away.

BROTH
1 teaspoon sesame oil
1 tablespoon light cooking oil
2 teaspoons crushed garlic
1 teaspoon crushed chilli
2 teaspoons grated fresh ginger
2 spring onions, chopped, green bits and all
2 litres good-quality chicken or vegetable stock (use a low-salt variety, if possible)
2 tablespoons fish sauce

2–3 chicken breasts, skinned, boned and cut into thin strips
150g dried flat rice noodles
2 tablespoons fresh coriander to garnish
extra fresh chilli to garnish (according to taste)
bean sprouts to garnish (optional)
lime wedges to garnish

To make the broth, heat the oils in a large pot and cook the garlic, chilli, ginger and spring onions on low–medium heat until the onions are soft. Add the stock and fish sauce and, when it is gently simmering, add the chicken. Poach the chicken for 8–10 minutes, skimming off any fat or other scum that rises to the surface to ensure a nice clear broth.

Meanwhile, cook the noodles according to the directions on the packet.

Drain the noodles and divide between four deep bowls. Add one-quarter of the chicken to each bowl and then pour in the broth. Garnish with coriander, extra chilli, bean sprouts (if using) and lime wedges.

SERVES 4

CHICKEN, PAWPAW AND MINT SALAD WITH SWEET CHILLI DRESSING

This simple salad is a fine example of the taste-tingling zingy freshness that is unique to Vietnamese food.

DRESSING
3 tablespoons lemon juice
1 teaspoon finely grated fresh ginger
2 large red chillies, deseeded and finely chopped
1 tablespoon fish sauce
1 tablespoon rice wine vinegar
1 tablespoon chopped fresh coriander
1 tablespoon toasted sesame seeds
2 tablespoons grated palm sugar (or 1 tablespoon brown sugar)

SALAD
400g chicken breasts, skinned, boned and thickly sliced
130g packet baby cos lettuce leaves
100g snow peas, blanched
1 pawpaw, peeled, deseeded and sliced
¼ cup fresh mint leaves

To make the dressing, put all the ingredients in a small bowl and stir until the sugar has dissolved. Set aside until required.

Heat a barbecue hot plate and cook the chicken until golden brown and cooked through. Toss the warm chicken with the dressing. Cover and chill for at least 30 minutes.

Place the lettuce on a serving platter. Add the snow peas, pawpaw and mint and toss gently to combine. Arrange the chicken on top and drizzle the dressing over. Serve immediately.

SERVES 4

CHICKEN SALAD WITH NUOC CHAM

Nuoc cham – a Vietnamese dipping sauce made with fish sauce (nuoc nam) – is like a decent tomato sauce. It's addictive and if you like it as much as I do, you'll end up having it with everything!

NUOC CHAM
1–2 red chillies, deseeded and finely chopped (according to taste)
1 clove garlic, crushed
2 tablespoons sugar
3 tablespoons lemon or lime juice
1 tablespoon rice vinegar
2 tablespoons fish sauce

MARINADE
2 tablespoons light cooking oil
1 teaspoon sesame oil
1 stalk lemongrass, finely chopped
3 spring onions, finely chopped
½ teaspoon salt
½ teaspoon freshly ground black pepper

400g chicken breast, skinned, boned and thinly sliced
extra oil for frying

SALAD
2 cups shredded Chinese cabbage
2 cups shredded lettuce
2 medium-sized carrots, cut into matchsticks
¼ cup bean sprouts
½ cup roughly chopped fresh coriander, mint and basil

To make the nuoc cham, place all the ingredients in a small bowl and stir to combine until the sugar has dissolved. Set aside until required.

To make the marinade, put all the ingredients in a bowl and stir to combine. Add the chicken and mix together, making sure the chicken is well coated. Cover and refrigerate for 30 minutes.

Heat the extra oil in a heavy-based frying pan over high heat. Add the chicken and stir-fry for 4–5 minutes until cooked. Set aside to cool slightly.

Place all the salad ingredients onto a large platter. Top with the warm chicken. Drizzle the nuoc cham over and serve immediately.

SERVES 4

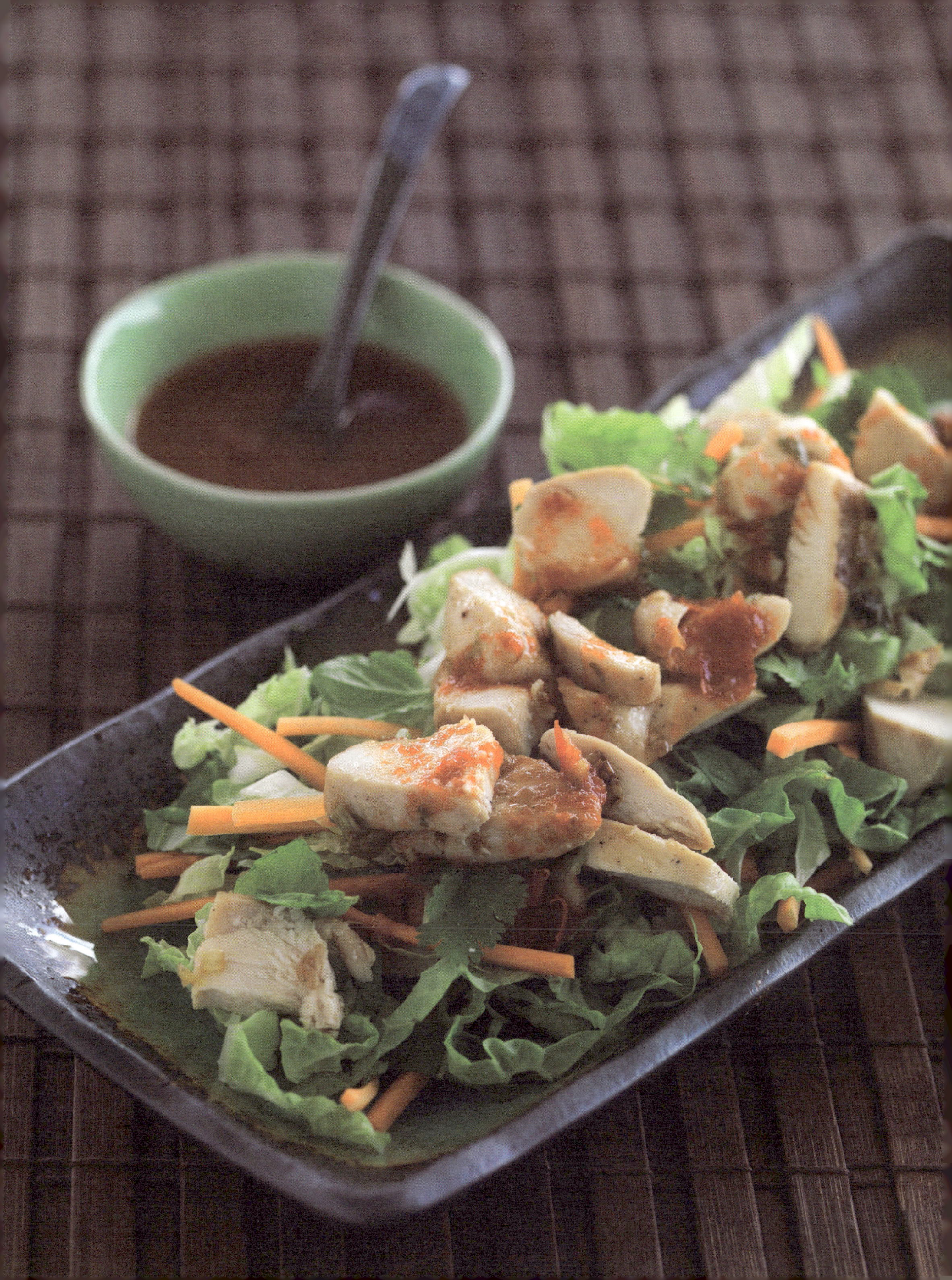

VIETNAMESE STEAMBOAT

This is a great dinner party idea – prepare the ingredients in advance and let your guests choose what they would like to poach in the broth provided, and eat as they go. You will need a steamboat, electric wok or a gas burner and a large saucepan.

BROTH
1½ litres good-quality chicken stock
2 tablespoons rice wine
3 lemongrass stalks, bruised
3 cloves garlic, crushed
3cm piece ginger, sliced
2 spring onions, thinly sliced on the diagonal

DIPPING SAUCE
1–2 red chillies (according to taste), deseeded and finely chopped
1 clove garlic, crushed
1 tablespoon sugar
¼ cup lemon or lime juice
1 tablespoon rice vinegar
2 tablespoons fish sauce

STEAMBOAT OPTIONS
1 tablespoon oyster sauce
1 tablespoon soy sauce
1 tablespoon rice vinegar
½ teaspoon sesame oil
1 clove garlic, crushed
600g chicken breasts, skinned, boned and thinly sliced
12 raw prawns, shelled
150g silken tofu, cut into cubes
Asian greens
sliced Chinese cabbage
asparagus
bean sprouts
sliced celery
sliced mushrooms
fresh coriander
Thai basil
Vietnamese mint

300g fresh egg noodles

To prepare the broth, put all ingredients in a saucepan and bring to the boil. Simmer for 20 minutes.

To prepare the dipping sauce, put all the ingredients in a bowl and stir until the sugar has dissolved. Set aside until required.

To prepare the chicken, place the oyster sauce, soy sauce, rice vinegar, sesame oil and garlic in a bowl. Add chicken and mix well making sure the chicken is well coated.

To prepare the steamboat options, arrange the prepared chicken, prawns, tofu, vegetables and herbs onto platters.

To serve, place the steamboat, electric wok or gas burner and saucepan in the centre of the table. Add the broth and bring to the boil then reduce the heat so the broth is simmering. Place the platters of steamboat options and a bowl of dipping sauce on the table and tuck in. Let your guests poach their selections in the steamboat and dip them in the dipping sauce. When they have finished, add the noodles to the broth and simmer until the noodles are cooked. Ladle the broth into serving bowls and eat straight away.

SERVES 6

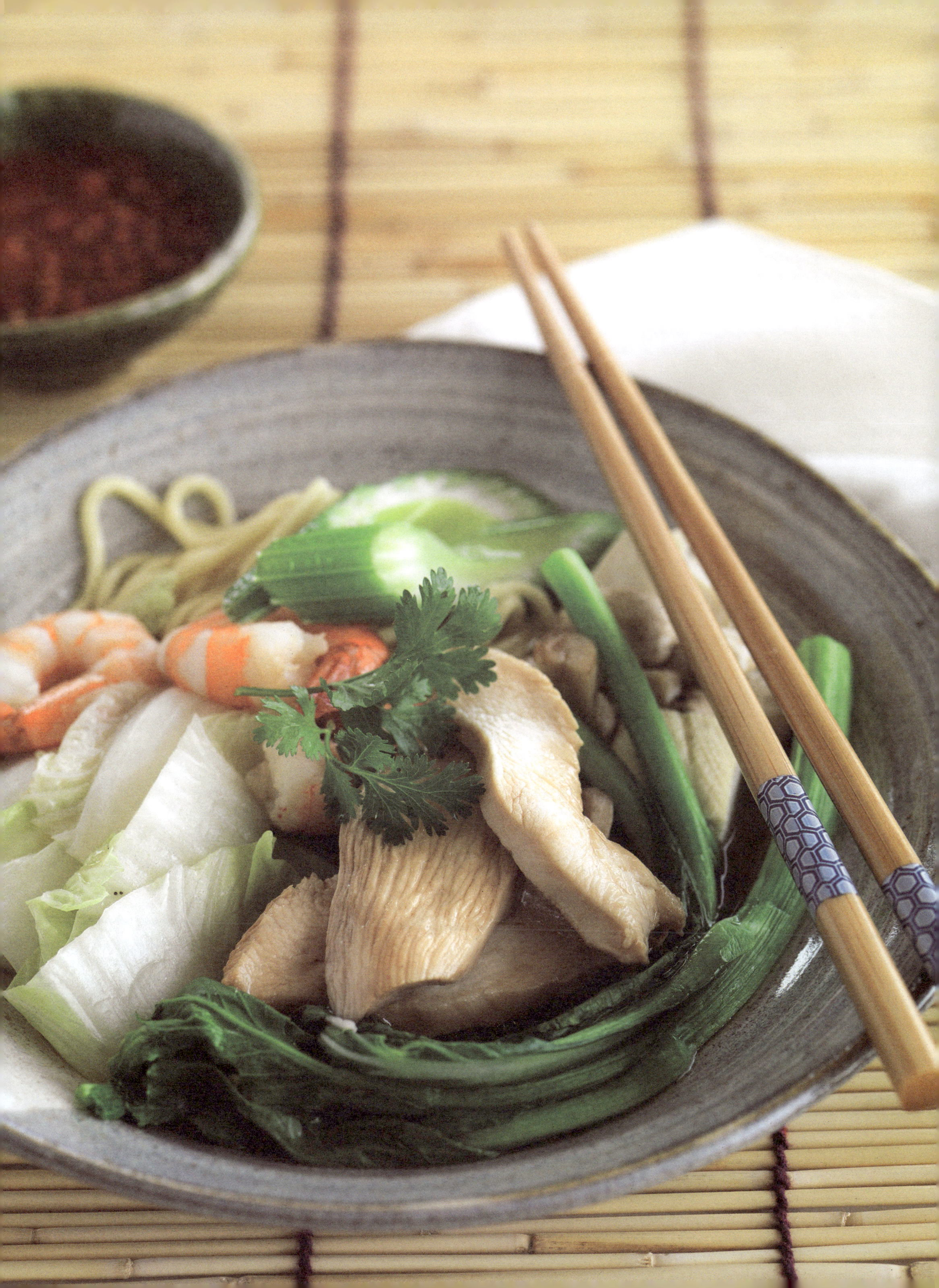

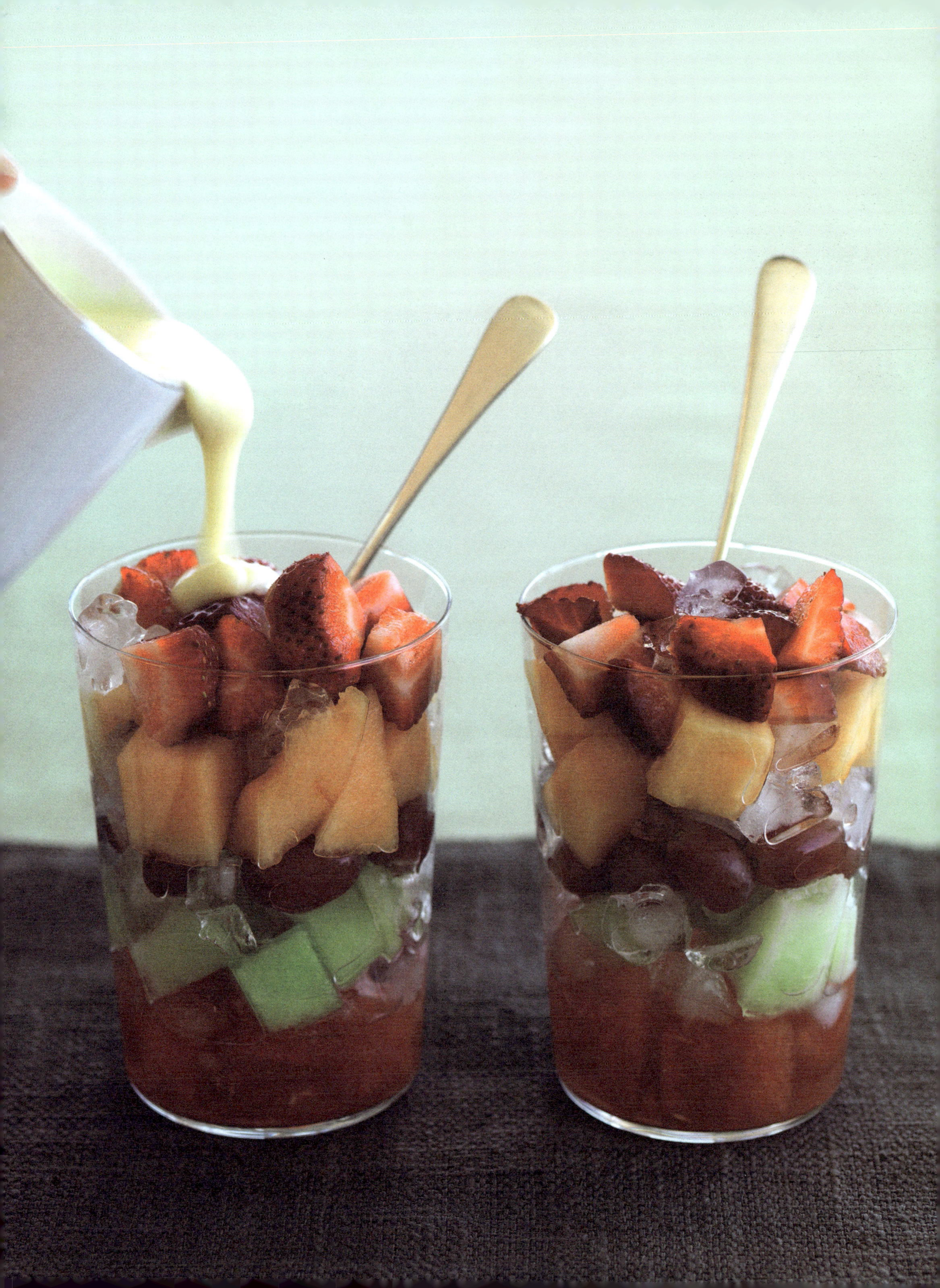

✻ ICED FRUIT CUPS

Simple, elegant and refreshing – there's nothing nicer on a hot day than an iced cup made with fresh fruit.

assorted fruits – melons, strawberries, grapes – chopped
crushed ice
sweetened condensed milk
coconut milk

Assemble fruit in a tall glass with crushed ice and drizzle condensed milk and coconut milk over.

The quantities depend on how big the glasses are and how sweet your tooth is!

✻ LYCHEE AND GINGER SORBET

The sweet and subtle flavour of lychees and the tanginess of ginger combine beautifully in this tasty cocktail. Reserve the juice from the lychees for use in another fruit cocktail later.

2 x 565g cans lychees, drained
2 tablespoons lime juice
2 teaspoons finely grated fresh ginger, strained

Place all the ingredients in a food processor and process until smooth. Pour into a large shallow dish and freeze for at least 1½–2 hours until frozen.

When ready to serve, transfer the mixture into a food processor and process until smooth. Serve immediately or freeze (although bear in mind that it does go rock solid when frozen – so you will need to thaw it slightly from frozen before serving).

SERVES 4

✻ VIETNAMESE-STYLE ICED COFFEE

When you go to Vietnam you need to leave behind your usual coffee-drinking habits and instead embrace the idea of having strong black coffee, hot or ice-cold, laced with sweetened condensed milk. Pure bliss once you get over the shock of it! Try serving the ice-cold version when you next have friends over for coffee – I guarantee it will be a hit.

3 cups strong espresso, cooled
¼ cup sweetened condensed milk
crushed ice

Half-fill three tall glasses with crushed ice and pour espresso to about two-thirds full.

Carefully drizzle sweetened condensed milk down the side of each glass so that it settles at the bottom in a milky white layer. Serve each with a long teaspoon.

SERVES 4

INDONESIA
TASTY FAVOURITES
FROM BALI

'Learning the phrase for "That looks delicious" has helped me in my quest and I see faces light up and more great food appear at the table everywhere I go.'

I was just 22 years old and on my first trip to an exotic location when Bali captured my heart. Backpacking through Indonesia with my boyfriend, I experienced a whole new world of food and taste sensations that I could never have imagined. Feeling very much the intrepid travellers, we ate at the local warung – small, family-owned, outdoor restaurants – or from the many and varied street vendors. Satay hot off the coals, rice wrapped in banana leaves, gado-gado with lashings of spicy peanut sauce and tangy nasi goreng . . . there were blissful bursts of flavour to be found around every street corner.

Since that first visit, I've returned many times to enjoy the gentle people, graceful rituals, incredible coastline and, most of all, the fantastic food that Bali has to offer. It's getting harder these days to find the real thing, but my rule of thumb is to get out of the tourist spots and look at where and what the locals are eating.

Learning the phrase for 'That looks delicious' and 'That was delicious' has helped me in my quest and I see faces light up and more great food appear at the table everywhere I go!

In Indonesian homes meals are often cooked at the start of the day and left out for family members who return from work or school throughout the day to graze on at their leisure. Unless it's a special occasion, or one of the many festival celebrations, there's not usually a sit-down meal in these relaxed households. That's why many of the dishes included here are perfect eaten not so hot. In fact, the flavours are often more pronounced when the food has cooled to room temperature.

Serving Indonesian food to guests certainly takes the stress out of getting everything to the table hot and at the same time!

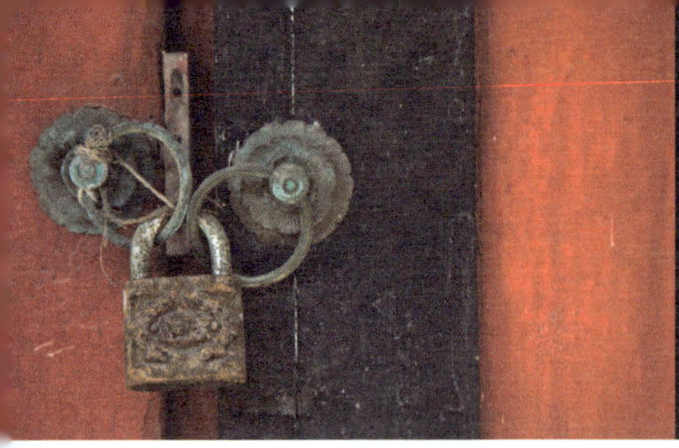
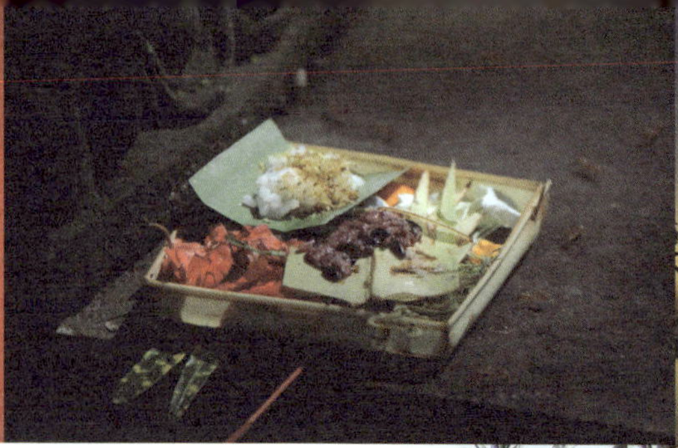
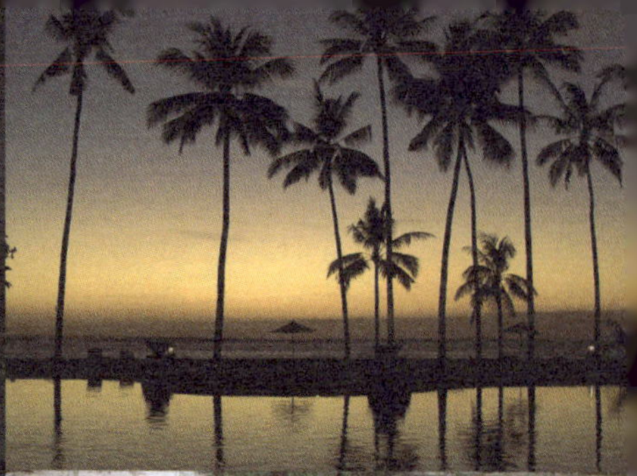
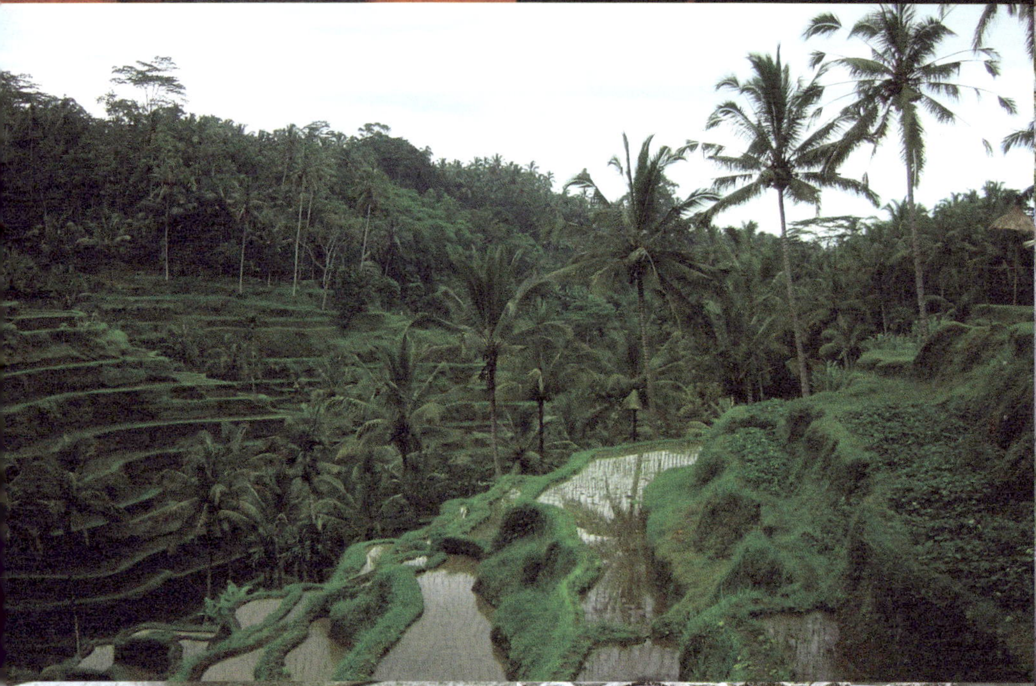
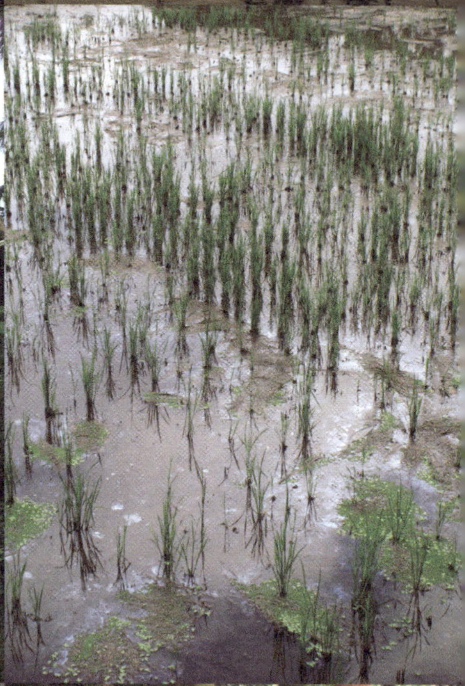
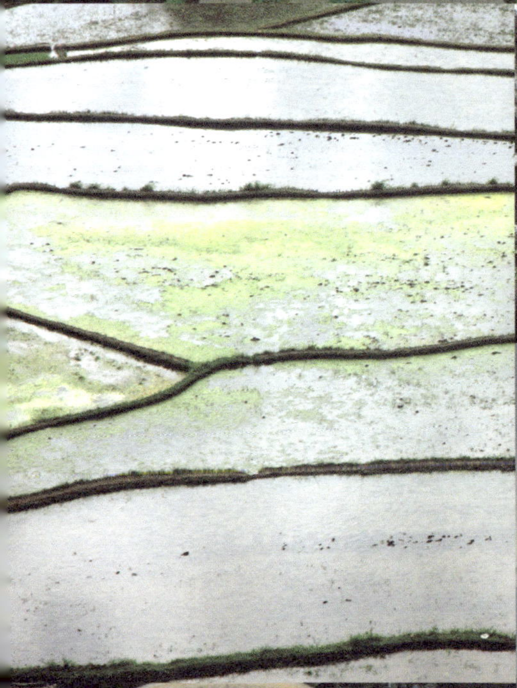
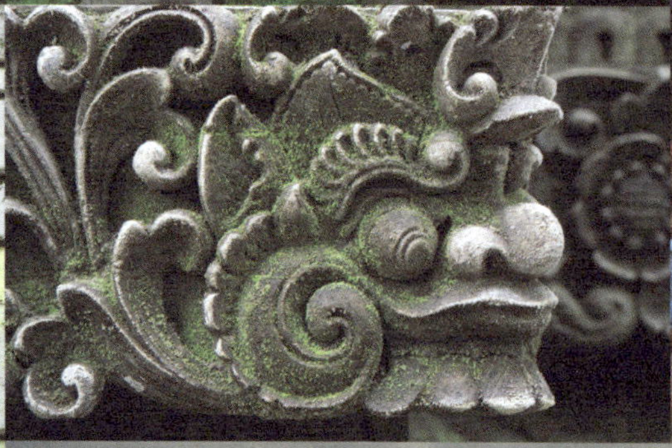
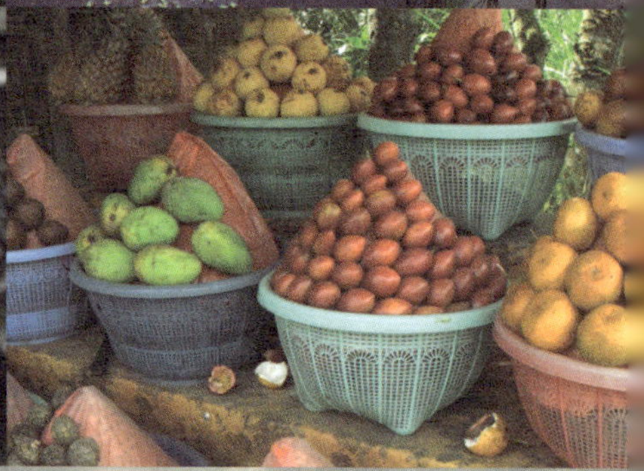
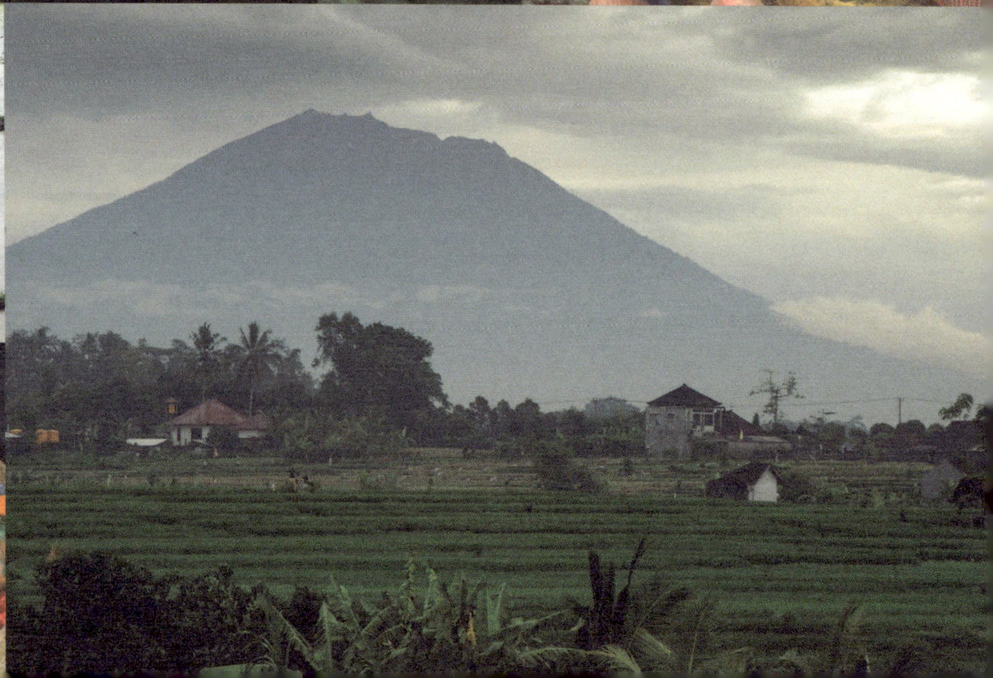
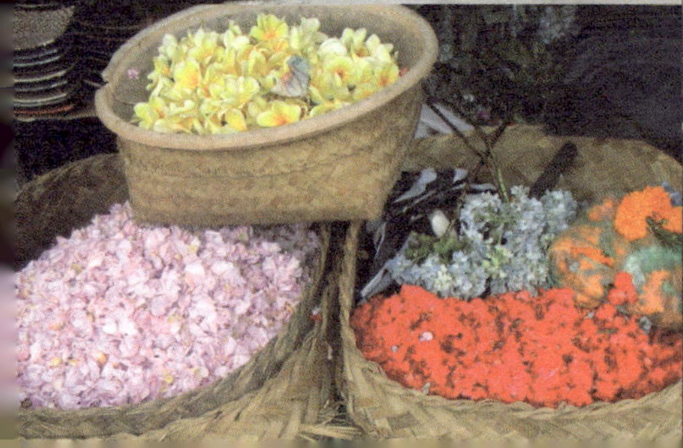

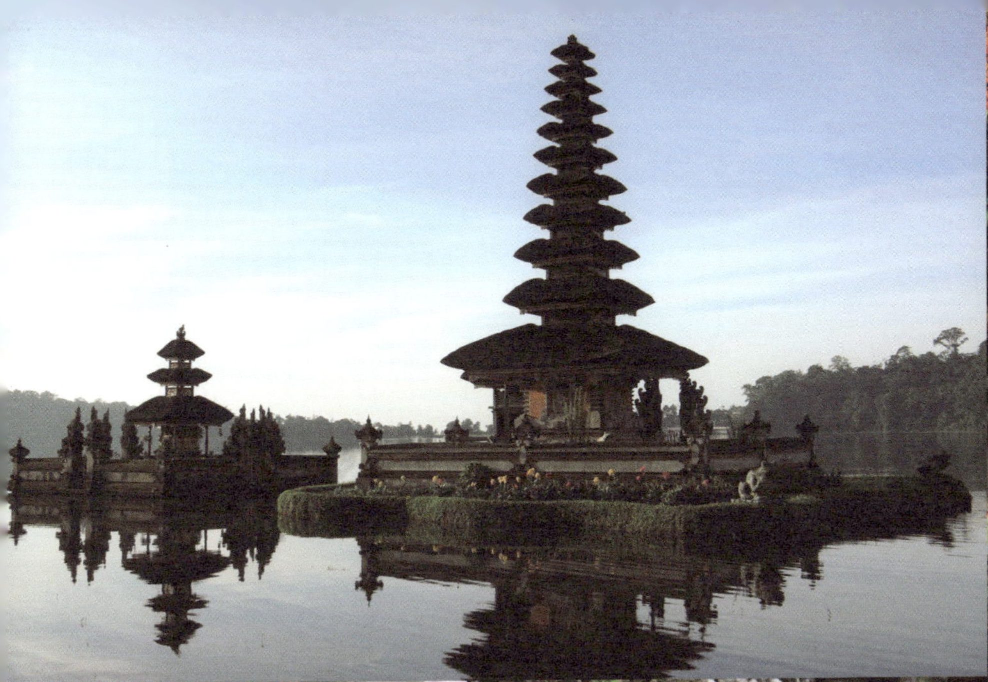
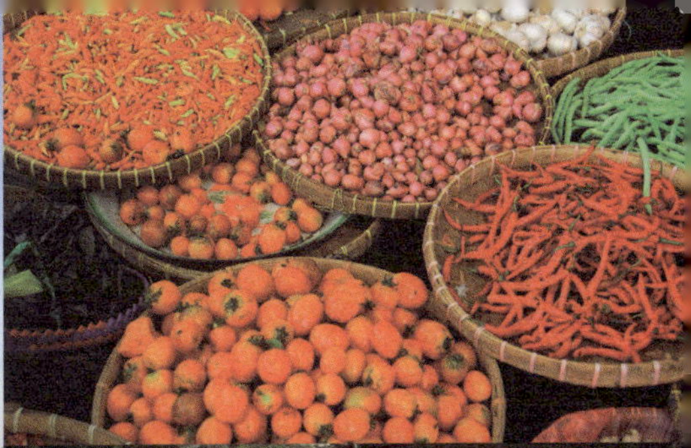
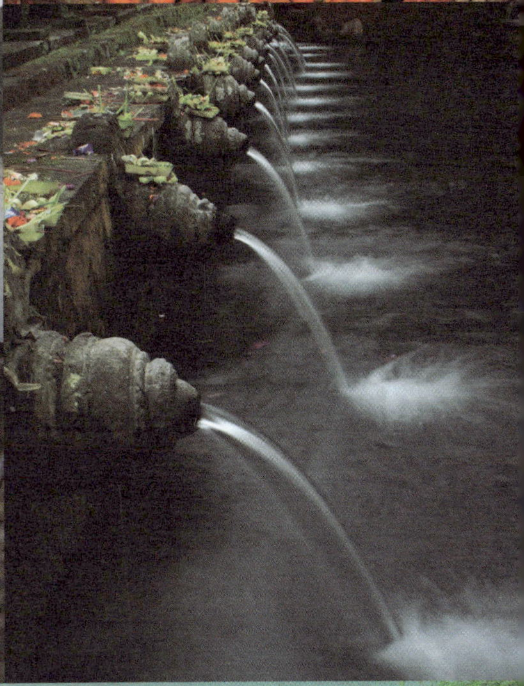
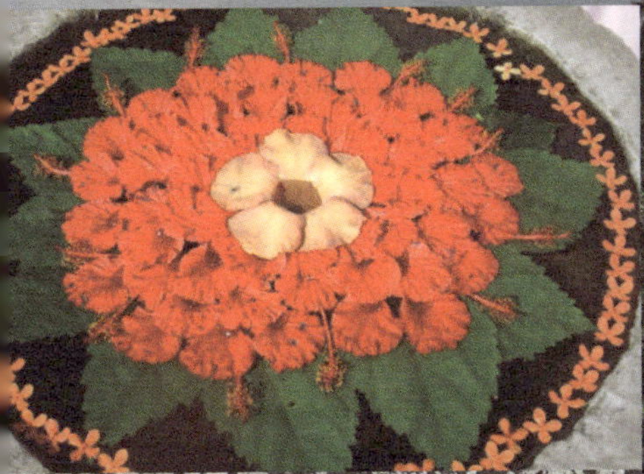
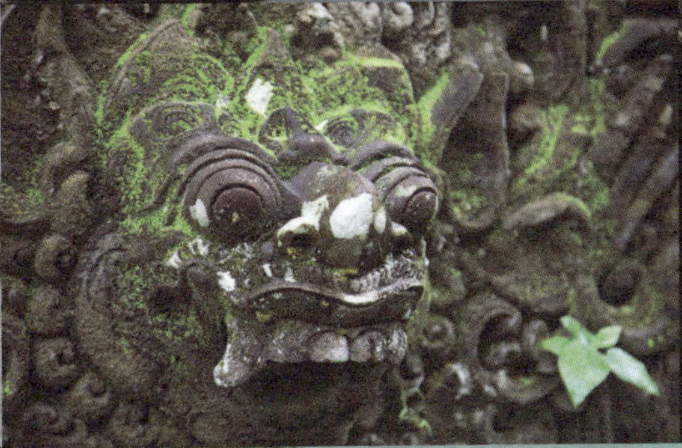
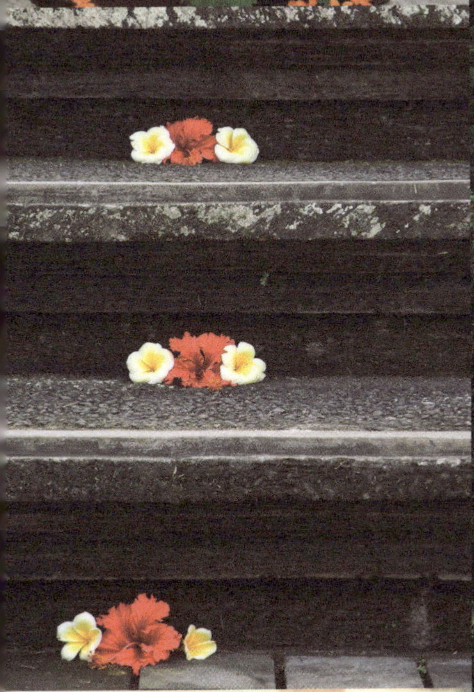
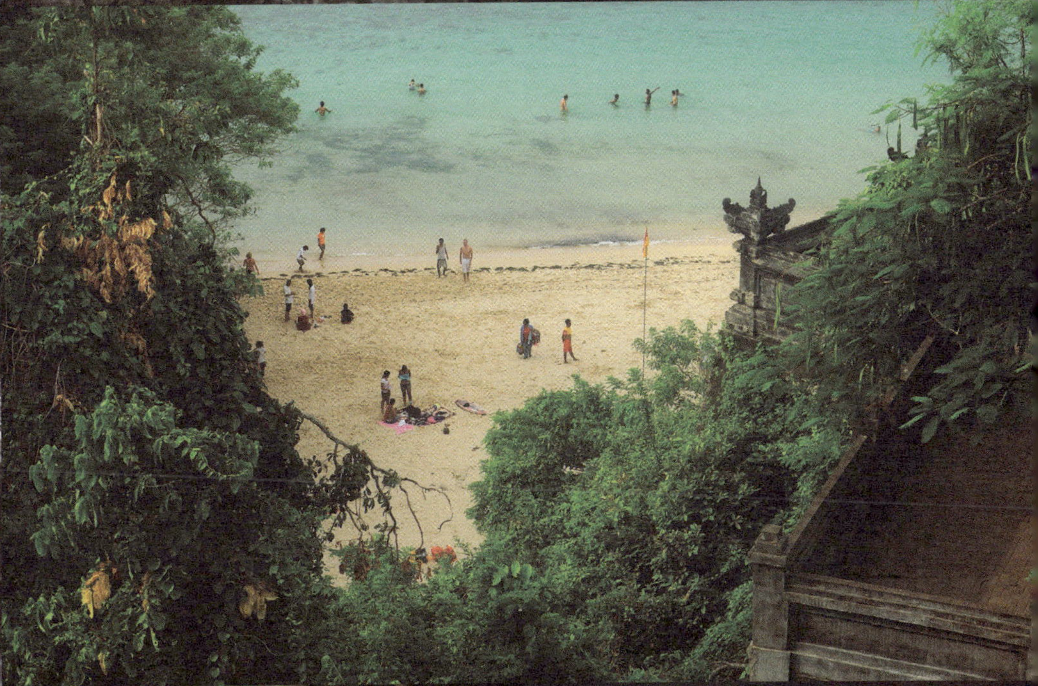
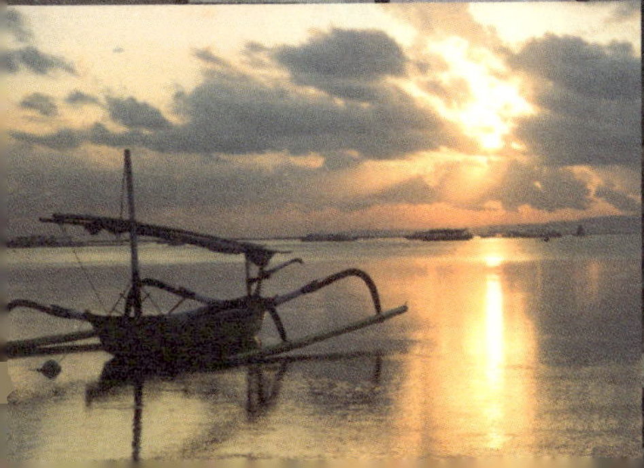
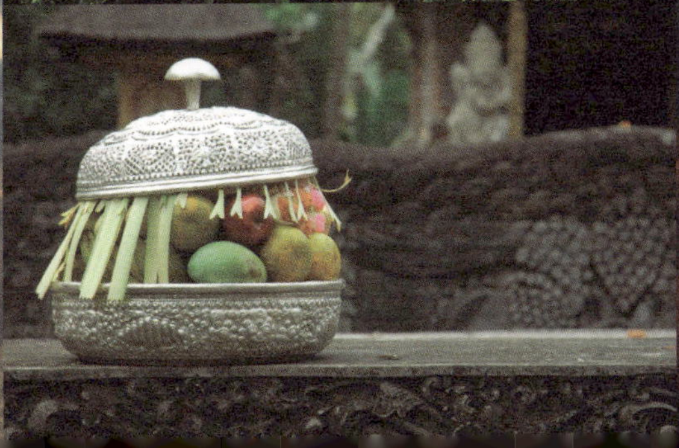
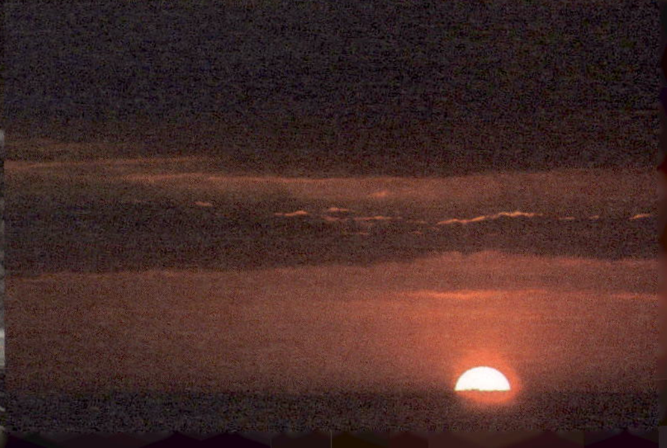

PEPES AYAM

There's something special about food that has been wrapped and cooked in little parcels – the aroma released when the parcels are opened gets me salivating every time. You can cut the wrappers from banana leaves, corn husks or baking paper and assemble the parcels up to 24 hours before required. Store in the fridge. Pepes ayam makes a great addition to a buffet.

400g chicken breasts or thighs, skinned, boned and diced
2 cloves garlic, crushed
1 onion, finely diced
1 tablespoon grated fresh ginger
½ teaspoon chilli powder
1 teaspoon salt
½ teaspoon white pepper
1 salam or bay leaf
2 tablespoons peanut oil
shrimp paste (optional, according to taste)

20 x 15cm square wrappers for cooking (see note above)
toothpicks

Mix all the ingredients together.

To make your parcels, spoon 1 heaped tablespoon of the chicken filling into the centre of each wrapper, fold in the sides and then the ends and secure with a toothpick to make a flat-bottomed parcel.

To steam the parcels, it's preferable to use a bamboo steamer, if you have one. Arrange the parcels in a single layer and steam for 15–20 minutes until the chicken is cooked through. You may have to do this in batches to prevent overcrowding, depending on the size of the steamer.

To serve, pile the cooked parcels onto a platter.

MAKES 16–20 TASTY MORSELS

DELICIOUS CHICKEN SATAY WITH PEANUT SAUCE

Traditionally, these are served with *Peanut Sauce* (see page 129) and rice.

MARINADE
¼ cup finely chopped lemongrass
1 small onion, finely chopped
2 cloves garlic
5cm piece fresh ginger, grated
½ teaspoon dried turmeric
3 tablespoons kecap manis
1 tablespoon fresh lime juice
1 teaspoon salt

8 chicken thighs, skinned, boned and cut into small pieces or thin strips
20 bamboo skewers, soaked in cold water for at least 1 hour

Put all the marinade ingredients in a bowl and stir to combine. Add the chicken and stir, making sure the chicken is well coated in the marinade. Set aside to marinate for up to 1 hour, covered, in the fridge.

When ready to cook, slide the pieces of meat onto the wooden skewers. Cook on a hot barbecue or under a hot grill for 10 minutes or until well browned on one side. Turn over and cook for 10 minutes or until browned and cooked through, but not dry.

Serve with steamed rice and peanut sauce.

SERVES 4–6

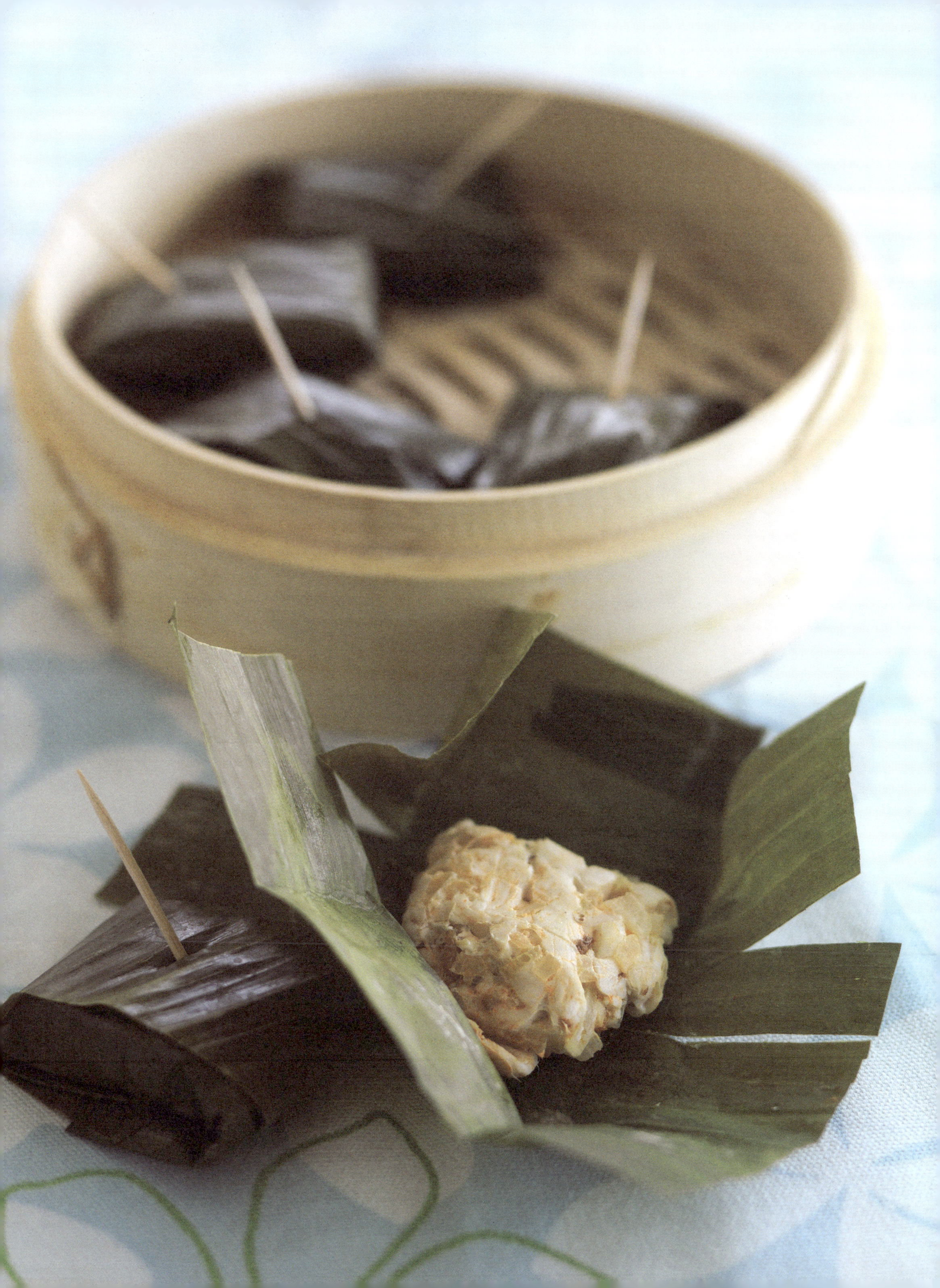

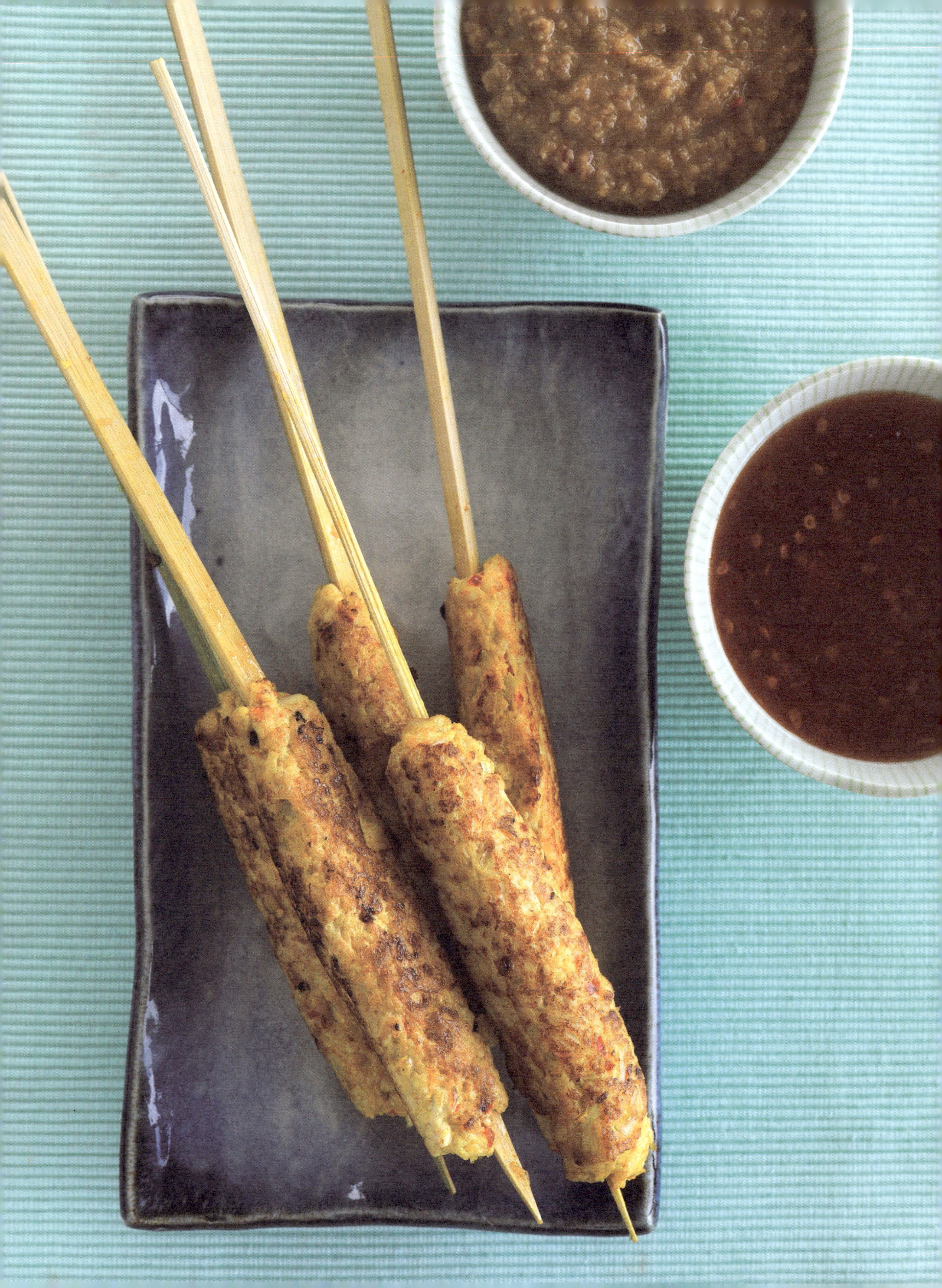

TRADITIONAL BALINESE SATAY

On Bali, traditional 'saté' is made with minced chicken and spices. The mixture is pressed around a wide stick and barbecued over hot embers – delicious!

2–3 chillies, deseeded
3 cloves garlic
2 teaspoons dried turmeric
1 onion, roughly chopped
5cm piece fresh ginger, chopped
1 teaspoon salt
1 teaspoon peanut or sesame oil
1 tablespoon palm sugar, grated
400g chicken mince

20–25 wide, flat bamboo skewers, soaked in cold water for at least 1 hour

Put all the ingredients, except the chicken mince, in a mortar and pestle or food processor and grind or process to form a thick paste. Put the paste in a bowl with the chicken mince and stir to combine.

Take 2 tablespoons of the mixture and wrap it around one-third of each skewer, pressing it on firmly. It can be tricky at first, but you'll get the knack with a bit of practice. Continue until all the mixture has been used.

Heat a barbecue or grill to hot and cook the skewers until cooked through, turning often.

Serve with a selection of dipping sauces, such as store-bought sweet chilli sauce and *Peanut Sauce* (see recipe below).

MAKES APPROXIMATELY 20

GORGEOUS GADO-GADO WITH PEANUT SAUCE

I discovered gado-gado on my first visit to Bali and was instantly hooked. This cooked vegetable salad served with spicy peanut sauce is ideal as a light meal or as a side dish served with simple barbecued meat.

Lots of versions of peanut sauce are made with peanut butter. Don't do it! It's far too sweet and has very little authenticity to it. The real deal, made with dry-roasted peanuts, is almost as quick to make and stores well in the fridge. I'm sure you'll agree that it's well worth the effort.

PEANUT SAUCE
1 cup dry-roasted peanuts
1/3 cup water
2 cloves garlic, crushed
1/2 teaspoon dark soy sauce
2 teaspoons sesame oil
2 tablespoons brown sugar
2 tablespoons fish sauce
1/2 teasoon tamarind purée
1–1½ teaspoons red chilli sauce
1 teaspoon fresh lime juice
2 tablespoons light cooking oil

SALAD
1/2 cup beans, cut into bite-sized pieces
1/2 cup small florets of cauliflower or broccoli
1/2 carrot, cut into matchsticks
1 cup finely shredded cabbage
1 cup bean sprouts
1/2 cup cucumber, sliced into half rounds
2 hard-boiled eggs, sliced
10 prawn crackers

To make the peanut sauce, put all the ingredients except the light cooking oil in a food processor and blend to make a smooth paste.

Heat the oil in a small heavy-based saucepan and add the paste. Stirring to avoid sticking, fry the paste on a medium heat and bring to the boil. Simmer for 5–10 minutes. Adjust the consistency by adding water, if required. Set aside to cool until required or store in the fridge, but serve at room temperature.

Bring a large pot of lightly salted water to the boil. Blanch the beans, cauliflower (or broccoli) and carrot for 2 minutes. They should be tender but still crisp – definitely not mushy. Drain and rinse in cold water.

Pile the cabbage, followed by the vegetables, in the middle of the serving dish with the bean sprouts on top and garnish with cucumber slices and boiled eggs and prawn crackers on the side.

Pour peanut sauce over the salad and serve.

SERVES 6

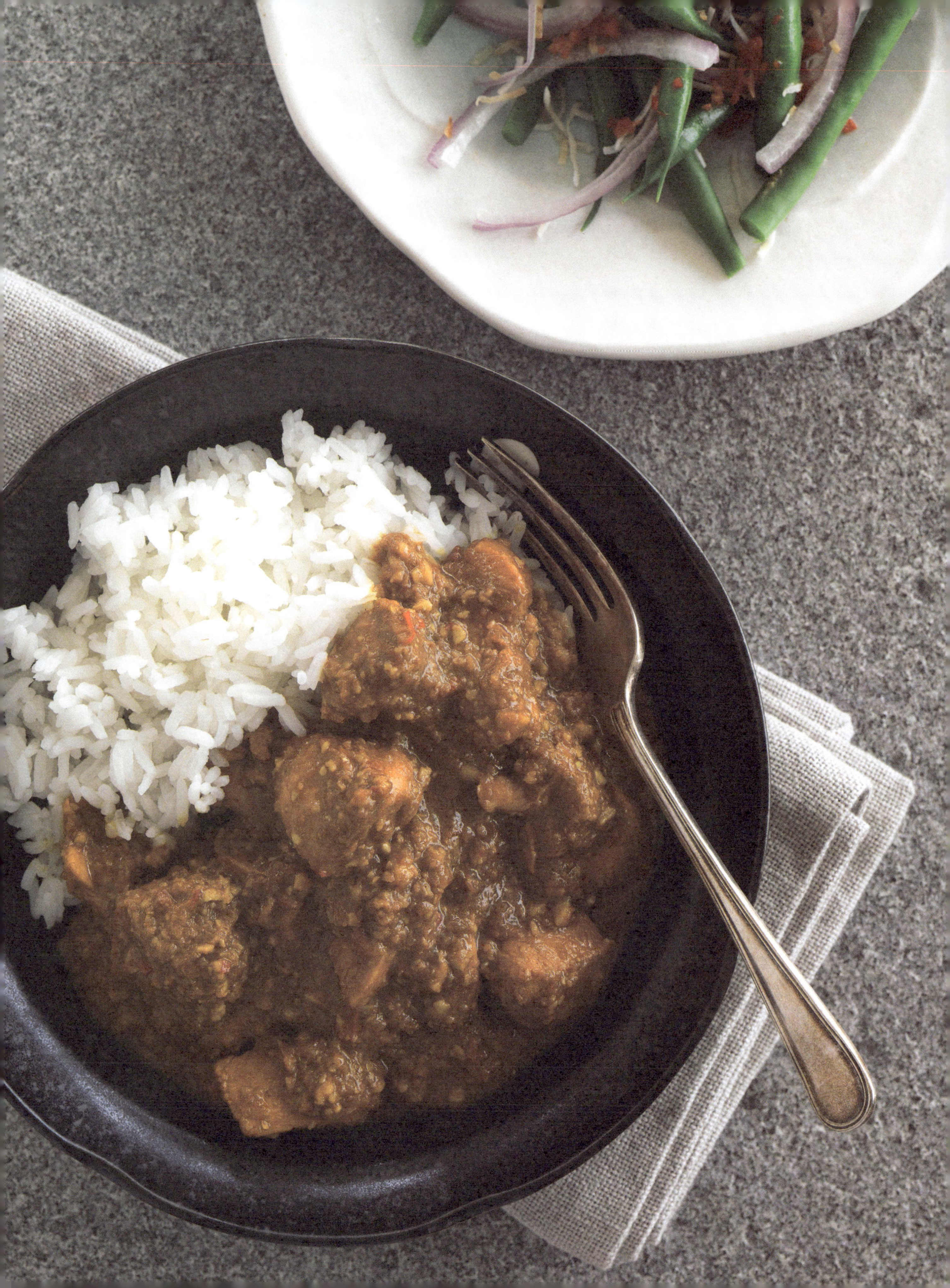

ZINGY BALINESE CHICKEN CURRY

This is a stand-out recipe and incredibly simple to make. It's not a hot curry but is extremely fragrant and tasty.

1 medium-sized onion, roughly chopped
3 cloves garlic, peeled
2 mild red chillies, deseeded
¼ cup cashew nuts
1 teaspoon dried turmeric
3 tablespoons lemon juice
1 tablespoon dark soy sauce
2 tablespoons grated palm sugar or 1 tablespoon brown sugar
1 tablespoon grated fresh ginger
1 tablespoon peanut oil
2 chicken breasts or 4 thighs, skinned, boned and cubed
½ cup coconut milk
½ cup water

Put the onion, garlic, chillies, cashew nuts, turmeric, lemon juice, soy sauce, sugar and ginger in a mortar and pestle or food processor and grind or blend to form a smooth paste.

Heat the oil in a heavy-based frying pan and add the curry paste. To allow the flavour to develop, and stirring to prevent sticking, cook for 4–5 minutes until the sugar caramelises. Add the chicken and cook for 15 minutes.

Add the coconut milk and water and turn the heat to low. Simmer uncovered for 10–15 minutes, stirring occasionally, until the chicken is tender and cooked through and the sauce has thickened.

Serve with rice or salad.

SERVES 2

GREEN BEAN AND ROASTED COCONUT SALAD WITH CHILLI LIME DRESSING

This is a delicious blend of crisp beans and coconut, charged with a tangy lime dressing that will make your taste buds tingle.

SALAD
200g green beans, blanched
½ red onion, thinly sliced
1 tablespoon long thread coconut (or desiccated coconut if long thread is unavailable), toasted

DRESSING
juice of 1 lime
½ teaspoon crushed red chilli
1 teaspoon sesame oil
1 teaspoon rice wine vinegar

To assemble the salad, put the beans, onion and coconut in a bowl.

To make the dressing, put all the ingredients in a bowl and stir to combine.

Pour the dressing over the salad and toss gently to combine. Serve immediately.

SERVES 2

Zingy Balinese Chicken Curry (front), Green Bean and Roasted Coconut Salad with Chilli Lime Dressing (rear)

AROMATIC CHICKEN CURRY WITH COCONUT CREAM

Don't be put off by the long list of ingredients – this curry is not that difficult to make and the aromatic combination of flavours showcases the very best of Indonesian cooking.

4 cloves garlic, roughly chopped
5cm piece fresh ginger, roughly chopped
3 shallots, roughly chopped
1–3 red chillies (according to taste), deseeded and chopped
2 teaspoons tamarind purée
1 tablespoon brown sugar
2 teaspoons soy sauce
3 tablespoons fish sauce
2 teaspoons ground coriander
2 teaspoons ground cumin
400ml can coconut milk
1 tablespoon light cooking oil
4 whole cloves
2 star anise
1 cinnamon stick
20 fresh curry leaves (optional)
750g chicken pieces, bone in
toasted shredded coconut to garnish
fresh coriander leaves to garnish

Place the garlic, ginger, shallots, chillies, tamarind purée, brown sugar, soy sauce, fish sauce, coriander, cumin and coconut milk into a food processor and process to form a purée.

Put the oil in a large heavy-based saucepan. Add the cloves, star anise, cinnamon stick and curry leaves, if using. Stir-fry for 1–2 minutes over medium heat.

Add one-third of the coconut milk mixture to the pan and bring to the boil. Add the chicken pieces and turn to coat them. Cook the chicken for 5 minutes then add the remaining coconut milk mixture. Bring to a simmer then lower the heat and continue to simmer uncovered for 50 minutes, stirring frequently to prevent it from sticking, until the chicken is cooked through. Continue to cook for a few more minutes, stirring every minute, until the sauce has reduced enough to form a thick coating on the chicken.

Garnish with toasted coconut and coriander leaves and serve with rice.

SERVES 4

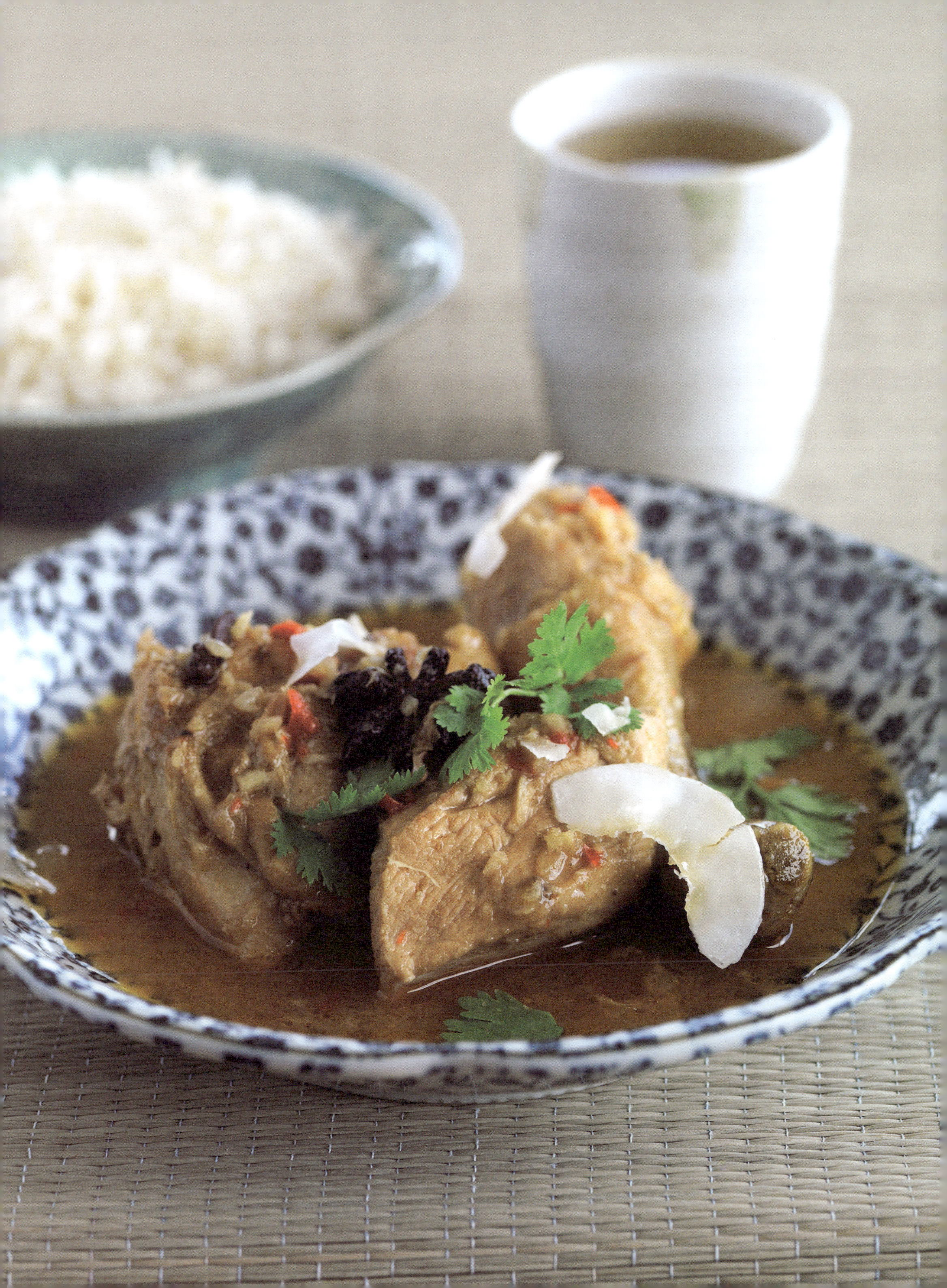

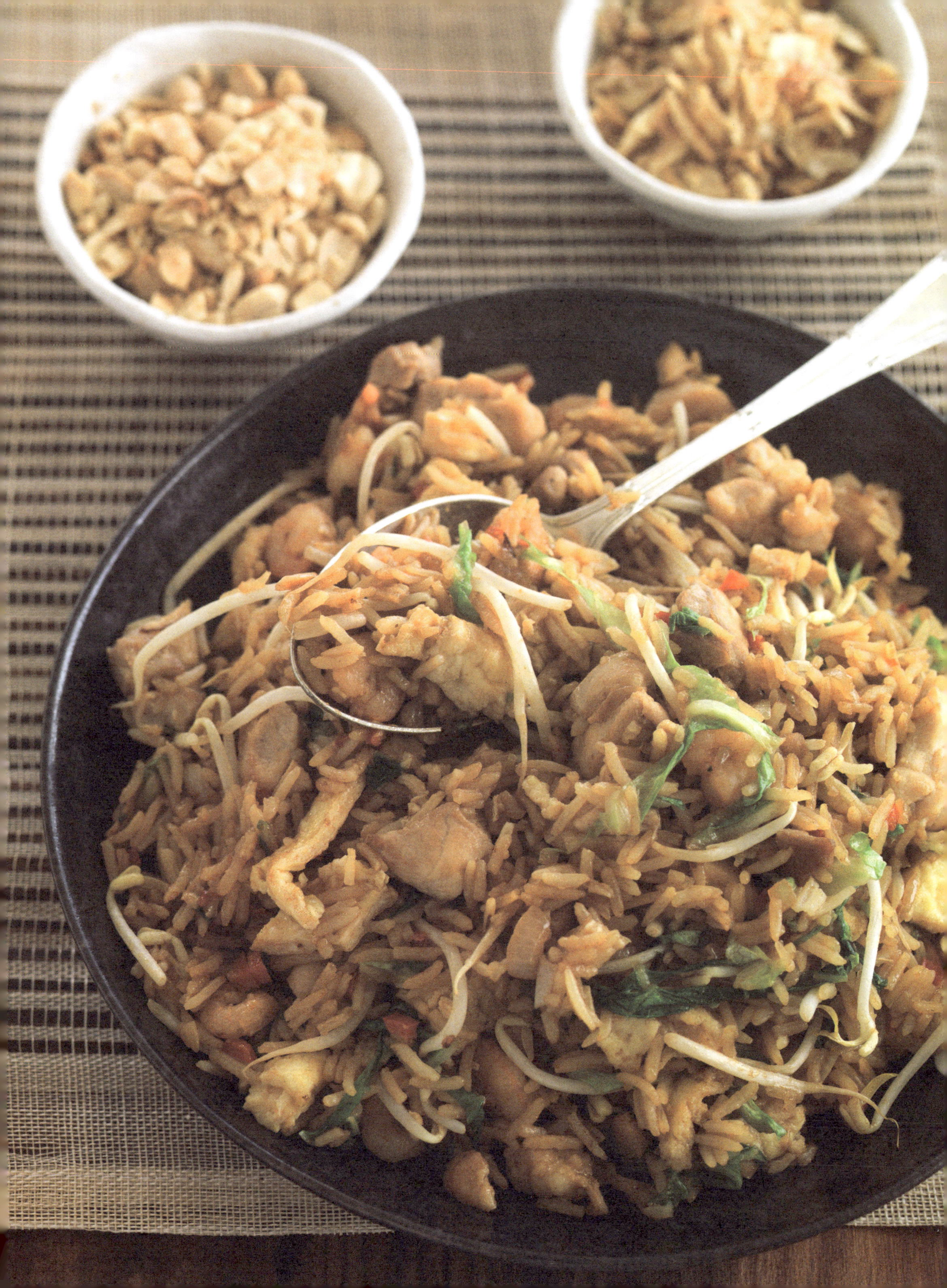

NASI GORENG

If I'm looking for a savoury start to my day in Indonesia, this traditional fried-rice dish is it.

1½ cups long-grain rice
2 tablespoons light cooking oil
2 eggs, lightly beaten
300g chicken thighs, skinned, boned and cut into small pieces
4 shallots, finely chopped
2 cloves garlic, thinly sliced
1 teaspoon shrimp paste
1–2 red chillies, deseeded and sliced
1 cup small cooked prawns
1 cup finely shredded Chinese cabbage
1 cup bean sprouts
2 tablespoons kecap manis
1 tablespoon soy sauce
fried shallots to garnish
chopped peanuts to garnish

Cook the rice according to directions on the packet until only just cooked – it will cook a bit more when added to the pan later. Spread the cooked rice in a thin layer on an oven tray to cool quickly.

Heat a frying pan over high heat. Add 1 tablespoon of the oil and quickly add the eggs, swirling them around the pan to make a thin layer. Once golden, flip the omelette. Cook for a few more seconds on the other side and remove it from the pan. Slice the omelette into small strips, ready to add to the rice when required.

Add the remaining oil and the chicken. Cook for 3–4 minutes or until the chicken is browned.

Push the chicken to one side of the pan. Add the shallots, garlic, shrimp paste and chillies to the pan and cook for 2–3 minutes until the mixture is fragrant. Add the rice, prawns and cabbage and mix all ingredients gently together. Cook until it has heated through and the cabbage has softened.

Add the strips of omelette, bean sprouts, kecap manis and soy sauce.

To serve, garnish with fried shallots and chopped peanuts.

SERVES 6

TOFU FRITTERS

This recipe has been adapted from one used at the Casa Luna Cooking School in Ubud and even if you're not a big fan of tofu you'll love these tasty treats.

2 cloves garlic
3 teaspoons grated fresh galangal
2 teaspoons dried turmeric
¼ teaspoon shrimp paste
1 large red chilli, deseeded
250g firm tofu, cubed
1 egg, lightly beaten
2 kaffir lime leaves, shredded
3 teaspoons grated palm sugar
1 tablespoon fried shallots
½ teaspoon sea salt
½ cup light cooking oil

DIPPING SAUCE
1 red chilli, deseeded and chopped
juice of 1 lime
¼ teaspoon salt
1 tablespoon grated palm sugar

Place the garlic, galangal, turmeric, shrimp paste and chilli in a food processor and process to form a smooth paste. Add the tofu and process to form a chunky paste. Stir in the egg, lime leaves, palm sugar, fried shallots and sea salt.

Heat the oil in a heavy-based frying pan over medium heat. Fry the fritters, a tablespoon at a time, until golden brown on both sides – you may need to do this in batches to prevent overcrowding and cooling of the oil.

Remove fritters from the pan and drain on paper towels.

To make dipping sauce, combine all ingredients in a small bowl and mix well.

Serve fritters immediately with dipping sauce on the side.

MAKES 15 FRITTERS

Nasi Goreng

BAMI GORENG

Wok-fried noodles is common street food in Indonesia. Sold from carts that do the rounds at lunchtime and into the afternoon, bami goreng is very popular with the locals and I'm a huge fan!

2 eggs, lightly beaten
3 tablespoons light cooking oil
2 cloves garlic, thinly sliced
3cm piece fresh ginger, grated
2 spring onions, chopped
1 chilli, deseeded and finely chopped
1 tablespoon coriander seeds, crushed
1 small red capsicum, deseeded and thinly sliced
8 peeled prawns
200g chicken breasts, skinned, boned and thinly sliced
300g dried egg noodles (instant noodles will do)
2 cups boiling vegetable stock or water
2 tablespoons soy sauce

Place a frying pan over high heat. Add 1 tablespoon of the oil and quickly add the eggs, swirling them around the pan to make a thin layer. Once golden, flip the omelette. Cook for few more seconds on the other side and remove it from the pan. Slice the omelette into small strips, ready to add to the noodles when required.

Heat 1 tablespoon of oil in a wok or thin-based frying pan and fry the garlic until it begins to colour. Add the ginger, spring onions, chilli and coriander seeds and fry for 2–3 minutes. Add the capsicum, prawns and chicken, and cook for 4–6 minutes until chicken is cooked through.

Break the noodles up and add to the wok or pan with 1 cup of hot stock or water. Turn the heat up, cover and allow to simmer, adding more stock or water if you need to, until the noodles are almost cooked – don't allow them to become soggy. Once the liquid is absorbed and the noodles are almost cooked, finish by adding the soy sauce, remaining oil and the strips of omelette. Stir through until all the flavours blend and cook for 1 minute more or until piping hot.

Serve immediately.

SERVES 4

LEMONGRASS SLUSHY

If you need a refreshing drink on a hot day it's hard to go past a lemongrass slushy.

2 discs palm sugar (or 4 tablespoons caster sugar)
¼ cup water
2 stems lemongrass, smashed with a rolling pin
crushed ice
1 litre soda water
lime wedges to serve

Put the sugar and water in a small saucepan and simmer until the water has reduced a little and the mixture has thickened slightly. Add the lemongrass and continue to simmer for 5 minutes. Set aside to cool.

Fill glasses with crushed ice and pour over soda water, add 1 tablespoon (or to taste) of syrup and stir. Top with lime wedges.

MAKES APPROXIMATELY 1 LITRE

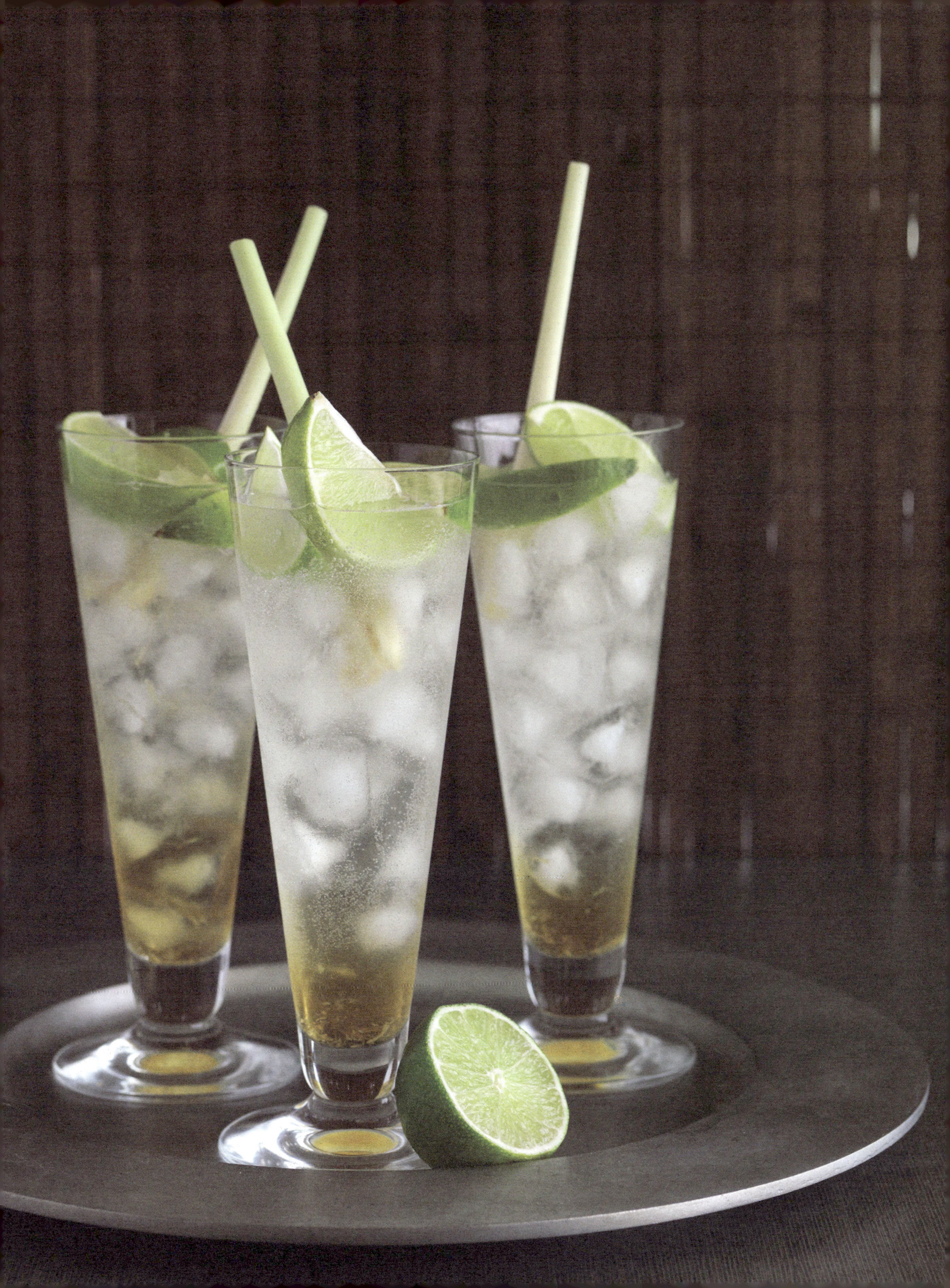

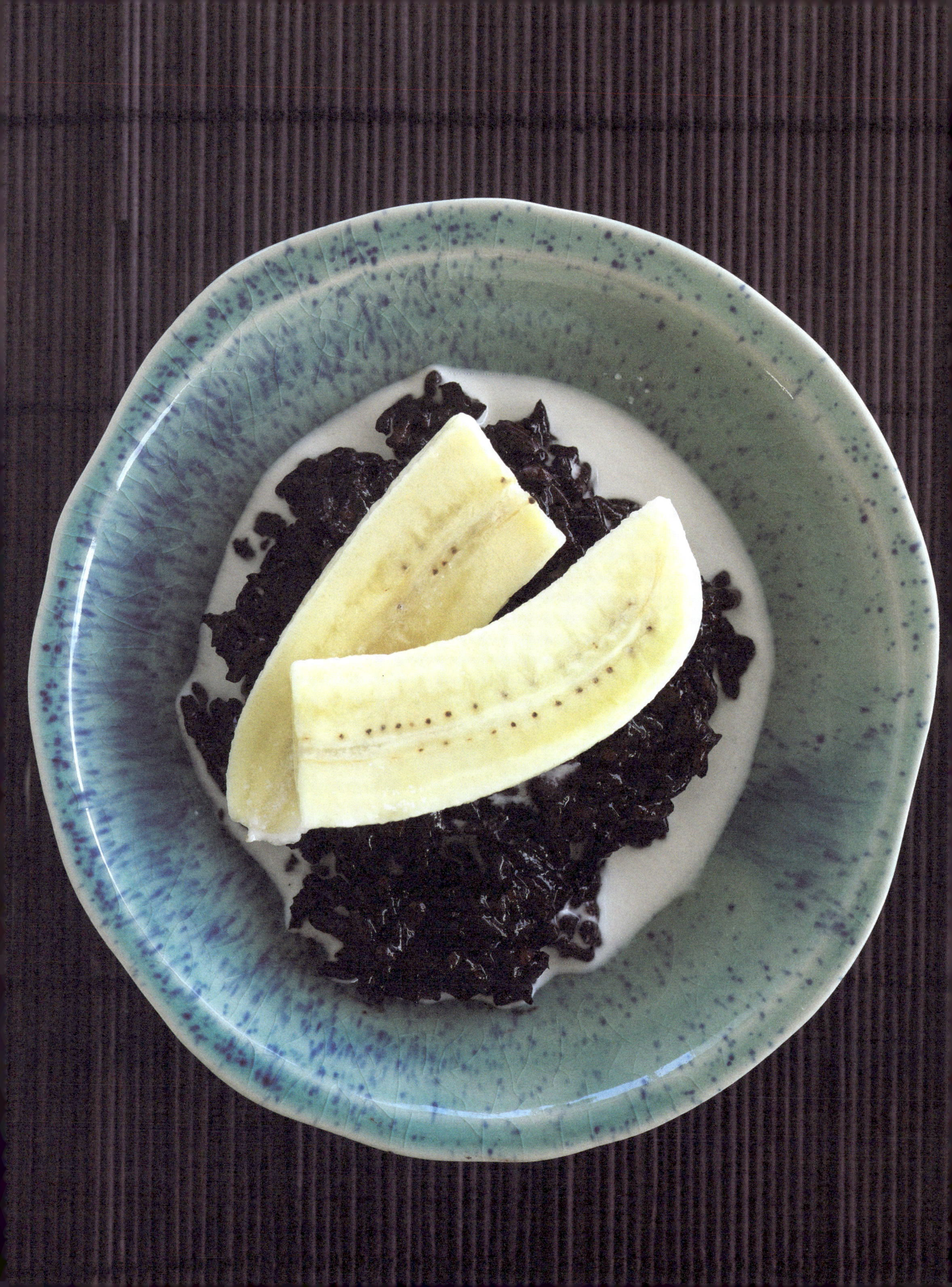

STICKY BLACK-RICE PUDDING

This sweet black-rice pudding with its nutty flavour and cooling coconut milk is an ideal way to kick-start your day.

½ cup glutinous black rice (must be glutinous not just wild rice)
⅓ cup glutinous white rice
1 vanilla pod
3¼ cups water
¼ cup grated palm sugar
1 cup thick coconut cream or coconut milk
chilled coconut cream or coconut milk to serve
fresh bananas to serve

Rinse the rice well under cold running water to remove starch. Place the rice, vanilla pod and 3 cups of water into a heavy-based saucepan and simmer, stirring occasionally.

Place the palm sugar and remaining water into a small saucepan and bring to a simmer. Continue simmering until the water has reduced by half.

When the rice has simmered for about 20 minutes, add the palm sugar syrup and thick coconut cream or milk to the cooked rice, and continue to simmer gently, stirring occasionally to prevent sticking, until most of the liquid has evaporated. Make sure the mixture does not boil dry and add more water, if required. The rice and syrup will now be a dark purple colour.

Serve cooled with fresh bananas and drizzled with chilled coconut cream or milk.

SERVES 4

LIME AND COCONUT ICE-CREAM WITH SESAME BRITTLE

Plain ice-cream gets an exotic make-over to become a gourmet treat! You can make the sesame brittle in advance, as it will keep for up to 2 weeks in an airtight container.

ICE-CREAM
4 scoops vanilla ice-cream (no need to go gourmet)
zest of 1 lime
2 tablespoons toasted coconut

SESAME BRITTLE
1 cup sesame seeds
½ cup brown sugar
water

To prepare the ice-cream, remove it from the freezer to soften. After 10 minutes, add the lime zest and toasted coconut. Stir through. Return the ice-cream to the freezer until required.

Preheat oven to 170°C. Line an oven tray with baking paper.

To make the brittle, mix the sesame seeds and sugar together with just enough water – start with 1 tablespoon – to moisten the mixture so that it forms a thick paste. Spread paste onto prepared oven tray and bake for 20 minutes or until it is bubbling and crackling. Check it frequently to make sure it does not burn.

Remove from the oven and, when it has cooled, break into pieces. Store in an airtight container until required.

Serve ice-cream and sesame brittle with grilled mango pieces if desired.

SERVES 2

Sticky Black-rice Pudding

GLOSSARY

ARBORIO RICE
A variety of short-grain rice commonly used in New Zealand to make risotto due to its ability to absorb liquid well yet still retain a creamy texture.

ASIAN GREENS
There are now many varieties of Asian greens widely available in New Zealand, including gai larn, bok choy (or pak choy) and Chinese cabbage. All are commonly used in stir-fries, soups and noodle dishes.

BANANA LEAVES
These are used instead of foil in Asian cooking. Use fresh leaves or purchase frozen leaves from Asian supermarkets.

BLACK SESAME SEEDS
Often used as a garnish, they have a slightly bitter flavour.

BLACK STICKY RICE
Dark brown, long-grain rice that has a sticky texture and nutty flavour when cooked. It is used throughout Asia for sweet snacks and desserts. Available from Asian supermarkets.

BUFFALO MOZZARELLA
Large balls of white mozzarella cheese produced from the milk of water buffalo. It is sold submerged in brine to keep it fresh.

CARNAROLI RISO SUPERFINO
Firm-textured medium-grain rice with a high starch content considered by the Italians to be the finest for making risotto.

CALASPARRA
Short-grain rice grown in the mountains of Murcia in Spain. It is used to make traditional paella. Available from specialist food stores.

CHINESE COOKING WINE
Wine brewed from grains, such as rice and wheat, with an intense flavour. Also known as shao hsing wine. Available from most Asian supermarkets. Substitute dry sherry.

CHORIZO
A coarse-textured, cured Spanish sausage made from pork and highly seasoned with garlic, chilli, herbs and spices. It is Spanish paprika that gives chorizo its distinctive flavour. Both Spanish and locally made chorizo are available in supermarkets.

COOKING OILS
There are many different cooking oils available. Refined oils are more commonly used in cooking as they have a high smoke point and longer shelf-life. Light cooking oils that are suitable for most sautéing, frying, deep-frying and stir-frying include rice bran oil, sunflower oil, canola oil, peanut oil, and soya bean oil. Unrefined oils, such as extra virgin olive oil and any cold-pressed oils, are fragrant, potently flavoured and ideal for salad dressings.

CRÈME FRAICHE
A naturally matured sour cream with a distinctive tangy flavour. It is slightly soured with bacterial culture, but is less sour, and thicker, than sour cream. Available from supermarkets.

CURRY LEAVES
Fresh leaves of the curry plant add a specific tangy flavour to curries. Available from Asian supermarkets and Indian food suppliers.

DIJON MUSTARD
A smooth, mild mustard made from black and brown mustard seeds. Available from supermarkets.

FINGER BANANAS
Also known as Lady Fingers, they are much smaller and sweeter than regular bananas.

FISH SAUCE
Also known as nuoc nam. Made from fermented small fish, it is used throughout South-east Asia. It is an essential ingredient in many curries and sauces. Available from supermarkets.

FRIED SHALLOTS
Crispy fried shallots are used as a garnish for rice dishes, salads and soups. They are available ready-to-use from Asian supermarkets.

GALANGAL
A rhizome similar in appearance to ginger, but with a milder flavour. It is used extensively in Thai cuisine. It is available frozen from Asian supermarkets.

GLUTINOUS RICE
A high-starch variety of short-grain rice – also known as sticky rice – that is used extensively in Thai cooking. When steamed, the grains stick together.

KAFFIR LIME LEAVES
The aromatic, double leaves of *Citrus hystrix* are used throughout Asia. Finely shredded or whole leaves are used to flavour soups, fish dishes and curries. Available from Asian supermarkets, but can also be grown in the garden.

KECAP MANIS
A sweet, thick, less-salty-than-usual, Indonesian soy sauce sweetened with palm sugar. Available from supermarkets.

LEMONGRASS
A grassy plant used extensively throughout South-east Asia to provide a tangy lemon flavour and aroma to many dishes. The white part at the base of the plant is finely sliced or pounded to break up the coarse fibres. It is sold fresh in long stalks or preserved in brine in jars. Available from supermarkets.

LONG-THREAD COCONUT
Coconut that has been shredded into long threads, as opposed to the shorter desiccated coconut that is often used in baking. Can use desiccated as a substitute.

MANCHEGO CHEESE
Aged, pressed sheep's milk cheese with a pale yellow colour. From the La Mancha region of Spain, it is name-controlled. Available from specialist food stores.

MASCARPONE
A smooth, high-fat Italian-style soft cream cheese. It has a velvety texture and a rich, creamy, slightly acidic flavour that is best used fresh. Locally made mascarpone is available from supermarkets.

ORZO
Also known as risoni. Rice-shaped silken-textured pasta that is perfect for salads.

PALM SUGAR
Small, solid discs of hard sugar made from the sap of the palmyra and sugar palm trees. They range from dark brown to creamy white in colour and are usually grated or dissolved in water before use. Used throughout South-east Asia to sweeten desserts and in sweet-and-sour dishes. Available from most supermarkets. Substitute with brown sugar.

PAPPARDELLE
Wide, flat ribbons of pasta. Great with meaty sauces.

PARMESAN
A hard, granular cheese with a rich flavour made from partially skimmed cow's milk. Both Italian Parmigiano-Reggiano and locally produced Parmesan are available in New Zealand.

PECORINO
A hard Italian sheep's milk cheese with a sharp, salty flavour. It is used in pasta and risotto dishes, soups and gratins. Available from specialist food stores.

POLENTA
Ground yellow cornmeal. It is a staple food in northern Italy. Available from supermarkets.

POTATOES
There are many different varieties widely available in New Zealand and all have slightly different uses. Floury potatoes, such as Agria, Red Rascal and Ilam Hardy, are ideal for mashing, frying and roasting. Waxy potatoes, such as Draga Nadine and Frisia, are best suited to boiling, casseroles and soups.

PROSCIUTTO
Salted and air-cured Italian ham. It is sliced paper thin and is typically served uncooked. Italian and locally produced prosciutto is available from supermarkets.

RICE BRAN OIL
Extracted from the inner husk of rice, rice bran oil has a mild flavour and very high smoke point, making it suitable for high-temperature cooking methods such as stir-frying and deep-frying.

RICE FLOUR
Raw white or brown rice is ground to a powder to make rice flour. It is most commonly used in rice noodles and as a thickening agent in Asian desserts.

RICE NOODLES
Made from rice flour and water, fresh noodles are available in white sheets that can be cut into ribbons of various widths. Dried rice 'stick' noodles are made from a paste of rice flour and water. They have a translucent appearance and need to be soaked in hot water until tender before use.

RICE-PAPER WRAPPERS
Wrappers made from dried, paper-thin sheets of dough made with rice flour. They need to be soaked in water before use. Available from most supermarkets.

RICE WINE VINEGAR
A mild, slightly sweet vinegar made from rice wine.

RISOTTO
A creamy rice dish made with special rice. Arborio, the main variety used to make risotto in New Zealand, is available from supermarkets. Carnaroli Riso Superfino is also available from specialist food stores and some supermarkets.

SAFFRON
The world's most expensive spice, made from the dried stigmas of *Crocus sativus*. Just a few strands infused in hot water will flavour and colour a dish. Available from supermarkets.

SALAM LEAVES
Similar to curry leaves, also known as Indonesian bay leaves, these may be difficult to find in New Zealand. Substitute with bay leaves.

SHRIMP PASTE
Ground from fermented and dried shrimps. Its pungent odour can be very strong but small amounts enhance the flavour of many Asian dishes. Also known as blachau and trasi, it should be fried before use.

SPANISH SHERRY VINEGAR
Vinegar made from grapes grown in the Jerez sherry region of Spain. Substitute with red wine vinegar.

SPANISH SWEET SMOKED PAPRIKA
A bright red spice made from sweet capsicums that are slowly smoked and dried then ground.

SPONGE FINGERS
Finger-shaped sponge biscuits – also known as ladyfingers – that are coated in sugar. Available from supermarkets.

SUNFLOWER OIL
Extracted from sunflower seeds and commonly used in stir-frying due to its high smoke point.

TAMARIND PURÉE
The tamarind is a large tropical tree that produces an acid-tasting fruit. The long pods contain small seeds and a sweet-and-sour pulp that is compressed into blocks. Before use, the blocks are soaked and strained to remove the seeds and stringy parts leaving a tamarind purée that is used to add a distinctive sour flavour to food.

TAPIOCA FLOUR
Tapioca is a starch extracted from the roots of the cassava plant. It is then cooked and finely ground into flour – also known as cassava flour. It is usually mixed with rice flour in order to give a silky, elastic texture to baked products.

THAI BASIL
An aromatic variety of basil used in Thai and Vietnamese cooking. Substitute with regular sweet basil.

VIETNAMESE MINT
A pungent-tasting herb that is used raw in salads. Substitute with mint.

WHITE RICE VINEGAR
Sweet, mild-tasting vinegar made from fermented white rice and used commonly in Asian cooking.

INDEX

(Numbers in bold indicate recipe photographs)

Almond Crust, Red Capsicum Chicken with an 18, **19**

Apple Tarts, Caramelised 76, **77**

Aromatic Chicken Curry with Coconut Cream 132, **133**

Artichokes and Cherry Tomatoes, Linguine with Chicken, 42, **43**

Asian Greens, Zesty Citrus Chicken Stir-fry with **97**, 99

Baked Chicken Pieces, Spicy 85

Baked Chicken with Eggplant, Tomato and Mozzarella 50

Baked Chicken with Garlic and Lemon, Spanish 29

Bami Goreng 136

Bananas, Fried Sesame 100, **101**

Bangkok Chinatown Noodles with Chicken and Pickled Squid 92, **93**

Barbecued Tuscan Chicken with Caramelised Lemons 40, **41**

Basil, Chicken Lasagne with Fresh 46, **47**

Bean and Roasted Coconut Salad with Chilli Lime Dressing, Green 131

Bean Sprouts and Bamboo shoots with Fragrant Noodles, Chicken, 111

Bikini, Chicken and Prosciutto 26

Black-rice Pudding, Sticky **138**, 139

Bruschetta, Garlic 36

Butterflied Citrus and Rosemary Roasted Chicken 70, **72**

Camembert, Galettes with Chicken, Mushroom and 66, **67**

Capsicum and Basil Stuffing, Chicken Schnitzel with Mozzarella, Red 50, **51**

Capsicum Chicken with an Almond Crust, Red 18, **19**

Capsicum Salad, Chicken, Orzo and Roasted Red 52, **53**

Capsicum Stuffing, Chicken Thighs with Green 40

Capsicum, Orange and Olive Salad, Red **21**, 22

Caramel Chicken 112

Caramelised Apple Tarts 76, **77**

Chargrilled Chicken with Green Olive and Orange Salsa 26, **27**

Chargrilled Chilli Chicken 84, **85**

Chicken and Mushroom Rice Balls 16, **17**

Chicken and Pistachio Terrine 70, **71**

Chicken and Prosciutto Bikini 26

Chicken, Bean Sprouts and Bamboo shoots with Fragrant Noodles 111

Chicken Curry with Tamarind and Kaffir Lime 92

Chicken Lasagne with Fresh Basil 46, **47**

Chicken, Lemon, Parmesan and Parsley Spaghetti 36, **37**

Chicken Liver Parfait with Onion Marmalade 65

Chicken, Orzo and Roasted Red Capsicum Salad 52, **53**

Chicken, Pawpaw and Mint Salad with Sweet Chilli Dressing 115

Chicken Salad with Nuoc Cham 116, **117**

Chicken Schnitzel with Mozzarella, Red Capsicum and Basil Stuffing 50, **51**

Chicken Soup with Coconut Cream and Lemongrass **82**, 83

Chicken Thighs with Green Capsicum Stuffing 40

Chicken Thighs with Oregano and Prosciutto 44, **45**

Chicken with Creamy Mushroom Sauce **68**, 69

Chicken with Lemon and Olives 45

Chicken with Tarragon Cream Sauce **62**, 63

Chicken with Tomatoes, Garlic and Olive Oil 69

Chilli Chicken, Chargrilled 84, **85**

Chocolate, Spanish Churros with Cinnamon-scented Liquid 30, **31**

Chorizo and Herb Stuffing, Whole Roasted Chicken with 28, **29**

Churros with Cinnamon-scented Liquid Chocolate, Spanish 30, **31**

Citrus and Rosemary Roasted Chicken, Butterflied 70, **72**

Citrus Chicken Stir-fry with Asian Greens, Zesty **97**, 99

Classic Sangria **12**, 13

Clay-pot Chicken, Heroic Hanoi **112**, 113

Coconut Cream and Lemongrass, Chicken Soup with **82**, 83

Coconut Cream, Aromatic Chicken Curry with 132, **133**

Coconut Cream, Sticky Rice with Mango and 100

Coconut Ice-cream with Sesame Brittle, Lime and 139

Coconut Salad with Chilli Lime Dressing, Green Bean and Roasted **130**, 131

Coffee, Vietnamese-style Iced 121

Coq au Vin **60**, 61

Coriander, Steamed Chicken with Tomatoes and **110**, 111

Creamy Mushroom Sauce, Chicken with **68**, 69

Creamy Pesto Chicken with Pappardelle 43

Creamy Polenta **48**, 49

Crème Brûlée 76

Crisp Chicken and Herb Rice Paper Parcels **106**, 107

Cucumber, Pineapple and Bean Sprout Salad 108

Curry Paste, Mild 95

Curry Paste, Red 95

Curry with Basil, Red Chicken **94**, 95

Curry with Coconut Cream, Aromatic Chicken 132, **133**

Curry with Tamarind and Kaffir Lime, Chicken 92

Curry, Zingy Balinese Chicken **130**, 131

Delicious Chicken Satay with Peanut Sauce 126

Easy Paella **24**, 25

Eggplant, Tomato and Mozzarella, Baked Chicken with 50

Eggplants Stuffed with Pumpkin, Pine Nuts and Spinach 19, **20**

Fragrant Lemongrass Chicken with Chilli and Pineapple Salsa 86, **87**

Fresh as Fresh Spring Rolls 108, **109**

Fried Sesame Bananas 100, **101**

Fritters, Tofu 135

Fruit Cups, Iced **120**, 121

Gado-gado with Peanut Sauce, Gorgeous 129

Galettes with Chicken, Mushroom and Camembert 66, **67**

Garlic Bruschetta 36

Ginger Sorbet, Lychee and 121

Ginger Chicken with Sugar Snaps, Stir-fried 86

Gorgeous Gado-gado with Peanut Sauce 129

Grapefruit Salad 89

Gratin, Potato **64**, 65

Green Bean and Roasted Coconut Salad with Chilli Lime Dressing **130**, 131

Grilled Nectarines with Vanilla Ricotta 55

Heroic Hanoi Clay-pot Chicken **112**, 113

Ice-cream with Sesame Brittle, Lime and Coconut 139

Iced Coffee, Vietnamese-style 121

Iced Fruit Cups **120**, 121

Kaffir Chicken on Spinach Leaves **98**, 99

Lasagne with Fresh Basil, Chicken 46, **47**

Lazy Tiramisu **54**, 55

Lemon and Olives, Chicken with 45

Lemongrass Chicken with Chilli and Pineapple Salsa, Fragrant 86, **87**

Lemongrass Slushy 136, **137**

Lemongrass, Chicken Soup with Coconut Cream and **82**, 83

Lemons, Barbecued Tuscan Chicken with Caramelised 40, **41**

Lettuce Cups, Vietnamese-style 107

Lime and Coconut Ice-cream with Sesame Brittle 139

Linguine with Chicken, Artichokes and Cherry Tomatoes 42, **43**

Liver Parfait with Onion Marmalade, Chicken 65

Lychee and Ginger Sorbet 121

Mango and Coconut Cream, Sticky Rice with 100

Meatballs, Skewered Smoky Chicken, with Roasted Tomatoes 12, **13**

Mild Curry Paste 95

Mozzarella, Baked Chicken with Eggplant, Tomato and 50

Mozzarella, Red Capsicum and Basil Stuffing, Chicken Schnitzel with 50, **51**

Mushroom and Camembert, Galettes with Chicken, 66, **67**

142 WORLD KITCHEN

Mushroom Rice Balls, Chicken and 16, **17**

Mushroom Sauce, Chicken with Creamy **68**, 69

Mustard Tart, Tomato and **73**, 75

Nasi Goreng **134**, 135

Nectarines with Vanilla Ricotta, Grilled 55

Nibbles, Parsley and Green Olive Chicken **14**, 15

Noodles with Chicken and Pickled Squid, Bangkok Chinatown 92, **93**

Noodles, Chicken, Bean Sprouts and Bamboo Shoots with Fragrant 111

Olive Chicken Nibbles, Parsley and Green **14**, 15

Olives, Chicken with Lemon and 45

Onion Marmalade, Chicken Liver Parfait with 65

Orange and Olive Salad, Red Capsicum, **21**, 22

Orange and Rosemary Chicken 22, **23**

Orange Salsa, Chargrilled Chicken with Green Olive and 26, **27**

Oregano and Prosciutto, Chicken Thighs with **44**, 45

Orzo and Roasted Red Capsicum Salad, Chicken, 52, **53**

Pad Thai, Perfect 90, **91**

Paella, Easy **24**, 25

Pappardelle, Creamy Pesto Chicken with 43

Parsley and Green Olive Chicken Nibbles **14**, 15

Pawpaw and Mint Salad with Sweet Chilli Dressing, Chicken, 115

Peanut Sauce, Delicious Chicken Satay with 126

Peanut Sauce, Gorgeous Gado-gado with 129

Pepes Ayam 126, **127**

Perfect Pad Thai 90, **91**

Pesto Chicken with Pappardelle, Creamy 43

Pesto Stuffing, Roast Chicken Breast with Sun-dried Tomato and 52

Pho Ga **114**, 115

Pineapple and Bean Sprout Salad, Cucumber, 108

Pistachio Terrine, Chicken and 70, **71**

Polenta, Creamy **48**, 49

Pot au Feu **74**, 75

Potato and Rosemary Tortilla, Sensational **14**, 15

Potato Gratin **64**, 65

Prosciutto Bikini, Chicken and 26

Prosciutto, Chicken Thighs with Oregano and **44**, 45

Pudding, Sticky Black-rice **138**, 139

Pumpkin and Pecorino Risotto **38**, 39

Pumpkin, Pine Nuts and Spinach, Eggplants Stuffed with 19, **20**

Ratatouille 61

Red Capsicum Chicken with an Almond Crust **18**, 19

Red Capsicum, Orange and Olive Salad **21**, 22

Red Chicken Curry with Basil **94**, 95

Red Curry Paste 95

Rice Balls, Chicken and Mushroom 16, **17**

Rice Noodle Salad with Tamarind Dressing, Tangy Chicken and 83

Rice Paper Parcels, Crisp Chicken and Herb **106**, 107

Rice with Mango and Coconut Cream, Sticky 100

Risotto, Pumpkin and Pecorino **38**, 39

Roast Chicken Breast with Sun-dried Tomato and Pesto Stuffing 52

Roasted Chicken, Butterflied Citrus and Rosemary 70, **72**

Roasted Chicken with Chorizo and Herb Stuffing, Whole 28, **29**

Roasted Chicken with Wine and Garlic, Tuscan-style, **48**, 49

Rosemary Chicken, Orange and 22, **23**

Salad, Chicken, Orzo and Roasted Red Capsicum 52, **53**

Salad, Cucumber, Pineapple and Bean Sprout 108

Salad, Grapefruit 89

Salad, Red Capsicum, Orange and Olive **21**, 22

Salad, Spicy Thai Chicken **88**, 89

Salad, Watercress 62, **63**

Salad with Chilli Lime Dressing, Green Bean and Roasted Coconut 131

Salad with Nuoc Cham, Chicken 116, **117**

Salad with Sweet Chilli Dressing, Chicken, Pawpaw and Mint 115

Salad with Tamarind Dressing, Tangy Chicken and Rice Noodle 83

Salsa, Chargrilled Chicken with Green Olive and Orange 26, **27**

Salsa, Fragrant Lemongrass Chicken with Chilli and Pineapple 86, **87**

Sangria, Classic 12, **13**

Satay with Peanut Sauce, Delicious Chicken 126

Satay, Traditional Balinese **128**, 129

Schnitzel with Mozzarella, Red Capsicum and Basil Stuffing, Chicken 50, **51**

Sensational Potato and Rosemary Tortilla **14**, 15

Sesame Bananas, Fried 100, **101**

Sesame Brittle, Lime and Coconut Ice-cream with 139

Skewered Smoky Chicken Meatballs with Roasted Tomatoes 12, **13**

Slushy, Lemongrass 136, **137**

Sorbet, Lychee and Ginger 121

Soup with Coconut Cream and Lemongrass, Chicken **82**, 83

Spaghetti, Chicken, Lemon, Parmesan and Parsley 36, **37**

Spanish Baked Chicken with Garlic and Lemon 29

Spanish Churros with Cinnamon-scented Liquid Chocolate 30, **31**

Spicy Baked Chicken Pieces 85

Spicy Thai Chicken Salad **88**, 89

Spinach Leaves, Kaffir Chicken on **98**, 99

Spinach, Eggplants Stuffed with Pumpkin, Pine Nuts and 19, **20**

Spring Rolls, Fresh as Fresh 108, **109**

Squid, Bangkok Chinatown Noodles with Chicken and Pickled 92, **93**

Steamboat, Vietnamese 118, **119**

Steamed Chicken with Tomatoes and Coriander **110**, 111

Sticky Black-rice Pudding **138**, 139

Sticky Rice with Mango and Coconut Cream 100

Stir-fried Ginger Chicken with Sugar Snaps 86

Sugar Snaps, Stir-fried Ginger Chicken with 86

Sun-dried Tomato and Pesto Stuffing, Roast Chicken Breast with 52

Tamarind and Kaffir Lime, Chicken Curry with 92

Tamarind Dressing, Tangy Chicken and Rice Noodle Salad with 83

Tangy Chicken and Rice Noodle Salad with Tamarind Dressing 83

Tarragon Cream Sauce, Chicken with 62, **63**

Tart, Tomato and Mustard **73**, 75

Tarts, Caramelised Apple 76, **77**

Thai Spicy Chicken Salad **88**, 89

Tiramisu, Lazy **54**, 55

Tofu Fritters 135

Tomato and Mozzarella, Baked Chicken with Eggplant, 50

Tomato and Mustard Tart **73**, 75

Tomatoes and Coriander, Steamed Chicken with **110**, 111

Tomatoes, Garlic and Olive Oil, Chicken with 69

Tomatoes, Linguine with Chicken, Artichokes and Cherry **42**, 43

Tomatoes, Skewered Smoky Chicken Meatballs with Roasted 12, **13**

Tortilla, Sensational Potato and Rosemary **14**, 15

Traditional Balinese Satay **128**, 129

Tuscan Chicken with Caramelised Lemons, Barbecued **40**, 41

Tuscan-style Roasted Chicken with Wine and Garlic **48**, 49

Vanilla Ricotta, Grilled Nectarines with 55

Vietnamese Steamboat 118, **119**

Vietnamese-style Iced Coffee 121

Vietnamese-style Lettuce Cups 107

Watercress Salad 62, **63**

Whole Roasted Chicken with Chorizo and Herb Stuffing 28, **29**

Zesty Citrus Chicken Stir-fry with Asian Greens **97**, 99

Zingy Balinese Chicken Curry **130**, 131

ACKNOWLEDGEMENTS

Putting a cookbook together is a huge task! It's like a never-ending buffet of ideas, images, recipes and proofs, and I am so grateful to everyone who has helped to navigate me through it and who stayed to do the dishes afterwards.

Thanks so much to Heather and the team at Zoomslide and to Martha and the crew who made finding and filming these recipes in their country of origin such absolute fun – you know who you are!

To all those who have helped to get this book to completion: Louise for hassling and editing me and making my 'first book' experience so easy, Shaun and Bronwyn for the gorgeous styling and photography of the food, Keely for the beautiful design and New Holland Publishers for the opportunity. And finally, a big thank you to the Tegel team who have been truly wonderful to work with, and who have trusted us so implicitly throughout this project. Thank you for your vision and commitment.

First published in 2009 by New Holland Publishers (NZ) Ltd
Auckland • Sydney • London • Cape Town
www.newhollandpublishers.co.nz

in association with Tegel Foods Ltd

World Kitchen was first broadcast in 2009 on TV3 (Mediaworks TV) at 5.30pm on Sundays.

New Holland Publishers (NZ) Ltd
218 Lake Road, Northcote, Auckland 0627, New Zealand
Unit 1, 66 Gibbes Street, Chatswood, NSW 2067, Australia
86–88 Edgware Road, London W2 2EA, United Kingdom
80 McKenzie Street, Cape Town 8001, South Africa

Copyright © 2009 in text: Tegel Foods Ltd
Copyright © 2009 in food photography: Shaun Cato-Symonds
Copyright © 2009 New Holland Publishers (NZ) Ltd

Front cover photographs: Shaun Cato-Symonds, Big Stock Photo, Flickr photographers: Yellow.Cat, Poguri, Jaume Meneses, Bernard Oh, Luca Venturelli
Photographs of Nici Wickes on front cover, back flap and p. 4: Shaun Cato-Symonds
pp. 9–10: Big Stock Photo, stock.xchnge, Flickr photographers: Yellow.Cat, Poguri, Detlef Schobert, Juanma Pérez Rabasco, Miikka Hoo, Jaume Meneses, Laura Kidd, Mariano Fotos, Berni Martin, Adrià García, Henry Burrows, Jaume Ventura
pp. 34–35: Big Stock Photo, Flickr photographers: Allan Harris, Glen MacLarty, Gwennypics, Austin Keys, fachxx00, Mimi_K, Augen.Blicke, Antonio Scaramuzzino
pp. 58–59: Big Stock Photo, Flickr photographers: Edwin Lee, Avril Lynn Dudley
pp. 80–81: Big Stock Photo, Flickr photographers: Stas Kulesh, Rene Ehrhardt
pp. 104–105: Big Stock Photo, stock.xchnge, Flickr photographers: Bernard Oh, Rachel Black, Eric Molina, Bastian Stein, Toby Forage, Nguyen Trung, Deadly Tedly
pp. 124–125: Big Stock Photo, stock.xchnge, Flickr photographers: Tiger Lily, Trent Strohm, Whitecat Singapore

Commissioned and project managed by Louise Armstrong
Publishing manager: Matt Turner
Editor: Fiona McRae
Designer: Keely O'Shannessy
Food stylist: Bronwyn Byrne

National Library of New Zealand Cataloguing-in-Publication Data

Wickes, Nici.
World kitchen : bringing great chicken recipes back home to New Zealand / author: Nici Wickes ; photography: Shaun Cato-Symonds.
Includes index.
ISBN 978-1-86966-257-8
1. Cookery (Chicken) 2. Cookery, New Zealand. I. Title.
II. World kitchen (Television program)
641.665—dc 22

10 9 8 7 6 5 4 3 2 1

Colour reproduction and printing by Craft Print Pte Ltd, Singapore on paper sourced from sustainable forests.

All rights reserved. No part of this publication may be reproduced, stored in a retrieval system, or transmitted in any form or by any means, electronic, mechanical, photocopying, recording or otherwise, without the prior permission of the publishers and copyright holders.

The recipes in this book have been carefully tested by the author. The publishers and the author have made every effort to ensure that the recipes and instructions pertaining to them are accurate and safe but cannot accept liability for any resulting injury or loss or damage to property whether direct or consequential.